The Family

An Introduction

EIGHTH EDITION

J. ROSS ESHLEMAN

Wayne State University

Allyn and Bacon

Boston   London   Toronto   Sydney   Tokyo   Singapore

Senior Series Editor: Karen Hanson
Editorial Assistant: Jennifer Jacobson
Marketing Manager: Joyce Nilsen
Editorial-Production Service: DMC & Company
Text Designer: Donna Merrell Chernin
Photo Researcher: Laurie Frankenthaler
Production Administrator: Susan Brown
Cover Administrator: Linda Knowles
Cover Designer: Studio Nine
Manufacturing Buyer: Megan Cochran
Composition and Prepress Buyer: Linda Cox

Copyright © 1997 Allyn & Bacon
A Viacom Company
160 Gould Street
Needham Heights, MA 02194
www.abacon.com

Eshleman, J. Ross.
      The family: an introduction / J. Ross Eshleman. — 8th ed.
            p. cm.
      Includes bibliographical references and indexes.
      ISBN 0-205-19147-9 (hardcover)
      1. Family. 2. Marriage. 3. Family—United States. I. Title.
HQ515.E83 1996
306.85'0973–dc20
                                                96–20213
                                                CIP

Printed in the United States of America
10 9 8 7 6 5 4 3 2   99 98 97

ISBN 0-205-19147-9

*To Janet, Jill, Sid, and Krishe,
and the persons and couples who so kindly agreed
to be interviewed for the case examples.*

The Family

An Introduction

EIGHTH EDITION

J. ROSS ESHLEMAN

Wayne State University

Allyn and Bacon

Boston   London   Toronto   Sydney   Tokyo   Singapore

Senior Series Editor: Karen Hanson
Editorial Assistant: Jennifer Jacobson
Marketing Manager: Joyce Nilsen
Editorial-Production Service: DMC & Company
Text Designer: Donna Merrell Chernin
Photo Researcher: Laurie Frankenthaler
Production Administrator: Susan Brown
Cover Administrator: Linda Knowles
Cover Designer: Studio Nine
Manufacturing Buyer: Megan Cochran
Composition and Prepress Buyer: Linda Cox

Copyright © 1997 Allyn & Bacon
A Viacom Company
160 Gould Street
Needham Heights, MA 02194
www.abacon.com

Eshleman, J. Ross.
    The family: an introduction / J. Ross Eshleman. — 8th ed.
        p. cm.
    Includes bibliographical references and indexes.
    ISBN 0-205-19147-9 (hardcover)
    1. Family. 2. Marriage. 3. Family—United States. I. Title.
HQ515.E83 1996
306.85'0973–dc20   96–20213
                                                                         CIP

Printed in the United States of America
10 9 8 7 6 5 4 3 2   99 98 97

ISBN 0-205-19147-9

To Janet, Jill, Sid, and Krishe,
and the persons and couples who so kindly agreed
to be interviewed for the case examples.

Contents

3   Marital, Family, and Kinship Organization 77

4   Marriage, Family, and Work 109

PART IV   SEXUAL NORMS AND RELATIONSHIPS

11   *Sexual Relationships in Social and Marital Contexts 319*

PART V   MARITAL AND FAMILY RELATIONSHIPS:
PATTERNS OF INTERACTION THROUGHOUT
THE LIFE CYCLE

PART VI   MARITAL CRISIS, DIVORCE, AND FAMILY POLICIES

16   *Family Crisis and Violence Among Intimates 489*

Preface

What should an introductory family textbook try to do? First, I believe it should provide a thorough and objective coverage of the basic concepts and ideas in the area of marriages, families, and intimate relationships. The ideas should be presented clearly and intelligibly. The coverage should include specific factual data as well as abstract principles and empirically supported findings as well as hypotheses for testing. Since this introduction to the family will be the only course on the family that many students take, the text should arouse a curiosity toward, and include tools for, an ongoing process of observation, understanding, and analysis of intimate relationships, marital and family systems, and organizations.

Second, and equally important, I believe an introductory family textbook should capture students' interest. The processes and organization of intimate relationships and family behavior should be conveyed to students in a manner that is understanding, readable, and interesting, yet realistic, without sacrificing accuracy. Given this foundation, students should be able to relate personal and familial values and behaviors to differing life-styles and patterns, both within their own society and in relationship to others. That is, students should be guided to see more clearly their places in the United States and the world.

I have tried to write a text that is both interesting and highly readable, that is relatively comprehensive in the coverage of topics, and that emphasizes the family in the United States and supplements this discussion with historical and cross-cultural referents. I have tried to make the text accurate yet contemporary, including nontraditional marital and family life-styles while keeping a realistic perspective relative to the more common, traditional family forms. I have tried to document extensively when presenting the study of the family as a scholarly discipline to encourage further thought and reading. Each chapter is documented throughout with footnote citations of sources, and each chapter ends with questions for discussion and an annotated bibliography of further reading materials. The latest research and census materials have been presented, and illustrative material has been inserted throughout the text.

Illustrative material is presented in the form of four types of boxed panels. Relevant to the topics in each chapter is one example of (1) *global diversity*—presenting an illustration from a culture or society other than the United States; (2) *U.S. diversity*—presenting an illustration of diversity with the United States; (3) a *news item*—selecting a journalistic writing or news event from the media;

and (4) a *case example*—a personal or couple illustration based on an interview or on a specific, existing organizational policy or program. All of the personal/couple interviews, representing true-life events or experiences, were completed by the author. Participants were shown the final write-up and gave their written permission for its use.

All of the writing effort was an outgrowth of several major objectives:

- to present an objective description and analysis of contemporary U.S. families within a world perspective
- to examine without condemnation or praise nontraditional family and marital life-styles
- to apply general theoretical schemes and frames of reference to family issues
- to present basic concepts and descriptive materials clearly and intelligibly
- to suggest questions and supplemental sources to stimulate discussion and reading beyond the textual materials
- to illustrate material with interest items of a personal and diverse nature
- to cultivate in students an increased awareness of their particular niche in the family and general social order.

Plan for the text

This eighth edition of *The Family* basically follows a sociological and social-psychological approach. Part I deals with understanding the family irrespective of time and place. Chapter 1 summarizes basic issues in families in the United States. Chapter 2 examines approaches to the study of families and establishes five basic frames of reference, or theories, central to understanding intimate relationships, family groups, and systems. The coverage of contemporary family theories includes sociobiological, humanist, and feminist approaches. Chapter 3 illustrates the boundaries of marital, family, and kinship organization; and Chapter 4 identifies the linkages between the family and other institutions, and focuses on the institution of work.

Part II looks at cultural and subcultural variations in family life-styles. Chapter 5 considers traditional and contemporary mainland Chinese families as well as Swedish families. Chapter 6 considers African American families and Chapter 7 examines Hispanic American, Asian American, and Native American families in the United States. Chapter 8 examines social-class variations in the United States, including an extensive look at single parents and the feminization of poverty.

Chapters 9 and 10 of Part III analyze structural variations and processes of selection in the formation of intimate relationships and marital and family status by examining mate selection in contemporary U.S. society and around the world. In Part IV, Chapter 11 addresses a range of sexual norms and relationships as major and significant social aspects of intimate relationships and marital/family systems.

Part V considers patterns of interaction throughout the family life course: marriage (Chapter 12), parenthood (Chapter 13), childrearing and socialization

(Chapter 14), and the middle and later years, including dying, death, and the post-marital family (Chapter 15).

Part VI addresses contemporary issues in the study of intimate relationships, marriages, and families. Chapter 16 examines the nature of family crisis and violence among intimates, and Chapter 17 examines divorce and remarriage. The book concludes with a discussion of the family and social policy in Chapter 18.

As a result of an extensive review of the literature as well as selected feedback from faculty and students who used previous editions, various changes and additions appear in this eighth edition of *The Family.* Two previous chapters on sexual interaction have been combined into one. Many chapters have been considerably reorganized. Extensive new and updated research material will be evident throughout the text, including significant research findings on topics involving intimate relationships beyond traditional marriage/family boundaries. Completely new sections have been added on Asian American and Native American families.   As in previous editions, selected theories and frames of reference are described and applied throughout the text. Extensive use is made of recent census data and research findings, and the previously described four types of boxed panels are provided to supplement and illustrate the basic textual material. Each chapter ends with several useful study aids: Summary, Key Terms and Topics, Discussion Questions, and Further Readings. A glossary and name and subject indexes are provided at the end of the book.

It is my hope that students and teachers alike will find the ideas presented in *The Family* stimulating and clearly explained. I hope the book is readable and interesting, that it presents an accurate portrayal of intimate relationships and family systems, that it allows flexible use, that it will stimulate thought and discussion, and, perhaps most important, that it will change behavior by expanding readers' awareness of and sensitivity to, self and others.

A final word about the language used in *The Family.* Efforts have been made in writing and editing this book to follow contemporary style guidelines for language describing people of cultural minority groups. For example, the terms *African American* and *black* are used as synonyms in most cases. The term *white* is used to designate people of Caucasian heritage. The general terms *Hispanic American* and *Asian American* are used to identify members of a number of cultural subgroups of Spanish or Asian heritage; more specific terms, such as *Mexican American* or *Japanese American,* are used in discussions of individual subgroups. The terms *American Indian* and *Native American* are used interchangeably to describe people native to the North American continent. Generally, when reporting results from a given source, a specific term has been used following the style used in the source. For example, in presenting data from U.S. census reports, the terms *black, white,* and *Hispanic origin* are most often used, since those terms are used in the actual reports.

Similarly, care has been taken to describe with sensitivity people with exceptionalities and people who have been victimized. The general idea is to acknowledge, first, that these individuals are people; the characteristics or experiences that make them exceptional are secondary. For example, the phrase *people with AIDS* has been used instead of *AIDS victims* and *disabled people* are described as *people with disabilities*. While labels are needed to identify special groups within the general population, these terms need not stigmatize the people to whom they apply.

Acknowledgments

It is difficult to know where to begin or end in expressing a deeply felt sense of gratitude and appreciation to many people. First, I want to convey my affection for and recognize the support received from my own primary intimates including my wife, Janet; my daughter, Jill; my son, Sid; and his wife, Kristie. Other primary relatives—including Claudett, Robert, Orpha, Effie and Jim, and Joyce and Jim—have been particularly influential in my life and in creating a personal awareness of the significance and importance of family. Close friends—such as John and Ginger Campbell, Millie and the late Milton Cudney, A. M. and Bebe Denton, Ralph and Zeddy Jordan, Joyce and Stewart Rhymer, and John and Chris Turner—are and were constant sources of encouragement, feedback, and meaningful relationships.

I also wish to acknowledge professional colleagues and students, namely, Marilyn Daniels, Donald Gelfand, Cassandra George, Katrina Henry, David Klein, Tamieka Lee, Lionel Matthews, Joe Sloan, Joe Therrien, Mary Jane VanMeter, Leon Warshay, and Leon Wilson who have made specific contributions with library resources, computer applications, editorial assistance, or ideas. And, of course, special thanks go to the persons and couples who agreed to be interviewed and share a segment of their personal life experiences: Andrea, Butch, Dal, Dee, Deloris, Duan, Effie, Jim, Joyce, Larry, Marsha, Mary, Phyllis, Richard, Stewart, Tonya, Yvonne, and others.

To single out others would require a more lengthy list. But several should be mentioned. Professionals in the field who used the last edition and the reviewers for this edition's manuscript—Larry Beckhouse, College of William and Mary; Professor Bedell, California State University, Fullerton; G.E. Bodine, Syracuse University; R.C. Busch; Sylvia Clavan; Marvin Kaller, Kent State University; David M. Klein, University of Notre Dame; Teresa G. Labov, University of Pennsylvania; David Kent Lee, Sacramento State University; Rich Miller, Kansas State University; Pyong Gap Min, Queens College; Larry R. Peterson, Memphis State University; and R. Stephen Schwartz, Winona State University—provided valuable reactions, comments, and suggestions for changes in this edition.

Finally, individuals such as Karen Hanson and Jennifer Jacobson at Allyn and Bacon, each fulfilling her professional tasks, were influential in getting this book into its final form. Donna Chernin of DMC & Company provided excellent editorial, design, and production assistance. To each of these individuals I extend my thanks and appreciation.

J. Ross Eshleman

The Family

An Introduction

Chapter 1

Introduction to the Family: Issues and Change

- **Ideal-Type Constructs**
    - Definition
    - Functions
- **Issues in U.S. Families**
    - Meaning of marriage and the family
    - Family organization
    - Family functions
    - Marital- and gender-role differentiation
    - Social class and social mobility
    - Partner selection
    - Love
    - Sexual relationships
    - Family size and family planning
    - Aged family members
    - Violence and abuse among intimates
    - Family permanence
    - Other contemporary issues
- **Characteristics of U.S. Families**
    - Numbers of families and households
    - Sizes of families and households
    - Marital status
    - Family income
- **Today's Families: Significant Changes**
- **Summary**
- **Key Terms and Topics**
- **Discussion Questions**
- **Further Readings**

The family? What is *the family*? Is the family comprised of one female legally married to one male? Does the family have children, born within wedlock; a husband, employed full time, serving as the primary provider and ultimate authority; and a wife who is a full-time mother and homemaker? Or is the family a single parent, divorced or never married, raising his or her children? Does the family include a wife who is employed full time and a husband who chooses to be the primary child-rearer? Is a childless couple a family? Is the family a cohesive, loving, sexually exclusive unit, bound until death do they part? Or is the family sometimes less than cohesive, even conflict-ridden and abusive? Do members of the family always live together?

Sociologically, **the family** is a social group, a social institution, and a social system. As a *social group*, it is a collection of persons who recognize one another as family members and interact in a sexually bonded, intimate, primary network. As a *social institution*, the family meets broad societal goals that center around intimate relationships and the reproduction and socialization of children. As a *social system*, it has many interdependent components with major differentiations by gender, race, class, age, size, and so forth.

Viewing selected patterns of behavior as fixed has led a number of scholars to question if the word *family* is even a meaningful concept, since it implies images of married couples, love, permanence, children, sexual exclusivity, homemakers, legal unions, and intergenerational continuity. Such scholars have questioned whether these images are more than perceived idealism that is inconsistent with the realities of today's relationships: remarriages, dual careers, childless couples, one-parent households, same-sex unions, gender inequalities, abusive partners, and intergenerational disruptions. Some writers have asked if it is time to begin thinking about *the family* as a social institution, and *families* as pluralistic or diverse units less in terms of structure and stability and more in terms of process and change, less in terms of traditional images and standards by which everything else is judged and more in terms of close relationships and sexually bonded primary relationships.[1] The former terms suggest a traditional view held by a select segment of the population, while the latter suggest a broader, comprehensive, more accurate portrayal of the reality of human, close, primary, sexually bonded relationships.

It is difficult to find terms or concepts that differentiate family from nonfamily relationships and experiences. Recently, the term *sexually bonded* has been suggested as a characteristic. Other scholars have suggested *family realm* as a term that differentiates familial types of human relationships from nonfamilial types such as political, economic, medical, educational, military, and artistic relationships.[2] Jan

---

[1] John Scanzoni, Karen Polonko, Jay Teachman, and Linda Thompson, *The Sexual Bond: Rethinking Families and Close Relationships* (Newbury Park, CA: Sage, 1989). See also: Jaber F. Gubrium and James A. Holstein, *What Is Family?* (Mountain View, CA: Mayfield, 1990); and Jan Trost, "Do We Mean the Same by the Concept of Family?" *Communications Research*, 17 (August 1990): 431–443.

[2] Ivan F. Beutler, Wesley R. Burr, Kathleen S. Bahr, and Donald A. Herrin, "The Family Realm: Theoretical Contributions for Understanding Its Uniqueness," *Journal of Marriage and the Family* 51 (August 1989): 805–816.

Trost proposes a system of *dyadic units* to define and conceptualize family.[3] Individuals might define what their own families consist of and may include two men who cohabit, an ex-spouse, parents-in-law, stepparents, siblings, friends, and even pets. Any dyad (two persons) or set of dyads could be considered family.

This book views the family as a social institution and assumes that every society in the world includes a wide range of patterns, structural arrangements, and behaviors that are defined as family or family-like. While the title *The Family* remains, it is with the recognition that the family as a social system includes marriages and families that do not fit traditional notions of what marriages and families are or should be. Many relationships (same-sex, cohabitors, fictive kin, unmarried parents, and the like) fulfill responsibilities and functions that are basic to family systems. This book proposes to examine a wide range of these family and family-like patterns that exist in the United States and around the world. Current research findings have been incorporated in an effort to understand the similarities as well as the differences among the norms, values, and behaviors that characterize marriage and family-type relationships.

Similarities and most differences in attitudes, behaviors, and organization create little conflict or controversy. In fact, most of these similarities and differences are not obvious to the majority of persons who have never undertaken systematic study of the family. Are parents, teachers, and businesspeople disturbed over changing divorce rates, over employment rates of mothers, or over the failure of Amish American families to use electricity or drive automobiles? Generally, not. However, social controversy does arise when property settlements and child placements cannot be agreed upon by divorced couples, when children of working parents are not provided adequate care, or when Amish buggies present a highway danger to fast-moving automobiles.

This introductory chapter will present selected major issues brought about by social change and will describe general characteristics of families and family-type relationships in the United States. Chapter 2 will discuss approaches used to examine these issues.

IDEAL-TYPE CONSTRUCTS

Definition

Many concepts, illustrations, and ideas used in this book are treated in ideal-type terms. Use of the word *ideal* is not meant to imply that which is good, best, valuable, perfect, or desirable. Rather, ideal types are hypothetical constructs based on pure, definitive characteristics.

---

[3] Jan Trost, "Family From a Dyadic Perspective," *Journal of Family Issues* 14 (March 1993): 92–104.

Ideal-type constructs always represent the ends, the extremes, or the poles of a continuum. Used hypothetically, ideal types provide contrasting qualities with which to characterize any social phenomenon. *Patriarchal/matriarchal, nuclear/extended, primary/secondary, individual/familial,* and *rural/urban* are examples of qualities of ideal types. The pure characteristics of *rural* might include geographical and social isolation, homogeneity, agricultural employment, sparse population, and a subsistence economy. Characteristics of *urban* are likely to include social heterogeneity, industrial employment, dense population, and impersonality. Any community in the world could be placed along this ideal-type continuum—between *rural* and *urban*—but none is likely to include all characteristics to the maximum degree. These terms accentuate, even exaggerate, reality rather than describe it specifically and accurately. On a *rural/urban* construct, Chicago would fall toward the *urban* end of the continuum. However, New York may be more characteristic of *urban* than Chicago, and Tokyo more so than both New York and Chicago. Few would argue against classifying Rough Creek, Arizona, or Mud Lick, Kentucky, as *rural,* but compared to the rain forests of Brazil or the Philippines, both are quite *urban.*

The concept *ideal type* was systematically developed by the German sociologist Max Weber.[4] He was careful to point out that, first, value connotations should be avoided. The prefix *ideal* denotes a constructed model, not evaluation or approval. This term makes no suggestion as to what ought to be or what norm of conduct warrants approval or disapproval. Second, an ideal type or ideal construct is not an average or a model. An *average* denotes a central tendency, whereas an *ideal* is an extreme. Third, as mentioned, an ideal type does not reflect reality. It is an abstraction, a logical construct, a pure form; thus, by nature, it is not found in reality.

Functions

An ideal-type construct performs several basic functions:

1. It provides a limiting case with which concrete phenomena may be contrasted.
2. It provides for analysis and measurement of social reality.
3. It facilitates classification and comparison.

In short, an ideal type provides a standard with which to assess what any phenomenon would be if it always or never conformed to its own definition. Thus, ideal types enable social scientists to make valid and precise comparisons among societies, institutions, and families separated in time and place. They enable peo-

---

[4] Max Weber, *The Methodology of the Social Sciences,* trans. and ed., Edward H. Shils and Henry A. Finch (New York: Free Press, 1949).

ple who are studying the family to have a methodological tool that provides assistance in examining, for instance, the upper or lower classes, African American or white American families, or arranged or free-choice mate selection. In the next section, ideal types will be used to examine selected issues affecting the U.S. family.

ISSUES IN U.S. FAMILIES

There is little dispute that the family in U.S. society has changed and will continue to change. This notion is widely acknowledged in the mass media and has been documented by empirical research. Arland Thornton, for example, examined three decades of changing norms and values concerning American family life from the late 1950s through the middle 1980s.[5] Using a broad range of data sets, Thornton documented a weakening of the imperatives to marry, to remain married, to have children, to restrict intimate relations to marriage, and to maintain separate roles for males and females. Such changes away from traditional attitudes and family forms are likely to continue. Trent and South suggested that as individuals have ever-widening experiences with different family forms (parental divorce, unmarried motherhood, maternal employment, etc.), they appear to be less committed to traditional family patterns.[6]

Changes such as these are not necessarily bad, disruptive, or suggest family decline and breakdown. This view, however, is in sharp contrast to that of social scientists who argue that the family in America is not merely changing but is declining, that the decline is extraordinarily steep, and its social consequences, especially for children, is serious and a cause for alarm.[7] Perhaps many of you share that perspective.

The intent of this chapter is not to take the value stance that family change means decline or breakdown but to note the diversity in family values and behaviors, to compare patterns of family life that were predominant in the past with patterns prevalent in the present, and to show how these differing perspectives may produce social and personal conflict. Thus a series of ideal-type constructs (extended family/conjugal family, patriarchal family/matriarchal family, arranged marriage/free-choice marriage, homogamous relationship/heterogamous relationship), are used to measure any quality of a given family system on a continuum at different points in time, and to observe the changes or trends that seem to be taking place.

---

[5] Arland Thornton, "Changing Attitudes toward Family Issues in the United States," *Journal of Marriage and the Family* 51 (November 1989): 873–893.

[6] Katherine Trent and Scott J. South, "Sociodemographic Status, Parental Background, Childhood Family Structure, and Attitudes Toward Family Formation," *Journal of Marriage and the Family* 54 (May 1992): 427–439. Note also: Julie DaVanzo and M. Omar Rahman, "American Families: Trends and Correlates," *Population Index* 59 (Fall 1993): 350–386.

[7] David Popenoe, "American Family Decline, 1960–1990: A Review and Appraisal," *Journal of Marriage and the Family* 55 (August 1993): 527–555.

In this chapter, discussion of selected issues in the family will follow the procedure just outlined. Namely, a continuum of traditional versus nontraditional will be used to measure qualities of family systems and compare changes over time. This type of dichotomization (see Table 1-1) is not meant to perpetuate myths, such as that traditional patterns were monolithic (having a uniform structure without variations) or stable, harmonious, and without problems. Rather, the increasing acceptance of nontraditional patterns offers the opportunity to contrast these variations or alternative patterns with accepted notions of traditional patterns.

Issues—that is, unresolved conflicts—exist because both traditional and nontraditional sets of norms and values exist simultaneously. In other words, certain groups and individuals resist nontraditional norms and cling vehemently to more traditional patterns; other groups and individuals find traditional patterns unacceptable and adhere to different sets of norms and values. Thus, major issues (conflicts) occur primarily because of social change. If no change occurs and everyone accepts traditional patterns of norms, values, and behaviors, no issue or conflict results; similarly, if everyone adopts a nontraditional set of norms, no conflict exists.

Several ideal-type constructs will be developed in the following sections to illustrate the conflicts that result when nontraditional sets of marital and family values coexist with traditional values inherited from the past. Both traditional and nontraditional patterns exist simultaneously in pluralistic societies. This results in conflict, confusion, and unsettlement in the family system.

The issues that follow are not listed in order of importance, with exception of the first. All other issues relate to or basically stem from the meaning given to marriage and the family itself.

Meaning of marriage and the family

The most basic issue in studying the family is the meaning of marriage and the family. This issue questions the sources of authority in marital and family decisions. It also questions whether marriage itself is necessary.

The most traditional social norm, which represents one extreme of the ideal-type construct, views marriage as a *sacred* phenomenon. That is to say, the family and marriage are divine and holy institutions, created and maintained by God, Yahweh, or some supreme being greater than men and women. The phrase "Marriages are made in heaven" is, in many ways, consistent with this perspective.

This traditional social norm was perhaps most widely prevalent prior to the turn of the twentieth century. In its extreme form, marriage is not only sacred but is a sacrament in itself. The Catholic church views marriage as one of the seven sacraments. This implies that human beings and their personal needs and wishes are of secondary importance to that which is God-created and God-given. Basic to this view is the idea that authority on all family and religious matters stems from God and is administered by church officials (popes, cardinals, bishops, and priests).

Table 1-1

Traditional family norms and nontraditional alternatives

Traditional family norms	Nontraditional alternatives
Legally married	Singlehood/Never married Nonmarital cohabitation
Married once	Remarriage Multiple marriages
Heterosexual marriage	Same-sex marriage
Endogamous marriage	Interfaith marriage Interracial marriage Interclass marriage
Two-adult household	Multiadult household Communal living Affiliated families
Children	Voluntarily childless
Two parents living together	Single parent Joint custody Stepfamilies (three or more parents)

Parent as key source of:
   education
   religion
   protection
   recreation
	Tasks fulfilled by:
	   schools
	   churches
	   government/police
	   clubs, professional sports

United until death	United until divorce or separation
Male as provider	Female as provider Dual careers Commuter marriage
Male as head of household/Authority Female as homemaker/Support	Female as head of household/Authority Androgynous relationship
Self-supporting, independent	Welfare Social Security
Premarital chastity	Pre- or nonmarital intercourse
Marital sexual exclusivity	Extramarital relationships Sexually open marriages Intimate friendships

A second traditional norm, one in widespread existence at the turn of the century and the early 1900s, views the meaning of marriage and the family as being rooted in *social* obligations. The social meaning of marriage, like the sacred meaning, represents traditional norms. Instead of God, authority stems from human beings, as represented by the kin group, community, church as a social institution, and society in general. In this context, primary values of marriage and the family are to maintain social respectability, conform to kin and community wishes, and maintain a proper image within society. Thus, what other people think is very important. Divorce, nonmarital sex, single parenthood, black/white intermarriage, and so forth, are not forbidden or approved per se, but vary from one racial, ethnic, community, or network to another. Conformity to the norms of one's social category or group brings approval and acceptance; nonconformity brings disapproval.

A third meaning of marriage suggests that families and marriages exist for the *individual.* Thus, the concern is not with God or with society but with *me.* If someone chooses to marry outside of his or her race, religion, ethnic group, social class, or educational level, that is his or her business. Likewise, choosing a marriage-like relationship by cohabiting, either heterosexually or homosexually, is also a private, personal decision. According to this view, being happy in a marriage or intimate relationship is what determines success. Neither God nor society can dictate personal behavior nor can they force someone to endure an unsuccessful marriage or relationship. Within this meaning, the source of authority is the person alone; each individual is responsible for his or her own success or failure, without regard to the community structure or the social conditions in which he or she operates.

Thus, there are at least three basic meanings of marriage and the family, all of which exist today. To some persons and groups, marriage is sacred; to others, marriage is a social contract, and success is viewed in terms of conformity to societal demands; and to still others, marriage is a highly personal, highly individualistic concern. The lack of uniformity in the source of authority on the meaning of marriage and how success is determined is basic to most issues and conflicts that exist in the contemporary U.S. marital and family system.

Family organization

Closely related to the basic meaning of marriage is what constitutes the proper form of marital and family organization. Traditionally, in the United States and in much of the world, the extended-family form was most common and most highly desired. Power resided in the elders, and they in turn were responsible for caring for other members of the kin group. Kin-group members were located in geographical proximity to one another. They followed and married other kin groups with similar norms and rules, maintained intimate emotional ties to one another, and were isolated from outside contacts. This type of family organization resulted in behavior patterns and values that remained constant from one generation to the next, in children being socialized basically to be duplicates of their parents in

Case Example:
Benefits for Same-Sex Domestic Partners

Effective September 1, 1995, Wayne State University enhanced employee benefits for same-sex partners. The benefits included medical insurance, dental insurance, reduced tuition, and designation of beneficiary on life insurance and the retirement plan.

Who is a domestic partner? Any two individuals of the same sex who:

- are both 18 years or older and
- have resided together continuously for at least six months and
- intend to reside together indefinitely and
- have agreed to be jointly responsible for each other's welfare and
- share financial obligations and
- are not involved in any other domestic partnership or marriage.

In order to obtain benefits for a domestic partner, an affidavit, attesting that the above conditions have been met, must be completed.

The University is of the opinion that records containing information on domestic partners are confidential, but indicated the law is uncertain in this area. They note that it is possible that a court or other adjudicative agency would decide such records must be made public by the University. Therefore, it is important to understand that there is risk of disclosure when signing up for domestic partner benefits at a public university.

Domestic partners be aware: benefits are taxable.

---

thought and in action, and, in Bernard Farber's terms, in having an **orderly replacement** among successive generations.[8]

In contrast to the orderly replacement concept is the idea of **pluralism**: many and varied forms of marital and family organization. The family organization that is preferred will vary both over time and from one individual to another. Some individuals may prefer to bypass a formal marriage contract and simply live together. Others may desire some form of communal family where, at least economically, labor and goods are shared equally among all members. Certain members may choose not to marry at all. Some members, whether married or not, may choose to be parents. Multiple forms of family organization may be preferred by different families and even within the same family at different times. Again in Farber's terms, the result would be **universal permanent availability**.[9]

The concept of universal permanent availability suggests that individuals are available for marriage with anyone at any time. Homogamous social characteris-

---

[8] Bernard Farber, *Family Organization and Interaction* (San Francisco: Chandler, 1964), Chapter 4.

[9] Ibid., 105

tics decline in importance, and marriage becomes a personal issue rather than a kinship one. Thus, free-choice marriages based on love rather than arranged marriages based on need become prevalent, the rates of divorce and remarriage increase, and the number of children per union declines. In addition, less emphasis is placed on premarital chastity and marital fidelity, and more emphasis is placed on competence and interpersonal relations. More married women enter the work force, and youth and glamour are emphasized. Thus, polygyny, polyandry, homosexual marriages, nonlegal voluntary associations, progressive monogamy, trial marriages, group marriages, communal families, single-parent families, and remaining unmarried all have a place within nontraditional forms of family organization.

A basic issue exists today over what constitutes the proper form of family organization. Those who view marriage as a sacred, monogamous, lifelong relationship and who insist that a family is a two-parent, permanent unit will find it difficult to accept and adjust to the multiple (mostly nontraditional) forms of family organization that are becoming increasingly common and public. It is not that these forms are totally new; rather, it is that they now occur with greater frequency, receive more publicity, and result in meaningful and realistic marital and family organizations for thousands of persons in the United States today. The multiple number of acceptable forms of marriage and family life are part of the pluralistic nature of U.S. society.

Family functions

Many critics of the American family assume the family has "broken down," and base their argument for this breakdown on the loss of family functions. Throughout history, the family has been the major social institution, serving functions such as protection, education, and recreation. Given the loss of functions that the family traditionally performed, the increasing specialization and complexity of modern society have led to a dehumanizing and fragmentizing process.

This issue is by no means a recent one. In the 1930s, William Ogburn argued that the dilemma of the modern family was its loss of functions.[10] It was his belief that, prior to modern times, the power and prestige of the family was due to the seven functions it performed.

1. *Economics* —Foremost was the economic function. The family was a self-sufficient unit whose members primarily consumed that which they produced. Thus, banks, stores, and factories were not needed.

2. *Prestige and status* —The family provided prestige and status to its members. The family name was important. Each person in the family was less an individual and more a member of the group.

---

10 William Ogburn, "The Changing Family," *The Family* (1938): 139–143.

3. *Education* —The family performed the basic function of education, not only of infants and children but also of youth, for vocational education, physical education, domestic science, and so on.

4. *Protection* —The family protected its members. Not only did the father provide physical protection for his family, but the children provided social and economic protection against the economic and psychological needs of their elders.

5. *Religion* —The family exercised a religious function, as evidenced by grace at meals, family prayers, and reading together passages in the Bible or other holy works.

6. *Recreation* —The recreation function was performed at the homestead of some family or within the family rather than at recreation centers outside the home provided by the school, community, or industry.

7. *Affection and procreation* —The final function was to provide affection between mates and to procreate.

Many people in U.S. society today are committed to the idea that these traditional functions of the family should be maintained. That is, families should be relatively self-sufficient, familism should have priority over individualism, education should be centered in the home, children should care for their aging parents, prayer and religious rituals should be basic parts of daily family life, recreation should involve the family as a unit, and affection should be shared relatively exclusively among family members.

Emergent norms suggest that many of these traditional family functions are now being performed by other agencies. The economic function has shifted to the factory and office. Prestige and status are associated more with performance or achievements of the individual family member than with the reputation of the family name. Teachers and day-care employees have become substitute parents and are responsible for educating children of all ages. Police, reform schools, Social Security, Medicare and Medicaid, unemployment compensation, and other types of social programs provided by the state have replaced the traditional protective function. Professional priests, rabbis, and clergy have assumed responsibility for the religious function. Little League baseball, company bowling teams, TV watching, and women's tennis groups, for example, have replaced the family as a source of recreation. Although many would argue that the family is still the basic source of affection among members and the primary setting for producing children, one does not have to look far to discover that both functions are easily served outside the boundaries of the family.

To be sure, not only losses have taken place in family functions; gains have occurred as well. The family and peer groups, for example, have increased in importance as sources of emotional support. Within these primary-group boundaries, members may increasingly find a therapeutic milieu for personal and physical health problems. Families increasingly may be responsible for developing members' competence in the use of community and nonfamily resources. Existence in complex, highly specialized societies requires a knowledge of the range of options available, an ability to make sound choices, and a flexibility toward new technologies and ideologies. Thus, a major new family function is that of *socialization*: teaching members competence in a changing, complex society and world. A further discussion of the concept and use of *function* as well as family functions will be presented in Chapter 2.

Marital- and gender-role differentiation

Marital and gender roles need to include masculine/feminine and male/female roles, as well. The confusion and uncertainty about role definitions of male and female genders become very evident when students are asked to define and list characteristics of masculinity. It is often difficult, first, to list characteristics and, second, to reach agreement about them. Traditionally, no such difficulty was likely to exist. The male/husband/father was the head of the family, its main economic support, and its representative in the community. The female/wife/mother provided support by caring for the children and maintaining the home, but she remained silent and even passive. In short, the male was the boss, the breadwinner, and the aggressive partner while the female was the subservient helpmate.

These traditional norms, which endorse a patriarchal family, are supported today by religious fundamentalist groups,[11] who take literally words such as those of the Apostle Paul in his letters to the Ephesians and the Colossians. To the Ephesians, Paul said:

> Wives submit yourselves unto your husbands…for the husband is the head of the wife…Therefore as the church is subject unto Christ so let the wives be to their own husbands in everything.[12]

To the Colossians, Paul was very clear on the proper hierarchy of power and authority within the family. He wrote:

> Wives submit yourselves unto your own husbands, as it is fit in the Lord. Husbands, love your wives and be not bitter against them. Children, obey your parents in all things: for this is well pleasing unto the Lord.[13]

This traditional role pattern is consistent with the sacred meaning of marriage. The source of authority is God, not human beings.

---

[11] Harold G. Grasmick, Linda Patterson Wilcox, and Sharon R. Bird, "The Effects of Religious Fundamentalism and Religiosity on Preference for Traditional Family Norms," *Sociological Inquiry* 60 (November 1990): 352–369.

[12] Ephesians 5: 22–24.

13 Colossians 3: 18–20.

An increasing number of women, wives, and mothers are entering the paid labor force with many obtaining positions in occupations and professions traditionally held only by men. No society in the world has achieved gender equality in the home or workplace, but increasingly in both areas, men and women are pursuing nontraditional roles and behaviors.

The traditional expectations of appropriate marital and gender roles are clear and unmistakable. Women are expected to make marriage, home, and children their primary concerns. Wives take their husbands' name, share their income, and rely on them for status and identity. Women should be sympathetic, caring, loving, compassionate, gentle, and submissive, which in turn makes them excellent wives, mothers, nurses, and teachers of young children. In American society, to be feminine the skin must be smooth and soft, and the body slim and erotic.

In contrast, men financially support their wives and children. To be masculine is to be self-reliant, strong, verbally and physically aggressive, dominant, and muscular. Men are risk takers, decision makers, and protectors. The ideal male is hardworking, responsible, achieving, and reliable. In addition, heterosexuality is greatly stressed in interests and activities, and departures from this life-style are strongly condemned.

This type of gender-role differentiation has benefits for both sexes, but it has great costs as well. For females, satisfaction may be derived from the emphasis on beauty, the lack of pressure to achieve professionally, the freedom of emotional expression, and the right to claim support. For males, satisfaction may be derived from the access to power, the ideology of male supremacy, the opportunities to develop skills and talents, the exercise of autonomy and independence, and the ability to be self-supporting. However, it is often at great cost to females that restrictions are placed on self-development, on training to cope with an increasingly complicated world, and on ability to achieve economic independence (obtain a loan, open a business, etc.). It is often at great cost to men that they are pressured to achieve, to assume responsibility for family members, to be in constant competition to excel, and to be unable to express themselves emotionally.

The traditional differentiation of male/female roles has come into serious question over the past few decades. While **androgyny** (a condition of no gender-role differentiation) has not been achieved, pressures exist to move in that direction. Factors such as nonfamilial roles being made available to women, increasing egalitarian emphasis in intimate family and nonfamily relationships, changing beliefs in both work and play, and changing patterns of socialization and education have led to nontraditional attitudes and behaviors as appropriate for males and females.

While the labels may vary—*androgyny, unisex, desegregation, new neuter*—the message is similar: Men and women increasingly are pursuing their similarities, experiencing the thrill of escaping from traditional gender-role stereotypes and choosing to behave as *persons* rather than as males or females. Both sexes are behaving in ways that are instrumental as well as expressive, assertive as well as yielding, and masculine as well as feminine.

The transition from gender-role differentiation to androgyny or from complementary- to egalitarian-type marriage is far from complete. But women's participation in the world of paid employment is growing, household and childrearing responsibilities are being shared by husbands and wives, and each sex is thinking and behaving more and more in ways traditionally linked to its opposite.[14] These changes will be described more fully throughout the book, particularly in Chapters 4–8, 11, 12, 14, 15, and 17.

Social class and social mobility

The issue of social class and social mobility centers around the extent to which it is desirable to have tremendous variations in wealth, status, and power among families in a given society and the extent to which it is possible for families to move from one social status to another. Should some families accumulate vast amounts of wealth in a society where countless other families live in poverty? This issue includes the distribution of resources (jobs, education, health care, and housing) as well as the ability to move from one status to another. It also includes the "American Dream" of going from rags to riches, from a log cabin to the White House.

---

[14] See, for example: Constance L. Shehan and John N. Scanzoni, "Gender Patterns in the United States: Demographic Trends and Policy Prospects," *Family Relations* 37 (October 1988): 441–450.

The polar extremes of an ideal-type construct would include an open-class society, where anyone could move up or down in the social structure strictly on the basis of personal effort and ability, versus a closed-class society, where all would remain in the position in which they were born, with no change possible through individual achievement or other means. The classic representation of a closed-class system is that of the caste system of ancient India. There, position was based on ancestry and was sustained by strict rules of same-caste marriage (endogamy), by religious beliefs, and by rigidly enforced legal and normative expectations.

No society has an absolutely open- or closed-class system. In U.S. society, family position exerts a major influence on one's chances for getting an education; for exposure to literature, travel, and the arts; for inheritance; for marriage choices; and the like. On the other hand, factors such as educational achievement, marriage possibilities, and business successes do provide opportunities for upward social mobility.

Traditionally, factors such as the extended-family system, the predominantly rural farming economy, the authority held by elders, and religious and ethnic ties appeared to make upward mobility extremely difficult. Even today, the lack of opportunity and resources available to people who are poor makes planning for the future and gaining social status exceedingly difficult, if not impossible. Yet the dream of upward social mobility, of "doing better than my parents," of economic success, and of obtaining a new and superior life-style remains popular among Americans. A further discussion of this issue and of the meaning and consequences of social-class position will be presented in Chapter 8.

Partner selection

The issue of partner selection centers around two questions: Who chooses? and Who is chosen? The polar extremes of an ideal-type construct include arranged marriage, with no voice given to the partners involved, versus absolutely free choice, where the decision is made solely by the partners involved. Around the world and traditionally in the United States, arranged marriages have been more prevalent than free-choice marriages.

In American society, traditional norms suggested that parents, in particular, give their approval to the partner chosen for their son or daughter. It is not uncommon today to find men in the fifty-and-older age group who formally and directly requested their wives' parents' permission for marriage. Permission to live together without marriage was rarely, if ever, an option for this age cohort. Although in the United States individuals' partners are no longer chosen by their parents (as they are in much of the Eastern world), partners are chosen with a clear consciousness of whether they will meet the approval of parents. And to many individuals, it would be unthinkable to marry someone who was not known by their parents or their kin group and community. Thus, who actually does the choosing? The most nontraditional norm, at the other extreme, is to have an absolutely free choice of partner without seeking or needing the approval of parents, friends, or others.

Closely related to who chooses is the question of who is chosen. Traditionally, in-group (endogamous) selection was extremely important. The ideal spouse was from one's own social class, religious, racial, ethnic, or neighborhood group. Outsiders were viewed with much suspicion, and marriage to an outsider portended future marital problems. That this traditional norm still exists today is very obvious when one looks at the type of material taught in marriage-preparation classes within the American education system, the position taken by most religious groups, and the advice of parents or columnists.

An emergent norm suggests that partner selection is increasingly coming under the control of youth themselves and that out-group (exogamous) selection is becoming increasingly common. How many people today would be willing to have their spouse chosen by their parents, relatives, or friends? How many would marry someone of a different religious background, ethnic affiliation, or social class? People who want to have the ultimate say in whom they choose to marry or who are willing to marry outside their religious, ethnic, or class group fail to conform to the most traditional partner-selection norms. (It might be interesting to inquire of married friends whether the husband asked the wife's parents for permission to marry. Or perhaps today, a more realistic question is whether either set of parents knew about their children's unmarried cohabitation prior to marriage.)

Consistent with the individualistic meaning of marriage and family is the idea that individuals should choose the people they want to love and perhaps live with or marry. That one's partner comes from a different community, social class, religion, or race is not the concern of relatives or church groups. These issues focusing on mate selection will be discussed in detail in Chapters 9 and 10.

Love

The issue of love, as related to marriage, considers several questions: Is love even necessary for marriage? If so, to what degree of intensity and to what extent of exclusiveness? On ideal-type continuums, the polar extremes are represented by (1) love not being a factor for consideration in marriage versus love being the sole and prime factor for marriage, (2) having no feelings of love versus having strong and complete feelings of love, and (3) loving only one person versus loving many people.

There is an obvious linkage among this issue of love, the previous issue of partner selection, and the next issue of sexual relationships. Traditionally in the United States and today in much of the world, kin, economic, and status considerations are still the key determinants for marriage. Love is expected to develop after marriage, not before. In contrast is the nontraditional idea that marriage without love is unthinkable. Romantic notions such as "Love makes the world go round" and "Love conquers all" are rooted in this idea.

Closely related to the issue as to whether or not love is necessary is that of the intensity of love. Clearly, feelings are subjective. The question is, How intense must

Global Diversity: Number of Marriage Partners

``Marry women of your choice,
Two, or three, or four;
But if ye fear that ye shall not
Be able to deal justly (with them),
Then only one..."

Source: The Holy Koran, Sura IV, Verse 3.

these subjective feelings be before they are real? Thus, references are made to "puppy love" or infatuation as feelings that are superficial and not the type upon which lasting relationships are built. Descriptions such as "romantic love," "conjugal love," "spiritual love" (agape), and "sexual love" (eros) have been used to identify different types of love or love conditions. In any case, attempts at understanding what love is, measuring how genuine or real it is, and analyzing its intensity have been basic problems for centuries and still engender debate and conflict today.

A final issue of love, particularly as it relates to marriage, is the exclusiveness of love relationships. Can someone love two people at once? Does loving one's partner or spouse eliminate the possibility of loving someone else? The traditional view of conjugal love demands devotion exclusively to one person, "in sickness and in health, for richer, for poorer," and so forth. This traditional relationship is all-absorbing and all-encompassing.

A conflicting view suggests that one person, spouse or otherwise, cannot and perhaps need not meet all of a partner's intimacy needs. Rather, an individual who is personally growing, developing, and changing will find that differing needs are fulfilled by different individuals. Thus, the fulfillment of various intimacy needs can be met outside of marriage without diminishing the love for a spouse. From this nontraditional perspective, if an individual is to grow and develop, one other person cannot fulfill all of his or her intimacy needs. This type of relationship allows each partner the right to new experiences and growth possibilities, both sexual and nonsexual. The result is more enriched relationships, with drastic reductions in feelings of possessiveness, rigidity of role expectations, and feelings of confinement.

As with the other issues, traditional and nontraditional views of love conflict. A person cannot have an exclusive love relationship and at the same time be open to other intimate relationships.

Sexual relationships

The central question surrounding the issue of sexual relationships is whether sexual relations (coitus) should be limited to marriage. Are there conditions or circumstances under which nonmarital, extramarital, or postmarital intercourse are legitimate? In addition, are there rational arguments for a so-called double standard, differentiating the sexual norms for men and women?

The traditional sacred norm is quite clear. Prior to the turn of the century, nonmarital, extramarital, postmarital, and even marital sexual relations for the purpose of pleasure were considered taboo. Officially, the mores allowed little deviation from this norm. Unofficially, a double standard existed, whereby sexual deviation by men, although not sanctioned, was understood and tolerated. Women were socialized to believe that sex was not important to them but was to their husbands, that sex should remain solely within the marital relationship, and that a good wife submitted to sex because that was her duty to her husband.

Various changes took place when the social meaning of marriage began to emerge. As established by the sacred meaning of marriage, sexual relationships outside of marriage were basically taboo, except among unmarried couples who were marriage-oriented or in love. The traditional social view of sex limited intercourse primarily to marriage; this also changed as sex became increasingly separated from reproduction and became a source of pleasure for both sexes. Anything occurring within the marital relationship was perfectly normal and satisfactory, as long as it was agreeable and not harmful to the couple involved. This latter view is the predominant position today.

The trend has been away from traditional sexual norms toward norms that question the double standard and the necessity of limiting sexual relationships to marriage. Most people enjoy sex. Why should this enjoyment be limited to a specific person (a spouse or fiancé) or certain circumstances (being in love)? If maturity and adulthood imply independence and the capacity to make one's own decisions, then two individuals—whether married or single, male or female—should have the choice as to when, where, and with whom to have sexual relationships. The publicity given to premarital cohabitation and same-sex liaisons documents the increasing prevalence of these sexual norms. As women seek equality with men, as it becomes increasingly possible to separate sex from parenthood, and as the primary informal means of control lessen, sexual independence and permissiveness are likely to result.

The implications of this sexual issue are far-reaching, affecting the family, the educational system, other social and legal institutions, and personal behavior. The conflict is again obvious. One cannot adhere to both extremes: namely, a sexual relationship within marriage primarily for reproductive purposes versus "sex as fun," in or out of marriage. These issues involving sexual relationships will be discussed in Chapter 11.

Family size and family planning

Closely related and directly limited to the issues of sexual relationships and marital and gender roles is the three-part issue of family size and family planning: (1) determining whether to have children, (2) determining how many to have and when, and (3) selecting the appropriate means to accomplish these ends. Several decades ago, extensive publicity on the population explosion and the need for zero population growth focused attention on family size. More recently, controversies over abortion (morality, use of public funds to pay for them), means of overcoming infertility (test-tube babies, surrogate parenting), and contraception (new methods, long-term effects) have raised new questions about how to have or prevent having children.

The most traditional norm, one highly consistent with the sacred meaning of marriage, suggests that the primary purpose of sex is reproduction, and the only approved context for reproduction is within marriage. (One biblical admonition is that families should be fruitful and multiply.) In the past, one-child families were not viewed as the ideal, and a mother who had only one or two children drew community concern. Even more problematic was pregnancy outside of marriage. The result was usually a forced, hasty marriage. A nonmarital pregnancy and birth brought shame to the family.

Traditionally, large families were an economic asset and contributed to the parents' security in old age; thus, children within marriage were highly valued. Few families consciously and successfully controlled family size. Many mothers took pride in proclaiming that they had produced and raised ten or fifteen healthy children. There may have been concern for the mother's health when one pregnancy occurred soon after another, but having a lot of children in close succession was not itself an issue.

As the social norms changed, so did the view of large families. Population shifts removed families from farms, which made children less of an economic asset. Increasingly, sex came to be viewed as being for pleasure as well as for reproduction. Children became a matter of choice rather than chance. The current norm pertaining to family size suggests that the maximum number of children should be two or three; to have four or six is to have too many, and to have ten or fourteen is disastrous. It is also socially acceptable for couples to have only one child or even no children.

The means of controlling the number of children has changed as well. The traditional norm suggests that only nonartificial or God-given means of fertility control are appropriate. Since each female naturally has a period of time each month when she cannot conceive, rhythm as a method of limiting family size is appropriate. This is consistent with the "will of God," since God created women. The traditional gender-role norm maintains that women are responsible for the prevention of pregnancy. Again, the timing of sexual relationships around the menstrual cycle is consistent with the sacred meaning attached to marriage.

The social meaning of marriage and perhaps the view most common among couples in U.S. society today suggests that any means of fertility control that is effective, nonharmful, and agreeable to both spouses is legitimate. As a result, the majority of both Catholics and non-Catholics in the United States today use some artificial contraceptive or birth-control method; the use of abortion to end unwanted pregnancies is also common. The social meaning of family planning agrees with the sacred meaning in that planning should be limited to the marital relationship; however, means of achieving family planning are not consistent between the two views.

The most nontraditional norms pertaining to family size, family planning, and childbirth in or out of marriage suggest that family-size limitation is an individual choice and the methods used to achieve it (rhythm, condoms, pills, diaphragms, IUDs, jellies, foams, Norplant, abortion, vasectomy, tubal ligation) should not be limited by laws or other measures of control. The current social norm places the responsibility for preventing conception on men as well as women, single as well as married. These issues of parenthood and family size (including unwed parenthood) will be presented in Chapter 11. Less attention will be focused on methods of birth control and means of family planning.

Aged family members

Traditional norms concerning the roles of people who are aged strongly suggest that these persons should be given deference, respect, and recognition. Traditionally, the eldest person had the most prestige, the widest experience, thus the greatest amount of wisdom. Elderly family members had various important roles to fulfill, particularly in advisory and leadership positions; enjoying and caring for children and grandchildren were also significant roles.

The changing social scene has also changed the role of the aged person in the American family. The number of persons over the age of sixty-five in the U.S. population has increased steadily throughout the twentieth century. Most men and women of this age are no longer employed at full-time jobs. For many, retirement means a lowered income, and for men, it means the loss of their major role as productive workers. Thus, the ascribed status of age per se no longer brings prestige.

The emergent norm suggests that elderly people must substitute play for work. This means a drastic shift in activities, self-definitions, and role performances. The basic issue for people who are aged is to create and maintain a meaningful way of life, which includes being able to contribute to life and to the society in which they live. The roles of older people, their marital patterns, retirement, and postmarital family styles will be discussed in Chapter 15.

Violence and abuse among intimates

The issue of violence and abuse among marriage and family members, while relatively new as a legitimate area of research, is not new to the U.S. or world scene. The traditional norms and values are well understood: Family members should care for one another, providing emotional support, understanding, and kindness. Of all social institutions, the family should be the haven where love, serenity, and security prevail in the midst of an often impersonal, uncaring, crime-filled, and violent world.

The nontraditional reality of violence and abuse in family life has been increasingly recognized. Reports of family members killing one another, husband and wife beatings, marital rape, incest, elderly and sibling abuse, and other variations of violence among intimates are common. Most attention has been focused on physical violence, including sexual abuse, although patterns of verbal, psychological, and emotional abuse are found in many families as well. Chapter 16 will examine these as well as other issues of violence among intimates.

Family permanence

The issue of family permanence addresses whether marriages and families are permanent, life-long commitments, or temporary, situational arrangements. If marriage and family are viewed as temporary, what criteria should be used to determine when one relationship should end and another begin? Also, what arrangements should be made to facilitate the change? For this issue, ideal-type constructs might include divorce/no divorce, total separation/no separation, or divorce for any reason/no reason.

The sacred view of marriage holds that marriage lasts until death (unless one happens to be a Mormon who marries in the temple, where the celestial marriage is for time and eternity). Thus, reorganizing the marital/family structure by means of divorce is not an option in resolving conflict. Marriage endures and remains legally intact, irrespective of personal unhappiness or conflict in the relationship. This traditional norm was especially prevalent prior to 1920 or 1930. Even today, this model is used when divorce is viewed as marital or family *disorganization,* or splitting up, rather than as *reorganization* to produce new forms, such as single-parent or reconstituted families involving at least one person who was previously married and divorced.

Less extreme than the idea of marriage as a permanent relationship, irrespective of persons or circumstances, is a second traditional norm that suggests certain conditions or reasons are legitimate for ending marital and family commitments. Adultery has long been a socially acceptable reason for ending a legal marital contract. Conditions that existed prior to the marriage, such as emotional instability and infertility, have also been considered grounds for dissolution. Even the Catholic church, which takes a sacramental view of marriage, accepts dissolution due to pre-existing conditions. *Annulment* is a type of marital dissolution recognized by the church and state; in effect, the marriage is deemed null and void, as if it never existed.

The most common means for ending a marital relationship (other than death) is divorce. The legal grounds for divorce are determined by individual states; thus, the reasons for permitting divorce vary. Traditionally, there was general agreement that one party had to be at fault. Over time, citing fault was deemed irrelevant; several states made legal changes and most states interpreted existing laws more leniently. While many people believe that a major reason for increased divorce rates has been legal changes that facilitate dissolution, it is more likely that greater tolerance toward divorce is responsible for higher rates. Although a widely held social norm maintains that divorce should come only as a last resort, after all other options have been considered, movement has been toward greater acceptance of divorce. In any case, the 1970s witnessed a major increase in divorce rates; levels in the 1980s exceeded any in U.S. history.

An emergent norm concerning family reorganization suggests that marital success stems less from permanence and more from the meaningful, dynamic interaction of persons, even if the partners may change. In fact, maintaining a relationship that is, for all practical purposes, broken may be considered less moral than getting a divorce. Thus, divorce may be viewed as a solution for other types of problems.

The result of these changing norms is that marriages may have become more vital and successful than ever before in American history. People today are married out of personal desire rather than social or sacred obligations. Norval Glenn, for one, has taken exception to this argument. He has claimed that, when people have the option or are encouraged to end unsatisfactory relationships, existing marriages become so insecure that rational people will not invest a great deal of time, energy, or money in such unions. Individuals will not make more than tentative, limited commitments in marriage or intimate pairings. This level of commitment is not enough to provide security and emotional support for its members; they will not attain maximum happiness and satisfaction.[15]

The same traditional/nontraditional issue exists in regard to remarriage. Prior to the Civil War, remarriage was a right held only by the "innocent party," or whoever was not at fault in the divorce. Many clergy refused to marry divorced persons. In certain fundamentalist denominations, this is still the situation today. Within the Catholic church, as well, canon law prohibits the remarriage of divorced persons previously married in the church unless that marriage has been annulled. In actual practice, some priests do overlook this requirement and perform marriage ceremonies for divorced persons. The remarriage rate of divorced persons is high.

The basic nature of the issue of marital and family reorganization should be evident. Conflicts exist between those who adhere to the sacred meaning of marriage, accepting no reasons for dissolution, and those who grant social approval to temporary marital relationships.

Other contemporary issues

There are an extensive number of issues that are not likely to be classified as marriage or family issues per se but that have direct bearing on family life. At the most general level, every social policy and social problem is family-related: pollution,

---

[15] Norval D. Glenn, "Continuity Versus Change, Sanguineness Versus Concern," *Journal of Family Issues* 8 (December 1987): 351.

U.S. Diversity: Marriage Vows: Before and After

He married her because among other things, her hair looked so beautiful.

He divorced her because she spent so much time fixing her hair.

She married him because his muscles rippled so much when he swam.

She divorced him because he spent more time in the bedroom doing sitting-up exercises than anything else.

He married her because she was such an adept conversationalist, never at a loss for a word.

He divorced her because she never got off the telephone.

She married him because he loved to take her dancing.

She divorced him because he was "tired" most of the time.

He married her because she was so "vivacious."

He divorced her because she was too restless.

She married him because he could support her in lavish style.

She divorced him because he had too firm a hold on the purse-strings.

He married her because their families shared a common background.

He divorced her because her family kept interfering in their affairs.

She married him because he had a robust masculine appetite and appreciated her cooking.

She divorced him because he never wanted to take her out to eat.

He married her because she was quick, neat, and intelligent.

He divorced her because she had absolutely no patience with the children, who were sometimes slow, slovenly, and stupid.

She married him because he was a "real sport."

She divorced him because he refused to give up the sporting life.

He married her because they shared the same intellectual and political beliefs.

He divorced her because she wasn't interested in anything but the house and the kids.

She married him because he was so courteous and attentive in all the little things that matter so to a woman.

She divorced him because he was so punctilious about little things, and so oblivious to important things.

He married her because all the other men were so impressed with her magnificent figure.

He divorced her, after the third child, because she had "let herself go."

Source: Sidney Harris, "Marriage Vows: Before and After," *Detroit Free Press,* 21 November 1966, p. 15-A. Copyright Publishers–Hall Syndicate. Used with permission.

international trade, taxation, immigration, affirmative action, student loans, school prayer, burning the flag, and so forth.

Families are instrumental in the socialization process (see Chapter 14), by which individuals learn what issues are important as well as how to view or approach them. Likewise, social events, social circumstances, and social policies tend to influence people's behaviors and life-styles. Three significant social issues of this type will be addressed briefly in the following sections.

AIDS

One prominent social issue is AIDS (Acquired Immune Deficiency Syndrome). First reported in 1981, the term AIDS has become a household word and a world-

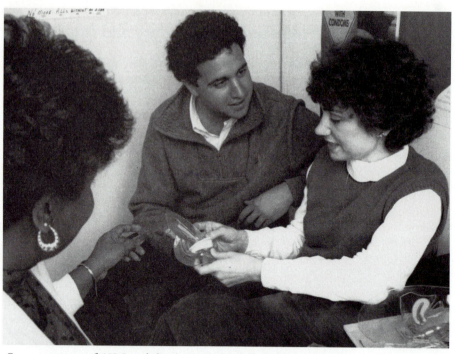

One consequence of AIDS and the transmission of the AIDS virus has been to sensitize couples to obtain contraceptive education and to practice "safe sex," particularly with the use of condoms.

wide health epidemic. Most people are aware that the virus is transmitted in three major ways: having sex with someone who has AIDS; sharing needles for drug use with someone who has AIDS; and transmission from an AIDS-infected mother to an infant before, during, or after birth. The AIDS virus can also be transmitted by blood transfusion.

The Centers for Disease Control and Prevention in Atlanta, states that as of June 1995, in the United States alone nearly 500,000 AIDS cases and 300,000 deaths have been reported.[16] Between 630,000 and 900,000 Americans were believed to be alive with HIV. Estimates are that 1 in every 92 American men ages 27 to 39 may be battling the AIDS virus. Black men are especially hard hit with 1 of every 33 young men estimated to be infected (compared to 1 in 60 Hispanic and 1 in 139 non-Hispanic white men). About 1 in 98 black women, age 27–39, are estimated to be infected (compared to 1 in 222 Hispanic and 1 in 1,667 non-Hispanic white women). The Centers for Disease Control and Prevention announced that AIDS has become the number one killer of people ages 25 to 44.

Because no cure has been found to date, AIDS presents to the world a crisis with profound implications for mate selection, sexual relationships, and

---

[16] U.S. Department of Health and Human Services, *HIV/AIDS Surveillance Report,* Atlanta: Centers for Disease Control and Prevention 7 (Mid-year edition): Tables 1 and 9.

parent/child interactions.[17] Although AIDS was originally perceived as a disease confined to homosexuals, current research has indicated that its incidence has increased greatly in the heterosexual population as well as among newborns. Even before AIDS, there were other sexually transmitted diseases, including syphilis, gonorrhea, and herpes. Most of these diseases can be cured; all can at least be controlled with treatment.

The traditional *sacred* norm in regard to sexually transmitted diseases was one of avoidance through sexual abstinence apart from marriage. The traditional *social* norm toward sexually transmitted diseases (and more specifically, toward AIDS) supports heterosexuality and, if one is sexually active, "safe-sex" practices, such as using condoms and limiting sexual relations to a love- or marriage-oriented partner. The contemporary reality with nontraditional norms includes gay communities, homosexual partners (including some who define themselves as married), sexually active adolescents, and adults who are not married and have no intent to marry. Another reality is that many people do not practice safe sex. The AIDS issue is very real and has profound implications for marriage and family life.

Abortion

Abortion, another highly visible social issue, has a direct impact on the family. It is related to the issues of sexual relationships, and family size and family planning, presented previously. Abortion involves a pregnancy and thus focuses on the meaning of life. The importance of choice and deciding one's own destiny is also a central issue. Thus, abortion is about more than sexual behavior and family planning; it focuses on a wide range of values.

The traditional *sacred* norm sees a pregnancy as a life, as God-given, and not to be destroyed out of social or personal concerns. This antiabortion (pro-life) stance advocates restrictive policies toward abortion. The traditional *social* norm may or may not define conception as the beginning of human life. The viability of that life on its own (depending on the length of time since conception) is an important factor. The traditional social norm supports abortion in certain situations, such as when there is a defective fetus, when there are complications due to the age or health of the mother, and in cases of rape or incest. This stance toward abortion advocates restrictive policies under certain conditions and permissive policies under others.

The nontraditional norm toward abortion focuses on individual and personal decisions. This pro-abortion (pro-choice) stance advocates a permissive policy, allowing a woman absolute choice. A number of questions must be considered: Was the pregnancy planned and desired? If born, would the child be properly supported and cared for? Will the pregnancy, birth, and parenthood disrupt college,

---

[17] See Eleanor Macklin (ed.), *AIDS and Families,* Birmingham, NY.: The Haworth Press, 1989; and Joan Huber and Beth E. Schneider (eds.), *The Social Context of AIDS* (Newbury Park, CA: Sage Publications, Inc.), 1992.

News Item: Personal Decisions on Church Teachings

As reported by the Associated Press (15 June 1992), a majority of U.S. Catholics think they should make up their own minds on such issues as abortion and birth control rather than follow church teachings.

In a poll of 1,250 respondents, conducted by Yankelovich Clancy Shulman in June 1992, 79 percent of Catholics disagreed with the statement "Using artificial means of birth control is wrong." Sixty-three percent said they favored allowing priests to be married.

Catholics have the same opinions on abortion as the public as a whole: 84 percent of Americans and 81 percent of Catholics favor abortion if the woman's life is in jeopardy. And while 47 percent of Americans favor allowing abortion for any reason during the first trimester of pregnancy, 45 percent of Catholics support this notion.

Only 14 percent of Catholics believe they should always obey church teachings.

marriage, and career plans? The most important question is about the right to choose: Should a court or a group of legislators (both usually male-dominated) or anyone else (be it a relative, a member of the clergy, or a physician) dictate what a woman does with her body and her life? Again, the abortion issue is one that impacts marriage and family life in significant ways.[18]

Homelessness

The third and final issue to be addressed at this point is that of housing and the homeless. A *house* provides physical shelter. A *home* anchors a family in a community and provides them with stability and a place with which each member identifies. Both shelter and stability could be argued to be essential basic human needs.

Homelessness involves more than isolated individuals; it is increasingly recognized as a family issue in U.S. society. One source claims that families with children represent the fastest-growing segment of the homeless.[19] The vast majority of families are homeless for economic reasons and most were poor before they became homeless. Others are unable to pay the rent, mortgage, or taxes: some lose

---

[18] Interested readers may want to examine H. W. Smith and Cindy Kronauge, "The Politics of Abortion: Husband Notification Legislation, Self-Disclosure, and Marital Bargaining," *The Sociological Quarterly* 31 (1990): 585–598; and Hyman Rodman, "Should Parental Involvement Be Required for Minors' Abortions?" *Family Relations* 40 (April 1991): 155–160.

[19] Elaine A. Anderson and Sally A. Koblinsky, "The Need to Speak to Families," *Family Relations* 44 (January 1995): 13–18. See also: Elliot Liebow, *Tell Them Who I Am* (New York: The Free Press, 1993).

the homes they rented, were buying, or even owned. Others are forced to move because their homes are sold from under them, destroyed by fire, or allowed by landlords to become uninhabitable. Some women and children, subjected to family violence, flee their homes. Most families stay with friends or relatives and exhaust all other options before they turn to shelters or the street.

It is not difficult to perceive the devastation homelessness causes parents and children. The toll on health, education, emotional development, and self-identity that results from being poor or in poverty is in itself major (see Chapter 7), but being homeless magnifies all issues. Even basic needs, such as having a place to sleep or bathe, are difficult to meet; needs for education and medical attention may be impossible to meet.

The traditional norm is that all persons deserve and need housing. But this norm is rooted in basic beliefs that anyone who tries hard enough can prosper and that rugged individualism is more important than commitment to community. The result is the nontraditional alternative of many families being poor, unable to afford even low-income housing, and forced, quite literally, into the street. Climbing rents, the lack of affordable housing, waiting lists for existing housing, and the retreat of the federal government from providing housing or legal assistance to the poor magnify this issue. The long-term underlying effects of the crisis of homelessness on U.S. society are only beginning to be understood. Discussion of family policy that can be applied to this and other issues will be presented in the final chapter.

CHARACTERISTICS OF U.S. FAMILIES

The United States Bureau of the Census is a primary source of numerical data about families in this country. To provide an introduction to the American family, a summary of various characteristics will be presented in the following discussion, as portrayed by census material. More specific characteristics, statements of relationships, and research findings will be presented throughout the book in the chapters appropriate to specific topic discussions.

In 1995, the total resident population of the United States was estimated at 263.4 million.[20] This included approximately 128.7 million males and 134.7 million females. By race, this included 218.3 million classified as white (82.9 percent), 33.1 million classified as black (12.6 percent), and 12.0 million classified as other races (4.5 percent). "Other races," as used by the Census Bureau, does not denote any scientific definition of biological stock. It is based on the self-identification of respondents and classification into one of fifteen groups that, in addition to white and black, include American Indian, Eskimo, Aleut, Japanese, Chinese, Filipino, Hawaiian, Samoan, Asian Indian, Korean, Vietnamese, Guamanian, and

---

[20] U.S. Bureau of the Census, *Statistical Abstract of the United States: 1995*, 115th ed. (Washington, DC: U.S. Government Printing Office, 1995), Table 12, p. 14.

other individuals. Persons of Hispanic origin (who may be of any race but who classified themselves as Mexican American, Chicano, Mexican, Puerto Rican, Cuban, Central or South American, or other Hispanic origin) number 26.8 million persons, or 10.2 percent of all households.

Numbers of families and households

The term *family*, as used in census reporting, refers to a group of two or more persons related by birth, marriage, or adoption and who reside together in a household.

In 1994, there were 68.5 million family households in the United States. Of these, 53.2 million were considered to be married couples (husband/wife families), 2.9 million were families with a male householder/no wife present, and 12.4 million were families with a female householder/no husband present.[21] Beginning with the 1980 *Current Population Report*, the Bureau of the Census discontinued use of the term *head of the family or household*, substituting the terms *householder* and *family householder*. This change resulted from a recognition that household or family responsibilities are frequently shared among the adult members of both genders. This significant classification shift discontinued a longtime practice of always classifying the husband as the reference person (head) when he and his wife are living together. Today's *head of family*—that is, *family householder*—is legitimately recognized as either female or male.

A *family* is different from a **household**. A household consists of all persons who occupy a housing unit. A house, an apartment or other group of rooms, or a single room is regarded as a housing unit when it is occupied or intended for occupancy as separate living quarters. A household includes related family members and all other unrelated persons, if any, such as lodgers, foster children, wards, and employees. A person living alone in a housing unit or a group of unrelated persons sharing a housing unit is also counted as a household.

Thus, not all households contain families. In 1994, there were 97.1 million U.S. households,[22] and, as illustrated by Figure 1-1, the proportion of nonfamily households has increased. In 1950, only about one in ten households (10 percent) was of the nonfamily type, but by 1994, about 30 percent were nonfamily units. In other words, changes over the past forty years show that an increasing number and proportion of people are living alone or with nonfamily members.

Sizes of families and households

Family size refers to the number of persons who are living together and are related by birth, marriage, or adoption. The average size of a U.S. family was 3.2 persons in 1994. The average size of a family with a married couple was 3.26 persons, com-

---

21 U.S. Bureau of the Census, *Current Population Reports* Series P20-483, Steven W. Rawlings and Arlene F. Saluter, "Household and Family Characteristics: March 1994" (Washington, DC: U.S. Government Printing Office, 1995), Table A, p. vii.

22 Ibid., Table A, p. vii.

Figure 1-1

Family and nonfamily households as percentage of all households:
1950–1994

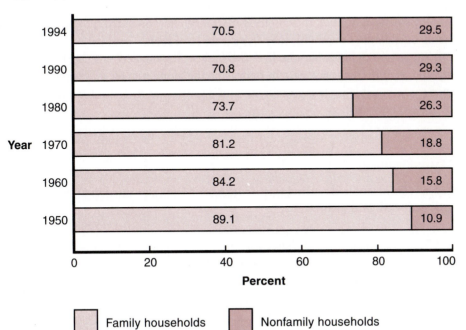

Year

Year	Family households	Nonfamily households
1994	70.5	29.5
1990	70.8	29.3
1980	73.7	26.3
1970	81.2	18.8
1960	84.2	15.8
1950	89.1	10.9

Percent

☐ Family households   ☐ Nonfamily households

Source: U.S. Bureau of the Census, *General Population Characteristics: United States Summary* (Washington, DC: U.S. Government Printing Office, 1983), Figure 18, p. 15; and U.S. Bureau of the Census, *Current Population Reports* Series P20-483, Steven W. Rawlings and Arlene F. Saluter, "Household and Family Characteristics: March 1994" (Washington, DC: U.S. Government Printing Office, 1995), Table B, p. vii.

pared to 2.79 for a family with a male householder and 3.05 for a family with a female householder. The average size of white families was 3.14 persons, compared to an average of 3.5 for black families and 3.93 for Hispanic-origin families.[23]

Households had fewer persons per unit than did families in 1994. The average number of persons per household was 2.67 compared to 3.2 for families. The number of persons per household has decreased considerably since the earliest census reports were taken. The average size of a household was 5.4 in 1790, 4.2 in 1900, 3.3 in 1940, and, 2.67 in 1994. Thus, the average household has 2.73 fewer persons today than it did at the end of the eighteenth century.

This decrease in average household size may have some positive influence on the interaction of its members and the social connectedness with others outside the household. However, while many households can adjust to include more members, others report increased instances of aggression, disagreement, frustration, and general dissatisfaction.

[23] Ibid., Table 1, pp. 1–4.

One national study found that a shortage of household space affected parental attitudes negatively; parents felt unable to control their children's actions, made more complaints, and were dissatisfied with leisure time.[24] Another national survey concluded that persons who live alone do not feel they are isolated and forced into the situation. Rather, they prefer this arrangement, provided they have attachments outside the household; they frequently have higher levels of social contact and integration than people who live with others. The smaller[25] average household size and even the large increase in persons living alone suggest a life-style preference made possible by rising affluence and a greater desire for autonomy among all age groups in society.

Marital status

Census classification of **marital status** identifies four major categories: single, married, widowed, and divorced.

- A *married couple* is a husband and wife who are counted as members of the same household and who may or may not have children living with them.
- A *single person* is one who has never been married.
- A *widowed person* is a female (widow) or a male (widower) who is no longer married due to the death of his or her spouse.
- A *divorced person* is one who is no longer married as a result of a legal decree that ended the marriage.

As shown in Table 1-2, approximately 91.2 million men and 98.8 million women were age eighteen or over in 1994. For men, 62.5 percent were married, 27.1 percent were single, 2.4 percent were widowed, and 7.9 percent were divorced. For women, 58.8 percent were married, 19.7 percent were single, 11.2 percent were widowed, and 10.3 percent were divorced. Thus, ignoring age differences, men are more likely than women to be married or single, and women are more likely than men to be widowed or divorced.

Marriage was and continues to be popular. About 80 percent of American men between the ages of forty-five and seventy-four and more than 72 percent of American women between the ages of thirty-five and fifty-four are currently married. That less than 5 percent of both men and women over age fifty-five are listed as *single* suggests that at least 95 percent (nineteen out of twenty persons) of these persons married at some point in their lives. These rates, however, are likely to drop.

---

[24] Mark Baldassare, "The Effects of Household Density on Subgroups," *American Sociological Review* 46 (February 1981): 110–118.

[25] Duane Y. Alwin, Philip E. Converse, and Steven S. Martin, "Living Arrangements and Social Integration," *Journal of Marriage and the Family* 47 (May 1985): 319–334.

Table 1-2

Marital status of the population, by sex and age: 1994 (persons 18 years old and over)

Sex and Age	Number of Persons (1,000)					Percent Distribution				
	Total	Single	Married	Widowed	Divorced	Total	Single	Married	Widowed	Divorced
Male	**91,222**	**24,727**	**57,028**	**2,221**	**7,245**	**100.0**	**27.1**	**62.5**	**2.4**	**7.9**
18 to 19 years old	3,462	3,375	80	2	5	100.0	97.5	2.3	0.1	0.1
20 to 24 years old	9,221	7,469	1,658	5	89	100.0	81.0	18.0	0.1	1.0
25 to 29 years old	9,765	4,910	4,422	9	424	100.0	50.3	45.3	0.1	4.3
30 to 34 years old	11,108	3,298	6,940	6	864	100.0	29.7	62.5	0.1	7.8
35 to 39 years old	10,892	2,094	7,603	31	1,164	100.0	19.2	69.8	0.3	10.7
40 to 44 years old	9,651	1,255	7,104	31	1,262	100.0	13.0	73.6	0.3	13.1
45 to 54 years old	14,454	1,185	11,362	137	1,770	100.0	8.2	78.6	0.9	12.2
55 to 64 years old	9,933	539	8,034	327	1,033	100.0	5.4	80.9	3.3	10.4
65 to 74 years old	7,924	390	6,353	695	486	100.0	4.9	80.2	8.8	6.1
75 years old and over	4,812	211	3,471	980	150	100.0	4.4	72.1	20.4	3.1
Female	**98,765**	**19,458**	**58,113**	**11,073**	**10,120**	**100.0**	**19.7**	**58.8**	**11.2**	**10.2**
18 to 19 years old	3,454	3,152	278	3	21	100.0	91.3	8.0	0.1	0.6
20 to 24 years old	9,338	6,162	2,931	11	234	100.0	66.0	31.4	0.1	2.5
25 to 29 years old	9,861	3,476	5,689	29	667	100.0	35.2	57.7	0.3	6.8
30 to 34 years old	11,212	2,228	7,703	80	1,202	100.0	19.9	68.7	0.7	10.7
35 to 39 years old	11,078	1,420	7,959	135	1,563	100.0	12.8	71.8	1.2	14.1
40 to 44 years old	9,906	909	7,358	146	1,492	100.0	9.2	74.3	1.5	15.1
45 to 54 years old	15,068	892	10,977	705	2,494	100.0	5.9	72.8	4.7	16.6
55 to 64 years old	10,805	440	7,500	1,501	1,364	100.0	4.1	69.4	13.9	12.6
65 to 74 years old	10,163	386	5,520	3,476	781	100.0	3.8	54.3	34.2	7.7
75 years old and over	7,880	393	2,199	4,986	302	100.0	5.0	27.9	63.3	3.8

Source: U.S. Bureau of the Census, *Statistical Abstract of the United States: 1995*, 115th ed. (Washington, DC: U.S. Government Printing Office, 1995), no. 59, p. 55.

The large numbers of nonmarried males and females at the young and old ends of the age spectrum reflect a premarital status for young single persons and a postmarital status (widowed or divorced) for older persons. Note the vast differences shown in the data (see Table 1-2) between widowed men and women between ages sixty-five and seventy-four (8.8 percent men versus 34.2 percent women) and after age seventy-five (20.4 percent men versus 63.3 percent women).

The percentage of men and women who are divorced in a given year holds fairly constant for persons between the ages of thirty-five and sixty-four (10.4 percent to 13.1 percent for men; 14.1 to 16.6 percent for women). Even in the maximum age category, only 16.6 percent of women and about 13.1 percent of men are divorced. Thus, in spite of all the talk and concern about "easy divorce," "marital breakdown," and "family decay," at any given time, most of the United States adult population is married, and, when divorced, most people remarry.

Family income

Family income refers to the total amount of earnings reported by related persons who were members of the family during the time specified. In the census, each family member fifteen years of age and over was asked the amount of income received in the preceding calendar year from sources such as wages or salaries, self-employment, unemployment compensation, Social Security, dividends, interest, rental income, child support, public assistance or welfare payments, and other periodic income. Income did not include amounts from sources such as the sale of property (stocks, bonds, a house, or a car) nor did it include borrowed money, tax refunds, gifts, or lump-sum inheritance or insurance payments. The total income of a family is the sum of the amounts received by all income recipients in the family.

Family income has increased considerably since 1970. The median family income in 1993 was $36,959 compared to $9,867 in 1970. This 375 percent increase appears impressive until the figures are adjusted for the changes in consumer prices and inflation. The median family income of $36,959, in constant 1993 dollars, was comparable to a 1970 value of $34,523, which is an increase of $2,436 in actual purchasing power.

As might be expected, rates of growth as well as median income for families varied widely by social categories. For example, in 1992, the median income of white families was $38,909, compared to $21,161 for black families and $23,901 for Hispanic families. Families with a male householder/no wife present had a median income much higher than those with a female householder/no husband present ($27,821 versus $17,221). Married couples with a wife in the paid labor force had a median family income of $49,984, while couples where the wife was not in the paid labor force had an income of $30,326. U.S. families living in the Northeast had a higher median income than those living in the South ($40,884 versus $33,028). Families with householders who had a college education of four years or more had a median income of about $51,000, compared to $34,000 for householders with a high school diploma and $18,000 for householders with less than an eighth-grade education.[26]

Many other examples could be given to illustrate the wide range of median incomes for families in the United States. In any case, it should be clear that family incomes differ dramatically by gender, race, marital status, employment of one or both spouses, educational attainment, and other factors.

TODAY'S FAMILIES: SIGNIFICANT CHANGES

Dramatic changes over time and diversity at any given point are illustrated by various **demographics**, or social statistics of a population. Consider the following factors, which are supported by data from the U.S. Bureau of the Census.[27]

- Throughout the 1980s and 1990s, the United States had one of the highest marriage and divorce rates among the world's industrialized countries.

- About 3.7 million unmarried couples lived together in 1994, seven times the 523,000 who lived together unmarried in 1970.

- By 1993, the median age of people at first marriage had increased about three-and-one-half years since 1970, from 23.2 to 26.5 for men and 20.8 to 24.5 for women; about two years of this increase occurred since 1980.

- In 1994, 66.0 percent of the women age twenty to twenty-four were never married, compared to 50.2 percent in 1980 and 35.8 percent in 1970. For men of similar age, 81.0 percent were never married, compared to 68.8 percent in 1980 and 54.7 percent in 1970.

- The number of divorced persons per thousand married persons in 1993 had increased more than three times since 1970 (from 47 in 1970 to 152 in 1993).

- Slightly more than one-fourth (26 percent) of the nation's 53.2 million married–couple families in 1994 had children under age eighteen in the home, compared to nearly half (49.6 percent) in 1970.

- One-parent families accounted for 26.7 percent of all families with children under age eighteen in 1993, up from 11.9 percent in 1970.

- In 1994, the most common household size was two persons (32 percent), but the next most common size was one person (24 percent). The average number of persons per household had decreased to 2.67 in 1994 from 2.76 in 1980 and 3.14 in 1970.

---

[26] U.S. Bureau of the Census, *Current Population Reports*, Series P-60, No. 184, "Money Income of Households, Families, and Persons in the United States: 1992 (Washington, DC: U.S. Government Printing Office, 1993, Tables 13 and 14, pp. 40–45.

[27] All figures in this paragraph and the section that follows were taken from U.S. Bureau of the Census, *Current Population Reports*, Series P-60, No. 184; *Statistical Abstract of the United States: 1995*; and *Current Population Reports*, Series P-20–477 and P-20–478 (Washington, DC: U.S. Government Printing Office, 1994).

- The number of persons living alone increased from 11 million in 1970 to nearly 24 million in 1994. This was about one of every nine persons in the United States.

- Between 1970 and 1994, the number of interracial married couples among the fifteen groups listed in the race item on the census questionnaire increased more than three times (from 310,000 to 1,283,000), but still made up only about 2.4 percent of all married couples. Black/white interracial married couples increased from 65,000 to 296,000 during those twenty-four years but made up only 0.5 percent of the total.

- Less than 5 percent of the people over age fifty had never married. While the number of people who remain single is increasing, statistics show that most men and women marry at some time in their lives.

- Approximately 17.5 percent of women aged fifteen to forty-four were childless in 1993, up from 16.4 percent in 1970.

- Approximately 21.4 million single (never married) women gave birth to a child in 1992, 12.7 million more than in 1970.

- Children born in 1995 had a projected life expectancy of about 76.3 years (79.7 for females, 72.8 for males). This figure was up from 73.7 in 1980, 68.2 in 1950, and 54.0 in 1920.

- The number of persons living below the official government poverty level was 39.3 million in 1993, or 15.1 percent of the U.S. population. In 1970, 25.4 million, or 12.6 percent of the population, lived below the poverty level.

- The number of families living below the poverty level in 1993 was 8.4 million, or 12.3 percent of all U.S. families. This included 9.4 percent of white families not of Hispanic-origin, 31.3 percent of black families, and 27.3 percent of Hispanic-origin families. Among female householders with no husband present, this included 28.1 percent of white women, 49.8 percent of black women, and 48.8 percent of Hispanic women.

Need more illustrations be given? Census data alone (apart from the countless number of completed research studies) illustrate quite clearly the pluralistic and changing nature of the U.S. family. More detailed breakdowns of characteristics such as these will be presented at appropriate places in the text.

SUMMARY

1. This first chapter introduces some basic issues and characteristics of U.S. families. While all family systems adhere to similar norms and values, great diversity exists in family structures, attitudes, and behaviors.

2. Ideal-type constructs provide a means of illustrating the range of perspectives between two extremes (along a continuum). This tool can be used to examine major issues in the U.S. family, evaluating traditional and nontra-

ditional norms. Each issue involves conflict as a result of social change; that is, traditional patterns coexist with nontraditional patterns. Were there no change or were there total change, no conflicts or issues would exist.

3. The most important family issue, that to which all other issues are related, is the meaning given to marriage and the family. The most traditional social norm holds that marriage and the family are sacred phenomena, created and maintained by God and thus beyond control of human beings. Less traditional is the norm that suggests that marriage is created and maintained by society: kin, community, and social institutions. The emergent norm suggests that marriage is created and maintained *by* the individual, *for* the individual. Thus, at least three meanings that are basically incompatible exist simultaneously. Only when individual meanings, social meanings, and sacred meanings are identical will there be no conflict.

4. Related issues include marital and family organization; functions of the family; marital- and gender-role differentiation; social class and social mobility; mate selection; the need for and degree of love; the limits of sexual relationships; family size and family planning; the role of people who are aged in society; violence and abuse among intimates; family permanence; and other contemporary issues such as AIDS, abortion, and homelessness.

5. It is impossible to state with certainty that one issue is more important than another. For young, single people, primary issues may be mate selection and sexual relationships. For married couples, primary issues may be family planning and marital roles. For elderly persons, primary issues may be the functions of the family and the roles of older people in society. The meaning given to marriage and the family, if maintained consistently from one issue to another, will influence, for example, whether one is for divorce or against it, for abortion or opposed to it, or for extramarital sex or opposed to it.

6. This chapter, while highly descriptive, presented an overview of issues and changes in the family within the United States, concluding with some demographic data about families in the United States: number of families and households, size of families and households, marital status, family income, and selected significant family changes that have taken place over the past 20 or 25 years. Chapter 2 will focus on disciplinary and theoretical approaches to family study.

KEY TERMS AND TOPICS

DISCUSSION QUESTIONS

1. How would you define marriages and families? Must persons be related legally? Biologically? Residentially? Psychologically? Explain.

2. Consult five married adults and ask about their perceptions of the most important issues in marriage and the family today. Do the same with five single adults. Compare results.

3. Which issue (of those listed in question 2 or another) do you perceive as the most significant or serious today? Why? How can this issue be resolved?

4. Why do marriages exist today? What is their purpose? What or who should be the ultimate authority?

5. If conflict exists between traditional and nontraditional marital and family norms, do the adherents of either position have a right to impose their view on the other? Take, for example, the couple who wants an abortion versus people who argue that abortion is wrong. Explain your answer.

6. Can a person love more than one person simultaneously? Can an intimate relationship with someone other than a person's spouse enrich his or her relationship with that spouse? Why?

7. Over the past thirty or forty years, has there been a greater change in gender norms for men or for women? Support your choice. Are conflicts over gender and marital roles primarily a thing of the past, or will these conflicts continue? Why?

8. Is an increase in the divorce rate indicative of a breakdown of marriage and the family in the United States? What about an increase in nonmarital and extramarital sexual relations, out-of-wedlock births, and interracial marriages? Why?

9. AIDS, abortion, and homelessness were discussed as contemporary family-related issues. What moral issues are also involved in each? To resolve these issues, what types of social policies need to be implemented and by whom?

10. This chapter ended with a section titled "Today's Families: Significant Changes." Select several of the changes given, and ask the question, Why?

For example: Why does the United States have some of the highest marriage and divorce rates among the world's industrialized countries? Why has there been an increase in median age at marriage over the last twenty years? Why has there been an increase in persons living alone over the same time period?

FURTHER READINGS

Acock, Alan C., and Demo, David H. *Family Diversity and Well-Being.* Thousand Oaks, CA: Sage, 1994. Based on the National Survey of Families and Households, the authors examine four family types: two-parent families, divorced mothers with children, remarried families, and unwed mothers.

Bird, Gloria W., and Sporakowski, Michael J., eds. *Taking Sides: Clashing Views on Controversial Issues in Family and Personal Relationships.* Guilford, CT: Dushkin, 1994. Opposing viewpoints are taken on seventeen controversial issues relating to family and personal relationships.

Brubaker, Timothy H., ed. *Family Relations: Challenges for the Future.* Newbury Park, CA: Sage Publications, 1993. Twelve articles explore selected current issues in the contemporary American family.

Conger, Rand, and Elder, Glen H., in collaboration with Lorenz, Frederick O., Simons, Ronald L., and Whitbeck, Les B., eds. *Families in Troubled Times: Adapting to Change in Rural America.* New York: A. de Gruyter, 1994. Based on the Iowa Youth and Families Project, thirteen chapters are organized around a specific theory of family economic issues.

Edgar, Timothy; Fitzpatrick, Mary Anne; and Freimuth, Vicki S., eds. *AIDS: A Communication Perspective.* Hillsdale, NJ: Erlbaum Associates, 1992. An examination of how theory informs our understanding of communication processes as they relate to the AIDS crisis around the world.

Goldscheider, Frances K., and Waite, Linda J. *New Families, No Families?* Berkeley: University of California Press, 1991. An examination of two revolutions confronting the family, one of changes inside and the other outside; presents a profound choice of creating new families or of being left with no families.

Gottfried, Adele Eskeles, and Gottfried, Allen W., eds. *Redefining Families: Implications for Children's Development.* New York: Plenum Press, 1994. Eight chapters dealing with some of the implications for children of new family arrangements, such as primary-caregiving fathers, dual-earner employment status, lesbian mothers, gay fathers, and custodial grandparenting.

Gubrium, Jaber F., and Holstein, James A. *What Is Family?* Mountain View, CA: Mayfield, 1990. An examination of family discourse with the theme that the everyday reality of the family is as much a way of thinking and talking about relationships as it is a concrete set of social ties and sentiments.

Jencks, Christopher. *The Homeless.* Cambridge: Harvard University Press, 1994. An examination of the steady increase in the number of homeless people in the United States, including how widespread homelessness is, how it happened, and what can be done about it.

Jones, Charles L.; Tepperman, Lorne; and Wilson, Susannah J. *The Futures of the Family.* Englewood Cliffs, NJ.: Prentice-Hall, Inc., 1995. A brief overview of changes in family life with a final chapter focusing on families in the future.

Kain, Edward L. *The Myth of Family Decline.* Lexington, MA: Lexington Books, 1990. A brief paperback that focuses on family change: ways of thinking about it and actual changes in U.S. families.

Seltser, Barry Jay, and Miller, Donald E. *Homeless Families: The Struggle for Dignity.* Urbana, IL: University of Illinois Press, 1993. Based on interviews with 100 homeless families living in shelters, the authors provide a glimpse of what it means to lose one's dignity and to be homeless.

Skolnick, Arlene S., and Skolnick, Jerome H., eds. *Family in Transition*, 7th ed. New York: HarperCollins, 1992. A book of readings, with major sections on the changing family, gender and sex, coupling, children in the family, and a wider perspective of families in society.

Chapter 2

Disciplinary and Theoretical Approaches to Family Study

■ Disciplines Involved in Family Study

■ Social Science Approach to the Family
  Sociology of the family
  Uses of family sociology

■ Nature of Research and Theoretical Frames of Reference
  Concepts and variables
  Conceptual frameworks
  Propositions and hypotheses
  Theories

■ Theories and Frames of Reference
  Structural-functional frame of reference
  Social conflict frame of reference
  Symbolic interaction frame of reference
  Social exchange frame of reference
  Developmental frame of reference

■ Appraisal and Expansion of Contemporary Family Theory
  Feminist frame of reference

■ Summary

■ Key Terms and Topics

■ Discussion Questions

■ Further Readings

Chapter 1 was a general introduction to the family, particularly families in the United States. It provided some descriptive material and then examined selected major issues in the American family system through the use of ideal-type constructs. This general overview was intended to provide the foundation for and introduce the various issues, topics, and themes that are considered in the following chapters. Many disciplines, approaches, and frames of reference can be used to study these family-related issues. These various perspectives will be examined in this chapter, with emphasis given to the basic approaches and orientations emphasized throughout this book.

DISCIPLINES INVOLVED IN FAMILY STUDY

The area of marriage and the family touches on a wide range of topics, lends itself to many types of research, and uses the results of the research in various ways. The orientation used in dealing with families will, in large part, determine the areas to be investigated and then, for each area, the questions to be asked, the research and theoretical approaches to be applied, and the results to be derived. Since no single discipline is able to ask all the questions, obviously none has all the answers.

The problem of disciplinary isolation is strikingly persistent. Anthropologists, who focus on families and family structures, often overlook the emotional dynamics of family life. Psychologists, who focus on child development and personal adjustment, often overlook aspects of cultural variation and social organization. Sociologists, who focus on the social order, often overlook historical and personal developmental factors.

Table 2-1 illustrates the wide range of disciplines that are concerned with families and family-related issues and the topics associated with each. Clearly, no one discipline or profession dominates the topic of marriage and the family. In fact, the subject itself is highly interdisciplinary.

The use of new interdisciplinary approaches may lead to closing some of the gaps that separate disciplines and may bring forth new concepts and thus new meanings; yet each discipline will continue to focus attention in a specific direction. The anthropologist will focus on family patterns in a cross-cultural and national context. The counselor, usually in an applied context, will attempt to assist individuals, couples, and groups in resolving conflicts and modifying attitude or behavioral problems. The educator will attempt to convey ideas and elicit thoughts on child development, preparation for marriage, sexual concerns, and parental functioning. The historian will examine family patterns, events, and changes over time. The politician will formulate policies and enact laws to deal with child care, marriage, and parenting. The social worker will direct knowledge and skills toward assisting families with problems of income, health, and behavior.

Neither the disciplines described nor the illustrations given in Table 2-1 present an exhaustive listing of approaches to family study. A feminist frame of reference (described at the end of this chapter) alerts the teacher, researcher, and fam-

Table 2-1
*Selected disciplines involved in study of the family
and family-related issues*

Discipline	Illustrative topics
Anthropology	Families in developing societies; cross-cultural studies; evolution; kinship
Biology	Human growth; genetics; conception and reproduction
Child development	Infant growth; learning; personality formation
Counseling	Family therapy; interpersonal relationships; vocational guidance
Demography	Marriage, birth, and divorce rates; mobility patterns
Economics	Family finance; consumer behavior; standards of living
Education	Family life; marriage preparation; child development; sex education
English	Family through literature and mass media
Gerontology	Family life of the elderly; intergenerational links; kin-support systems
History	Family origins, trends, and patterns over time
Home economics	Housing; nutrition; ecology; child development
Law	Marriage; divorce; abuse; adoption; welfare; child custody
Psychology	Interpersonal relationships; learning; human development
Public health	Venereal disease; maternal and infant care; preventive medicine
Religion	Morality; marriage vows; love; sex; religious training
Social work	Family, child, maternal, and aging assistance
Sociology	Family systems; interpersonal relationships; social change

ily practitioner to existing values and assumptions in their professions that ignore the perspectives of women. Scholars from the humanities have long been interested in the family realm. For centuries, poets, theologians, philosophers, linguists, artists, musicians, and others have portrayed images of various aspects of intimate relationships and family life. All forms of media—from magazines and newspapers to soap operas and situation comedies on television to dramas in movies—convey values about families and family life.[1]

---

[1] See for example: Muriel G. Cantor, "The American Family on Television: From Molly Goldberg to Bill Cosby," *Journal of Comparative Family Studies* 22 (Summer 1991): 205–216; and Jennings Bryant (ed.), *Television and the American Family* (Hillsdale, NJ: Lawrence Erlbaum Associates, 1990).

A sociobiological or biosocial approach to family study is an interdisciplinary perspective that cannot be ignored. Reproductive technologies alone (in vitro fertilization, artificial insemination, freezing embryos, sperm banks, genetic engineering, ovum transfer, cloning, surrogacy) have profound implications for the family.[2] Other scientific advances have similar potential to alter personal well-being and interpersonal interactions in dramatic ways, including the ability to select the sex of an offspring or even manipulate the child's appearance and capacities, the donation and transfer of organs from one person to another, and the availability of mind-altering drugs to treat most pains and illnesses.

The point is that a student could take a large number of family courses and encounter different ideas, approaches, and interests. Some courses would include theories and findings from other disciplines; other courses would not have an interdisciplinary focus. The question becomes less Which is better or correct? than Which fulfills the objectives or purposes desired? The student interested in how mothers are portrayed in the mass media may not find much satisfaction in a course on child growth and development. Likewise, the student interested in sex education may not care much about insurance plans or budgeting patterns of nineteenth-century English households.

Textbooks, like disciplines and courses, approach the family with a particular focus and orientation. Although this book gives minimal attention to human anatomy, childhood diseases, and family nutrition, that does not mean these areas are unimportant. Rather, the frame of reference of this book basically follows that of the social sciences and, more specifically, that of sociology.

SOCIAL SCIENCE APPROACH TO THE FAMILY

As with the other subject areas mentioned and perhaps to a greater extent, the social sciences have a primary interest in the family. Generally, the social sciences include sociology, anthropology, psychology, economics, and political science. Sometimes, history, geography, and linguistics are added to this list. Each discipline examines the same subject matter (viz., the behavior of human beings), employs the same body of general principles, and shares similar aims and methods. Science is determined by its aims and methods, not by its results.

Regardless of the topic studied, be it the family or the economy, the social scientist is obligated to follow certain standards of inquiry:

1. *Objectivity* — The personal biases and values of the person doing the research must never influence reporting of data or interpretation of results.
2. *Replication* — Research should be conducted and reported in such a way that someone else can duplicate methods and findings.

---

[2] See John N. Edwards, "New Conceptions: Biosocial Innovations and the Family," *Journal of Marriage and the Family* 53 (May 1991): 349–360; and Eric E. Filsinger, *Biosocial Perspectives on the Family* (Newbury Park, CA: Sage Publications, Inc., 1988).

3. *Precision of measurement* — The phenomenon being studied should be measured in precise, reliable, and valid ways.[3]

All phenomena, including social phenomena, have certain regularities and uniformities that operate independently of the researcher or observer. These patterns can be discovered through objective observation. Science is predicated on the assumption that there is a real world, that things exist and happen naturally and consistently. These things can be demonstrated and verified; thus, they are empirically knowable.

The aims and goals of a social science approach to the family are to establish more or less general relationships. These relationships must be based on empirical observation, and findings must be considered tentative and open to multiple interpretations. Within the social science framework, the following sections examine the sociological approach to the family.

Sociology of the family

Sociology per se is devoted to the study of how society is organized, including its social structures and social processes. The primary units of investigation include human groups, social systems, and institutions.

A sociology of the family seeks to explain the social order and disorder of the family by examining family systems and family groups. A sociology of the family is interested in many related topics: how the family is organized; how the family as a social system is sustained and modified; how family relationships are formed and changed; how the components within the family are interrelated; and how the family as a unit is interdependent with other groups or systems.

A sociological approach to the family differs from both psychological and social psychological approaches to the family. While both of these approaches are primarily concerned with the behavior of individuals, sociology is interested in the social forms and structures within which this behavior takes place. The separation of **psychology, social psychology,** and **sociology** is not always distinct, but each of the three branches of social science has a different emphasis. According to Eshleman, Cashion, and Basirico:

> Psychology is concerned with individuals. Social psychology is the study of how an individual influences his or her social interactions with other individuals or with groups, and of how social behavior influences the individual. Sociology deals primarily with groups and social systems.[4]

A sociology of the family does not focus on the motivations and perceptions of individuals. It does not emphasize how each individual is unique or has experiences that are different from those of anyone else. Rather, the sociological focus is

---

[3] J. Ross Eshleman, Barbara C. Cashion, and Laurence Basirico, *Sociology: An Introduction,* 4th ed. (NY.: HarperCollins, 1993): 65–66.

[4] Ibid., 14.

on the context in which those individual experiences operate and how individual thinking and behavior are shaped by social and cultural forces. All people, as social human beings, exist in a larger structural and organizational network that exerts powerful influences on their lives. The languages people speak, the things that make them feel good or guilty, and the way they respond to the opposite gender are highly patterned. In their efforts to understand social life, sociologists question the obvious, seek patterns and regularities, and look beyond individuals to social interactions and group processes.

Uses of family sociology

Of what use is a sociological approach to the family, particularly since most people have no intention of becoming either sociologists or family specialists? First of all, family sociology does with families what sociologists do with social life: It questions the obvious, seeks patterns and regularities, and assesses individual behavior in the context of a larger society. Thus, family sociology becomes useful in understanding existing behaviors, in presenting new ways of viewing life, and in acquiring knowledge about relationships and families in the United States and around the world. This has traditionally been used to describe a *basic* or *concrete* approach to family study. The emphasis of this approach is less on applying or using the knowledge and more on obtaining it. On a purely applied basis and operating within an ideal-type framework (see Chapter 1), persons involved in the acquisition of knowledge do not devote their time and attention to the direct, day-to-day application of the knowledge. Knowledge, from this extreme, is sought for its own sake.

What about the opposite extreme of application, performance: working with couples, solving family problems, and so forth, without the knowledge? Uninformed intervention, no matter how well intended, can be both dangerous and damaging; taking family social science or family sociology courses can help prevent this. Certainly, no one would want to drive a car across a bridge built by someone with no training in the basic principles of physics or be treated by a physician with no training in the biological sciences. So, too, "do-gooders" in the family realm, who have no training in the social sciences, should be regarded with skepticism. Thus, a second important use of family sociology is in applying the knowledge gained within a framework of sound theory and research.

How can this knowledge be gained? One way to acquire knowledge about families is through basic or applied social research done by oneself or others. Here, one might use knowledge of research methods and sampling, interviewing, analytical, and statistical skills to design and carry out a study on single parents, family conflicts, or a similar issue. The results may be:

1. *Descriptive*, presenting how many problems exist or what the problems are
2. *Explanatory*, demonstrating why the problems exist
3. *Evaluative*, recommending what programs or policies are effective

Most often, however, knowledge is gained by studying the research of others.

How can this knowledge be used? Most importantly, it can affect one's performance in any profession that deals with people. Some of these professionals focus directly on work with families: counselors, clergy, and social workers. Other professionals work with members of families in less direct ways: business- and salespeople, teachers, health care workers, law enforcement personnel, and the like. Anyone associating with people can put to use the knowledge obtained in a course on the family. Would knowledge about African American families, children of divorced parents, or sexual activities of children and adolescents be helpful to a teacher or member of the clergy? Would an understanding of male and female roles or of marital power and decision making be helpful to a salesperson? Would knowledge about never-married parents or divorced parents be helpful to legislators or politicians who establish policy on welfare or child custody? Would an understanding of nontraditional life-styles help anyone accept and work with people whose values and behaviors may differ from one's own? The answer to each of these questions is clearly *yes*.

The third and perhaps most important use of family sociology is at a personal level. All people are brought up in a social context (poor, only child, single parent, Hispanic American), which plays a major part in who and what they are and will become. Many people want and have intimate relationships and specific ideas as to what they want and need from parents, partners, and children. While sociology cannot provide answers and solutions to all personal problems, it can provide some assistance and direction in dealing with the complex social world in which people live. How can this be done?

A knowledge of family theories and awareness of research findings can add to one's *critical-thinking* and *problem-solving* skills. Critical-thinking skills include the ability both to analyze a situation or information and to arrive at a careful, precise judgment. Problem-solving skills include the ability to resolve a conflict or difficulty. Family sociology can add to one's *interpersonal* skills, which help in managing everyday life and dealing with others in interactional settings. To understand the values, roles, norms, and behaviors common to people of a particular ethnic group or who practice a nontraditional life-style can improve one's interaction with them. Family sociology can also improve individual *communication* skills. Most assignments in family sociology, written and oral, are concerned not only with giving correct answers but with developing and presenting an argument and getting the point across logically and clearly. The perpetual interplay of ideas provides practical experience at a personal level in "thinking on your feet" and communicating individual thoughts and ideas to others.

Finally, family sociology can help people *understand* themselves. People are social animals and can only understand themselves by studying the social context in which they live. It is true that knowledge of the social constraints that hinder people can make them feel trapped, frustrated at their inability to control their lives, and angry at the social injustices and inequalities that surround them. But only through understanding the society and the social context in which they exist can people truly understand themselves.

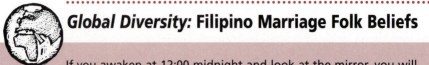

Global Diversity: Filipino Marriage Folk Beliefs

If you awaken at 12:00 midnight and look at the mirror, you will see your future partner or sweetheart.

A person with dimples will marry someone from a place far away from his place.

It is not good for a girl or woman to sit at the head of the table because she won't get married and will eventually end up as an old maid.

A layman who goes through life without being married will not be admitted in heaven. He lacks the sacrament of matrimony and fails to comply with the commandment of God.

If a man marries a woman who is one year older than him, their whole married life always meets problems and difficulties.

A girl who is always fainting should get married and she will be cured.

Marriage should be held at a date when the moon is getting big—half moon or full moon—for abundance of children.

If a husband can cut a banana plant with just one stroke of the blade (bolo), he is the master of the house. If he cannot, he is a henpecked husband.

Source: Francisco Demetrio y Radaza, S.J., ed., *Dictionary of Philippine Folk Beliefs and Customs,* Book III (Cagayan de Oro City, The Philippines: Xavier University, 1970), 619–22, 624–25.

Hopefully, reading this book will increase individual knowledge about existing situations, present frameworks for analysis and action, and suggest alternate life-styles and directives. After studying the available knowledge and various interpretations of what that knowledge means, the reader will be in a sound position to make his or her own choices and judgments on social policy and social action. Toward that goal, the next section will examine the nature of research and theoretical frames of reference common in literature on the family.

NATURE OF RESEARCH AND THEORETICAL FRAMES OF REFERENCE

Like theoreticians in most other fields, family scholars are increasingly attempting to organize their accumulated knowledge in the forms of concepts, generalizations, and theories. Specialists in the family area have been conscious of the need to organize concepts, develop hypotheses and propositions, and interrelate these propositions in a meaningful fashion in order to explain particular aspects of marital or family organization and behavior.

Family theories are neither right nor wrong but are basically ways of looking at and rationally explaining phenomena related to the family. Understanding the most widely used frames of reference can enable the student to study and analyze family behavior in a way that is organized and logical. Thus, behavior within the family context becomes patterned, regular, and predictable under certain conditions rather than remaining idiosyncratic and inconsistent.

Concepts and variables, conceptual frameworks, propositions and hypotheses, and theories are important in that they tell scholars where to focus their attention. Each of these topics will be addressed separately.

Concepts and variables

Basic to all theory and to all sociological research tools are **concepts.** A family concept, as in any area, is a miniature *system of meaning*, that is, a symbol, such as a word or phrase, that enables a phenomenon to be perceived in a certain way. Concepts are tools by which one can share meanings. They are unitary (parts of a whole) and thus do not explain, predict, or state relationships. Concepts are abstractions that are used as building blocks for the development of hypotheses, propositions, and theories. In family analysis, concepts are used to identify qualities, attributes, or properties of social behavior. Examples of concepts within the family area include *nuclear family, monogamy, sex ratio, roles, norms, values, cohabitation, birth order, intermarriage, stepfamilies,* and so on.

Concepts that represent degrees or values are referred to as **variables.** *Husband* is a concept; *years married* is a variable. A variable may be classified as *independent* (the presumed cause) or *dependent* (the presumed effect). The independent variable is antecedent to or simultaneous with the dependent variable. For instance, *family income* (a variable) may be dependent (the presumed effect) on the number of years of education (the presumed cause).

Concepts and variables undergo continuous revision and refinement. Frequently, new concepts must be invented to symbolize new ideas or to identify social properties that have not previously been seen. Thus, *family* may in itself serve as an adequate term for use by laypeople, but the professional differentiates among families of *orientation* or *procreation* and *nuclear, conjugal, extended, consanguine, stem,* and *joint* families. New concepts, such as *sexually bonded relationships, family realm,* and *dyadic units,* were introduced in the first chapter.

Because use of a particular concept will affect what is seen, concepts must be constructed in ways that will not distort reality. An extremely difficult task for the family scholar is to label phenomena in ways that will avoid undesired connotations. Consider the suggestions made by a book on the family that uses titles such as *honky, WASP,* and *paleface.* Also notice the obviously different connotations of labels or concepts such as *nigger, colored, Negro, black,* and *African American.* Research by Hallord Fairchild testified to this argument that the differences are crucial.[5]

---

[5] Hallord H. Fairchild, "Black, Negro, or Afro-American? The Differences Are Crucial," *Journal of Black Studies* 16 (September 1985): 47–55.

Conceptual frameworks

When a set of concepts is interrelated to describe and classify phenomena—in this case, phenomena relative to the family—the concepts are generally defined as a **conceptual framework.** In a strict sense, a conceptual framework is not a theory. A framework is more frequently descriptive rather than explanatory and is generally employed as a classification scheme or taxonomy.

Considerable changes have occurred in the identification of current conceptual frameworks. In 1957, seven basic frameworks or approaches were defined by Hill and others: institutional-historical, interactional-role analysis, structural-functional, situational-psychological habitat, learning theory-maturational, household economics-home management, and the family-development or family life-cycle approach.[6]

In 1960, in what has become a classic article by Hill and Hansen, the chief conceptual properties and basic underlying assumptions of five frameworks were provided in taxonomic tables.[7] The frameworks delineated included these approaches: interactional, structural-functional, situational, institutional, and developmental.

These two initial works have stimulated a large number of articles and chapters on conceptual frameworks, frames of reference, and theories that are particularly applicable to study of the family but seldom unique to it. These frameworks include conflict, legal, economic, institutional, exchange, evolutionary, biological, psychoanalytic, behavioristic, balance, game, ecological, and general systems frameworks, among others.

Five frameworks are covered in this chapter, namely, structural-functional, social conflict, symbolic-interactional, social exchange, and developmental. These five tend to appear regularly in the family literature.[8] These frames of reference are not to be substituted for nor are they to replace an interest in the creation of hypotheses, propositions, and theories.

Propositions and hypotheses

Conceptual frameworks can be used to generate or establish propositions, hypotheses, and theories. A **proposition** is a statement about the nature of some phenomenon. It generally involves a statement of the relationship among two or more concepts. For example, "Young marriage is related to marital conflict" is a proposition. If this or another proposition were formulated for empirical testing, it would be considered a **hypothesis.** Thus, a testable hypothesis would be "The younger the age at marriage, the higher the rate of divorce."

---

[6] Reuben Hill, Alvin M. Katz, and Richard L. Simpson, "An Inventory of Research in Marriage and Family Behavior: A Statement of Objectives and Progress," *Marriage and Family Living* 19 (February 1957): 89–92.

[7] Reuben Hill and Donald A. Hansen, "The Identification of Conceptual Frameworks Utilized in Family Study," *Marriage and Family Living* 22 (November 1960): 299–311.

[8] For example, these same five frameworks constitute the book by Chester A. Winton, *Frameworks for Studying Families,* Guilford, CT: Dushkin Publishing Group, Inc., 1995.

Hypotheses and propositions are identical, with the exception that hypotheses carry clear implications for testing or measuring the stated relations. Hypotheses serve as an important branch between theory and empirical inquiry. Hypotheses and propositions are formed by combining concepts into statements that set forth meaningful relationships.

Frequently, a proposition states that, if one variable changes in some regular fashion, predictable change will take place in another variable. For example, it has been suggested that "As industrialization increases, extended-family ties decrease." Thus, in this proposition, the two variables, *industrialization* and *the extended family*, are stated as being inversely related (as one increases, the other decreases).

Theories

When it is possible to interrelate logically and systematically a series of propositions that explain some particular process, the result is a **theory**. A good theory should be testable, abstract, and cumulative; have wide application; and give grounds for prediction. Thus, a theory is far more than mere speculation or a random collection of concepts and variables. It is a set of logically interrelated propositions that explain some process or related phenomena in a *testable* fashion.

It should be clear that theory and research are and need to be closely linked. Lavee and Dollahite suggested that, if the best is to be made of research, researchers must make themselves more familiar with theories about families. These researchers contended that scholars must sensitize themselves and teach their students to "think theory" while doing research and to be clear and explicit about theory when research is reported. It is theory that gives meaning to research findings and enables the development of systematic, consensual explanations.[9]

The application of theory—or perhaps more accurately, *theoretical frames of reference*—is emphasized throughout this book. While no independent chapters exist on theory per se, subsections within chapters use particular frames of reference. For example, the structural-functional frame of reference is applied extensively to analysis of family life-styles in Chapters 5, 6, and 7. The social conflict frame of reference is applied to social class, the marital system, violence, and divorce in Chapters 8, 12, 16, and 17, respectively. The symbolic interaction frame of reference is applied throughout the book to analyses of mate selection, sexual relationships, marital interaction, and childrearing (socialization). The developmental framework is applied from Chapters 10 through 13 in viewing marriage over the life cycle. Social exchange theory is applied throughout the book to mate selection and the marital system. Likewise, feminist theory, a recent development, is applied to a wide range of issues that range from inheritance patterns and lineage systems to gender inequality and marital violence.

---

[9] Yoav Lavee and David C. Dollahite, "The Linkage between Theory and Research in Family Science," *Journal of Marriage and the Family* 53 (May 1991): 361–373.

News Item: Should Parents Be Punished When Their Children Break the Law?

When children break the law, should parents be punished? The assumption supporting this action is based on the theory that parents are the sole and primary sources of socialization and control of their children. This notion gained increasing attention when, in 1989, federal drug czar William Bennett said in a speech that parents and live-in boyfriends and girlfriends should face stiffer legal liability in drug-related juvenile crimes.

The *Charlotte Observer* reported that the Charlotte Housing Authority told a thirty-four-year-old mother that her Fairview Homes public housing lease would be terminated because her sixteen-year-old son was convicted of dealing cocaine in the complex. The previous week, the Los Angeles police, using a ground-breaking California law that holds parents responsible for the crimes of their children, arrested the mother of a seventeen-year-old rape suspect and gang member. She was charged with ``failure to exercise reasonable care, supervision, protection, and control" of her son. She was freed on $20,000 bail pending arraignment on the charge, which carries a penalty of up to one year in jail and a $2,500 fine.

Are these laws fair, reasonable, and workable? Can parents be responsible for the behavior of teenagers and older children, the ones most likely to commit the crimes? Should the law go a step further and punish their siblings and friends, as well? Or maybe teachers, who may spend more time with a child than a parent?

Other theories (frames of reference) not specifically summarized in this chapter are presented where appropriate throughout the text to offer explanations of particular aspects of the family: an orderly replacement theory of change, a complementary need theory of mate selection, a learning-behaviorist and psychoanalytic theory of socialization, an ABCX model of crisis, and the like. From this list alone, it becomes obvious that many theories exist that explain a variety of processes or sets of phenomena. Those more directly pertinent and widely used in a sociology of the family will be summarized in the section that follows.

THEORIES AND FRAMES OF REFERENCE

Structural-functional frame of reference

The structural-functional frame of reference, sometimes called *functional analysis*, is a major and dominant theoretical orientation in sociology. Within the family area, the scope of this approach is very broad; it provides a framework for dealing with relationships within the family (husband, wife, sibling, etc.) as well as influences on the family from other systems within society (educational, religious, occupational, etc.).

The structural-functional frame of reference stems from the functionalist branch of psychology (especially the gestalt position), from social anthropology, and from sociology (especially as seen by social systems theorists such as Talcott Parsons).[10] A *gestalt* is an organized entity or whole in which the parts, although distinguishable, are interdependent. The gestalt position focuses on the relation between a whole and its parts. Functionalism is identified with the study of interrelationships among the structures of any system. Numerous social anthropologists have stressed the impossibility of studying any particular aspect of life detached from its general setting.

To talk about social structures is to talk about social organizations, social systems, norms, values, and the like. Cultural structures, social structures, structural interrelations, and other structure-related terminology refer to the interdependence of parts in a definite pattern of organization. Within this framework, societies (and families) are composed of interdependent parts that are linked together in a boundary-maintaining whole and are basically in harmony with each other. Since the parts of a system need each other, there is a social bond and high degrees of order, cohesion, stability, and persistence. The implication is that groups, systems, and behaviors are not purely random, individualistic, or unpredictable. Family groups and systems and the individuals that comprise them, similar to the other components of a society, are orderly and predictable units that must be viewed in a social context.

The social structure of a family refers to the arrangement of social units, the interrelationship of the parts, and the patterns of organization. These patterns differ greatly around the world, but, given a particular type of organization, definite recurrent consequences occur. Linda Bryan and others, for example, found that a family structure consisting of stepparents and stepchildren appeared to lend itself to negative stereotypes. Bryan et al. hypothesized that family structure is a cue by which stereotypes are formed and that stepparents and stepchildren are seen more negatively than married or widowed parents and their children but less negatively than divorced or never-married parents and their children. All hypotheses were supported.[11]

To extend this argument—namely, that structure produces or results in patterned, recurrent consequences—suggests that different outcomes will result if norms or values permit one wife or several, if newlyweds establish a residence with or separate from parents, if the husband makes the basic decisions or both husband and wife share in making them, and if inheritance is given to the oldest child or to all children equally. *Nuclear, polyandry, patriarchy, avunculocal, bilineal, primogeniture, exogamy, arranged marriage,* and *consanguine* are all words that define specific structural arrangements of given family systems. Most of these terms will be described and illustrated in Chapter 3.

---

10 Talcott Parsons, *The Social System* (Glencoe, IL: The Free Press, 1951).

11 Linda R. Bryan, Marilyn Coleman, Lawrence Ganong, and S. Hugh Bryan, "Person Perception: Family Structure as a Cue for Stereotyping, *Journal of Marriage and the Family* 48 (February 1986): 169–174.

The concepts *structure* and *function* can be discussed separately, although they are interrelated and one implies the other. Speaking in circular terms, *social structures* are units of society that carry out or result in one or more basic functions, and *functions* are results or consequences of given social structures.

What specifically is meant by *function*? This term is generally used in one of two related ways. To determine function, one can ask, What does it do? That is, to describe functions of the family in the United States or any given society, one can ask what the family does: Why does it exist? What purposes does it serve? Functions may be *manifest,* that is, intended and recognized, or *latent,* that is, neither intended nor recognized. Functions may be performed for the individual, for a particular social system or social institution, or for the wider society.

It has been suggested that, for individual members, some manifest functions of the family are to provide basic personality formation, basic status ascription, nurturant socialization, and tension management. For the larger society, some manifest functions are to replace members, to socialize the members to the norms and values of the society, and to act as an agent of social control.

More than forty years ago, Talcott Parsons and Robert Bales suggested that there are two basic and irreducible family functions: (1) the primary socialization of children so that they can truly become members of the society into which they have been born and (2) the stabilization of the adult personalities of the society.[12] Evidence has shown that these two functions remain basic to the institution of the family today as well.

Families also perform latent functions for persons and society. While latent functions are real in the sense that they take place, by definition, they are neither intended nor recognized. They may include socializing children to be abusive adults or instilling in children negative feelings of self-worth. For the larger society, some latent functions may be to keep women in inferior positions to men or to perpetuate inequality from one generation to the next. Generally, families are not intended to fulfill such functions; nevertheless, such latent functions (some may say *dysfunctions*) exist.

A second way in which the term *function* is used is related to the first. Function may be used to describe consequences or results of activities. Thus, given a certain type of structural pattern—for example, working mothers—one could ask, What are some of the consequences (results) of the employment of mothers? Note that the question is not What do working mothers do? but rather What are some of the results or consequences of this type of behavior pattern? Are smaller family size, improved levels of mental health, delinquency among children, and marital instability consequences of mothers working? Do families in societies that permit mothers to join the labor force have higher standards of living, closer parent/child relationships, or more egalitarian decision-making patterns? Are the con-

---

[12] Talcott Parsons and Robert F. Bales, *Family Socialization and Interaction Process* (New York: The Free Press, 1955): 16–17.

sequences similar, irrespective of cultural context, time, or location? How does this structure (working mothers) interrelate with other structures? Does it lead to the maintenance or breakdown of a particular system?

Three examples, of many that could be cited, illustrate how variations in family structure lead to differing consequences for children. In one study, data from a nationally representative sample of more than 17,000 children under age eighteen revealed that the health and well-being consequences for children were quite different, depending on whether the parental structure included both biological parents or single but once-married mothers. Those children living with single mothers (or with mothers and stepfathers) were more likely to have repeated a grade of school, been expelled, been treated for emotional problems, been at increased risk of accidental injury, and even been at increased risk of asthma.[13]

Another study examined the relationship between family structure and homicide victimization rates of infants and children in seventeen developed nations. Infant homicide rates were higher when rates of births to teenage mothers were high. Child homicide rates were higher under structural arrangements of illegitimacy, teenage motherhood, and divorce.[14]

A third study reinforced the view that child poverty and racial inequality cannot be separated from the issue of changing family structure in the United States. Increases in divorce rates, female headship rates, and nonmarital fertility rates over the past several decades were some of the changes in family structure that fueled the growing proportion of children living in poverty.[15]

Note some of the implications of these ideas for social policy. That is, if consequences for children (or anyone) vary by type of family structure, conditions can be improved or changed by supporting certain types of structural arrangements rather than only focusing on the individuals who suffer the consequences. In other words, if children's emotional problems occur less frequently when they live with two biological parents, where should the focus be: solely on the children with the problems or also on the types of economic, educational, and community support that can be given to keep parents together? If infant homicide rates are higher among teenage mothers, what can be done to delay parenthood? If childhood poverty increases with female headship and nonmarital fertility rates, how can the number of these types of family structures be decreased?

These arguments should not blind one to the reciprocal and perhaps interactional nature of *cause*. Consider whether changing family structure is a cause of poverty or whether poverty is a cause of changing family structure. Perhaps both are operative. It is not always easy to answer this type of question, but that does

---

13 Deborah A. Dawson, "Family Structure and Children's Health and Well-Being: Data from the 1988 National Health Interview Survey on Child Health," *Journal of Marriage and the Family* 53 (August 1991): 573–584.

14 Rosemary Gartner, "Family Structure, Welfare Spending, and Child Homicide in Developed Democracies," *Journal of Marriage and the Family* 53 (February 1991): 231–240.

15 David J. Eggebeen and Daniel T. Lichter, "Race, Family Structure, and Changing Poverty Among American Children," *American Sociological Review* 56 (December 1991): 801–817.

not take away the argument for creating social policies that best support the types of structures that have the most positive consequences.

On an ideal-type continuum, the type of policy or the level of analysis ranges from macroanalysis to microanalysis. The distinction between the two is made purely in terms of the size of the unit chosen for analysis. *Macrofunctionalists* are concerned with the analysis of relatively large-scale systems and institutions. The *microfunctionalists* are concerned with the analysis of individual families and relatively small-scale systems (often designated as *group dynamics*). Both positions conceive of their units of analysis as important to and interrelated with the other parts of the larger system.

Today, a major thrust of the structural-functional approach is to explain the parts (structure) of a society and the manner in which these parts interrelate, both within and outside the particular system under study. Each component of society must be seen in relationship to the whole, since each component acts on and reacts to other components. Thus, the task of structural-functional analysis is to explain the parts, the relationship among the parts, the relationship among the parts and the whole, and the functions (both manifest and latent) that are performed by or result from the relationship formed by the parts.[16]

Social conflict frame of reference

Perhaps the most basic assumption of a social conflict frame of reference is that conflict is natural and inevitable in all human interaction. Thus, rather than stressing order, equilibrium, consensus, and system maintenance, as does functionalism, the focus of a social conflict frame of reference is conflict management. Conflict is not viewed as bad and disruptive of social systems and human interaction; instead, conflict is viewed as an assumed and expected part of all systems and interactions.

At a macrolevel, the conflict may be between the family system and the work/employment/economic system, between sexes (males and females), between social classes, or between age groups. At a microlevel, the conflict may be between a husband and wife, a son-in-law and mother-in-law, or two sisters. Since within this frame of reference conflict is quite natural and to be expected, the issue is not

---

[16] Key concepts in structural-functional theory in sociology are social system, social structure, social function, dysfunctions, manifest and latent functions, functional requisites and prerequisites, equilibrium and order, status and norms.

Some of the leading advocates of this perspective include Talcott Parsons, Robert Merton, Kingsley Davis, Wilbert Moore, Robin Williams, Charles Loomis, Harry Johnson, Emile Durkheim, George Homans, Marion Levy, William Goode, and Robert Winch.

For information on structural-functional theory from the perspective of the family, examine the following: Norman W. Bell and Ezra F. Vogel, *A Modern Introduction to the Family*, rev. ed. (New York: The Free Press, 1968); William J. Goode, *The Family*, 2d ed. (Englewood Cliffs, NJ: Prentice-Hall, 1982); and Chester A. Winton, *Frameworks for Studying Families*, Guilford, CT: Dushkin Publishing Group, Inc., 1995, Chapter 2, 44–85.

how to avoid conflict but how to manage and/or resolve it. In so doing, the conflict, rather than being disruptive or negative, may force change and perhaps make relationships stronger and more meaningful than they were before.

The classic case for social conflict theory stems from Karl Marx, who assumed that economic organization, especially the ownership of property, generates revolutionary class conflict.[17] Marx believed that, as the exploited and oppressed members of the proletariat become aware of their oppression and their true interests, they will revolt and form a revolutionary political organization aimed at overthrowing the dominant, property-holding bourgeoisie.

Basic to Marx and influential in the thinking of contemporary conflict theorists are ideas such as the following: (1) Social relationships are rife with conflicting interests; thus, (2) social systems systematically generate conflict, which (3) is an inevitable and pervasive feature of all social systems and (4) tends to be manifested in the opposition of interests that (5) occurs over the distribution of scarce resources, most notably power and material wealth, which (6) results in change in social systems.[18]

Hypotheses stemming from these assumptions suggest that:

1. The more unequal the distribution of scarce resources, the greater the conflict between the dominant and the subordinate.

2. As the subordinate become aware of their collective interests, they increasingly question the legitimacy of existing patterns.

3. The more the subordinate question inequities, the more likely they are to join in overt conflict against the dominant group.

4. The more overt or violent the conflict, the greater the change and the redistribution of resources that will result.

From this Marxian economic conflict perspective, the family serves to support the capitalistic system that exploits working-class workers by paying them low wages. Similarly, capitalism exploits women, not merely by paying lower wages to those who are employed but by encouraging them to perform unpaid housework and child care so that husbands can devote their full time to their capitalist employers.

In brief, from a social conflict perspective, the family is not the haven posited by an order perspective such as functionalism (see Table 2-2). Functionalists, who see the family as the primary socialization agent of youth, are seen by conflict theorists as promoting a false consciousness by teaching youth to accept the inequities between the sexes and classes as natural. Functionalists also see the family as perpetuating the same "life chances" from one generation to another (the rich stay

---

17 Karl Marx, *The Communist Manifesto,* trans. Samuel Moore (Baltimore: Penguin, 1967), originally published in 1849 with Friedrich Engels; C. Wright Mills, *The Marxists* (New York: Harcourt, Brace, 1948); and Rolf Dahrendorf, *Class and Class Conflict in Industrial Society* (Stanford: Stanford University Press, 1959).

18 See Jonathan H. Turner, *The Structure of Sociological Theory,* 4th ed. (Chicago, IL: Dorsey, 1986): 135.

rich and the poor stay poor), whereas conflict theorists feel this perpetuation maintains and promotes inequality based on ascription rather than achievement. Functionalists believe that the isolated nuclear family is consistent with the mobility needs of a capitalist society; conflict theorists believe that mobility is disruptive to individual members and their emotional needs. Finally, functionalists, who see the modern family as tranquil, passive, and in a state of equilibrium with other units of society, are seen by conflict theorists as promoting a system fraught with potential and actual conflict. Conflict, which is inevitable in society, in the family, and in interpersonal relationships, leads to change.

Issues related to conflict theory—such as power, decision making, marital adjustment, economic factors, and the like—are discussed elsewhere, particularly in Chapters 8 and 12.[19]

Symbolic interaction frame of reference

Symbolic interactionism describes a particular and distinctive approach to study of the group life and personal behavior of human beings. As a social-psychological frame of reference, symbolic interactionism addresses two issues—socialization and social interaction—both of which are of central concern to the family. The first issue, socialization, focuses on how a newborn becomes social and on how human beings obtain and internalize the behavior patterns and ways of thinking and feeling of the society and culture in which they live. The second issue, social interaction, is basic to socialization itself and to all aspects of life; it focuses on self in relation to others and on the social interchanges between individuals and groups.

Within social psychology, symbolic interactionism constitutes both a theoretical perspective and a methodological orientation. Its theoretical uniqueness lies in the extent to which covert activity is a crucial dimension in understanding behavior and society. That is, *like* Pavlovian and Skinnerian radical behaviorism, symbolic interactionism includes the observable actions of individuals; *unlike* radical behaviorism, symbolic interactionism stresses the importance of meanings, definitions of situations, symbols, interpretations, and other internalized processes.[20]

---

[19] Key concepts in conflict theory are conflict, competition, negotiation, patriarchy, resources, scarcity, interests, change, power, and class.

   Some of the leading advocates of the perspective include Karl Marx, Georg Simmel, Rolf Dahrendorf, Lewis A. Coser, and Pierre van den Berghe.

   For information on conflict theory from the perspective of the family, examine the following: Marie Withers Osmond, "Radical-Critical Theories" in Marvin B. Sussman and Suzanne K. Steinmetz, *Handbook of Marriage and the Family* (New York: Plenum Press, 1987), Chapter 5, pp. 103–125; Jetse Sprey, "Conflict Theory and the Study of Marriage and the Family," in Wesley Burr, Reuben Hill, F. Ivan Nye, and Ira L. Reiss, *Contemporary Theories About the Family*, vol. 2 (New York: Free Press, 1979): 130–159; and Chester A. Winton, *Frameworks for Studying Families*, Guilford, CT: Dushkin Publishing Group, Inc., 1995, Chapter 3, 86–108.

[20] Pavlovian and Skinnerian radical behaviorism, parallel to classical and operant conditioning, are described in Chapter 14 under the heading, "Learning-Behaviorist Frame of Reference."

Table 2-2
Duality of social life: Assumptions of the order and conflict models of society

	Order model	Conflict model
Question:	What is the fundamental relationship among the parts of society?	
Answer:	Harmony and cooperation	Competition, conflict, domination, and subordination
Why:	The parts have complementary interests. Basic consensus on societal norms and values.	The things people want are always in short supply. Basic dissensus on societal norms and values.
Degree of integration:	Highly integrated	Loosely integrated. Whatever integration is achieved is the result of force and fraud.
Type of societal change:	Gradual, adjustive, and reforming	Abrupt and revolutionary
Degree of stability:	Stable	Unstable

Source: D. Stanley Eitzen and Maxine Baca Zinn, *In Conflict and Order: Understanding Society,* 7th ed. (Boston: Allyn and Bacon, 1995), 51. Used with permission.

Interaction among socialized human beings is mediated by the use of symbols and by interpreting meanings from the actions of others. Methodologically, the world of reality is known by any means or set of techniques that offers a likely possibility of ascertaining what is going on: making direct observations, conducting interviews, listening to conversations, securing life history accounts, using letters and diaries, consulting public records, arranging for group discussions, and other allowable procedures that lead to obtaining subjective meanings. Basically, symbolic interactionism involves a *phenomenological* approach, where preferred techniques include use of participant observation, personal documents, and ethnomethodological accounts. The use of quotations from personal interviews is also consistent with this particular frame of reference.

The interactionist approach makes a number of basic assumptions:

• Marriages and families must be studied at their own levels; that is, the behavior of humans, human interactions, and social systems cannot be inferred from the study of nonhuman or infrahuman forms of life, such as animals.

Families, irrespective of how they are structured, are the most important of all social institutions in fulfilling the function of nurturing and rearing the young. Various theories explain the socialization process; most are based on the necessity of an intimate network of caring adults who serve as caretakers, providers, and role models for children.

- Marriages and families and their components can only be understood in the context of the social setting in which each exists. For instance, the language spoken, the definitions given to situations, and the appropriateness of given activities only make sense within specific social contexts.

- The human infant at birth is neither social nor antisocial but asocial. He or she learns through interaction with others what is good and bad, acceptable and unacceptable behavior.

- A social human being is an actor as well as a reactor; that is, he or she can communicate symbolically and share meanings. Thus, individuals do not merely respond to objective stimuli but select and interpret them. Individuals can interact with themselves, can take the roles of others, and can respond to symbolic stimuli.

These assumptions, spelled out in more detail in Chapter 14, are basic to understanding the significance of the symbolic interaction framework as applied to both marital and parental interaction and to human behavior in general.

Concepts from the social interaction framework are used extensively throughout this book. For example, the concept *role* is used both within a structural-functional framework and an interactionist framework. However, its use varies significantly. An institutional or structural concept of *role* attaches societal expectations to statuses that people occupy. Certain statuses—such as sex, age, and race—are generally ascribed, whereas marital, occupational, and parental statuses are likely achieved. Each of these statuses or status sets carries with it expected, appropriate behaviors. These expectations of what is appropriate for men or women, married or single, homosexual or heterosexual, are termed *roles*. *Roles* are culturally defined expectations and exist independently of any given person.

Role, as used within an interactionist framework, does not deny the institutional usage, but, rather than dealing with a package of behavioral expectations wrapped up in a set of rules, it deals with a relationship between what one person does and what others do. The expectations (roles) are developed in interaction. The emphasis here is on process. The interactionist concept of *role* describes the processes of cooperative behavior and communication. It involves the idea of *role taking*. Role taking as a process involves actors adjusting their behavior and reactions to what they think the other person is going to do. Perhaps a simple example may clarify the difference in the use of these two schools of thought, functionalism and interactionism.

Suppose there are two students, one male and one female. The fact that they occupy student and gender statuses implies that certain expectations or roles are associated with these statuses. But for the moment, concentrate on the students as male and female. Some of the rules or expectations traditionally associated with the status *male* in relationship to *female* are that he walk on her outside (along the curb), that he open doors and generally permit her to proceed first, that he assist her with a chair, and that he pay the bills. Thus, the institutional concept of *role* emphasizes society's prescribed expectations for behavior. Whether these rules are actually followed is secondary. The roles (expectations) exist independently of a given individual's fulfillment of them. Failure to conform to the expectations appropriate to status does not eliminate the normative expectations.

In contrast to the institutionalized concept of *role,* the interactionist concept involves the process of determining appropriate behavior in interaction with others. Now, the actor is not the occupant of a position for which there is a standardized set of rules; he or she is a person whose expectations for behavior are supplied in part by his or her relationship to another person or persons. Since the expectations of the other person can only be inferred and not directly known, there is a continuous process of testing. The clues given by the other person in part determine the expected behaviors (roles) appropriate to that situation.

Getting back to the example male and female, as they interact, the expectations (roles) for appropriate and approved behavior may vary widely from socially ascribed expectations. The female may quite appropriately pay the bills, open the doors, be the aggressive sexual partner, drive the automobile, and the like. But these roles, too, become patterned and recurrent. This inevitability is what makes behavior predictable and interaction possible with either strangers or intimate, lifelong friends.

These two conceptions of *role* are not totally independent and separate, for one never escapes the norms or roles established by a given society. At best, how-

Case Example:
Unfulfilled Marital Role Expectations

Mary has been married for 15 years. She was raised a Catholic and knew that marriage and children were things she wanted in life. She got married and had two children but the marriage has never fulfilled her expectations.

"I wanted to be a good wife, was happy being a housewife, and worked hard at it. As a matter of fact, I was a superwife, doing everything for my husband and was shocked when he told me I'm not the kind of wife he wanted. For years, I knew that to focus on a career would be a detriment to my marriage. I don't feel that way anymore.

"My husband was always emotionally distant from me and has a hard time showing affection. In fact, we sleep in different rooms and haven't had sex for about five years. But that's as much my doing as his since I feel angry and really don't love him anymore.

"Our expectations as to what I feel I should do and what he feels I should do are so different. The same is true for him. For example, I already spoke of the lack of affection. I believe that is an essential part of a marriage but not if you don't care for each other. But differences are equally evident when it involves money, kids, discipline, work, or simply following through on anything. To him, money is the bottom line and I believe he'd respect me more if I had a job. In his view, I have never worked. When he stays with the kids, he lets them do anything they want. He is the buddy type while I must do the disciplining.

"What really gets me is how he never follows through on anything. He's a quitter in everything he starts. Once he got into a computer certificate program but dropped out. Although he makes good money at his automobile company job, he feels he never achieved much. But why doesn't he make any effort to do something about it?

"Why do I stay? It's strictly for economic reasons and for the benefit of the kids. He says he wants me as a wife, but after all I've been through, he really frightens me emotionally. I'm too willing to give in. Now I'm back in college. This makes him all the more insecure because he knows that when I become financially able to care for myself, our marriage is over for sure."

ever, the expectations associated with a given status offer only generalized guidelines; they do not determine specific behavior patterns for every situation. Thus, even though the norm prescribes that intercourse is not appropriate on a first date, as the couple interacts, the result may be coitus. The gestures, the clues, the symbols, the verbal communications, and the clarity of shared meanings may lead to intercourse as a highly appropriate role expectation for the dating partners within the interactionist concept of *role*. The behavior of intercourse on a first date within the institutional concept of *role*, however, is inconsistent with the culturally prescribed rules for unmarried couples in the United States.

Other concepts that are key to the understanding of this frame of reference include the *social self, significant other, reference group,* and generalized other. Each will be clarified and illustrated in various chapters throughout the text; a more extensive discussion of the symbolic interaction frame of reference will be presented in Chapter 14. At this point, the family will be recognized as a "unit of interacting personalities"[21] involved in a never-ending, never-completed, or never-fixed process.[22]

Social exchange frame of reference

Seldom does a day pass in which certain social exchanges do not take place. Work, gifts, cards, affection, and ideas are given in hopes of getting something in return. Certain exchanges, such as many economic ones, are institutionalized and predetermined, clarified in precise terms prior to the exchange. For instance, one can exchange 50 cents for a newspaper or 80 dollars for a membership in the National Council on Family Relations. Other exchanges, including the type found in the social exchange frame of reference, leave unspecified the exact nature of the return, although a return—an expectation of reciprocity—does exist. For example, neighbors who lend tools, friends who buy dinner, and politicians who promise lower taxes all expect something in return. That exact something is often unspecified.

Social exchange or social choice theory rests on the belief that human beings attempt to make choices that they expect will maximize their rewards and/or minimize their costs. Social exchange theory seeks to explain why certain behavioral outcomes occur (marriage, sex, employment), given a set of structural conditions (age, race, gender, class) and interactional potentialities. The following assumptions are made:

- Most types of human gratification originate in the actions of other humans (spouse, children, friends, colleagues, fellow workers).

- New associations are entered into because they are expected to be rewarding, and old associations continue because they are rewarding.

---

[21] Ernest W. Burgess, "The Family as a Unit of Interacting Personalities," *Family* 7 (1926): 3–9.

[22] Key concepts in symbolic interaction theory are symbols, interaction, process, status, role, role playing, role taking, role conflict, meaning, reference group, significant other, generalized other, social self, "I," "me," socialization, actor, and identity.

Some of the leading advocates of this perspective include George Herbert Mead, Charles Cooley, William James, Herbert Blumer, Tomatsu Shibutani, Alfred Lindesmith, Anselm L. Strauss, Erving Goffman, and Sheldon Stryker.

For information on symbolic interaction theory from the perspective of the family, examine the following: Sheldon Stryker, "Symbolic Interaction Theory: A Review and Some Suggestions for Comparative Family Research," *Journal of Comparative Family Studies* 3 (Spring 1972): 17–32; Wesley R. Burr, Geoffrey K. Leigh, Randall D. Day, and John Constantine, "Symbolic Interaction and the Family," in *Contemporary Theories About the Family,* vol. 2, ed. Wesley Burr, Reuben Hill, F. Ivan Nye, and Ira L. Reiss (New York: Free Press, 1979), 42–111, and Chester A. Winton, *Frameworks for Studying Families,* Guilford, CT: Dushkin Publishing Group, Inc., 1995, Chapter 5, 131–156.

- As people receive rewards or benefits from others, they are under obligation to reciprocate by supplying benefits in return.
- Earning social credit through giving is preferable to building social debt through receiving.

While it may be true that persons exist who selflessly work for others with no thought of reward, such "saints" are rare, and even they seek social or perhaps spiritual approval. In brief, social exchange refers to voluntary social actions that are contingent upon receiving rewarding reactions from others. These actions cease when the actual or expected reactions are not forthcoming.

Social exchange theory has followed two differing schools of thought, best represented by George Homans[23] and Peter Blau.[24] Homans, the recognized initiator of exchange theory, represented a perspective consistent with that of behavioral psychologists who believe in psychological reductionism and reinforcement theory, where the focus is on actual behavior that is rewarded or punished by the behavior of other persons. Humans, like animals, react to stimuli based on need, reward, and reinforcement. It is expected that, in exchange relationships, the rewards will be proportional to the cost (a notion of distributive justice).

Blau differed considerably from Homans and represented a perspective consistent with that of the symbolic interactionist. That is, not all exchange is explained in terms of actual behavior of individuals. Exchange is more subjective and interpretative. Exchange, like interaction, is a creative process that occurs between actors. While humans want rewards, the choices and decisions they make are affected by social influences, such as friends or kin. The human mind responds subjectively to stimuli through conceptualizing, defining, valuing, reflecting, and symbolizing. As a result, explaining behavioral outcomes (the goal of social exchange theory) is a function of the actors who interact symbolically, have social selves, and can take roles.

Both Homans and Blau agreed that what is important is that each party in the exchange receive something perceived as equivalent to that which is given (to Homans—*distributive justice,* to Blau—*fair exchange*). All social exchange involves a mutually held expectation that reciprocation will occur.[25] If resources or exchange criteria are unequal or imbalanced, one person is at a distinct disadvantage and the other has power over the relationship. Specific resources (money, position, physical assets, personality) may be more applicable in one exchange than in another and may have different values in different exchanges. The worth of a resource can only be accurately assessed through participation in actual social

---

[23] George C. Homans, *Social Behavior: Its Elementary Forms* (New York: Harcourt, Brace, and World, 1961); George C. Homans, "Social Behavior as Exchange," *American Journal of Sociology* 63 (May 1958): 597–606.

[24] Peter M. Blau, *Exchange and Power in Social Life* (New York: Wiley, 1964); Peter Blau, "Justice in Social Exchange," *Sociological Inquiry* 34 (Spring 1964): 193–206.

[25] Alvin W. Gouldner, "The Norm of Reciprocity," *American Sociological Review* 25 (April 1960): 161–178.

markets. Therefore, socialization in exchange and bargaining skills is vital to maximizing the use of available resources.

The family literature is filled with many examples of social exchange. In the chapter on partner selection, Willard Waller suggested, in his *principle of least interest,* that interest is exchanged for control of the relationship in that the person who is least interested in continuing the dating relationship is in a position to dominate. (See Chapter 9 on partner selection.) In arranged marriages, for instance, labor, gifts, or a bride price are often exchanged for the right to marry. Robert Winch spoke of complementary needs, involving an exchange of needs that provide maximum gratification. The higher incidence of premarital sexual behavior by engaged females has been explained as an exchange of sex on the part of the female in return for commitment on the part of the male. Throughout the text, note the value of different types of resources and the exchange processes at work in understanding authority and power, husband/wife interaction, mate selection, kin relationships, sexual patterns, parent/child conflict, and the like.[26]

Developmental frame of reference

Originating in the 1930s, the family development approach to family study attempts to join together various parts of previously delineated theories. Hill and Hansen, who discussed the characteristics of the developmental framework, indicated that this approach is not a precisely unique framework but an attempt to transcend the boundaries of several approaches through incorporation of their compatible sections into one unified theme.[27]

> From rural sociologists [the developmental frame of reference] borrowed the concept of stages of the family life cycle. From child psychologists and human development specialists came the concepts of developmental needs and tasks. From the sociologists engaged in work in the professions it incorporated the concept of the family as a convergence of intercontingent careers. From the structure-function and interactional approaches were borrowed the concepts of age and sex roles, plurality patterns, functional prerequisites, and the many concepts associated with the family as a system of interacting actors.[28]

---

[26] Key concepts in social exchange theory are exchange, reciprocity, negotiation, transaction, dependence, resources, cost, distributive justice, fair exchange, and power.

Some of the leading advocates of this perspective include George C. Homans, Peter M. Blau, Kingsley Davis, Alvin W. Gouldner, John W. Thibaut, Harold H. Kelley, John N. Edwards, and John Scanzoni.

For information on social exchange theory from the perspective of the family, examine the following: John N. Edwards, "Familial Behavior as Social Exchange," *Journal of Marriage and the Family* 31 (August 1969): 518–526; F. Ivan Nye, ed., *Family Relationships: Rewards and Costs* (Beverly Hills: Sage Publications, 1982); John Scanzoni, *Sexual Bargaining: Power Politics in the American Marriage,* 2d ed. (Chicago: University of Chicago Press, 1982), and Chester A. Winton, *Frameworks for Studying Families,* Guilford, CT: Dushkin Publishing Group, Inc., 1995, Chapter 4, 111–130.

[27] Hill and Hansen, "The Identification of Conceptual Frameworks Utilized in Family Study," pp. 299–311.

[28] Ibid., 307.

The developmental approach covers a very broad area and tends to be both macro- and microanalytic in nature. The peculiar character of this approach lies in its attempt to account for changes in the family system over time as well as changes in patterns of interaction over time. Traditionally, the major conceptual tool among family scholars for this time analysis has been termed the *family life cycle.*[29] Today, frequent reference is made to the term *life course* in dealing with changes and differences over time.

The most systematic, widespread, and long-term use of the family life-cycle idea has been provided by Evelyn Duvall, who attempted to provide a link between life-cycle stages[30] and the developmental-task concept.[31] A *developmental task* is one that arises at or about a certain period in the life of an individual. Successful achievement of the task leads to individual happiness, social approval, and success with later tasks, while failure leads to unhappiness, disapproval, and later difficulties. Developmental tasks have two primary origins: (1) physical maturation and (2) cultural pressures and privileges.[32] The number of developmental tasks an individual faces over a lifetime are innumerable. Many of them are delineated in human development textbooks.

The developmental theory contends that, like individuals, families also face tasks at given stages in the family life cycle. A family's developmental task is "a growth responsibility that arises at a certain stage in the life of a family, the successful achievement of which leads to present satisfaction, approval and success with later tasks whereas failure leads to unhappiness in the family, disapproval by society, and difficulty with later family developmental tasks."[33] For a family to continue to grow as a unit, they need to satisfy, at a given stage, (1) biological requirements, (2) cultural imperatives, and (3) personal aspirations and values.

Duvall recognized and depicted the family life cycle as consisting of eight stages:

Stage 1 Married couples (without children)

Stage 2 Childbearing families (oldest child, birth–30 months)

Stage 3 Families with preschool children (oldest child, 2 1/2–6 years)

---

[29] For a discussion and empirical evaluation of this concept, see Paul C. Glick, "The Family Life Cycle and Social Change," *Family Relations* 38 (April 1989): 123–129; Graham B. Spanier and Paul C. Glick, "The Life Cycle of American Families: An Expanded Analysis," *Journal of Family History* 5 (Spring 1980): 97–111; and Joan Aldous, "Family Development and the Life Course: Two Perspectives on Family Change," *Journal of Marriage and the Family* 52 (August 1990): 571–583.

[30] See, for example, Gunhild O. Hagestad, "Demographic Change and the Life Course: Some Emerging Trends in the Family Realm," *Family Relations* 37 (October 1988): 405–410; and Tamara K. Hareven and Kanji Masaoka, "Turning Points and Transitions: Perceptions of the Life Course," *Journal of Family History* 13 (1988): 271–289.

[31] Evelyn M. Duvall and Brent C. Miller, *Marriage and Family Development,* 6th ed. (New York: Harper and Row, 1985): Chapter 3.

[32] Ibid., 47.

[33] Ibid., 61.

Stage 4   Families with school children (oldest child, 6–13 years)

Stage 5   Families with teenagers (oldest child, 13–20 years)

Stage 6   Families as launching centers (first child gone to last child leaving home)

Stage 7   Middle-aged parents ("empty nest" to retirement)

Stage 8   Aging family members (retirement to death of both spouses)[34]

These stages are determined by the age and school placement of the oldest child up to the launching stage (6), after which the situation facing those remaining in the original family is the determinant. This type of scheme explicitly fails to recognize multiple-child families, overlapping stages, the death of a spouse, and many other variations in families. But this scheme, as most developmental schemes, views stages as distinct periods in the life course of the family group, with certain events (birth of a child, child entering school, etc.) triggering transitions to different stages.

Examples of empirical studies using family life-cycle categories can be seen in Chapter 12, which includes a section on marital quality over the family life course. Chapters 12 through 15 in general follow a family life-cycle model.[35]

APPRAISAL AND EXPANSION OF CONTEMPORARY FAMILY THEORY

The reader should not think that the structural-functional, social conflict, symbolic interaction, social exchange, and developmental theories are the only frames of reference in family sociology. In fact, the 1990s may be a time of theoretical synthesis: an integration of macro and micro ideas, a joining of structural and exchange theories into a network theory, or a blurring of distinct theoretical boundary lines, as theories borrow heavily from one another and new or revived ideas come to the fore.

What ideas? Notions of rationality are once again being challenged. Humanists are pressing for the involvement of social scientists in efforts toward

---

[34] Ibid., 26.

[35] Key concepts in the developmental approach are life cycle, developmental tasks, family transitions, family stages, family careers, life events, norms, roles, and role relationships.

Some of the leading advocates of this perspective include Joan Aldous, Evelyn Duvall, Robert J. Havighurst, Reuben Hill, Roy H. Rodgers, and James M. White.

For information on the developmental approach from the perspective of the family, examine the following: James M. White, *Dynamics of Family Development, A Theoretical Perspective* (New York: The Guilford Press, 1991); Evelyn M. Duvall and Brent C. Miller, *Marriage and Family Development*, 6th ed. (New York: Harper and Row, 1985); Roy H. Rodgers, *Family Interaction and Transaction: The Developmental Approach* (Englewood Cliffs, NJ: Prentice-Hall, 1973); and Chester A. Winton, *Frameworks for Studying Families*, Guilford, CT: Dushkin Publishing Group, Inc., 1995, Chapter 1, 9–43.

achieving social justice and improving social conditions. Many critical and feminist scholars have no desire to subject their theories and ideas to the positivistic (recognizing only matters of proof and fact) principles of science.

Jetse Sprey, who presented an appraisal of current theorizing about the institutions of marriage and the family, raised three concerns that might be labeled "unfinished business."[36] First is the integration of existing conceptual schemes into broader, more flexible vocabularies. Sprey would suggest, for example, that the five frames of reference listed in this chapter be viewed not as competitive or unique in their own right but as attempts to incorporate ideas—a conceptual and theoretical integration. The second concern is about modes of explanation. Basically, this involves linking and integrating conceptual vocabularies with appropriate questioning and levels of explanation. Sprey's third concern is the ongoing ambiguous relationship between conceptualization and theory building. Theoretical models, while abstract, can be constructed with "ordinary language or mathematics," either of which may provide a way to think about reality.

Sprey emphasized that theorizing cannot be considered static or unchanging. He proposed three alternatives to current mainstream family theorizing, which he termed hermeneutic, critical, and feminist orientations.[37] **Hermeneutics** refers to the art or theory of interpretation. It goes beyond the methods of science to any mode of experience in which truth is communicated. Subjectivity is not the opposite of objectivity but an essential human way of interpretative understanding and of managing one's social life. **Critical social science** approaches societies and families in terms of both what exists and what is possible in the future. It questions what types of social change are feasible and desirable as well as how they can be achieved. This orientation links the actual with the possible. **Feminist theorizing** is aimed at recognizing the absence of women in the history of social and political thought. It challenges patriarchal and sexist notions about the family, such as that it is natural or biological or that it is monolithic (having a single structure). This chapter will conclude with an expansion of the feminist frame of reference.

Feminist frame of reference

Feminist theories and perspectives assert that gender is basic to all social structures and organizations. The impetus for contemporary feminist theory is a simple question: And what about women?[38] Answers to this question are based on ideas that the experiences of women are *different* from those of men, are *unequal* (less privileged) to those of men, and are actively *oppressed* (restrained, subordinated, used, and abused) by men.

---

[36] Jetse Sprey, "Current Theorizing on the Family: An Appraisal," *Journal of Marriage and the Family* 50 (November 1988): 881–882. See also: Jetse Sprey (ed.), *Fashioning Family Theory: New Approaches* (Newbury Park, CA: Sage Publications, 1990).

[37] Sprey, "Current Theorizing," 882–886.

[38] Patricia Madoo Lengermann and Jill Niebrugge-Brantley, "Contemporary Feminist Theory," in George Ritzer, *Contemporary Sociological Theory* (New York: Alfred A. Knopf, 1988): 282–325.

Feminist theory alleges that women are not merely different from men but are less privileged and subordinate to them. The National Organization for Women is one key formal organization that works to acknowledge women and enhance their position.

Related to these ideas are basic assumptions of feminist thought, as discussed in an article in a special issue of *Family Relations* on feminism and family studies:

1. Women—or any group that is defined on the basis of age, class, race, ethnicity, disability, or sexual preference—are oppressed.

2. The *personal* is *political.* In other words, nothing is exclusive to women's personal lives; everything has social ramifications. The social system imposes a reality on everyday life and is not separate from it. Social structure must be taken into account.

3. Feminists have a double vision of reality: They need to be successful in the current system while working to change oppressive practices and institutions.[39]

Myra Marx Ferree challenged family studies to rethink two notions: (1) that families can be understood separately from the economic, political, and other systems of male power and (2) that families are unitary wholes where conflicts of

[39] Alexis J. Walker, Sally S. Kees Martin, and Linda Thompson, "Feminist Programs for Families, *Family Relations* 37 (January 1988): 17–22. See also Katherine R. Allen and Kristine M. Baber, "Starting a Revolution in Family Life Education: A Feminist Vision," *Family Relations* 41 (October 1992): 378–384; and Linda Thompson, "Conceptualizing Gender in Marriage: The Case of Marital Care," *Journal of Marriage and the Family* 55 (August 1993): 557–569.

U.S. Diversity: A Phenomenological Analysis of Female Sexuality

Phenomenological approaches seem to be highly appropriate for understanding how people construct their own reality. It is often used to examine meanings and experiences about which little is known or that are fraught with erroneous assumptions and misinformation. Thus Judith Daniluk, writing in the *Psychology of Women Quarterly* (1993: 53–69) revealed how she interviewed women in a group setting for 2–3 hours once a week for 11 weeks to determine how they experience their sexuality and what meanings they associate with these experiences.

All the women struggled with the reality that to be female, as defined in our culture is to be unworthy, flawed, and somehow deficient. Four primary contextual sources were identified as highly disenabling in defining and constructing their experiences of their sexuality. These included the influence of medicine, religion, sexual violence, and the media.

The experience of these women with *medicine* and medical professionals was one of having their power and dignity undermined, resulting in feelings of anger, loss, and helplessness. Normal female functions were pathological and the women felt blamed for their illnesses. Their experience with *religion* was one of making them feel guilty. Religious conceptions of the female body and bodily processes

left the women feeling dirty and shameful: punishment was viewed as God's response to female sexual desire and expression.

The women's experience with *sexual violence* in the form of rape, incest, verbal abuse, and sexual harassment resulted in all participants feeling victimized. Male ownership and prerogative was perceived as the guiding principle in a society that seems to discount women's needs for and right to safety. Fear, combined with feelings of betrayal, anger, violation, and self-blame characterized many of their memories. The *media* was a more subtle but pervasive source of influence in the women's experience of their sexuality. Television, music, movies, magazines, and videos all represented unrealistic standards of beauty and behavior.

In spite of these themes of cultural oppression, the women were able to access positive life- and self-affirming experiences. Areas of central importance to women for experiencing their sexuality included sexual expression, reproduction, body image, and intimate relationships. Rather than de-emphasizing differences between men and women, the perceived road to sexual self-esteem was viewed as a celebration of differences and the experiences unique to women.

interest between men and women are disregarded.[40] The first notion questions the *separateness* between public and private, where fundamentally different social relations exist in families more than in the rest of society. This idea supports the false notion that the family is a private world, where women take center stage, appear to have unlimited power, and are held responsible for everything—from the quality of the marital relationship to the mental health of the children and even to the prevention of male violence.

The second notion questions the *solidarity* myth, according to which the family is a unitary whole in which everyone shares a standard of living, class position, and set of interests. The reality is that conflicts of interest exist by gender, and fem-

---

[40] Myra Marx Ferree, "Beyond Separate Spheres: Feminism and Family Research," *Journal of Marriage and the Family* 52 (November 1990): 866–884.

inist thought recognizes this. In the words of Ferree, the feminist perspective "redefines families as arenas of gender and generational struggles, crucibles of caring and conflict, where claims for an identity are rooted, and separateness and solidarity are continually created and contested."[41]

Feminist theorists, while not denying the economic inequalities argued by Marxian theorists, do not blame all male/female inequalities on economic systems. Some feminists have substituted the word *patriarchy* for *bourgeoisie* and even for *sex roles*. *Sex roles*, with its theme of different but equal tasks and power, downplays the structured inequality (male dominance) that is pervasive. Male dominance exists in its own right and cuts across all economic and class lines. In addition, male dominance implies female oppression and sexism. The source of this oppression and sexism is in the home, where women, employed or not, find that housework and home are part of the same system. Until women increase their independence from men and gain resources (power, money, education, job opportunities, etc.) that improve their status, the family will never be an egalitarian institution.

What does a feminist frame of reference suggest for family studies and research? Linda Thompson has argued that a feminist agenda for family studies "includes experience embedded in broader context, the struggle to adapt to the contradictions of family life, a vision of nonoppressive families, diversity among women and families, and rethinking the discipline."[42]

Rethinking the discipline means moving beyond simple refining or revising existing concepts to generating new concepts and theories based on women's work and experiences. It means continually grappling with concepts such as truth, reality, and objectivity. It means believing that science, including family science, is a social activity embedded in a sociohistorical context. It means acknowledging that the questions asked (or not asked) about relationships and families are as significant as the answers given (or withheld). It means viewing theory, research, education, and all other aspects of family life from a perspective of social justice, where everyone is treated equally and differences are respected.

SUMMARY

1. A wide range of disciplines, approaches, and selected frames of reference are used in the study of the family. The marriage and family area is highly interdisciplinary; no single discipline either asks all the questions or provides all the answers. This book uses a social science orientation, with a major concentration focused on a sociology of the family.

2. Of what use is a sociology of the family? It alerts one to question the obvious and assess individual behavior in the context of the larger society. It enables one to obtain a body of knowledge about persons, relationships, and

---

[41] Ibid., 880.

[42] Linda Thompson, "Feminist Methodology for Family Studies," *Journal of Marriage and the Family* 54 (February 1992): 3.

family structures. It assists one in applying this body of knowledge to work with persons and families. It can be very useful to one on a personal level in improving critical-thinking and problem-solving skills, interpersonal skills, and communication skills. And finally, family sociology should help people understand themselves and the social context in which they live.

3. As the foundation for the entire book, this chapter summarized the nature of conceptual frameworks, frames of reference, and theories in general and provided an overview of five basic approaches: structural-functional, social conflict, symbolic interaction, social exchange, and developmental.

4. In this chapter and several that follow, considerable attention is given to concepts and their definitions. Although definitions of concepts seldom make very interesting reading, they are important. Namely, concepts are miniature systems of meaning that permit viewing a phenomenon in a certain way and sharing that view with others. In addition, concepts are basic to the development of hypotheses, propositions, and theories.

5. One of the most dominant theories or frames of reference in sociology is the structural-functional theory. This frame of reference uses the social system as the basic autonomous unit of which the family is a subsystem. All systems have interdependent parts (structures) that do certain things for the individual or society and have various social consequences (functions). The basic task of functional analysis is to explain the parts, the relationship among the parts and the whole, and the functions that are performed by or result from the relationship formed by the parts.

6. A second frame of reference is that of social conflict. Two significant issues in this perspective are the view of conflict (a) as natural and inevitable and (b) as a major factor that can lead to social change. Conflict theory is particularly applicable to a further understanding of marital relationships, power, the division of labor, and conflict at both macro (societal) and micro (interpersonal) levels.

7. The symbolic interaction frame of reference addresses two basic issues, both of central concern to the family: socialization and social interaction. The basic premises of this approach are (a) that human beings act toward things on the basis of the meanings things have for them, (b) that these meanings are derived from interaction with others, and (c) that these meanings are modified through an interpretive process. Each human being is unique unto himself or herself, understood only in his or her social context, is neither inherently good nor bad, and responds to self-stimulating or symbolically interpreted stimuli.

8. The social exchange framework helps explain why certain behavioral outcomes occur given a set of structural conditions and interactional potentialities. Two different approaches to exchange were examined in this chapter: one consistent with a behavioral frame of reference and the other with an interactionist frame of reference.

9. The developmental frame of reference has the peculiar characteristic of attempting to account for change in the family system and change in patterns of interaction over time with the use of concepts such as the *family life cycle* and *family life course.* The general outline of this book from Chapters 8 through 13 will follow broad stages of the life cycle, moving from premarital processes to marital and parental systems to the middle and later years.

10. An expansion of family theory includes alternatives to mainstream approaches such as those described. Alternatives include, among others, a feminist frame of reference that recognizes that the experiences of women are different, unequal, and oppressed as compared to those of men. Families cannot be understood apart from other systems of male power nor are families unitary wholes, where conflicts of interest between men and women can be disregarded.

11. Chapter 3 will turn to the family as a social institution, establishing the boundaries of marital, family, and kin groups and systems and examining selected structural features of this basic institution.

KEY TERMS AND TOPICS

Disciplines involved in family study p. 42

Social science approach to the family p. 44

Psychology, social psychology, and sociology p. 45

Uses of family sociology p. 46

Concepts p. 49

Variables p. 49

Conceptual frameworks p. 50

Propositions p. 50

Hypotheses p. 50

Theories p. 51

Structural-functional frame of reference p. 52

Social conflict frame of reference p. 56

Symbolic interaction frame of reference p. 58

Social exchange frame of reference p. 63

Developmental frame of reference p. 65

Hermeneutics p. 68

Critical social science p. 68

Feminist theorizing p. 68

Feminist frame of reference p. 68

DISCUSSION QUESTIONS

1. Examine two of the family and marriage books suggested in "Further Readings" (following). What disciplines are represented? How do they differ in their content and approach to the family?

2. Since no one discipline has all the answers to any family-related question, why isn't all research of an interdisciplinary nature? What problems exist in interdisciplinary research?

3. Of what value is a social science approach to the family? Within the social sciences, compare and contrast how psychology, social psychology, social anthropology, and sociology approach the family as an area of study.

4. Identify folklore that relates to mate selection, weddings, sexual behavior, childbirth, successful marriage, and so on. Which tales are likely to be challenged by science?

5. Differentiate between terms in the following pairs: concepts and variables; hypotheses and propositions; and conceptual frameworks and theories.

6. Discuss the major functions of the family in the United States. How are these different from the functions of families thirty years ago? What functions will the family likely perform thirty years from now?

7. Is conflict natural and inevitable in all marriages and families? Is conflict essential for change? Explain.

8. What types of assumptions and issues are basic to a symbolic interaction frame of reference? What difference does it make to assume that humans must be studied on their own levels, that the human infant is asocial, and the like? Relate these ideas to marriage and the family.

9. Write a paragraph on "Who I Am." Begin by listing the statuses you occupy. Take this list of statuses, and write one or two social expectations appropriate to each status. After reflection, write about the following: Which role expectations do you personally find displeasing? Are there conflicts between different expectations or between your personal preferences and social expectations? How do you handle them?

10. What exchanges can you identify in explaining male/female sexual behaviors, husband/wife spending patterns, and parent/child disciplinary behaviors? What is given and received in each exchange? Can you think of examples where no reciprocity is expected or given in return for a favor or gift? If so, what are they?

11. Identify what stage of the family life cycle your family is currently in (either you and your parents and siblings *or* you and your spouse and/or children). Identify the central problems, concerns, and tasks of a family at this particular stage.

12. Describe some basic assumptions of the feminist perspective. What contributions does this approach make to family studies and how people think about families?

FURTHER READINGS

Aldous, Joan. *Family Careers: Rethinking the Developmental Perspective.* Thousand Oaks, CA: Sage. 1996. A new version of family development that explores couple relations over time, parent-child relations over time, and sibling relations over time.

Baber, Kristine M., and Allen, Katherine R. *Women and Families: Feminist Reconstructions.* New York: Guilford Press, 1992. An examination from a feminist perspective of realms of family life that matter most to women: intimate relationships, sexuality, childbearing, caregiving, and work.

Boss, Pauline G.; Doherty, William J.; LaRossa, Ralph; Schumm, Walter R.; and Steinmetz, Suzanne K. *Sourcebook of Family Theories and Methods: A Contextual Approach.* New York: Plenum Press, 1993. A sociohistorical contextual approach to family theories, tracing their origins, assumptions, major concepts, research examples, and application to families.

Broderick, Carlfred B. *Understanding Family Process: Basics of Family Systems Theory.* Newbury Park, CA: Sage, 1993. An examination of the foundations of family process theory, including an exploration of relational space and the socialization of children within the family system.

Collins, Randall. *Four Sociological Traditions.* New York: Oxford University Press, 1994. An expanded edition of his earlier theoretical work, *Three Sociological Traditions* (conflict, Durkheimian, and microinteractional) with the addition of a rational/utilitarian tradition.

Collins, Randall, and Coltrane, Scott. *Sociology of Marriage and the Family; Gender, Love, and Property.* 4th ed. Chicago: Nelson-Hall, 1995. A sociology text that incorporates conflict and feminist perspectives into family issues and studies.

Cowan, Philip A.; Field, Dorothy; Hansen, Donald A.; Skolnick, Arlene; and Swanson, Guy E., eds. *Family, Self, and Society: Toward a New Agenda for Family Research.* Hillsdale, NJ: Lawrence Erlbaum Publishers, 1993. While the title suggests a new agenda for family research, the book includes 21 chapters focusing heavily on conceptual models and family theory that emphasize a contextual approach to the study of family relationships.

Grieve, Norma, and Burns, Ailsa, eds. *Australian Women: Contemporary Feminist Thought.* New York: Oxford University Press, 1994. Twenty-four articles cover the context of Australian feminism, feminist theory, and contesting male power.

Klein, David M., and White, James M. *Family Theories: An Introduction.* Thousand Oaks, CA: Sage, 1996. Six theoretical frameworks from the perspectives of sociology and family studies are presented: exchange, symbolic interaction, family development, systems, and ecological.

Rosenblatt, Paul C. *Metaphors of Family Systems Theory: Toward New Constructions.* NY: Guilford Press, 1994. Theoretical metaphors, where one kind of action or idea is used in place of another, are explored as the basis for thinking about family systems and for use in family therapy.

Sprey, Jetse, ed. *Fashioning Family Theory: New Approaches.* Newbury Park, CA: Sage, 1990. A book aimed at furthering communication and mutual understanding among scholars of differing theoretical perspectives.

Thorne, Barrie, with Marilyn Yalom. *Rethinking the Family: Some Feminist Questions.* Boston: Northeastern University Press, 1992. An introduction to feminist thinking on selected issues about the family as it has evolved over the last two decades.

Winton, Chester A. *Frameworks for Studying Families,* Guilford, CT: Dushkin Publishing Group, Inc., 1995. An examination of five theories central to studying families: developmental, structural-functional, conflict, social exchange, and symbolic interaction.

Chapter 3

Marital, Family, and Kinship Organization

Chapter 2 presented a variety of interdisciplinary, social science, and theoretical approaches to family study. Basic to any approach are selected concepts that provide systems of meaning to an aspect of the world in which people live. Consider the various ways in which the term *function* is used by family scholars; the dual perceptions of *role*, depending on its use in a structural or interactional frame of reference; and the different schools of thought evident in the social exchange framework.

Families take on new and varied perspectives when viewed in institutional terms; when seen as social groups or social systems; or when differentiated according to marriage and kin, orientation and procreation, nuclear and extended, and the like. This chapter will make note of these and other conceptual distinctions in studying and understanding the family.

FAMILY AS A SOCIAL INSTITUTION

Frequent reference is made to the family as the most basic of all social institutions. It is most closely linked to the supporting institution of marriage. What is meant by this?

The concept *institution* refers to specific areas of human social life that have become broadly organized into discernible patterns. *Institution* refers to the organized means whereby the essential tasks of a society are organized, directed, and carried out. In short, it denotes the system or norms that organize human behavior into stable patterns of activity.

Institution is a noun; *institutionalize* is a verb. The noun *institution* refers to "a system of norms, values, statuses, and roles that develop around a basic social goal."[1] All societies must deal with sexual activity and the social relations established by sexual union as well as the birth and care of dependent children. The institutional norms concerned with these matters constitute familial or kinship institutions.

The verb *institutionalize* means to establish patterned and predictable behavior; thus, noninstitutionalized behavior is spontaneous and irregular. Typically, a husband/wife fight is noninstitutionalized behavior; a professional boxing match is institutionalized. When an activity such as dating, sexual behavior, or childrearing becomes institutionalized, it becomes accepted by society as a necessary, proper, and predictable activity. At this time, although extramarital intercourse is common in American society, it has not been institutionalized; that is, it has not been accepted as standardized, approved, and culturally safeguarded behavior.

Several basic social institutions can be identified in all societies. Familial and kinship, educational, economic, political, and religious institutions appear to have existed in some form in all societies throughout history. Each of these institutions performs certain functions that are basic for the existence of a given society.

---

[1] J. Ross Eshleman, Barbara G. Cashion, and Lawrence Basirico, *Sociology: An Introduction*, 4th ed. (New York: HarperCollins, 1993): 109.

However, other areas have also become institutionalized. In American society, marriage, business, communication, medicine, law, science, and recreation have become institutionalized and thus basic to the way of life.

Few institutions have received more recognition and criticism than the family. It has been claimed to be the solution of most problems, on the one hand, and the basic cause of most problems, on the other. The family has been looked on with hope and dismay. Scientists, clergy, politicians, newspaper columnists, parents, and even stockbrokers speak out with authority on this institution. This book is intended to examine the diverse nature of family groups and family systems. Hopefully, the reader will be prompted to examine and redefine his or her understanding of this particular social institution: the family.

FAMILIES AS GROUPS AND SYSTEMS

Family and marital **groups and systems** are basic to a sociology of the family and to understanding the family as a social institution. Family systems are used in sociology much as physicists and biologists speak of solar or biological systems. In each instance, the word *system* means a configuration of interdependent parts. All systems, whether living or nonliving, have characteristic organizations and patterns of functioning. All major systems have subsystems that are part of the larger systems.

To treat the family as a social system is to note the forms of social organization and its modes of functioning. The family system is one example of interrelated statuses that fulfill certain basic functions. The family is a subsystem of the larger society that is related to and interdependent with other subsystems in society. The family fulfills selected tasks for society that are highly patterned, recurrent, and organized. Within the family system are subsystems (marital systems, partner-selection systems, sexual systems, childrearing systems) that are also highly patterned, recurrent, and organized in order to fulfill selected tasks. Although people are part of the system, it is the statuses, roles, norms, ways of ranking, means of social controls, and values (all abstractions) of those people that are significant in examining social systems.

The basic units, therefore, of a marital or family system are not persons but the interrelated statuses (positions) and the expectations (roles) that accompany those statuses. The interrelated statuses in the family system include, among others, parent/child, husband/wife, uncle/aunt, grandparent/grandchild, father/mother, and brother/sister. The norms (folkways and mores) and roles and also the expectations and values that accompany these statuses are of primary concern to the sociologist. Thus, a married male occupies the status of *husband.* He interacts with a married female who occupies the status of *wife.* These interrelated statuses, *husband* and *wife,* comprise the marital system. This system, like the family system or any other system, also has sets of norms and expectations that prescribe appropriate and inappropriate behaviors for the specific persons involved. Thus, systems are abstractions, forms of social organization composed of interrelated statuses.

Family and marital groups, in contrast to systems, are composed of people. These people are realities, rather than abstractions, who are physically present and who interact with one another in terms of their ascribed or achieved statuses. A person who is married belongs to a two-person marital group. The family group would consist of the married partners, the children, plus any other relatives included in the extended-family context. A marital or family group can have a specific address, a specific number of members, a specific income, and specific shared rituals. Marital and family groups are temporary, disbanding when their members depart. The system of which they are a part may continue for centuries, long after the departure or death of any specific member or specific family group.

It is the task of a sociology of the family to examine the nature of marital and family groups within societies and to understand the organizational patterns of marital and family systems that provide order within and among the groups involved.

Primary groups

Sociologists view groups as the core of their attention. They speak of in- and out-groups, primary and secondary groups, formal and informal groups, large and small groups, minority and majority groups, open and closed groups, organized and unorganized groups, independent and dependent groups, voluntary and involuntary groups, and others. Some of these ideal-type constructs are more useful to understanding family groups than others. One that appears to be particularly important is that of primary-group relationships.

A **primary group** consists of a small number of people who interact in direct, personal, and intimate ways. Primary-group relationships are facilitated by (1) face-to-face contact, (2) smallness of size, and (3) frequent and intense contact. Most families in the Western world operate under these conditions. Unlike most primary groups, the family is special because it is so essential, both to individuals and to society, and its formation is usually legitimized by the community through religious and legal rituals. While most other primary groups can disband voluntarily, the dissolution of the family group is generally accomplished through institutionalized means.

Much of the importance of marital, family, and kinship groups lies in their function as primary groups.[2] What functions does a primary group serve?

1. For most individuals, the primary group serves as the basic socializing agent for the acquisition and internalization of beliefs and attitudes.

2. The family, as a primary group, constitutes the chief focus for the realization of personal satisfaction. Perhaps more than any other source, the family provides everyone with a general sense of well-being, companionship, ego worth, security, and affection. Most people, when away from home for

---

[2] Note in particular: William Marsiglio and John H. Scanzoni, *Families and Friendships: Applying the Sociological Imagination.* New York: HarperCollins, 1995.

U.S. Diversity: Suicide and the Family

In 1992, according to information supplied by the U.S. Bureau of the Census, approximately 29,800 persons in the United States committed suicide. This number was equal to 12.0 suicides per 100,000 persons, down slightly from 12.4 in 1990. Since 1970, the increase in suicide rates has been most dramatic among persons under age thirty-five.

Is it possible that the increase in the number and rate of suicide, particularly in the fifteen- to thirty-five-year age group, is a result of less familial support, that is, a decrease in the family as a primary group? As first suggested by Emile Durkheim, in his classic study of suicide first published in 1897, explanations focusing on the psychology of the individual are inadequate. Second, suicide, most likely the most individual act that anyone is capable of, can only be fully understood in a social and societal context. Third, the rate of suicide varies inversely with the degree of social integration that a society (or a family?) provides.

Steven Stack attempted to determine the impact of divorce on suicide, namely, whether the strength of the relationship would change over time. He tested two opposing explanations: status integration theory and the Durkheimian perspective. Given that divorce became more frequent from the 1960s to the 1980s, status integration theory would predict a decline in the effect of divorce on suicide. The Durkheimian perspective, based on a state of anomie (not being integrated into a cohesive social group), would predict no change or an increase in suicide.

Stack's research, like that of others, found that populations with high divorce rates are marked by higher rates of suicide even when controlled by factors such as economic conditions. His research found, as well, some support for both perspectives. That is, as divorce has become more common, so has the gap narrowed between suicide rates of the divorced and married. The gap is, however, still substantial, given the high anomie of the divorced.

These findings lend additional support to the importance of the family and the social integration provided by being part of an intimate primary group.

Source: U.S. Bureau of the Census, *Statistical Abstract of the United States: 1995,* 115th ed. (Washington, DC: U.S. Government Printing Office, 1995) no. 136, p. 100; Emile Durkheim, *Suicide* (New York: Free Press, 1966; originally published in 1897); and Steven Stack, "New Micro-Level Data on the Impact of Divorce on Suicide, 1959–1980: A Test of Two Theories," *Journal of Marriage and the Family* 52 (February 1990): 119–27.

the first time, experience homesickness, or a nostalgia for the primary group from which their immediate ties have been severed.

3. The family also serves as a basic instrument of social control. The family has an extraordinary capacity to punish deviation and reward conformity, since most people depend on other group members for meeting psychological needs and for realizing meaningful social experiences.

Secondary groups

The opposite of the primary group is the **secondary group.** Many if not most of people's involvements with school, work, and the community are not characterized by the intimate, informal, and personal nature of primary groups but rather are characterized by impersonal, segmental, and utilitarian contacts. Secondary groups are basically goal oriented rather than person oriented. For instance, the personal life of the bus driver, or a classmate in a lecture, or the insurance sales-person is not of major significance in fulfilling the goals established for interactions with these people.

In a society dominated by secondary-group relationships, family groups, time and again, provide the primary relationships that are vital to individual health and happiness. Cochran et al., in a book dealing with the social networks of parents and children in several countries, suggested that important social support is given by primary sources such as friends, neighbors, workmates, and organizational/agency contacts. But the *primary* support network—that is, the people who are the most important—is, consistently, relatives.[3]

An absence or loss of familial networks as primary sources of social support has been linked to a wide range of negative outcomes: school truancy, accidents, suicides, commitment to mental hospitals, pregnancy disorders, coronary disease, and even lack of recovery from all types of illnesses. An argument could be made that, without primary-group relationships or the presence of intimate family bonds, survival itself would be doubtful. This idea has been fairly well substantiated with infants and adults who have no family or close friends.

One possible conclusion from all of this is that, rather than being in a state of decay, or losing its significant functions and becoming obsolete, the U.S. family may be fulfilling a primary-group function that has seldom been more crucial and important in maintaining personal and social stability and well-being.

CHARACTERISTICS OF MARRIAGE, FAMILY, AND KINSHIP GROUPS

Marriage, family, and kinship groups are institutionalized social arrangements in all known societies. However, the nature of the arrangement differs greatly across societies, over time, and even within a given society at a specific time.

Frequently, legal and social norms themselves lack clarity as to what does or does not constitute a marriage, family, or kinship group. For example, is it a marriage if two males live together and recognize each other as spouses, or if a male and female live together but have no marriage contract or never experience a wedding ceremony, or if a male and female go through a marriage ceremony and then almost immediately separate permanently? Can any group of persons constitute a marriage, a family, or a kinship group? Consider the boundaries of each.

Boundaries of marriage

Throughout the world, marriage is an institutional arrangement between persons, generally males and females, who recognize each other as husband and wife or inti-

---

[3] Moncrieff Cochran, Mary Larner, David Riley, Lars Gunnarsson, and Charles R. Henderson, Jr., *Extending Families: The Social Networks of Parents and Their Children*, Cambridge: Cambridge University Press, 1990.

Definitions and meanings of marriage and intimate relationships are changing. Marriages are no longer defined or labeled as being traditional, singular, or static; rather they are being defined as nontraditional, pluralistic, and dynamic. Many gay men and lesbian women are forming primary, intimate, long-term relationships and seek the rights and privileges enjoyed by marriages and families.

mate partners. Marriage is a social institution that is strictly human and assumes some permanence and conformity to societal norms.

About thirty-five years ago, William Stephens, an anthropologist, said that marriage is (1) a socially legitimate sexual union, begun with (2) a public announcement, undertaken with (3) some idea of performance, and assumed with a more or less explicit (4) marriage contract, which spells out reciprocal obligations between spouses and between spouses and their children.[4] For the most part, these same normative conditions exist today, although many marriagelike relationships are not defined by everyone as socially legitimate, are not begun with any type of announcement, are not entered into with the idea of permanence, and do not always have clearly defined contracts (written or nonwritten) as to what behaviors are expected. Thus, debate exists as to whether certain types of intimate relationships (such as among same-sex partners or unmarried cohabitors) are socially and legally recognized as marriages or families.

Any definition of marriage or family is, in a certain sense, arbitrary. Most current definitions of marriage exclude persons in same-sex relationships, persons such as children, and persons who do not meet the social or cultural norms that specify what marriage is and who the legitimate partners are. In fact, many phenomenological, conflict, and feminist theorists call into question the very use of labels such

---

[4] William N. Stephens, *The Family in Cross Cultural Perspective* (New York: Holt, Rinehart and Winston, 1963): 7.

as *marriage, family,* and *kin.* The suggestion is that the very use of a label reifies (makes real or concrete) a reality that ignores the historic origins and the range of meanings given to marriage and family by persons in their day-to-day lives.

Recognizing the danger of reifying the concept, let us turn our attention to historical and cross-cultural variations in marriage patterns, particularly as related to the number of persons involved.

Marriage and number of spouses

Marital status (single, married, separated, widowed, divorced) and number of spouses (none, one, more than one) are two major components of the boundaries of marriage. With a change in marital status and the number of spouses comes variations in marital interaction patterns; living and sleeping arrangements; exclusivity of sexual interactions; the likelihood of and number of children; patterns of support, decision making, and authority; and male/female roles, to mention a few.

Obviously, never to have had a spouse is to have a nonmarital status. The never-married single can be expected to share certain characteristics of other single statuses yet in many ways differs from the widowed or divorced single. The latter two single statuses (widowed and divorced) are discussed in Chapters 15 and 17, respectively.

Singlehood

In 1994, more than 24.7 million males and 19.5 million females in the United States, age eighteen and over, were never-married singles.[5] These numbers comprised 27.1 percent of all males and 19.7 percent of all females. White males and white females (24.9 and 17.1 percent, respectively) were less likely to be single than black males (42.4 percent), males of Hispanic origin (35.4 percent), black females (36.2 percent), and females of Hispanic origin (24.2 percent). As expected, the number and percentage of never-married individuals dropped sharply with increasing age. About 98 percent of the men and 91 percent of the women, age sixteen and under, were single (had never been married). By age forty-five, only 8.2 percent of the men and 5.9 percent of the women were not and had never been married.

Since 1970, the percentage of those who have never been married has risen sharply. This increase is particularly apparent in the age groups where most men and women have traditionally married. In the group age twenty to twenty-four, for example, there has been an 84.4 percent increase in the number of single women (from 35.8 percent in 1970 to 66.0 percent in 1994) and a 48.1 percent increase in the number of single men (from 54.7 percent in 1970 to 81.0 percent in 1994).[6] The increase in the twenty-five to twenty-nine age group is even more dramatic: 235 percent for women and 163 percent for men (see Figure 3-1).

Whether the tendency among younger groups to refrain from marrying represents merely a postponement of first marriage or development of a trend toward

---

[5] U.S. Bureau of the Census, *Statistical Abstract of the United States: 1995,* 115th ed. (Washington, DC: U.S. Government Printing Office, 1995), no. 59, p. 55.

[6] Ibid.

News Item: Can Lesbians and Gays Marry, Divorce, Adopt Children, and Be Families?

Case 1

An article in the *New York Times,* "Gay Marriages: Make Them Legal," cited the case of two women who exchanged vows and rings, pledged their love and lifelong devotion to one another, and were spouses for several years in every respect except the legal. However, one of the women was severely injured when her car was struck by a truck. She lost the capacity to walk or to speak more than several words at a time. She needed constant care. The partner sought a court ruling granting her guardianship. But the parents of the injured woman opposed the petition and obtained sole guardianship, moved their daughter three hundred miles away from her partner, and forbade all visits between the two women. Were they allowed to be legally married, which as of early 1996, all fifty states deny to millions of gay and lesbian Americans, this type of forced separation would not have been allowed.

Case 2

Two men in Pennsylvania sought a divorce. But the Pennsylvania state superior court ruled that people of the same sex could not contract a common-law marriage and thus were not eligible to divorce.

The judges ruled that marriage was a heterosexual activity that dated back to the nation's beginnings, when statutes spoke, as they do now, of husband and wife and bride and groom, which are interpreted to mean male and female.

Case 3

Florida and New Hampshire have laws prohibiting lesbians and gays from adopting children under any circumstances. New York, California, Oregon, Washington, Alaska, Vermont, and the District of Columbia permit same-sex, second-parent adoptions. That is, if both members of a same-sex couple want to be a child's parents, the partner of the legal parent may adopt the child and become a second parent (much as stepparents adopt the children of their spouses).

Case 4

The San Francisco Board of Supervisors approved a law that allows unmarried partners to register their relationships with the city. San Francisco thus joins other cities and governments that are considering domestic partnership laws in legal recognition of diverse family structures.

lifelong singleness is not clear. However, just as cohorts (people born during a similar time period) of young women who have postponed childbearing for an unusually long time seldom make up for the child deficit as they grow older, so may young people who delay marriage never make up for the marriage deficit.

Apparently, a new style of singlehood is emerging that represents one of choice and a status that has positive outcomes for happiness, career, and social mobility. Take happiness, for example. Studies in the United States have consistently reported considerably higher levels of personal happiness for married persons than for persons in any unmarried category (never married, divorced, or widowed). But these married/nonmarried differences in happiness appear to have lessened over the past several decades.[7] The overall change has been due primarily to an increase

[7] Norval D. Glenn and Charles N. Weaver, "The Changing Relationship of Marital Status to Reported Happiness," *Journal of Marriage and the Family* 50 (May 1988): 317–324.

Figure 3-1
Individuals never married, by selected age groups: 1970, 1980, and 1994

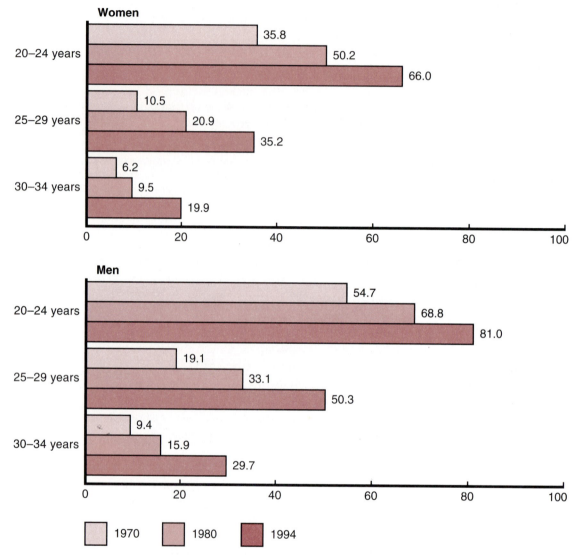

Source: U.S. Bureau of the Census, *Statistical Abstract of the United States: 1995,* 115th ed. (Washington, DC: U.S. Government Printing Office, 1995), no. 59, p. 55.

in the reported happiness of never-married males and a decrease in the reported happiness of married females. Findings such as these have led the authors to question the strong statements about the continued importance of marriage and the widely held belief that the institution of marriage in the United States is as strong and viable as ever.

Such a decrease in single/married differences is not universal, however. For example, in contemporary Japan, it was found that the levels of mortality experienced by single Japanese is staggeringly high in comparison with those of married Japanese.[8] Not only is discrimination and stigma associated with those who do not marry but unmarried individuals experience relatively high rates of dying and presumably much poorer health. For example, mortality data for the mid-1990s indicates that a 20-year-old Japanese man or woman who remains single can expect to live as much as 15 years less than his or her married counterpart.

This recent finding, while perhaps extreme, supports the hundreds of research studies over the past one hundred years that have shown that married men and women throughout the world tend to live longer and experience better health than do never-married, widowed, and divorced persons. Marriage may serve to increase social networks that facilitate access to medical information and services, constrain risk-taking behavior, and act as a buffering mechanism in stressful situations.

Returning to the United States, for females at least, being single has a number of consequences that most might view as positive. For example, being single is associated with having a higher educational level, a higher median income, a higher occupational status, and in general a higher level of achievement. As demonstrated in the discussion of the dual-career marriage in Chapter 4, marriage seems to impede career advancement for females. What is unclear is the extent to which the single status results from educational and economic success or the extent to which these successes result from the single status.

What is clear is that as the median age at marriage increases, so does a longer period of singlehood. With later marriage comes an increased likelihood of remaining in the family home. National data revealed that 29 percent of never-married adult children live with their parents (as do 13 percent of divorced adult children).[9] Thus both delayed marriage and high divorce rates increase parents, long-term, day-to-day responsibility for their children.

On the other hand, with later marriage and a longer period of singlehood comes the potential for an increased period of independent living away from the parental home. Some consequences of remaining single for a longer time, particularly for women, are that they are more likely to plan for employment, lower their expected family size, be more accepting of the employment of mothers, and be more nontraditional on sex roles than those who live with parents.[10]

Monogamy

To most Americans, the most traditional as well as the most proper form of marriage is **monogamy: one man to one woman** (at a time). Throughout the world, this form of marriage is the only one universally recognized and is the predomi-

---

8 Noreen Goldman, "The Perils of Single Life in Contemporary Japan," *Journal of Marriage and the Family* 55 (February 1993): 191–204.

9 Lynn White and Debra Peterson, "The Retreat from Marriage: Its Effect on Unmarried Children's Exchange with Parents," *Journal of Marriage and the Family* 57 (May 1995): 428–434.

10 Linda J. Waite, Frances Kobrin Goldscheider, and Christina Witsberger, "Nonfamily Living and the Erosion of Traditional Family Orientation Among Young Adults," *American Sociological Review* 51 (August 1986): 541–554.

nant form even within societies where other forms exist. In these societies, most men are too poor to have more than one wife. However, it should be noted that historically, on a societal basis, only a small percentage of societies in the world have been designated as strictly monogamous (monogamy is the required form).[11]

Although the United States is designated as strictly monogamous, it is possible for Americans to have more than one husband or one wife. Since monogamy has never achieved perfect stability, certain married persons end their relationships and most of them remarry. Thus, the second spouse, although not existing simultaneously with the first, is sometimes referred to as fitting into a pattern of **sequential or serial monogamy,** or *remarriage* (see Chapter 15). Thus, in U.S. society, it is both legally and socially approved to have more than one wife or more than one husband, as long as they occur sequentially and not simultaneously.

To a sizeable proportion of the population, replacing marriage partners in a sequentially monogamous fashion is a variation on the lifelong, same-spouse, monogamous pattern. In addition, most nontraditional marital life-styles occur within the context of monogamy or sole partners. Childless marriage, sexual equality, dual careers, and androgynous role patterns are more likely to occur in a one-male/one-female marriage than in any other type. These marital life-styles are discussed elsewhere throughout this book, usually as found within monogamous situations.

Polygamy

Polygamy is distinguished from monogamy. The suffix -*gamy* refers to marriage or a union for propagation and reproduction. Thus, *monogamy* (single), *bigamy* (two), *polygamy* (several or many), *allogamy* (closely related), *endogamy* (within), and *exogamy* (outside or external) describe the nature of marriage. Polygamy refers to marriage to several or many individuals. Theoretically, there could be several or many wives (**polygyny**), several or many husbands (**polyandry**), or several or many husbands and wives (**group marriage**). Each of these is a polygamous marriage, as distinguished from a monogamous (one) or bigamous (two) marriage.

The frequency with which marriage to a plural number of spouses occurs normatively (as an expected or desired type of marriage) was investigated in the late 1950s in a classic study by George Murdock. In a world sample of 554 societies, polygyny was culturally favored in 415 (77 percent), whereas polyandry was culturally favored in only 4 (less than 1 percent): Toda, Marquesas, Nayar, and Tibet.[12] Research over the years has never uncovered a society in which group marriage was clearly the dominant or most frequent form.

Several words of caution are needed concerning polygamy. First, it is necessary to maintain a clear distinction between ideology and actual occurrence. Occasionally in the United States, a group advocates the right to have as many or

---

[11] George P. Murdock, "World Ethnographic Sample," *American Anthropologist* 59 (August 1957): 686.
[12] Ibid.

as few spouses as desired. Also, when multiple-spouse marriages or communes are located and studied, the results are exploited by the mass media and given considerable attention. It seems that the uniqueness or rarity of the situation attracts the attention, rather than any commonality.

Second, multiple spouses (except in group marriage) are only possible on a large scale when an unbalanced **sex ratio** (number of males per 100 females) exists. Only if the sex ratio is either high or low will polygamy be possible without increasing the number of single persons of one sex.

Third, polygamy, where it exists, is highly regulated and normatively controlled, as are all forms of marriage. Rarely does it involve a strictly personal or psychological motive. Rather, polygamy is likely to be supported by the attitudes and values of both sexes and linked closely to the sex ratio, economic conditions, and belief systems.

Fourth, polygamy itself has many forms and variations of normative structure that determine who the spouse should be. For example, in some cases, all the multiple husbands are considered brothers *(fraternal polyandry)* or all the multiple wives are sisters *(sororal polygyny)*. A levirate and sororate arrangement existed in the ancient Hebrew family. The *levirate* was a situation (technically, sequential monogamy) in which the wife married the brother of her deceased husband, whereas the *sororate* was a situation in which the preferred mate for a husband was the sister of his deceased wife.

From the perspective of families in North America, each of the preceding patterns represents a nontraditional family form. Polygyny and polyandry will be examined in greater detail.

Polygyny **Polygyny** is the marriage of one man to more than one woman at the same time, and is the most frequent form of polygamy. Although not rare throughout the world, researchers and writers often ignore contemporary polygyny. Charles Welch and Paul Glick suggested that this oversight is due in part to the fact that systematic study is hampered by the persistent absence of adequate amounts of readily accessible and reliable data.[13] However, Welch and Glick selected fifteen African countries to illustrate its incidence (polygynists per hundred married men), intensity (number of wives per polygynist), and general index (number of wives per married man). The incidence of polygyny per hundred men was typically between twenty and thirty-five; that is, from about one in five to one in three married men had more than one wife. The intensity ranged from 2.0 to 2.5, which indicates that most polygynists had two wives rather than three or more. And for each country as a whole, the general index (number of wives per married man) ranged from 1.1 to 1.6, which indicates that most men, even in highly polygynous countries, had only one wife.

13 Charles E. Welch, III and Paul C. Glick, "The Incidence of Polygamy in Contemporary Africa: A Research Note," *Journal of Marriage and the Family* 43 (February 1981): 191–193.

Global Diversity: How About a Temporary Marriage—or Several Simultaneously?

Temporary marriage, or *muta,* is a contract under Islamic law between a man and an unmarried woman. Both the period that the marriage shall last and the amount of money to be exchanged are specified in advance. In *muta,* witnesses are not required and the marriage need not be registered. By mutual agreement of the partners, the marriage can last from one hour to ninety-nine years; at the end of the specified period, the temporary spouses part without having a divorce ceremony.

A Moslem man may contract simultaneously as many temporary marriages as he desires. This is in addition to the four wives he is legally allowed. An unmarried woman—virgin, divorcee, or widow—is permitted to marry only one man at a time, whether in a temporary or permanent union.

Religious leaders say that *muta* is positive and acknowledges human needs. The Islamic regime joins these leaders in advocating the benefits of temporary marriage, extolling its roots in the Koran and its positive effects for social and moral health. The public drive to encourage *muta* has become particularly intense as a result of the deaths of thousands of men in the Iran-Iraq War. Critics condemn the practice as nothing more than legalized prostitution that debases and abuses women.

Source: World Press Review, July 1990.

In Nigeria, the number of plural wives was found to be related to the stability of marriage.[14] Unions with two wives were more stable than those with three or more wives. Despite an ideology of equity among all the wives, it is likely that, when there are more than two, differentiation increases among the wives on the bases of age, education, family wealth, and so on. Marriage to a third or fourth wife thus seems to intensify co-wife conflict and economic constraints.

Polygyny appears to be a privilege of the wealthy. Often, having several wives is a mark of prestige, distinction, and high status. The chiefs, the wealthy, the best hunters, and the leaders get second and third wives. Even in Israel, throughout the Old Testament period, polygyny was practiced but often restricted to men who were rich, occupied leading positions, or had some other claim to distinction. Even today in the Middle East, the common man has only one wife.

Why have more than one wife? Many circumstances and motives contribute to polygyny. The prestige and status dimension has been mentioned. Beyond that, there is sometimes a need or desire to facilitate procreation, particularly that of male children. Interestingly, while a plural number of wives increases the chances for a

---

[14] Anastasia J. Gege-Brandon, "The Polygyny-Divorce Relationship: A Case Study of Nigeria," *Journal of Marriage and the Family* 54 (May 1992): 285–292.

male child, it reduces fertility for women in these marriages.[15] That is, women in polygynous marriages have a lower rate of pregnancy than do women in monogamous marriages. Warren Hern claimed that polygyny is almost universally linked with postpartum sexual abstinence, lactational amenorrhoea (absence or suppression of menstruation while breastfeeding), and long birth intervals.[16] The final factor—long birth intervals—is closely and causally related to low fertility, better child survival, and lower maternal mortality. Lower fertility may be a consequence as well of the mother's age at marriage, of added wives having previous marital disruptions, of senior wives insisting on sexual abstinence later in life, and of husbands being considerably older at the time second and third wives are added.

Other reasons given for polygyny include wife capture (where the men from one village literally take wives from another village), economic value of wifely services, and, in some instances, religious revelation. The frequently cited example of Mormon polygyny originated in a religious revelation to Joseph Smith, the founder of the Church of Jesus Christ of the Latter-day Saints (the Mormon religion). Interestingly, some of the very factors that led to the occurrence of polygyny in this religion were the same factors that led to its being outlawed. Namely, the Mormon faith was begun and maintained by devout conviction to carrying out God's will; it was ended by a revelation from God to the president of the church, forbidding continuation of polygyny.

Christianity stamped Western society in a similar manner by outlawing polygyny. Polygyny was frequent among the pre-Christian tribes of Europe as well as in Old Testament Hebrew accounts. Gideon, the Israelite judge, had many wives who bore him seventy sons (Judges 8:30). King David had several wives (Samuel 25:39, 43; II Samuel 3:2 ff., 5:13), and King Solomon had a huge number of wives (I Kings 9:16; Song of Solomon 6:8).

Most people who have been socialized in the Western world and frequently in the Judeo-Christian tradition (including readers of this text) would not likely favor polygyny as a personal life-style. They would suspect jealousy, competition, and conflict as disruptive factors among the multiple wives. In contrast, a study from Ibadan, Nigeria, where polygyny is very common, indicated that co-wives get along fairly well. When wives were asked how they would feel if their husbands took another wife, some 60 percent said they would be pleased to share the housework, husband care, and childrearing and to have someone to gossip and "play" with.[17]

Jealousy among co-wives, however, does seem to be considerably more frequent than jealousy among co-husbands, for several reasons. The greater likelihood

---

15 See Douglas L. Anderton and Rebecca Jean Emigh, "Polygamous Fertility: Sexual Competition versus Progeny," *American Journal of Sociology* 4 (January 1989): 832–855; Nan E. Johnson and A. M. Elmi, "Polygamy and Fertility in Somalia," *Journal of Biosocial Science* 21 (1989): 127–134; and Alfred A. Adewuyi, "Marital Fertility in Polygamous Unions in Nigeria," *Journal of Biosocial Science* 20 (1988): 393–400.

16 Warren M. Hern, "Polygyny and Fertility among the Shipibo of the Peruvian Amazon," *Population Studies* 46 (1992): 53–64.

17 Helen Ware, "Polygyny: Women's Views in a Traditional Society, Nigeria 1975," *Journal of Marriage and the Family* 41 (February 1979): 188.

of jealousy among co-wives may stem from the fact that women are more fre-quently *chosen*, whereas men more likely *choose* to have co-spouses. Understandably, having less choice in the matter of being married may contribute to much greater potential for jealousy. In addition, it has been suggested that co-husbands are more likely to be brothers than co-wives are likely to be sisters. If this is the case, it is possible that jealousy would be less among siblings than among nonsiblings.

Anthropologists have observed that, if co-wives are sisters, they usually live in the same house; if co-wives are not sisters, they usually live in separate houses. Thus, for some reason, it seems that siblings can better tolerate, suppress, and live with a situation of sexual rivalry than can nonsiblings.

What about polygyny in the United States today? The most frequently cited sources of polygyny are those of certain Mormon fundamentalists living in "under-ground" family units in Utah and neighboring states. The number of these mar-riages is unknown.

Polyandry   **Polyandry** is the marriage of one woman to more than one man at the same time, and appears to be quite rare. Stephens has made several generalizations about polyandry. First, polyandry and group marriage tend to go together; where one is found, the other will likely be found.[18]

Second, co-husbanding is fraternal. In the few cases in which the husbands are not brothers, they are clan brothers; that is, they belong to the same clan and are of the same generation. Among the Todas, a non-Hindu tribe in India, it is under-stood that when a woman marries a man, she becomes the wife of his brothers at the same time. Among the Yanomama Indians living in northern Brazil, a wife may have other recognized sexual unions with the consent of her husband. The most frequent union is with the husband's younger brother, who, until he acquires his own wife, has a quasi-right to his older brother's wife. The husband may also consent to share his wife with other males, kin or nonkin, who may be recognized as secondary husbands throughout their lives.[19]

Third, an economic inducement is often mentioned. A man tries to recruit co-husbands so they will work for him. In other instances, co-husbandry is prac-ticed for economic security or as an answer to a land shortage. When several men marry one woman, the fragmentation of holdings, especially land, is avoided. Cassidy and Lee argued that economic factors are the key to understanding the very existence of polyandry.[20] That is, the two most important antecedents to polyandry appear to be (1) extreme societal poverty with harsh environmental conditions and (2) limited roles for women in the productive economy.

---

[18] Stephens, *The Family in Cross Cultural Perspective*, pp. 39–49.

[19] John D. Early and John F. Peters, *The Population Dynamics of the Mucajai Yanomama.* (New York: Academic Press, 1990), p. 40.

[20] Margaret L. Cassidy and Gary R. Lee, "The Study of Polyandry: A Critique and Synthesis," *Journal of Comparative Family Studies* 20 (Spring 1989): 1–11.

Where polyandry does exist, there is frequent mention of female infanticide. It is a curious anomaly that male infanticide is rarely, if ever, mentioned in the literature. Female infanticide eliminates the wife surplus among polyandrous families; however, male infanticide does not seem to be used to eliminate the husband surplus in polygynous societies.

Group marriage Group marriage exists when several males and several females are married simultaneously to each other. Except on an experimental basis, this is an extremely rare occurrence and may never have existed as a viable form of marriage for any society in the world.

The Oneida Community of upstate New York has been frequently cited as an example of a group marriage experiment (see "Oneida Today" panel p. 94). In the mid-1800s, the Oneida practiced economic and sexual sharing based on spiritual and religious principles. The group was an experimental religious community and not representative of U.S. society at the time. In addition, similar to most group marriages on record, the time span of this experiment was limited. Rarely do such arrangements endure beyond one or two generations.

Group marriage has various difficulties that include, among others, getting all members to accept each other as spouses; avoiding jealousy over status, privileges, affection, and sex; and problems related to housing, income, children, privacy, and division of labor in general. What's more, when group marriage does exist, the strong negative reactions of outside persons who are aware of it force anonymity and secrecy. Thus, it seems reasonable to assume that group marriage will never become very popular.

Boundaries of the family

The family signifies a set of statuses and roles acquired through marriage, procreation, adoption, or a recognition and inclusion of certain persons as family members. The primary relatives, such as parents and children, tend to share a common residence but the residence may include many other persons as well. Generally, the members assume reciprocal rights and obligations to one another. One key function of families that appears to be a cultural universal centers around the socialization of children.

It could be said that all marriages are families but not all families are marriages. And certain functions expected in the marital relationship (coitus or sexual intercourse) are taboo among certain family members (such as between brothers and sisters). As marriages differ structurally in the number of spouses, so do families differ structurally in size and composition.

Typology of family structures

One controversy in the family literature has focused on the extent to which families, particularly in the United States, are small, isolated, independent units as

Case Example:
Oneida Today: Group Marriage Out—Profits In

The Oneida community began in New York in 1848 with approximately twenty-five members. The leader, John Humphrey Noyes, gave up law to enter the ministry. He preached that human beings were capable of living sinless lives based on a spiritual equality of all persons: materially, socially, and sexually. Monogamy was a sign of selfish possessiveness.

Under the charismatic leadership of this man, the group grew and prospered. The emphasis was on *we* rather than on *I*. Economically, there was self-sufficiency and equal ownership of property. The Oneida made traps, marketed crops in cans and glass jars, did silk spinning, and manufactured silverware. To eliminate feelings of discrimination and sexual inequality, jobs were rotated.

The group differed from most other communal groups in their *group marriage*, or pantogamous (marriage for all), relationship. It was felt that romantic love made spiritual love impossible to attain and gave rise to jealousy, hate, and the like; therefore, everyone should literally love everyone else. Requests for sexual relationships were made to a central committee. A go-between, usually an older woman, would get the consent of the requested female (women rarely made requests), and, if agreed upon, the couple would go to the woman's bedroom.

Any discord or problem among the Oneida was handled daily in a practice known as *mutual criticism,* where the followers would subject themselves to criticism by the rest of the group. The criticized member would sit quietly while the others listed his or her good and bad points. The result was said to be a catharsis, a spiritual cleansing, with remarkably successful outcomes.

When Noyes left the group for Canada in 1879, for whatever reason (outside pressures, age, health, intracommune strife), the group marriage practice came to an end. However, the economically successful venture continued.

On November 20, 1880, the group incorporated as Oneida Community, Ltd., to succeed Oneida Community. The present title, Oneida Ltd., was adopted in 1935.

Today, Oneida Ltd. can be found listed on the New York Stock Exchange. A recent chairman of the board was Peter T. Noyes, a grandson of John Humphrey Noyes, founder of the Oneida Community. The company makes flatware, silverplated and pewter holloware, jewelry, and gift items. It also markets tableware products and makes cookware and industrial wire products. This international corporation has plants in Arkansas, New York (three), Massachusetts, Kansas, England (three), Canada, and Northern Ireland. In early 1996, the stock was selling at sixteen dollars per share, paid a forty-eight cent dividend per share, and had yearly sales of over 500 million dollars.

Thus, Mr. Noyes would be proud. His children and grandchildren have prospered well. While group marriage is out, profits are in.

opposed to large, interdependent networks. The extremes are usually represented by a nuclear/extended dichotomy, with modified nuclear and modified extended as intermediate positions. The major characteristics of these family types are outlined in Table 3-1.

Nuclear and conjugal families **Nuclear and conjugal families** both characterize the family unit in its smallest form. Generally, this form includes the husband, the wife, and their immediate children. The terms *nuclear* and *conjugal* are at times used interchangeably; however, they are not truly synonymous. A conjugal family must include a husband and wife. A nuclear family may or may not include the marriage partners but consists of any two or more persons related to one another by blood, marriage, or adoption, assuming they are of the same or adjoining generations. Thus, a brother and sister or a single parent and child are both nuclear families but would not, technically speaking, be conjugal families.

Since most persons marry, it is likely that, during their lifetime, they will be members of two different but overlapping nuclear families. The nuclear family into which someone is born and reared (consisting of self, brothers and sisters, and parents) is termed the **family of orientation.** This is the family unit where the first and most basic socialization processes occur. When an individual marries, he or she forms a new nuclear (and conjugal) family: a **family of procreation.** This family is composed of self, spouse, and children.

Table 3-1
Typology of family structures

Nuclear-conjugal	Modifed-nuclear and Modifed-extended	Extended
Small size	Intermediate size	Many kin
Geographic isolation	Kin within easy visiting distance	Geographic proximity
Minimal kin contact	Regular contact	Daily contact
Family autonomy	Family autonomy with kin influences in decision making	Intergenerational authority
Self-sufficient economically	Considerable exchange of goods and services	Economic interdependence
Nonkin models of socialization	Kin, friendship, nonkin models of socialization	Kinship network as model for socialization
Emotional support and protection from nonkin	Emotional support and protection from kin and nonkin	Kinship completed source of emotional support and protection

The controversy over whether the family system in the United States and Canada is nuclear centers on questions related to geographical isolation, economic independence, and social autonomy. Do families live separately from kin? Do other relatives outside the nuclear unit provide financial assistance or aid in times of need? Do kin provide significant emotional support, visiting patterns, and social activities? And if the nuclear family is isolated, independent, and autonomous, does this lead to high divorce rates; to the need for more public assistance programs for people who are aged, for single parents, or for families in poverty; and to an increase in personal instability (alcoholism, suicide, mental illness, and the like)? Whatever the actual state of the family, questions such as these seem highly relevant to individual health as well as societal functioning.

Modified-nuclear and modified-extended families A number of writers have suggested that the isolated nuclear family is largely fictitious. That is, families of procreation as well as never-married single, widowed, and divorced persons actually function within a network of other nuclear families and social networks, offering services and gifts and maintaining close contact.[21] Thus, the idea of a modified form of nuclear or extended family has developed.

In a **modified-nuclear** or **modified-extended** family structure, the nuclear family retains considerable autonomy yet maintains a coalition with other nuclear families with whom they exchange contacts, goods, and services. Modified-nuclear and modified-extended families take intermediate positions between the isolated, independent, small nuclear unit and the interdependent kin network of the extended family (see Table 3-1).

One indicator of the prevalence of the modified-extended family in the United States was provided by a fifteen-year study of extended households among middle-aged black and white women.[22] At some time over the fifteen-year period, nearly one-third of white, middle-aged women and two-thirds of black women of the same age lived in modified-extended families. This led researchers to conclude that, contrary to popular perception, extended families are a relatively common form of living arrangement for adults in the United States, if only for short periods of time.

Extended families The term **extended family** refers to family structures that extend beyond the nuclear family. As stated, there may be a multiple number of nuclear family groupings within the extended family. Sometimes the terms *consanguine families* and *joint families* are used interchangeably with *extended families*. Both consanguine and joint families are extended families; however, the emphasis in the consanguine family is on blood ties rather than marital ties. Thus in a consan-

---

[21] Eugene Litwak and Stephen Kulis, "Technology, Proximity and Measures of Kin Support," *Journal of Marriage and the Family* 49 (August 1987): 649–661; and Naomi Gerstel, "Divorce and Kin Ties: The Importance of Gender," *Journal of Marriage and the Family* 50 (February 1988): 209–219. See also the classical article on this topic by Marvin B. Sussman, "The Isolated Nuclear Family: Fact or Fiction," *Social Problems* 6 (Spring 1959): 333–340.

[22] Rubye W. Beck and Scott H. Beck, "The Incidence of Extended Households Among Middle-Aged Black and White Women," *Journal of Family Issues* 10 (June 1989): 147–168.

guineous marriage, the two partners have at least one ancestor in common, such as a marriage with a third cousin or closer relative.

It is generally assumed that consanguineous marriages between relatives has and will decline with forces of modernization and industrialization. But some recent evidence from Iran suggests that may not always be the case. Factors such as an increased pool of cousins may actually lead to an increase in consanguinity when modernization takes place.[23]

The term **joint family** is not used as frequently today as in times past. The term has most often been used to describe large families in India, where at least two brothers, with their own wives and children, lived together in the same household. The joint family was consanguine in that the brothers were related by blood and extended in that the wives of the brothers (sisters-in-law) and their children (nephews, nieces, and cousins) lived together. The family was joint in that there existed a common treasury, common kitchen and dining room, and common deities. This Indian form of joint family was usually patrilineal and patrilocal and emphasized filial and fraternal solidarity.

The smallest variety of extended family is the **stem family**. Normally, a stem family consists of two families in adjacent generations, joined by economic and blood ties. This type of family is quite common in Japan, where, despite rapid urbanization, approximately 25 percent of middle-aged married couples live with one spouse's parents.[24] These stem families were most common if the marriage was arranged, the husband was the oldest son, and/or the wife was the oldest daughter and had no brothers.

Another example of the stem family is found in rural Ireland, where the family consists, for example, of a father and mother living in the same household with a married son, his wife, and their children. This type of family is a common device for maintaining the family estate. In contrast to the joint family, in the stem family, the male members of the original family do not pool their resources. Rather, the estate belongs only to the son to whom it is given by the father. The father continues to live in the place, contribute his labor, and derive his living from it. The other sons are given cash settlements in lieu of their shares of the land, and they then leave the family place.

Irrespective of the specific structure of the extended family, kin have both instrumental and psychological value. Close emotional relationships, especially between grandparents and grandchildren, can be quite important and can serve to relieve parents from being the sole sources of affection, care, and general socialization. Economically, the advantages of living in an extended household or family include having a number of active members share the work and costs as well as the resources. Kin serve as well as important sources of identification and as important in the stable transmission of ideologies and value systems.

---

[23] Benjamin P. Givens and Charles Hirschman, "Modernization and Consanguineous Marriage in Iran," *Journal of Marriage and the Family* 56 (November 1994): 820–834.

[24] Yoshinori Kamo, "Husbands and Wives Living in Nuclear and Stem Family Households in Japan," *Sociological Perspectives* 33 (1990): 397–417.

Extended-family networks exist in all societies. Even in the United States, the transmission of property, the proximity of residence, and the formal and informal contacts made through calls, visits, and gifts demonstrate the presence and importance of extended-kin networks. Some families even have reunions on a regular basis to bring old and new members together.

Given the importance of these extended relationships, it is logical that, as ties with extended kin weaken or disappear, people will increasingly experiment with new family forms that incorporate extended-kin features. These forms may include communes, with common ownership of goods and sharing of tasks; family networks, where three or four nuclear families join together to share problems and exchange services; and affiliated families, where a nuclear family accepts (socially adopts) one or more nonrelated older persons and recognizes them as part of the kin network.

The following section will look more closely at the boundaries of the kinship network and the major importance it holds for most people today.

Boundaries of kinship

The kinship system, like marital and family systems and groups, involves special ties, bonds, and linkages among its members. However, family groups and systems are units upon which kinship systems are built. Kinship systems are regulated by patterns of social norms. These norms vary widely from one society to another; thus, it is impossible to categorize all of them. However, certain norms exist universally among kinship relationships.

The most widely used example of a universal norm is a taboo on **incest.** All societies forbid sexual relations between persons in certain kinship positions, particularly those within and closest to the nuclear family: father and daughter, mother and son, brother and sister, stepfather and stepdaughter, and the like. Violations of these norms arouse strong feelings among the kinship group as well as in the larger society.

It is unsettling to imagine the confusion of statuses and role expectations that would result if fathers and daughters or mothers and sons had offspring. Consider, for example, a female child born to a mother/son relationship. The child would be a daughter to her brother, a sister to her father, a granddaughter to her own mother, a stepdaughter to her grandfather, and so forth. Should her father, who is also her brother, discipline her as a parent or treat her as a sibling? Could she marry her stepfather, who is her grandfather, if he divorced her mother?

In the United States incest occurs in all social classes and in urban as well as rural environments. The most frequent target is a daughter, and the most frequent perpetrator is a biological father; often, however, a step- or foster father or even a boyfriend or lover of the mother may be the perpetrator.

Interestingly, an analysis of narrative accounts of incest perpetrators revealed that almost all of them defined incest as love and care and their behavior as considerate and fair.[25] Some even described their experience as mutual romantic love. These professed notions of love and care, however, were contradictory in many ways, including their refusal to stop when children wanted them to. Another account, focusing on the meaning surrounding incestuous relationships, reported that both fathers and daughters saw the sexual activity growing out of already existing family interactions such as backrubs, wrestling, reading before bed, or watching TV.[26] Few verbal interactions occurred, leaving the children to rely on their interpretations of what was happening. Many distrusted what they felt and ,if they felt it was wrong, blamed themselves.

As might be expected, the thoughts of the fathers and daughters differed. The fathers' thoughts were dominated by themes of sexual gratification and/or curiosity. More than half of the men reported thinking that the child enjoyed what was happening. None of the children concurred and spoke instead of disbelief, confusion, guilt, and anger. Many saw no way to end the situation. Only as the children reached adolescence, did many of them tell a friend or their mother.

In interviews with a random sample of more than nine hundred adult women in San Francisco, Diana Russell found that, although the most frequent incest perpetrators were biological fathers (since, as girls, most women lived with and were accessible to biological fathers), the next largest group of perpetrators was stepfathers.[27] The likelihood of incestuous abuse was far greater if a stepfather was the

---

[25] Jane F. Gilgun, "We Shared Something Special: The Moral Discourse of Incest Perpetrators," *Journal of Marriage and the Family* 57 (May 1995): 265–281.

[26] Patricia Phelan, "Incest and Its Meaning: The Perspectives of Fathers and Daughters," *Child Abuse and Neglect* 19 (1994): 7–24.

[27] Diana E. H. Russell, "The Prevalence and Seriousness of Incestuous Abuse: Step-fathers vs. Biological Fathers," *Child Abuse and Neglect* 8 (1984): 15–22.

principal figure in the woman's childhood years (17%, or one out of approximately every six women) than if a father was the principal figure (2%, or one out of approximately forty women). And perhaps more significantly, when stepfathers sexually abused their stepdaughters, they were much more likely than any other relative to abuse the girls seriously, namely, performing forced penile/vaginal penetration, oral/vaginal/penile sex, or anal intercourse. In contrast, other less serious experiences involved digital penetration of the vagina; touching of breasts, buttocks, thighs, and legs; forced kissing; and so forth.

Russell explained these differences by suggesting that stepfathers, who are not biologically related to stepdaughters, may feel less bound by the normative taboo on incest. Another explanation is that the bonding that commonly occurs between biological fathers and daughters may often be absent between stepfathers and stepdaughters. A third explanation is that the daughter, often feeling betrayed by her mother who remarried, may compete with the mother for the attention of the stepfather. Whatever the explanation, the far greater prevalence and seriousness of stepfather/stepdaughter incest over biological father/daughter incest suggests that daughters in parental remarriages face substantial risks of incestuous abuse.

In addition to kinship sexual restrictions, all societies also forbid intermarriage between certain kinship group members. The circle of prohibited relatives for marriage does, however, vary widely in different societies. One extreme, in ancient Egypt, permitted brother/sister and father/daughter marriages. The other extreme may be represented by the traditional clan system of China and by certain extended families in India, where the prohibition extended to a very wide group of relatives, including cousins to the sixth degree.

Social norms tend to treat members of the kinship group differently. In most societies, women are accorded lower status than men. The eldest male or the eldest son may be accorded greater prestige, power, and responsibility than younger men. In general, status positions in the kinship network are differentiated by rights, privileges, and obligations; by inheritance; and by general social expectations.

In some societies, kinship is such an integral part of all aspects of the society that it is difficult to differentiate it from other nonkinship institutions and relationships. Particularly in primitive and peasant societies, the political, educational, religious, economic, and property units are so interlinked and meshed with the kinship system that it becomes impossible to separate kinship networks from nonkinship networks. That is, other institutions are part of the kinship system itself. In contrast are the kinship systems known in most Western societies, where kinship is separate and clearly distinguished from other institutions and relationships. The economic system, while not totally independent of kinship networks or influences, exists separate from and is distinguishable from the kinship system. This differentiation is also true for other institutionalized patterns of norms and activity.

Functions of kinship systems

Kinship groups and systems tend to fulfill certain functions even when the kinship network is indistinguishable from other institutions. Key functions include:

1. Property holding and inheritance
2. Housing and residential proximity
3. Obligation to help in time of need
4. Affection, emotional ties, and primary relationships

A brief examination of each of these four basic characteristics of kinship groups follows.

Property holding and inheritance The holding, ownership, and control of property and the transmission of this property from one owner to another is an issue of central concern to family sociologists and anthropologists, in general, and to conflict theorists and feminists, in particular. Property tends to indicate wealth and power. Inheritance tends to indicate how wealth and power are transmitted. Within family systems, this transference is directly linked to inheritance and the rules of descent.

At birth, each person inherits two separate bloodlines; thus, a key issue in most societies (less so in the United States) is whose bloodline, the mother's or the father's, is the most important. If the descent pattern is *unilineal*—as is true in most societies in Asia, India, and Africa—the name, property, authority, and marriage controls are traced through one line, usually that of the father and his bloodline. This pattern is **patrilineal.** A **matrilineal** pattern, a unilineal system that traces the lineage through the female line, is found much less frequently. The system of descent most prevalent in the United States is the **bilateral** system, where power and property are transferred through both the mother's and father's lines to both males and females.

One key exception to this pattern is name; both genders tend to assume the names of their fathers, and wives take their husbands' family names upon marriage. This too, may be in a process of changing, albeit slowly. Female college students were found to be far more accepting of nontraditional name choices and more tolerant of choices made by others than males.[28] Even so, more than 80 percent of females said that if they marry, they plan to change their last name to that of their husband. Women planning to marry at a later age and expecting nontraditional work roles were less likely than other women to want to change their last name to that of their husband.

Patterns of descent take on special significance to many feminists and conflict theorists, for several reasons. First of all, most family systems throughout the world tend to perpetuate power and wealth through successive generations—that is, the rich stay rich and the poor stay poor. Also, most family systems differentiate this power and wealth between the sexes, with males receiving preferential treatment.

---

[28] Laurie K. Scheuble and David R. Johnson, "Marital Name Change: Plans and Attitudes of College Students," *Journal of Marriage and the Family* 55 (August 1993): 747–754. Note also: David R. Johnson and Laurie K. Scheuble, "Women's Marital Naming in Two Generations: A National Study," *Journal of Marriage and the Family* 57 (August 1995): 724–732.

The result is that class and sexual inequalities are built into most family systems, such that the inequalities come to be viewed as natural and legitimate. In other words, some families have the right to be wealthier than others, males are expected to be dominant, and females are supposed to submit to their male counterparts.

Housing and residential proximity All family systems have rules of residence that establish who lives where and with whom. Since husbands and wives come from different families and most spouses choose to share the same residence, to achieve this, one or both individuals must move.

The most common residential pattern is **patrilocal**, in which the bride changes residence and lives with the parents of the groom. In the **matrilocal** pattern, which is much less frequently found, the newlywed couple lives with the parents of the bride. In the United States, far more common than either of the preceding are the **bilocal** system, in which the couple lives near the parents of either spouse, and the **neolocal** system, in which the couple lives in a home of their own that may be located apart from both sets of parents.

The pattern of residence takes on a special significance as one looks at the third and fourth aspects of kinship, namely, obligation and emotional ties among kin. Helping patterns and showing affection to grandparents, parents, and siblings take on a different character when the people involved share the same building, live in the same neighborhood or community, or reside hundreds of miles apart.

Residence patterns in the United States show a surprising degree of local concentration. In the study of Middletown, for example, taking any resident of the city at random, the odds were one in five that a brother or sister also lived in the city; one in three that one or both parents lived there; and two in five that a more distant relative (a grandparent, aunt, uncle, or cousin) lived there.[29] The respondents' immediate families were especially concentrated, with 54 percent of the grown children, 43 percent of the parents, and 31 percent of the brothers and sisters living right in Middletown.[30] These percentages increased considerably when a fifty-mile radius was used to establish residence. Thus, while a newlywed couple may establish a residence separate from their parents, it tends to be in geographical proximity to parents and siblings. Other studies have indicated a similar finding.

Obligation to help in time of need A range of kinship obligation patterns can be identified. One kin obligation is to communicate, or keep in touch, particularly with parents, to a lesser extent with siblings, and even less so with other relatives such as aunts, uncles, and cousins. One study found that many extended families had a person who could be considered a "kinkeeper," usually a female, who worked at keep-

---

[29] Theodore Caplow et al., *Middletown Families* (New York: Bantam Books, 1982): 206.
[30] Ibid., p. 203.

ing the family members in touch with one another.[31] Another kin obligation is to share services or gifts as gestures of goodwill and kindness. A third obligation is to help or assist kin members in need.

It is likely that all three obligation patterns are observed by most families throughout the world. What are likely to differ are the amounts and types of contact, sharing, and helping patterns and the ranges of kin or relatives included.

In Middletown, almost everyone agreed that people ought to keep in touch with relatives and seemed to regard this as more of a pleasure than a duty. Obligations to parents were more widely held than obligations to siblings.

The main determinants of the amount of interaction between relatives in Middletown were the distance between their homes and the closeness of their relationships. With increasing distance, visiting was replaced by telephone calls, which was replaced by letter writing. Almost no one corresponded regularly with cousins, except perhaps through exchanging Christmas cards. Consistently, women did more joint activities with parents and other kin than did men. Again, while Middletown was cited, it appears that these patterns are highly representative of kin obligations elsewhere in the United States.[32]

Affection and primary relationships Affection and primary relationships are the emotional dimensions of visits, calls, and letters. *Affection* means being emotionally close to kin. Women seem to be the "specialists" in affectionate kin relationships. In Middletown, as elsewhere, women expressed more affection than men did for every category of relative. The distribution of affection was highest for mothers, next highest for fathers and near siblings, and lowest for best-known cousins.

The affection dimension between children and parents seems to increase with age but seems to weaken with kin such as cousins. In Middletown, the increased closeness to parents was attributed to children's own maturity, their own parental experience, the belated recognition of the emotional debt they owe, the relaxation of parental authority, the increased needs of parents, and the expectation of bereavement. It can be said that, in Middletown, as well as elsewhere, most people feel good about their parents, love them, and make sacrifices for them when necessary.[33] And surprising to many, there has been little evidence of any weakening of kinship ties during the past fifty years.

---

[31] Carolyn J. Rosenthal, "Kinkeeping in the Familial Division of Labor," *Journal of Marriage and the Family* 47 (November 1985): 965–974.

[32] See Geoffrey K. Leigh, "Kinship Interaction over the Family Life Span," *Journal of Marriage and the Family* 44 (February 1982): 197–208; Susan M. Essock-Vitale and Michael T. McGuire, "Women's Lives Viewed from a Revolutionary Perspective. II. Patterns of Helping." *Ethology and Sociobiology* 6 (1985): 155–173.

[33] Caplow et al., *Middletown Families*, 220.

Family ambiguity

This chapter first focused on the family as a social institution and as a group or system. It then explored the boundaries of marriage, family, and kin. The reader who desires to segment and isolate these three interrelated components is likely to face many difficulties, for the boundaries of each are seldom precise and distinct. This is true both conceptually and in real life.

Pauline Boss and Jan Greenberg, for example, wrote about **family boundary ambiguity** as a new variable in understanding family stress.[34] They defined *boundary ambiguity* as not knowing who is in and out of the family system. New and old spouses, stepparents and stepchildren, in-laws, distant relatives, and others may or may not be fully recognized as part of a particular family network. While families' perceptions of boundaries will differ from one cultural context to another, the central notion is that a high degree of boundary ambiguity over time will lead to a high level of stress in the family system. Determining who is in and who is out of the family becomes a major issue in determining task performance and inheritance as well as visiting, communicating, and helping responsibilities.

SUMMARY

1. The family, as a social institution, is an organized, formal, and regular system of carrying out certain essential tasks in society. The family is defined by a wide system of norms that organize family units into stable and ongoing social systems. This chapter presented numerous ways in which marital, family, and kin groups and systems are organized to fulfill certain tasks.

2. The family system is an abstract network of interrelated statuses and the social expectations that accompany them. The family group is a concrete set of persons who interact with one another. The primary family group, which is small in size and has frequent and intense contact among members, is distinguished from the secondary group, which is more formal and involves the impersonal contacts that characterize much of an individual's life.

3. The boundaries of marriage are not always precise and clearly defined. Generally, marriage includes a heterosexual union of at least one male and one female. It grants legitimacy to children and approval to sexual relationships. Marriage is usually a public affair and establishes reciprocal rights and obligations between the spouses. Finally, marriage is usually a binding relationship that assumes some permanence.

4. The variations in marriage and number of spouses include singlehood, monogamy, and polygamy (polygyny, polyandry, and group marriage). The number of people in the United States choosing to remain single has risen dramatically over the past several decades. Available data have indicated

---

34 Pauline Boss and Jan Greenberg, "Family Boundary Ambiguity: A New Variable in Family Stress Theory," *Family Process* 23 (1984): 535–536.

some extreme differences among males and females who choose or involuntarily experience this particular nonmarital life-style.

5. Polygyny and polyandry, two forms of polygamy, occur in a wide range of contexts and take numerous forms. The plural spouses may be brothers or sisters, may marry simultaneously or sequentially, and may perform various functions. Polygyny is very common, but polyandry is quite rare. Group marriage, as well, occurs extremely infrequently and may never have existed as a viable and lasting form of marriage for any society in the world.

6. As do those of marriage, the boundaries of the family vary considerably. Usually, a family results from marriage and includes people united by marriage, blood, and adoption. The members, some of whom share a common residence, have reciprocal rights and obligations to one another. This institutionalized pattern fulfills certain basic functions for society, particularly as related to socialization and primary relationships.

7. One typology of family structures differentiates the nuclear/conjugal unit from a variety of extended units. Some of these include families of orientation and procreation; modified-nuclear and modified-extended families; and consanguine, joint, and stem families.

8. The boundaries of kinship serve as an extension of those of the marital and family units. A universal taboo in incest consists of norms that specify who is an eligible sexual and marital partner.

9. Kinship systems have key functions and characteristics that include property holding and inheritance, housing and maintenance of residential proximity, obligation or helping in time of need, and affection and emotional ties.

10. The next chapter will address how the marital, family, and kin systems are interrelated with other major systems, particularly the economic, employment, and work-related systems. The employment of none, one, or both spouses is a key factor in better understanding the functioning of marital, family, and kin networks.

KEY TERMS AND TOPICS

DISCUSSION QUESTIONS

1. What is meant by the phrase *family as a social institution*? Are factors such as homosexuality, children born to unwed mothers, and child support part of this institution?

2. Differentiate *family groups* from *family systems*. Since systems are abstractions, of what relevance are family systems to understanding the family?

3. Describe what would likely happen to a person who was removed from all primary-group relationships. Why are such relationships so crucial?

4. Define the terms *marriage* and *family* in a way that would be comprehensive enough to include marriages and families in most societies in the world. How are the two terms similar and different? How do marriage and family differ from other groups and relationships? Should gays and lesbians be able to marry, divorce, adopt children, and be families (see the box on p. 85)? Why?

5. Is it likely that the trend will continue that an increasing percentage of people will choose to remain single? Is this trend the same for males and females? Explain.

6. Why is monogamy so strongly stressed in the United States as the appropriate form of marriage? What advantages or disadvantages do polygyny, polyandry, and group marriage have for adults in the United States?

7. In societies where polygamy is culturally approved, polygyny appears to be far more common than polyandry. Why? What factors explain exceptions that occur?

8. Think of your own kin group. How many persons in it do you know (uncles, cousins, and so on)? With how many kin do you interact on a regular basis (say, at least yearly)? What differentiations do you make between kin on your mother's side and kin on your father's side?

9. How would you explain the universal norm of a taboo on incest? Within your own kinship system, what relatives (second cousins, step-siblings, and so forth) would be considered to be legitimate sexual or marital partners?

10. What arguments will feminists and conflict theorists likely make about traditional unilineal descent and inheritance systems?

FURTHER READINGS

Cochran, Moncrieff; Larner, Mary; Riley, David; Gunnarsson, Lars; and Henderson, Charles R., Jr. *Extending Families: The Social Networks of Parents and Their Children.* Cambridge, England: Cambridge University Press, 1990. A focus on personal family-child networks, how they are influenced by race, class, and culture, how they change over time, and the impact they have on human development.

Farber, Bernard. *Conceptions of Kinship.* New York: Elsevier, 1981. An empirical study of kinship from the central perspective of collaterality, with considerable evidence of kinship as a significant element in maintaining social continuity.

Goode, William J. *World Revolution and Family Patterns.* Glencoe, Illinois: Free Press, 1963. A description and interpretation of the main changes in family patterns that have occurred over the past half-century in various cultures.

Gordon, Tuula. *Single Women: On the Margins?* New York: New York University Press, 1994. A study of single women in London, Helsinki, and San Francisco: how they have constructed their lives and notions about femininity and how they have dealt with pressures toward marriage and maternity.

Jacobs, Janet Liebman. *Victimized Daughters: Incest and the Development of the Female Self.* New York: Routledge, 1994. A study of white, African American and Latina incest survivors with a focus on the identification with the incestuous father and its impact on the identity formation.

Kephart, William M., and Zellner, William W. *Extraordinary Groups: An Examination of Unconventional Life-Styles.* 5th ed. New York: St. Martin's Press, 1994. A look at eight different cultural groups and life-styles that exist in the United States: the old-order Amish, the Oneida Community, the gypsies, the Church of Christ—Scientist, the Hasidim, the Father Divine Movement, the Mormons, and the Jehovah's Witnesses.

Lee, Gary L. "Comparative Perspectives." In *Handbook of Marriage and the Family,* edited by Marvin B. Sussman and Suzanne K. Steinmetz, Chapter 3, 59–80. New York: Plenum Press, 1987. A cross-national, comparative look at the commonality and variations in family structure, marital power, and socialization.

Marsiglio, William, and Scanzoni, John H. *Families and Friendships: Applying the Sociological Imagination.* New York: HarperCollins, 1995. A focus on primary relationships with a particular emphasis on families and friendships.

Milardo, Robert M., ed. *Families and Social Networks.* Newbury Park, CA: Sage, 1988. A systematic look at social relationships as they change during the transition to motherhood, during later stages of the life course, following separation and divorce, and so forth.

Murdock, George P. *Social Structure.* New York: Free Press, 1965. Although recommended reading for a general and excellent cross-cultural perspective on family structure, the book also extensively analyzes sexual patterns and incest.

Simon, Barbara Levy. *Never Married Women.* Philadelphia: Temple University Press, 1987. A look at the lives of fifty women who have never been married.

Westerlund, Elaine. *Woman's Sexuality After Childhood Incest.* Scranton, PA: W. W. Norton, 1992. A study of the sexual attitudes and practices of women with incest histories, including both statistical and anecdotal findings.

Chapter 4

Marriage, Family, and Work

Chapter 3 provided an examination of how marriage, family, and kin groups and systems are organized, showing variation in the number of spouses, presenting a topology of family structures, and noting some of the basic functions of kinship networks. As noted in that chapter, in many societies, family/kin networks are such an integral part of society that it is difficult to separate and differentiate the family system from other major institutions.

One example of these institutionalized linkages in the United States is the Amish subculture, in which family roles and responsibilities often are inseparable from other aspects of everyday life: Anabaptist religious teachings; home-oriented educational training for appropriate adult male/female responsibilities; and a community-oriented political system, where neighbors and friends provide protection, insurance, welfare, and justice. In the wider U.S. society and in most of the Western world, it is much easier to separate the family system from work, school, church, politics, health, communication, military, recreation, and other systems.

Although this chapter will focus primarily on linking marriages and families to work and the economic system, the first topic will be how religion, politics, and education affect and are affected by the family. Many of these institutionalized linkages will be reemphasized throughout the text, as in discussions of economic and social-class matters (Chapter 8), interfaith marriage (Chapter 9), the significance of formal education (Chapters 6, 7, 8, 13, and 17), and government policies (Chapter 18).

LINKAGES BETWEEN THE FAMILY AND OTHER SYSTEMS

It appears obvious that linkages exist between family systems and other systems, yet at a macrolevel of analysis, these linkages are frequently ignored in family studies. A structural-functional frame of reference establishes the interdependence of the parts of a system. As the economy changes, so do employment rates and family spending patterns. As wars affect international relations, so do they affect divorce rates. As political decisions determine policies related to health and welfare, so do they affect attitudes toward one-parent families and child-support responsibilities. And as education, employment, and the advancement of fertility-control methods modify the opportunities and options available to women and men, so do these changes affect male/female, husband/wife, and parent/child interactions and expectations.

Religion and the family

Cross-culturally as well as historically, the relationship between the religious system and the family system has been reciprocal.[1] In most societies, many family celebrations are religious in nature. Religious norms also influence speech patterns, nonmarital as well as marital sexuality, male and female roles, husband/wife and parent/child relations, and so forth. Marriage contracts, baptisms, and death rituals frequently involve the clergy and religious organizations.

The pathbreaking study of the relationship between family and religion in the United States was done by Gerhard Lenski in the 1950s.[2] In comparing religious groups, he found, for example, that Protestants had higher divorce rates than Catholics, that Catholics had more children than Protestants and Jews, that Jews and Protestants were more likely than Catholics to see personal autonomy as the key value in preparing children for life, and that Catholics were less mobile than Protestants and Jews.

More recently, an increasing body of evidence has suggested a general converging of values and behaviors among major religious/ethnic groups in the United States. Duane Alwin documented substantial changes in the social experiences of groups such as U.S. Catholics to the point that few, if any, differences were found among religioethnic groups in their orientation to the extended family.[3] In dealing specifically with childrearing, Alwin supported earlier predictions of a decline in differences in values and orientations among these groups, possibly to the point of nonexistence.

What *has not* changed is the linkage between the religious system and the family system, between religiosity and familism, and between religious beliefs and practices and family beliefs and practices. What *has* changed is the extent of denominational differences. Today, differences between churchgoers and nonchurchgoers are more pronounced than those between people of particular religious groups, such as Protestants and Catholics. Churchgoers, for example, are more likely to be married; to have more children; to be more conservative on issues relating to sexuality, such as abortion, homosexuality, and nonmarital sex; to stress traditional gender roles; and so forth.

In spite of widely held assumptions about the weakening and decline of both religion and family, evidence from Middletown (mentioned in Chapter 3) suggested that family ties in the late 1970s were at least as strong as they were in the 1920s, and citizens seemed to be at least as religious. Judging from recent statements about what people believe, how much money they donate to churches, and how often they attend church, Americans take their religion at least as seriously today as their grandfathers did fifty years previously.[4] The message is clear: "Families that pray together, stay together," irrespective of religioethnic orientation. Differences are linked more closely to intensity of religious participation than to denominational differences.

---

[1] See, for example, Darwin L. Thomas and Marie Cornwall, "Religion and Family in the 1980s: Discovery and Development," *Journal of Marriage and the Family* 52 (November 1990): 983–992; Arland Thornton, William G. Axinn, and Daniel H. Hill, "Reciprocal Effects of Religiosity, Cohabitation, and Marriage," *American Journal of Sociology* 98 (November 1992): 628–651; and Gene H. Brody, Zolinda Stonemen, Douglas Flor, and Chris McCrary, "Religion's Role in Organizing Family Relationships: Family Process in Rural, Two-Parent African American Families," *Journal of Marriage and the Family* 56 (November 1994): 878–888.

[2] Gerhard Lenski, *The Religious Factor* (Garden City, NY: Doubleday, 1961).

[3] Duane F. Alwin, "Religion and Parental Child Rearing Orientations: Evidence of a Catholic-Protestant Convergence," *American Journal of Sociology* 92 (September 1986): 412–440.

[4] Howard M. Bahr and Bruce A. Chadwick, "Religion and Family in Middletown, USA," *Journal of Marriage and the Family* 47 (May 1985): 407–414.

Many contemporary examples of the linkage between the religious and family systems are provided throughout the text. These examples present issues related to abortion, prayer in the schools, sex education, parental notification when dispensing contraceptives and contraceptive information to minors, discipline and corporal punishment, and so forth. All these issues have been of particular concern to certain fundamentalist and right-wing religious groups, whose stated purpose has been the general good of protecting, solidifying, and reestablishing the traditional family. While it is yet unclear how successful any of these movements has been or will be in the future, the reciprocal linkage between the religious and family institutions is very clear.

Politics and the family

A study of politics and the family examines the relationship between the family and the state (or government). The *state* is defined by civil laws and policies created by legislators that the citizenry has elected; these laws and policies are enforced by agents of local, state, and federal governments. The state (political system) influences families through laws that regulate and support families.

For instance, families are regulated through laws that govern marriage, including the choice of spouse, the number of spouses, the age at which marriage is permissible, the necessity of a blood test, the acceptance or nonacceptance of common-law marriages, the prohibition or acceptance of same-sex marriages, what relationships are seen as incestuous, and the soundness of the mental condition. Families are also regulated through laws that specify the rights and duties of parenthood, such as those that relate to contraception, pregnancy, and abortion; custody of children; and abuse. Other regulations of families relate to factors such as divorce and separation as well as economic factors, such as the distribution of property. Some of these laws are very general and establish guidelines or boundaries of permissible behavior; others are very precise and specific and carry legal and civil sanctions.

The state not only regulates families; it supports them, as well. The extent to which the state has this responsibility is an ongoing controversy. Homelessness, for example, was mentioned in Chapter 1 as a contemporary issue of concern. Should the government assume the responsibility of providing housing for people who are homeless and poor? Is the government responsible for guaranteeing adequate housing for everyone or simply serving as a "safety net," a last resort when all else fails? Do welfare programs generate a positive response from people who believe that government is fulfilling its responsibility to the poor, or do such programs generate feelings of anger from people who feel that tax dollars are being distributed to those who haven't contributed their fair share in work or money? A variety of government programs provide support for families: AFDC (Aid to Families with Dependent Children), OASDI (Old Age, Survivors, and Disability Insurance), Social Security, Medicare (medical care for the elderly), Medicaid (medical care for the poor), food stamp coupons, school lunch programs, subsidized student loans, energy allowances, and tax breaks for children and the elderly. Granted, all sorts of regulations specify conditions of eligibility for these programs; nonetheless, the focus is on the assistance (support) of families and family members in need. How this support is given, who gets it, and how much is enough are topics of debate in every election. These issues clearly separate the liberals from the conservatives.

Most governmental programs and laws that affect families are not established for or directed specifically at them. Examples include laws directed at drug use, discrimination, driving, unemployment, draft registration, health, and the environment. What should be clear at this point is the extent to which the family is related to and influenced by the state or government. The political system represents power, determining who gets what in society.

Does the family have any recourse or power against the state? Many would argue that, in most of the world, including the United States, the power of an individual or family against the government is extremely limited. Generally, this may be the case. Yet the people eventually have their say. Even factors such as marital status seem to affect voting outcomes; for example, single voters favor Democrats in greater numbers than do married voters.[5] In addition, kin networks and the solidarity of family ties can be vital forces in political activities, demonstrated by candidate support and voting patterns. The stability of family systems takes on a symbolic importance to political figures, who attempt to present themselves and their families as moral citizens and in support of strong family life. Thus, often in subtle and even deceptive ways, families are important in the political arena. Issues of social policy are addressed more explicitly in Chapter 18.

Education and the family

Just as family structures and processes affect educational achievement, so also do schools and the educational system affect the lives of families and their members.[6] Socialization, employment, and vacations are affected by the schools. Schools group students according to their ages and sometimes their abilities. Family life changes when young children enter school, become active in school endeavors, and move through the K–12 system. Schools take children through an established curriculum of academic subjects, yet schools focus heavily on the so-called *hidden curriculum,* teaching civic and moral responsibility, obedience to rules, respect for authority, punctuality, success through competition, conscientiousness, and other areas traditionally believed to be in the family domain. The extent of social literacy and social competence are clearly linked to the educational system.

---

[5] Eric Plutzer and Michael McBurnett, "Family Life and American Politics: The "Marriage Gap" Reconsidered," *Public Opinion Quarterly* 55 (1991): 113–127.

[6] William J. Weston (ed.), *Education and the American Family: A Research Synthesis* (New York: New York University Press, 1989).

Family and educational systems tend to supplement one another in teaching selected cultural values, norms, and skills. One intended function of education is to supplement family socialization. The schools use experts (teachers) to teach children knowledge, values, and selected skills that parents frequently are incapable of teaching and that are necessary for individuals to function successfully in a changing world. The close relation between the family and educational systems appears in many studies that show educational training in the home to be directly linked to the success of training in the school. Why, then, have schools?

Participation in the educational system from early childhood through late adolescence is expected to increase the individual's level of knowledge and mental and interpersonal skills. Ideally, having these skills will improve the individual's marital and parental performance in addition to employment performance. Sometimes, the training provided adolescents in schools is at odds with parents' values or perhaps exceeds the level of training that parents have had. Thus, the authority of the family may be undermined or the skills of the parents may be less than those of the child. In such instances, parental authoritarianism may give way to more egalitarian parent/child relations or may set the stage for emancipation from the household. Again, the linkages between the educational and family systems are evident.

Economy and the family

Perhaps as much as any other institution, the economic system influences family organization and interaction. The economy is the component of society concerned with the creation, distribution, and consumption of goods and services. The family contributes labor and skills and in turn receives wages or other forms of compensation (prestige, insurance, services, etc.). Stress is a well-documented result of receiving inadequate wages or other compensation. And financial stress, in turn, has pernicious consequences for both adults and children.[7] Poor mental health, erosion of self-image, increased risk of suicide, alcohol-related disease, divorce, and child abuse are a few of the negative consequences for adults. Children have also been found to exhibit a range of emotional and behavioral problems.

At a macrolevel of analysis, the economic system includes issues ranging from rates of employment and unemployment to indices of depression and inflation. Inflation, for example, affects all families but has a worse impact on those people least often employed or on fixed or low incomes: female heads of families; children; people who are retired, elderly, or disabled; and so forth.[8]

---

[7] Patricia Voydanoff, "Economic Distress and Family Relations: A Review of the Eighties," *Journal of Marriage and the Family* 52 (November 1990): 1099–1115; and David T. Takeuchi, David R. Williams, and Russell K. Adair, "Economic Stress in the Family and Children's Emotional and Behavioral Problems," *Journal of Marriage and the Family* 53 (November 1991): 1031–1041.

[8] Joan Aldous, Rodney Ganey, Scott Trees, and Lawrence C. Marsh, "Families and Inflation: Who Was Hurt in the Last High-Inflation Period?" *Journal of Marriage and the Family* 53 (February 1991): 123–134.

According to Marxian conflict theorists, the economic system is the key to understanding all inequality within or outside the family system. More than one hundred years ago, Karl Marx's co-writer, Friedrich Engels, argued that marriage represents a class antagonism in which the well-being and development of one group are attained through the misery and repression of the other.[9] In marriage, as in the economy, the dominance of husbands and the suppression of wives is evident, making the linkage between the two unmistakable.

This dominance/suppression issue is at the heart of gender-role discussions. Conflict theorists link the male/female division of labor to economic specialization and domination. Traditional norms state that men are expected to "bring home the bacon," or support the family, thus constituting the basic employed, paid labor force. Women "belong in the home," doing domestic chores such as cooking, cleaning, and child care. Household labor, according to one branch of conflict theory, is intricately linked to a capitalistic type of economic system in that the free and unpaid labor of the woman makes it possible for the man to leave home to work, earn wages, and support the family. His wages, in turn, contribute to his dominant position and make the wife/mother dependent on him. Hence, the employed male can play the role of capitalist within his own household.

In light of this discussion, one can understand why the phrase *working wives* describes those who are employed outside the home. Housework is not considered "real work" and, as will be shown later in this chapter, remains the task of women whether they are full-time homemakers or paid employees outside the home.

WORK ROLES OF FAMILY MEMBERS

Women as full-time homemakers

Traditionally, few roles of women have held a higher priority than that of wife and homemaker. The full-time homemaker has been relatively neglected by social scientists as a central topic for research. The attention granted women in paid employment has clearly overshadowed that given to women who are *not* in the paid labor force. In 1994, 41.2 percent of the female population age sixteen and over and 39.4 percent of married women with a husband present did not work outside the home.[10]

The qualifications for the role of homemaker are only two: female or male and married. Factors such as age, education, skills, hours, and productivity are basically ignored in job performance, as are benefits such as sick days and bonuses. The role of homemaker is generally categorized as a low-status position, earning both

---

[9] Friedrich Engels, *The Origin of the Family, Private Property, and the State* (New York: International Publishing, 1942). Originally published in 1884.

[10] U.S. Bureau of the Census, *Statistical Abstract of the United States: 1995*, 115th ed. (Washington, DC: U.S. Government Printing Office, 1995), nos. 628 and 639, pp. 400 and 406.

low prestige and low economic value. Research findings of Bird and Ross suggest that housework is more routine than paid work, is the least fulfilling of any type of work examined, and provided the least recognition for work well done.[11] "I'm only a housewife" is a phrase that captures the sentiment of many women.

The fact is that homemakers perform tasks that are economically valuable to society and would be costly for a family to purchase. At times, the homemaker serves as cook, baker, waitress, teacher, sexual partner, seamstress, housekeeper, bookkeeper, secretary, chauffeur, nurse, therapist, tutor, counselor, hostess, and recreation director. Exactly what is the productive value of housework and of being a homemaker? Specific data are difficult to obtain, since payroll checks and dollar expenditures seldom document homemakers' efforts. But the cost of purchasing all the services mentioned would be extremely expensive. Certainly, the work a woman does contributes to the family economy and thus to the society's total economic output. Without the services performed by the full-time homemaker, the family's standard of living would be lowered drastically.

How much work do homemakers do compared to employed wives? And how much are men or husbands involved in household and child-care tasks? It appears that women in most countries, even when employed, do most of the housework and child care with the gender gap widest among married persons.[12] That is, the time women spend doing housework is highest among the married and lower among the never-married, divorcees, and widows. Divorced and widowed men do substantially more housework than any other group and are especially more likely than their married counterparts to spend time in cooking and cleaning. Women who are employed spend somewhat less time doing household work than homemakers do. Husbands spend some additional time doing housework when their wives work outside the home but equity exists only as an ideal, not in actual practice.

Consistent with other research, a national sample found that the average husband's contribution to housework is small.[13] For example, the mean number of hours per week devoted by the average husband to the five tasks of cooking, washing dishes, cleaning, shopping, and laundry was 8.6. Of the husbands in the survey, about half contributed less than six hours of housework per week, and fewer than one in ten (8.4 percent) performed twenty or more hours. In contrast, eight of ten wives (82.9 percent) performed twenty or more hours of housework per week, with one-third devoting forty or more hours to these tasks. Factors that

---

[11] Chloe E. Bird and Catherine E. Ross, "Houseworkers and Paid Workers: Qualities of the Work and Effects on Personal Control," *Journal of Marriage and the Family* 55 (November 1993): 913–925.

[12] Arne L. Kalleberg and Rachel A. Rosenfeld, "Work in the Family and in the Labor Market: A Cross-National, Reciprocal Analysis," *Journal of Marriage and the Family* 52 (May 1990): 331–346; Scott J. South and Glenna Spitze, "Housework in Marital and Nonmarital Households," *American Sociological Review* 59 (June 1994): 327–347; and David H. Demo and Alan C. Acock, "Family Diversity and the Division of Labor: How Much Have Things Really Changed," *Family Relations* 42 (July 1993): 323–331.

[13] Scott Coltrane and Masako Ishii-Kuntz, "Men's Housework: A Life Course Perspective," *Journal of Marriage and the Family* 54 (February 1992): 43–57. Note also: Beth Manke, Brenda L. Seery, Ann C. Crouter, and Susan M. McHale, "The Three Corners of Domestic Labor: Mothers', Fathers', and Children's Weekday and Weekend Housework," *Journal of Marriage and the Family* 56 (August 1994): 657–668.

Global Diversity: **Italian Homemakers Want Salaries**

As reported in the *Charlotte Observer* (July 5, 1995), the Italian National Housewives Federation is asking for salaries for women who stay at home the first five years of the children's lives. In addition, they want state-sided pension plans to be run by homemakers for the benefit of homemakers.

The 800,000-member National Housewives Federation was started in the early 1980s as a social action group. Recently, following a constitutional court ruling that the economic value of housework is equivalent to work outside the home, they decided to unionize. And now the union, arguing that home-makers, mothers, and children are a resource vital to Italy's interest, is asking for funds to support them. Italian women overwhelmingly approve of the idea. A poll revealed that 70 percent of working women said they would be willing to put their careers on hold to stay home with their young children if they were paid a salary.

Maybe it is time to ask the U.S. government to build and support fami-lies rather than orphanages and prisons. What do you think?

increased the husband's proportionate contribution to housework were the wife having greater resources, the wife having less traditional values, the husband hav-ing greater time availability, the wife having less time availability, and an increase in childcare demand. In other words, the average woman does most of everything, but the average husband's involvement is influenced by employment schedules, time availability, relative resources, and role ideology.[14]

Catherine Ross and others also found that the household division of labor is shaped by the husband's values and the relative power of husband and wife.[15] Well-educated husbands and husbands with less traditional gender-role beliefs are more likely to participate in household tasks. Ross also found that the smaller the gap between the husband's and wife's earnings, the greater the husband's relative contribution. In other words, the more the husband's earnings exceed the wife's, the less housework he does.

The role of children in the performance of household tasks should not be overlooked. In particular, children have been found to do increasing amounts of housework with age. Daughters do more than sons and children in one-parent households do more than in two-parent households. As might be expected, chil-dren do more housework when a parent is in poor health.[16]

---

[14] Harriet B. Presser, "Employment Schedules Among Dual-Earner Spouses and the Division of Household Labor by Gender," *American Sociological Review* 59 (June 1994): 348–364; and April Brayfield, "Juggling Jobs and Kids: The Impact of Employment Schedules on Fathers' Caring for Children," *Journal of Marriage and the Family* 57 (May 1995): 321–332.

[15] Catherine E. Ross, "The Division of Labor at Home," *Social Forces* 65 (March 1987): 816–833; and Yoshinori Kamo, "Determinants of Household Division of Labor," *Journal of Family Issues* 9 (June 1988): 177–200.

[16] Glenna Spitze and Russell Ward, "Household Labor in Intergenerational Households," *Journal of Marriage and the Family* 57 (May 1995): 355–361.

Table 4-1 documents how often household and child-care tasks are performed by men and women, based on findings from a survey done in the United States and a study done in Australia. In both countries, the breakdown of duties was fairly traditional: Women more often performed housework and child-care tasks, whereas men more often did yardwork and home repairs. Interestingly, in both countries, disciplining and punishing children was the task for which men's and women's performance levels were most comparable.

From a conflict and feminist perspective, housework serves as a prime example of an unequal division of labor between men and women that generates tension, conflict, and change. Women as homemakers augment the power of men. As stated earlier, the fact that female homemakers are excluded from paid employment and an opportunity to support themselves reinforces their dependence on their husbands. The family remains a primary arena where men exercise their patriarchal power over women's labor.

The literature in general suggests that, when wives' and husbands' views of marriage are compared, "his" marriage is considerably better than "her" marriage.[17] Jessie Bernard stated this most explicitly by reporting that more wives than husbands expressed marital frustration and dissatisfaction, negative feelings, and marital problems; considered their marriages unhappy; regretted getting married; sought marital counseling; initiated divorce proceedings; felt they were going to have a nervous breakdown; had more feelings of inadequacy in marriage; and blamed themselves for their own lack of general adjustment. Bernard described *housework* as menial labor, isolating, and a dead-end job with no chance of promotion. According to Bernard, "In truth, being a housewife makes women sick."[18]

Given these findings, one must ask about women who are employed outside the home: Are they more satisfied than homemakers? Evidence from six large national surveys consistently failed to support the hypothesis that women with jobs outside the home are generally happier and more satisfied with their lives than full-time homemakers.[19] Working outside the home and being a full-time homemaker each was found to have benefits and costs. The net result was that no consistent or significant differences were found in patterns of life satisfaction between the two groups. Constance Shehan, as well, surveyed employed wives and homemakers and found no significant difference between the two groups in feelings of depression, health anxiety, or life satisfaction. The majority of respondents in both groups were "well-off" psychologically.[20]

While research has tended to present the homemaker's status as negative (low prestige, heavy workload, no salary or fringe benefits), it should not be overlooked

---

[17] Jessie Bernard, *The Future of Marriage* (New Haven: Yale University Press, 1982): 26–53.

[18] Ibid., 48.

[19] James D. Wright, "Are Working Women Really More Satisfied? Evidence from Several National Surveys," *Journal of Marriage and the Family* 40 (May 1978): 301–313. See also Myra Marx Ferree, "Class, Housework, and Happiness: Women's Work and Life Satisfaction," *Sex Roles* 11 (1984): 1057–1074.

[20] Constance L. Shehan, "Wives' Work and Psychological Well-Being: An Extension of Gove's Social Role Theory of Depression," *Sex Roles* 11 (1984): 881–899.

Table 4-1
Who performs **all** *or* **most** *of selected household and child-care chores?
A comparison of men and women in the United States and Australia
(in percent)*

	United States		Australia		
	Women	Men	Wife More	Husband More	About Equally
Doing laundry	79%	27%	88%	3%	9%
Preparing meals	78	26	81	6	13
Grocery shopping	72	26	73	5	22
Cleaning house/Vacuuming	69	22	78	7	15
Washing dishes	68	31	63	9	28
Caring for children (U.S.)/	72	12	—	—	—
Taking them to activities (Aust.)	—	—	60	5	35
Disciplining/punishing children	42	28	23	9	68
Working in the yard	21	63	9	74	17
Making minor home repairs	16	74	7	81	12

Source: United States data were selected from *The Gallup Poll Monthly* 293 (February 1990): 31;
and Australian data were selected from Helen Glezer, "Juggling Work and Family Commitments,"
Family Matters 28 (April 1991): 3.

that many women find satisfaction in the performance of this role. The job is not competitive. The work schedule is highly flexible. The position may even be one of choice. Some women prefer housekeeping to other types of work. Some women define their highest contribution as service to their husbands and children. And as suggested by Ahlander and Bahr, perhaps the time has come to conceptualize housework and family work less in terms of technical, economic, or political dimensions and more in terms of a moral context that encourages attention to the cultural and personal meanings of activity, interaction, and sentiment.[21] They propose reappropriating the image of family work as a calling that is essential to the physical, mental, and spiritual maintenance of a family group. Among the products of this fundamental and inescapable work are strong bonds of kinship, linking of persons to one another, and transmitting the aspirations and skills that make up human cultures.

---

21 Nancy Rollins Ahlander and Kathleen Slaugh Bahr, "Beyond Drudgery, Power, and Equity: Toward an Expanded Discourse on the Moral Dimensions of Housework in Families," *Journal of Marriage and the Family* 57 (February 1995): 54–68.

A report from the national surveys, conducted by the Survey Research Center at the University of Michigan, indicated that 50 percent of homemakers had a positive opinion of housework and 44 percent had a neutral or ambivalent opinion.[22] Only 6 percent perceived housework as negative. Positive views were inversely related to level of education; that is, homemakers with more formal education were less likely to respond positively to housework. Educated women were also most likely to want careers. The group least likely to favor housework was college-educated, young wives.

Have the attitudes of homemakers changed over the past few decades? Apparently they have but not entirely in the direction one might assume. National surveys of homemakers from 1972 to 1986 revealed that they were increasingly likely to hold traditional attitudes regarding marital roles, mothers' employment outside the home, sexuality, and abortion.[23] Attitudes of part-time workers/homemakers were very similar to those of full-time homemakers. But a widening attitudinal gap was found between women who were full-time homemakers versus full-time workers. The latter group was younger, better educated, had fewer children, and had more income than the homemakers. Even when the survey controlled for these differences, attitudes differed sharply on topics such as abortion for married women and the effects of mothers' employment on children.

The political implications of this polarization of women's attitudes may be profound, particularly on issues such as the future socialization of children. Disparate attitudes between homemakers and employed wives about having children may also have profound social consequences. Namely, there may be an increased concentration of childrearing in fewer but less affluent and more traditional households.

Employed wives and mothers

In 1994, 58.8 percent of all females age sixteen and over (a total of 60.2 million) were employed in the labor force. This level was up from 51.5 percent (or 45 million) in 1980 and up from 43.3 percent in 1970 (see Table 4-2). Of these 60 million females, 25.4 percent were single, 54.6 percent were married, and 20.0 percent were widowed, divorced, or separated. Thus, both the number and proportion of females in the paid labor force have increased dramatically, and well over half of these women are married. This marital distribution has changed very little over the past thirty-five years (again, note Table 4-2).

---

[22] Alfreda P. Iglehart, "Wives, Work, and Social Change: What About the Housewives?" *Social Service Review* 54 (September 1980): 317–330.

[23] Jennifer Glass, "Housewives and Employed Wives: Demographic and Attitudinal Change, 1972–1986," *Journal of Marriage and the Family* 54 (August 1992): 559–569. Note also Karen A. Schroeder, Linda L. Blood, and Diane Maluso, "An Intergenerational Analysis of Expectations for Women's Career and Family Roles," *Sex Roles* 26 (1992): 273–291.

Table 4-2
Marital status of women in the U.S. civilian labor force, 1970-1994
(persons 16 years and over)

	1970	1980	1990	1994
Female labor force (thousands of persons)				
Total	31,543	45,487	56,554	60,239
Single	7,265	11,865	14,229	15,333
Married, husband present	18,475	24,980	30,970	32,888
Widowed, divorced or separated	5,804	8,643	11,354	12,018
Distribution of female labor force (in percent)				
Single	23.0%	26.1%	25.2%	25.4%
Married, husband present	58.6	54.9	54.7	54.6
Widowed, divorced or separated	18.4	19.0	20.1	20.0
Female labor force as proportion of female population (in percent)				
Total	43.3%	51.5%	57.5%	58.8%
Single	56.8	64.4	66.9	66.7
Married, husband present	40.5	49.8	58.4	60.7
Widowed, divorced or separated	40.3	43.6	47.2	47.5

Source: U.S. Bureau of the Census, *Statistical Abstract of the United States: 1995,* 115th ed. (Washington, DC: U.S. Government Printing Office, 1995), no. 637, p. 405.

The implications of these trends for both the economic system and the family system are dramatic. Today's economy is highly dependent on the tasks performed and roles fulfilled by women. And that the majority of the female labor force is married raises questions about dual incomes, dual careers, fertility, child-rearing, and various other marital and family factors.

One particularly significant family issue is related to the employment of mothers. Traditionally, and for many people today, a wife's/mother's primary responsibility was to her husband and children. A single woman was expected to work to support herself, and as can be seen from the table, two-thirds of single women are in the paid labor force (Table 4-2). A divorced or separated woman, including one with children, was "allowed" to work if she needed the income. A married woman without children could also work to supplement the family income. But the married woman with children, particularly young children (preschool), was expected to assume the responsibility for rearing those children with economic support provided by her husband.

Figure 4-1 illustrates trends over the past thirty-plus years in rates of paid employment of mothers with children under age eighteen. The top line shows that, for several decades, divorced mothers with children of school age have had higher employment rates than other mothers; only slight increases have been observed. The most dramatic increases have been shown by married women, with

Figure 4-1

Labor force participation rates of mothers with children under eighteen years old: 1960–1994

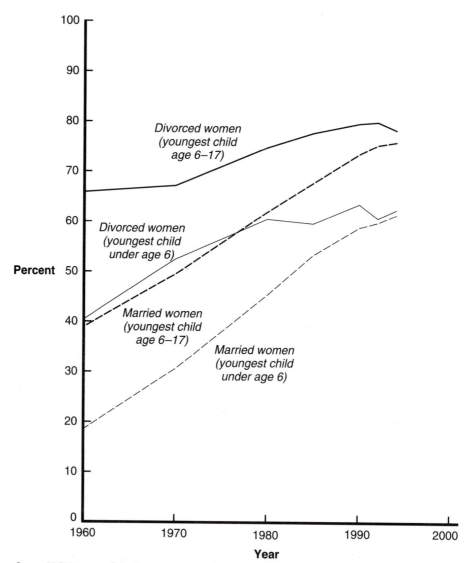

Source: U.S. Bureau of the Census, *Statistical Abstracts of the United States: 1995,* 115th ed. (Washington, DC: U.S. Government Printing Office, 1995), no. 638, p.406.

the single biggest increase (bottom line—18.6 percent in 1960 to 61.7 percent in 1994) coming from married women with at least one child under age six.

It is likely that rates of employment of mothers with young children will continue to increase. Data suggest that mothers who contribute all or a lot of the total family income are more likely to remain employed, exit from employment more slowly, and return to employment more quickly after childbirth.[24] Given the decreased relative contribution of the husband/father to the total family income, the need for the wife/mother to be (and remain) employed is high.

What are the social implications of these changes in the paid employment of women with children? Need society be concerned about the divorced mother, namely, her support and the care of her children? Need society be concerned about women who face the multiple responsibilities of being wife, mother, and employee? Need society be concerned about the marriage or the children of an employed wife and mother? These and a number of other issues will be addressed in the sections that follow.

Reasons for wives'/mothers' employment

Why do wives and mothers work? They work for the same reasons that husbands and fathers work (although men are much less likely to be asked the question). The most frequently articulated reason for working is money, or financial need. But clearly, many other factors also influence the decision to seek paid employment.

Results from a study of North Carolina women suggested that the best predictor of a wife's employment was her husband's emotional support.[25] That is, the relationship between the husband and wife seems to take precedence over financial considerations in determining the wife's employment.

In addition to income and the support of a husband, a long list of factors influence the employment likelihood for a wife and mother, including:

- The availability of jobs
- The number and age of her children
- Her age and level of education, work experience, and work skills
- The income level of her husband
- Status maintenance and status enhancement
- A range of attitudinal variables, including those of her husband[26]

---

[24] Deeann Wenk and Patricia Garrett, "Having a Baby: Some Predictions of Maternal Employment Around Childbirth," *Gender and Society* 6 (March 1992): 49–65.

[25] Becky L. Glass, "A Rational Choice Model of Wives' Employment Decisions," *Sociological Spectrum* 8 (1988): 35–48.

[26] See, for example, David J. Eggebeen, "Determinants of Maternal Employment for White Preschool Children: 1960–1980," *Journal of Marriage and the Family* 50 (February 1988): 149–159; Cedric Herring and Karen Rose Wilson-Sadberry, "Preference or Necessity? Changing Work Roles of Black and White Women, 1973–1990, *Journal of Marriage and the Family* 55 (May 1993): 314–325; and Joan Z. Spade, "Wives' and Husbands' Perceptions of Why Wives Work," *Gender and Society* 8 (June 1994): 170–188.

News Item: Women and the Changing Job Market

When I was a child, Dad and Mom sometimes engaged in minor skirmishes. I listened and learned a thing or two. Thing One: My parents might seem to be arguing about money or what color to paint the porch swing, but the true subject in contention was probably power. As Dad sometimes bellowed, "Just who do you think wears the pants in this family?"

Thing Two: "Pants" has nothing to do with wearing apparel. It is a metaphor for privilege, I decided.

The responsibility, it seemed to me, was one of earning income to pay bills. Men did that and wore pants in the doing. Women tended children and kept house. There were exceptions. But not many.

In my youth, wives were expected to defer to husbands in all major decision-making, even minor decision-making if the husband insisted. Whether he or she was better at making these choices didn't matter. Rank has privilege.

So when Dad hurled the pants question at Mom, there was only one acceptable response: "Of course, dear, you still wear the pants." Unconditional surrender! Buoyed by this reaffirmation of his role, Dad would decide the issue. Or he would let Mom decide. All the heated debate was suddenly irrelevant.

Grown-ups were sure weird when I was a kid. They still are. The gender wars continue.

Many women wear pants today, on jobs and off. According to U.S. government figures, 80 percent of women between the ages of 16 and 65 now have full- or part-time jobs outside their homes. This nontraditional women's work has been blamed by some critics for most of America's social woes, including children's poor performance in schools, juvenile crime, and teen-age pregnancies. Of course, it's the reason for our high divorce rates. Any fool can see that.

Women would be much happier letting men wear the pants and earn the bread, this argument goes. It's

continued

For instance, it is easier for a woman to work in her middle years, when she does not have young children. Generally, it is easier to find a job if one has training, skills, and experience. The woman who does not have a husband or who has a part-time employed husband or a husband with a low income may be forced to work outside the home. Generally, an *inverse* relationship exists between the husband's level of income and the likelihood the wife will be employed.

Interestingly, a *direct* relationship exists between women's economic attainment and unmarried status. In many cases, the employed single woman is less a "marriage reject" than one who has rejected marriage. The higher the woman's income, the more likely she is to be and remain single.

Employed women and motherhood

Few sociocultural factors are as strong as the inverse relationship between female participation in the labor force and having children. Simply, working women have

the dread feminists who have told them they should have jobs. This is all wrong, and women are beginning to understand how wrong it is. Perhaps you've heard the argument, popular among many political and religious conservatives.

The Women's Bureau of the U.S. Department of Labor recently circulated a questionnaire among working women nationwide. More than 250,000 women responded. These responses were augmented by information gathered from a telephone survey of 1,200 additional working women.

More than half of America's working women, cutting across all income and occupational categories, complain of too much work-associated stress. It's not the job that causes the stress, however. Four out of five working women reported they either "love" or "like" their jobs. I doubt so many men feel so warmly disposed toward their employment situations.

What women find most stressful is the pay scales, still lagging behind the pay for men doing the same or comparable work. And the lack of opportunities for advancement, promotion, on-the-job training and job-related education. And the lack of adequate health and pension benefits. And the difficulty of finding convenient, affordable, and high-quality child care.

Women love their jobs and are not likely to quit even if they can afford to do so. The problem for them is that the American workplace and benefits systems were designed for their fathers and grandfathers.

Since women make up half the nation's workforce and are likely to grow in numbers as the female majority grows, industries, corporations and businesses need to rethink their concept of family and its breadwinners. Forget pants. Think bottom line.

Source: Nickie McWhirter. *The Detroit News,* 5 November 1994, p. 12-C.

fewer children. Employment of married females before childbearing is associated with lower fertility levels later, longer first-birth intervals, and earlier use of birth control.[27] There has also been a dramatic increase in labor force participation of women with school- and preschool-age children (see Figure 4-1). Having young children remains a slight deterrent to women's labor force participation but only minimally so in contrast to thirty years ago (again, see Figure 4-1).

Pregnancy and first birth clearly have a major impact on female employment. A national longitudinal survey of over 19,000 high school seniors, beginning in 1972 with four follow-up surveys, reported that the majority of women who have been married have jobs prior to pregnancy. Most leave these jobs as the pregnancy progresses, so that only one woman in five remains employed in the month that

---

[27] H. Theodore Groat, Randy L. Workman, and Arthur G. Neal, "Labor Force Participation and Family Formation: A Study of Working Mothers," *Demography* 13 (February 1976): 115–125.

the child is born.[28] Following the birth, some women return to work, but employment rates only rise to about 60 percent of their previous levels. Had these women not become mothers, the proportion of those employed would have steadily increased. Thus, motherhood does lead to an employment deficit. The study found that even women who retain their jobs show some decline in hours at work.

It is often assumed that maternal employment has many effects on a child—all bad. However, endorsement of this belief has declined, especially among women, and research in the last several decades has seriously challenged this view. Few recent studies have reported meaningful differences between the children of working mothers and the children of nonworking mothers. When differences do exist, they are often explained less by the mother working than by other factors: social class, part- or full-time employment, age of the child, mother's attitude toward employment, and other social and psychological factors.

Various positive outcomes of maternal employment are found in the research literature. For example, mothers who hold high status jobs leads to positive effects on children's schooling.[29] Both sons and daughters are more likely to do better in school, complete high school, enter college, and complete a degree. It was found as well that occupational complexities and the resources that employed mothers bring to the home and family environment lead to positive outcomes for children.[30] Doing complex work enhances one's intellectual flexibility and provides more opportunity for autonomy and self-direction. For a mother, this in turn leads to her placing greater value on her children's self-direction and having less concern for behavior conformity per se. Personal resources that employed mothers bring to childrearing—such as high levels of self-esteem, educational attainment, the delay of childbearing, and older age and maturity—also have positive effects on their children's home environments.

Jay Belsky, who has done extensive research on parental and nonmaternal child care and the socioemotional development of young children, found that children whose mothers were employed full time, beginning in the first or second year of the child's life, scored more poorly on a compliance component of adjustment than did children whose mothers were not employed.[31] *Compliance* referred to items such as whether the child would eat the food given, protest going to bed,

---

[28] Linda J. Waite, Gus W. Haggstrom, and David E. Kanouse, "Changes in the Employment Activities of New Parents," *American Sociological Review* 50 (April 1985): 263–272. See also: Sonalde Desai and Linda J. Waite, "Women's Employment During Pregnancy and After the First Birth: Occupational Characteristics and Work Commitment," *American Sociological Review* 56 (August 1991): 551–566.

[29] Matthijs Kalmijn, "Mother's Occupational Status and Children's Schooling," *American Sociological Review* 59 (April 1994): 257–275.

[30] Elizabeth G. Menaghan and Toby L. Parcel, "Determining Children's Home Environments: The Impact of Maternal Characteristics and Current Occupational and Family Conditions," *Journal of Marriage and the Family* 53 (May 1991): 417–431.

[31] Jay Belsky and David Eggebeen, "Early and Extensive Maternal Employment and Young Children's Socioemotional Development: Children of the National Longitudinal Survey of Youth," *Journal of Marriage and the Family* 53 (November 1991): 1083–1110; and Jay Belsky, "Parental and Nonparental Child Care and Children's Socioemotional Development: A Decade in Review," *Journal of Marriage and the Family* 52 (November 1990): 885–903.

The increasing employment of mothers has created a need for day care far beyond what can be provided by spouses, grandparents, in-laws, or other family members. Many corporate, university, community, and private centers have been established to help fill this gap, but costs and the availability of competent staff are still major concerns.

or turn off the TV when told. However, other areas of adjustment (behavior problems, insecurity, sociability, inhibition) showed no negative effects of maternal employment.

Belsky's review of the effects of mothers' working on children's socioemotional development has suggested that maternal employment per se is less important than the degree to which child care (by parents or nonparents) is sensitive and responsive. Childrearing that is sensitive and responsive seems to promote security in the infant and toddler and cooperation, compliance, and even achievement in the older child. Conversely, inconsistent, unsupportive, and unresponsive care fosters uncooperative and problematic behavior, irrespective of the employment of the mother.

In brief, maternal employment as an isolated factor is too broad a concept to produce major distinctions in effects on children. However, the number of women and mothers who work does focus attention on other areas, such as the need for day-care services. Attention is also focused on the husband/wife relationship and the balance of power between them, which will be discussed next.

Employed women and marriage

The effects of female employment on marriage, intimate partnerships, and other relationships varies considerably, depending on whether the woman's employment is full time or part time, on whether she has preschool children, on the ages of her and her husband, on their stage in the life cycle, and on many other factors.[32]

One of these factors that affects marriage negatively is when women hold nontraditional gender ideologies. Greenstein found that hours employed per week did not have a significant effect on a marriage if the wife held traditional gender ideologies. But it has a strong negative effect on marital stability for nontraditional women.[33] As shown earlier in this chapter, husbands tend not to share equally in the division of household labor. This is not perceived as a major problem for women who hold traditional gender ideologies. Nontraditional women, on the other hand, have normative expectations of an egalitarian relationship and the inequality of household labor seems to manifest itself in a decrease in marital satisfaction, increase in marital conflict, and ultimately in an increased probability of marital disruption.

Various other female employment factors appear to have a significant impact on marital dissolution. Data from the United States and countries such as Thailand and Puerto Rico show that the greater the number of hours worked, transitions in female employment status, and wage increases, all increase the probability of marital instability, divorce, or both.[34]

In contrast, a female employment factor that affects marriage positively is the extent to which the family experiences accommodate the wife's employment. The marriage is improved when a woman has her husband's support of her working and has some freedom from childrearing responsibilities.[35]

The most important conclusion from a review of twenty-seven studies, spanning over thirty years and exploring the relationship between employment status and marital adjustment, was that the wife's employment status alone appears to have little or no effect on marital adjustment.[36] This finding challenged the common belief that employment of wives per se places the marital relationship in jeopardy.

Considerable shifts in power in the husband/wife relationship seem to occur when the wife is employed. In general, the wife's power tends to increase. (In Chapter 12, a resource theory is used to explain shifts in power.) Thus, as the wife becomes employed, she gains income, independence, and new contacts (resources)

---

[32] An excellent review of the effects of women's employment on families can be seen in Glenna Spitze, "Women's Employment and Family Relations: A Review," *Journal of Marriage and the Family* 50 (August 1988): 595–618.

[33] Theodore N. Greenstein, "Gender Ideology, Marital Disruption, and the Employment of Married Women," *Journal of Marriage and the Family* 57 (February 1995): 31–42. Note as well: Darlene L. Pina and Vern L. Bengston, "The Division of Household Labor and Wives' Happiness: Ideology, Employment, and Perceptions of Support," *Journal of Marriage and the Family* 55 (November 1993): 901–912.

[34] John N. Edwards, Theodore D. Fuller, Sairudee Vorakitphokatorn and Santhat Sermsri, "Female Employment and Marital Instability: Evidence from Thailand," *Journal of Marriage and the Family* 54 (February 1992): 59–68; and Karen Price Carver and Jay D. Teachman, "Female Employment and First Union Dissolution in Puerto Rico," *Journal of Marriage and the Family* 55 (August 1993): 686–698.

[35] Dana Vannoy and William W. Philliber, "Wife's employment and Quality of Marriage," *Journal of Marriage and the Family* 54 (May 1992): 387–398.

[36] Drake S. Smith, "Wife Employment and Marital Adjustment: A Cumulation of Results," *Family Relations* 34 (October 1985): 483–490.

that increase her contribution to the marriage. This increase in power among employed wives appears not only in the United States but cross-culturally, as well.

Employment of mothers affects far more than children and marriage. It affects the women, as well. In one study, paid employment was found to have a substantial liberalizing effect on women's roles and responsibilities but only a small effect on their support of feminist positions (support for the Equal Rights Amendment, approval of legal abortion, approval of sexual behavior between consenting adults, etc.).[37] Employed mothers were likely to enjoy their activities and relationships with children, reveal positive feelings about themselves, project an image of stability and confidence, and evaluate their communities as satisfactory places to live.[38]

In her middle years, when her children are gone from home, the interests of the employed mother are no longer divided between motherhood and employment. At this time, some women turn from part-time to full-time employment. Some begin work for the first time or, at least, the first time since marriage or having children. Employment may take on new meaning to the middle-aged woman, presenting perspectives on the world and her own values considerably different from those known previously.

Employed husbands and fathers

In 1994, 75.1 percent of all males aged sixteen and over (a total of 70.8 million) were employed in the labor force. This level was down slightly from 77.4 percent (61.5 million) in 1980 and down from 80.0 percent (51.2 million) in 1970.[39] These figures show that, while the number of males in the employed labor force has increased over the last twenty years, the proportion of employed men relative to the total male population has decreased. These data are unlike those presented for females, which showed both number and proportional increases.

Apart from number differences in the employment of males and females, the significant differences center around social norms and expectations. As suggested earlier in the section on employed wives and mothers, questions as to why men work and what effects paternal employment have on family size, marriage, and the like seem less important. Are children, especially preschool-age children, affected by their fathers' working? Are single, career-oriented males considered "marriage rejects"? If a boy is asked what he wants to be when he grows up, what is the "correct" answer: "married" or "a father" or rather some employment status, particularly one of a prestigious nature, such as "doctor," "lawyer," "banker," or "president." In short, does work define men's worth, their success or failure? Is work their major source of identity?

---

[37] Eric Plutzer, "Work Life, Family Life, and Women's Support of Feminism," *American Sociological Review* 53 (August 1988): 640–649.

[38] See Ronald C. Kessler and James A. McRae, Jr., "The Effect of Wives' Employment on the Mental Health of Married Men and Women," *American Sociological Review* 47 (April 1982): 216–227.

[39] U.S. Bureau of the Census, *Statistical Abstract of the United States: 1995*, no. 628, p. 400.

If the answers to these last two questions are yes, it can be assumed that unemployment is a crucial dimension in men's lives. Studies of the Depression in the 1930s found that the husband's unemployment had a negative effect on his self-esteem, personal functioning, and marital and family relationships. Similar results have appeared in studies since then. Jeffry Larson, looking at blue-collar families, reported that the unemployment of husbands corresponded to significantly lower marital adjustment, poorer marital communication, and lower satisfaction and harmony in family relations.[40]

The length of time that married men are unemployed, when compared to single men, is yet another indicator of the negative effect of unemployment and of how seriously married men take their role as economic providers. One study indicated that in any given month, married men are between 50 to 100 percent more likely to take a job than single men.[41] That is, if men do become unemployed, married men spend significantly less time without a job than single men.

Among the employed, job insecurity as well as stress on the job have been found to have negative effects on the husband, wife, and other family members.[42] The research by Larson and others indicated that job insecurity stress was significantly related to lower marital adjustment, poorer overall family functioning, less family role clarity, less family affective responsiveness, and more marital and family problems. The research by Rook and others found that job stress experienced by husbands detracted from the psychological health of their wives. It was suggested that the wives' increased symptomatology in response to their husbands' job problems may be rooted in the nature of their emotional involvement with their husbands. That is, concern for a loved one may increase one's own vulnerability to emotional stress. Or it may be that the time and energy expended in support of someone else tends to jeopardize one's own well-being.

Men, like women, work for financial reasons. But the emphases on having a job, getting ahead, and gaining prestige or achieving power are stressed in sex-role socialization far more for men than for women. For men, work often becomes their "home away from home." The boss or the corporate hierarchy tends to serve as a surrogate parent in holding authority, defining duties, and dispensing rewards or punishments. Workmates serve as siblings with their competition, rivalry, friendship, and relatively equal status.

In brief, while women are likely to gain status and identity through marriage, men are often "married to their work" and gain their status and identity accordingly.

---

[40] Jeffry H. Larson, "The Effect of Husband's Unemployment on Marital and Family Relations in Blue-Collar Families," *Family Relations* 33 (October 1984): 503–511.

[41] Jay D. Teachman, Vaughn R. A. Call, and Karen Price Carver, "Marital Status and the Duration of Joblessness Among White Men," *Journal of Marriage and the Family* 56 (May 1994): 415–428.

[42] Jeffry H. Larson, Stephan M. Wilson, and Rochelle Beley, "The Impact of Job Insecurity on Marital and Family Relationships," *Family Relations* 43 (April 1994): 138–143; and Karen Rook, David Dooley, and Ralph Catalano, "Stress Transmission: The Effects of Husbands' Job Stress on the Emotional Health of Their Wives," *Journal of Marriage and the Family* 53 (February 1991): 165–177.

U.S. Diversity: Husband Roles Among the Amish

Amish family organization and expected gender roles are centered around the father. This patriarchal structure is shown by the extent to which his wife and children are subject to him. However, the line of authority is not rigid; the wife is consulted, particularly about childrearing, family problems, and decisions relating to home purchases. The children may also be consulted in planning farming matters. However, the husband's word is regarded as final.

The husband's way of life, as with most Amish behavior, stems from the scriptures. As stated in I Corinthians 11:3, "The head of the woman is the man." Thus, both husband and wife are well aware that the husband is the head of the house, although age, too, is a significant status factor. The oldest male, or grandfather, is respected as the patriarch, and his social status increases at least until he reaches the age where he simply moves into the *Gross Dawdy* (grandfather) house and the younger generation takes over.

The husband's major activities center around farming. He purchases the equipment and livestock without seeking the advice of his wife. He performs the majority of the farming activities with the assistance of his wife and children. Only on occasion does the husband assist his wife in household tasks.

Personal relationships between husband and wife are quiet and sober, with no apparent demonstration of affection. Irritation between mates, expressed in a variety of ways, is conditioned by informally approved means of expression: the tone of voice, a gesture, or a direct statement. The husband may express disapproval by complete silence at the dinner table, leaving the wife to guess what is wrong.

Men as full-time homemakers

Work, to men, is generally defined in terms of labor force employment, not in terms of housework and child care. Traditionally, husbands and fathers were not responsible for any substantial amount of housework and child care. The husband's responsibility to the family was to provide economic support through paid employment. In terms of *role differentiation*, the male held primary responsibility for relationships and needs external to the family; the female held responsibility for relationships and needs internal to the family. In terms of exchange, the husband exchanged his work and economic services for the wife's companionship and household services. In terms of *resources* (see Chapter 12) relative to housework and childcare, the wife/mother supposedly had time for these activities whereas the full-time employed husband/father did not.

Are these traditional ideas changing? Some would say yes but not much. As suggested previously, some argue that male avoidance of housework and child care is a deliberate strategy to maintain power over women. Studies reported earlier in this chapter revealed that (1) the husband's performance of housework is small in tasks and time relative to the wife's, and, more significantly, that (2) husbands of employed wives do not spend much more time doing housework than husbands

While male homemakers are still not prevalent in the United States, men have proven to be effective parents and housekeepers. Relatively few men, married or single, give up employment to serve as full-time homemakers, as women have traditionally done, but men appear to be assuming more responsibility for the care of their children.

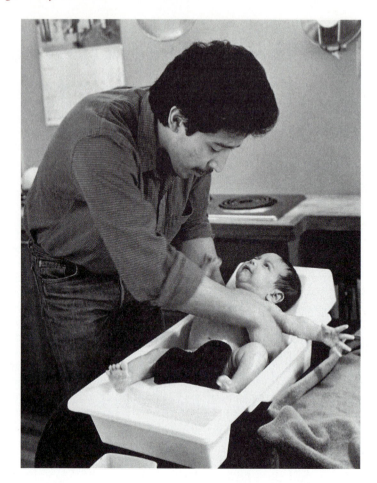

of nonemployed wives. (That is, employed wives do less housework than nonemployed wives, but husbands do about the same amount, irrespective of the employment status of the wife.) What these two findings reveal is a substantial work overload for the woman in a combined homemaker/employed worker role. There exists a substantial lag between the slower rate of change in men's participation in housework and the more rapid rate of change in women's attaining paid employment.

Some evidence for greater change is seen in subgroups such as single-parent fathers, fathers deliberately holding part-time jobs, single adoptive fathers, and full-time male homemakers; in these situations, men assume major household and child-care duties. What is not known is the extent to which contemporary male homemakers relinquish traditional male roles. A small study of Hispanic male homemakers, for example, revealed that their homemaker role was brought about by external economic circumstances and viewed as a temporary status.[43] They did, however, report greater involvement in family life, increased insight into their spouses' experiences, and as a result, closer relations with their spouses and children.

---

[43] Sharon Kantorowski Davis and Virginia Chavez, "Hispanic Househusbands," *Hispanic Journal of Behavioral Sciences* 7 (1985): 317–332.

While there is no question that wives continue to hold the primary responsibility for housework and child care and that the pace of change may seem both slow and minimal, in fact, men's behavior appears to be changing. There is currently no major trend toward full-time male homemakers, but there is increased participation of men in household and child-care tasks, as revealed in studies of dual-employed and dual-career marriages.

Dual-employed and dual-career marriages

Dual-employed marriages have become common in the United States, particularly increasing since World War II. The **dual-career marriage**, however, is a much newer life-style. The term *career* is distinguished from *work* or *paid employment* to designate a level of commitment and continuous development that offers both personal and material rewards. A job taken primarily for additional income is less likely to have such rewards. The dual-career life-style is rooted in assumptions of increasing female access to high-level professions and managerial positions, of norms of gender equality, and of employment motivations centering on self-development and interpersonal relationships more than on economics alone.

An interesting reality is that women in professional and management positions are far more likely than comparable men to be single, married with no children, or divorced as a consequence of their career involvement. And married women with professional and managerial positions are still basically in the traditionally female, lower-paid professions of teaching and nursing.

Existing literature on dual-earner marriages has suggested a range of common problems related to stress, role strain, and work overload.[44] Many such problems result from time pressures in completing simultaneous work and family obligations. One remedy for this time bind is a reduced work week for one or both parents. One study found that over half of mothers and two-thirds of fathers preferred this arrangement.[45] But the discrepancy between *actual* work hours and *desired* work hours, combined with being locked into a job where hours are fixed, only increased the role strain. Strain resulting from difficulty in meeting work and family demands was found to be associated with more depression, more pessimism, less marital bonding, and more family conflict.[46]

---

[44] Shelley L. Paden and Cheryl Buehler, "Coping with the Dual-Income Lifestyle," *Journal of Marriage and the Family* 57 (February 1995): 101–110; and Rosalind C. Barnett, "Home-to-Work Spillover Revisited: A Study of Full-Time Employed Women in Dual-Earner Couples," *Journal of Marriage and the Family* 56 (August 1994): 647–656.

[45] Phyllis Moen and Donna I. Dempster-McClain, "Employed Parents: Role Strain, Work Time, and Preference for Working Less," *Journal of Marriage and the Family* 49 (August 1987): 579–590.

[46] Nancy L. Galambos and Rainer K. Silbereisen, "Role Strain in West German Dual-Earner Households," *Journal of Marriage and the Family* 51 (May 1989): 385–389; and Patricia M. Ulbrich, "The Determinants of Depression in Two-Income Marriages," *Journal of Marriage and the Family* 50 (February 1988): 121–131.

This overload situation is what Karen Fox and Sharon Nickols referred to as the "time crunch."[47] The day is precisely twenty-four hours long, which may or may not be enough time to perform multiple roles and tasks—dual careers or not. Many couples alleviate the time crunch by having the employed wife spend less time in housework. Consistent data (some reported earlier in this chapter) have shown that husbands do not provide a corresponding increase in time doing housework to offset the wife's decrease.

Another related issue in dual-career or dual-earner marriages involves the relationship between parents and children. When the mother, married or single, is employed, her place is not exclusively in the home. Thus, concerns about latchkey children and child care take on increased importance. **Latchkey** ("self-care") **children** come home after school to an empty house, let themselves in with a "latch key," and remain home alone until a working parent gets home. Virginia Cain and Sandra Hofferth suggested that there are fewer latchkey children than popularly believed (about 2.4 million); that they are home alone for only a short period of time each day (most for two hours or less); and that they are not the children of low-income, single parents who cannot afford stable child-care arrangements.[48] Latchkey children are an important concern for some dual-career parents, but the more significant issue is child care.

How can dual-career or dual-employed couples both work outside the home and rear their children? The obvious answer is that they make alternative child-care arrangements for the hours they are employed. For many parents, child care is a great economic cost. An analysis of data from the National Consumer Expenditure Survey revealed that when work-related costs (the largest of which is child care) are taken as a portion of the dual-career family's income, their advantage over single earners is decreased by as much as 68 percent.[49]

One way to reduce the high cost of child care is shift work on the part of parents. Harriet Presser documented a remarkably high prevalence of nonday shifts among dual-earner spouses, with the result being high rates of parental child care, including father care.[50] For many dual-career families, however, shift work is not a possibility and the whole issue of **day care** takes on increased importance (as it does for single parents). Both day-care and after-school care are currently in great need in the United States. The availability of group care is limited, and costs are often high.

---

[47] Karen D. Fox and Sharon Y. Nickols, "The Time Crunch: Wife's Employment and Family Work," *Journal of Family Issues* 4 (March 1983): 61–82.

[48] Virginia S. Cain and Sandra L. Hofferth, "Parental Choice of Self Care for School-Age Children," *Journal of Marriage and the Family* 51 (February 1989): 65–77.

[49] Sandra L. Hanson and Theodora Ooms, "The Economic Costs and Rewards of Two-Earner, Two-Parent Families," *Journal of Marriage and the Family* 53 (August 1991): 622–634.

[50] Harriet B. Presser, "Shift Work and Child Care Among Young Dual-Earner American Parents," *Journal of Marriage and the Family* 50 (February 1988): 133–148. For the negative effects of shift-work on marital quality, see: Lynn White and Bruce Keith, "The Effect of Shift Work on the Quality and Stability of Marital Relations," *Journal of Marriage and the Family* 52 (May 1990): 453–462.

Employer-supported benefits and policies can be of great assistance in alleviating costs associated with child care, work/family stress, division of labor conflicts, and the like. A sample of Louisiana businesses revealed that a small percentage of companies have personnel policies that include flextime, an option to work at home, job sharing, parental and maternal leave, parenting seminars, and family counseling; financial aid programs with vouchers to subsidize child-care expense, on-site or near-site child care centers, and cafeteria plans; and information and referral services that include educational materials and lists of child -care providers.[51] Many of these benefits and policies do not require large capital investments but have been shown to have positive benefits in areas such as productivity, absenteeism, morale, tardiness, turnover, and recruiting.

Recognizing that very few companies include policies such as these just mentioned, and after reading about the dilemmas and resultant strains produced by dual careers, one could ask, Why dual careers? Clearly, this type of life-style provides gains beyond economic ones, including satisfaction derived from creating something, achieving recognition, expanding energies beyond home and children, and enriching marriage. Some research results have suggested that men respond less positively to the dual-earner arrangement than women.[52] It appears that the husband of an employed wife loses part of his active support system when she no longer functions exclusively as spouse, homemaker, and mother. Employed wives, on the other hand, expand into roles that have more positive value for them.

While the professional employment of women is gaining increasing respectability and acceptance, true gender equality has not and perhaps will not be achieved. Wives are still generally expected to give up their own jobs for the sake of their husbands and to shoulder the primary responsibility for housework and child care. The structure of the U.S. family may make it virtually impossible for the married woman to have career goals like those of her male counterpart.[53] The pressures of both family responsibilities and career obligations for the married career woman may result in the increased separation of work and family. Or perhaps integration is only possible later in life, when child-care responsibilities are lessened.

In brief, today's aspiring married professionals face difficult choices: lowering career aspirations, consciously rejecting parenthood, divorce, withdrawal of one spouse from the top professional tier, and for some, commuter marriages.

Commuter marriages

One form of dual-career life-style is where the husband and wife live separately. The pattern of one spouse leaving home temporarily is nothing new, and the

---

[51] Dian L. Seyler, Pamela A. Monroe, and James C. Garand, "Balancing Work and Family: The Role of Employer-Supported Child Care Benefits," *Journal of Family Issues* 16 (March 1995): 170–193.

[52] Sandra C. Stanley, Janet G. Hunt, and Larry L. Hunt, "The Relative Deprivation of Husbands in Dual-Earner Households," *Journal of Family Issues* 7 (March 1986): 3–20.

[53] Mary C. Regan and Helen E. Roland, "Rearranging Family and Career Priorities: Professional Women and Men of the Eighties," *Journal of Marriage and the Family* 47 (November 1985): 985–992.

Case Example:
A Commuter Marriage

Butch has a full-time job and lives in Toledo, Ohio. Marsha has a full-time job and lives in Pontiac, Michigan. Since their marriage more than three years ago, nearly 100 miles have separated them, causing each to experience many lonely days apart from each other and many nights sleeping in separate cities. They are both in their mid-40s and in their second marriage. Why don't they live together and how does this marriage work?

Marsha has been employed by the State of Michigan for many years and has a teenage daughter living at home. She would like to live with Butch but has seniority in her job and would lose her excellent benefit package were she to move out of state. Plus, her daughter wants to complete high school in the city she lived in all her life. Butch has a good-paying supervisory job in tool and die making. After extensive searching, he has been unable to find any comparable job near Pontiac. So, they visit on week-ends and converse on the phone several times each day.

Butch says he owns the phone line between their homes. Last month his phone bill was $249.00 and that wasn't one of the high ones. To Butch, the only advantage of a commuter marriage is to make their moments together more precious. Marsha doesn't see any advantages but many disadvantages. She says it creates a lot of stress. "He's not around when I need and want him the most." Maintaining two homes, the cost of commuting, fixing separate meals, getting to children's events, and so forth, is very expensive and time con-suming. Marsha said when she married, she believed their separate residences would be a very temporary thing but that it hasn't worked out that way.

Both Butch and Marsha mentioned the difficulty in such a living arrange-ment and neither would recommend it to others. They agreed that it takes a lot of trust and faith in one another. For a time, Butch was ready to give it up. He was frustrated with living alone and was tempted to engage in other relationships. He stated how Marsha was the stronger one who really wanted their marriage to work. So she did (and continues to do) all sorts of little things, like sending cards, gifts, and surprise activities of an intimate nature that add spice to their relationship. He too, on occasion, surprises her with flowers, extra money, or an unannounced visit.

Today, they define their relationship as a good one and both believe it will get better when they can live together. Marsha's advice to others is to weigh carefully where you'll live before you get married. You have to really be com-mitted to each other and take your marriage vows seriously. She says it defi-nitely is not for everyone and should only be done if there is no other way.

amount of separation varies both by occupation or profession as well as distance. Politicians, professional athletes, and salespersons routinely spend time apart from their spouses. In addition, military service, imprisonment, and seasonal work in selected occupations force the separation of husbands and wives.

Today, the decision for family members to live apart increasingly results from the woman's career aspirations and an unwillingness either to divorce or relocate one spouse in the community of employment of the other. This pattern stands in sharp contrast to the traditional one of the married couple and their children living and moving where the husband has employment. Now, however, the wife's career may require her to spend the weekdays in Los Angeles or Chicago while the husband's career may require him to be in Atlanta or Boston.

The traditional option was for one spouse—usually, the wife—to give up his or her job to live with the other spouse. Newer options include marital separation or divorce, with each person pursuing careers independently, or remaining married but establishing separate residences, with commuting between residences possible. Neither option has much social or cultural support. Popular views of both divorce and a commuting life-style are generally pessimistic. Marriage, as defined by most people, includes sharing a common residence. Friends and relatives are prone to question the couple's satisfaction with or commitment to a marriage when the husband and wife live apart.

Yet several examinations of the quality of life of commuting couples compared to single-residence, dual-career couples revealed both benefits and costs to both types of arrangements.[54] Commuters were more satisfied with their life work and the time they had for themselves. They reported significantly less overload and a less stressful life-style than did their single-residence counterparts. Commuters listed as benefits increased independence, greater self-sufficiency, and enhanced appreciation for spouse and family. On the other hand, commuters were more dissatisfied with family life and with the lack of emotional support and companionship from their partners. Most saw commuting as a temporary life-style.

For many commuter couples, the telephone becomes a means of regular contact. Time together becomes well planned and is not spent in meaningless socializing with uninterested others. A number of factors appear to make the separation easier: strong career commitment by both parties, having adequate financial resources to meet the expense of maintaining two residences, making phone calls, traveling to see one another, living short distances apart, and maintaining established patterns of interaction.

SUMMARY

1. This chapter began by briefly looking at selected linkages between the family and other institutions. Cross-culturally as well as historically, major connections have existed at a macrolevel between basic systems within all societies. Families are linked to religion, not only at weddings and funerals but also in terms of sex roles, sexual behaviors, and family size. Families are linked to politics in terms of social policy and legislation, ranging from tax-

---

[54] Barbara B. Bunker, Josephine M. Zubek, Virginia J. Vanderslice, and Robert W. Rice, "Quality of Life in Dual-Career Families: Commuting Versus Single-Residence Couples," *Journal of Marriage and the Family* 54 (May 1992): 399–407; and Melissa M. Groves and Diane M. Horm-Wingerd, "Commuter Marriages: Personal, Family and Career Issues," *Sociology and Social Research* 75 (July 1991): 212–217.

ation deductions for dependents to providing income for people who are elderly through Social Security. Families are linked to education in terms of learning social norms, skills, and mobility patterns.

2. The focus of the chapter was the link between work and family systems. Conflict theorists, in particular, view the economic system as the key to understanding inequality within or outside the family. Even household labor is intricately linked to a capitalist type of system that enables men to hold a dominant position over women.

3. A primary role for most married women is that of homemaker. This role is often accorded low status, involves long hours, has high productive value, and produced an inequitable assignment of marital tasks. Yet being a homemaker is a source of satisfaction for many women, particularly those adhering to traditional marital-role expectations.

4. The number and proportion of wives and mothers in the paid labor force has increased yearly for several decades. Women work for many of the same reasons men work, especially income, but derive many other rewards from employment as well: status, prestige, recognition, and feelings of success and achievement. Very few negative effects on children are directly attributable to employment of the mother. Women's working has similar effects on marriage. While employment of wives affects husband/wife relationships, no signs of marital discord and stress can be attributed to wives' working per se.

5. The number of employed husbands and fathers has also increased in recent decades, but the proportion of men working relative to the total male population has decreased. There is widespread agreement on the expectation that men should be employed. Work appears to be a key source of identity and self-worth for men.

6. Being a male homemaker, unlike being a female homemaker, is rarely a full-time job. There is some evidence of change in the amount of time and frequency with which men engage in household tasks, but the rate of change is slow.

7. The increasing employment of women combined with the constant high employment of men has resulted in a large number of dual-employed and dual-career marriages. Numerous assumptions about these marriages run counter to basic realities. These life-styles involve both rewards and costs, but various strains for both sexes often force difficult choices between family and career.

8. The increase in employment of both parents or of a single parent has focused attention on the care of children in the parents' absence. Latchkey, or "self-care," children, who come home from school to a parentless house, are of concern to society in general, as well as parents in particular. The more significant issue, however, is child care. For some parents, shift work

is a possibility, but for single parents and many two-parent households, it is not. Day care for children is a major need in the United States. Group care is limited in availability, and costs for all types of care are often high.

9. Another marital life-style is the commuter marriage where the husband and wife live separately. For some, this type of living arrangement serves as the compromise between giving up the marriage or the career.

10. Chapters 1 through 4 have provided an introduction to marriage and the family: namely, family issues and change; disciplinary and theoretical approaches to the family; marital, family, and kinship organization; and the linkages among marriage, family, and work. Chapters 5 through 8 will focus on variations in American family life-styles, with chapters on Chinese and Swedish families (5), African American (6), and Hispanic, Asian, and Native American families (7). Chapter 8 will address social-class variations in family life-styles.

KEY TERMS AND TOPICS

Linkages between the family
    and other systems p. 110

Religion and the family p. 110

Politics and the family p. 112

Education and the family p. 113

Economy and the family p. 114

Women as full-time homemakers p. 115

Employed wives and mothers p. 120

Reasons for wives'/mothers'
    employment p. 123

Employed women and
    motherhood p. 124

Employed women and marriage p. 127

Employed husbands and fathers p. 129

Men as full-time homemakers p. 131

Dual-employed marriage p. 133

Dual-career marriage p. 133

Latchkey children p. 134

Day care p. 134

Commuter marriages p. 135

DISCUSSION QUESTIONS

1. Discuss linkages among the family system and other systems, such as religion, politics, and education. What does each system contribute to and receive from the other?

2. Discuss the statement that "Differences between churchgoers and nonchurchgoers are more pronounced than differences between denominations or particular religious groups."

3. Why is the assumption made that *housework* is not really work when wives and mothers are asked, "Do you work?" What arguments can be made linking housework to male/female roles, to the dominance/submission issue, and to a capitalist-type society?

4. One writer (Jessie Bernard) stated that "being a housewife makes women sick" (*The Future of Marriage*, p. 48). What did she mean by this? What does other research suggest in this regard?

5. What social factors most influence who will work, male or female? Explain reasons for the increase in female paid employment.

6. Discuss what consequences being employed may have for a woman in terms of her marriage, her children, and her own self-image. Do the negative consequences outweigh the positive in any circumstances?

7. Discuss what consequences being employed may have for a man in terms of his marriage, his children, and his own self-image. Do the negative consequences outweigh the positive in any circumstances?

8. Examine the various perspectives on male roles in relation to housework and child care. Have significant changes occurred in men's roles in the United States or around the world? What is the current outlook for change?

9. What strains may occur in dual-career marriages that are less likely to occur in one-career marriages? What rewards exist in each type of marriage?

10. Discuss the pros and cons of commuter marriage. What conditions may increase or decrease the strain living apart has on the couple's relationship?

FURTHER READINGS

Gerson, Kathleen. *No Man's Land: Men's Changing Commitments to Family and Work*. New York: Basic Books, 1993. A look at how and why men's lives are changing, the differences among men, and the varied ways men are reassessing their commitments to family and work.

Gilbert, Lucia Albino. *Two Careers/One Family: The Promise of Gender Equality*. Newbury Park, CA: Sage, 1993. An analysis of the interplay between work and family in the lives of dual-career couples.

Googins, Bradley K. *Work/Family Conflicts: Private Lives—Public Response*. New York: Auburn House, 1991. An overview of work/family conflicts examined at four levels: individuals, families, corporations, and governments.

Hood, Jane C., ed. *Men, Work, and Family*. Newbury Park: CA: Sage, 1993. Fourteen writings on ways men are negotiating commitments to work and family, using comparative contexts and a variety of methodological tools.

Lerner, Jacqueline. *Working Women and Their Families*. Thousand Oaks, CA: Sage, 1994. An overview of maternal employment including its impact on children's development: intellectually, emotionally, and vocationally.

Moen, Phyllis. *Women's Two Roles: A Contemporary Dilemma*. New York: Auburn House, 1992. An examination of the meshing of work and family roles, both as the private dilemma of individual women and as a public dilemma for the nation.

Percel, Toby L., and Menaghan, Elizabeth G. *Parents' Jobs and Children's Lives*. Hawthorne, NY: Aldine de Gruyter, 1994. A comprehensive examination of parental work and family influences on the well-being of children.

Rubin, Rose M., and Riney, Bobye J. *Working Wives and Dual-Earner Families.* Westport, CT: Praeger, 1994. Descriptive and empirical research is presented on the economics of dual-earner families and their central role in the economy and society.

Silberstein, Lisa R. *Dual-Career Marriage: A System in Transition.* Hillsdale, NJ: Lawrence Erlbaum, 1992. Examining a small sample of dual-career marriages, the author looks at how gender roles have shifted in the worlds of work and family.

Voydanoff, Patricia. *Work and Family Life.* Beverly Hills, CA: Sage, 1987. An examination and review of current knowledge on the relationship between work and family.

Wheelock, Jane. *Husbands at Home: The Domestic Economy in a Post-Industrial Society.* New York: Routledge, 1990. An attempt to integrate and present a model of monopoly capitalism, the domestic economy, and the changing nature of work.

Zedeck, Sheldon, ed. *Work, Families, and Organizations.* San Francisco: Jossey-Bass Publishers, 1992. A multidisciplinary collection of articles on work, family, and organizational issues, including separate chapters on work and families in Israel and the United Kingdom.

Chapter 5

Life-Styles Among Chinese and Swedish Families

Much can be gained by examining family systems—in this chapter, Chinese and Swedish—other than one's own. While it may be fascinating to examine the bizarre or sensational, a more fruitful outcome would be to gain insight into the variety of family patterns and practices around the world. In doing so, it is equally important to discover the threads of commonality among family systems: the prevalence of monogamy; the strong ties between mother and child, particularly during the child's early years; the lack of unregulated promiscuity; the status affiliation afforded by the family; and the significance of the kin networks as systems of support.

An examination of families other than one's own may help eliminate ethnocentric and provincial orientations, as one learns to question the obvious and destroy false stereotypes. Such an examination may also enable one to consider alternatives to traditional practices. One might better understand the close linkages between families and the larger social/cultural contexts within which they operate by looking at other families and other societies. In addition to *describing* life-styles and social patterns, examining other families may help one in *explaining* human behavior and social organization, which may lead to discovery of more general propositions and principles.

The first part of this chapter considers the Chinese of mainland China; namely, both traditional and contemporary Chinese family systems will be examined. The second part of this chapter considers the contemporary Swedish family system.

CHINESE FAMILY SYSTEM

Mainland China has a land area about equal to that of the United States but has a population more than four times as large. Indeed, China is a massive country, with more than 1.2 billion inhabitants; about 22 percent of the world's population are Chinese. China opened its borders and allowed observers to enter in the early 1970s. Today, the country is making a transition from a patriarchal family system, based on ancient techniques of agricultural labor, to a more egalitarian system, based on a developing and modernizing economy.

Until the early part of this century, the Chinese family avoided extensive change for nearly two thousand years.[1] The end of the Ch'ing Dynasty in 1911, the culmination of the Chinese Revolution in 1949, and the Marriage Laws of 1950 and 1980 brought about dramatic changes in the lives of Chinese families of all classes and in the lives of women in particular.

The Chinese family, as it currently exists under an authoritarian political regime, is often thought of as a relatively uniform entity. As will be shown in this chapter, there are many exceptions to a monolithic pattern. In addition to gender and rural/urban differences, which will be described in some detail, differences

---

[1] See Rubie S. Watson and Patricia Buckley Ebrey (eds.), *Marriage and Inequality in Chinese Society* (Berkeley, CA: University of California Press, 1991).

also existed in the traditional family among clans, villages, and regions of the country. For example, women were not expected to work in fields in the North, but the practice was acceptable in the South. Women were described as severely oppressed, yet some were highly educated and became known for their music, art, or poetry. Suicide was held to be a socially acceptable solution to a variety of problems, yet its practice was not considered widespread.

Traditional Chinese family

In a broad sense, the term **traditional Chinese family** refers to the type of general system that existed in China up to approximately 1900 or even 1950. Two important status distinctions need to be understood in this traditional system: (1) class differentiation, as demonstrated particularly within the clan, and (2) gender differentiation, as demonstrated in the father/son relationship and the oppression of women.

Clans

The clan system of traditional China was extremely important to maintenance of ancestral linkages and group solidarity. A **clan**, sometimes referred to as a **tsu**, included all persons with a common surname who traced descent from a common ancestor. The tsu operated through a council of elders; it often involved several thousand persons—sometimes entire villages—and was composed of everyone from gentry to peasants. The **gentry** were intellectuals who did no manual labor but who received income from being landlords or from holding government offices or academic positions. The **peasants**, who comprised the bulk of the population, cultivated the land and were generally very poor. In a country greatly overpopulated, in the sense that there was not enough cultivated land to give the average peasant an adequate livelihood, infant and general mortality rates were high. Widespread conditions of poverty contributed to undernourishment and lack of medical care. Indirect consequences of poverty, particularly for females, including infanticide, abandoning and selling children, and out-adoption (placing children for adoption); women often married late or not at all.

The significance that this large clan group, comprised of gentry and peasants, had for the family can be seen in the functions the clan performed: lending money to members, helping individual families pay for extravagant weddings and funerals, establishing schools, exercising judicial authority, acting as a government agent in collecting taxes, and maintaining ancestral graves and tsu property.[2] The clan performed most of the functions generally associated with government: taxes, law enforcement, schools, welfare, and so on. As one might guess, the tsu came under serious attack when the revolutionary government came into power.

The clan network was maintained in a variety of ways. One widely described practice was **ancestor worship**. An individual existed by virtue of his (not her)

---

[2] Paul Chao, *Women Under Communism: Family in Russia and China* (Bayside, NY: General Hall, 1977): 123.

ancestors, who, in turn, continued to exist through their descendants. In life, parents cared for children and children took on caring for their parents in old age. After a parent's death, while the form of care changed, the duty did not. In life, parents were served and respected. In death, they were served and worshipped. If, when alive, the parents needed food, clothing, shelter, and money, then even when they were dead, the children supplied them with these essentials. The transfer of goods from this world to the next was achieved primarily by burning. Food, however, could be offered directly. In return, the ancestors gave blessings and assistance through their supernatural powers. As could the Greek gods, Chinese ancestors could bless warfare, hunting, or agriculture or punish with famine, defeat, sickness, or death. Thus, there was a continuing reciprocal relationship between living and dead clan members.

Closely related to ancestor worship was the principle of **filial piety**, or the duty and subordination of a son to his father. Giving proper deference to parents and other ancestors tended to perpetuate and maintain property within the family, to grant universal authority to the male elders, to serve as a major source of both formal and informal social control, and perhaps above all, to maintain stability and continuity (preventing drastic change).

Gender roles

As the principle of filial piety alone suggests, males held an extremely favorable position relative to females in the traditional Chinese system. In traditional Chinese cosmology, the world was composed of two complementary elements. The **yin**, the female, stood for all things dark, weak, and passive; the **yang**, the male, stood for all things bright, strong, and active.

Following this philosophy, women were oppressed. Paul Chao noted that a wife had to obey three persons: her father before marriage, her husband after marriage, and her son after her husband died.[3] At all stages of life, recognition of women never approached that of men. Female infanticide was common, especially among the poorest peasants; a girl was an expense to raise and would later need a dowry to marry.

Marriages were not based on love and free choice but were arranged by parents through matchmakers. Since persons with the same surname (from the same clan) could not marry, marriage usually meant that the female would be completely removed from her family, friends, and community and go away to live with her husband. In addition, a woman often met her husband for the first time on their wedding day and then entered a husband/wife relationship that was considered subordinate and supplementary to the parent/son (particularly father/son) relationship.

The traditional Chinese wife's chief responsibilities were to bear male children and to aid in the work. Failure of a wife to bear male children could lead to repudiation and gave her husband the right to take a concubine or additional wives, among

---

[3] Chao, *Women Under Communism*, p. 124.

the gentry, at least. A woman could have only one husband, and if he died, she was not allowed to remarry. A wife or mother had few legal or property rights but could wield some power over other women, particularly her daughters-in-law. The latter peacefully endured harsh treatment until they, in turn, became mothers-in-law.

Not all women tolerated these oppressive conditions. Margaret Wolf observed that, for peasant women, suicide was a socially acceptable solution to a variety of problems that were otherwise unsolvable.[4] A young widow, particularly a childless one, could expect little from the future. Even among the gentry women, suicide was considered a proper response for a woman whose honor had been stained or who in any way brought dishonor or disgrace to her husband's family.

Another indication of the oppression of women is the traditional practice of binding their feet. Bound from early childhood, women's feet were reduced to three inches in length from toe to heel; the result was permanent crippling. **Footbinding**, which extends back to the tenth century, was prevalent among the upper classes, not so much as a sign of beauty but to restrain women's movement. Peasant women, heavily involved in agriculture and production, were exempted from this practice. Footbinding as well as other oppressive practices came under heavy attack in the Chinese Revolution.

Traditional Chinese family in a process of change

It is difficult to distinguish any single, major influence behind the dramatic changes that occurred in the Chinese family during the twentieth century. Events in Russia and the Western world as well as within China itself combined to force new patterns of existence in all social areas, including the family.

Major changes in the Chinese family were affected by the Russian Revolution and the Bolshevik party. Following the revolution, between 1917 and 1927, the Soviet government passed laws aimed at revamping marriage and divorce laws, granting free abortion on demand, and giving women legal equality with men. The ideas of Friedrich Engels clearly provided a basis for the formulation of official family policy in both the Soviet Union and mainland China.[5] Of prime significance was Engels' assertion that ownership of private property leads to men's domination over women. Engels also believed that family property elevates a man's position, that monogamy was instituted for women only, that the married woman sells her body once and for all into slavery, and that a woman becomes the slave of a man's lust and a mere instrument for the production of children.[6]

Because the system of family property and the concept of traditional family solidarity were incompatible with communist ideals, it became mandatory to make a major effort to change the traditional system. A Chinese Communist Party

---

[4] Margaret Wolf, "Women and Suicide in China," in Margaret Wolf and Roxanne Witke, *Women in Chinese Society* (Stanford: Stanford University Press, 1975): 111–141.

[5] Friedrich Engels, *The Origin of the Family, Private Property and the State* (New York: International Publishers, 1942). Originally published by Charles H. Kerr, Chicago, 1902.

[6] Ibid., pp. 49–51, 56, 65.

conference in 1922 called for voting rights for all persons, regardless of sex, and the abolishment of all legislation restricting women. The traditional low status of women and the maltreatment of wives, daughters-in-law, and domestic maids were branded as vestiges of the evils of the old family system. According to Chao, the communist government attempted to bring about a fundamental, drastic revolution in the family system by means of the Marriage Law of 1950. The purpose of this law was to plant in the minds of people, especially youth, new ideas regarding marriage and the family and to dismiss the Confucian virtue and ethics of the family.[7] Further changes were implemented in a second marriage law in 1980.

Marriage Laws of 1950 and 1980

The first marriage law was officially promulgated by the Chinese Communist Central Government in Peking on May 1, 1950. The two major principles of that law were:

1. The abolishment of the feudal marriage system, which was based on arbitrary and compulsory arrangements and the supremacy of men over women and which disregarded the interests of children. Enacted instead was a new, democratic marriage system based on free choice of partners, monogamy, equal rights for both sexes, and protection of the lawful interests of women and children.
2. The prohibition of bigamy, concubinage, child betrothal, interference in the remarriage of widows, and the extraction of money or gifts in connection with marriage.[8]

The Marriage Law of 1950, in defining the rights and duties of husbands and wives, gives them equal status in the home. The marital pair are in duty bound to love, respect, assist, and look after each other; live in harmony; and engage in productive work. Both spouses have the right to a free choice of occupation and free participation in social activities. They have equal rights to possess or manage property. Each has the right to use his or her own family name.

The law also defines the relations between parents and children; namely, it prohibits infanticide and mandates parents' duty to rear and educate their children and children's duty to support and assist their parents. Children born out of wedlock enjoy the same rights as children born in lawful wedlock. With the consent of the mother, the natural father may have custody of the child.

Divorce is granted when husband and wife both desire it. When only one party insists on divorce, the district People's Government may try to effect a reconciliation. If this fails, the county or People's Court makes a decision without delay after assurance that appropriate measures have been taken for the care of children and property. Interestingly, the law prohibits a husband from applying for

---

[7] Chao, *Women Under Communism*, p. 126.

[8] These principles are derived from Chao, ibid., appendix II, pp. 221–226.

a divorce when his wife is pregnant; after the birth of a child, the husband must wait one year.

Following divorce, no matter which parent gets custody of the children, they remain the children of both parties. Both parents have the duty to support and educate their children. If a divorced woman remarries and her husband is willing to pay the cost of maintaining and educating the children, the natural father is entitled to have his cost reduced or eliminated.

The need for further changes in family life led to the Marriage Law of 1980. This law differs in several respects from the old one. For example, the 1980 law raises the minimum legal marriage age from eighteen to twenty for women and from twenty to twenty-two for men. The law also relaxes restrictions on divorce. The twelfth article of the new law stipulates that both the husband and wife are obligated to practice family planning.[9]

Wei Zhangling described a number of dramatic effects of the 1950 and 1980 marriage laws:

1. Monogamy has become a reality. Before, there were many cases of polygamy, especially among the rich.

2. There has been a shift from arranged marriages to free-choice marriages, especially in the cities.

3. Young people tend to marry at a later age.

4. Family size has been reduced.

5. More and more women are participating in social production; many former homemakers have obtained jobs. Generally, women have become more self-confident and independent than ever before.

6. Household work has been partly socialized. For example, in cities, many people take their meals in work-unit dining halls. Many kindergartens and nurseries have been set up to lighten the burdens of housewives.

7. The great inequality between men and women prevalent before the revolution has been reduced. For example, when women get married, they do not change their surnames. Some children even adopt the surnames of their mothers.[10]

Contemporary Chinese family

The preceding overview highlighted a number of general changes in families and characterized the **contemporary Chinese family**. Many oppressive traditional norms have been abandoned, liberating women to some degree. But among families and individuals, inequalities and differences remain in areas such as gender, rural/urban residence, and mate selection.

---

[9] Wei Zhangling, "The Family and Family Research in Contemporary China," *International Social Science Journal* 126 (November 1990): 497.

[10] Ibid., p. 497.

U.S. Diversity: **Chinatowns and Beyond**

As will be noted in Chapter 7, Asian Americans are better educated and have higher median incomes than the U.S. population as a whole. And Chinese Americans rank among the top of Asian American groups in population size, in the percentage of young people enrolled in school, and in their rich heritage of organizational membership in associations such as clans (the *tsu,* based on common ancestors), benevolent associations (*hui kuan,* based on district of origin in china), and secret societies (*tongs,* based on specific interests such as drugs, gambling, and prostitution).

Not only do Chinese Americans differ from other Asian American groups, they differ dramatically among themselves. Despite Chinese Americans' remarkable achievements as a group, life in Chinese American settlements such as Chinatown's are faced with economic inequality including many living in poverty. Within most Chinatowns is found a wide array of social problems, including poor health, a high suicide rate, run-down housing, a rising crime rate, poor working conditions, and inadequate care for the elderly. An increase in Chinese immigration only exacerbates these problems.

Diversity is seen in other areas as well. Several dialects exist and different languages separate Chinese not only from each other but from the rest of U.S. society. *Occupational profiles* indicate a bipolar structure of a clustering of workers in both high-paying professional occupations and low-paying service jobs with relatively few in between. Changes in family life include the questioning of parental authority and the intrusion of values more American than Chinese among the youth. Religious differences now include Christianity in addition to Confucian, Buddhist, and Taoist beliefs. Chinatowns themselves represent a paradox between the bright lights, unique sights, exotic sounds, and tasty foods witnessed by the tourist and the reality of high-density populations located in older, poorer, deteriorating sections of cities such as San Francisco, Chicago, and New York.

Gender-role differences

While women in China have made significant progress toward emancipation, aspects of traditional gender-role differentiation still persist. Women's lower position in the gender hierarchy is reflected in the continued preference for sons, in women's double burden of full-time paid employment and major responsibilities for child care and housework, in the lack of representation of women in political affairs, in violence against women in the form of infanticide and wife battering, and in attitudes about the proper qualities of husbands and wives.[11]

A study examining the role of gender in family businesses in rural China revealed that men are about three times more likely than women to work in the household business and women are more than twice as likely as men to work exclusively in agriculture.[12] Part of this difference is explained by women having considerably less schooling than men (another gender difference) which puts them at a disadvantage in their ability to bargain well. The difference is explained as well

---

[11] John Bauer, Feng Wang, Nancy E. Riley, and Zhao Xiaohua, "Gender Inequality in Urban China," *Modern China* 18 (July 1992): 333–370; and Nan Lin and Yanjie Bian, "Getting Ahead in Urban China," *American Journal of Sociology* 97 (November 1991): 657–688.

[12] Barbara Entwisle, Gail E. Henderson, Susan E. Short, Jill Bouma, and Fengying Zhai, "Gender and Family Business in Rural China," *American Sociological Review* 60 (February 1995): 36–57.

by the patrilocal and exogamous character of marriage in rural China: rural women typically become "outsiders" when they marry.

Inequality between the sexes is very evident in issues related to patriliny, patriarchy, and patrilocal residence.[13] Most unions involve the transfer of the bride to her husband's household (estimated at 80 percent in rural areas), where she is often under the rule of her husband's father. The children women raise, the fields they tend, and the elderly they support don't belong to their birth families but rather to the families into which they marry. Daughters are expendable (as will be illustrated in the discussion later of an imbalanced sex ratio and "missing" daughters).

Other gender differences are still evident, as well. After years of communist rule, the traditional protective attitude toward females seems to have survived. Most of the important jobs in politics, education, agriculture, factories, and hospitals are held by men. In the political arena, only a small proportion of the persons elected to the Central Committee of the Chinese Communist Party are women. In household tasks, most responsibilities remain women's.

Rural/urban differences

Historically, as well as in contemporary Chinese families, major rural/urban differences exist. In Chinese cities, clan organizations were never as important as in villages. The family patterns found in contemporary cities also seem somewhat more varied than those found in the countryside. Patrilocal residence (in the man's father's house) after marriage is less the general rule in cities than it is in villages. Urban youth marry later than rural youth. Urban parents play a less central role in choosing mates for their children. Marriage finance is negotiated less between the two families in urban areas. In husband/wife relations, it appears that, while all women—urban and rural—do more domestic chores than men, this factor is more pronounced in rural areas. Urban divorce is said to be more equitable or even biased in favor of women.

The continuation of and changes in rural/urban differences are documented in terms of the average number of children born per Chinese family. As recently as 1955, the average number of children per family was 6.39 in rural areas compared to 5.67 in urban areas. Twenty years later, in 1975, these figures were 3.95 (rural) and 1.78 (urban). In 1987, the comparable figures were 2.45 (rural) and 1.38 (urban).[14] These figures reveal both the long-standing discrepancy in number of children between urban and rural families as well as the powerful impact of the one-child policy (discussed later).

Even in death, rural/urban differences are evident. In cities, cremation has become the norm, but in the countryside, burial remains common, although the

---

[13] Watson and Ebrey, *Marriage and Inequality in Chinese Society*, p. 350.

[14] Xiangming Chen, "The One-Child Population Policy, Modernization, and the Extended Chinese Family," *Journal of Marriage and the Family* 47 (February 1985): 193–202; and Griffith Feeney, Feng Wang, Mingkun Zhou, and Baoyu Xiao, "Recent Fertility Dynamics in China: Results from the 1987 One Percent Population Survey," *Population and Development Review* 15 (June 1989): 297–322.

place of burial is often viewed as a waste of land. And since the land no longer belongs to the family, it has become increasingly difficult to maintain kin loyalty, totally irrespective of any religious significance. Under communism, religious beliefs in general have been labeled as superstitious, and religious practices have been discouraged.

Partner selection

Major changes are taking place in Chinese patterns of partner selection, moving dramatically from the arranged pattern to one of greater freedom and personal choice. In the past, marriages were predominantly arranged by parents or another third party. The party who made the arrangements (usually, the bride's parents) would demand and receive substantial gifts from the family of the groom as a precondition for marriage. The nature of the betrothed's gifts (sometimes referred to as **brideprice**) included money or goods and were often used to prepare the bride's dowry. The **dowry** included any material possessions the bride brought with her into marriage, including clothes, jewelry, and land.[15] Under the traditional system, the couple to be married usually did not have the chance to see each other before marriage. Increasingly, however, young women are insisting on self-determination and love relationships.

Interview data, gathered from two surveys of Chinese women from three age groups, revealed that the percentages of arranged marriages by year of marriage declined from 83 percent in 1946 to 38 percent in 1953 to 2 percent in 1986. The free choice of marriage partners increased from none in 1946 to 14 percent in 1953, to 22 percent in 1986.[16] Yet, it is clear that parents continue to have a major influence on the decisions made for marriage. Riley notes that housing shortages, the continuing strong family ties, the proximity of younger and older generations, and the lack of dating culture all have contributed to the continuing decision-making cooperation between parents and children.[17]

Wolf interviewed three hundred Chinese women in both cities and rural communes about various aspects of their lives, including courtship and marriage. Even among women in cities, love was an ideal, but few could define it and few had had an opportunity to develop it or other intimate feelings before marriage. Wolf claimed that the sad thing about many contemporary marriages is that couples often seem as mismatched as they were in the old days, when marriages were arbitrarily arranged by parents. In Wolf's words:

> The young person who is taught that his or her spouse will be a friend and lifelong companion often finds "after the rice is cooked, that they have very

---

[15] For an extensive discussion of women and property, see Watson and Ebrey, *Marriage and Inequality in Chinese Society*, Chapter 10, pp. 313–346.

[16] Dai Kejing, "The Life Experience and Status of Chinese Rural Women from Observation of Three Age Groups," *International Sociology* 6 (March 1991): 5–23.

[17] Nancy E. Riley, "Interwoven Lives: Parents, Marriage, and Guanxi in China," *Journal of Marriage and the Family* 56 (November 1994): 791–803; and Xu Xiaohe and Martin King Whyte, "Love Matches and Arranged Marriages: A Chinese Replication," *Journal of Marriage and the Family* 52 (August 1990): 709–722.

little in common." Even though marriage is delayed until parties are in their mid or late twenties, both are usually sexually inexperienced, and, from all reports, many women wish they had stayed that way.[18]

Case Example: Dating and Marriage in China

Lixin (pronounced Lee Shin) is a 25-year-old student in postgraduate study at Shanghai Foreign Languages University in Shanghai, China. She served as a translator for the author and several others at a population and environment conference at East China Normal University in May 1995, and was interviewed at that time. Following are selected excerpts from that interview.

"I had my first love when I was in my third year at the University. He was very nice but his living style was very different from mine. So, after two months, I wrote him a letter explaining that we were different but that I would like to remain his friend. He came to see me and we talked. He is still my friend, and we send one another cards on birthdays.

"Now I have another boyfriend. I met him at the University. He is Japanese and is now in Japan but he is hoping to return to China. I think I would like to marry him someday. If he does ask to marry me, it would be my decision to accept, but I would ask for my parents' permission. They are both educators and understand that things are different today.

"When my boyfriend and I were together, we would send notes to one another, talk, discuss many things, or listen to music. I know that some of my friends have kissed their boyfriends but I'm conservative. Things like that are not very common but is happening more than in the past, especially in cities or at the universities.

"When I do marry, I would like just one child—a girl. Why? They are more considerate and closer to their mothers when getting old. Boys are more removed. Plus I want a child like me—female. If I were to go to Japan, maybe two children would be nice. But here in China, I could get a full salary for one full year to keep the child, but my husband would not get off work at all. And later my child would get priority in schooling and we would get extra money. If I were to get pregnant a second time, abortion would be encouraged but not enforced. But in the city I would have to pay a fine—a lot of money.

"Here in China, men do little housework like cooking, cleaning, or laundry. But I would want my husband to help with these things or stand by to assist. I would want his help with child care but that is primarily the responsibility of the mother. That's another reason I want a girl.

"Now I am still in school. I pay nothing for medical care, housing, or tuition and my books are free. My meals and clothes are excluded. Also, I get a small amount of money to cover incidentals. When I am working, I expect to help care for my parents as they grow old."

---

[18] Margaret Wolf, "Marriage, Family, and the State in Contemporary China," in Norval D. Glenn and Marion Tolbert Coleman (eds.), *Family Relations: A Reader* (Chicago: The Dorsey Press, 1988): 106.

Age at marriage seems to be increasing as well. In the study cited previously by Kejing, the average age at marriage of women under age thirty-eight was nearly twenty-four years; that of women ages thirty-nine to forty-five was twenty-two; and that of women over age forty-five was nineteen.[19] An increase in the average age at marriage is consistent with other data from China. Today, marriage and husband/wife relationships are greatly influenced by the very tight housing situation in many urban areas. Wolf cited one woman as saying that, if a couple wants to have an argument, they either take a walk or resign themselves to involving the whole family.

Still, the control of the family is far greater in rural areas than in urban areas. Rural couples are less influenced and controlled by the state but more controlled by their families and extended kin. In short, the new marriage decree, while granting couples increased freedom of choice and male/female equity in relationships, has for the most part had minimal impact on rural Chinese families.[20]

One-child family policy

A family policy, perhaps unparalleled in the world, was a **one-child family policy** introduced in China in 1979. This policy urged women to cease childbearing after the birth of the first child and followed earlier policies of the 1970s that stressed later marriage, longer intervals between births and fewer children. The result of these policies was a decrease in fertility and increase in one-child families of such magnitude across educational levels for a short period and for such a large population that some writers claimed it was probably unprecedented, apart from periods of famine, epidemic, war, and other disasters.[21]

As a result of an intensive Chinese family-planning program (called *birth planning* by the Chinese), the birthrate was reduced from 34 per 1,000 in 1970 to 20.9 in 1981 to 17.5 in 1984. In 1986, however, the birthrate rose to about the 1981 level.[22] While some of this increase was due to a shift in the age structure (more women in the peak childbearing ages of 21–30), much was due to an increase in fertility. Chinese leaders became concerned about rumors that the policy had changed to allow couples to have two children and about evidence that family-planning work had not been stringently implemented in many areas of China in the mid-1980s. By 1987 and 1988, Chinese leaders had issued commentaries that stated that party committees at all levels must never lower their

---

[19] Keijing "The Life Experience and Status of Chinese Rural Women…," p. 9.

[20] For an extensive analysis of marriage and domestic relations see: Emily Honig and Gail Hershatter, *Personal Choices: Chinese Women in the 1980s* (Stanford: Stanford University Press, 1988): Chapters 4–6; and Ming Tsui, "Changes in Chinese Urban Family Structure," *Journal of Marriage and the Family* 51 (August 1989): 737–747.

[21] Ronald Freedman, Xiao Zhenyu, Li Bohua, and William Lavely, "Local Area Variations in Reproductive Behavior in the People's Republic of China, 1973–1982." *Population Studies* 42 (1988): 57.

[22] Karen Hardee-Cleveland and Judith Banister, "Fertility Policy and Implementation in China, 1986–88," *Population and Development Review* 14 (June 1988): 247, Table 1.

The one-child policy of contemporary mainland China is one of the most dramatic national family policies ever instituted in the world. A couple who agree to have only one child receive financial rewards and can expect their child to be given preferential treatment in school and later in employment and housing.

guard and become negligent; the population must be strictly controlled. The population target of 1.2 billion by the end of the twentieth century was still in effect.[23]

The one-child policy included the innovation of a one-child pledge. Those individuals who promised to have no more children had the option of receiving *single-* or **one-child certificates**. For the first five years or so, the certificate acceptance rate was quite high; the rate declined sharply in later years because of women who wanted second children.[24] Those couples who did accept the certificates were entitled to increased income, lower-cost health care, better nursing, larger pensions, and eventually preferential treatment in schooling and employment for their only children. In some areas, a slightly larger monetary bonus was allowed if the couple's first child were a girl rather than a boy. In rural areas of many provinces, couples today can have two children if their first child is a girl, recognizing the preference for a son and providing a practical way of dealing with its implications. Couples who have more than two children face penalties.

The Chinese government not only tells couples that they must practice birth control; it also often tells them what type of contraceptive they must use. For example, one government announcement was that a woman with one child should use an IUD, that a couple with two children should have one partner sterilized, and that a woman with an unauthorized pregnancy should undergo an abortion. While the official position is that induced abortion should be performed only in

---

[23] Ibid., p. 249.

[24] Rosemary Santana Cooney, Jin Wei, and Mary G. Powers, "The One-Child Certificate in Hebei Province, China: Acceptance and Consequence, 1979-1988," *Population Research and Policy Review* 10 (1991): 137–155; and Rosemary Santana Cooney, and Jiali Li, "Household Registration Type and Compliance with the 'One-Child' Policy in China, 1979–1988," *Demography* 31 (February 1994): 21–32.

the event of a contraceptive failure, it appears that nearly 50 percent of induced abortions are performed among nonusers of contraception.[25] This practice of performing abortions, by the way, led the U.S. government to withhold all contributions from the United Nations Fund for Population Activities.

To overcome traditional Chinese desires for a son to provide support for parents in old age, the government has designed additional incentives for the one-daughter family. Today, property can be distributed to a daughter as well as a son; a daughter is legally responsible for the parents' welfare in the same way as a son; and a daughter as well as a son may take over the father's job when he retires. These practices may not, however, eliminate parental fear about security in old age, especially in rural areas, where the welfare of the aged is closely tied to the economic well-being of the commune.

The one-child policy has had both positive and negative effects. Some positive effects mentioned by Zhangling include a higher standard of living, increased social development that eliminates the patriarchal/feudal clan system and the inferior position of women, enhanced quality of life, and increased social assistance.[26] Some negative effects include social and psychological pressures associated with having only one son or daughter, an increased incidence of divorce, and an unbalanced sex ratio. The sex ratio at birth appears to have increased from 105 before 1970 to about 114 in the 1990s, well above the biologically normal level of 105 to 106 boys at birth per 100 girls. One study of three villages in 1993 suggests that during the period of strong enforcement between 1988 and 1993, the sex ratio in these villages for first births was 133, for second births 172, and for third and higher births was 1100.[27]

Numerous studies have examined these unusually high sex ratios among live births. These studies of the "**missing girls**" of China tend to focus on three explanations: female infanticide, an underreporting of births of girls, and gender-specific abortion.[28] *Female infanticide*, a traditional practice in China, may have accounted for the high sex ratios of cohorts prior to the 1950s but does not appear to be a significant factor today. The second explanation, the *underreporting of female births*, appears to be related to the incidence of adoption. Adoption (which often goes unreported) increased greatly during the 1980s, with female adoptions outnumbering males by three to one. This may account for half of the "missing girls" in China in the late 1980s.

The third explanation, *gender specific abortion*, seems to be the major reason for the escalation in the proportion of young females missing in China. Since the mid-1980s, China has manufactured a large number of high-quality ultrasound

[25] Virginia C. Li, Glenn C. Wong, Shu-Hua Qiu, Fu-ming Cao, Pu-quan Li, and Jing-Hua Sun, "Characteristics of Women Having Abortion in China," *Social Science and Medicine* 31 (1990): 445–453.

[26] Wei Zhangling, "The Family and Family Research in Contemporary China," pp. 498–499.

[27] Susan Greenhalgh and Jiali Li, "Engendering Reproductive Policy and Practice in Peasant China: For a Feminist Demography of Reproduction," *Signs: Journal of Women in Culture and Society* 20 (Spring 1995): 601–641.

[28] Sten Johansson and Ola Nygren, "The Missing Girls of China: A New Demographic Account," *Population and Development Review* 17 (March 1991): 35–51.

News Item: Sex for the Chinese—Quick and Clothed

Liu Dalin, a scholarly pioneer in the study of human sexuality in China, published an 844-page document titled "Sexual Behavior in Modern China: A Nationwide Survey on 20,000 Subjects." For Liu, one of the shocking aspects of the survey was the respondents' lack of knowledge about sexual matters. For example, one in three married women reported never having had an orgasm and not even knowing what the question meant until they were asked if they feel any pleasure from sex. Because of the absence of foreplay, many wives found sex bothersome and painful. When sex did occur, it was restricted to less than a minute.

The study also found that 25 percent of the men and 20 percent of the women had had intercourse before marriage—a revelation that evaporated the government-promoted legend of a China where premarital sex had been eliminated by the love for socialism. In contrast, thousands of survey participants confirmed the proverbial modesty of Chinese couples. According to Liu's statistics, only 13 percent of married couples had made love naked. In addition, 80 percent of the Chinese considered any form of masturbation wrong.

Source: Reported by Uli Schmetzer, *Chicago Tribune,* and published in the *Detroit Free Press,* 4 November 1992, p. 17A.

machines that are intended for the diagnosis of fetal defects, locating previously inserted IUDs, and for various health purposes. Identification of a embyro's sex is strictly forbidden by government authorities but when the technician (typically a local resident), observes the sex on the machine, the parents (usually friends) are likely to be notified.[29] An East–West Center report suggests that as of 1992, this sex-specific abortion resulted in a sex ratio of 119 males per 100 females.[30] This factor, however, is not unique to China as the same report suggests a sex ratio of 114 in South Korea, 112 in India, and 110 in Taiwan. Only when broken down by birth order do findings suggest any preference for girls. Families with two or more older brothers and no older sisters provided a sex ratio of 74 males per 100 females: a strong preference for girls.[31]

What are the consequences of the one-child policy to Chinese children, who grow up without siblings? In an examination of the academic and personality outcomes of only children, Dudley Poston and Toni Falbo found remarkable similarities to the outcomes of children with siblings.[32] The few differences were con-

[29] Ansley J. Coale and Judith Banister, "Five Decades of Missing Females in China," *Demography* 31 (August 1994): 459–479.

[30] Sidney B. Westley, "Evidence Mounts for Sex-Selective Abortion in Asia," *Asia-Pacific Population and Policy* 34 (May–June 1995): 1–4.

[31] Barbara A. Anderson and Brian D. Silver, "Ethnic Differences in Fertility and Sex Ratios at Birth in China: Evidence from Xinjiang," *Population Studies* 49 (1995): 211–226.

[32] Dudley L. Poston, Jr., and Toni Falbo, "Academic Performances and Personality Traits of Chinese Children: Onlies versus Others," *American Journal of Sociology* 96 (September 1990): 433–451.

centrated in academic areas, where only children, particularly those living in urban areas, had the advantage. Perhaps this advantage is explained by parents' additional opportunities to spend time with the only child, which may well facilitate intellectual development. Consistent with studies of children in the West, Chinese only children did *not* appear to differ from children with siblings in terms of personality dimensions representing childhood adjustment.

Divorce

Prior to the Marriage Law of 1980, divorce could be granted to a Chinese couple after mediation by the courts if *legitimate* reasons existed. What appeared to be the most legitimate were reasons of political differences. Following the law of 1980, the absence of love became a primary criterion in divorce cases.

Divorce cases are typically of two types: those where both husband and wife desire divorce and those where only one partner desires it. Procedures for divorce in the first category, referred to as *divorce by agreement*, are simple and without cost to the applicants. The couple simply goes to the local marriage registration office and completes an application. If no coercion is involved and the couple is able to reach agreement on custody of the children and the division of family property, a divorce certificate is issued. When only one partner wants a divorce, he or she will go to the marriage registration office and apply. Application is followed by mediation, attempting reconciliation. If that fails, the case goes to the People's Court, which decides for or against the divorce and, if there are children, who gets custody.

Have the marriage laws and changes in family size and gender roles led to an upsurge in divorce? In percentage terms, yes, but the numbers involved appear to be very small. For example, an increase from 341,000 divorces in 1980 to 800,000 in 1990 is an increase of 135 percent.[33] But in China, a country of 1.2 billion people, this is equal to 0.8 cases per 1,000 population. Viewed from a global perspective, this rate is very low, particularly when compared with rates of most countries in the industrialized West. Without a doubt, today most marriages in China are stable, most individuals expect to stay married for life, and both the local kinship structure and government policy favor such stability.

Overview of Chinese familism

It appears that the statements of Marx and Engels regarding family property, monogamy, marital love, sexuality, and the like have not reached fruition in mainland China. The communist government is making major efforts to renovate housing, maintain stability in monogamous marital relationships, and provide for the care and protection of children by responsible parents. For all intents and purposes, important roles are assigned to the family system, which is adapting but

---

[33] Sheryl Wu Dunn, "Divorce Rate Soars as Chinese Decide Love Is Part of Marriage, *The New York Times,* April 17, 1991, p. B1.

remains strong. Many aspects of Chinese family life demonstrate a melding of the traditional and the contemporary.

SWEDISH FAMILY SYSTEM

Unlike China, which is about equal in size to the United States, Sweden is only slightly larger than the state of California. China has more than 1.2 billion inhabitants and more than one in five persons in the world, whereas Sweden has a population of about 8.5 million, or less than that of the state of Michigan. The Swedish have a life expectancy about ten years longer than that of the Chinese. In China, people adhere to Confucianism, Buddhism, Atheism, and folk religions; 95 percent of Swedes are Lutheran, the official religion of the country.

Sweden has a constitutional monarchy type of government. The educational system is strong. The literacy rate among Swedes is 99 percent; they complete twelve years of compulsory schooling. The infant mortality rate in Sweden is about 6 per 1,000 live births—one of the lowest in the world.

As one of the world's most affluent nations, Sweden is one of the best places to examine new models of families and relationships. No other society in the world has more effectively addressed the meshing of childrearing and motherhood. Few societies in the world parallel Sweden in its efforts toward achieving gender equality, in its frequency of unmarried cohabitors, in its low marriage rate, in its extensive movement of women into the paid labor force, or in its focus on parents and children.

Marriage and marriage rates

David Popenoe, who presented a statistical portrait of the changing family in Sweden, noted that, until recent decades, Sweden had not shown any remarkable differences in marriage rates from comparable European nations.[34] Beginning in the mid-1960s, the picture in Sweden changed with startling rapidity. The marriage rate decreased in a seven- or eight-year period by about 40 percent, a decrease that Jan Trost, one of the leading family scholars in Sweden, believed to be unprecedented.[35] The rate continued to drop even further, so that, by 1980, the Swedish rate of 78 marriages per 1,000 women in the 25- to 29-year age group compared to rates of 99 in Denmark, 109 in Japan, 117 in France, 127 in the United States, and 168 in England and Wales. These low figures for Sweden reflect a rising average age at marriage as well as an increase in the number of Swedes who do not marry at all.

---

[34] David Popenoe, "Beyond the Nuclear Family: A Statistical Portrait of the Changing Family in Sweden," *Journal of Marriage and the Family* 49 (February 1987): 173–183. Selected portions of this section are derived from this source.

[35] Jan Trost, "Marriage and Nonmarital Cohabitation," in John Rogers and Hans Norman (eds.), *The Nordic Family: Perspectives on Family Research* (Uppsala: Uppsala University, 1985).

Today, Sweden has the lowest marriage rate in the industrialized world and, at the same time, one of the highest mean ages of first marriage. Figures from the mid-1980s showed the median age at first marriage to be about 27 for women and nearly 30 for men.[36] These figures are somewhat unrepresentative because marriage in Sweden is being replaced by nonmarital cohabitation.

Nonmarital cohabitation

Nonmarital cohabitation (discussed more fully in Chapter 10) is the life-style of couples who form *consensual unions*, or who live together but are not legally or officially married. In Sweden, these people are classified as living in "marriage-like relationships." It is estimated that, today, about one in four, or 25 percent, of Swedish couples live in this type of arrangement, and it is generally recognized that virtually all Swedes now cohabit before marriage.

For several decades, literature in the family area has recognized that Sweden is more permissive about nonmarital sex than most of the Western world. As a result, in years past, many Swedish couples who did eventually marry included a pregnant bride. Today, a major change is that nonmarital cohabitation and pregnancy are not necessarily a prelude to marriage but are a legally and culturally accepted alternative to it. Children are less and less viewed as an incentive to get married.

Given these norms, is the rate of illegitimacy high in Sweden? Is this a significant social problem? The answer is no to both questions. First, despite high rates of cohabitation, fertility control has given Swedish women a low unplanned pregnancy rate and a higher age of first childbearing. And second, even if the pregnancy rate were not low, the characterization and stigma would not occur. The term *illegitimacy* was dropped in Sweden in 1917 and the concept of children born out of wedlock was dropped from all Swedish legislation in the early 1970s.[37] Today in Sweden, to be born to an *unmarried* parent does not necessarily mean being born to a *single* parent. Rather, to be born out of wedlock in Sweden usually means being born to nonmarital cohabitors but two parents nonetheless. (This is in contrast to the typical meaning in the United States of being born to a single parent, discussed more extensively in Chapter 13.) Jan Trost, in his previously mentioned article, maintained that, in Sweden, marriage and nonmarital cohabitation are equally acceptable life-styles.

Couple/marital/family dissolution

Given the incidence of nonmarital cohabitation in Sweden, the divorce rate is not a very adequate indicator of marital dissolution. A better measure is one that shows the breakup rate of couples who are either married or living in a consensual union.

---

[36] Britta Hoem and Jan M. Hoem, "The Swedish Family: Aspects of Contemporary Developments," *Journal of Family Issues* 9 (September 1988): 397–424.

[37] Popenoe, op. cit., "Beyond the Nuclear Family," p. 176.

As one might suspect, if it is difficult to know how many consensual unions form, it is even more difficult to know how many break up. What does seem clear is that, in Sweden and around the world, nonmarital cohabitation does not have the stability of marital cohabitation. Thus, to add a nonmarital cohabitation dissolution rate to the divorce rate in Sweden (about one-half that of the United States) may give Sweden the highest breakup rate in the industrialized world. The subject of couple/marital dissolution in Sweden, however, has not received much attention.

Single parents

Of the many children in Sweden who live with unmarried parents, not all live with both parents. A number of children live with single parents.

In Sweden, about 15 percent of families are headed by a single mother and 3 percent by a single father.[38] Although Swedish single-parent families have more difficulties than two-parent families, the former are not characterized by the high levels of poverty and relative deprivation that characterize single-parent families in the United States (see Chapter 8).

Why is this so? For one, in Sweden, most women participate in the labor force, regardless of whether they are married or have children of any age. Also, Sweden guarantees single-parent families a minimum amount of child support (maintenance), regardless of whether the absent parent pays at a low level, fails to pay, or pays irregularly.[39] The results of this policy are twofold: (1) Earnings still provide the core of the family income and (2) the family's standard of living is protected. Even though providing maintenance is a burden on the public purse, single parents have an incentive to work, since the maintenance benefit is not enough for a family to live on.

Gender roles

The roles of males and females and their interrelationship is one of the most widely discussed and studied aspects of intimate relationships in Sweden. Considerable evidence supports the claim that this country is one of, if not the most egalitarian, in the world.

Sweden has the highest percentage of women in the labor force in the Western world and the lowest percentage of full-time homemakers. On comparable-worth issues, women who supervise day care, for example, are paid on roughly the same wage scale as men in industrial employment. In Sweden, while men's use of family leave remains modest, men take employment leave to care for their newborn children to a greater extent than perhaps anywhere in the world.

---

[38] Karin Sandqvist, "Swedish Family Policy and the Attempt to Change Paternal Roles," in Charles Lewis and Margaret O'Brien, *Reassessing Fatherhood* (Newbury Park, CA: Sage Publications, 1987), p. 147.

[39] Soren Kindlund, "Sweden," in Alfred J. Kahn and Shela B. Kamerman (eds.), *Child Support: From Debt Collection to Social Policy* (Newbury Park: CA: Sage Publications, 1988), pp. 74–92.

Swedish social policy toward couples and families is very unique when viewed from a global perspective. Policies favoring sex education, supporting male and female parental leave from paid employment, and condemning corporal punishment are a few of the progressive legal and program aspects. Gender differences still exist, but egalitarianism is the goal.

Linda Haas, in a number of writings, revealed how Swedish couples engage in parenting and domestic role sharing to a greater extent than American couples.[40] Yet Haas found that the *practice* of gender-role equality in the home still lags considerably behind the official ideology. This may change as younger couples appear to be markedly more egalitarian than older ones. Two important obstacles to an egalitarian division of labor appear to be having children and attitudes toward the man's role as breadwinner. In most countries of the world, even if the woman is gainfully employed, she is still primarily responsible for home and child care.

These ideas have been supported by studies that show how experiences on the job spill over into family life. A national study of working parents in Sweden revealed that, despite the efforts of the labor movement and the Social Democratic Party to reduce class- and gender-based inequalities, mothers and fathers had different employment conditions and experiences.[41] Men were more likely than women to be engaged in physical labor and to supervise subordinates, while women were more likely than men to have jobs where they perform monotonous tasks. A majority of mothers of young children worked less than full time, where-

---

[40] Linda Haas, *Equal Parenthood and Social Policy: A Study of Parental Leave in Sweden* (Albany, NY: State University of New York Press, 1992); and Linda Haas and Philip Hwang, "Company Culture and Men's Usage of Family Leave Benefits in Sweden," *Family Relations* 44 (January 1995): 28–36.

[41] Phyllis Moen, *Working Parents: Transformations in Gender Roles and Public Policies in Sweden* (Madison, WI: The University of Wisconsin Press, 1989). Note also: Toni M. Calasanti and Carol A. Bailey, "Gender Inequality and the Division of Household Labor in the United States and Sweden: A Socialist-Feminist Approach," *Social Problems* 38 (February 1991): 34–53.

Global Diversity: **Spanking Illegal in Sweden**

Sweden has outlawed the old adage "Spare the rod and spoil the child." It is illegal for Swedish parents to spank their children or treat them in a humiliating way.

A 1979 law, passed in the Swedish Parliament by an overwhelming majority of 259 to 6, says that "the parent or guardian should exercise the necessary supervision in accordance with the child's age and other circumstances. The child should not be subjected to corporal punishment or other injurious or humiliating treatment."

A member of the justice ministry in Stockholm said that this law is an attempt to change people's attitudes toward the physical punishment of their children and to show them that society does not approve of this sort of behavior. It is based on the belief that the reaction of children when hit by parents is one of revenge, not one of respect, and that physical punishment of children stimulates fear instead of love.

as the great majority of fathers continued to put in a standard work week. Public policies leading to reduced working hours and mandating **parental leave** of absence have gone a long way to balance work with family roles for women; however, these policies seem to have produced little change in the work involvement of fathers. Regardless of the measure used, Swedish mothers consistently reported lower levels of well-being than did fathers.

Even at the professional level, evidence of gender inequality is available. A national sample of nearly 1,400 members affiliated with the Swedish Confederation of Professional Associations (SACO), the major professional union in the country, revealed some surprising statistics.[42] For example, women earn 77 percent of what their male counterparts earn. And female professionals, regardless of industrial sector or age, hold only 68 percent of the supervisory positions that men have. The major factor explaining these gaps is occupational segregation: men and women continue to follow gender-typed patterns of employment. Men's patterns of employment tend to provide resources and structural positions that reward them with higher earnings and access to positions of authority. Of women who are in professional positions, a distinct marriage and family pattern emerges. Female professionals are less likely to be married than their male counterparts and have fewer children at home than men do. These findings support the stereotypical picture of women who give up marriage and children to be successful in the professional world.

In spite of such examples of gender inequality, another writer noted that Sweden's complex of social policies and programs must be admired for having eliminated poverty and for having produced a basic level of economic security for all

---

[42] Charles W. Mueller, Sarosh Kuruvilla, and Roderick D. Iverson, "Swedish Professionals and Gender Inequalities," *Social Forces* 73 (December 1994): 555–573.

citizens. But clearly, these programs and policies have not succeeded in fully eliminating social and economic disadvantages for women. Gender-role divisions remain rather entrenched, despite women's high participation in the workforce and specific policies that encourage men to participate more actively in child-care tasks.[43]

Overview of Swedish familism

According to Popenoe, the case for Sweden's world-leading move away from the traditional nuclear family is based on five main factors:

1. A low rate of marriage
2. A high rate of cohabitation
3. A high rate of family dissolution
4. A small household size
5. The extensive move of mothers into the labor force[44]

In spite of these changes, Popenoe suggested the Swedish family is strong and established. Most men and women want to live as couples and have not turned against the idea of permanent, monogamous dyads. Most women still want to have and do have children. Children are born into a society that has an enviable record in its public child-care policies. Fathers and mothers, in greater numbers than anywhere in the Western world, may take parental leave from employment for up to nine months at nearly full salary and another three months at partial salary (note parental leave box in Chapter 18, p. 579).

The degree of Swedish familism is shown as well by the extent to which social life continues to revolve strongly around gatherings of relatives. It seems that the Swedish women's movement has never had much of the antifamily sentiment found in the U.S. movement. In short, while the form or structure of the family has changed and will likely continue to do so, families are alive and well in Sweden.

SUMMARY

1. This chapter on family life-styles in mainland China and Sweden examined three drastically different systems: the traditional Chinese family, which existed for several thousand years; the contemporary Chinese family, which has emerged since 1950; and the contemporary Swedish family.

2. The traditional Chinese family was characterized by sharp class and gender distinctions. The gentry, who were well educated and owned the land,

---

[43] Marguerite G. Rosenthal, "Sweden: Promise and Paradox," in Gertrude Schaffner Goldberg and Eleanor Kremen, *The Feminization of Poverty: Only in America?* (Westport, CT: Praeger, 1990), pp. 129–155. Note also: Karen Sandqvist, "Sweden's Sex-Role Scheme and Commitment to Gender Equality," in Susan Lewis, Dafna N. Izraeli, and Helen Hootsmans *Dual-Earner Families* (Newbury Park, CA: Sage Publications, 1992).

[44] Popenoe, op. cit., p. 181.

stood in contrast to the poor peasants who cultivated it. Similarly, the male, who was highly valued and privileged from birth on, stood in contrast to the female, whose purpose was to serve, honor, and bear male children for the men.

3. The traditional Chinese family changed dramatically with the passage of the Marriage Laws of 1950 and 1980, which sought to abolish the supremacy of men over women, the arrangement of marriages, female infanticide, foot-binding, and the like. In turn, these laws created a family system that gave men and women equality in jobs and in the home, allowed women to own and hold property, raised the minimum legal age of marriage, relaxed restrictions on divorce, and demanded family planning.

4. The contemporary Chinese family system, while incorporating many aspects of the traditional system, clearly stands apart. The contemporary family is characterized by monogamous marriage, more freedom of choice of marriage partners, small family size, and greater participation of women in all aspects of life. Full gender equality, however, has not been achieved. Similarly, major rural/urban differences remain. Traditional values are still more widely held in rural areas.

5. Mate selection is another area of significant change, as major strides have been made in moving from an arranged pattern to one of greater freedom of choice. Chinese couples are marrying later in life; the tight housing situation in urban areas also affects marital relationships.

6. The one-child family policy in China—enforced by birth-control measures, sterilization, and abortion—has both positive and negative consequences. One positive aspect is a higher standard of living; negative aspects include more divorce and an unbalanced sex ratio resulting from the preference for boys.

7. The Swedish family system stands in sharp contrast not only to the Chinese family but to most family systems in the Western world. Over the past three decades, the marriage rate in Sweden has dropped sharply, as the number of consensual unions (unmarried cohabitations) has increased sharply. When the divorce rate is combined with the rate of nonmarital dissolutions, Sweden may have the highest rate of couple breakup in the industrialized world.

8. Even though cohabitation rates are high, Sweden does not have a problem with children born out of wedlock. First, rates of such births are low, due to fertility control and delayed childbearing. And second, children who are born to unmarried parents are accepted and cared for. Government maintenance for single-parent families ensures a certain standard of living.

9. While gender roles in Sweden are often considered the most egalitarian in the world, the practice of gender-role equality in the home and in employment lags considerably behind the official ideology.

10. The contemporary Swedish family is characterized by a low marriage rate, a high cohabitation rate, a high family dissolution rate, small household size, and the extensive move of mothers into the labor force. The family system remains strong as it deals with continual change.

11. Chapter 6 will return to discussion of selected racial and ethnic families in the United States. Each of these family systems stands in sharp contrast to those of the Chinese and Swedish.

KEY TERMS AND TOPICS

Traditional Chinese family p. 145

Clan, or tsu p. 145

Gentry p. 145

Peasants p. 145

Ancestor worship p. 145

Filial piety p. 146

Yin and yang p. 146

Footbinding p. 147

Marriage Laws of 1950 and 1980 p. 148

Contemporary Chinese family p. 149

Gender-role differences p. 150

Rural/urban differences p. 151

Partner selection p. 152

Brideprice p.152

Dowry p. 152

One-child family policy p. 154

One-child certificates p. 155

"Missing girls" p. 156

Divorce p. 158

Overview of Chinese familism p. 158

Swedish family system p. 159

Marriage and marriage rates p. 159

Nonmarital cohabitation p. 160

Couple/marital/family dissolution p. 160

Single parents p. 161

Gender roles p. 161

Parental leave p. 163

Swedish familism p. 164

DISCUSSION QUESTIONS

1. What value exists in studying family life-styles other than one's own?

2. How is it possible that the traditional Chinese family system withstood extensive change for several thousand years? Is it possible for any family system to resist change in the twentieth century? Why or why not?

3. Why were women so oppressed in the traditional Chinese family? What justifications were given for practices such as female infanticide, footbinding, arranged marriage, and prohibition of widows remarrying?

4. What degree of success did the Marriage Laws of 1950 and 1980 have, based on what is known about the contemporary Chinese family? Give examples of positive changes as well as continued setbacks.

5. Discuss some of the implications of China's one-child policy in terms of population control, family interaction, preference for a male child, and effects on the only child.

6. Should populations be "controlled" by sterilizing people who are mentally retarded, allowing deformed infants to die, or terminating pregnancies of women who exceed an allotted number of births? Who should make such decisions? Should national concerns supersede individual ones?

7. What similarities exist between the contemporary Chinese family and the contemporary Swedish family? Address gender roles, childrearing, divorce, and religion in making this comparison.

8. With the sharp drop in marriage rates, the increase in nonmarital cohabitation, and high couple-dissolution rates, is the family disappearing in Sweden? Why or why not?

9. Contrast the consequences of single parenthood in the United States versus Sweden. What welfare policies exist in each country and with what results?

10. Is it possible to achieve egalitarian gender roles in the home if they do not exist in the workplace? Sweden possibly leads the world in gender-role equality yet has failed to achieve full male/female equality. Why?

FURTHER READINGS

Davis, Deborah, and Harrell, Steven (eds.), *Chinese Families in the Post-Mao Era.* Berkeley: University of California Press, 1993. Eleven sociologists and anthropologists explore the effects of policy shifts on families in China following Mao Zedong's death.

Haas, Linda. *Equal Parenthood and Social Policy: A Study of Parental Leave in Sweden.* Albany: State University of New York Press, 1992. An analysis of the parental-leave policy in Sweden, with a unique focus on fathers.

Ho, David Y. F. "Continuity and Variation in Chinese Patterns of Socialization," *Journal of Marriage and the Family* 51 (February 1989): 149–163. A discussion of two central issues regarding Chinese patterns of socialization: continuity versus change through time and variation across geographic locations.

Iwao, Sumiko. *The Japanese Woman: Traditional Image and Changing Reality.* New York: The Free Press, 1993. A contemporary look at Japanese women that depicts the nature of their lives and roles in marriage, as mothers, and in professions.

Moen, Phyllis. *Working Parents: Transformations in Gender Roles and Public Policies in Sweden.* Madison: University of Wisconsin Press, 1989. A time-series study of several thousand working parents of preschoolers in Sweden, with a focus on the interconnections between work and family.

Popenoe, David. "Beyond the Nuclear Family: A Statistical Portrait of the Changing Family in Sweden," *Journal of Marriage and the Family* 49 (February 1987): 173-183. A portrayal of the changing structure of the Swedish family, with evidence of a move away from the ideal/typical nuclear form.

Tsai, Wen-Hui. "Mainland Chinese Marriage and Family Under the Impact of the Four Modernizations," *Issues and Studies: A Journal of China Studies and International Affairs* 24 (March 1988): 100–119. A readable overview of changes in Chinese marriages and families, from the traditional family to the family under Mao to the current form.

Watson, Rubie S., and Ebrey, Patricia Buckley. *Marriage and Inequality in Chinese Society.* Berkeley: University of California Press, 1991. An explanation of the social and historical bases of marriage and inequality in China.

Chapter 6

Life-Styles Among African American Families

- Significant Social Transitions of African Americans
    - From Africa to the United States
    - From slavery to emancipation
    - From rural/southern areas to urban/northern areas
    - From negative to positive social status
    - From negative to positive self-image

- Patterns of African American Family Life
    - Matricentric female-headed family pattern
    - Middle-class two-parent family pattern
    - Patriarchal affluent family pattern

- Summary

- Key Terms and Topics

- Discussion Questions

- Further Readings

This chapter will examine the life-styles and family patterns of the largest racial and minority population in the United States: African Americans. To be labeled as a member of a particular minority group has major implications for the extent of access to power and resources. In addition, to be labeled as a member of a specific racial or ethnic group may further add to variations in opportunities and social interactions.

African, or black, Americans[1] constitute a racial, ethnic, and minority group in the United States. A *racial* group is a socially defined group distinguished by selected, inherited physical characteristics. An *ethnic* group is distinguished by a sense of peoplehood or "consciousness of kind" based on a common national origin, religion, or language.[2] If one's racial or ethnic group is subordinate to the majority in terms of power and prestige (not necessarily in terms of number of members), he or she occupies a *minority* status, as well.

The key characteristics of any racial or ethnic group centers around self and social definitions. In Hawaii and Jamaica, for example, the social meaning of *black* is very different than in Kansas and Georgia. To have a particular skin color, speech pattern, or manner of dress may lead others to perceive and label someone, correctly or incorrectly, as a member of a specific racial or ethnic group.

The four racial, ethnic, or minority families in the United States that are examined in this and the next chapter are basically more similar than dissimilar to the dominant family forms that exist in the larger U.S. society. For black Americans, Hispanic Americans, Asian Americans, or Native Americans, social status is positively related to marital stability; children receive their basic identity and status subscription within the family context; and parents ascribe to the basic achievement and mobility values that exist within the larger society. Of course, there are also clear variations in family structures, behaviors, and values, many of which are due to unique geographical and historical experiences. Immigration policies, slavery, job circumstances, legal and social segregation, and personal and institutional discrimination have resulted in differences in life-styles and value patterns between groups and within each group. In the sections that follow in this chapter and the next, some of these factors will be examined.

SIGNIFICANT SOCIAL TRANSITIONS OF AFRICAN AMERICANS

The African American population is the largest racial/ethnic minority group in the United States. Because of unique historical and social experiences, many African Americans have life-styles and value patterns that differ considerably from those of

---

[1] In this chapter, the terms *African American, black American,* and *black* will be used interchangeably.

[2] J. Ross Eshleman, Barbara C. Cashion, and Laurence Basirico, *Sociology: An Introduction* 4th ed. (New York.: HarperCollins, 1993): 224.

the European-American majority. The relations between whites and blacks in the United States has been the source of a number of major social issues in the past several decades: busing, segregation, job discrimination, and interracial marriage, to mention a few.

Perhaps these issues can be understood more fully by examining five social transitions that have affected or continue to affect African Americans. These include transitions from:

1. Africa to the United States
2. Slavery to emancipation
3. Rural and southern areas to urban and northern areas
4. Negative to positive social status
5. Negative to positive self-image

From Africa to the United States

Three factors in the transition from Africa to the United States have profound relevance for blacks. First is *color*, the factor that is the most influential characteristic of African American people in U.S. society. Color identifies blacks as such. Black Americans who can "pass" as white due to fair coloring are confronted with a different set of interactions than those with dark coloring who cannot "pass." In fact, it appears that color is not merely a question of black or white. Skin tone (complexion) itself has been found to have significant effects on educational attainment, occupation, and income among African Americans.[3] Darker-skinned blacks are at a continuing disadvantage and experience more discrimination than fair-skinned blacks in the contemporary United States.

The second factor in the transition from Africa to the United States is *cultural discontinuity*. The system of behavior that was socially learned and shared by members of African society was not applicable to the social conditions they faced in the United States. It is perhaps difficult, if not impossible, to find any other group who came or were brought to the United States and faced such a disruption of cultural patterns. Yet many African cultural patterns were maintained. Thus arose the concept *African American*.

The third factor is *slavery*. Again, unlike almost all other groups in the United States, the Africans did not choose to come. With few exceptions, Africans came only as slaves. The impact that slavery had on family patterns and norms at the time it occurred as well as the significance slavery has for understanding African American families today has become an issue of controversy.

For example, some writers have emphasized the instability of marriage and family ties, the disruption of husband/wife and kin networks, the extent of

---

[3] Verna M. Keith and Cedric Herring, "Skin Tone and Stratification in the Black Community," *American Journal of Sociology* 97 (November 1991): 760–778.

Global Diversity: Women's Work Among the Masai Tribe in Tanzania

In the Masai tribe, men live as supervisors and women perform most of the work, including the heavy work. Men leave all the everyday activities for the women to do. It is not unusual to see a woman, even if she is pregnant, looking after cattle, sheep, and goats or taking donkeys to fetch cornmeal from very distant shops.

It was traditional for Masai women to allow men to be free as warriors, defending territory and raiding cattle. The warrior days are now over, but rather than assist with the domestic chores, men typically spend their days drinking alcohol or playing bao, a popular board game. When men have money, they often spend it on homemade liquor. But when women have money, they spend it on cornmeal for their children and on helping the family.

Masai custom says that if a wife does not perform her chores, the husband must beat her. One man said that if the roof leaks, a husband must beat his wife or the other men will laugh.

Such a disproportionate division of labor is by no means confined to Masai culture. The World Bank estimated that about 70 percent of the food crops in Africa are cultivated by women. Efforts by international organizations to improve the lot of the African woman have met with meager success, largely because many of the continent's national economies are weak, putting women in even more vulnerable positions.

Source: New York Times, 2 December 1991.

matrilocality, and the lack of authority of fathers. Others suggest that the slave family was considerably stronger than has been believed. It was not patterned by instability, chaos, and disorder but rather by two-parent households. While a somewhat higher proportion of African American families were headed by females than was true for other racial and ethnic groups, slavery was not the sole explanation. Economic conditions, in general, had a significant impact on the black family structure. Black males had high mortality rates, and females with children faced extreme difficulties in marrying or remarrying.

Although there has been disagreement about the nature of the slave family, most scholars would agree that the history of slavery in the United States continues to have a major impact on the African American family today. In the United States, slavery assumed inferiority. The slave had no legal rights, marriages were not licensed, many female slaves were sexually used or abused, and miscegenation (which violated the social norms of the times) was frequent.[4]

---

[4] Miscegenation refers to marriage and interbreeding between members of different races, especially in the United States between whites and blacks.

From slavery to emancipation

In 1863, the Emancipation Proclamation, issued by Abraham Lincoln, freed the slaves in all territories still at war with the Union. No longer could individuals be sold away from their families. Marriages among blacks were to be legalized and recorded. At least in theory, the slave was free from servitude, bondage, and restraint. For thousands of African Americans, however, emancipation brought with it freedom to die of starvation and illness. In many ways, this transition presented a crisis for many black families.

At least three patterns of family life emerged from this crisis.

1. The majority of African Americans remained on plantations as tenants of their former owners, receiving little or no wages for their labor.

2. Families that had been allowed to establish common residence worked common plots of ground for extra food for the family. Families where the man was an artisan, preacher, or house servant made the transition with the least difficulty.

3. In situations where only loose and informal ties held a man and woman together, those ties were severed during the crisis of emancipation, even despite the presence of children. In search of work, many men banded together and wandered around the countryside. Females were established as the major productive and dependable family element. This pattern was perhaps the most disruptive of family life.

Ruggles, in tracing the origins of the contemporary pattern of single parenthood in the African American family, suggests several historical explanations. First, it could have been a response to the socioeconomic conditions of extreme poverty and inadequate employment opportunities faced by newly freed blacks after the Civil War and by free blacks in 1850. Second, the pattern could reflect a difference in social norms between blacks and whites developed either through the experience of slavery or could have its roots in differences between European and African culture.[5]

From rural/southern areas to urban/northern areas

In 1994, there were 33.0 million African Americans (referred to in the U.S. Census material as *black*) in the United States, comprising 12.7 percent of the 259.7 million total population. Geographically, blacks were overrepresented in the South (where they comprised 20.0 percent of the total population) and underrepresented in the other three regions (10.9 percent in the Northeast; 10.9 percent in the Midwest; and 4.4 percent in the West).

The movement of African Americans from rural areas and from the South has, in general, followed that of the rest of the population; however, very few African

---

[5] Steven Ruggles, "The Origins of African-American Family Structure," *American Sociological Review* 59 (February 1994): 136–151.

Americans have migrated to western states, with the exception of California. In 1930, about four-fifths of all African Americans lived in the South, compared to slightly more than half (54.9 percent) in 1994. Likewise, a change has occurred in the transition to metropolitan areas. In 1960, 64.8 percent of all black families lived in metropolitan areas. By 1970, this figure had increased dramatically to 79.1 percent, and by 1994, it had increased to 86.3 percent. Fifty-six percent of all African American families currently live in central cities, 30 percent live in the rings around central cities, and 14 percent live in rural (nonmetropolitan) areas.[6]

The significance of these migration patterns largely evolves around their selectivity: Not all ages of African Americans were caught up in the movement to urban areas or to the North, nor were complete families. The industrial pool preferred young men, which had a tremendous impact both on the community left behind and on the community into which African Americans migrated. Family life was affected by disrupting the nuclear family and by geographically separating extended family ties. The educational/occupational structures of both communities were affected, which had an effect on other factors, such as housing, ghetto life, and patterns of discriminatory behavior. African American males, in particular, brought with them to the city or the North aspirations for economic improvement; for many, these dreams were not fulfilled. Unlike a person from the middle class, who will relocate due to a job offer, the lower-class male is more likely to migrate because of current unemployment or an irregular work schedule.

On the other hand, the consequences of the shift from rural/southern to urban/northern areas have not all been negative. Many stabilizing factors and positive aspects have resulted. Although the city is often portrayed as a center of evil in U.S. society, in a very real sense, it has been the center of hope for some African Americans: better schools, better social welfare services, better medical and public health facilities, and more tolerance for racial minorities.

In some ways, these geographical transitions have produced a generation gap among African Americans. On the one hand, there is a sizable number of transplanted parents who were reared in rural Mississippi or Alabama in a highly segregated society and moved north; they would likely be considered blue-collar class or are living below the poverty level. On the other hand, there is an increasing number of children of these parents living in large urban centers; they have integrated into the school systems, have aspirations and hopes for a college education, and have occupational and earnings achievements considerably higher than those possible in southern states. Their life-style is equivalent to persons born in the North.

From negative to positive social status

Some would argue that the single most important variable to understanding the African American family today is social class. Many family forms are more likely

---

[6] U.S. Bureau of the Census, *Current Population Reports*, Series P20-480, Claudett E. Bennett, "The Black Population in the United States: March 1994 and 1993" (Washington, DC: U.S. Government Printing Office, 1995), Table 3, p. 35.

to be the consequence of class rather than either race or ethnicity. Major differences seem to exist within the African American family if a distinction is made between those living below the poverty level and those living in the middle class of the subculture. It is the African American middle class that is seldom publicized. This is a stratum of two-parent units in which most marriages are stable and where husbands have a high school education or better and occupy positions in business, government, or education. These families are basically more similar than dissimilar to the dominant white family form that exists in U.S. society.

The shift from a negative to a positive social status has prompted a shift in the approach to and the interpretation of African American families. The *traditional model* of the African American family projected a negative stereotype, one of the family as a monolithic lower-class entity, as a social problem in itself, as a pathology of out-of-wedlock births and broken homes, as centering around the female as a dominating matriarch, and as including males with low self-esteem. The *emerging model* challenges these negative views, stressing that the African American family comprises a variety of types at different social-class levels; rejecting the social problem and pathology orientation as an expression of middle-class ethnocentrism; viewing the family as having strengths such as egalitarianism, self-reliant males, strong family ties, and high achievement orientations; and finally, being worthy of study as a form of social organization in its own right.

The old model of the African American family was vividly portrayed twenty-five years ago by Daniel Patrick Moynihan in his now classic **Moynihan Report**.[7] It was his contention that there had been a serious weakening in the African American social structure and that there was a trend away from family stability in lower socioeconomic levels. Moynihan concluded in his report that the structure of family life in the African American community constitutes a "tangle of pathology" and that at the heart of the deterioration of the fabric of African American society is the deterioration of the family. The major block to equality centers around the matrilocal family. The implication is that young African American children grow and are reared in mother-centered families without the helpful influence of both parents. This, in turn, Moynihan argued, was a major reason that African Americans were making only limited gains during the prosperous 1960s.

Billingsley and others disagreed directly and strongly with Moynihan's central tenet.[8] They contended that the African American family is not a cause of the "tangle of pathology" but rather that it is an absorbing, adaptive, and amazingly resilient mechanism for the socialization of its children and the civilization of its society.

Have specific shifts occurred for African Americans, from a negative to a positive social status, as portrayed primarily by census data in regard to employment, income, and education? Note particularly (1) the tremendous gains made in recent years in the United States for both black males and females and (2) the major disparities that still exist between blacks and whites.

---

[7] Daniel P. Moynihan, *The Negro Family: The Case for National Action* (Washington, DC: U.S.Government Printing Office, U.S. Department of Labor, 1965).

[8] Andrew Billingsley, *Black Families in White America* (Englewood Cliffs, NJ: Prentice-Hall, 1968): 33.

Table 6-1
*Unemployment rates by race, sex and age: 1994
(annual averages in percent)*

	White	Black	Hispanic
Adult males	5.4	12.0	9.4
Adult females	5.2	11.0	10.7
Teenage males*	16.3	37.6	26.3

Source: U.S. Bureau of the Census, *Statistical Abstract of the United States, 1995,* 115th ed. (Washington, DC: U.S. Government Printing Office, 1995), no. 640, p. 407.

*Teenagers include persons sixteen to nineteen years old

Employment

An increasing number of African Americans have entered positions of leadership in the professions, in business, and in government. These gains have been over-shadowed, however, by the number and rate of African Americans who are not employed. For many years, the unemployment rate among blacks was double the rate of the population as a whole. That is, if the national unemployment rate were 5 percent, one could assume a 10 percent rate for blacks. In 1994, the annual average unemployment rate was 5.4 for white males and 12.0 for black males (see Table 6-1). The unemployment rate for black females, like that of black males, was more than twice that of white males or females. For the population as a whole, evidence has not supported the widespread belief that a double-negative status (being both black and female) provides an occupational advantage. And most black females who are employed are overrepresented in service, clerical, and blue-collar jobs that generally are low status and pay low wages.

The unemployment rate for black teenagers is most dramatic: 39.9 percent in 1994. Employment opportunities for uneducated, unskilled, young blacks are not sufficient to meet the employment and income needs of these youth during times of economic prosperity; this group also suffers disproportionately during times of economic recession.

These high levels of unemployment—more than one in ten of all black males and more than one-third of all black teenage males—are dire predictors for stable marriage and family life.

Income

There is no doubt that the African American population has made substantial social status gains over the past thirty years in terms of occupation, education, and income. Yet irrespective of absolute gains, blacks remain significantly deprived when compared to whites at the same income level. The economic gap that separates whites and blacks in the United States is growing, despite all efforts of recent years.

Table 6-2

Median incomes of white, black, Hispanic, and Asian families,
1970–1993 (in current dollars)

Year	White	Black	Ratio: black to white*	Hispanic	Asian
1993	$39,300	$21,542	55	$23,654	$44,456
1990	36,915	21,423	58	23,431	42,246
1985	29,152	16,786	58	19,027	(NA)
1980	21,904	12,674	58	14,716	(NA)
1975	14,268	8,779	62	9,551	(NA)
1970	10,236	6,279	61	(NA)	(NA)

Source: U.S. Bureau of the Census, *Statistical Abstract of the United States, 1995,* 115th ed.
(Washington, DC: U.S. Government Printing Office, 1995), no. 732, p. 474.

* *Ratio* means black income as a percentage of white income.

NA = Not available.

According to census data (see Table 6-2), the dollar gap between blacks and whites actually grew in the last quarter century. In 1970, the median white family income was $10,236 and the median black family income was $6,279, a dollar gap of $3,957. By 1980, after widely heralded social reforms, white income doubled to $21,904 and black income doubled to $12,674, with the constantly increasing dollar difference reaching $9,230. As of 1993, the median income for white families was $39,300 and for black families, $21,542, a dollar difference of over $17,700.

The ratio of black-to-white income was 55 in 1993. (That is, the median income of blacks was 55 percent that of whites.) However, ratios mean very little when dollar amounts are insufficient to maintain families. In 1993, the poverty threshold for a family of four was $14,763 (see Table 8-1), only about $7,000 less than the median family income for blacks. Thus, one-third (33.3 percent) of the total black population lived below the poverty level.

What implications do figures such as these have for family life among African Americans? Broman has shown that blacks are significantly less likely than whites to feel their marriages are harmonious and black women are less likely to be satisfied with their marriages than white women.[9] One key explanation for these patterns centered on financial factors: increased marital well-being was associated with satisfaction with the family's financial well-being. In general, an established sociological finding positively relates socioeconomic status to marital stability. Thus, based strictly on economic factors, we could expect a high rate of marital disruption among black families (shown in Chapter 17) to have support.

[9] Clifford L. Broman, "Race Differences in Marital Well-Being," *Journal of Marriage and the Family* 55 (August 1993): 724–732.

Table 6-3

Persons twenty-five years and over completing four years of high school or more by sex and race: 1970–1994 (in percent)

Year	White		Black		Hispanic	
	Male	Female	Male	Female	Male	Female
1994	82.1	81.9	71.7	73.8	53.4	53.2
1990	79.1	79.0	65.8	66.5	50.3	51.3
1980	69.6	68.6	50.8	51.5	47.3	45.8
1970	54.0	55.0	30.1	32.5	37.9	34.2

Source: U.S. Bureau of the Census, *Statistical Abstract of the United States, 1995,* 115th ed. (Washington, DC: U.S. Government Printing Office, 1995), no. 239, p. 157.

Education

Transition from a negative to a more positive social status can also be seen by examining the percentages of African Americans ages twenty-five years and over who have obtained at least a high school education. In 1994, 71.7 percent of black males and 73.8 percent of black females had completed four years of high school or more. These figures are considerably more than double the comparable 1970 percentages of 30.1 and 32.5 for black males and females, respectively, and show greater percentage increases than those for whites (see Table 6-3). These changes are quite dramatic for the time span involved and may be equally dramatic in understanding mate selection and marriage for African American men and women.

If an equal or greater number of black females than males is completing high school, it may be increasingly difficult for black women to find mates with education or income levels equal to or better than their own. This trend may also result in increased strain and conflict for marriages in a society that stresses a male provider role. Addressing these issues directly, Paul Secord and Kenneth Ghee suggested that strain in black marriages would be somewhat relieved if black men had better employment prospects, more occupational mobility, and higher educational attainment relative to black women.[10] The educated black woman who still expects her husband to be the primary provider is likely to be dissatisfied with his performance. The educated black woman, who is more likely than the less educated woman to expect her husband to be sensitive, emotionally nurturant, and companionable may have difficulty finding the black man who can fulfill her expectations. Factors such as these help explain the high incidence of divorce and separation among black couples.

---

[10] Paul F. Secord and Kenneth Ghee, "Implications of the Black Marriage Market for Marital Conflict," *Journal of Family Issues* 7 (March 1986): 21–30.

The educational attainment of African American women has had a dramatic effect on partner-selection and marriage patterns. As black women become more educated, they are less likely to find partners with education and income levels equal to or better than their own.

Study of blacks in the United States suggest that the difficulties many black men have in providing adequately for their families often lead to difficulties in spousal relationships and satisfaction with their own lives. Marital difficulties may be attributed to the disparities in education, with women marrying less educated men, and the low sex-ratio issue, where black women have a more restricted field of eligible partners than do white women.[11]

Generally, as economic conditions improve, the incidence of family disorganization decreases, family life becomes increasingly stable, aspirations for children become higher, and conformity to the sexual mores of society increases. However, when black American families are compared to white American families, the prognosis for blacks is not good. Among blacks, higher rates of unemployment and underemployment, low family income, lack of education such as college, and male/female disparities in education and eligible marital partners will likely lead to continued change: fewer marriages, more single parents, higher rates of divorce, and the like.

From negative to positive self-image

A basic tenet of social psychology states that people develop themselves, their identities, and their perceptions of self-worth in interaction with others. As black chil-

---

[11] Richard E. Ball and Lynn Robbins, "Marital Status and Life Satisfaction Among Black Americans," *Journal of Marriage and the Family* 48 (May 1986): 389–394; and Scott J. South and Kim M. Lloyd, "Marriage Opportunities and Family Formation: Further Implications of Imbalanced Sex Ratios," *Journal of Marriage and the Family* 54 (May 1992): 440–451.

dren grow up in a society that encourages feelings of inferiority and degrades self-worth, it might be expected that a self-fulfilling prophecy will be operative: Growing black children will believe and act out the societal messages bestowed upon them.

The prevailing view of African Americans over the years has been that they suffer from negative self-esteem manifested in feelings of self-hate and a lack of self-actualizing behavior. But numerous studies have called into question this view. Although it cannot be denied that racism and discrimination abound and take their toll on African Americans, empirical evidence has not supported the view of negative self-evaluation. Studies comparing blacks and whites on measures of self-esteem concluded that the level of self-esteem among blacks does not differ significantly from that of whites or may actually be higher than that of whites.[12]

A Detroit study considered whether levels of self-evaluation vary among blacks, based on demographic characteristics and satisfaction with internal and external factors in their lives.[13] It was found that older blacks tended to appraise themselves more positively than did younger blacks. High self-evaluation was strongly associated with family life satisfaction, particularly for women. This finding further strengthened the notion that the family plays an important role in shaping blacks' attitudes about themselves. For African Americans, the family has been one of the primary sources of support and a major reference group for boosting self-pride.

How is it possible that African Americans have positive concepts of themselves in spite of oppressive social and economic conditions? Foster and Perry provided several explanations.[14] One is that, over the past few decades, black organizations and social interactions have served to bolster self-pride, identification with blackness, and appreciation of black culture and life. Also, historical black writing and poetry "damn as a falsehood" the concept of inferiority. Third, the family, church, fraternal groups, friendships, and general social relationships provide positive support systems that influence blacks' self-evaluations. Numerous other writings have supported a number of these views on the importance of friends and the affective bonds among extended family members to the well-being of black Americans.[15]

Thus, it seems that the African American community, church, and family teach their children to act, feel, and think positively and to be proud. This factor may explain the finding, surprising to many, that suicide rates in the United States

---

[12] See Michael Hughes and David H. Demo, "Self-Perceptions of Black Americans: Self-Esteem and Personal Efficacy," *American Journal of Sociology* 95 (July 1989): 132–159; and Castellano B. Turner and Barbara F. Turner, "Gender, Race, Social Class, and Self Evaluations Among College Students," *The Sociological Quarterly* 23 (Autumn 1982): 491–507.

[13] Madison Foster and Lorraine R. Perry, "Self-Evaluation Among Blacks," *Social Work* 27 (January 1982): 60–66.

[14] Ibid., 65.

[15] See Christopher G. Ellison, "Family Ties, Friendships, and Subjective Well-Being among Black Americans," *Journal of Marriage and the Family* 52 (May 1990): 298–310; and Jon B. Ellis and Lillian M. Range, "Differences Between Blacks and Whites, Women and Men, in Reasons for Living," *Journal of Black Studies* 21 (March 1991): 341–347.

News Item: **What Does It Feel Like to Be White?**

I wonder what it feels like to be white. I have no idea, but I am, on occasion, curious.

I've never, on the other hand, found myself wondering what it feels like to be male, although I have wanted in times of stress to have bulging biceps so I could knock an adversary flat on his back.

But white is something else again. I wonder if the collective white experience, if indeed there is such a thing, can be probed, explored, and subjected to the same kinds of generalizations that routinely are applied to the collective black experience?

I doubt it. Still, I can't resist the temptation to ask, in a general way, some questions that come from my experience.

I wonder if little white girls played with little black dolls whose hair had to be oiled and straightened into submission? Of course, that's an unfair question. Little black girls didn't play with those dolls either. We played with pink or brown cloth-bodied babies whose hair could be brushed and teased into big fat curls.

Kinky hair, mahogany skin, thick lips, and a wide nose were not things you paid money for. No. You paid money to straighten your hair, to lighten your skin, to buy a lip liner to make your lips look smaller. I started thinking about all of this after I was given a new face by an extremely nice makeup artist who brushed dark powder down the sides of my nose to narrow it and then outlined my lips in brown to give them less substance and more form.

Somehow I never thought my lips would become a metaphor for life.

The usual questions

In any event, I wonder what it would feel like to walk into the Free Press one day and be a member of the majority population?

I wonder what it would feel like to walk into a General Motors management meeting or to go into a restaurant in Traverse City and see your skin tone repeated over and over again throughout the room?

I wonder what it feels like to walk into an office or store filled with white shoppers and not feel out of step, if only for a second?

I wonder what it feels like never to have been told: "I never think of you as black."

I wonder what it feels like to go through an entire week at work without being asked:

My opinion on a black political or social situation.

The name of a black expert on a particular subject.

If a story is racially significant.

I wonder what it feels like to go on vacation, get a deep tan, walk up to a black person and put your tanned arm next to that black arm and say: "See how dark I am? We're almost the same color."

I wonder what it feels like to have someone ask what nationality your parents are?

Are there answers?

I wonder what it feels like to be able to go to almost any movie at any time and see people who look like you up on the screen—to see loving, laughing, fighting, heroic, or cowardly people, each one reflecting an aspect of humanity. I've often thought that the controversy over "The Color Purple" really stemmed from the fact that blacks are woefully underrepresented in movies. Thus, every "black" movie becomes a statement about black life and is given greater significance than it deserves.

I wonder what it feels like to set up a lunch date with a stranger at a fancy restaurant in some upscale suburb and have to give a detailed description about what you'll be wearing and the color of your hair?

Perhaps there are no answers to these questions. Perhaps the inherent generalizations make them meaningless.

Still, I do wonder…about the questions and about the responses I'll get from those folks, black and white, who think they know the answers.

Source: Susan Watson, *Detroit Free Press,* 18 June 1986, p. 3A. Used with permission.

Table 6-4

Suicide rates by race and sex: 1970, 1980, 1990, and 1992 (deaths per 100,000 population)

| | Black | | White | |
	Male	Female	Male	Female
1992	12.0	2.0	21.2	5.1
1990	12.0	2.3	22.0	5.3
1980	10.3	2.2	19.9	5.9
1970	8.0	2.6	18.0	7.1

Source: U.S. Bureau of the Census, *Statistical Abstract of the United States, 1995,* 115th ed. (Washington, DC: U.S. Government Printing Office, 1995), no. 136, p. 100.

(certainly an extreme index of depression and low self-esteem) are consistently lower for blacks than for whites. For example, in 1992, the suicide rate per 100,000 population was 12.0 for black males and 21.2 for white males; the rate was 2.0 for black females and 5.1 for white females (see Table 6-4). For many years, suicide rates have been higher for males than for females. When controlled for race, the rates are much higher for white males than for black males and for white females than for black females. Clearly, not all blacks have high self-concepts and self-esteem, but evidence has suggested a highly positive self-image among black Americans.

PATTERNS OF AFRICAN AMERICAN FAMILY LIFE

At least three distinct patterns of African American family life have emerged from the social transitions described:

1. The matricentric female-headed pattern
2. The middle-class, two-parent pattern
3. The patriarchal affluent pattern

Although these patterns refer primarily to the nuclear family unit, they do not exclude other relatives. Not uncommon among African American nuclear families is the presence of nephews, aunts, grandparents, cousins, and other adult relatives. These extended kin, plus unrelated kin living in as roomers, boarders, or guests, exert a major influence on the life-styles of African American families.

Two points must be made at this juncture in the discussion: (1) There is a wide range of family structures beyond the matriarchal, egalitarian, and patriarchal family patterns, and (2) the African American family institution is extremely resilient. Neither the mother-centered nor any other type of family is necessarily "falling apart"; the black family is capable of major adaptations to the historical and contemporary social conditions confronting it.[16]

Matricentric female-headed family pattern

Today, the most predominant family pattern among African Americans is the single-parent family with the vast majority of these being female- or mother-headed families. Nearly 54 percent of all families are male or female households with no spouse present. In 1994, of the 7.99 million African American families in the United States, 3.7 million (46.5 percent), were female households with no husband present and another 450,000 (5.6 percent) were male households with no wife present (see Table 6-5). The female household has an average number of 1.28 children compared to 0.83 children for male households.

The matricentric female-headed family pattern, the least stable of the three patterns, is one in which the female is the dominant member. The female may be a mother or grandmother who resides with children, usually without the continuous presence of a husband or father. Early motherhood, lack of education, and insufficient income lead to the characterization of this family pattern as "multiproblemed." Families living below the level of poverty are most likely to fit this pattern.

There were 10.9 million African Americans and 26.2 million white Americans living below the poverty level in 1993.[17] Low-income blacks comprised 33 percent of the black population, nearly three times the comparable proportion of low-income whites (12 percent). Families headed by females without husbands comprise a sizable proportion of low-income families. In 1993, 65.9 percent of all black female households with no husband present were below the poverty level. Among white female households, 45.6 percent were below the poverty level.[18] Clearly, irrespective of race, female-headed households and poverty are highly interrelated. It is debatable whether the family structure of the female householder with no husband present explains the family's poverty or whether the poverty explains the family's structure. This issue is discussed more extensively in Chapter 8 under the headings of "Feminization of poverty" and "Single parents and poverty." Most likely, each contributes to the other, and governmental policies contribute to both.

---

[16] For two reviews of black family studies, see Robert Joseph Taylor, Linda M. Chatters, M. Belinda Tucker, and Edith Lewis, "Developments in Research on Black Families: A Decade Review." *Journal of Marriage and the Family* 52 (November 1990): 993–1014; and Vasilikie Demos, "Black Family Studies in the *Journal of Marriage and the Family* and the Issue of Distortion: A Trend Analysis," *Journal of Marriage and the Family* 52 (August 1990): 603–612.

[17] Families are classified as being above or below the poverty level by using a poverty index based on a sliding scale of money income that is adjusted for such factors as family size, composition, and farm-nonfarm residence. The poverty threshold for a family of four was $14,763 in 1993 (see Chapter 8 and Table 8–1).

[18] U.S. Bureau of the Census, *Current Population Reports,* Series P60-480, "The Black Population in the United States: March 1994 and 1993" (Washington DC: U.S. Government Printing Office, 1995), Table O, p. 26.

Table 6-5

Selected characteristics of white, black, Hispanic-origin and Asian family households, 1994

Characteristic	White	Black	Hispanic-origin	Asian
Total number of family households in the U.S. (in thousands)	57,870	7,989	5,940	1,737
Married couple families (in thousands)	47,443	3,714	4,033	1,426
Percentage of total	82.0%	46.5%	67.9%	82.1%
Female householder, no husband present (in thousands)	8,130	3,714	1,498	232
Percentage of total	14.0%	47.9%	25.2%	13.4%
Male householder, no wife present (in thousands)	2,297	450	410	79
Percentage of total	4.0%	5.6%	6.9%	4.5%
Average number of children under age 18 per married-couple family, total	0.87	0.97	1.45	(NA)
Female householder	0.99	1.28	1.40	(NA)
Male householder	0.65	0.83	0.74	(NA)

Source: U.S. Bureau of the Census, *Current Population Reports,* Series P20-483, "Household and Family Characteristics: March 1994" (Washington, DC: U.S. Government Printing Office, 1995, Tables E and 1, pp. xiii and 2–5.

NA = Not available

Robert Staples indicated that the proliferative growth of female-headed households has probably been the most significant change in the black family in the last thirty years.[19] One of the most visible reasons for the dramatic increase in households headed by women has been a corresponding increase in out-of-wedlock births. While the rates of nonmarital sexual activity of black and white women are converging, the black female initiates intercourse at an earlier age, is more likely to

---

[19] Robert Staples, "Changes in Black Family Structure: The Conflict Between Family Ideology and Structure Conditions," *Journal of Marriage and the Family* 47 (November 1985): 1005–1013. Note also: Ann M. Nichols-Casebolt, "Black Families Headed by Single Mothers: Growing Numbers and Increasing Poverty," *Social Problems* 33 (July/August 1988): 306–313.

One of the most significant changes over the past several decades among African American families is the growth of single-parent, primarily female-headed households. Yet the family, regardless of structure, remains the key agent of childhood socialization and source of meaningful relationships.

have unprotected intercourse, and is less likely to marry or have an abortion if she becomes pregnant.

A less visible reason than out-of-wedlock births for the increase in female-headed households is related to the shortage of men relative to the number of women during the marriageable years (a low sex ratio). A greater prevalence of men (higher sex ratio) was found to be associated with higher marriage prevalence for black women, higher prevalence of husband-wife families, higher percentages of children living in husband-wife families, and higher percentages of marital births.

In addition to the negative effect of a shortage of men on marriage and two-parent families was the positive effect of men's economic status on marriage prevalence and marital births for black women. For women, however, higher economic status was associated with lower marriage prevalence and fewer marital births.[20] In brief, fewer marriages and more out-of-wedlock births seem to be related to (a) a shortage of black men, (b) a lower socioeconomic status of black men who are available, and (c) a higher educational and economic status for black women.

---

20 Mark A. Fossett and K. Jill Kiecolt, "Mate Availability and Family Structure Among African Americans in U.S. Metropolitan Areas," *Journal of Marriage and the Family* 55 (May 1993): 288–302; and Richard A. Bulcroft and Kris A. Bulcroft, "Racial Differences in Attitudinal and Motivational Factors in the Decision to Marry," *Journal of Marriage and the Family* 55 (May 1993): 338–355.

U.S. Diversity: Adoption Patterns in the United States

Slightly more than 2 percent of ever-married women ages fifteen to forty-four adopt a child. Those most likely to adopt are older women, sterile women, and women who have never had their own children. Both the proportion of U.S. women who adopt children and the proportion of U.S. women who place their babies for adoption appear to have remained relatively stable since the mid-1970s. This apparently ended the sharp down-trend in adoptions prior to 1975, which reflected the wider availability of abortion as a means of resolving unwanted pregnancies.

Who places their child for adoption? In this report, 88 percent of the mothers had never been married. White women were much more likely to place their babies for adoption (12 percent) than black women (less than 1 percent). Unmarried women who placed their babies for adoption were less likely to be receiving some form of public assistance, less likely to be poor, and more likely to have completed high school than unmarried women who kept their babies.

What are the material consequences for adopted children? They have overwhelmingly greater economic advantages than do children who remain with their never-married mothers. Only 2 percent of adopted children were living below the poverty level compared with 62 percent of children who remained with their never-married mothers.

Source: Family Planning Perspectives, January/February 1987.

Black women desire marriage but appear to be resistant to marrying men with fewer educational and economic resources than they have.

How much of a shortage of men exists and how is it accounted for? According to the U.S. Bureau of the Census, in 1993, there were 1.89 million more black women than black men. Since there is an excess number of black males at birth, the shortage of adult males is attributed both to their higher infant mortality rate and a considerably greater mortality rate of young black males through homicide, accident, suicide, drug overdose, and war casualty. In addition, black males who are divorced or separated due to military service, unemployment, or institutional confinement (such as prison or mental hospitals) and those with serious alcohol or drug problems are also removed from the "marriage market." Factors such as these magnify the serious disadvantages of black women in choosing from the eligible and desirable males in the marriage pool or in staying married.

A generally unrecognized reason for the increase in female-headed households was referred to by Andrew Billingsley as the impact of technology.[21] He cited three levels of technological development since World War II that have had relevance to African American families, in general, and to female-headed families, in particular.

---

[21] Andrew Billingsley, "The Impact of Technology on Afro-American Families," *Family Relations* 37 (October 1988): 420–425.

The first level is *domestic technology* associated with the home. The most dramatic impact comes from television, which robs parents of their capacity to think critically and inundates children with a glorification of violence, irresponsible sexual behavior, and unbridled materialism.

The second level is *construction technology* associated with community development. The automobile, the superhighway, and the construction industry combined to produce suburbia. Suburbia provided an escape from the problems of the city, drained resources from the city, and became synonymous with middle-class white flight. Social forces such as these were responsible for the expansion of black underclass neighborhoods, poverty, and fear in the central cities of the nation.

The third level is *industrial technology* associated with the production of goods and services in the wider society. The launching of spacecraft, the decline in manufacturing jobs and the explosion of service jobs, the accompanying high unemployment rates for blacks (again, note Table 6-1), and the acceleration of the civil rights movement were four major events driven by changes in industrial technology. All of the factors—unemployment, the exploitation of African American women in low-paying jobs, poor housing, homelessness, and policies that fail to retrain workers or provide job skills for the school dropout—had major impacts on the African American family and particularly on increasing the number of one-parent, mother-only families.

In U.S. society, it has been assumed that adults cannot maintain family stability unless they are married and living with their spouses. It has also been assumed that children cannot be adequately socialized unless they are reared in two-parent families. Willie alerts us to overcome ethnocentrism and to be conscious of an approach (such as phenomenology) that recognizes that the behavior and family structures of individuals and groups tend to be functions of the situations and circumstances in which they find themselves.[22] And if black populations are subdominant in the power structure, this situation may require or result in adaptive forms that differ from that found among whites or the dominant group in power. Thus comes an assertion that all behavior or any structural arrangement (such as single parent) is lawful and appropriate when viewed as coping strategies in response to existing situations or statuses. This does not detract from research that shows positive outcomes stemming from a two-parent family structure but broadens our view that stability in and positive outcomes from African American families can result from marital/family patterns other than one that includes two parents.

Middle-class two-parent family pattern

Family stability, life satisfaction, and personal happiness do not depend on a two-parent family pattern, but marriage itself appears to contribute to the life satisfaction of black adults. Generally, married black persons tend to be happier and more satis-

---

22 Charles V. Willie, "Social Theory and Social Policy Derived From the Black Family Experience," *Journal of Black Studies* 23 (June 1993): 451–459.

Case Example:
Father of Three, Husband to None

"I'm Larry, a 23-year-old African American male, high school graduate, and full-time employee as a security and electrical technician. I have never been married but have three children, ages 7, 4, and 3, by three mothers. I was responsible for two other pregnancies, both of which ended before birth. Prior to the first pregnancy, I guess I had sex with about 20 different women.

"My oldest boy was conceived when I was 15. The mother was 18. I only slept with her one time in my life and she got pregnant. I wanted her to have an abortion but she refused. I accepted paternity, pay child support each month, and see my son regularly.

"Several years later, I had a daughter by my first love and the only woman I was ever committed to. We were in high school together and I was very happy about her pregnancy. Since she was only 16, we both agreed not to get married but continued to see each other for another year or so. During this time, I continued to have sex with other women, and my third child, a son, was conceived before my daughter was born.

"I gave money to the mother of my third child to have an abortion, but she wouldn't do it. I'm not close to her at all and while I provide support to my two oldest children, I don't help financially with this child. Anyway, she makes more than I do.

"No, none of the five pregnancies by me were planned. And although I have had sex with probably 130 to 150 women, the last two years I have always carried a condom and have used one every time I had sex. I don't want any more children, and the disease thing is real scary. About one-third of the women I've had sex with have come on to me. I respect women, and if they want sex, so do I. I'll do whatever they want. But I will never sleep with a woman who doesn't want to. I've never picked up a prostitute but have agreed to give some money to several women to move the relationship along a bit faster. I'd have to spend it on them anyway.

"My goal is to get a college education and degree. I'll probably get married within the next three years to the mother of my second child. None of the mothers of my children have ever been married, but this one is real nice. I do a lot with my daughter, with the other child she has, and with my oldest son and want them all to do well in school."

fied with life than unmarried black persons. National survey data from several studies found this relationship to hold regardless of gender, age, education, or structure of the respondents' family of orientation (reared by both parents, one, or neither).[23]

As indicated previously, 47.5 percent of African American households are two-parent, married-couple families. In contrast to single-parent families, married-couple families are more likely to be middle-class or higher-income working-class families. Males are likely to have more stable employment and assume an active role in decision-making and childrearing responsibilities.

---

[23] Ann Creighton Zollar and J. Sherwood Williams, "The Contribution of Marriage to the Life Satisfaction of Black Adults," *Journal of Marriage and the Family* 49 (February 1987): 87–92; and Clifford L. Broman, "Satisfaction Among Blacks: The Significance of Marriage and Parenthood," *Journal of Marriage and the Family* 50 (February 1988): 45–51.

For example, one study of black families in a predominantly lower-class urban area focused on intact (husband/wife) families and found little, if any, evidence that husbands/fathers renounced their positions in the family or of reversed husband/wife roles, where the female assumed traditional male responsibilities. The results overwhelmingly indicated that, in these intact families, the husbands were the main providers for their families, were positive role models for their children, participated actively in childrearing, and were active participants with their spouses in the decision-making process.[24]

The two-parent intact African American family has been relatively neglected by most social scientists. Perhaps this family pattern has been ignored because these families are relatively stable, conforming, achieving, and cause few problems to anyone. The presence of two parents increases the likelihood of having two adult wage earners, which improves levels of income and other economic resources. As indicated previously, a direct link appears to exist between economic resources and family structure, including among African American families.

It appears that families in which both husband and wife are present are those from which African American leaders emerge. A three-generation analysis of the social origins of contemporary black leaders in the United States revealed that most of these individuals were reared in stable families; 67.8 percent lived with both parents (15.3 percent lived with their mothers, 4.1 percent with their fathers, 5.6 percent with relatives, and 4.9 percent with other people).[25] Interestingly, these eminent blacks were also predominantly the descendants of families characterized by antebellum (before the Civil War) freedom, lighter skin, urban residence, and higher educational and occupational attainment. It is in the two-parent family pattern that the father plays a more dominant role and that the children develop a greater identification with him. The role of the father as playmate, teacher, and disciplinarian to his children is less likely to be fulfilled in the matricentric form of family organization, even when the father is present.

Once again, the point made at the beginning of this chapter can be reiterated: Families are not isolated groups, existing independently from the society in which they function. The success or failure of a two-parent pattern or a matricentric pattern relates very closely to the opportunity structure that is provided to the family.

Patriarchal affluent family pattern

The patriarchal affluent family pattern can perhaps more accurately be illustrated by using Willie's concept of "affluent conformists."[26] This type of two-parent family is

---

24 Bernice McNair Barnett, Ira E. Robinson, Wilfred C. Bailey, and John M. Smith, Jr., "The Status of Husband/Father as Perceived by the Wife/Mother in the Intact Lower Class Urban Black Family," *Sociological Spectrum* 4 (1984): 421–441; and Ira E. Robinson, Wilfred C. Bailey, and John M. Smith, Jr., "Self-Perception of the Husband/Father in the Intact Lower Class Black Family," *Phylon* 46 (1985): 136–147.

25 Elizabeth I. Mullins and Paul Sites, "The Origins of Contemporary Eminent Black Americans: A Three-Generation Analysis of Social Origin," *American Sociological Review* 49 (October 1984): 672–685.

26 Charles V. Willie, *A New Look at Black Families*, 2nd ed. (Bayside, New York: General Hall, 1981): 58.

heavily represented among professional and high-income African Americans. Both spouses are likely to have college or graduate degrees, and the husband/father is likely to take primary responsibility for most major decisions. Among these families, the problems so often associated with blue-collar or poverty-level families are almost nonexistent.

Endogenous marriages are highly encouraged. Much of a given generation's wealth has been inherited from the previous generation. These wealthier African Americans in large part tend to isolate themselves from the majority of black families. For instance, many college graduates from this background do not engage actively in black organizations.

A study of black married couples from an urban North Carolina area demonstrated that the husband-led power pattern was associated, in general, with the highest level of marital quality.[27] Egalitarian and wife-led couples both reported lower levels of marital quality. In this research report on black couples, the husband-dominant family was suggested as the goal to be obtained rather than egalitarianism. Namely, husband/wife equality in power could be construed to be the effect of the financial and social discrimination that prevents black husbands from clearly surpassing their wives in income and education and thus assuming undisputed leadership of their families.

For the purposes of this discussion, perhaps the most noteworthy features of the patriarchal affluent pattern of family life are its stability and strict patterns of socialization and social control. And when economic factors are held constant, black American families, particularly at higher socioeconomic levels, differ little from white American families. One difficulty with this economically based perspective, however, is that it ignores the influence of social/cultural forces and transitions in the lives of American blacks, such as those described earlier in this chapter. And African American families in the United States cannot be understood without acknowledging the importance of historical factors as related to race and culture.

SUMMARY

1. The African American family in U.S. society, like any family system, is not a uniform entity, nor is it isolated and separate from other social systems within the community and society. The basic structural patterns, the interpersonal processes, and the personal value positions can only be understood within the context in which they exist.

2. African American families have been and still are affected by numerous major social transitions. The transition from Africa to the United States is relevant to understanding factors such as the influences of skin color, slavery, and cultural discontinuity.

---

[27] Bernadette Gray-Little, "Marital Quality and Power Processes Among Black Couples," *Journal of Marriage and the Family* 44 (August 1982): 633–646.

3. The transition from slavery to emancipation had a major influence on the emergence of multiple family forms, occupational patterns, kin relationships, and the forms of families.

4. The transition from rural and southern to urban and northern areas, while presenting the opportunities for better wages, schools, and health services, also tended to disrupt kin ties and community linkages.

5. The transition from negative to positive social status refers to changes in employment, income, and education. The controversial Moynihan Report placed the blame for changes in the black community on the deterioration of the family. Other writers strongly disagreed and argued that the family is a key force in stability and socialization. What is clear is the direct linkage between socioeconomic status and family life.

6. The transition to a positive self-concept and self-evaluation appears to be one area where African Americans excel. Numerous studies have suggested a higher level of self-esteem and self-evaluation exists among black Americans than among white Americans. The family and other primary and secondary groups provide positive support systems that influence blacks' self-evaluations.

7. From these major social transitions, distinct patterns of African American family life have emerged. The matricentric female-household is the family type where multiple problems are most frequently found. Those families with a female householder and no husband present most likely have low incomes, have greater numbers of children than white families or other black families, and appear to face the greatest difficulties in meeting the daily demands of existence.

8. The middle-class, two-parent family, the most prevalent type among African Americans, is one in which both husband and wife live together and have distinctive and complementary roles. These families, often ignored in the social science literature, are relatively stable, conforming, and achieving.

9. The patriarchal affluent family pattern, although less common than the other forms, is heavily represented among African Americans in high socioeconomic levels. In this family, the father is present, makes most major decisions, and is dominant in most respects. Noteworthy features of this pattern are its stability and strict patterns of socialization and social control.

10. The next chapter will continue our examination of American ethnic families, focusing specifically on Hispanic Americans, Asian Americans, and Native Americans.

KEY TERMS AND TOPICS

Significant social transitions of African Americans p. 170

From Africa to the United States p. 170

From slavery to emancipation p. 172

From rural/southern areas to urban/northern areas p. 173

From negative to positive social status p. 174

Moynihan Report p. 175

From negative to positive self-image p. 179

Matricentric female-headed family pattern p. 183

Middle-class, two-parent family pattern p. 187

Patriarchal affluent family pattern p. 189

DISCUSSION QUESTIONS

1. Is there a unique African American family in the United States today? Explain.

2. What contemporary family characteristics can be traced directly to African heritage? How does understanding slavery in the United States contribute to understanding current patterns of African American family life?

3. Compare African American with white families on dimensions such as family size, educational level, rural/urban residence, and marriage rate. How can differences be explained? What differences exist if one controls for social class?

4. Using state census data, contrast the demographic characteristics by race of a county or state with national data. Explain similarities or differences that may exist.

5. Examine the Moynihan Report. What data are presented that are subject to interpretations other than those given? Why did this report cause such alarm and controversy?

6. What significance for families is attached to mobility, for example, among states (such as from South to North), between rural and urban areas, or between countries (such as from Mexico or Cuba to the United States)?

7. What factors explain the high level of self-evaluation among African Americans? What place does the family hold in this explanation?

8. What dangers lie in characterizing African American families as homogeneous groups? Describe variations in life-styles and marital patterns within the African American community.

FURTHER READINGS

Davis, Richard A. *The Black Family in a Changing Black Community.* New York: Garland Publications, 1993. A discussion of how the black family evolved into a multi-ethnic socioeconomically diverse institution.

Dickerson, Bette J. (ed.). *African American Single Mothers: Understanding Their Lives and Families.* Thousand Oaks, CA: Sage Publications, 1995. The writers examine the history, legal dilemmas, media images, and religious values of African American single mothers.

Jackson, James S. (ed.). *Life in Black America.* Newbury Park, CA: Sage, 1991. An interdisciplinary reporting of a national survey of black Americans that includes chapters on family life, women and men, work, joblessness, and the black American life course.

McAdoo, Harriette Pipes (ed.). *Family Ethnicity: Strength in Diversity.* Newbury Park, CA: Sage, 1993. A look at the diversity found in five major cultural groups in the United States: African, Hispanic, Native, Muslim, and Asian Americans.

Stack, Carol B. *All Our Kin: Strategies for Survival in a Black Community.* New York: Harper, 1974. An anthropologist who lived in the Flats—the poorest section of a black community in a midwestern city—reports on men, women, kin, and domestic networks.

Staples, Robert, and Johnson, Leanor Boulin. *Black Families at the Crossroads: Challenges and Prospects.* San Francisco: Jossey-Bass, 1992. A picture of the black family, including its changing structures, roles of its members, and how it has been influenced by other systems.

Taylor, Robert Joseph; Chatters, Linda M.; Tucker, M. Belinda; and Lewis, Edith. "Developments in Research on Black Families: A Decade Review." *Journal of Marriage and the Family* 52 (November 1990): 993–1014. A literature review of topics and issues of importance to black families in the 1980s.

Wilkinson, Doris. "Ethnicity." In *Handbook of Marriage and the Family*, edited by Marvin B. Sussman and Suzanne K. Steinmetz, Chapter 8, 183–210. New York: Plenum Press, 1987. An overview of demographic patterns, regional variations, and marital and kinship relationships of ethnic groups with major sections on African Americans, Hispanic Americans, Asian Americans, and American Indians.

Wilson, William J. *The Truly Disadvantaged: The Inner City, the Underclass and Public Policy.* Chicago: University of Chicago Press, 1987. A description of inner-city neighborhoods, causes of the deterioration of the ghetto underclass, and the recommendation of a comprehensive public policy agenda to address these groups; Chapter 3 on poverty and family structure is particularly pertinent.

Chapter 7

Life-Styles Among Hispanic American, Asian American, and Native American Families

The previous chapter examined various life-styles and family patterns of African Americans. This chapter will focus on family patterns and life-styles of three ethnic and minority populations: Hispanic Americans, Asian Americans, and Native Americans. The groups are *ethnic* in that they share a sense of identity based on a common national origin and cultural traditions. The groups are *minority,* not merely in numbers of persons or families, but primarily in terms of power and prestige relative to more dominant groups.

As with African Americans, a key factor in dealing with any racial, ethnic, or minority group focuses around self and social definitions attached to the members. In Arizona or Puerto Rico, the social definition of *Hispanic* is very different than in Kansas or Vermont. The social definition of *Asian* is very different in California or Hawaii than in Michigan or North Carolina and the social definition of *Native American* is very different in Alaska or on the reservations of New Mexico than in cities such as Chicago or Atlanta. Not defining oneself or not being defined by others as black, Mexican, Chinese, or Indian (either Asian or Native American) influences everything from interaction patterns, to occupational opportunities, to clothing and food preferences.

Our attention is directed first at Hispanic Americans. Note the diversity that exists between them and other subculture and ethnic groups as well as the diversity that exists within Hispanic American groups.

HISPANIC AMERICAN FAMILY SYSTEM

As of 1993, about 8.9 percent of the U.S. population (22.8 million) claimed Hispanic origins.[1] While the U.S. population as a whole increased by about 10 percent in the past decade, the Hispanic American population increased by 48 percent. The category *Hispanic American* includes those who classify themselves as Mexican American (14.6 million), Puerto Rican (2.4 million), Cuban (1.1 million), Central and South American (3.1 million), and other Hispanic (1.6 million) from Spain or other Spanish-speaking countries (see Figure 7-1). Also included in this category are those who simply identify themselves as *Spanish American, Hispanic,* or *Latino.*

Social status characteristics

As with African American families, Hispanic American families can be better understood by examining unemployment, income, and educational information. It was stated earlier that the unemployment rate for African American males and females is generally more than twice that of white Americans. For Hispanic

[1] U.S. Bureau of the Census, *Current Population Reports,* Series P20-475, Patricia A. Montgomery, "The Hispanic Population in the United States: March 1993" (Washington, DC: U.S. Government Printing Office, 1994), Table 1, pp. 10–11.

Figure 7-1

Sizes of subgroups within Hispanic American population: 1993

Source: U.S. Bureau of the Census, *Current Population Reports,* Series P20-475, Patricia A. Montgomery "The Hispanic Population of the United States: March 1993" (Washington, DC: U.S. Government Printing Office, 1994), p. 2.

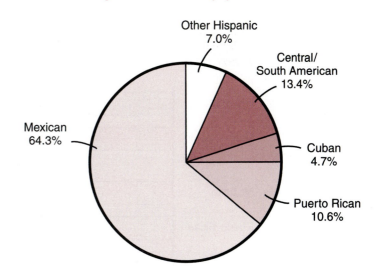

Other Hispanic 7.0%

Central/ South American 13.4%

Mexican 64.3%

Cuban 4.7%

Puerto Rican 10.6%

Americans, the unemployment rate tends to fall between the rates for whites and blacks (review Table 6-1 in the previous chapter). As with other groups, the unemployment rate for Hispanic teenage males was more than double that of Hispanic adult males (26.3 percent versus 10.7 percent).

As of 1993, the median income of Hispanic families ($23,912) was about 59 percent of the median income of non-Hispanic families ($38,015). Among Hispanic subgroups, median family incomes varied from $20,301 for Puerto Rican families to $23,714 for Mexican families to $31,015 for Cuban-origin families.[2]

The poverty rates of families (1992 data) are shown in Figure 7-2. The overall Hispanic rate (26.2 percent) was about two-and-one-half times that of the non-Hispanic rate (10.4 percent), with considerable variation by region of origin. Poverty rates were very high for Puerto Ricans (32.5 percent) and lowest for Cubans (15.4 percent); about one-fourth of Mexican and other Hispanic families lived in poverty.

A report by the *Urban Institute* indicated that in spite of persistent and growing Latino poverty, most national policy discussions fail to address poverty issues relevant to the Latino/Hispanic experience.[3] Why? Five reasons are given.

1. Misperceived identity. Even though 64 percent of U.S. Latinos are native-born, most are perceived as immigrants, thus being temporary or seen as competing for scarce resources.

2. No attention to the working poor. Most reform efforts have been directed to the "underclass" of nonworking poor, overlooking the problems of the Latino poor, most of whom are working.

---

[2] Ibid., 18–19.

[3] Maria Enchautegui, "Policy Implications of Latino Poverty," *The Urban Institute/Policy and Research Report* 25 (Winter/Spring 1995): 10–12.

Figure 7-2

Hispanic American families (and subgroups) living below poverty level: 1992

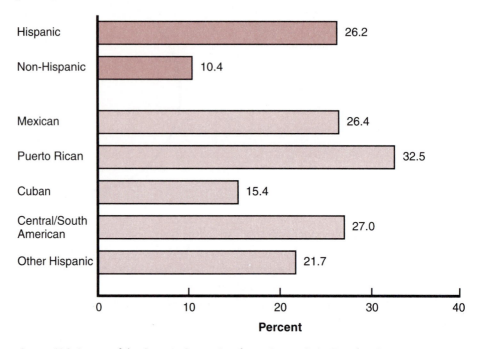

Source: U.S. Bureau of the Census, *Current Population Reports,* Series P20-475, Patricia A. Montgomery "The Hispanic Population of the United States: March 1993" (Washington, DC: U.S. Government Printing Office, 1994), Table 4, pp. 18–19.

3. Geographic concentration. Three-fourths of all Latinos live in five states (California, Florida, Illinois, New York, and Texas), thus directives are toward local rather than national efforts.

4. Political participation. Only one-third of Latinos were registered to vote in 1992 (compared to 64 percent of African Americans and 70 percent of white non-Hispanics.

5. Differences among sub-groups. By highlighting differences among ethnic groups in employment, welfare use, female-headed households and the like, larger underlying themes common to the poverty experience of Latinos have been overlooked.

Yet, as indicated, the poverty rate, particularly among subgroups such as Puerto Rican–origin families is very high. This appears to be related, at least in part, to two factors:

1. There is a heavy concentration of Puerto Ricans living in cities and working in low-paying full-time jobs, part-time jobs, or without a job at all. In

New York City, for example, initially the city provided access to jobs that required few skills and little education; however, many of these types of manufacturing industries have left New York.

2. In greater numbers than other Hispanics, Puerto Ricans form families without benefit of marriage; the result is a high proportion of families maintained by females with no spouses present. In 1993, about 60 percent of the Puerto Rican families maintained by a female without a spouse present lived in poverty.[4]

These two factors, parental work/employment patterns and family structure/ female-headed households as related to poverty were examined among Latino children.[5] Daniel Lichter and Nancy Landale suggest that Puerto Rican and black children pay a high price for the "breakdown of the family" if measured strictly in terms of economic well-being. Family structure alone accounted for 55 percent of the differences between Puerto Ricans and whites in child poverty, and when family structure was combined with parental work patterns, 78 percent of the difference in child poverty was explained. The lack of parental work and the low rate of labor force participation among Puerto Rican women has exacerbated the child poverty problem.

The Lichter/Landale analysis indicates that policies designed to "strengthen the family" or to promote maternal employment without regard to wage levels will neither eliminate inequality nor have significant effects on reducing child poverty across racial and ethnic groups. Without policies such as earned income tax credits, minimum-wage legislation, job training, child support assurance, and the like, earnings from work will remain insufficient to raise families above the poverty level.

Of course, low paying jobs and single-parent households are not the only explanations for the high poverty rate among Puerto Ricans. Large families, the time children are in the home, the age of the children, and restricted or nonexistent welfare benefits affect it as well.[6]

As poverty rates vary by Hispanic group, so do infant mortality rates. Research in Florida showed that Puerto Ricans and Mexicans have higher rates of infant mortality than either Cubans or the resident group of other Hispanics.[7] Infant mortality rates per 1,000 births was 13.46 for Puerto Ricans, 12.46 for Mexicans, 9.20 for Cubans, and 8.07 for other Hispanic groups. Differences were especially marked among exogenous causes of death (related to the environment and external factors) in contrast to endogenous causes (due to the genetic makeup of the

---

[4] Ibid., 19.

[5] Daniel T. Lichter and Nancy S. Landale, "Parental Work, Family Structure, and Poverty Among Latino Children," *Journal of Marriage and the Family* 57 (May 1995): 346–354.

[6] Robert Aponte, "Urban Hispanic Poverty: Disaggregations and Explanations," *Social Problems* 38 (November 1991): 516–528. See also: "The Puerto Rican Exception" in Linda Chavez, *Out of the Barrio* (New York: Basic Books, 1991), Chapter 7.

[7] Robert A. Hummer, Isaac W. Eberstein, and Charles B. Nam, "Infant Mortality Differentials among Hispanic Groups in Florida," *Social Forces* 70 (June 1992): 1055–1075.

infant, circumstances of life in utero, or conditions of labor). Exogenous mortality rates for Puerto Ricans and Mexicans were three and four times higher than those of Cubans and other Hispanics. The two former groups had the highest percentages of nonmetropolitan residents, the highest percentages of births to teens, the highest percentages of prior deaths, the latest onset of prenatal care, and the lowest mean levels of education. Each of these factors seems to relate to higher incidences of infant mortality.

What about the educational attainment of Hispanic Americans? As was shown in Table 6-3, about eight of ten white persons and nearly three-fourths of black persons ages twenty-five years and over have completed four years or more of high school. For Hispanic Americans, the rate drops considerably to slightly over one-half (53.4 percent for females; 53.2 percent for males as of 1994).

Given this information on unemployment, income, infant mortality, and education, the following sections will address the marital status of Hispanic Americans and then, specifically, the Mexican-American subgroup, who constitute approximately 64 percent of the Hispanic American population.

Marital status

As illustrated in the previous chapter (Table 6-5), in 1994, about 68 percent of all Hispanic-origin family households consisted of married couples. Another one-fourth (25.2 percent) of households were maintained by females with no husbands present. Both the married-couple and the female-householder figures for Spanish-origin families fall between those of the white and black populations.

Again, considerable differences can be seen by country of origin. About three-fourths of Cuban and Mexican families consisted of married couples, while only slightly over half of Puerto Rican families were such. This may be due to the prevalence of nonmarital cohabitation among Puerto Rican women. A study in New York City suggested that these informal unions resemble marriages.[8] While not legal marriages, the study showed that women in these unions were more similar to married women than single women in respect to childbearing behavior and employment and educational pursuits. The high rate of poverty (review Figure 7-2) and the low median family income for Puerto Ricans is directly linked to the low number of married-couple households. In fact, 60 percent of Puerto Rican families with no husband present live below the poverty level (compared to 48.8 percent of all Hispanic Americans and 33.7 percent of the non-Hispanic population).[9] (These figures will have additional meaning in the discussion of the feminization of poverty in Chapter 8.)

---

[8] Nancy S. Landale and Kathrine Fennelly, "Informal Unions Among Mainland Puerto Ricans: Cohabitation or an Alternative to Legal Marriage?" *Journal of Marriage and the Family* 54 (May 1992): 269–280.

[9] U.S. Bureau of the Census, *Current Population Reports*, Series P20-175, Table 4, pp. 18–19.

Mexican American families

Mexican Americans are also identified by the term *Chicanos,* a contraction of *Mexicanos* (pronounced "meschicanos" in the ancient Nahuatl language of Mexico). Over one million Mexican Americans are descendants of the native Mexicans who lived in the Southwest before it became part of the United States following the Mexican American War. These natives became Americans in 1848, when Texas, California, New Mexico, and most of Arizona became U.S. territory. These four states plus Colorado contain the largest concentrations of Mexican Americans today. Most urban Mexican Americans live in California, especially Los Angeles.

Other Mexican Americans who have come from Mexico since 1848 can be classified into three types: (1) legal immigrants; (2) **braceros,** or temporary workers; and (3) illegal aliens. Large-scale migration in the early 1900s was caused in part by the Mexican Revolution and unsettled economic conditions in Mexico as well as by the demand for labor on cotton farms and railroads in California. Before the minimum wage law was passed, agricultural employers preferred *braceros* to local workers because the Mexicans could be paid less and were not a burden to the federal government (as they returned to Mexico when their services were no longer needed). These Mexican nationals (who live in Mexico) need to be distinguished from Mexican Americans (who live in the United States).

Changes in traditional families

Traditional Mexican American culture is characterized by strong family ties. The extended family has long been recognized as the most important institution in the Chicano community. **Familism** (*la familia* among Hispanics) appears to remain a more typical feature of Mexican-American families than of non-Hispanic white families.[10] Familism involves a spatial dimension of living near nuclear and extended family members, includes an expressed identification with the interests and welfare of the family unit, and means behaving in ways that incorporate an attachment and affinity with the family. In brief, the needs of the family collectively supersede individual needs. Familism may explain why many young people of parents with a low level of education drop out of school to take jobs, a decision that has immediate financial benefits for the family but is detrimental to the individual in the long run. Among higher-educated parents, however, familism may be beneficial to staying in school and getting good grades.

The theme of family honor and unity occurs throughout Mexican American society, irrespective of social class or geographical location. This theme extends beyond the nuclear family unit of husband, wife, and children to relatives on both sides, including grandparents, aunts, uncles, married sisters and brothers and their children, and even to godparents and to ties of *compadres* or *compadrazgo* (co-parenthood).

---

[10] Angela Valenzuela and Sanford M. Dornbusch, "Familism and Social Capital in the Academic Achievement of Mexican Origin and Anglo Adolescents," *Social Science Quarterly* 75 (March 1994): 18–36.

Case Example:
A Mexican American Daughter

Yvonne, age 20, lives at home with her father (Mexican in America but not a citizen) and her mother (Mexican American) who became a citizen two years ago. Her parents were born and married (25 years ago) in Mexico and came to the United States one year after they married. Yvonne has one older brother who married a Mexican girl and is living in Laredo, Texas.

As Yvonne said, "Spanish is the only language spoken in the home. I seldom speak English to my parents. Fortunately, I went to a school which had a bilingual program. At home, almost all of our cooking is Mexican but we do eat steak fajitas and pizza.

"My dad is clearly the head of our family. He represents all the qualities of machismo. He is very protective of me and needs to know who I am going out with, where I am going, and tells me when I need to be home. But he doesn't communicate openly and directly to me. For example, when I was developing physically, he became concerned about what I was wearing and, through my mother, made me return some clothes I bought because they were too tight. Because I am a girl, he is embarrassed to talk about sex or about how I look. For a long time, he even wanted my mother to wear only dresses, not jeans.

"If my father had his way, I wouldn't be in college. My brother was encouraged to go so as to be able to support a family. But for me, he allows me to go just in case of a divorce or widowhood and not to be fully dependent on a man. In many ways, my brother was not overprotected like I was. He could go away to school but Dad won't allow me to live away from home, even in a dorm. I dropped hints about renting an apartment with my friends but he didn't take too kindly to that idea. I know I'm old enough to do what I want, but I obey my parents. I don't go to parties without their permission. When I'm out, I'll call them to let them know I'm fine. Last week, when they weren't home, I left a note telling them where I was going. They would have a fit if they didn't know where I was.

"My dad wants me to date Hispanics (preferably Mexicans) or white Americans. I had a regular boyfriend but my dad refused to meet him or let him in our home. It wasn't that he objected to me going with him but if he were to come in, the boy might get too comfortable. And he's afraid of what the neighbors would say. He's also afraid of losing his daughter. He doesn't talk to me about it, but I know he wants me to remain a virgin until I get married. And if I were to get pregnant, as a few of my friends have done, I would not only embarrass my parents but disgrace the family name."

The general patterns of **compadres** and **compadrazgo** are associated primarily with infant baptism but may also apply to first communion, marriage, and other rituals. At these times, ties are established between parents and godparents and child and godparents. Traditionally, expectant parents selected a married couple from among close friends or an extended-family member to be the child's sponsors. An invitation to be a sponsor was a special honor that was not to be refused. Through the baptism ceremony, a major social bond was established between the parents and godparents (co-parents), which brought them into a relationship that was expected to last a lifetime. The godparent was expected to take care of the physical and spiritual needs of the child in the event the parents could not perform these essential duties. Williams determined, however, that today the *compadrazgo* ceremony no longer serves to sustain the "fictive kinship system," as traditionally defined.[11] Many of its elements have disappeared or been modified.

Mexican American women have traditionally played (and somewhat still continue to play) the active role in the home. A "good woman" was one who married, had children, and stayed home to care for her children and her husband. Wives and daughters were subordinate to their husbands and fathers, a role pattern highly reinforced by the religious belief system, that of the Roman Catholic Church.

Conversely, Mexican American men have traditionally adhered to an ideal of manliness (*machismo*) equated with authority, strength, and sexual virility and prowess. The man was the patriarch who made the important decisions. He was strong and brave. He could seek other sexual partners, but his wife could not. The cultural practice of machismo has been found, for example, to have an effect on condom use and the prevention of AIDS.[12] The concept goes beyond how men treat women in stereotypical dominating ways such as being "macho" but also includes viewing men as providers, protectors, and representatives of their families. Manly characteristics include being courageous and being respectful of women. Since the use of condoms appears to be more a male prerogative than a female one, condom use was found to depend on how well males took charge of obtaining and using condoms in fulfilling certain aspects of the machismo role.

Williams found that decision making in the Mexican American family has become increasingly egalitarian in nature.[13] While husbands and wives often replied in rather traditional terms to questions about gender- or sex-role expectations, their behaviors did not necessarily conform to traditional notions. Modern couples saw their marital relationship and household division of labor as very different from those of their parents. In particular, professional women have come to participate more fully in decision making, and husbands have made significant adjustments as well.

What type of general conclusions can be made? When compared to non-Hispanic American families, it seems that Mexican American husbands still exert power over wives and that women still fulfill the majority of child-care and household tasks. Husbands and fathers, however, have been shown to have a definite interest in their child's behavior, placing great importance on being independent,

---

[11] Norma Williams, *The Mexican American Family: Tradition and Change* (Dix Hills, NY: General Hall, 1990): 44.

[12] James K. Mikawa, Pete A. Morones, Antonio Gomez, Hillary L. Case, Dan Olsen, and Mary Jane Gonzales-Huss, "Cultural Practices of Hispanics: Implications for the Prevention of AIDS," *Hispanic Journal of Behavioral Sciences* 14 (November 1992): 421–433.

[13] Williams, *The Mexican American Family: Tradition and Change:* Chapters 5 and 6.

exercising self-control, obeying, getting along with others, and succeeding in athletics.[14] When compared to the traditional patterns of their Mexican American parents and grandparents, change is very real for contemporary families.

Family size

One of the most distinctive characteristics of Mexican American families today is their unusually high fertility. It is not unusual for Mexican American families to have five or more children; most other American families have two or three. In 1993, for example, Hispanic-origin families had an average of 3.78 persons (compared to 3.08 in non-Hispanic families) but Mexican American families had an average of 4.01 persons. One-third (33 percent) of Mexican American families had five or more members (compared to 12 percent of non-Hispanics).[15]

Given this family size, along with the minimal skills and low levels of income that characterize Mexican Americans, it is increasingly difficult for these people to make social and economic gains and to have the life enjoyed by the dominant groups in American society. To improve the educational and income levels of the Mexican American family, several Mexican American social movements have emerged over the past three decades. One movement was directed at introducing bilingual instruction at the elementary school level. Bilingualism became such a politically controversial issue that, in 1986, California passed a resolution (joining six other states) making English the state's official language.

Another movement was led by César Chávez, one of the best-known Chicano leaders. In 1962, he formed the National Farm Workers Association (later the United Farm Workers Union) and organized Mexican migrant farm workers, first, to strike against grape growers and later, against lettuce growers. These strikes included boycotts against these products, which carried the struggles of low-paid Chicano laborers into the kitchens of homes throughout the United States.

One thing seems very clear: Mexican and other Hispanic Americans are continually changing, adapting to new situations and opportunities. This change causes numerous conflicts between one class and another, the foreign born and the native born, new immigrants and old ones. Vestiges of tradition remain while new patterns emerge. Therefore, it is very difficult to write or speak about *the* Hispanic American or Mexican American family.

ASIAN AMERICAN FAMILY SYSTEM

As of 1995, about 3.3 percent of the U.S. population (9.8 million) were characterized by the U.S. census as Asian or Pacific Islanders.[16]

---

[14] Teresa W. Julian, Patrick C. McHenry, and Mary W. McKelvey, "Perceptions of Caucasian, African-American, Hispanic, and Asian-American Parents," *Family Relations* 43 (January 1994): 30–37.

[15] U.S. Bureau of the Census, *Current Population Reports,* Series P20-475, Table 4, pp.18–19.

[16] U.S. Bureau of the Census, *Statistical Abstract of the United States, 1995,* 115th ed. (Washington, DC: U.S. Government Printing Office, 1995), no. 12, p. 14. Specific country figures are for 1990 from no. 31, p. 31.

U.S. Diversity: Age at Marriage and Fertility Among the Hmong

About 90,000 Asian Americans are identified as Hmong. Since WW II, Hmong families have undergone 25 years of constant warfare in their Laotian homeland, years of confinement in resettlement camps in Thailand, and finally relocation in countries such as Australia, France, and the United States. Evidence suggests that in spite of war, resettlement camps, and foreign relocation, the Hmong have retained many of their traditional family values and characteristics.

These traditional characteristics include an early age of marriage for female children, high levels of fertility, and a narrow set of circumscribed roles for females. Traditional Hmong society was organized in a patrilineal clan system and marriage occurred only between persons from different clans. Men married between the ages of 18 and 30 but women married between the ages of 14 and 18. With a young age at marriage came many children, described by one writer as at "the highest level possible."

What about Hmong residents in the United States? Data from San Diego revealed fertility levels among the Hmong to be higher than any other immigrant group. The Hmong reported a child-woman fertility ratio of 1,750 children under the age of four per 1,000 Hmong women between the ages of 15 and 44. This compares to 575 for non-Chinese Vietnamese refugees and only 300 for the general United States population. Hmong women had the youngest age of marriage of all Southeast Asian refugee groups ranging from 13 to 18 years of age.

Data from St. Paul, Minnesota, of Hmong adolescents revealed that girls married at a young age, to husbands several years older, with high levels of early fertility. More than half of the girls had married by their senior year in high school and two-thirds of these had one or more children (half had two or more). Interestingly, the majority of those who were married did not drop out of school, a deviation from the traditional patterns associated with early marriage and pregnancy.

Source: Ray Hutchison and Miles McNall, "Early Marriage in a Hmong Cohort," *Journal of Marriage and the Family* 56 (August 1994): 579–590.

Like Hispanic Americans, Asian Americans are not a homogeneous group but are a diverse collection of ethnic minorities. The groups most often classified under the category of Asian include persons who identify as Chinese (1.6 million), Filipino (1.4 million), Japanese (848,000), Asian Indian (815,000), Korean (799,000), Vietnamese (615,000), Laotian (149,000), Cambodian (147,000), Thai (91,000) and Hmong (90,000).

The term Pacific Islanders appears as a subcategory in the U.S. census, on affirmative-action forms, and the like, but Pacific Islanders are not an ethnic group.[17] Almost no persons wake up thinking of themselves as a Pacific Islander. Some may think of themselves as Polynesian, Melanesian, or Micronesian but most identify as Tongas, Samoans, Maoris, or Fijians and even they are multiethnic within each person. But according to the census, Pacific Islander Americans include persons who identify as Hawaiians (211,000), Samoan (63,000), and Guamanian (49,000). Relatively few of the Pacific Islanders are foreign born; of course, Hawaiians are native to the United States.

---

17 Paul R. Spickard and Rowena Fong, "Pacific Islander Americans and Multiethnicity: A Vision of America's Future," *Social Forces* 73 (June 1995): 1365–1383.

In spite of tremendous diversity among Asian American families, childrearing patterns tend to emphasize obligation to family, obedience, and a desire for educational achievement.

Without exception, each of these groups differs in ancestry, language, culture, and recency of immigration. Some groups, like the Chinese and Japanese, have had sizable numbers of members in the United States for several generations while others, such as the Vietnamese, Laotians, and Cambodians, are comparatively recent immigrants. Asian Americans are heavily concentrated in California and Hawaii, with sizable proportions of the total in New York, Texas, Illinois, and New Jersey as well. More than 90 percent live in metropolitan areas.

Social status characteristics

As with African Americans and Hispanic Americans, Asian American families can be better understood by examining a number of general social-status characteristics. Asian Americans are younger than the population as a whole. As of 1991, their median age was about 30.4 compared to 33.9 for the U.S. population.[18]

Asian Americans are better educated than the population as a whole. Those with four years or more of high school were 85 percent in 1994 compared to about 82 percent for white, 72 percent for black, and 53 percent for Hispanic. The image of Asians as good students seems to be supported by higher-than-average

---

[18] Many of these figures come from U.S. Bureau of the Census, *Current Population Reports,* Series P20–459, Claudette E. Bennett, "The Asian and Pacific Islander Population in the United States: March 1991 and 1990" (Washington, DC: U.S. Government Printing Office, 1992), and *Statistical Abstract: 1995.*

Scholastic Achievement Test scores in mathematics, for example. And with a higher level of education tends to come a higher median family income (see Table 6-2). In 1993, the median family income for Asian Americans was $44,456, about $5,000 more than whites and double that of blacks.

Given these higher levels of education and median family income, we would expect a relatively low percentage of families below the poverty level. This appears to be the case with about 13 percent of all Asian American families below the level of poverty as of 1994 (compared to about 29 percent for Hispanics and 31 percent for blacks. For other group, jump ahead to Figure 8-2). But the rate of poverty of Asian Americans is increasing as factors such as job discrimination and exclusion from high-earning occupations lead to a lower return on their education than exists for their European American counterparts.

Marital/family patterns

In 1994, Asian and Pacific Islanders in the United States had a married couple rate (82.1 percent), the same as the white population (82.0 percent) but considerably higher than the Hispanic (67.9 percent) and black (46.5 percent) populations (see Table 6-5 in the previous chapter). Likewise, the rate of female households with no husband present was quite low at 13.4 percent when compared with Hispanics at 25.2 percent and blacks at 47 percent.[19]

Particularly among Chinese, Japanese, and Filipino marriages, there is a high level of family stability and a greater degree of permanence than that found among Hispanic American and African American marriages. Divorce rates are low and strong kinship associations are high. Most Asian American populations have entrenched norms and role expectations pertaining to caring for older relatives, particularly parents, many of whom live in the same household as their adult children.

Some of the traditional cultural norms such as speaking the native language, patriarchal authority, rigid role expectations for wives and children, and the heavy emphasis on childhood obedience and loyalty to parents bring with it intergenerational strains. Second and third generation children tend to accept English as their dominant language, adopt the dress codes and musical preferences of their peers (many of whom are not of Asian descent) and pick up various dating and sexual patterns that are at odds with traditional and parental values.

One indication of these changes is seen in the significant increase in the degree of intermarriage between Asian Americans of different Asian nationalities and with non-Asians. As is noted in the next chapter, the most common types of interracial marriage are between Japanese American women and white men and Filipino American women and white men. While wars such as in Korea and Vietnam brought with it numerous marriages of Korean and Vietnamese women

---

[19] U.S. Bureau of the Census, *Current Population Reports,* Series P20-483, Steve W. Rawlings and Arlene F. Saluter, "Household and Family Characteristics: March 1994" (Washington, DC: U.S. Government Printing Office, 1995), Table E, p. xiii.

Global Diversity: Frugality in Japanese Households

The changing economy of Japan has led to some major changes in many Japanese households. *The New York Times* (September 15, 1995) cites the case of Yumiko Sakurai who has not suddenly become poor but worries that she could. So she violates a cardinal principle of Japanese cooking by refrigerating unused rice from one meal and then reheating it in the microwave. She keeps a thermos of iced tea on the counter so her children will not keep opening the refrigerator door. She turns off the lights when she goes out. The leftover bathwater is poured on the plants or splashed on the garden.

The news article suggested that frugality is sweeping the nation. Magazines offer many suggestions as to how a few yen can be saved by using microwave cooking rather than gas-burning cooking, taking baths rather than showers, or watching a 14-inch television which costs half that of a 25-inch one.

In Japan, women often control the household purse strings and one sign of the times is the smaller allowances that wives give to their husbands. For example, a stockbroker who saw his income drop this year used to get 50,000 yen a month. Now his wife gives him 20,000 yen, forcing him to eat meat kabobs at cheaper places rather than eating traditional Japanese meals at Ginza. Another wife started to make a box lunch for her husband rather than having him eat at restaurants. And another wife said she would like to cut her husband's allowance to zero, but all hell would break loose if she did.

to white and black American servicemen, these "war brides" were a small proportion of the total Asian intermarriages.

What about the ethnic identity of the children of these Asian American intermarried couples? Do most children define themselves as Asian or as American? Data from California suggest that the majority of Asian American couples tend to be defined by Anglo ethnic identities, yet a significant portion of children (about 38 percent) are viewed as Asians.[20] However, these ethnic-identification patterns are related to various characteristics of the child, the Asian parent, and the Asian ethnic-specific community. Children who hold an Asian identity tend to be those who are foreign-born, speak a language other than English at home, have fathers who are Asian, and live in areas having large Asian populations and low degrees of ethnic heterogeneity. In contrast, children with an American identity tend to be those born in the United States and have a foreign-born Asian parent, who speak English at home, have mothers who are Asian, and live in areas with a small Asian population but high degrees of ethnic heterogeneity.

Birth characteristics

A special report issued by the National Center for Health Statistics revealed the diverse nature of Asian and Pacific Islanders in regard to birth characteris-

---

[20] Rogelio Saenz, Sean-Shong Hwang, Benigno E. Aguirre, and Robert N. Anderson, "Persistence and Change in Asian Identity Among Children of Intermarried Couples," *Sociological Perspectives* 38 (1995): 175–194.

tics.[21] With data from seven states, which accounted for 72 percent of all Asian/Pacific Island births, several findings appear to be of interest.

First, the Asian American population more than doubled between 1980 and 1991, representing the fastest-growing minority population in the United States. Most of this growth was the result of immigration, and accordingly, only 17 percent of Asian and Pacific Islander mothers giving birth in 1992 were themselves born in one of the 50 states. The proportion of mothers born elsewhere varied widely among the Asian American groups. Almost all Vietnamese, Asian Indian, or Korean mothers (97–99 percent) were born elsewhere, as were the vast majority of Chinese (90 percent). Less than half of all Japanese mothers (45 percent) and almost no Hawaiian mothers (2 percent) were born elsewhere.[22]

Second, the heterogeneity of Asian Americans can be seen in the age distribution of the mothers giving births. Teenage childbearing ranged from less than 1 percent of all births for Chinese mothers to 19 percent for Hawaiian mothers. Very few Korean mothers (1 percent) and Asian Indian mothers (2 percent) were teenagers while teenage mothers from Guam (17 percent) and Samoa (11 percent) were more common. In contrast, almost two-thirds of Japanese and Chinese births were to mothers at least 35 years of age.

Third, and closely related to teenage mothers, were births to unmarried women. The lowest proportion of out-of-wedlock births was for Korean women (4 percent) and the highest for Pacific Islanders (Hawaiian, 47 percent; Samoan, 36 percent; and Guamanian, 35 percent). Interestingly, Asian American mothers born in the United States were almost three times as likely to be unmarried as were mothers born elsewhere.

As indicated, Asian Americans are a very diverse collection of ethnic groups. Immigration patterns to the United States have varied widely by time period, numbers, and reasons for migrating. Languages spoken, employment numbers, including those of wives and mothers, levels of education of parents and children, religious identities and practices, number of children born and in the household, extended-kin relationships, childrearing practices, and the like differ considerably between Americans of Asian descent and identity such as the Chinese, Japanese, Korean, Vietnamese, Filipino, Asian Indian, Hawaiian, and others. For specific information on the family life and characteristics of many of these groups, the reader is directed to edited books by Taylor, Kephart and Zellner, and McAdoo.[23]

---

[21] National Center for Health Statistics, *Monthly Vital Statistics Reports,* vol. 43, no. 10, Joyce A. Martin, "Birth Characteristics for Asian or Pacific Islander Subgroups, 1992" (Hyattsville, MD: Public Health Service, 11 May 1995).

[22] Contrast these figures with non-Asian American mothers from outside the 50 states: Hispanic, 65 percent; black, 14 percent; and white non-Hispanic, 7 percent.

[23] Ronald L. Taylor (ed.), *Minority Families in the United States: A Multicultural Perspective* (Englewood Cliffs, NJ: Prentice-Hall, 1994); William M. Kephart and William W. Zellner (eds.), *Extraordinary Groups.* (New York: St. Martin's Press [5th ed.], 1994); and Harriette Pipes McAdoo (ed.), *Family Ethnicity: Strengths in Diversity* (Newbury Park, CA: Sage, 1993).

NATIVE AMERICAN FAMILY SYSTEM

Suzan Shown Harjo notes that for over 500 years, Native Americans were referred to as "Indians."[24] They were, and remain, several hundred tribes or nations with 300 separate languages and dialects. The population at the time Columbus landed in 1492 was estimated to be about 10 million (compared to about 2.2 million today).

As of 1995, about 0.8 percent of the U.S. population claimed American Indian and Alaska Native origins.[25] According to U.S. census data, more than half (54 percent) of these Native Americans live on reservations, trust lands, or tribal designated areas. Federal American Indian **reservations** are areas established by treaty, statute, or court order and are recognized as territories in which the tribes have jurisdiction. **Trust lands** are properties associated with a particular tribe but are located outside of reservation boundaries and held in trust by the Federal Government. **Tribal designated statistical areas** have no specific land base or trust lands but provide statistical areas upon which census data are tabulated. The other 46 percent of Native Americans live in cities or communities apart from the designated areas listed. Growing numbers are leaving the reservations and rural areas for urban employment and schooling.

Within the American Indian population are hundreds of distinct tribes or nations. The largest group, the Cherokees, comprise about 16 percent of the Native American population. The second largest, the Navaho, comprise about 12 percent. Other large groups ranging from 6 to 2 percent of the Indian population, include the Chippewa, Sioux, Choctaw, Pueblo, Apache, Iroquois, Lumbee, and Creek tribes.[26] As might be expected, the majority live in the western regions of the United States: California, Arizona, Oklahoma, New Mexico, Washington, and Alaska.

Exact patterns of growth are difficult to determine but census data suggest the Native American population may be increasing at a rate four times the national average. This is due to factors such as a rise in the birthrate, a reduction in infant mortality, and a greater number of persons identifying themselves as having Native American ancestry. Eschbach claims that over the past few decades, an increasing portion of the American Indian population has not been enumerated historically as Indian and is not native to the regions where most reservation Indians live. The recent growth of this Indian population is treated most appropriately as a new emergence of ethnic identification, or at least of changes in the expression of an ethnic identification.[27]

---

[24] Suzan Shown Harjo, "The American Indian Experience," in Harriette Pipes McAdoo, *Family Ethnicity: Strengths in Diversity* (Newbury Park, CA: Sage, 1993): 199.

[25] Statistical Abstract of the United States, 1995, no. 12, p. 14.

[26] Ibid., no. 55, p. 50.

[27] Karl Eschbach, "Changing Identification Among American Indians and Alaska Natives," Demography 30 (November 1993): 635–652.

Social status characteristics

Like African Americans, Hispanic Americans, and Asian Americans, it is inaccurate to view Native Americans as a homogeneous people. While sharing many values in common, they have distinct languages, tribal customs, family forms, life-course rituals, patterns of lineage, and kinship relationships. For example, many tribes have a kinship descent pattern that is patrilineal, but among the Hopi Indians the pattern is matrilineal. Many tribes have a postmarital residence pattern that is patrilocal, but again, the Hopi are matrilocal. But as with the other major racial/ethnic/minority groups, some general characteristics of Native Americans will be presented.

One startling characteristic is the median age and life expectancy of Native Americans. The median age is 26.4 (compared to the white median age of 34.4) and the life expectancy is estimated to be less than 50 (compared to the white life expectancy of about 75). A high rate of infant mortality, alcoholism, tuberculosis, diabetes, and other diseases, psychological distress, suicide, crime, and accident deaths all contribute to this low life expectancy.

Although the majority of Native American population was enrolled in school, the drop-out rate tends to be high. In 1992, only about 5 percent of the Native American population was enrolled in college with females making up about 58 percent of the students. The majority of these (54 percent) were attending a two-year institution. In general, low educational achievement, combined with a large proportion of men and women relegated to service and unskilled jobs, results in Native Americans having one of the lowest median family incomes of any ethnic minority in the United States.

The Native American experience

How does one understand the low life expectancy, the high school drop-out rate, or the low family incomes? While the experience of most minorities in the United States involved a struggle to gain a place in the melting pot—social acceptance, economic power, and equal rights—the experience of the American Indian was the opposite, involving a struggle to avoid being subjugated and to reserve their land, water, traditions, and unique legal rights.[28] Unlike any other minority group in the United States, Native Americans have negotiated over 600 treaties with the United States Government and have ceded billions of acres of land and untold natural resources.

Harjo states that assimilation for Indian people meant cultural genocide—a concerted effort to destroy Indian languages, traditions, customary laws, dress, religion, and occupations. This was done in three major ways: (1) through federal franchising on Indian nations to Christian denominations; (2) through an

---

[28] Harjo, "The American Indian Experience," pp. 199–207. The information in this section comes primarily from this source.

Native American families maintain strong patterns of inter- and intra-family cooperation and sharing. Conceptions of time and living in harmony with nature illustrate departures from Western norms.

imposed educational system designed to separate child from family and instill non-Indian values; and (3) through federal efforts to break up tribal landholdings, turn Indians into individual landowners, and impose taxes on their lands.

Dealing with the educational system extends back to the early 1800s when a congressional appropriation for Indian education was set aside in a "civilization fund." In 1871, President Grant delegated specific reservations to churches which had the aim of stripping Indian people of their religious ceremonies (including the Sun Dance and the Ghost Dance), forbidding them to speak their native languages, and separating children from their parents (for up to 12 years) by sending them to off-reservation boarding schools or to place them in foster homes. Harjo notes that until recently, educational efforts were based on the premise that Indian people are inferior to white people. Children were taught that their traditions were savage and immoral.

Only in the past couple of decades have efforts been made to reestablish traditional family values, including an extended family with sharing of child care among relatives. The Indian Child Welfare Act of 1978 was designed to stop the practice of removing Indian children from their homes. Harjo notes that from 1969 to 1974, 25 to 35 percent of Indian children were separated from their families and placed in non-Indian homes.

Today, Indian education is increasingly under tribal control as a result of educational reform acts passed in the 1970s. But U.S. history books used by most students in grade schools, high schools, and colleges relegate Indian matters to a few pages or at best a chapter. Thanksgiving is when schools set aside a day or week for "Indian awareness."

Many issues other than education are pertinent to understanding Native Americans and their family life today. Take land, for example. Not only was their land decreased dramatically but major efforts were made to allocate land to individual families, to make them farmers, and therefore to have them become more civilized. Promises were made to irrigate these lands (much of which was desert or semiarid and not suitable for cultivation), most of which were never fulfilled.

Perhaps the issues surrounding the Native American experience can be summed up by Harjo, who wrote:

> the taking of land, forced relocation, an institutionally racist educational system, removal of Indian children from their homes, U.S. government paternalism, obstacles to self-governance, stripping of tribal recognition, and denial of religious freedom—continue to place great stress on Indian families. Symptoms of these policies are, not surprisingly, high unemployment and alcohol and drug abuse.[29]

Marital/family patterns

About 66 percent of all Native American family households are comprised of married couple families.[30] This is below that of Hispanic Americans, Asian Americans, and white Americans but above that of blacks (note Table 6-5 in the previous chapter). Another 26 percent were female households with no husband present, well below that of blacks but higher than that of white Americans, Asian Americans, or Hispanic Americans. The remaining 8 percent of family households were classified as male households with no wife present, a figure slightly higher than for any of the other three ethnic/racial groups considered. This may be somewhat misleading because a strong norm of family helping and exchange is very common, especially on reservations and trust lands.

Despite tribal differences, kinship ties are of supreme importance, and extended family networks remain as a constant regardless of specific life-style patterns. These networks often include several households of significant relatives operating within a community context. These members engage in obligatory mutual assistance and actively participate in important ceremonial events.

Elders play a special role in Native American communities and families. Children are taught to respect and assist them. Grandparents participate actively in the training of grandchildren, nephews/nieces, and other extended relatives and assume much of the responsibility for passing on the cultural heritage, including language, tribal rituals, and family traditions. Of particular relevance is the teaching of living in harmony with nature and having respect for the land. Other values, many that depart from the European-American culture, include a conception of time as a blend of the past and future.

As with Asian Americans, interracial marriage is common. Eschbach identified six regions as having high rates of intermarriage: the Northeast, Northwest,

---

[29] Ibid., pp. 206–207.

[30] *Statistical Abstract of the United States, 1995*, no. 52, p. 50.

News Item: Wind Trees Follows in Footsteps of Father

Wind Trees moved from New Mexico to Old Fort, North Carolina, to continue the work of her late father, Bear Clan Chief Two Trees. Two Trees was a Cherokee Indian medicine man who treated those who visited him with natural herbs and vitamins and, according to his daughter, a lot of common sense.

Chief Two Trees (Kenneth Cannon was his Americanized name) arrived in Old Fort about ten years ago and established his nonprofit Native American Institute of Health. He never charged for his services but accepted donations.

In May of 1995, Chief Two Trees died of cancer at the age of 68. His only heir was a daughter, Wind Trees (whose Americanized name is Darlene). Wind Trees, a single mother, knew her father was ill and moved with her son to be with him. Wind Trees said that regardless of sex, it is Indian tradition to carry on the work of their father. She believes the land her father left her is sacred and has plans to make natural medicines from the native plants and flowers that grow wild on the institute's 30 acres.

As a registered nurse, Wind Trees plans to offer counseling in spiritual and emotional healing through holistic teachings in addition to the natural medicines. She believes that healing a sickness involves the entire body, including the mind. And like her father, she will not charge for her services but will accept donations.

Source: Adapted from *The Charlotte Observer,* 3 July 1995, pp. 1-C and 5-C.

South, California, Prairie, and Midwest.[31] In these areas in 1990 more than three-fourths of married Indians were married to non-Indians. Nearly 80 percent of married Indians under the age of 25 were racially intermarried. Eschbach notes an irony in these figures in that this is an Indian population that by and large did not self-identify as such in census responses just thirty years ago. In 1960, the Indian population in these areas was 151,000. By 1990, the Indian population had increased to 928,000—more than a sixfold increase. (Migration from other areas played only a small role in this population growth.) In contrast, a pattern of a relatively high degree of endogamy and ethnic homogeneity (low intermarriage rates) characterizes the Southwest, North Carolina, Alaska, and the Northern Plains. In these areas in 1990, about one-fourth of married Indians were married to non-Indians.

Wilkinson[32] suggests these intermarriage alliances, other than changes in identification, are a result of a number of social conditions: residence in metropolitan areas, new occupational opportunities, frequency of contact with other ethnic groups, higher educational status, and the desire for and perceptions of the possibility of assimilation.

Because of major social changes in the larger society, continuing changes can be expected in the Native American Community and family. As more Native

---

[31] Karl Eschbach, "The Enduring and Vanishing American Indian: American Indian Population Growth and Intermarriage in 1990," *Ethnic and Racial Studies* 18 (January 1995): 89–108.

[32] Doris Wilkinson, "Family Ethnicity in America," in Harriette Pipes McAdoo, *Family Ethnicity: Strengths in Diversity* (Newbury Park, CA: Sage, 1993): 44.

Americans move off the reservations to urban areas, values of time, sharing, cooperation, and responsibility for one another is likely to lessen. As more women are employed outside the home, traditional gender roles are likely to break down. As some members are successful in obtaining higher levels of education and income, the gap between the haves will contrast even more sharply with the have-nots who live in substandard housing and rely on government assistance just to survive. These and other changes will lead to continuing diversity, not only between tribal groups and families but within them as well.

SUMMARY

1. The Hispanic American population is made up of groups with ties to Mexico, Puerto Rico, Cuba, Central and South America, and other Spanish-speaking countries. Major differences exist among these groups in factors such as unemployment, income, and education. For example, the poverty rate for Hispanic Americans is about two-and-one-half times that of non-Hispanic Americans, with particularly high rates among Puerto Rican Americans.

2. Data on household types of Hispanic Americans have shown that numbers of married couples and female householders fall between those of the white and black populations. As with other groups, the proportion of female-headed families that live below the level of poverty is very high.

3. Mexican Americans are the largest subgroup of Hispanic Americans. Most are in the United States as legal immigrants, temporary workers, or illegal aliens. Families have traditionally been characterized by strong family ties as well as close linkages to *compadres,* or godparents.

4. Male and female roles in the Mexican American family, while still highly traditional, are exhibiting change. Particularly among professional women, marital decision making appears to be becoming more egalitarian, and the traditional *machismo* pattern among men seems to be lessening.

5. One of the most distinctive characteristics of Mexican American families today is their high fertility. Large family size combined with low levels of education and income make upward social mobility extremely difficult.

6. As with Hispanic Americans, Asian Americans are a very diverse collection of ethnic minorities. Chinese and Filipinos are the largest groups with sizable numbers of Japanese, Asian Indian, Korean, Vietnamese, Hawaiian, Laotian, Cambodian, Thai, Hmong, Samoan, and Guamanian as well.

7. Asian Americans, when compared with the other groups considered, have higher levels of education and median family incomes. Select groups, such as the Chinese, Japanese, and Filipinos, have high levels of family stability and low rates of divorce.

8. Rapid growth of the Asian American population stems primarily from immigration. With exceptions among the Pacific Islanders, teenage childbearing and births to unwed mothers among the Asian American groups is very low.

9. Native Americans or American Indians are made up of several hundred tribes. The majority reside in western regions of the United States but Native Americans can be found in any state and most cities. Compared to the other groups considered, Native Americans have a lower median age and shorter life expectancy.

10. Despite tribal differences, kinship ties, the role of the elders, and the sacredness of the land are values shared among most Native Americans. Adherence to many traditional values becomes more difficult as increasing numbers intermarry and move to urban areas.

11. Chapter 8 will expand on many of the ideas presented in this and the last chapter, particularly as related to income, poverty, and single-parent differences within and between groups. Our attention is directed in the next chapter to variations in family life-styles based on social class.

KEY TERMS AND TOPICS

Hispanic American family system p. 196

Social status characteristics p.196

Marital status p. 200

Mexican American families p. 201

Braceros p. 201

Familism p. 201

Compadres and *compadrazgo* p. 201

Machismo p. 203

Family size p. 204

Asian American family system p. 204

Social status characteristics p. 206

Marital/family patterns p. 207

Birth characteristics p. 208

Native American family system p. 210

Reservations, trust lands, and tribal designated statistical areas p. 210

Social status characteristics p. 211

Marital/family patterns p. 213

DISCUSSION QUESTIONS

1. Research this question: Why does such diversity exist among subgroups of Hispanic American families, including Mexicans, Puerto Ricans, Cubans, Central and South Americans, and others?

2. Discuss the traditional role of godparents in the lives of Mexican American families. How were they selected? What did they do?

3. Examine the unique role and status of the wife and mother in the Mexican American family. What special duties does she perform? Why does she have so many children? Why does she have a subordinate status to her husband?

4. Examine the role and status of the husband and father in the Mexican-American family. What are his primary responsibilities? Does the *machismo* pattern still exist? How might this concept influence behavior such as condom use?

5. How would you explain the higher levels of education and median family income among Asian Americans than among other groups considered?

6. Explain how the rapid growth in numbers of Asian Americans and Hispanic Americans differ from that of African Americans and Native Americans. Should policies, such as related to family planning and births or to numbers permitted to immigrate, be established and enforced?

7. Why are births to Asian American unmarried mothers, who were born in the United States, about three times as high as for mothers born elsewhere?

8. What images do you hold about Native Americans? Are they accurate? Were they obtained from personal experience, from formal schooling, or from the mass media?

9. It was suggested that one major factor in the Native American rapid population growth is due to a surge in persons who identify themselves as such. Explain. Why are more now claiming Native American roots?

10. Explain the low median age and shorter life expectancy among Native Americans.

FURTHER READINGS

Gelfand, Donald E. *Aging and Ethnicity.* New York: Springer Publishing Co., 1994. An investigation of the aging process among ethnic elderly with considerable data on ethnic families.

Kitano, Harry H. L., and Daniels, Roger. *Asian Americans: Emerging Minorities.* Englewood Cliffs, NJ: Prentice-Hall, 2nd ed., 1995. An excellent source detailing Asian immigration to the United States, including the Chinese before and after 1943, the Japanese before and after 1946, Filipinos, Asian Indians, Koreans, Pacific Islanders, and Southeast Asians.

Kunitz, Stephen J.; Levy, Jerrold E.; and collaborators. *Navajo Aging: The Transition from Family to Institutional Support.* Tucson: University of Arizona Press, 1991. An investigation of Navaho aging and the aged, with a particular focus on health and mortality and health care utilization.

Lamberly, Gontran, and Coll, Cynthia Garcia. *Puerto Rican Women and Children: Issues in Health, Growth, and Development.* New York: Plenum Press, 1994. A presentation of current knowledge and issues surrounding the health and development of Puerto Rican mothers and children living on the mainland of the United States.

Taylor, Ronald L. (ed.), *Minority Families in the United States: A Multicultural Perspective.* Englewood Cliffs, NJ: Prentice-Hall, 1994. Chapters are devoted to a range of minority families in the United States, including Mexican, Puerto Rican, Cuban, Chinese, Japanese, American Indian and others.

U.S. Bureau of the Census, *Current Population Reports,* Series P23-183, "Hispanic Americans Today" (Washington, DC: U.S. Government Printing Office, 1993). A total of 57 figures on Hispanic Americans covering everything from family composition to income and labor participation to housing and business ownership.

Vega, William A. "Hispanic Families in the 1980s: A Decade of Research." *Journal of Marriage and the Family* 52 (November 1990): 1015–1024. A literature review showing both the typical features of as well as the diversity in Hispanic families.

Williams, Norma. *The Mexican American Family: Tradition and Change.* Dix Hills, NY: General Hall, 1990. A look at changes in the extended and conjugal family arrangements in the Mexican American working and professional classes.

Zambrana, Ruth E. (ed.). *Understanding Latino Families: Scholarship, Policy, and Practice.* Thousand Oaks, CA: Sage, 1995. An integrated focus on the Hispanic/Latino family with particular attention devoted to Latino subgroups and a theoretical direction for the study of Latino families.

Chapter 8

Social-Class Variations in Family Life-Styles

- Meaning of Social Class
- Determination of Social Class
- Consequences of Social Class to Families
- Social Categories of Families
  - Wealthy families
  - Middle-class families
  - Blue-collar families
  - Families living in poverty
- Social Mobility: Changing Family Life-Styles
  - Likelihood of vertical social mobility
  - Extent of vertical social mobility
  - Consequences of social mobility
- Summary
- Key Terms and Topics
- Discussion Questions
- Further Readings

The discussions in the three previous chapters on Chinese, Swedish, African American, Hispanic American, Asian American, and Native American families included many aspects of social class. Among traditional Chinese families, for example, the life-styles of the gentry were radically different from those of the peasants. Among contemporary Chinese and Swedish families, class extremes have been diminished, but class and power distinctions still exist. Life-styles between two-parent and one-parent African American and Hispanic American families reflect different class levels within the larger American society.

In this chapter, the class dimension will be examined: what it means, how it is determined, and how families who comprise general class categories experience and express differing life-styles. The chapter will end with a discussion of family mobility—changing life-styles by moving from one class category to another.

MEANING OF SOCIAL CLASS

The concept of **social class** refers to an aggregate of individuals who occupy a broadly similar position on a scale of wealth, prestige, and power. As even the most untrained observer can note, some kinds of work, some styles of life, and some types of homes, automobiles, and dress are viewed as more prestigious than others. All persons, families, and societies differentiate some roles and positions as more important, more powerful, more privileged, more prestigious, and more highly rewarded than others. This differentiation in power, prestige, money, and the like results in inequality among persons and families and even racial and ethnic groups. The ranking of persons and groups in a hierarchy of social positions is referred to in sociology as **social stratification.** The term *stratification*, borrowed from geology, refers to an arrangement of different strata, or layers. *Social stratification* is the ranking of people into positions of equality and inequality.

Two of the theories described in Chapter 2, the **structural-functional** and the **conflict** theories, are particularly relevant to understanding social class and the stratification system. A structural-functional perspective views stratification as both an inevitable and a necessary feature of society. The assumption is that all societies have a wide range of tasks that need to be performed. These tasks are essential for the stability and maintenance of that society but carry different levels of prestige and rewards. Some individuals must collect garbage, repair plumbing, and assemble automobiles, while others must teach students, plan defense strategies, and perform heart surgery. Those tasks that require greater levels of skill and training are likely to be more highly rewarded. This unequal distribution of social rewards is defined as *functional* for society because it enables all roles and tasks to be completed, with those that demand the most scarce talents being performed by the most able and skilled persons.

For many years, this structural-functional perspective was the predominant one among sociologists, and for many, it remains so today. However, other people have questioned why some families are highly rewarded with inherited fortunes when they perform little of value to society; why film stars and athletes earn millions each year for doing work that is viewed as less important than that done by social workers, scientists, and even the president (who may not earn as much in a lifetime); and why poor families live in poverty from one generation to the next. Sociologists have also raised value-oriented questions about the justice of unequal rewards and the fairness of assignment by birth of certain groups to positions of low prestige, wealth, and power. An awareness of these and other inequities among persons and families led conflict theorists to reject the structural-functional view of a stratified society.

Conflict theorists believe that a stratified society leads to dissatisfaction, alienation, and exploitation, not stability and order. The differentiation of economic rewards led one of the classical theorists of nineteenth-century sociology, Karl Marx, to suggest that conflict would result in capitalist countries between those who have and those who have not; between those who control the means of production and those who serve as the instrument of production; between management and labor; between the bourgeoisie, who use capital, natural resources, and labor for profit, and the proletariat, who sell their labor to buy the products they produce.

Translated into family terms, conflict will likely occur between the families who own and control the wealth and means of production and the families who work for wages and produce the products or provide the services. Translated into gender terms, conflict may exist between the males (husbands), who are employed, who receive higher wages, and who are the order givers, and the females (wives), who are less likely to be employed, who receive lower wages, and who are the order takers.

DETERMINATION OF SOCIAL CLASS

The discussion presented thus far suggests that class is determined by examining who manages, oppresses, and controls in contrast to who is managed, oppressed, and controlled. Traditionally, class determination and categorization of both husband and wife were based on an examination of the husband's class identification. The results shown by Baxter in an analysis of the United States, Sweden, Norway, and Australia, suggest that even today, the husband's class location is a significant predictor of husband's and wife's class identifications with no significant differences among countries.[1] Others have argued that the employment and occupational prestige of the wife and other family members must be considered as well.[2]

Their argument is that given the increasing number of women in the paid labor force, the class-identification process will differ for men and women; thus,

[1] Janeen Baxter, "Is Husband's Class Enough? Class Location and Class Identity in the United States, Sweden, Norway, and Australia," *American Sociological Review* 59 (April 1994): 220–235.

[2] Yoshinori Kamo, Lynn M. Ries, Yvette M. Farmer, David G. Nickinovich, and Edgar F. Borgatta, "Status Attainment Revisited," *Research on Aging* 13 (June 1991): 124–143; and Robert Erikson and John H. Goldthorpe, "Individual or Family? Results from Two Approaches to Class Assignment," *Acta Sociologica* 35 (1992): 95–105.

U.S. Diversity: What Class Are You?

Some 1,225 respondents in the United States were surveyed and asked if they consider themselves to be rich, upper income, middle income, lower income, or poor. How did they respond?

Almost 60 percent said "middle income." Even among those with high incomes, relatively few described themselves as "rich" and only 7 percent as "upper income."

While most Americans would like to be rich, most don't think they presently are or ever will be. However, they were quite willing to apply the label to others. The respondents described 21 percent of all Americans as "rich" and 33 percent as "poor." The less money a respondent made, the more he or she thought other people were rich.

What constitutes "rich"? To some respondents, particularly those who didn't earn much money themselves, making $50,000 a year or more qualified one as rich. To others, especially those with high incomes, a person needed to earn more than $1,000,000 a year to be rich. The most frequent response was that it takes an annual income of $100,000 or more to be rich.

Source: George Gallup, Jr., and Frank Newport, "Americans Widely Disagree on What Constitutes 'Rich,'" *Gallup Poll Monthly* 298 (July 1990): 28–29.

be gender specific.[3] Conclusions from research on the effects of workplace and occupational variables asserted that:

1. Working wives do not simply borrow class identification from their husbands. Work experiences are a core part of the class-identification process of employed wives, just as is true for husbands.

2. The workplace and occupational variables related to class identification differ for men and women, without any overlap. For men, the identification variables are whether they do manual or nonmanual work and whether they are subordinated in a chain of command. For women, the identification variables are work in a female occupation, self-employment, and membership in unions. The result is that a middle- or working-class identification differs for a man and a woman.

3. The class identification of men is much more based on the workplace than the class identification of women, which is more occupationally based. Factors such as type of work done and place in the chain of command shape men's classifications; factors such as working in a female-oriented occupation, being self-employed, and being a union member shape women's.[4]

---

[3] Randall Collins, "Women and Men in the Class Structure," *Journal of Family Issues* 9 (March 1988): 27–50; and Ida Harper Simpson, David Stark, and Robert A. Jackson, "Class Identification Processes of Married, Working Men and Women," *American Sociological Review* 53 (April 1988): 284–293.

[4] Simpson et. al., op. cit., pp. 284–293.

These gender-specific variables were not used in earlier studies. In those studies, class identification was determined by taking one or several prestige indicators (occupation, income, education, wealth, self-ranking, etc.), placing them on a continuum from high to low, and dividing them into any number of categories or strata. The studies of Middletown (Muncie, Indiana), which are among the most famous community studies in sociology, used two classes: the business class and the working class.[5] Most people think in terms of three classes: upper, middle, and lower. The classic work by August Hollingshead, entitled *Elmtown's Youth*, subdivided the community into five classes: upper, upper middle, lower middle, upper lower, and lower lower.[6]

If social-class or -stratification systems represent systems of inequality, who makes the objective determination that there are two, five, or seventeen classes of strata? Perhaps few distinct and separate strata exist at all; rather, perhaps there is a continuum of inequalities of wealth, income, prestige, power, age, sex, and race. What is clear is that differences exist between men and women and among families in income and spending power, in owning and serving production processes, in recognizing wealth and power, and in the consequences these differences have.

CONSEQUENCES OF SOCIAL CLASS TO FAMILIES

The real significance of class structure stems from some of its consequences. In addition to influencing one's chances to live (including the likelihood of being born in the first place), to live through the first year, and to reach retirement, social class influences one's early socialization, role expectations and role projections, values, standards of appropriate behavior, and likelihood of mental illness. In addition, class affects educational opportunities (type of education available, the motivation to get it, the likelihood of doing so) and outcomes (the ends for which education is meant). Dropout rates, scores on intelligence tests, grades, occupational/vocational aspirations, and almost all other factors related to education are also related to class. Most significantly, social class both determines and results in important differences in influence, power, and opportunities.

Similar consequences of class hold true for marriages and families. Social class affects that age at which one is likely to marry, the success of that marriage, the meanings attached to sexual behavior, the size of family, the recreation engaged in, the type of food eaten, the discipline and care given to children, sleeping arrangements, and contraceptive use. Irrespective of race, ethnicity, or gender, differences in behaviors are evident at varying class levels.

Although it is true that no sharply defined boundaries separate one class from another, many normal life experiences are highly similar among people who share

---

[5] Robert S. Lynd and Helen Merrell Lynd, *Middletown* New York: Harcourt, Brace and World, 1939); Robert S. Lynd and Helen Merrell Lynd. *Middletown in Transition* (New York: Harcourt, Brace and World, 1937); and Theodore Caplow et al., *Middletown Families* (New York: Bantam Books, 1982).

[6] August B. Hollingshead, *Elmtown's Youth* (New York: Wiley, 1949).

a class subculture. For example, where polygyny is practiced, men of high social or economic position are most likely to have a number of wives. In the United States, the divorce rate goes up as class level goes down (with the exception of professional women). The birthrate increases as the social-class level drops. Upper-social-strata young persons are granted less freedom of choice of mates than are lower-social-strata persons. In the Western world, particularly, the age of men at marriage rises with class position. If class lines are crossed in marriage, the woman is more likely to be upwardly mobile (hypergamy). Higher-social-strata couples are more likely to use contraceptives than are lower-social-strata couples.

One could continue indefinitely with a list of family variables that is highly related to class position. This list is not meant to be complete nor has each relationship been established to hold true cross-culturally. The key point is that, within a culture as well as between cultures, significant regularities occur between a family's attitude and behavior patterns and the class position that that family occupies.

SOCIAL CATEGORIES OF FAMILIES

Wealthy families

Wealthy families have been identified as the *very rich*, the *upper class*, and the *ruling class*. Compared to other categories of families, relatively little recent data are available on the wealthy. This group of families, while small in number relative to other groups, is large in power and influence. They possess enormous economic and social resources. They have a network of affiliations on important boards in banking, insurance, and manufacturing. The wealthy are the elite who own and control the means of production and make the rules for workers to follow.

The family structure of the very rich is interesting. Families are described by researchers as extremely lineal and concerned with who they are, rather than what they do. They are quite ancestor-oriented and conscious of the boundaries that separate the "best" families from the others. Families are obviously the units within which wealth is accumulated and transmitted.

Women in the wealthy class serve as "gatekeepers" of many of the institutions of the very rich. They launch children, serve as board members at private schools, run social and service clubs, and facilitate marriage pools through events such as debuts and charity functions. Susan Ostrander conducted interviews with thirty-six upper-class women and found that they held a clear preference for being with people like themselves (such as through private and exclusive clubs, by invitation only), felt a sense of being better than other people (materially, morally, and in terms of volunteer work and contributions to the community), and conveyed an awareness that people define and judge them by who they are rather than by what they do.[7]

---

[7] Susan A. Ostrander, *Women of the Upper Class* (Philadelphia: Temple University Press, 1984).

Global Diversity: Can You Afford Both a Querida and a Wife?

Polygyny is not permissible for the Christian Filipino male, but those who can afford it have a *querida.* In the Philippines, the querida system involves a married man, usually of higher status, seeing, supporting, and possibly having children by a woman other than his wife. While a mistress relationship is frowned upon, the civil code provides for the maintenance of his illegitimate children.

The double standard is seen in that equal privileges do not exist for the wife. The husband can separate from the wife for adultery on her part, but she cannot do likewise. Nor can the wife bring an action for legal separation against the husband unless he maintains his mistress in the same dwelling as his legitimate wife. The wife can, of course, simply leave him or refuse to cohabit, which would be a separation de facto. But doing so would simply create additional problems of support and custody of the children.

The frequency of this keeping a mistress, "second wife" (not legally), or querida is unknown. But an informal survey of priests from twenty-two dioceses suggested that the percentage of men with queridas is about 1 or 2, although, in certain urban social strata, it is probably much higher.

The querida often represents a serious threat to a wife and children in diminishing their man's affection and support. Thus, while a wife may know about her husband's querida, she may pretend not to. As long as the man adopts some measure of self-control and fidelity, his morality is secure and his role adequately discharged. The wife, in turn, avidly participates in religious life and, in effect, prays for two: Her piety supposedly makes up for both her own and her husband's failings.

Ostrander noted that these wives, like traditional wives in other social classes, held a subordinate position to their husbands, had an unequal voice in family decisions, and maintained sole responsibility for home and family. But at this class level, women did not perform the nitty-gritty tasks of housework and child care. Women of other races and classes did such work for them. At this class level, women did not need—economically, personally, or socially—to seek paid work outside the home. At this class level, women's accommodative and supportive function to their husbands enabled the men to manage the economic and political affairs of society and to perpetuate the dominance of the upper class.

Without doubt, the upper class is very gender segregated. Interestingly, this gender separation is an accepted fact, virtually unchallenged by upper-class women. Why? Ostrander suggested that perhaps the gains of *gender* equality are not enough to balance the losses of *class* equality.

By any measure, this category of wealthy persons is the smallest numerically of all social classes in the United States but has the highest prestige and influence. Since the wealthy are at the very top of the class hierarchy, the members maintain their positions by preserving symbols of status, such as genealogies, biographies of ancestors, heirlooms, and records of ancestral achievement. The wealthy also maintain their position by carefully controlling the marriage choices of their children.

Middle-class families

When most Americans are asked to what class they belong, they will likely respond "middle" (see "What Class Are You?" box, p. 222). Relatively few people can honestly respond "wealthy," and few people want to admit to being "poor," even if it's true. Furthermore, a response of "middle class" generally carries positive connotations, implying that, while some people occupy higher occupational statuses and more prestigious positions, other people obviously occupy lower positions.

Middle-class families form the linkage between powerful, wealthy families and the working-class, less powerful, poorer families. For those residing in the middle position, the possibilities exist of moving upward as well as downward. Perhaps consequentially, the middle class is very conscious of social values, involved in the major issues brought on by social change, and relatively rigid in moral standards. Some middle-class families closely resemble wealthy families in their economic status and degree of influence. Other middle-class families vary little from blue-collar workers in terms of family patterns. Thus, analysis of the middle class as a distinct family type or life-style is extremely difficult and will produce highly ambiguous results.

From a Marxian perspective, the middle class is composed of the **bourgeoisie,** those people who own small amounts of productive resources and have control over their working conditions in ways not found among the **proletariat,** those working-class people who work for wages. Today, the term *middle class* is more likely to refer to people employed as professionals or corporate and government bureaucrats. In Middletown, this group was categorized as the business class: those who made their living by selling or promoting ideas and by arranging the goods and services produced by the working class. They wore suits to their jobs in offices, banks, and businesses.[8]

Middle-class families are likely to receive salaries rather than hourly wages, which are prevalent among blue-collar and working-class families. This more stable income resource base appears to be one key factor in differentiating the middle class from those below it. With this stable resource base is likely to come a range of amenities that lessen the shock of unanticipated crisis events: medical coverage, pension and retirement plans, bank credit, investment income, and the like. Higher levels of income and greater job security also allow for some discretionary spending and leisure activities.

Given these opportunities for a stable resource base, high levels of education, and professional careers, value systems are promoted among the middle class that

---

[8] Caplow et al., *Middletown Families*, p. 86.

emphasize personal autonomy and the ability to develop and carry out rational plans. This ability to control and logically plan one's own life seems to be highly characteristic of the middle class and may partially explain the belief of many members that people of all classes should be able to do likewise.

Beliefs in self-determination and autonomy may also explain why employed professional women in the middle class tend to express reactions against full-time mothering and give work a higher priority in their lives.[9] In both the workplace and the home, these women have structural advantages, such as greater job flexibility and available child care. In contrast, working-class women experience more structural disadvantages (limited family income, inadequate child care, inflexible jobs), such that family roles must be given higher priority. Working-class women are more likely to enjoy full-time motherhood and to give family roles higher priority than work roles.

The nuclear family of the middle class espouses the ideal of equality between husband and wife and seems to be an important indicator of marital conflict if not shared. In contrast, for working-class wives, a more consistent indicator of frequency of marital conflicts is not equity but the division of feminine tasks. In other words, for a working-class wife, conflict is avoided when she does "the women's work" whereas for a middle-class wife conflict arises when her husband is not taking on, in her view, his "fair share" of family work.[10]

A widely studied area showing differences between the middle class and those below them is in parent/child relations and childrearing practices. About thirty-five years ago, Melvin Kohn suggested that, in terms of discipline, middle-class parents were more likely to use reason, verbal threats, or withdrawal of rewards to punish a child or solicit the child's compliance.[11] In contrast, blue-collar parents were more likely to rely on physical punishment. Kohn's reasoning was that, by virtue of experiencing different conditions of life, members of different social classes come to see the world differently and to develop different conceptions of social reality and desirable personality characteristics as well as different aspirations. The middle class (white-collar occupations), in contrast with the lower class (blue-collar occupations), requires the individual to (1) deal more with the manipulation of ideas, symbols, and interpersonal relations; (2) be involved in work that is more complex and requires great flexibility, thought, and judgment; and (3) be less closely supervised. From these occupational differences come different values, which are reflected in patterns of discipline. Middle-class values are likely to include self-direction, freedom, individualism, initiative, creativity, and self-actualization. Thus, parents encourage in their children *internal* standards, such as

---

[9] Beverly H. Burris, "Employed Mothers: The Impact of Class and Marital Status on the Prioritizing of Family and Work," *Social Science Quarterly* 72 (March 1991): 50–66.

[10] Maureen Perry-Jenkins and Karen Folk, "Class, Couples, and Conflict: Effects of the Division of Labor on Assessments of Marriage in Dual-Earner Families," *Journal of Marriage and the Family* 56 (February 1994): 165–180.

[11] Melvin Kohn, "Social Class and Parent-Child Relationships: An Interpretation," *American Journal of Sociology* 68 (January 1963): 471–480; and Melvin Kohn, *Class and Conformity* (Homewood, IL: Dorsey, 1969).

consideration, curiosity, and self-control. Discipline is based on the parents' interpretation of a child's motive for a particular act.[12]

Kohn's ideas in regard to parent/child interaction by social class have received widespread attention, and attempts have been made at extension and replication. Most studies have found that, since Kohn's original survey in the early 1960s, clear trends have existed in self-direction values among middle-class parents and that social class is a primary differentiation in childrearing values. Even studies done outside the United States (such as in Germany and the Netherlands) tend to confirm the effect of social class on childhood socialization; the middle-class tendency is to use psychological rather than physical approaches to discipline.[13] This class effect appears to be due largely to the higher level of educational attainment of middle-class parents.

Blue-collar families

Blue-collar, or working-class, families are made up of individuals classified in the U.S. Bureau of Census as employed in (1) precision production, craft, and repair; (2) machine operating, assembling, and inspecting; (3) transportation and material moving; and (4) handling, equipment cleaning, helping, and laboring. Service jobs are generally also classified as blue-collar occupations. Most women fit into this categorization.

Randall Collins argued that most women are either white-collar working class or blue-collar working class because, in terms of the power of the position, women are order takers, not order givers.[14] Women in paid employment as secretaries, clerks, retail sales personnel, operators of machines, and the like are order takers. Even nurses, Collins claimed, in spite of their professional classification, tend to be assistants (order takers) to physicians (order givers). Ironically, women married to middle-class men, who are assumed to take their husbands' class positions, still provide the services of cooking, cleaning, and emotional support for men and children.

The job of a blue-collar worker generally requires some sort of manual skill. The "elite" of the blue-collar workers—usually male electricians, plumbers, and highly skilled operators—frequently earn more than members of the middle class. For example, public school teachers, generally assigned to the middle class, are likely to average $3,000 to $6,000 a year less than certain blue-collar workers.

---

[12] In contrast, lower-class or blue-collar workers deal more with the manipulation of physical objects, require less interpersonal skill, have more standardization of work, and are more closely supervised. This leads to values of conformity to external standards such as orderliness, neatness, and obedience. Discipline is based on the consequences of the child's behavior rather than on the interpretation of motive for the behavior.

[13] Robert C. Williamson, "A Partial Replication of the Kohn-Gecas Nye Thesis in a German Sample," *Journal of Marriage and the Family* 46 (November 1984): 971–979; and Maja Dekovic and Jan R. M. Gerris, "Parental Reasoning Complexity, Social Class, and Child-Rearing Behaviors," *Journal of Marriage and the Family* 54 (August 1992): 675–685.

[14] Randall Collins, "Women and Men in the Class Structure," *Journal of Family Issues* 9 (March 1988): 27–50.

Blue-collar families tend to conform closely to traditional images of husband and wife roles, such that the husband is the principal provider and final authority. Since work is highly influenced by swings in the business climate, families often suffer great hardship during economic downturns.

Formal education beyond a high school or trade school is not generally required to learn the manual skills necessary for members of the working class. Physical health is quite crucial to blue-collar workers, since many jobs depend on the ability to perform physical labor. Blue-collar groups are often represented by trade unions. A great amount of faith is placed in the union to protect workers from those above them in the hierarchy, to provide help with family medical expenses, and to prevent dismissal.

Members of the working class are almost completely dependent on the swings of the business cycle in the U.S. wage/price/profits system; thus, the economic stability enjoyed by middle-class families is less prevalent among working-class families. Most income is received from wages earned by the hour, the piece, the day, or the week. To supplement the incomes of husbands, many wives are employed outside the home. Unlike a sizable proportion of working wives from the middle class, blue-collar wives are more likely to work out of economic necessity than desire for a career.

The strains associated with life's uncertainties for members of the working class lead to a high degree of family instability. Divorce occurs with greater frequency among this class group than among any of the higher income, education, or occupational groups.

Members of the blue-collar family, more than any other, conform to the traditional roles of husband and wife. The husband's role is to be a good provider, and as the primary wage earner, he is the final authority and disciplinarian. The wife's role is to do the housework and rear the children; she is often employed, too. If the family is broken by divorce or separation, the children will remain with the mother. It is expected that the wife will remain faithful to her husband as long as he remains faithful to her. If these obligations are broken, the offended party is likely to seek separation or divorce.

The role of children is definitely subordinate to that of parents. Unlike middle-class parents, who stress that children stay in school and who make major sacrifices to keep them there (including college), working-class parents are more likely to expect that children will leave school after fulfilling the minimum legal requirements or, at most, after completing high school. Boys and girls are taught to be self-sufficient, to be tough-minded, and to be able to compete for personal rights and privileges. Working-class boys have heterosexual experiences earlier and have intercourse more frequently than do boys from middle-class families. Working-class girls marry early, often because of premarital pregnancy. While these girls may desire love, they get babies.

Mirra Komarovsky's book *Blue Collar Marriage*, now more than thirty-five years old, offered a vivid glimpse into the lives of these families.[15] Using a case-study approach, fifty-eight "stable" families with children were interviewed. The respondents were chosen from a community the author called *Glenton*.

Husbands and wives in Glenton knew what was expected of them and generally agreed about marital ideals. However, role consensus (the clarity of role definition) was not necessarily suited to the conditions of life under which Glenton families had to live. Transitions to new roles were often hindered by circumstances such as the poverty of some young couples; the poor occupational adjustment of young, unskilled workers; and the need to reside in the parental home after marriage. The following illustration of a thirty-two-year-old husband, taken from

---

[15] Mirra Komarovsky, *Blue Collar Marriage* (New York: Random House, 1962).

Komarovsky's book, illustrates how unfavorable these circumstances can be. This quote might well have come from a blue-collar worker in the 1990s.

> You keep thinking you can do almost anything and get away with anything when you're still young. There had been a couple of big layoffs when we got married, but work was still pretty good and I thought I could do anything and that I was going places and I was going to be somebody. Nothing was good enough for my wife, and we didn't think nothing of charge accounts and buying things. We hadn't been married long and I got my first layoff. They said I was young. They laid off others and they said they was old. We couldn't keep up our payments on the furniture, and we lost every stick of it, and she was pregnant. …We went and stayed at her ma's for a few days, and then up to my ma's for a while. …We must have stayed there about a month while I was looking for work and then I got it, and then we moved out again. And then this time, we got one thing by paying the whole money on it that we borrowed the money for. We borrowed it from people, and not the bank. And we bought a bed. We figured we could sit on that, and we had our cooking pots and could eat out of them. But we didn't want to think of sleeping on the floor anymore. It would have been alright if it was summer and she wasn't pregnant.[16]

The majority of men and women Komarovsky interviewed saw the principal marital ties as sexual union, complementary tasks, and mutual devotion. Within the working class, functions of modern marriage such as friendship and sharing hurts, worries, and dreams with one's spouse are not fulfilled.

Families living in poverty

How are figures on poverty derived? How is it determined whether a family lives below the poverty level? Cannot a three-person family live on much less than a seven-person family? Obviously, the small family can live on less than the large one and family size is a key factor in determining the poverty threshold.

The **poverty index,** developed by the Social Security Administration, is based solely on money income and does not reflect noncash assistance or government benefits, such as food stamps, Medicaid, or public housing. The poverty index is based on the Department of Agriculture's Economy Food Plan and reflects the different consumption requirements based on family size and composition. Operating on the assumption that a family of three or more persons spends approximately one-third of their income on food, the poverty level is set at three times the cost of the Economy Food Plan.

---

[16] Ibid., p. 47. Reprinted by permission.

Table 8-1

Weighted average poverty thresholds: 1993

Size of family unit	Poverty threshold
1 person (unrelated individual)	$7,363
Under 65 years	7,518
65 years and over	6,930
2 persons	9,414
Householder under 65 years	9,728
Householder 65 years and over	8,740
3 persons	11,522
4 persons	14,763
5 persons	17,449
6 persons	19,718
7 persons	22,383
8 persons	24,838
9 persons or more	29,529

Source: U.S. Bureau of the Census, *Statistical Abstract of the United States: 1995,* 115th ed.
(Washington, DC: U.S. Government Printing Office, 1995), no. 746, p. 481.

Poverty thresholds are updated every year to reflect changes in the Consumer Price Index. Thus, as is illustrated in Table 8-1, the average poverty threshold for a family of four in 1993 was $14,763. For one person, it was $7,363, and for a family of eight, it was $24,838.

According to data supplied by the U.S. Bureau of the Census, in 1993, 39.3 million persons (15.1 percent) in the United States lived below the poverty level.[17] This included 8.4 million families, or 12.3 percent of all families. In short, one in every eight families in the United States was classified as having an income below the poverty level.

In 1992, the poverty rate for white families was 9.1 percent compared to 11.0 percent for Asian families, 26.2 percent for Hispanic-origin families and 30.9 percent for black families. Among families with a female householder with no husband present, the percentages increased to 22.3 for Asian families, 28.6 for white families, 48.8 for Hispanic-origin families, and 49.8 for black families. The single-parent family is discussed later in this chapter. The female-headed, single-parent family is one important aspect of the feminization of poverty.

[17] U.S. Bureau of the Census, *Statistical Abstract of the United States: 1995,* 115th ed. (Washington, DC: U.S. Government Printing Office, 1995), nos. 749 and 752, pp. 482 and 484.

Figure 8-1
Poverty rates for persons and families with selected characteristics: 1992

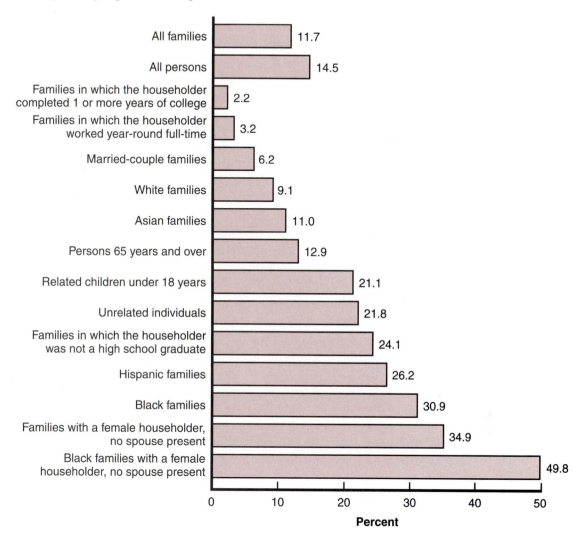

Source: U.S. Bureau of the Census, *Current Population Reports,* Series P60-185, "Poverty in the United States: 1992" (Washington, DC: U.S. Government Printing Office, 1993), Tables 1, 2, 11, and 19, pp. 1, 3, 71, and 113; Asian data is from *Current Population Reports,* P20-459, Table 8, p. 38.

Feminization of poverty

A look at sex differences in poverty has provided strong evidence that the feminization of poverty is not a myth. In a study of the gender poverty gap in eight
industrialized countries, only Sweden revealed poverty rates of men to be higher
than those of women. The key to the low gender poverty ratio in Sweden is
employment where men and women have very similar rates of labor force partic-

ipation. Gender differences were slight in Italy, with high rates of marriage being the key, and in the Netherlands, where a generous welfare system appears to be the key. The United States led all eight countries in both the rate of poverty as well as in the male-female difference. In all countries with large gender-poverty differences, employment and parenthood (including single parenthood) were the most important factors.[18]

In the United States, women's poverty rates have increased relative to men's across all age groups and among blacks and Hispanics as well as whites. Much of this increase is due to changes in parental obligations. Women more than men have been likely to live with children and to have greater parental responsibilities, both in terms of finances and domestic labor. This situation does not seem to be improving. Many women today must rely on their own incomes or on social welfare to support themselves and their children. Doing so is difficult, as the jobs that are available are low-paying and the public benefits to single mothers have declined.

A variety of interwoven demographic and socioeconomic trends are evident in the feminization of poverty. First is the trend just mentioned: the female-headed family where a woman lives independently and has custody and primary responsibility for her dependent children. A second trend, related to the first, is a decreasing marriage rate and a continuing high divorce rate. A third trend is the rise in teen and young parenting, where economic self-sufficiency is difficult. Fourth, income inequality remains prevalent, such that women earn much less than their male counterparts in the labor market. A fifth trend is the inadequate level of personal and child support available from absent husbands, social assistance, and other programs.

It is clear that poverty is linked to family structure. For example, an analysis of national data indicated that (1) the income of the poorest children declined absolutely in the 1980s while growing rapidly among the richest children, and (2) changes in family structure—namely, increases in the numbers of single parents and female-headed families—have exacerbated the decline in the economic status of children.[19] Changing family structure has accounted for nearly 50 percent of the increase in child poverty rates since 1980. Racial divergence in family structure has exacerbated the persistent black/white differences in children's economic status; blacks are far more likely to live in poverty. Changing family size differentials between poor and nonpoor households have also increased child poverty rates: the poor have more children. Changes in the family, such as greater freedom of sexual expression and decisions to enter and exit marital and nonmarital relationships, may have been partly achieved at the expense of children's well-being.

---

[18] Lynne M. Casper, Sara S. McLanahan and Irwin Garfinkel, "The Gender-Poverty Gap: What We Can Learn From Other Countries," *American Sociological Review* 59 (August 1994): 594–605; and Marjorie E. Starrels, Sally Bould, and Leon J. Nichols, "The Feminization of Poverty in the United States: Gender, Race, Ethnicity, and Family Factors," *Journal of Family Issues* 15 (December 1994): 590–607.

[19] Daniel T. Lichter and David J. Eggebeen, "Rich Kids, Poor Kids: Changing Income Inequality among American Children," *Social Forces* 71 (March 1993): 761–780; and David J. Eggebeen and Daniel T. Lichter, "Race, Family Structure, and Changing Poverty among American Children," *American Sociological Review* 56 (December 1991): 801–817.

Poverty and public assistance

As one might expect, a decrease in the well-being of children leads to an increase in the need for **public assistance.** And the greatest amount of public assistance does go to households below the poverty level. In 1992:

- 81.0 percent of the families below the poverty level lived in households that received means-tested assistance[20] (compared to 24.1 percent of all families—including those in poverty).
- 63.1 percent of the families in poverty included one or more members receiving Medicare (compared to 15.9 percent of all families).
- 58.9 percent of the families in poverty received food stamps (compared to 10.9 percent of all families).
- 20.1 percent of those in poverty lived in public or subsidized housing (compared to 4.2 percent of all families).[21]

Speculation about public assistance often takes the position that the majority of welfare recipients have been raised in households that also received welfare, that is, welfare continues from one generation to the next. Data from a large national representative sample revealed that three-quarters of welfare recipients did not grow up in households that received welfare.[22] On the other hand, those who were raised in households that received welfare were more likely to receive welfare when they became adults. The authors suggest that this intergenerational connection has little to do with welfare per se but has much to do with economic class. Children coming from families who have relied on welfare are generally coming from lower-income families. As a result, parents are limited financially in terms of the opportunities and resources they can offer their children.

Clearly, cuts in governmental food, housing, and health benefits hit those living below the poverty level the hardest and will likely increase the need for assistance across generations. Yet, in the mid-1990s, the United States House of Representatives had a "Contract with America" that aimed to decrease the national debt. There was no emphasis on getting persons and families out of poverty but rather on getting people and families off welfare. An attempt to increase the minimum wage was defeated and cuts in spending for educational and training programs were proposed. This was in spite of national data showing that higher wages for those working as well as investments in education are two very important factors in getting people off welfare and on to economic independence.[23]

---

[20] Means-tested assistance is that provided to recipients who have demonstrated need, namely, that they lack the means to support themselves.

[21] U.S. Bureau of the Census, *Current Population Reports,* Series P60-185, "Poverty in the United States: 1992." (U.S. Government Printing Office, Washington, DC, 1993), Table F, p. xviii.

[22] Mark R. Rank and Li-Chen Cheng, "Welfare Use Across Generations: How Important Are the Ties That Bind?" *Journal of Marriage and the Family* 57 (August 1995): 673–684.

[23] Kathleen Mullan Harris, "Work and Welfare Among Single Mothers in Poverty," *American Journal of Sociology* 99 (September 1993): 317–352.

News Item: Welfare Reform

Leslie Winner, a Democratic member of the North Carolina senate, wrote a column for the *Charlotte Observer* (July 5, 1995) about the political debate surrounding welfare reform. She makes the argument that almost all welfare reform advocates agree that:

- welfare dependency is bad for the recipients, their children, and society.
- it is not good for children to be the parents of babies.
- men who father children should support them.

She argues as well that many critical questions underlie the debate over reform. Welfare reform advocates disagree about:

- the goal of welfare reform. Is it to get people off welfare or to get them out of poverty? Even a full-time minimum wage job grosses only about $8,800 a year and carries few benefits.
- the care of children. To what extent are we willing to punish children because their parents don't conform to society's expectations? Two-thirds of welfare recipients are children.
- how best to invest taxpayers' money. Are we willing to invest in people to promote self-sufficiency, or is our primary goal to save money?
- the role of government toward families and the poor. Is it a government responsibility to assure that families have food and a roof over their heads or is that the role of religious organizations and private charities?

State Senator Winner says she is guided by two primary goals.

1. Proposals should be designed to lead welfare recipients to long-term economic self-sufficiency, and
2. The proposals must be cycle-breaking. They must make it more likely that the next generation will grow up healthy and productive, less likely to have babies too young, and more likely to be self-sufficient.

Should these governmental cutting efforts and actions be of concern? Is it not true that **welfare** and other government "handouts" simply increase dependency and breed additional poverty? This is a perspective that goes beyond "blaming the victim," the poor person, to "blaming the program." This argument suggests that welfare benefits and government programs simply make living in poverty a meaningful option for the poor, thus increasing poverty, maintaining dependency, and decreasing the need for self-support or employment.

Strong evidence has defied such arguments. Kathryn Edin contended that the welfare system actually prohibits dependence by paying too little to make this possible. The "welfare trap" is less one of behavioral dependency than one of economic survival. In Edin's words:

In a society where single mothers must provide financially for their children, where women are economically marginalized into unreliable jobs that pay little more than the minimum wage, where child-support is inadequate or nonexistent, and where day-care costs and health insurance (usually not provided by employers) are unaffordable for most, it should surprise no one that half the mothers supporting children on their own choose welfare over reported work.[24]

The obvious solution to the feminization of poverty is to increase income. But how?[25] This may be achieved by either expanding benefits or increasing income. Given federal and state budget deficits and shortfalls, it is more likely that benefits will be reduced rather than expanded. And winning the lottery or marrying a wealthy spouse are not likely means of increasing income. Realistic solutions include jobs and employment but employment that pays well enough to lift the family and the children within it out of poverty.

Most people believe that mothers in poverty and on welfare should work. About one-third of welfare mothers are working, and half of all single mothers have some contact with the labor market. But national data reveal that only very large and unrealistic increases in maternal employment would significantly reduce child poverty rates.[26] The solution to the poverty problems reside not only in encouraging parent work but in creating jobs that pay a family wage. The "welfare trap" is not one of dependency but one where welfare pays better than low-wage work. Thus it is essential that those who do work can earn a living wage, can be secure in their jobs, and can avoid future pregnancies and births. This means removing barriers to employment by assuring affordable child care, health insurance coverage, fair and favorable tax policies, child-support payments, and the like.

Do women on welfare have more children to receive more benefits? The idea that women receiving governmental assistance have a high fertility rate is often implicitly accepted by social and policy analysts. Such beliefs are simply not supported. In fact, Mark Rank found that women on welfare have a rate of fertility considerably below that of women in the general population. Furthermore, the longer a woman remains on welfare, the less likely she is to give birth.[27] The women themselves suggested that their financial and social situation is not conducive to having more children. The economic, social, and psychological costs of becoming pregnant and having a child are perceived as clearly outweighing the benefits. Given these findings, one could ponder the economic, social, and psychological implications of formulating policy, as many states have done, that eliminates public funding for pregnant women (particularly those in poverty) to obtain abortions.

---

[24] Kathryn Edin, "Surviving the Welfare System: How AFDC Recipients Make Ends Meet in Chicago," *Social Problems* 38 (November 1991): 462–474.

[25] See Alvin L. Schorr, "Ending Poverty," *American Behavioral Scientist* 35 (January/February 1992): 332–339; and Catherine S. Chilman, "Working Poor Families: Trends, Causes, Effects, and Suggested Policies," *Family Relations* 40 (April 1991): 191–198.

[26] Daniel T. Lichter and David J. Eggebeen, "The Effect of Parental Employment on Child Poverty," *Journal of Marriage and the Family* 56 (August 1994): 633–645.

[27] Mark P. Rank, "Fertility among Women on Welfare: Incidence and Determinants," *American Sociological Review* 54 (April 1989): 296–304.

Survival of families in poverty

Households and family life are unstable among people who are poor. In human terms, not only do the poor pay more, but they also share more, as well. One national study of African Americans found both family and friends to be important sources of assistance.[28] Stack's monograph of more than twenty years ago, which looked at strategies of survival in a black community, provided vivid descriptions of the cliché "What goes round comes round."[29] That is, clothing, furniture, food, appliances, money, and kids are shared among individuals and households. People give what they can and take what they need.

These exchange patterns result in a **fictive kinship**, by which friends are turned into family. The swapping of goods and services results not merely in the norms of reciprocity that seem prevalent in most social exchanges but also in stable friendships that pattern those of kin. As Stack found:

> Non-kin who live up to one another's expectations express elaborate vows of friendship and conduct their social relations within the idiom of kinship. Exchange behavior between those friends "going for kin" is identical to exchange behavior between close kin.[30]

Poverty in black, white, Hispanic American, Asian American, and Native American families is directly linked to unemployment and underemployment; since employment is irregular, income is irregular. Thus, a considerable amount of insecurity exists in regard to food, clothing, shelter, transportation, and other essential items. Children may be forced or encouraged to contribute to the financial needs of the family, and few remain in school beyond the minimum legal age. These conditions contribute to and are highly related to other concerns. For example, families in poverty have the highest rates of divorce, psychoses, and physical disabilities; the least amount of dental and health care; the largest proportion of people on public welfare; the greatest rejection rate from the armed services; the highest crime rate; the largest number of children; the highest rate of venereal disease; the most unemployment; and, as perceived by many middle-class persons, "the most of the worst."

The majority of persons and families who live below the level of poverty typically do so for intermittent periods. Researchers at the Survey Research Center at the University of Michigan found that, over a fifteen-year period, children had frequent transitions in and out of poverty.[31] Although about one-third of the chil-

---

28 Robert Joseph Taylor, Linda M. Chatters, and Vickie M. Mays, "Parents, Children, Siblings, In-laws, and Non-Kin as Sources of Emergency Assistance to Black Americans," *Family Relations* 37 (July 1988): 298–304; and Linda M. Chatters, Robert Joseph Taylor, and Harold W. Neighbors, "Size of Informal Helper Networks Mobilized during a Serious Personal Problem among Black Americans," *Journal of Marriage and the Family* 51 (August 1989): 667–676.

29 Carol B. Stack, *All Our Kin: Strategies for Survival in a Black Community* (New York: Harper & Row, 1974), Chapter 3, pp. 32–44.

30 Ibid., p. 40.

31 Greg J. Duncan and Willard L. Rodgers, "Longitudinal Aspects of Childhood Poverty," *Journal of Marriage and the Family* 50 (November 1988): 1007–1021.

Case Example:
Survival on Public Assistance

Dal is a 30-year-old single mother of four children between the ages of 6 and 12. She has been off and on AFDC several times since age 18 but has been on steadily for the past five years. While married for several of those years, her husband got involved in drugs and was not financially or emotionally responsible to her or the children.

According to Dal, public assistance provided the help she needed to raise her children and serve as a stepping-stone for her to eventually become financially able to manage on her own. How was this done? As she said:

"Finances were always a problem, but thanks to AFDC we were always able to have a home, food, and clothes. I knew that I was poor but seldom felt totally helpless. I was able to get the things the children really needed and I don't believe they feel they are worse off than others. While the amount we got has increased, it typically has been about $600 a month. Of that, $325 would go for rent, $60 for electric and gas, and I would have about $200 after those expenses were taken out. This I used for transportation to a part-time job, phone, some child care, and household items like cleaning stuff. We also got medical coverage for the children and about $340 in food stamps which they would reduce if I earned too much. I can understand them doing that but it does upset me because it takes away any incentive for me to work more. But I feel good knowing I earn money and gain work experience I can use.

"Thanks to the help I got from my aunt, grandmother, mother, and an elderly church friend, I was able to do a lot better than most. They would help sometimes with money, transportation, or with the children. My friend from church was, and is, especially important in providing emotional support and encouraging me when I am ready to give up. We pray together a lot. It is because of her that I hope to complete my degree in social work and go into gerontology.

"I really appreciate the assistance I've been given. I believe mothers should be encouraged to work but they must be given the tools to accomplish it. If cuts are made and more programs are eliminated, a lot of people, myself included, will never be able to go to school or get out of poverty."

dren in the United States actually fell below the official poverty line, nearly half found themselves in a vulnerable economic position at least once during their childhood. The researchers claimed that the average black child could expect to spend more than five years in poverty before reaching the age of fifteen; the comparable average for white children was about nine months. A surprising result of the research was that the single most important event associated with the transition in and out of poverty, for both black and white children, was substantial changes in the labor supply of secondary earners in the family other than the head.

Entrenched underclass

While poverty for many U.S. families is not a persistent condition (they move in and out of it), this is not the case for millions of children and adults. Within the U.S. population is an **underclass** characterized by persistent poverty and a variety of associated problems, such as welfare dependency, joblessness, crime, and substance addiction. The underclass is geographically concentrated in inner-city neighborhoods, namely, the ghettos of cities. Its members participate considerably in the underground economies that flourish in the neighborhood. While the underclass is a multiracial/multiethnic phenomenon, it is particularly prevalent among African American and Puerto Rican families.[32]

Robert Kelly argued that underclass crime and welfare dependency, while overdetermined by objective economic circumstances, are also influenced by stress mediated at the social and psychological levels, primarily through family, kinship, and informal social networks.[33] A key point is that extended and fictive kin networks are critical intervening variables in the analysis of economic- and stress-related behaviors among the underclass.

It is difficult for most people—students and teachers included—to describe life-styles of families in poverty without imposing middle-class evaluations upon them. The very use of terms such as *poor, impoverished, lower class,* and *underclass* may impose negative connotations and interpretations on persons and families who occupy this group. To describe families in terms of unemployment, welfare, illegitimacy, venereal disease, crime, and disabilities is to repeatedly apply negative labels and convey an impression of fault and blame.

It is particularly ironic that the ideology of family, so important to people who are poor, is used by people who are privileged to blame the poor for their own condition. A middle- or ruling-class view sees underclass families not merely as inadequate but as deviant or even pathological, as well. Perhaps the family is less inadequate or pathological than the relationship between the family or household and the productive resources available to them. Few people rationally choose or consciously desire the life-styles that accompany poverty. The single parent in poverty is no exception.

Single parents and poverty

The fact that this section on single parents is included in the section on poverty should not lead readers to assume that all one-parent families are poor. They are not. But by most objective measures, the vast majority of these families are socially disadvantaged relative to other family types.

---

[32] Garry L. Rolison, "An Exploration of the Term Underclass as It Relates to African Americans," *Journal of Black Studies* 21 (March 1991): 287–301; and Joan Moore, "Is There a Hispanic Underclass?" *Social Science Quarterly* 70 (June 1989): 265–284.

[33] Robert F. Kelly, "The Family and the Urban Underclass," *Journal of Family Issues* 6 (June 1985): 159–184. Note also: Robert F. Kelly and Sarah H. Ramsey, "Poverty, Children, and Public Policies," *Journal of Family Issues* 12 (December 1991): 388–403.

Along a social class continuum, many families in the inner city can be described as belonging to the underclass. At this level, families are characterized by persistent poverty and its accompanying problems: substandard housing, unsanitary living conditions, high rates of unemployment, and high incidences of crime and substance abuse.

Single-parent families are characterized by a high rate of poverty, a high percentage of minority representation, more dependents, relatively low education, and a high rate of mobility. Survey studies have consistently revealed that, psychologically, single parents are more depressed, are more anxious, have poorer self-images, and are less satisfied with their lives. In short, single parents generally have little equity or stature in U.S. society. They constitute a group with pressing social and economic needs.

These needs are most acute among African American and Hispanic American female-headed families, half of whom fall below the poverty level. Census data indicated that, in 1992, the median income of female-householder families with no husband present was $17,221. This is about 62 percent of the $27,821 median income of male-householder families with the wife absent and about 41 percent of the $42,064 median income of married-couple families.[34]

That same year, using the poverty index developed by the Social Security Administration (described in a previous section of this chapter), more than one-third (34.9 percent) of all families with a female householder and no husband

---

[34] U.S. Bureau of the Census, *Current Population Reports,* Series P60-184, "Money Income of Households, Families, and Persons in the United States: 1992" (Washington, DC: U.S. Government Printing Office, 1993), Table 13, p. 40.

present were below the poverty level. As indicated previously, this included 22.3 percent of Asian, 28.1 percent of white, 48.8 percent of Spanish-origin, and 49.8 percent of black female-householder families without a husband present. With inadequate incomes, many of these mothers are less able to plan for their lives or control their own destinies and are forced to go on welfare.

Who are these single parents? How many children in the United States reside in this type of family structure? Drawing from 1994 census data, more than 21.4 million children under the age of eighteen, or close to one in three (30.8 percent), did not live with two parents. As the data in Table 8-2 show, this included 23.8 percent of white, 66.7 percent of black, and 36.6 percent of Hispanic-origin children. Most children lived with their mothers only (17.7 percent white, 53.5 percent black, and 28.0 percent Hispanic-origin), but about 3 percent lived with their fathers only. The remaining 4 percent did not live with either parent.

The number of children in a single-parent context is quite dramatic when children's actual living arrangements are examined over an extended period rather than considered for a given year or at a single point in time. In one study, Sandra Hofferth drew data from the Panel Study of Income Dynamics, interviews with a national probability sample of about five thousand families that have been followed longitudinally since 1968. Hofferth projected that 70 percent of white children born in 1980 would spend at least some time with only one parent before they reach age eighteen; for black children born in 1980, the projection was 94 percent.[35] These figures stand in sharp contrast to the 19 percent of white children and 48 percent of black children born between 1950 and 1954 who have lived with one parent.

Why the dramatic increase? How is it possible that 70 percent of white and 94 percent of black children will live in a single-parent household before they reach age eighteen? An overly simplified but partial answer to this question can be obtained by examining the marital status (never married, married but spouse absent, widowed, or divorced) of single parents by race and ethnicity (black, white, Hispanic-origin), as presented in the lower third of Table 8-2.

Of all white single parents, nearly one-half are divorced (45.9 percent) and another one-fourth are married but with a spouse absent (24.1 percent). Thus, most white children under age eighteen come from two-parent households but, as a result of divorce or an absent parent, find themselves in one-parent contexts.

Black children, in contrast, are much more likely to be born into single-parent situations because their mothers have never married (55.7 percent). Less than one-fifth of black children enter one-parent situations because of divorce. Why do such a high percentage of African American mothers never marry? In Chapter 6 on African American families, one explanation focused on the low sex ratios which meant there was a decreased availability of marital partners for females. Other explanations focused on the educational levels and unemployment

---

[35] Sandra L. Hofferth, "Updating Children's Life Course," *Journal of Marriage and the Family* 47 (February 1985): 93–115.

Table 8-2

Living arrangements of children under eighteen years: 1994

Living arrangement of children/ marital status of parent	Racial/ethnic group			
	All groups	White	Black	Hispanic*
All children under age eighteen (numbers in thousands)	69,508	54,795	11,177	9,496
Living with two parents	48,084	41,766	3,722	6,022
Living with one parent	18,590	11,434	6,384	3,019
Living with neither parent (Numbers in thousands)	2,834	1,594	1,071	455
Living with two parents (percent)	69.2%	76.2%	33.3%	63.4%
Mother only	23.5	17.7	53.5	28.0
Father only	3.2	3.1	3.7	3.9
Other relatives	3.1	2.1	8.0	3.4
Nonrelatives only	1.0	0.9	1.5	1.3
Percent	100.0%	100.0%	100.0%	100.0%
Marital status of single mothers (percent)				
Never married	36.7%	24.8%	55.7%	40.9%
Married, spouse absent	23.5	24.1	22.7	31.4
Widowed	4.3	5.2	2.5	5.7
Divorced	35.5	45.9	19.1	22.0
Percent	100.0%	100.0%	100.0%	100.0%

Source: U.S. Bureau of the Census, *Current Population Reports,* Series P20-484, Arlene F. Saluter, "Marital Status and Living Arrangements, March 1994" (Washington, DC: U.S. Government Printing Office, 1996), Appendix A, Table A-5 and Table 5, pp. 31–34.

Note: Data exclude persons under eighteen years old maintaining households or family groups.

* Persons of Hispanic origin may be of any race.

or underemployment numbers for black men which make them less attractive marriage partners. A study of more than one thousand African American mothers residing in Chicago high-poverty neighborhoods revealed as well that household income, time on Aid to Families with Dependent Children (AFDC), and number of children were strong predictors of nonmarriage.[36] Their findings indicate that never-married mothers living in areas of concentrated poverty have great potential for perpetuating the growth of an urban *underclass* in American cities.

---

[36] Donna L. Franklin, Susan E. Smith, and William P. McMiller, "Correlates of Marital Status Among African American Mothers in Chicago Neighborhoods of Concentrated Poverty," *Journal of Marriage and the Family* 57 (February 1995): 141–152.

While white one-parent families typically result from divorce and black one-parent families typically result from never-married parents, Hispanic-origin one-parent families result from several circumstances: divorce (22.0 percent), married but absent fathers (31.4 percent), and never-married mothers (40.9 percent).

Among all three racial/ethnic groups, relatively few one-parent situations result from widowhood; this might be expected, since widowhood most often occurs when mothers are older and their children are no longer under age eighteen. In sum, several trends—the increase in births to unmarried women, the frequency of divorce, and the number of married couples with a spouse absent—seem to ensure that the vast majority of children born in the 1980s and 1990s will experience one-parent living arrangements.

As could be expected, most literature on single-parent households has dealt with the mother/child unit. What's more, rather than consider the mother who is present, this literature has considered the father who is absent. Thus, it seems the real topic has been the fatherless family.

To avoid this oversight, the following sections will consider these two single-parent situations: the mother/child family (the father-absent family) and the father/child family (the mother-absent family).

Mothers as single parents In 1994, over 16.3 million children under the age of eighteen lived in homes with their mothers only. As illustrated by the figures in Table 8-3, that number has increased over the last twenty years from 7.4 million (1970) to 11.4 million (1980), to 16.3 million (1994). Today, close to one child in four (24.5 percent) lives with his or her mother only.

The largest *number* of children under age eighteen who live with their mothers are white (9.7 million in 1994). But the greatest concern tends to focus on African American children because *over half* of them (6.0 million, or 59.0 percent, in 1994) live in mother-only households. This concern is heightened by (1) the widely held view that every child needs a father or his social equivalent, (2) the financial plight of female-headed families, (3) the welfare expenditures that go to support these families, and (4) the effects on children who have no father or adult male influence in the home.

Sara McLanahan and Karen Booth addressed issues such as these in an essay focusing on problems, prospects, and politics in mother-only families.[37] When compared with two-parent families, the authors found that mother-only families were much more likely to be poor, to have higher levels of stress, and to have lower levels of social integration. Economic insecurity, the authors suggested, was high in mother-only families because of low earning capacity, lack of child support from nonresidential parents, and meager public benefits. The authors also found evidence of negative intergenerational consequences. Children living in mother-only families were more likely to be poor in adulthood than children who lived

---

[37] Sara McLanahan and Karen Booth, "Mother-Only Families: Problems, Prospects, and Politics," *Journal of Marriage and the Family* 51 (August 1989): 557–580.

Table 8-3

Children under eighteen years old living with mothers only: 1970-1994

	1970	1980	1990	1994
Number (in thousands)				
All races/ethnic groups	7,452	11,406	13,874	16,334
White	4,581	7,059	8,321	9,724
Black	2,783	4,117	5,123	5,967
Hispanic	(NA)	1,069	1,943	2,624
Distribution (in percent)				
All Races/ethnic groups	10.8%	18.0%	21.1%	24.5%
White	7.8	13.5	16.2	18.3
Black	29.5	43.9	51.2	59.0
Hispanic	(NA)	19.6	27.1	29.3

Source: U.S. Bureau of the Census, *Statistical Abstract of the United States: 1995,* 115th ed., no. 78, p. 65 and *Current Population Reports,* Series P20-450, Arlene F. Saluter "Marital Status and Living Arrangements, March 1990" (Washington, DC: U.S. Government Printing Office, 1991), Table E, p. 5.

with both parents. Children living with single mothers were also more likely to become single parents themselves.

How well mother-only families manage seems to be closely linked to their living arrangements. The poorest households are those in which mother-only families live alone followed closely by those in which two related single mothers and their families (typically a mother and her daughter) double up. Single mothers who live in married-couple households (such as with the mother's parents) fare better from an economic perspective. And data suggest that single mothers cohabiting with unrelated males where income is fully shared do best of all and appear to differ little from the average-income household of a young married couple with children.[38] Findings such as these tend to support the argument of Bumpass and Raley that definitions of single-parent families should be based on living arrangements rather than on the marital status of the parent.[39] A growing proportion of premarital births into assumed single-parent families are, in fact, born into two-parent cohabiting families.

Patterns of assistance to single mothers vary by race and kin networks. One nationally representative sample confirmed that single mothers have better access to kin than married mothers and that kin access is better among blacks than

---

[38] Anne E. Winkler, "The Living Arrangements of Single Mothers with Dependent Children: An Added Perspective," *The American Journal of Economics and Sociology* 52 (January 1995): 1–18.

[39] Larry L. Bumpass and R. Kelly Raley, "Redefining Single-Parent Families: Cohabitation and Changing Family Reality," *Demography* 32 (February 1995): 97–109.

among whites.[40] In this sample, black mothers were more likely to reside with their kin, more likely to have free child care provided by kinfolk (most often grandmothers), and more likely to receive at least one-half of their income from individuals other than husbands. Even though these informal support networks were especially important for black mothers, they seldom provided support adequate to fully compensate for the costs of single motherhood.

As stated before, the children of mother-only households are themselves more likely to be poor and to be single parents. What other consequences do they face? A simple comparison of two-parent and one-parent families documents many differences. Children who grow up in single-parent families are less likely to complete high school and attend college[41] and more likely to smoke cigarettes, use drugs, and have sexual intercourse.[42] Children from the two groups also differ on many other dimensions.

What are the findings when factors such as socioeconomic status are controlled? That is, are the differences among children due more to family structure (one parent or two) or to social class (level of poverty)?

Barbara Cashion reviewed the social-psychological research pertaining to female-headed families published over a decade and concluded that children in mother-only families are likely to have good emotional adjustment, high levels of self-esteem (except when they are stigmatized), intellectual development comparable to that of others in the same socioeconomic status, and a rate of juvenile delinquency comparable to that of others in the same socioeconomic status.[43] Major problems in mother-only families stem from *poverty* and *stigma*. Poverty, as a general social problem, may be associated with the child's problems in school and juvenile delinquency as well as the mother's poor attitude about her own situation and her sense of not being in control. The stigma of being without a father causes lowered self-esteem in children; they may also be labeled or defined problematic even in situations where problems are minimal or nonexistent. Overall, Cashion concluded that the majority of single female-headed families, when not plagued by poverty, raise children comparable to those from two-parent families.

Fathers as single parents The father/child family, like the mother/child family, is a result of widowhood, divorce, separation, nonmarriage, and, more recently, single-parent adoption. While only 3.4 percent of all children under age eighteen live with their fathers only (review Table 8-2), that number has increased from

[40] Dennis P. Hogan, Ling-Xin Hao, and William L. Parish, "Race, Kin Networks, and Assistance to Mother-Headed Families," *Social Forces* 68 (March 1990): 797–812; and Sara McLanahan and Gary Sandefur, *Growing Up with a Single Parent* (Cambridge, MA: Harvard University Press, 1994).

[41] Nan Marie Astone and Sara S. McLanahan, "Family Structure, Parental Practices and High School Completion," *American Sociological Review* 56 (June 1991): 309–320.

[42] Robert L. Flewelling and Karl E. Bauman, "Family Structure as a Predictor of Initial Substance Use and Sexual Intercourse in Early Adolescence," *Journal of Marriage and the Family* 52 (February 1990): 171–181.

[43] Barbara G. Cashion, "Female-Headed Families: Effects on Children and Clinical Implications," *Journal of Marital and Family Therapy* (April 1982): 77–85.

748,000 in 1970 to 1.1 million in 1980 to 2.3 million in 1993. This increase is likely to continue as a result of more divorced fathers who desire to continue parenting, greater economic resources available to fathers than to mothers, and more favorable opinions of single fathers.

Research on fathers as single parents has been relatively infrequent and generally limited to small nonprobability samples. Yet father/child studies may prove to be more insightful than mother/child studies in light of the extreme importance placed upon the mother as the key agent of socialization. Can men "mother"?

This question was posed by Barbara Risman, who surveyed fathers about their experiences as homemakers, the nature of the father/child relationship, and their overall role satisfaction.[44] Risman's major finding was that most men felt comfortable and competent as single parents, regardless of the reason for custody or their financial status. This was true even though four out of five single fathers had no outside housekeeping help, either paid or volunteer. These men felt very close to and very affectionate toward their children, were glad to be fathers, and had little trouble fulfilling either the instrumental or expressive functions of single parenthood. Clearly, successful mothering is not an exclusively female skill. Men *can* "mother."

Similar support for men as single parents came from a study that examined whether significant differences exist between children reared in single-mother and single-father families. Factors examined included self-perception, self-esteem, social competencies, and the frequency and severity of reported behavioral problems. The historical assumption that single mothers are more effective parents than single fathers was not supported.[45] In a number of ways, fathers who maintain families alone are better situated than their female counterparts. Single-parent fathers typically have higher levels of education, are in the labor force, and as shown earlier, are well situated economically.

Do males do better in single-father households and females do better in single-mother households? That is, are there advantages to living with the same-sex parent in single-parent households? Apparently not. In a national study of several thousand eighth-graders living in mother-only and father-only homes, of 35 social psychological and educational outcomes, not even one revealed significant benefits from living with the same-sex parent as contrasted with the opposite-sex parent.[46] This research casts doubt on the advocacy of same-sex custody determinations.

Overview of single parenthood   Can any conclusions be drawn from the data available? It does seem clear that, just as growing up in a two-parent family does not

---

[44] Barbara J. Risman, "Can Men 'Mother'? Life as a Single Father," *Family Relations* 35 (January 1986): 95–102. Note also: Geoffrey L. Greif, "Lone Fathers in the United States: An Overview and Practice Implications," *British Journal of Social Work* 22 (1992): 565–574.

[45] A. Reuben Schnayer and R. Robert Orr, "A Comparison of Children Living in Single Mother and Single Father Families," *Journal of Divorce* 12 (1989): 171–184.

[46] Douglas B. Downey and Brian Powell, "Do Children in Single-Parent Households Fare Better Than Living With Same-Sex Parents?" *Journal of Marriage and the Family* 55 (February 1993): 55–71.

guarantee happy, well-adjusted, and well-behaved children, growing up in a one-parent family does not ensure the opposite. But neither can the findings be understood to imply that the absence of a father or mother has no effect whatsoever. Single parents assess their options, and mothers in particular make choices that allow them to forge meaningful lives despite harsh economic conditions in which they and their children find themselves.[47]

Single parents have definite limitations on the time and energy to do various tasks. Children in single-parent families are assumed to have more responsibility than children in two-parent families and engage in more gender-stereotyped chores. Single parents are often forced to exhibit both masculine and feminine behaviors which may tend to socialize their children in more nontraditional and flexible gender-role values and behaviors.

Parent-absent families

What about parent-absent families: those 7.4 percent of African American children, 3.7 of Spanish-origin children, and 1.9 percent of white children who, in 1993, lived with neither parent (see Table 8-2)? Apparently, most of these children live with relatives, especially grandparents. As the children get older, they are more likely to live in families with brothers or sisters or with other relatives. White children are more likely than black children to be placed in public agencies and institutions.[48]

The conditions that result in children living separately from their parents, the effects of parent absence on the children, and the existing support services for these children are questions in need of research.

SOCIAL MOBILITY: CHANGING FAMILY LIFE-STYLES

One fundamental characteristic of families and social stratification is the extent to which there is opportunity to move from one class to another. Although **social mobility** is often thought to mean *social improvement*, mobility can be upward, downward, or lateral. The first two types (upward and downward) are referred to as *vertical social mobility*, and the latter (lateral) is referred to as *horizontal social mobility*.

Generally, horizontal social mobility is used to refer to movement to a different occupation within a similar social strata or class. A residential or geographical move may be social mobility of a horizontal nature as well and one that has significant consequences. For example, children who live with only one parent or with stepparents were found to experience both (1) more residential mobility and (2) a higher school drop-out rate than children living in two-parent families.[49] As

---

[47] Robin L. Jarrett, "Living Poor: Family Life Among Single Parent, African American Women," *Social Problems* 41 (February 1994): 30–49.

[48] Raymond Montemayor and Geoffrey K. Leigh, "Parent Absent Children: A Demographic Analysis of Children and Adolescents Living Apart from Their Parents," *Family Relations* 31 (October 1982): 567–573.

[49] Nan Marie Astone and Sara S. McLanahan, "Family Structure, Residential Mobility, and School Dropout: A Research Note," *Demography* 31 (November 1994): 575–584.

much as 30 percent of the difference in the risk of dropping out of school between children from stepfamilies and children from intact families was explained by residential mobility.

Likelihood of vertical social mobility

The likelihood of vertical social mobility is a function of three separate phenomena. First is the *opportunity structure* to which the individual has access. This is the organizational structure of a society that defines the ultimate achievement possibilities for the individual as well as the channels available to realize achievement. Different opportunity structures apply to different individuals, groups, and subcultures within the same society. However, the structure of the society—including the presence or absence of jobs, the availability of educational and training programs, and other social characteristics—will, in large part, determine the extent to which mobility occurs.

The second component of the likelihood of vertical social mobility is the *individual*. Personality characteristics—such as intelligence, motivation, motor skills, and value systems—determine the individual's capacity for exploiting the opportunity structure and will influence the likelihood of mobility.

The third component may be termed the *frictional factor*. That is, two identically equipped individuals who confront the same opportunity structure may nevertheless attain disparate levels of mobility. These factors, inherent in neither the individual nor the opportunity structure, may be referred to as chance, luck, or fortune.[50]

The first factor in the likelihood of vertical social mobility, the opportunity structure, seems more crucial to understanding the low achievements of poor children and families than either psychological factors (such as personality type and motivation) or simple good fortune. What are the chances for mobility?

Extent of vertical social mobility

The American dream suggests that, in this land of opportunity, anyone can go from "rags to riches." The widespread belief is that hard work, endurance, and motivation will enable anyone to move up on the social-class ladder. The fact is that social mobility and equal opportunity have probably never been as attainable as U.S. citizens have believed. But recent data have suggested that social mobility in U.S. society is increasing.

It has been estimated that one of every four or five persons moves up at least one social-class level during his or her lifetime. The greatest amount of upward

---

50 Bradley R. Schiller, "Stratified Opportunities: The Essence of the 'Vicious Circle,'" *American Journal of Sociology* 76 (November 1970): 427.

mobility occurs among blue-collar workers. What is less frequently recognized and studied is downward mobility.

Patricia Smith, in two articles (one with the subtitle "Sinking Boats in a Rising Tide") notes that over two separate three year periods, in spite of a growing economy, a substantial minority of Americans (5 to 20 percent) experienced downward income mobility.[51] A large share of the downward mobility came from the middle and lower classes. Women who separated or divorced faced the highest risk of downward mobility. The factors that increased the odds of downward mobility included male headship, minority headship, family dissolution, nest leaving, and having a household head who works in mining, construction, manufacturing, transportation, trade, or farming. The factors that lowered the odds included having a college-educated head of household, retaining the same household heads, and having them working in a professional, technical, or operative occupation or in the finance, insurance, and real estate industry.

Downward mobility involves more than a loss of job and drop in income. It includes a loss of occupational prestige and demotion from one's place in society, as well. Marriage, childrearing, divorce, widowhood, and employment of wives all affect families and the status they hold. The experience of family disruption during childhood substantially increases men's odds of ending up in a lower occupational stratum,[52] and as stated before and will be shown in Chapter 16, divorce, in particular, is a traumatic event, leading to the downward mobility of women. Most victims of downward mobility, male or female, express feelings of anger, dismay, and injustice.

Empirical studies of social mobility have suggested several general conclusions:

1. Most children will ultimately live at the same class level as their parents.
2. A substantial proportion of sons and daughters will experience some mobility.
3. Upward mobility is more prevalent than downward mobility.
4. When mobility does occur, it will likely be a shift to a class level adjacent to that of the individual's parents; that is, short-distance mobility is more common than long-distance mobility.

Consequences of social mobility

Few people are immune to the possibility of downward social mobility, and many would likely embrace the opportunity for upward social mobility. With this oppor-

---

[51] Patricia K. Smith, "Recent Patterns in Downward Income Mobility: Sinking Boats in a Rising Tide," *Social Indicators Research* 31 (1994): 277–303; and Patricia K. Smith, "Downward Mobility: Is It a Growing Problem?" *American Journal of Economics and Sociology* 53 (January 1994): 57–72.

[52] Timothy J. Biblarz and Adrian E. Raftery, "The Effects of Family Disruption on Social Mobility," *American Sociological Review* 58 (February 1993): 97–109.

tunity comes a better job, a higher income, a more luxurious home, a more prestigious neighborhood, opportunities to travel, better clothes, a new car, freedom from debt—in short, a more luxurious and refined life-style. Many, if not most, people believe that education is one means to obtain these rewards. Within U.S. society, with its fairly open-class system and its increasing requirements for specialized and highly trained technicians and experts, "brain power" frequently means higher status. But a closer investigation of the open-class system shows that not all consequences of mobility, even upward social mobility, are positive. In various ways, the costs of upward social mobility may be great and the penalties quite severe.

Many students discover that their increased education (a potential contribution to upward social mobility) has some disruptive effects. The most obvious is likely to be an increasingly estranged relationship with parents. Many students find that, as they become more educated, their beliefs and values change in ways that may conflict with those of their parents, particularly if their parents are working-class people of limited formal education. The paradox of this situation is that these are frequently the type of parents who make major sacrifices to provide college education for their children. The painful consequence is that their children become socially distant from them.

In some instances, marriage itself may be threatened by upward social mobility. The wife who works to assist her husband in completing his education may find that his value system and life-style changes while hers remain more static. Success in business may encourage certain husbands to seek the friendship of more sophisticated or like-minded females. Career-oriented wives may discover that, with increased economic and social opportunities, they can be self-sufficient and independent, perhaps eliminating the need or desire for a husband. Career women may discover men whose values and behavior patterns are more to their liking than those of their husbands. These and many other examples of upward social mobility illustrate how this supposedly desirable phenomenon may disrupt husband/wife relationships.

Obviously, not all social mobility has negative consequences. In a relatively open-class system, a high rate of social mobility may tend to stabilize the social order by providing outlets for change to persons with particular skills or talents who are dissatisfied with their present social status. The possibility for upward social mobility may obviate rebellious and revolutionary tactics from such frustrated persons. Families may receive new recognition and social prestige from "social climbing." Thus, the question is not so much whether social mobility is good or bad but rather what consequences to individuals and families result within societies that have closed- or open-class systems.

SUMMARY

1. The term *social class* refers to an aggregate of individuals who occupy a similar position on a scale of wealth, prestige, and power. Ranking of different classes results in inequalities among persons and families.

2. Two theories particularly relevant to understanding social class are the structural-functional and conflict theories. Functionalist theory asserts that a stratified system is inevitable and necessary for the fulfillment of tasks needed to maintain a society. Conflict theory holds that a stratified system leads to dissatisfaction and conflict between the laborers who are the instrument of production and the owners and managers who control the means of production.

3. The determination of social-class position varies widely, from examining who owns, manages, and controls production to noting differential rankings of occupational prestige, income, and education. Four general social categories of families were described: wealthy, middle-class, and blue-collar families and families living in poverty.

4. Wealthy families have been identified as the *very rich*, the *upper class*, and the *ruling class*. This elite group owns and controls the means of production. Wealthy families are concerned with who they are and seek to protect their names and resources.

5. Middle-class families serve as the link between the small group of wealthy families and the group of working-class, blue-collar families. At this class level, married couples tend toward the ideal of equality between the spouses but, in reality, perform highly segregated roles. In childrearing, middle-class parents use reason, verbal threats, and withdrawal of rewards to punish their children, instilling belief in self-determination.

6. Blue-collar families do not have the economic stability found in middle-class families, since the working class is more highly dependent on the swings of the business cycle in the U.S. wage/price/profits system. Marriages are more unstable than among the higher social groups, husband/wife roles are highly traditional, and children are subordinate to parents. Early marriage and parenthood are frequent.

7. Nearly one in nine U.S. families is living in poverty. Evident in the feminization of poverty is the growth in female-headed families and the rise in teen and young parenting, income inequality, and inadequate personal and child support. Most people live in poverty on a transitional basis. However, a U.S. *underclass* is characterized by persistent poverty and a variety of associated problems, including crime and welfare dependency.

8. A disproportionate number of single-parent families lives in poverty. This is particularly true of female-headed households, in which no husband or father is present. Clear differences exist between mothers as single parents and fathers as single parents; in short, the fathers fare much better. Children from single-parent family structures compare well with those from two-parent structures when socioeconomic status is controlled. Children raised by single parents are likely to have more nontraditional and flexible gender-role values and behaviors.

9. What are the chances for and consequences of family social mobility, upward or downward? Upward social mobility in the United States has probably never been as widespread as has been widely believed, but it seems to be increasing. While seen as desirable by most persons, upward mobility can result in new recognition and social prestige or may bring rejection and social isolation.

10. Chapters 5 to 8 have examined structural and subcultural variations in family life-styles. Chapter 9 will examine structures and processes that deal primarily with partner selection. In a general sense, the next eight chapters follow the marital and family life cycle, from the point of selecting a partner or spouse through cohabitation or marriage, parenthood, the middle years, and, finally, the later years. A variety of frames of reference, or theoretical approaches (structural-functional, exchange, conflict, psychoanalytic, behaviorist, symbolic-interactional, feminist, and others), are used in examining organizational and process patterns at various stages of the life cycle.

KEY TERMS AND TOPICS

Social class p. 220

Social stratification p. 220

Structural-functional theory of
   stratification p. 220

Conflict theory of stratification p. 220

Determination of social class p. 221

Consequences of social class
   to families p. 223

Wealthy families p. 224

Middle-class families p. 226

Bourgeoisie and proletariat p. 226

Blue-collar families p. 228

Families living in poverty p. 231

Poverty index p. 231

Feminization of poverty p. 233

Public assistance p. 235

Welfare p. 236

Survival of families in poverty p. 238

Fictive kinship p. 238

Underclass p. 240

Single parents and poverty p. 240

Mothers as single parents p. 244

Fathers as single parents p. 246

Parent-absent families p. 248

Social mobility p. 248

DISCUSSION QUESTIONS

1. What is meant by *social class*? How many classes exist in U.S. society? How can that be determined?

2. Compare and contrast the structural-functional perspective of class with the conflict perspective of class.

3. Discuss the notion that "All men (women, families) are created equal." Namely, are Americans born into equal socioeconomic situations? Given one's start in life, what opportunities exist for mobility, upward or downward?

4. Make a class-stratification study of the families in a community with which you are familiar. Where do they live, work, play, and worship? Where do or will their children attend college (if at all)? What kinds of cars do they drive? What hobbies do they pursue? What are their family sizes, attitudes toward childrearing, and the like? Outline the style of living that characterizes each class.

5. Discuss these two statements: "When college students from middle-class families take jobs in a factory, they become members of the working class" and "When the same students become unemployed, they enter the poverty level." Are these ideas valid? Why or why not?

6. Define *fictive kin* and the *feminization of poverty*. Explain reasons for the existence of each. How are they related?

7. What kinds of programs or policies may be effective in helping families rise above the level of poverty? Should food stamps, subsidized housing, welfare programs, and the like be cut or eliminated? Why or why not?

8. What factors explain the increase in the number of one-parent families? Why is this increase of concern to policymakers and to the general public?

9. What differences exist between one- and two-parent situations? What differences exist between single-father and single-mother situations? Why?

10. What factors foster upward social mobility? Downward social mobility? Why are many consequences of upward social mobility disruptive to kin and community ties?

FURTHER READINGS

Bane, Mary Jo, and Ellwood, David T. *Welfare Realities: From Rhetoric to Reform*. Cambridge, MA: Harvard University Press, 1994. Five chapters that examine welfare, its recipients, its providers, as well as policy proposals.

Danziger, Sheldon H.; Sandefur, Gary D.; and Weinberg, Daniel H. (eds.). *Confronting Poverty: Prescriptions for Change*. Cambridge, MA: Harvard University Press, 1994. A work that documents trends in poverty and income inequality, reviews government programs, and analyzes the public's attitudes toward these policies.

Goldberg, Gertrude Schaffner, and Kremen, Eleanor. *The Feminization of Poverty: Only in America?* New York: Praeger, 1990. Eight chapters on the feminization of poverty in seven industrialized nations: the United States, Canada, Japan, France, Sweden, Russia, and Poland.

Hanson, Shirley M. H.; Heims, Marsha C.; Julian, Doris J.; and Sussman, Marvin B. (eds.). "Single Parent Families: Diversity, Myths and Realities," *Marriage and Family Review* 20 (1995): 1–550. The entire 1995 volume includes 25 chapters on single-parent families and provides an excellent resource for persons interested in this topic.

Jencks, Christopher, and Peterson, Paul E. *The Urban Underclass*. Washington, DC: Brookings Institute, 1991. A series of essays on the urban underclass that attempts to separate the truth about poverty and family life from the myths that have become contemporary folklore.

Kissman, Kris, and Allen, JoAnn. *Single-Parent Families.* Newbury Park, CA: Sage, 1993. An overview of single-parent families with particular attention devoted to interviews with mother-headed families.

McLanahan, Sara, and Sandefur, Gary D. *Growing Up With a Single Parent: What Hurts, What Helps?* Cambridge, MA: Harvard University Press, 1994. Drawing on four national surveys and a decade of research, the authors show how race, gender, and class influence children's chances for well-being.

Ostrander, Susan A. *Women of the Upper Class.* Philadelphia: Temple University Press, 1984. Interviews with thirty-six upper-class women about their lives as wives, mothers, club members, and volunteers.

Rubin, Lillian B. *Families on the Fault Line: America's Working Class Speaks about the Family, the Economy, Race, and Ethnicity.* New York: HarperCollins, 1994. An insightful, very readable book about what Rubin refers to as invisible Americans: working-class families in a contracting economy.

Wilson, William Julius. *The Ghetto Underclass: Social Science Perspectives.* Newbury Park, CA: Sage, 1993. Wilson and other leading social scientists cover family patterns, sexual behavior, immigration and homelessness of the urban underclass.

Chapter 9

Homogamy and Endogamy in the Selection of Intimate Partners

With this chapter, the discussion shifts from family institutions and variations in family life-styles to structures and processes in selecting intimate partners and creating marriages. Whenever the term *marriage* is used, it is meant to include marriage-like relationships, that is, those in which the partner relationship is bonded, intimate, and relatively exclusive and committed. This chapter will examine five normative structures in partner selection in the United States: age, residence, class, religion, and race/ethnicity.

DEFINING HOMOGAMY AND ENDOGAMY

The terms generally employed to describe the selection of a primary intimate partner from among those who share similar characteristics are **homogamy** and **endogamy.** *Homogamy* denotes likenesses or similarities among couples. *Endogamy* describes marriages and relationships within specific groups of almost any kind. That people choose partners like themselves more often than could be due to chance is known as **assortive mating.** The "assorted" mates are matched on specific structural dimensions.

Most of us in the United States believe that we are free to marry anyone we choose. But in the real world of partner choice, all kinds of restrictions exist. How free are you to choose someone of the same sex, someone already married, a child, a sibling, certain ethnic/racial groups, and so forth. Clearly, free choice is only "free" from within selected socially appropriate categories. And no society in the world leaves the selection of an intimate or marriage partner unregulated and indiscriminate.

Studies throughout the world have reported high rates of racial/ethnic, religious, class, educational, and age homogamy. Homogamy appears to exist even among persons with anxiety disorders and alcohol or drug dependence.[1] An analysis of explanations for intimate partners sharing these homogamous characteristics revealed support for some type of assortive mating: the selection of partners like themselves more often than could be due to chance. Whether the choice is made by the persons themselves, by parents, by relatives, by delegated persons or groups, or by specific social agencies, it is always subject to regulation by social and cultural controls.

One should not be led into believing that endogamy and homogamy are the preferred or required norms in all respects. The most universal of all norms regarding marriage and sexual relationships—the incest taboo—is an *exogamous* norm. **Exogamy** describes marriages and relationships with persons who are outside of specifically defined social groups. Thus, all marriages are exogamous in that they do not occur between members of the same nuclear-family unit. The terms *exogamy* and **heterogamy** are often used interchangeably. However, exogamy

---

[1] Jane D. McLeod, "Social and Psychological Bases of Homogamy for Common Psychiatric Disorders," *Journal of Marriage and the Family* 57 (February 1995): 201–214.

focuses on group factors whereas heterogamy focuses on any differences. If both exogamy and heterogamy are used to indicate marriage between persons of different social groupings or who are in any way different, then no purely endogamous or homogamous relationships exist.

This discussion of homogamy, exogamy, or both in the selection of intimate partners will be confined to specific group characteristics that are culturally relevant to the choice of a spouse or partner. For instance, a relationship could conceivably be endogamous in regard to race/ethnicity, exogamous in regard to kin, heterogamous in regard to height and eye color, and homogamous in regard to values and personality traits.

Intermarriage

Before leaving this introductory discussion of homogamy and endogamy, several general questions need to be addressed: How is **intermarriage** defined? Who is included or excluded in determining whether a relationship is actually mixed? How are rates of intermarriage influenced by reporting, particularly when using statistics of couples as opposed to individuals? What social and cultural factors are likely to foster or affect the likelihood of intermarriage?

Defining intermarriage

How much of an age difference must there be between two people before their relationship is age exogamous? Is a marriage between a Methodist and a Lutheran (both Protestants) an interfaith marriage? At what point does any difference or characteristic determine homogamy or heterogamy, endogamy or exogamy?

Obviously, in any study or in any reporting of rates, some definition must be used to determine whom to include and exclude. In research, *operational definitions* are used; in other words, variables are defined according to the way they will be measured. As a result, an age difference of more than four years may be arbitrarily defined as age exogamous. Or an interracial/interethnic relationship may be defined as any in which the couple defines themselves as such, irrespective of color or lineage. This problem of what is or is not an intermarriage is a serious one in determining rates and in comparing studies. Greater attention is devoted to this issue in dealing with specific social dimensions.

Reporting intermarriage

Specifically, can intermarriage rates be influenced by the reporting of couples as opposed to individuals? Most published rates of mixed marriage (or intermarriage) are based on the total number of *marriages*. But some rates are interpreted as if they were based on the number of individuals who marry. A **marriage rate** refers to the percentage of marriages that are mixed of all marriages involving individuals in a specific category. A **marriage rate for individuals** refers to the percentage of married individuals in a specific category who enter a mixed marriage.

Suppose there are ten couples, four that are black/white (interracial) and six who are white/white (intraracial). Is the mixed (interracial) rate 40 percent or 25 percent? Consider that four of the ten relationships (40 percent) are interracial, but four of the sixteen white persons (25 percent) entered interracial relationships.

Unless none or all of the relationships are mixed, the rate for marriages is always greater than the rate for individuals. Thus, if one's objective is to prove that mixed marriages are occurring in greater frequency, one would use the mixed-marriage rate for *marriages*. If one wanted to prove that the incidence of mixed marriage is declining, one would use the mixed-marriage rate for *individuals*. Statistically, both figures would be accurate. Thus, a way to "lie" with statistics (but honestly) is to use the rate that best fits one's purpose or interest.

In addition to distinguishing rates between marriages and individuals, it is also possible to distinguish a group's **actual rate** of intermarriage from its **expected rate.** The ratio between the two is important in determining if intermarriage rates are greater than could be expected to occur by chance or if partners had been chosen randomly. The expected intermarriage rate is the percentage of people who would have selected a mate outside their own group if they had chosen their marriage partners randomly, knowing the frequency distribution of the particular groups in the population. The actual rate refers to those marriages that do take place. Norval Glenn, for example, illustrated that, based on the relative sizes of religious categories, 68 percent of Protestants, 26 percent of Catholics, and only 2.3 percent of Jews could be expected to be endogamous with random mating. In actuality, as will be shown later, an overwhelming majority of Protestant, Catholic, and Jewish members marry endogamously.[2]

Clearly, assortive mating processes are operative for religious as well as most social groups. People marry endogamously far more often than could be expected simply by chance or at random.

Factors that foster intermarriage

Actual rates of intermarriage are influenced by various factors, many of which center around the normative eligibility rules for partner selection, such as role compatibility, value consensus, and similarity in age, class, religion, and race/ethnicity. However, apart from these normative rules are non-normative factors that favor endogamous marriages. Consider, for example, factors such as group size, community heterogeneity, sex ratio, group controls, cultural similarities, the romantic love complex, and influences of certain psychological factors.

Group size The size of a group relative to that of the larger population is likely to influence the extent to which the actual intermarriage rate is larger or smaller than would be expected by chance. Generally, the larger the group, the lower its intermarriage rate; the smaller the group, the faster its rate goes up with each intermarriage. For example, in Utah, the heart of the Mormon population in the

---

2 Norval D. Glenn, "A Note on Estimating the Strength of Influences for Religious Endogamy," *Journal of Marriage and the Family* 46 (August 1984): 725–727.

United States, marriages are highly endogamous. But in Florida, where Mormons constitute less than 1 percent of the population, research shows that about two-thirds of the Mormons living there had married non-Mormons.[3] That such a difference exists between the proportions of Mormons in Utah and Florida who marry outside their faith stems far less from differences in religious conviction than from the probability of meeting and interacting with persons from a Mormon background.

Heterogeneity Peter Blau and others proposed that, in addition to group size, the degree of heterogeneity in the community will influence the rate of intermarriage.[4] That is, intermarriage is more likely to occur when people reside in communities with many persons who are different from them. On the other hand, evidence has supported the idea that inequality is antagonistic to homogamy.[5] Thus, a paradox exists. People in heterogeneous communities are more likely to meet, interact with, and marry persons different from themselves. Yet inequality in education and socioeconomic status exerts constraints on intermarriage and increases the desire for status homogamy.

Sex ratio The sex ratio (number of males per 100 females) is likely to influence the rate of intermarriage. In a community or setting where one sex outnumbers the other, traditional barriers are crossed with increased frequency as the sex with greater numbers selects from the smaller pool of available partners. In other words, for the population as a whole, traditional age, class, religious, and other barriers are likely to decline in importance as the ratio of men to women drops with advancing age.

Group controls Intermarriage rates are likely to be influenced as well by the extent of social or group controls over the individuals involved. The Amish and Jewish, both religious minorities in the United States, maintain group sanctions through teachings and religious practices that discourage marriage with outsiders.

Cultural similarities Another factor that influences intermarriage rates is the development of cultural similarities and the elimination of differences. As ethnic minorities attend public schools, work in diverse social environments, and identify with the new or larger society, the differences in language, dress, and traditional practices decrease. As a result, the likelihood of intermarriage increases.

Romantic love complex Intermarriage rates also increase as a result of what might be called the *romantic love complex*: the idea that love is more important than group controls, cultural differences, and homogamous characteristics. Related to this complex is a personal choice ideal that suggests each person has the right to choose whom to marry, with minimal interference from others.

---

[3] Brent A. Barlow, "Notes on Mormon Interfaith Marriages," *The Family Coordinator* 26 (April 1977): 148.

[4] Peter M. Blau, Terry C. Blum, and Joseph E. Schwartz, "Heterogeneity and Intermarriage," *American Sociological Review* (February 1982): 45–62.

[5] Steven Rytina, Peter M. Blau, Terry Blum, and Joseph Schwartz, "Inequality and Intermarriage: A Paradox of Motive and Constraint," *Social Forces* 66 (March 1988): 645–675.

News Item: Young and Beautiful Marries Old and Wealthy

On June 27, 1994, Anna Nicole Smith, age 26, married J. Howard Marshall II, age 89. Smith is a six-foot- tall, former Guess jeans model, 1993 Playboy Playmate of the year, Naked Gun 33 1/3 actress, and former waitress and topless dancer. Marshall was an ailing, wheelchair-bound Houston oilman believed to be worth about $500 million. Following a courtship that began several years ago, Smith entered her second marriage and Marshall his third.

On August 4, 1995, J. Howard Marshall II, at the age of 90, died of pneumonia. This raised the question as to who would inherit his fortune as his son, E. Pierce Marshall, had held the power of attorney over his father's wealth.

The split between his wife and his son became obvious immediately with separate funeral arrangements. Pierce, the son, held a dignified private funeral. Anna Nicole, the wife, held a showy memorial service at a Houston funeral home. She appeared wearing a white dress with a plunging neckline and her wedding veil. Her son wore a white tuxedo and held a small black dog.

Another immediate fight developed over Marshall's remains. This ended in a settlement in which he was cremated and his ashes divided between the two sides. The battle over who gets what and how much of the estate is just beginning at the time of this writing.

Psychological factors Finally, intermarriage rates are likely to be influenced by certain psychological factors: rebellion against one's own group, feelings of alienation, emotional immaturity, and other psychological characteristics. As is the case with all factors mentioned, no given individual influenced by any of these factors will necessarily intermarry. But probabilities of intermarriage increase under conditions or circumstances such as those described.

SOCIAL/STRUCTURAL CHARACTERISTICS

The discussion that follows will examine selected social/structural characteristics that affect interpersonal relations and the selection of a marriage partner. These characteristics include age, residence, social class, religion, and race/ethnicity. Obviously, this list does not include all social structures relating to selection of a mate. However, discussion of these characteristics will clearly demonstrate the extent to which endogamous marriages are predominant in the United States.

Age at marriage

The age at which people marry is an important social/structural characteristic in most countries. It influences family/kin networks, birthrates, and educational

Table 9-1

Median age at first marriage, by sex: 1880–1994

Year	Male	Female	Difference	Year	Male	Female	Difference
1994	26.7	24.5	2.2	1980	24.7	22.0	2.7
1993	26.5	24.5	2.0	1970	23.2	20.8	2.4
1992	26.5	24.4	2.1	1960	22.8	20.3	2.5
1991	26.3	24.1	2.2	1950	22.8	20.3	2.5
1990	26.1	23.9	2.2	1940	24.3	21.5	2.8
1989	26.2	23.8	2.4	1930	24.3	21.3	3.0
1988	25.9	23.6	2.3	1920	24.6	21.2	3.4
1987	25.8	23.6	2.2	1910	25.1	21.6	3.5
1986	25.7	23.1	2.6	1900	25.9	21.9	4.0
1985	25.5	23.3	2.2	1890	26.1	22.0	4.1

Source: Adapted from *Current Population Survey* and U.S. Bureau of the Census, *Current Population Reports,* Series P20-484, Arlene F. Saluter, "Marital Status and Living Arrangements: March 1994" (Washington, DC: U.S. Government Printing Office, 1996), Table A-2, p. A-3.

advancement and, in turn, is influenced by social class, women's roles, occupational and educational opportunities, and countless other factors. The general trend in age at marriage around the world—in countries such as Ireland, Japan, Australia, and the United States—seems to be upward: a delay in or shift away from marriage.[6] What about the homogamy, or age similarity, factor?

Age homogamy

Most couples are relatively homogamous in terms of the age at which they marry. Although in many countries a person is free to marry someone considerably older or younger, most often a single person selects someone from a closely related age group. In the United States, in 1994, the median age at first marriage was 26.7 for males and 24.5 for females, an age difference of 2.2 years (see Table 9-1).

An examination of the data in Table 9-1 shows that the median age at first marriage as well as the age difference between males and females has changed considerably since the turn of the century. From 1890 until the 1950s, the trend in the United States was toward a younger age at marriage and a narrowing of the age difference between bride and groom at first marriage. Data for 1890 show the

[6] James A. Schellenberg, "Patterns of Delayed Marriage: How Special Are the Irish," *Sociological Focus* 24 (February 1991): 1–11; Kenji Otani, "Time Distribution in the Process to Marriage and Pregnancy in Japan," *Population Studies* 45 (1991): 473–487; and Peter McDonald, "The Shift Away from Marriage Among Young Australians," *Family Matters* 30 (December 1991): 50.

Most marriages are relatively age homogamous, which means that the partners are very similar in age. In the United States, when marriages are age exogamous, the most common pattern is for an older male to marry a younger female.

median ages at first marriage to be 26.1 years for males and 22.0 for females, an age difference of 4.1 years. In 1956, the median age at first marriage reached an all-time low: 22.5 for men and 20.1 for women. Since that time, there has been a gradual, though not continuous, increase in the median age at first marriage for both men and women. In the last twenty years, there has been more than a three-year increase in the median age at first marriage for both males and females. Today's median ages for marriage may be the highest that ever existed in the United States.

What explains this incredible increase in just one generation? Are people delaying marriage because they are spending more time in school? Is the delay due to increased job opportunities or the lack of them? Do people delay marriage until they attain a satisfactory level of income? Or are delays in marriage due to macrolevel factors, such as unemployment, military service, and other social and economic opportunity structures, that people experience over their life course?[7] Does an increase in cohabitation cause a delay in or replacement of marriage? Or might the "marriage squeeze," relating to a shortage of marital partners, be a contributing factor? (The "marriage squeeze" is described in the next section.)

Age homogamy is itself a function of age at marriage. Without exception, the median age at marriage for grooms is always higher than that for brides. It is esti-

---

[7] Teresa M. Cooney and Dennis P. Hogan, "Marriage in an Institutionalized Life Course: First Marriage among American Men in the Twentieth Century," *Journal of Marriage and the Family* 53 (February 1991): 178–190.

mated that, in six out of seven marriages in the United States, the male is as old or older than his bride. And an empirical study of marital-age heterogamy showed that, in 1980, 27 percent of males were five or more years older. In contrast, only 3.1 percent of males were five or more years younger.[8] For both types of age-heterogamous marriages (husband older as well as husband younger), when compared with age-homogamous marriages (operationally defined as plus or minus four years), a tendency existed for the heterogamous marriages to be characterized by lower educational levels, multiple marriages, lower family incomes, and lower occupational statuses of the husbands.

Why the overwhelming likelihood that males will be older than females? Several explanations have been offered, including the male's slower physiological and psychological maturity compared to that of the female, the traditional responsibility of the husband to be the major breadwinner (which requires more preparation time), the slight excess of males through the early twenties, the mating gradient (described later in this chapter), and the continued subjugation of women. This last gender argument is consistent with the proposition that female/male marital age differences narrow as societies become more egalitarian.

Age differences in marriage are the smallest at young ages and increase with age. Although the usual pattern is for men to choose women younger than themselves, the difference in their ages increases with the age at first marriage for the male. This indicates that, as men get older, they marry increasingly younger women. And as women get older, while nonmarriage is an increasingly popular option, another option is to redefine the "field of eligibles." Delayed marriage for women is associated with age hypergamy (women marrying older men), entry into the market of previously married men, and educational-status hypogamy (women marrying men with less education).[9]

One study found that age differences in marriage affected how long women live: that women married to younger men tended to live longer than expected, while women married to older men tended to die sooner than expected.[10] These results can be explained in two ways. One explanation suggests a mate-selection factor. That is, healthy and active women select or are selected by younger men and will live longer whomever they marry. The second explanation bases women's longevity on the biology, psychology, and sociology of marital interaction. Combinations of genetic factors, interpersonal interactions, and social norms lead partners to develop similar activities, interests, appearances, emotional states, and so forth. The causal factor of age difference in marriage and longevity may be related to the literal chemistry that people create in close relationships.

---

[8] Maxine P. Atkinson and Becky L. Glass, "Marital Age Heterogamy and Homogamy, 1900–1980," *Journal of Marriage and the Family* 47 (August 1985): 685–691.

[9] Daniel T. Lichter, "Delayed Marriage, Marital Homogamy, and the Mate Selection Process among White Women," *Social Science Quarterly* 71 (December 1990): 802–811.

[10] Laurel Klinger-Vartabedian and Lauren Wispe, "Age Differences in Marriage and Female Longevity," *Journal of Marriage and the Family* 51 (February 1989): 195–202.

A final question dealing with age homogamy is whether age differences affect the quality of marriage. Are age-dissimilar marriages, problem-ridden and unstable? Most evidence suggests that they are not, but some contradictory evidence does exist. A review of age-dissimilar marriages[11]cited some research showing that marital satisfaction does not differ between age-heterogamous and age-homogamous couples and that age differences do not impact negatively on marital quality. On the other hand, research was cited that showed age-discrepant unions to be more susceptible to dissolution, especially if the wife is older. It appears that the longer a couple is married, the more the effects of age heterogamy diminish.

"Marriage squeeze"

The "**marriage squeeze**" is used to describe the effects of an imbalance in the sex ratio, or the number of males and females available for marriage. Any shortage of marriageable males (a low sex ratio) or shortage of females (a high sex ratio), for whatever reason, will produce a marriage squeeze.

The squeeze (a low supply of either sex) may be due to wealth, power, status, level of education, age, or other factors. As will be noted in the discussion of the mating gradient, later in this chapter, women at the top and men at the bottom of a class or professional hierarchy have lower marriage rates. This type of marriage squeeze exists not only in the United States but in other countries, as well. High-caste women in India are a good illustration of this trend.[12]

Age is the characteristic considered most often in examining the marriage squeeze. Consider the hypothetical population, where males age twenty-seven typically marry females age twenty-four. If the annual number of births decreases each year, twenty-seven-year-old males will be looking for brides among the smaller cohort (an age-specific group) of females born three years later. The males will be caught in a marriage squeeze because they will encounter a shortage of females. Conversely, if a population experiences a substantial increase in the annual number of births, the same process will operate, but the females will be caught in the marriage squeeze. (That is, the male population born three years earlier will be smaller than the female population born three years later.)

The marriage squeeze phenomenon is a significant factor in marriage behavior. In the 1950s, men faced a shortage of women. The situation reversed in the 1980s, when women faced a shortage of men. It will reverse again at the turn of the century, when there will be a shortage of women. How are these imbalances and shifts explained?

Basically, the 1950s marriage squeeze was the result of a decline in the absolute number of births each year during the late 1920s and early 1930s, combined with the fact that men tended to marry women two or three years younger than themselves. Because there were more men born in 1930 than women born in

---

[11] Felix M. Berardo, Jeffrey Appel, and Donna Berardo, "Age Dissimilar Marriages: Review and Assessment," *Journal of Aging Studies* 7 (1993): 93–106.

[12] Michael S. Billig, "The Marriage Squeeze on High-Caste Rajasthani Women," *The Journal of Asian Studies* 50 (May 1991): 341–360.

1932 and 1933, the pool of women two or three years younger from whom to choose was smaller. Thus, a male marriage squeeze existed. A reverse female marriage squeeze resulted in the 1970s and early 1980s due to the increased number of births during the post–World War II "baby boom" of the 1950s. And finally, given the sharp decline in the birthrate in the 1960s and 1970s, it is safe to predict a return to the male marriage squeeze in the 1990s. Assuming a two- or three-year difference between men and women in marriage age, the smaller female population born several years later than the larger male population will have a larger pool from which to select.

Graham Spanier and Paul Glick demonstrated how the marriage squeeze affected black females far more than white females in the mid-1970s.[13] While the ratio of white males to females remained fairly close to 100 in the marriage-age group, the ratio for black males to females was lower. In the twenty- to twenty-four-year age group, there were 11 percent more black females than black males. This difference increased to 16 percent in the twenty-five- to twenty-nine-year age group and to more than 19 percent among those thirty to thirty-four. This marriage squeeze resulted in a restricted field of eligible partners for black women, causing an unusually large proportion of black women to remain unmarried or to marry men who were older, who had lower educational attainment, or who had previously been married.

Similar effects of the marriage squeeze are found in Israel where African Asian women born to cohorts who faced severe marriage squeezes were more likely to remain single and those who did marry were more likely to out-marry, that is, marry exogamously.[14]

Law and age at marriage

The legal control of age, marriage, and divorce in the United States lies with the states rather than the federal government. Most state laws have parental consent provisions regarding age at marriage; differences are based on the ages at which people may marry with or without parental consent.

To be married *without* parental consent, most states require that the bride and groom be eighteen. (Sixteen in Georgia and Hawaii, seventeen for males and fifteen for females in Mississippi, nineteen in Nebraska, and in Utah, counties are authorized to provide for premarital counseling as a requisite to issuing licenses to persons under nineteen). To be married *with* parental consent, the minimum age is typically sixteen for both sexes but California has no age limits at all. (The minimum age is fourteen in states such as Alabama, Massachusetts, New Hampshire, and Texas.) Numerous states have no age limit for marriage with parental consent and/or the permission of a judge, and some states give exceptions to parental con-

[13] Graham B. Spanier and Paul C. Glick, "Mate Selection Differentials Between Whites and Blacks in the United States," *Social Forces* 58 (March 1980): 707–725.

[14] Haya Stier and Yossi Shavit, "Age at Marriage, Sex-Ratios, and Ethnic Heterogamy," *European Sociological Review* 10 (May 1994): 79–87.

U.S. Diversity: Planning a Wedding? Check Out the Folkways

Somewhere I've read or heard that more marriages occur in December than in June; nevertheless, given their druthers, few prospective brides would turn down the sixth month if opportunity beckoned.

Why? Possibly because June is conceived as a sunny month, and, indeed, "happy the bride the sun shines on today." Further, if the wedding day be Wednesday or if the dates of June 1, 3, 11, 19, or 21 be feasible, the chances for a happy marriage are very good.

And why not a rainy day? No bride, of course, would wish to have her wedding dress ruined, but there's more to it than that. After all, raindrops are a symbol for tears: so many raindrops, so many tears in a marriage.

In addition, there is the matter of the blue sky on a sunny day—the color of the heavens and thus a divine assurance of good luck. Thus also the inclusion of "something blue" in the couplet, "Something old, something new/Something borrowed, something blue."

The idea of blue for good luck also carries over into possible early conception: it may also bring the fortune of a male child to the couple. Can this be the basic reason the young male is first dressed in blue?

Many other superstitions surround the custom of marriage, the why of each often forgotten with time.

Generally the bride should effect no color other than a touch of blue, since white (representing innocence and purity) is the traditional garb.

Neither should the bride wear pearls, for these, like raindrops, symbolize tears.

Silk should be the bride's first choice of material for her gown, for satin and velvet are deemed unlucky. Bridesmaids, on the other hand, have much more freedom of choice as to color and material, though the luckiest colors are supposed to be blue, pink, and gold.

Red and green are frowned on, the first being associated with blood and the second with jealousy (unless, of course, one is Irish).

A veil is absolutely necessary for the bride to protect her from the evil eye or from evil spirits, who, finding her attractive, might try to carry her away. As a matter of fact some say the reason the bridesmaids were originally included in the wedding ceremony was to help protect the bride.

Incidentally, when after the ceremony the groom raises the veil in order to kiss the bride, she is supposed to muster up a few tears—of joy or triumph.   Otherwise she is reserving tears to be spread throughout her married life.

The throwing of rice on the married couple as they leave the church is a time-honored fertility exercise, and occasionally one also sees an old shoe tossed after the couple as a guarantee of both fertility and happiness.

More often than not, however, shoes are tied to the wedding car, along with pots, pans, and other symbols of the married state.

As for the cutting of the wedding cake, the custom of the bride and groom cutting the first slice together results from its symbolizing the sharing of all things in their marriage.

In fact, should the groom attempt the cutting by himself, he may be facing the possibility of a childless marriage.

The best part of the wedding cake ceremony, however, is reserved for the young, unmarried female attendants. Rather than eat their cake, they must sleep with it under their pillows.

An absolute guarantee of sweet dreams and a vision of their own future mates!

Source: Rogers Whitener, "Folkways," *Watauga Democrat,* 29 May 1989, p. 14A. Used with permission.

sent if the minor was previously married, for a pregnancy or birth, or with a physician's approval if the parents are ill. No state has a legal age at marriage for females that is older than that for males; however, at least nine states permit females to marry younger than males with parental consent.[15] Over the past two decades, a majority of states have lowered the legal minimum age for marriage. Interestingly, this has come at a time when the median age at marriage has increased sharply, lessening the need for concern over young marriages.

Young marriage

Data presented about the median age at marriage show that close to half of all males and females marry for the first time below the ages of twenty-six and twenty-four, respectively. Some of these marriages occur among teenagers, an age category that most people view as too young for marriage. The consequences of teenage marriages are fairly well known: high incidence of dropping out of school,[16] high unemployment rates (refer to Table 6-1), higher-than-average fertility rates (the consequences of young parenthood are discussed in Chapter 13), lower-than-average lifetime earnings, and a high divorce rate (from two to four times that for persons who marry after age twenty).

Certainly, all of these consequences are serious and have negative long-range effects. It is likely that people who marry young are unprepared for the mate-selection process and marital-role performance, experience relatively low marital satisfaction as a result, and therefore appear disproportionately in divorce statistics.

Beyond this young age group, age at marriage does not appear to be a major point of difficulty in family life. Considering the upturn in the divorce rate in the late 1960s and in the 1970s and considering the stabilization or increase in age at marriage, it is not likely that any rise in the divorce rate can be accounted for by age at marriage.

Residential propinquity

Well established in the literature on sociology of the family is the idea that mate selection involves a *propinquity factor.* (Propinquity means "proximity.") A lengthy list of studies over the last thirty years has established the general conclusion that, in the United States, persons tend to marry people who live within fairly limited distances of their homes. Evidence to support this idea usually takes the form of a frequency distribution or cumulative percentage of marriages in some community, classified by the distance separating the bride's residence from the groom's residence just prior to marriage.

---

[15] These figures came from *The World Almanac and Book of Facts: 1995* (Mahwah, New Jersey: Funk and Wagnalls Corp., 1995): 727.

[16] Douglas M. Teti and Michael Lamb, "Socioeconomic and Marital Outcomes of Adolescent Marriage, Adolescent Childbirth, and Their Co-occurrence," *Journal of Marriage and the Family* 51 (February 1989): 203–212.

Since most propinquity studies were completed two or three decades ago, it is difficult to determine whether place of residence is as significant a factor in mate selection today. One might also expect considerable variations among different groups, such as rural dwellers, college students, and people who are elderly. However, it seems that people tend to marry those who live near them.

Explanations of propinquity

How can one account for the propinquity factor in mate selection? An obvious explanation is that people meet and interact with others who live nearby and attend the same schools, churches, and social events. While the pool of potential mates increases dramatically with increasing distance, proximity facilitates contact. People are less likely to meet and get to know intimately those who don't live near them. And obviously, people are not likely to fall in love with or marry people they don't meet.

Another explanation for propinquity has been called the **norm-segregation theory,** which suggests that people marry others who adhere to similar cultural norms and that these people reside in segregated clusters. People of similar normative categories of race/ethnicity, class, religion, and educational level tend to cluster together residentially. Neighborhoods and communities often tend to be characterized by norm-homogamous groupings. Thus, the combination of norm similarity and geographical proximity provides an additional explanation of residential propinquity in mate selection.

In a highly mobile society, one might expect nearness of residence less relevant in mate selection. For certain groups and persons, this is likely true. Higher-status groups may be less proximal than lower-status groups because money and time may be more readily accessible. Higher-status individuals may also be willing to travel farther. Propinquity differences among class and occupational groups can be ascribed to differences in time and resources.

One final point is that *propinquity* does not mean *nonmobility.* As an individual moves about for college, employment, military service, or whatever, he or she becomes increasingly more likely to marry someone currently living close by. Past ties will likely be broken. The individual who spent his or her childhood and adolescent years in Pennsylvania but goes to school and takes a job in Los Angeles may well marry someone from southern California. Most people do not become intimately acquainted with many eligible persons of the opposite sex, but those they do know are likely to be those who live near each other. Again, time and cost factors are operative.

Social status

Class endogamy, in U.S. society and around the world, is a desirable social norm, particularly for higher-status parents in regard to their children. Whether mates are selected by the individuals themselves, by parents, or by someone else, conditions supporting class endogamy are essential to preserve family lineage and status.

On the other hand, persons from lower statuses have much to gain by marriage to persons of higher standing. Irrespective of the desired or preferred circumstances, most marriages are class endogamous.

Class endogamy

Numerous studies in the past fifty years have found that both men and women marry persons within their own classes with greater consistency than could be expected simply by chance. As early as 1918, an analysis of marriages in Philadelphia showed that intermarriage between men and women in the same industry was distinctly more common than chance expectancy, revealing something of an endogamous trend.[17]

Like occupational endogamy, educationally endogamous or homogamous marriages occur more often than could be expected by chance. What's more, educational endogamy has been found (1) to be more important than social-class origins and (2) to have increased between the 1930s and the present.[18] Educational endogamy is common among all groups but particularly for highly educated persons and for those who marry shortly after leaving school. This intraclass pattern is often viewed by exchange theorists as a process in which individuals attempt to achieve the best possible bargain for themselves and their children by weighing marital resources and alternatives. If this is true, it would be highly surprising if the class origin/occupation/ education endogamy pattern were not the most prevalent. It is at similar class levels where marital resources will most likely be similar.

If this is the case, what does a person of lower social class have to "trade" with someone of higher social status? The following discussion will examine some patterns of marriage across class lines.

Mesalliance

Marriage with a person of a lower social position has been termed **mesalliance.** Special cases of mesalliance are **hypergamy,** denoting the pattern wherein the female marries into a higher social stratum, and **hypogamy,** where the female marries into a lower social stratum.

With particular reference to the United States, a number of writers have concluded that hypergamy is more prevalent than hypogamy; that is, women marry men of higher status more frequently than men marry women of higher status. On the basis of an exchange theory argument, the social advantages of hypergamy seem to exist primarily for low-status women. For equity to occur, this type of exchange would require that the woman be exceptional in those qualities defined as desirable by the culture into which she marries. Depending on the society, qualities in women that determine status might include shade of skin, facial and morphological features, and relative age.

---

[17] D. M. Marvin, "Occupational Propinquity as a Factor in Mate Selection," *Publications of the American Statistical Association* 16 (1918–1919): 131–150.

[18] Matthijs Kalmijn, "Status Homogamy in the United States," *American Journal of Sociology* 97 (September 1991): 496–523.

Men in the United States rank physical attractiveness at or near the top among the qualities they desire in women. Women, on the other hand, appear to be concerned with the socioeconomic status of potential spouses.[19] Thus, it would be expected that a male who achieves status through his occupation will exchange his social rank for the beauty and personal qualities of a female. Certain ideas related to mesalliance have been confirmed. One is that when males marry outside their class, they more frequently marry down than up. And the higher the occupational stratum of the male, the more commonly he marries down. Conversely, when females marry outside of their class, they more frequently marry up than down.

In brief, hypergamy is more prevalent than hypogamy. This notion extends to dating, as well, and is referred to as the mating gradient.

Mating gradient

If, as stated, when persons marry outside their social class, men tend to marry down and women tend to marry up, then it can be assumed the same patterns occur prior to marriage. Thus, when men and women date or engage in intimate personal interaction, women seek men of similar or higher status and men seek women of similar or lower status. This tendency has been called the **mating gradient.** It is rooted in the notion that men at the top have a wider range of mate choice than do men at the bottom, with the reverse being true for women; namely, women at the top have a more narrow range of choice than those at the bottom.

One interesting consequence of these choices is an excess number of unmarried men at the bottom of the socioeconomic ladder and an excess number of unmarried women at the top. Lower-status men must compete against other lower-status men as well as against higher-status men for the lower-status woman. Conversely, the higher-status women compete against other higher-status women as well as those below them for the higher-status man. Thus, unmarried men are likely to be disproportionately of lower-status and unmarried women are likely to be disproportionately of higher status. For women, however, as will be shown later in the discussion on marriage, higher-status or professional women who are more economically independent, increasingly choose not to marry (or remain married) in spite of the smaller pool of eligible men. And as was shown in Chapter 6, the lower marriage rate among African American women seems to be related to the smaller pool of higher-status eligible men.

The mating gradient also seems to operate in dating on college campuses. For example, the freshman male and the senior female have the smallest choice of probable dating partners. The freshman girl is the choice of college males at any class ranking, whereas the freshman male must, to a greater extent, limit his choices to freshmen females. Among seniors, the situation is reversed: The male can

---

[19] Scott South, "Sociodemographic Differentials in Mate Selection Preferences," *Journal of Marriage and the Family* 53 (November 1991): 928–940; and Susan Sprecher, "The Importance to Males and Females of Physical Attractiveness, Earning Potential, and Expressiveness in Initial Attraction," *Sex Roles* 21 (1989): 591–607.

Global Diversity: Alienation Among Unmarried Japanese Career Women

As reported in the *Wall Street Journal* (July 16, 1995), alienation is common among Japanese career women. They don't fit in the professional world or in the world of wives. They face powerful norms that dictate women belong in the kitchen, not in the top ranks of the workplace. But when in the home, they receive little help from their husbands whose lives revolve around the office. So where does that leave the independent-minded, highly paid, professional women?

The case was cited of Emiko Muto whose job as an account executive of an ad agency was changed from full time to a contractual position and her salary cut 30 percent. Unable to find another full-time job, she pursued marriage. Not meeting an unmarried prospect, she registered with a dating service, paying the equivalent of $3,000 for referrals to prospective spouses. But the husband search was as depressing as the job search. The several dozen men referred to her were looking for "servants to cook and clean and support them." None wanted an egalitarian independently minded partner.

The article reported that a poll of 1,000 Japanese women revealed that 56 percent agreed that the husband should be the breadwinner and the wife should stay at home. And for women who want a career, few female mentors exist—as only one percent of working women hold managerial posts and only 14 percent have professional and technical jobs. Many career women find themselves answering phones, greeting visitors, operating elevators, and serving tea—that is until they marry. But marriage too becomes difficult for a highly paid, highly skilled professional career woman. As is the case in the United States, in Japan the mating gradient appears to be alive and well.

select from any of the class rankings of females, whereas the female is more limited to senior and junior men.

Class heterogamy and marital conflict

What are the consequences of social-class heterogamy (hypergamy or hypogamy) in terms of marital conflict and divorce? One literature search of social-class heterogamy and marital success revealed great inconsistencies regarding the hypothesis that marrying someone of a higher or lower social-class background leads to marital incompatibility and divorce.[20] Women, in particular, strive to marry up and frequently do so. Status inequalities may become an important force in marital relations only when combined with certain status values, such as marrying down while striving to move up. From an exchange perspective, when status consciousness invades marriage, exchange equivalence is difficult to maintain.

---

[20] Norval D. Glenn, Sue Keir Hoppe, and David Weiner, "Social Class Heterogamy and Marital Success: A Study of the Empirical Adequacy of a Textbook Generalization," *Social Problems* 21 (April 1974): 539–550.

Religion and intermarriage

In the United States, religious endogamy is strong. The number of people who marry within their own religion is far greater than chance occurrence can explain. National data have suggested that the rate of endogamous Protestant marriage varies from 80 percent to 90 percent. For Catholics, the rates are somewhat lower, varying from 64 percent to 85 percent. For Jews, the rate is generally higher, about 90 percent. If marriages occurred at random, about 70 percent of Protestants, 25 percent of Catholics, and less than 4 percent of Jews in the United States would marry within their religions.

Yet, in spite of high rates of endogamy, Kalmijn showed how the social boundary between people from Catholic and Protestant backgrounds has declined over the course of this century, resulting in dramatic increases in Catholic/Protestant intermarriage.[21] It is Kalmijn's contention that education has become a more significant factor than religion in spouse selection.

Glenn, too, reported a substantial decrease in religious homogamy. He concluded that norms of religious endogamy have not been as strong as most writers addressing the topic have thought them to be. The apparent fact is that, in many cases, the individual is now willing to marry a person of a different religion and to change his or her own religion to that of the spouse. This fact led Glenn to state that "marriage in the United States has become very largely a secular institution, with religious institutions exerting only weak influences on marital choice."[22]

It is interesting to note that endogamy is not merely the predominant pattern when the broad Protestant/Catholic/Jewish classification is used; it is also the predominant pattern among Protestant denominations, as well. Protestants still marry other Protestants, as previous studies have shown, but they marry Protestants who share the same denominational affiliation (Lutheran, Methodist, etc.). The ratio of mixed marriages does not vary much across denominational lines. Interfaith marriages are most frequent among those persons who are religiously less devout.

Defining interfaith marriage

Determining what is within one's religion can be an extremely complex problem. To even define, much less measure, an interfaith (mixed religious) marriage involves problems that few persons have satisfactorily resolved. For example, is a Methodist/Lutheran marriage an intra- or interfaith union? If a devout Catholic married a person reared in the Catholic tradition but presently indifferent to religion, would they have a mixed marriage? If an atheist married an agnostic, would their marriage be endogamous or exogamous? If a Protestant married a Catholic and then the Protestant converted to Catholicism, would this be an inter- or intrafaith marriage?

---

[21] Matthijs Kalmijn, "Shifting Boundaries: Trends in Religious and Educational Homogamy," *American Sociological Review* 56 (December 1991): 786–800.

[22] Norval D. Glenn, "Interreligious Marriage in the United States: Patterns and Recent Trends," *Journal of Marriage and the Family* 44 (August 1982): 555–566.

How interfaith is defined influences the incidence as well as the consequences. Sander, for example, illustrated that the incidence of Catholic–mixed marriage rates are much lower if current religion is used rather than religious upbringing.[23] Yet most studies of interreligious marriage are limited to three broad categories—Catholic, Protestant, and Jewish—with little differentiation between religious upbringing, intensity of religious belief, extent of religious activity, or differences within categorical groups.

For example, Catholics tend to be viewed as quite homogamous. In Judaism, even though definite differences regarding interfaith and intra-Jewish marriages have been found to exist among the three major branches—Orthodox, Conservative, and Reform—studies distinguish among them relatively infrequently. The same is true among some of the major denominations of Protestantism: Methodist, Presbyterian, Lutheran, Baptist, and the like. This lack of differentiation is very unfortunate, for even the most untrained persons in religious thought recognize differences in beliefs and practices *among* Protestant denominations to say nothing of the differences *within* denominations.

Consequences of interfaith marriage

The general opposition to interfaith marriages stems from the widespread belief that they are highly unstable and create a multitude of problems that intrafaith marriages do not. Some empirical evidence has supported the belief that interreligious marriages are less satisfying and less stable than religiously homogamous marriages.[24] Those homogamous partners with no religious identification, however, are the least stable of all. Couples of the same denominational affiliation as well as those who attend church frequently are more likely to have happy, stable marriages than those whose religions are different or those who claim no religion.

Findings from these cross-sectional, homogamous/heterogamous comparisons must be interpreted cautiously, even if the reports are accurate. Marriages that were unhappy and have already ended in divorce do not contribute to unhappiness in the currently married population. Nevertheless, even taking this factor into account, it is likely that lower levels of happiness and slightly higher rates of divorce occur among interreligious marriages than among intrareligious, homogamous marriages. That the highest rates of divorce and marital instability occur among those with "no religion" underscores the importance of religion whether inter- or intrafaith.

What about the children of interfaith marriages? It has been argued that these children, compared to children of homogamous marriages, are subjected to less intense and less consistent religious socialization, such that they are weakly religious themselves. In other words, the assertion is that interfaith marriages have a secularizing effect on the children.

---

[23] William Sander, "Catholicism and Intermarriage in the United States," *Journal of Marriage and the Family* 55 (November 1993): 1037–1041.

[24] Evelyn L. Lehrer and Carmel U. Chiswick, "Religion as a Determinant of Marital Stability," *Demography* 30 (August 1993): 385–404; and Tim B. Heaton and Edith L. Pratt, "The Effects of Religious Homogamy on Marital Satisfaction and Stability," *Journal of Family Issues* 11 (June 1990): 191–207.

Case Example:
An Interracial, Interfaith Relationship

Richard and Tonya are in a committed dating relationship. He is white and Jewish. She is African American and Christian. Both are 26 years old and employed full time as social workers in foster care but affiliated with separate agencies. They met through their work more than three years ago.

As they described their love for one another, neither race nor religion was mentioned. Tonya liked his sense of humor, personality, outgoing nature, and the way he is always a gentleman with her. Richard described her as beautiful, ambitious, thoughtful, caring, and available when he needed her.

Neither seemed to be very concerned about their racial differences. Richard had attended a public school that he said was, at best, ten percent white. Tonya grew up in an integrated but mostly black community. Tonya's mother (her father is deceased) was very understanding about their relationship as she too had dated white men. Richard's parents accepted Tonya but he expressed concern as to how they would accept a marriage. More of a problem was his brother, with whom he is currently living, who talks openly of his belief in the inferiority of blacks.

The religious differences appeared to be of greater concern than racial differences. Tonya is a devoutly committed Christian in a nondenominational church while Richard is a nonpracticing Jew. Because of her belief, living with him without marriage is out of the question. Also, it was a key factor in delaying an intimate sexual relationship. Were she to become pregnant, which to both seemed highly unlikely, abortion would not be an option.

Tonya indicated that she would have a problem with children being raised in any faith but Christian. While she had no interest in attending a synagogue, he would consider going to church with her. Both agreed they are struggling with the religious issue but felt they would be able to work it out. As Richard said, she is a "beautiful, wonderful, and considerate woman. We love each other dearly and we will find a way to resolve any problems as they arise in the future."

For the most part, this assertion has not been found to be true. Larry Peterson, in studying over one thousand adult Catholics, claimed that, contrary to the secularization hypothesis, interfaith marriages have relatively inconsequential effects on religious commitment.[25] In this study, offspring from interfaith marriages did not consistently score lower on general religiosity measures than did offspring of homogamous marriages. Catholics who were the offspring of interfaith marriages and Catholics who formed them were as firmly committed to Christianity, in general, and Catholicism, in particular, as were Catholics in homogamous families.

---

[25] Larry R. Peterson, "Interfaith Marriage and Religious Commitment among Catholics," *Journal of Marriage and the Family* 48 (November 1986): 725–735.

In sum, the negative consequences often assumed of interfaith marriages regarding the success of the marriage and the secularization of the children do not have much empirical support.

Race/ethnicity and intermarriage

Of all the norms involving intermarriage, few are more widely held or rigorously enforced than those pertaining to race and ethnic origins. Despite scientific findings and the removal of legal barriers, the restrictions concerning interracial marriage still remain the most inflexible of all mate-selection boundaries.

The intermingling of people of different races and ethnic origins is nothing new in world affairs. Based on historical and biological evidence, the idea of a "pure race" or a "pure ethnic group" is totally inaccurate. Racial and ethnic mixture has been evident throughout recorded history; some evidence has suggested that racial/ethnic intermingling occurred even in prehistoric times. As there is no evidence to support the notion of a pure race, neither is there evidence to support the idea that racial/ethnic mixtures result in biologically inferior offspring. Biologically, there is nothing to prevent marriage of or procreation between persons of different races or ethnic groups.

Removal of the legal prohibition against interracial marriage in the United States came in 1967, when the U.S. Supreme Court struck down as unconstitutional a 1924 Virginia law, forbidding marriage between persons of different races. According to the Court, laws of this type violate rights guaranteed to all persons under the Fourteenth Amendment to the Constitution. Irrespective of the Supreme Court's decision declaring such laws unconstitutional, the social mores and the disfavor placed on interracial marriage by all major racial, religious, and ethnic groups are so strong in most areas that relatively few interracial marriages take place.

A Gallup poll asked the question, Do you approve of marriage between blacks and whites? Forty-eight percent responded they approved, 42 percent said they disapproved, and 10 percent had no opinion. Blacks were more likely to approve than whites (70 percent to 44 percent), males were more likely to approve than females (52 to 44 percent), and people under 30 were more likely to approve than those over 50 (64 to 27 percent). People from the western United States and large cities as well as people who were well educated and who had no religious preference were likely to approve of intermarriage.[26]

While the trend over several decades has been toward greater approval of interracial marriage, the strength of the prohibition—particularly against black/white marriage—remains high. Interestingly, a major discrepancy exists between verbal approval of interracial marriage and its actual occurrence.

---

[26] George Gallup, Jr., and Frank Newport, *The Gallup Poll Monthly* 311 (August 1991): 62.

Black-white intermarriage, while increasing, still constitutes a very small proportion of all marriages. When they do occur, a disproportionate number of couples include a black male and a white female.

Frequency of interracial/interethnic marriages

Determining the frequency of mixed or interracial/interethnic marriage is exceedingly difficult. As with religion, there is the matter of classification. If an African, Asian, or Native American is able to "pass" for white and marries a white American, is this an intermarriage or an endogamous marriage? Given the laws in various states, where a person who has one-eighth or one-sixteenth African blood is deemed black (an empirical impossibility), would it not be an intermarriage, irrespective of which race the individual married? Even if a categorization could be precisely determined and agreed on, it could be argued that social sanctions against certain types of interracial/interethnic marriage are so severe in most parts of the United States that the reported number of such marriages would be less than the actual number.

Since 1960, the United States census has been tabulated to show the number of husbands and wives who have the same or different racial backgrounds. This information, like all census information involving race, does not denote any clear-cut scientific definition of biological stock. Rather, it is based on self-identification by respondents. The data represent self-classification into one of fifteen groups listed on the census questionnaire.[27]

Table 9-2 presents census data from over the past several decades. In 1994, of the 54.3 million married couples in the United States, 1,283,000, or 2.4 percent of the total, were classified as interracial. Only 296,000, or 0.5 percent of the total number of married couples, were classified as black/white.

Thus, most interracial marriages in the United States do *not* occur between blacks and whites. Rather, intermarriages between Native American women and white men, Japanese American women and white men, and Filipino American women and white men are most common. Although census figures on interracial marriages must be interpreted with caution because they are based on self-reports and thus devoid of reliability or validity checks, such data do provide a valuable source of information on frequency, the increase over time, and the husband/wife differential.

Several findings in Table 9-2 are of interest. For example, while the number of married couples increased by 11.5 percent between 1970 and 1980 and by 9.1 percent between 1980 and 1994, the number of interracial couples increased by 110 percent between 1970 and 1980 and by 97.1 percent between 1980 and 1994. Thus, the number of reported interracial marriages increased at a much higher rate than did the number of all marriages.

Yet the number of interracial marriages relative to the total number of marriages remained small: 2.4 percent of all marriages were interracial and only 0.5 percent were black/white marriages. This figure, although small, more than doubled in the decade of the 1970s (a 157 percent increase) but increased by only 77.2 percent between 1980 and 1994. The percent of the total changed from 0.3 to 0.5 percent between 1980 and 1994). This suggests (1) that the occurrence of interracial marriages of any type and particularly of black/white marriage is infrequent and (2) that the political and social conservatism of the 1980s and 1990s was manifest in the number of interracial marriages, as well. If the frequency of interracial marriage and the percent of increase or decrease is one indicator of racial integration and equality, the years since 1980 have shown little improvement.

Interracial marriage rates vary widely from one region and state to another but precise data are hampered by the infrequency of such unions, the accuracy of defining what is or is not an interracial marriage, and the lack of consistent vital statistical data or any data at all from various states. For example, as many as seventeen states do not include race on their marriage licenses.

What is known is that fewer interracial marriages occur in the south. Kalmijn, using marriage license data, shows that while black/white intermarriage has increased in both the south and the non-south, rates in the south are well below

---

[27] These fifteen groups listed in the race item on the census questionnaire included: white, black, American Indian, Eskimo, Aleut, Chinese, Filipino, Japanese, Asian Indian, Korean, Vietnamese, Hawaiian, Samoan, Guamanian, and "other."

Table 9-2

Interracial married couples: 1970, 1980, 1990 and 1994

	1970	1980	1990	1994
Total married couples	44,598,000	49,714,000	53,256,000	54,251,000
Interracial married couples	310,000	651,000	946,000	1,283,000
Percentage of total	0.7%	1.3%	1.8%	2.4%
Black-white married couples	65,000	167,000	211,000	296,000
Percentage of total	0.1%	0.3%	0.4%	0.5%
Husband black, wife white	41,000	122,000	150,000	196,000
Wife black, husband white	24,000	45,000	61,000	100,000

	Percent Increase		
	1970–80	1980–90	1980–94
Total married couples	11.5%	7.1%	9.1%
Interracial married couples	110.0	45.3	97.1
Black-white married couples	156.9	26.3	77.2
Husband black, wife white	197.6	22.9	60.7
Wife black, husband white	87.5	35.6	122.2

Source: U.S. Bureau of the Census, *Statistical Abstract of the United States, 1995,* 115th ed. (Washington, DC: U.S. Government Printing Office, 1995), no. 61, p. 55.

half those outside the south with the increase among black grooms outside the south being the most dramatic.[28] This trend is seen as due partly to population composition. Although the north does not have the southern legacy of slavery and miscegenation laws, and even though racial attitudes there are generally more favorable, blacks in the north also have fewer opportunities to marry within their group than blacks in the south. As shown at the beginning of the chapter, group size does make a difference. There is an inverse relationship between group size and outmarriage: the smaller the proportion of blacks in a state, the greater the percentage of blacks who marry whites.

Interracial/interethnic marriages are sociologically important because they serve as an indicator of the relationship among various racial and ethnic groups. If full equality were achieved and social norms were favorable, the rate of interra-

---

[28] Matthijs Kalmijn, "Trends in Black/White Intermarriage," *Social Forces* 72 (September 1993): 119–146. Note also: M. Belinda Tucker and Claudia Mitchell-Kernan, "New Trends in Black American Interracial Marriage: The Social Structural Context," *Journal of Marriage and the Family* 52 (February 1990): 209–218.

cial/interethnic marriage would be high. The very low rate of black/white inter-marriage, for example, serves as a stark indicator of the separation of the races and the disapproval accorded to interracial marriage in the United States.

Male/female interracial differences

As indicated, census data have shown that most interracial marriages in the United States occur between Native American, Japanese, and Filipino women and white men. However, many articles and books have addressed black/white intermarriage, finding that black males marry white females more frequently than white males marry black females. This black husband/white wife pattern has also been strong-ly supported by census data (see Table 9-2). Of the 296,000 reported black/white marriages in 1994, 196,000, or 66.2 percent, were between a black husband and a white wife. Only 100,000, or 33.8 percent, of the total had a black wife and a white husband.

There is a lack of consensus on the reasons for different incidences of interra-cial marriage by sex. Research attempts aimed at establishing a race/class exchange have failed to find consistent support. For example, when education has been used as an indicator of class, highly educated black men are more likely to marry inter-racially. But this tendency is less true for highly educated black females and white males. Availability has also been ruled out as an answer, for the greater number of black females than black males would lead one to expect more intermarriage by black females.

Randall Collins and Scott Coltrane suggested that one possible explanation for the sex difference may be that there is a particularly strong distinction between male and female cultures in the African American community.[29] Black women have a tradition of independence (not being very subservient to men), which may account both for their own lower rate of intermarriage and for the tendency of black males to seek wives elsewhere.

One could hypothesize as well that differential norms operate for white and black males in relation to females. For example, for both races, males are more likely than females to initiate mate selection and marriage. In addition, due to his-torical and socioeconomic differences, it may be more prestigious for a black male to initiate interaction with a white female than for a white male to initiate inter-action with a black female. Other factors or explanations may be operative, as well.

Success of interracial/interethnic marriages

Do interracial and interethnic marriages succeed? A generally accepted view is that people who enter a racially or ethnically mixed marriage are more likely to get divorced. However, evidence supporting this view is conflicting. For example, data from Hawaii showed that interethnic (mixed) marriages more often resulted in divorce than intraethnic marriages. However, a sizable portion of these intermar-

---

[29] Randall Collins and Scott Coltrane, *Sociology of Marriage and the Family: Gender, Love, and Property,* 4th ed. (Chicago: Nelson-Hall, 1995): 268.

riages in Hawaii were between nonresidents. When the proportion of divorces to resident marriages was examined, intraethnic (within-group) marriages were more at risk than interethnic marriages. Other mixed results came from an analysis of differing groups. Some cross-ethnic combinations appeared more at risk for divorce than others. For example, marriages in which the bride was from a higher income group than the groom were at a significantly greater risk for divorce than marriages in which the bride came from a lower income group than the groom.[30]

In sum, the success or failure of an interracial or interethnic marriage is not dependent solely on the fact that it is mixed; as with other marriages, success is influenced by age, religious beliefs, educational level, residence location, first marriage or remarriage, and many other factors. Recognizing that Hawaii may be a unique case, recognizing that interracial/interethnic marital success depends upon which races or ethnic groups are intermarrying and the circumstances surrounding the marriage, and recognizing different methodological and research problems, findings should certainly lead one to seriously question the negative aspects of interracial/interethnic marriage per se to the couple themselves.

But what about the children of interracial and interethnic couples? Are they at risk for personality and adjustment problems?

Popular literature, often based on speculation or unrepresentative case histories, has been strongly biased toward the notion that offspring of cross-racial/cross-ethnic marriages are likely to suffer from adjustment problems. Data from Hawaii and New Mexico, at least, have suggested that this literature is incorrect.[31] In these states, positive effects of bicultural socialization were found for intergroup contact and attitudes, language facility, and enjoyment of the culture of minority groups. In contrast to their single-heritage peers, students of mixed heritage did *not* have lower self-esteem or feel more alienated nor did they experience greater stress. Mixed-heritage students appeared to have better relations with single-heritage groups than the single-heritage groups had with one another. Results such as these may be due to the low level of community-wide stigma associated with mixed marriages in Hawaii. If that is true, then pressures outside the marriage and the parent/child relationship are the key dimensions in producing negative effects of such marriages on offspring.

Whether dealing with husband/wife, parent/child, or employer/employee relationships, the success of the relationship depends on the total situation and not merely on the fact that the partners have different skin colors or ethnic heritages. Interpersonal relationships of any sort are clearly affected by external forces. Parents, kin, neighbors, teachers, politicians, and society in general lend either support or opposition with varying degrees of pressure on the marriage, family, or job situation. Success is relative to the social/cultural context, extending far beyond the boundaries of any two persons—whether their skin color is alike or different.

---

[30] Fung Chu Ho and Ronald C. Johnson, "Intra-ethnic and Inter-ethnic Marriage and Divorce in Hawaii," *Social Biology* 37 (Spring/Summer 1990): 44–51.

[31] Walter G. Stephan and Cookie White Stephan, "Intermarriage: Effects on Personality, Adjustment, and Intergroup Relations in Two Samples of Students," *Journal of Marriage and the Family* 53 (February 1991): 241–250.

Intermarriage trends

As was evident from the data in Table 9-2, the trend in interracial/interethnic marriage is upward. Yet the total incidence (1,195,000) is still so low that these marriages, relative to all marriages (54.2 million), are not likely to have any major effect in achieving assimilation and racial integration, in decreasing social distance among ethnic groups, or even in affecting black/white relationships in general.

It is hard to imagine a set of conditions under which black/white marriage rates would increase so rapidly as to achieve any large intermingling within the foreseeable future. It would be more likely that interacting forces would achieve this goal. For example, if schools were to become integrated, if educational opportunities were to become available to blacks, and if job opportunities for minorities were to increase, then it would be likely that the incidence of interracial/interethnic marriage would also increase. And if the incidence of black/white marriage would continue to increase, this would perhaps play some role, albeit small, in improving the relationship between black and white Americans.

SUMMARY

1. The terms *homogamy* and *endogamy* refer to the extent of intermarriage among people who share similar characteristics. This chapter examined the nature of intermarriage and five normative structures surrounding the selection of intimate partners in the United States: age, proximity of residence, social status, religion, and race/ethnicity.

2. Reporting and interpreting types of intermarriage are difficult. The boundaries of race/ethnicity, class, and religion are rarely clear-cut and precise. Rates for individuals are often confused with rates for marriages. Actual rates of intermarriage vary according to numerous social factors, such as group size, heterogeneity, sex ratio, controls over marriage, development of cultural similarities, the romantic love complex, and influence of certain psychological factors.

3. Most couples in the United States are relatively homogamous in the age at which they marry. Since the turn of the century, the tendency has been for the male/female age difference at the time of marriage to narrow.

4. The "marriage squeeze" is used to describe the effects of an imbalance in the sex ratio, or the number of males and females available for marriage. Based on age alone, this squeeze resulted in a shortage of women in the 1950s and a shortage of men in the 1980s and will predictably result in a shortage of women at the turn of the next century. The marriage squeeze is particularly acute among black women.

5. Partner selection involves a *propinquity factor.* Studies have concluded that people choose mates who live within fairly limited distances of their own homes. Explanations for propinquity center around the opportunity to meet, a norm-segregation theory, and a time/cost factor.

6. Mate-selection studies have concluded that marriages are highly endogamous by social class, more so than could be expected to occur simply by chance. When marriage occurs with someone from a lower social position (mesalliance), it may denote hypergamy or hypogamy. The general tendency for men to date and marry downward more frequently than upward has been termed the *mating gradient*.

7. Religious endogamy, although less rigid than racial/ethnic endogamy, remains an important factor in mate selection. There seems to be consensus that people who are religiously devout marry endogamously in greater frequency than those who are religiously less devout and that endogamous marriages have higher levels of happiness and slightly lower rates of divorce than interfaith marriages.

8. In the United States, racial/ethnic—endogamous norms are more rigorously enforced than any others described in this chapter. Findings have suggested that black males marry white females more frequently than white males marry black females. While the trend in interracial/interethnic marriage is upward, the incidence is low and the number will, in all probability, have little effect on integration.

9. In general, intermarriage of all types appears to be on the increase, but endogamous marriage continues to occur in a frequency far greater than could be expected to occur by chance alone.

10. Chapter 10 will continue to concentrate on mate selection, but the frame of reference will shift from a structural orientation to a more processual and interactional orientation. What explanations are offered for choosing one mate over another? What processes are followed from meeting someone to marrying him or her? These and related issues will be addressed.

KEY TERMS AND TOPICS

DISCUSSION QUESTIONS

1. Differentiate between terms in the following pairs: *endogamy/exogamy* and *homogamy/heterogamy.* What is meant by *assortive mating?* What constitutes *intermarriage* or *mixed marriage?*

2. Discuss factors that are likely to increase the incidence of intermarriage in the United States. What factors operate most strongly to discourage or prohibit intermarriage?

3. What trends are likely regarding age at marriage, place of residence, social class, religion, and race/ethnicity? Why?

4. Describe the "marriage squeeze." What factors account for a shift from a shortage of women to a shortage of men and vice versa? Why is the marriage squeeze so significant for black women?

5. Discuss *hypergamy* and *hypogamy*—how likely each is to occur, why it occurs, and what consequences result from its occurrence.

6. Is the mating gradient a common phenomenon in your school? Why or why not? Is the basic pattern among college students likely to change in ten years?

7. To what extent is a social exchange theory adequate in explaining interclass and interracial marriages? What factors are offered in exchange (for example, between a black male and white female)? How are exceptions handled?

8. In regard to black/white interracial marriages: Why do they occur so infrequently? What explains the predominance of black husband/white wife marriages? Why is the reverse pattern uncommon? What objections to interracial marriages likely lack empirical support?

FURTHER READINGS

Mayer, Egon. *Love and Tradition: Marriages Between Jews and Christians.* New York: Plenum Press, 1985. A look at Jewish/Christian marriages within a historical and cultural context based on survey data and personal interviews over a ten-year period.

Minow, Martha, ed. *Family Matters: Readings on Family Lives and the Law.* New York: The Free Press, 1993. Approximately 60 readings cover a broad range of topics of concern to family law from defining who is in or out of a family, who may marry, custody, divorce, violence, and the courts.

Rosenblatt, Paul C., Karis, Terri A., and Powell, Richard D. *Multiracial Couples: Black and White Voices.* Thousand Oaks, CA: Sage Publications, 1995. Using a qualitative research design, the authors explore the interpersonal dynamics of 21 interracial couples in committed relationships.

Schneider, Susan Weidman. *Intermarriage.* New York: Free Press, 1989. A focus on intermarriage between Christians and Jews: who "marries out," living with differences, raising children, and so forth.

Spickard, Paul R. *Mixed Blood: Intermarriage and Ethnic Identity in Twentieth-Century America.* Madison: University of Wisconsin Press, 1989. A historical look at ethnicity and intermarriage, with a focus on Japanese Americans, Jewish Americans, and African Americans.

Surra, Catherine A. "Research and Theory on Mate Selection and Premarital Relationships in the 1980s." *Journal of Marriage and the Family* 52 (November 1990): 884-865. A decade review article of major research and theory about mate selection and relationship development.

Chapter 10

Selection of Intimate Partners: Explanations and Processes

As was demonstrated in Chapter 9, selection of an intimate partner is not simply a matter of preference or free choice. Despite the increases in freedom and opportunities available to people both young and old to choose anyone they please, many factors well beyond the control of the individual severely limit the number of eligible persons from whom to choose. The taboo on incest and the restrictions placed on age, sex, marital status, class, religion, and race/ethnicity in most societies narrow considerably the "field of eligibles."

ARRANGED MARRIAGE VERSUS FREE CHOICE OF MATE

A sizable volume of research has suggested that all societies have systems of norms and sometimes specific rules about who may marry whom and how marriage partners are selected. These norms are likely to vary from one culture to another and to differ for a first marriage and a remarriage, for males and females, for wealthy and poor people, and so forth. However, norms, rules, and controls appear in all societies.

On an ideal-type continuum, these norms may vary from totally arranged marriages, at one extreme, to totally free choice of mate, at the other. Where marriages are arranged, the couple has nothing to say about the matter. The selection is usually but not always made by parents or kin. The other extreme, totally free choice, is so rare that to discuss it would simply be conjecture. The United States is, however, one of the few societies of the world that approaches this end of the continuum. In its extreme form, parents and kin are not consulted and in some instances not even informed of the impending marriage.

Between these two extremes are various combinations of arranged/free-choice possibilities. Parents may arrange a marriage and give their son or daughter veto power. The sons or daughters may make their own selection and give the parents veto power. One of the persons to be married, usually the son and his parents, may select the bride. Regardless of the method of mate selection, every society has a set of norms that prescribe the appropriate procedure.

The family is generally the chief and only source of employment for the selected partner; rather than establishing a new family, marriage is a means of providing for the continuity and stability of the existing family. Arranged marriage has the effect (function) of providing elders with control over younger family members and control over who from the outside may enter and become part of the family unit. In addition, arranged marriage preserves family property, furthers political linkages, protects economic and status concerns, and keeps the family intact from one generation to another.

As a result, almost without exception, the chosen partners in an arranged marriage must share similar group identities. Racial/ethnic, religious, and particularly economic statuses must be similar. Arranged marriage is not based on criteria such as romantic love, desire for children, loneliness, and sexual desire; rather, it will likely be based on factors such as a dowry or the size of the bride's price, the reputation of the potential spouse's kin group, levirate and sororate obligations, and traditions of prescribed marriage arrangements.

A contemporary example of arranged marriage comes from Japan where about 25 to 30 percent of all marriages are arranged.[1] A "marriage drought" makes it very difficult for young people to find desirable partners. As a result, professional "go-betweens services," modeled after the more traditional type of arranged marriage, have arisen. The objective criteria for mate selection through an arranged marriage are based on family standing such as reputation, social rank, or lineage and also the selected person's schooling, salary, or attractiveness. The match between the two persons must be that of equals to avoid embarrassment to either family.

After the couple meets, if the date was agreeable to both persons involved, the go-between gives out phone numbers and leaves it up to the couple to decide if they wish to continue. It is estimated that less than 20 percent of the first meetings are successful. But among those couples who after about three months decide to get married, the go-between is notified. He or she then makes arrangements for the families to meet. The groom's family sends a betrothal gift in the form of cash (about two to three months' income) to the family of the bride.

Arranged marriages result in a commitment among the selected partners that is, in many instances, as binding as the marriage itself. Since the marriage exists primarily to fulfill social and economic needs, concerns such as incompatibility, love, and personal fulfillment are not relevant. As a result, divorce is practically unknown or occurs only infrequently. Instances where marriages must be terminated frequently bring a great sense of shame and stigma to the entire family and kin group.

Evidence has suggested that, as traditional cultures are exposed to Western models of modernization and as they industrialize and adopt new technology from the outside world, marriage patterns will change. Namely, those segments of traditional cultures with the greatest exposure to outside influences tend to increasingly depart from an arranged-marriage pattern to free-choice or love-matched marriages.

As suggested, total free choice is practically nonexistent in the world. This pattern implies freedom to choose a partner for marriage without regard to the wishes of anyone else, certainly not parents or kin. Also, free choice implies that instrumental considerations such as money, power, social rank, occupation, education, age, incest, family ties, and even sex are not major considerations in the choice. A limited free-choice pattern takes these factors into consideration and permits choice of mates by the spouses themselves within the limits of permitted social groupings. Given this choice, then, love and prestige ratings become significant, as do the processes of getting to know one another and of moving the relationship toward increasing commitment. Personal needs and values also become significant.

---

[1] Kalman D. Applbaum, "Marriage with the Proper Stranger: Arranged Marriage in Metropolitan Japan," *Ethnology* 34 (Winter 1995): 37–51.

Global Diversity: Dowry Deaths in India

Many family systems throughout the world include a dowry as an essential aspect of the marriage arrangement. A dowry includes gifts given by the bride or her family to the husband and his family. Without a good dowry, a higher class woman was not very marriageable.

The *Wall Street Journal* (25 August 1994) reported that brides are increasingly being killed in India for providing dowries deemed inadequate by their husband's families. The number of deaths rose from 4,836 in 1990 to 5,582 in 1993 and over that four-year period was said to total 20,537.

These so-called dowry deaths meant the bride was put to death by being set on fire or by injuries or poisoning. The reasons for death usually included an inability by the family of the wife to meet the post-marriage demands for gifts or cash that was agreed upon prior to marriage or that the dowry given was not to the satisfaction of the groom's family. Though India outlawed dowry payments in 1961, the practice is still widespread among Hindus, who account for about 80 percent of the country's 900 million people.

The reader with an interest in this issue may want to see: B. Devi Prasad, "Dowry Related Violence: A Content Analysis of News in Selected Newspapers," *Journal of Comparative Family Studies* 25 (1994): 71–89.

INDIVIDUALISTIC EXPLANATIONS OF PARTNER SELECTION

With a decrease in kinship control over mate selection, particularly in Western societies, has come a freedom that has brought about an enormously complex process. This process clearly begins long before the first date. And for many, the selection process never ends, since, in the United States, it is possible to have more than one marriage partner (although legally, only one at a time). Most psychological and other individualistic theories explaining the choice of mate are based on a wide range of experiences, along with a variety of subconscious drives and needs.

Instinctive and biological theories

One of the oldest and perhaps most radical explanations of partner selection suggests that what guides a man to a woman (rarely is it thought to be the other way around) is *instinct*. Instinct is established by heredity and deals with unlearned behavior. Some sociologists would argue that there is no such thing as human instinct, but many biologists and psychologists would counter that instinct is basic to human behavior.

Related to the instinct theory is that of genetic similarity.[2] The idea is that genetically similar others, be they strangers or kin, have a tendency to seek each

---

[2] J. Philippe Rushton, Robin J. H. Russell, and Pamela A. Wells, "Genetic Similarity Theory: Beyond Kin Selection," *Behavior Genetics,* 14 (1984): 179–193.

other and provide supportive environments. In contrast, genetically dissimilar others have a tendency to form natural antipathies and provide mutually hostile environments. Assortive mating in both animals and humans is based on genetic similarity.

As far as is known, no one has ever discovered any instinctive, unconscious, or purely biological determinant for mate selection. Of course, the fact that such motivations are unconscious or innate makes them difficult if not impossible to discover. In short, to attribute selecting a mate to the unconscious adds little more to understanding basic processes involved in mate choice than does attributing it to spirits, fairies, or supernatural powers.

Parental image theory

Closely related to the instinct theory is the psychoanalytic idea of Sigmund Freud and his followers, which suggests that a person tends to fall in love with and marry a person similar to his or her opposite-sex parent. This, too, is generally a theory rooted in the unconscious.

According to the **Oedipus complex,** early in a male child's life, his mother becomes his first love object. But the presence of his father prohibits him from fulfilling his incestuous desire. As a result, the male infant develops an antagonism toward his father for taking his love object from him. This, in turn, results in an unconscious desire to kill his father and marry his mother. The male infant's desire for his mother and fear of his father becomes so great that he develops a fear of castration, or, as Freud called it, *castration anxiety*—a fear that his father wants to emasculate him by removing his penis and testes. But since the father is also protective and helpful and respected by the mother, a great amount of ambivalence exists for the son, which is resolved only by a primary type of identification with his father. The Oedipus complex is thus temporarily resolved for the male, but the repressed love for his mother remains. By adolescence, when the male is free to fall in love, he selects a love object that possesses the qualities of his mother.

The opposite but parallel result occurs for the female. At an early age, the girl becomes aware that she does not have a male sexual organ and develops *penis envy.* Feeling castrated, her feelings are transformed into the desire to possess a penis, especially the father's. These feelings for the forbidden object remain repressed throughout childhood, but her love for her father, known as the **Electra complex,** culminates in marriage when she selects a mate with the qualities of her father. (Both the Oedipus complex and the Electra complex are discussed more fully in Chapter 14.)

Although it seems very reasonable to believe that young people, in selecting mates, would be keenly aware of the qualities of their parents and the nature of their marriage, no clear evidence has supported the hypothesis that the boy seeks someone like his mother and that the girl seeks someone like her father.

Complementary needs theory

The theory of complementary needs in mate selection was developed and enhanced by Robert F. Winch about forty years ago. It was his belief that, although mate selection is homogamous with respect to numerous social characteristics—age, race/ethnicity, religion, residential propinquity, socioeconomic status, education, and previous marital status—when it comes to psychic level and individual motivation, mate selection tends to be complementary rather than homogamous. The idea grew out of a modified and simplified version of a need-scheme theory of motivation, but the needs tend to be complementary rather than similar.

To test his hypothesis of mate selection, Winch subjected to intensive study twenty-five husbands and their wives. In each of three early papers, Winch claimed that the bulk of the evidence from these couples supported the hypothesis that mates tend to select each other on the basis of complementary needs.[3] Conversely, Winch claimed that support is not available for the conflicting hypothesis that spouses tend to be motivationally similar.

Several years later, Winch published his book on mate selection.[4] For mate selection to take place on the basis of love—that is, due to complementary needs—it is understood that both man and woman must have some choice in the matter. The theory would not be operative in settings where marriages are arranged (as by parents, marriage brokers, or others). Thus, love will likely be an important criterion only under cultural conditions where (1) the choice of mates is voluntary, (2) the culture encourages premarital interaction between men and women, and (3) the marital friendship is culturally defined as a rich potential source of gratification. Since love is defined in terms of needs, the general hypothesis is that when people marry for love, their needs will be complementary.

Reports by Winch and his colleagues led to a constant flow of articles attempting to retest the complementary needs hypothesis. The results were basically negative, failing to provide empirical support for the idea that people tend to choose mates whose needs complement their own.

Various interpretations have been presented to explain why the complementary needs theory refutes popular opinion and fails to gain research support. Perhaps there are problems in the measurement of needs. Perhaps the basic theoretical considerations of the complementary needs theory are incorrect. Perhaps, like findings of endogamous factors presented in the previous chapter, needs also are more homogamous than heterogamous, more similar than different. Perhaps "likes do marry likes" rather than "opposites attract."

---

[3] Robert F. Winch, Thomas Ktsanes, and Virginia Ktsanes, "The Theory of Complementary Needs in Mate Selection: An Analytic and Descriptive Study," *American Sociological Review* 19 (June 1954): 241–249: Robert F. Winch, "The Theory of Complementary Needs in Mate Selection: A Test of One Kind of Complementariness," *American Sociological Review* 20 (February 1955): 52–56; and Robert F. Winch, "The Theory of Complementary Needs in Mate Selection: Final Results on the Test of the General Hypothesis," *American Sociological Review* 20 (October 1955): 552–555.

[4] Robert F. Winch, *Mate Selection* (New York: Harper, 1958).

Any or all of these reasons may be correct. What is clear is that relatively little empirical support exists for the theory of complementary needs, as originally formulated. In fact, most of the research that has attempted to explain mate selection on the basis of personality traits—whether similar, different, complementary, or some combination thereof—seems to have bogged down into a morass of conflicting results. Most findings have suggested the probable futility of further pursuits of personality matching. Perhaps instincts, drives, needs, complexes (including Oedipus ones), and personality traits all fail to find empirical support because they are based within persons rather than resulting from interactions. The cultural contexts and social situations in which these needs, drives, and traits are expressed are not considered.

In spite of the research, unsupported theories—whether instinctive, mother image, complementary needs, or personality traits—die hard. Further research on these ideas is sure to follow.

SOCIOCULTURAL EXPLANATIONS OF PARTNER SELECTION

Age, residential propinquity, class, religion, and race/ethnicity are sociocultural factors that influence mate selection. Any factor in which social norms and endogamous factors play a part in who marries whom falls into this category. Values and roles, although basic to norms of endogamy, can also be viewed as interaction processes that explain the choice of a mate.

Value theory

A value theory of mate selection suggests that interpersonal attraction is facilitated when persons share or perceive themselves as sharing similar value orientations. Values define what is good, beautiful, moral, or worthwhile. They are the criteria or conceptions used in evaluating things (including objects, ideas, acts, feelings, and events) as to their goodness, desirability, or merit. Values are not concrete goals of action but criteria by which goals are chosen.

A value theory of mate selection suggests that when persons share similar values, this in effect validates each person, thus promoting emotional satisfaction and enhancing the means of communication. When a value is directly attacked or is ignored under circumstances that normally call it to one's attention, those who hold the value are resentful. Because of this emotional aspect, it seems reasonable to expect that persons will seek informal social relations with others who uncritically accept their basic values and thus provide emotional security. Such compatible companions are most likely to be those who feel the same way about important things (those who possess similar values). This accounts for the tendency to marry homogamously and explains why friendships (homophily) and marriages involve people with similar social backgrounds.

Partner selection and the quality of family life are greatly influenced by sharing common values. Amish families preserve a life-style that is distinct from the ways of the larger U.S. society. They do not use electricity or drive automobiles, and they dress in simple clothing. A gemeinschaft type of community, based on strong religious convictions, reinforces Amish values.

In brief, the theory posits that:

1. Persons with similar backgrounds learn similar values.
2. The interaction of persons with similar values is rewarding, resulting in effective communication and a minimum of tension.
3. Rewards leave each person with a feeling of satisfaction with his or her partner and thus a desire to continue the relationship.

The inverse is equally true. Persons from different backgrounds learn different values; interactions among such persons are less rewarding and will likely result in feelings of tension and dissatisfaction and little desire to continue the relationship. Suppose, for example, a woman places a high value on heterosexual dating, marriage, and sexual activity. Would she accept as a dating or marriage partner someone who is known to have engaged in homosexual activities? Value theory suggests (predicts) that she would not, and research has strongly supported this very example.[5]

---

[5] John D. Williams and Arthur P. Jacoby, "The Effects of Premarital Heterosexual and Homosexual Experience on Dating and Marriage Desirability," *Journal of Marriage and the Family* 51 (May 1989): 489–497.

U.S. Diversity: Bundling as a Mate-Selection Process

Bundling is frequently associated with the Amish courtship system. A practice that was started in Northern Europe, brought to America, and practiced in the New England colonial family, bundling has been known to take several forms. The most common was using a bed with a "bundling board." (The bed was divided by a board down the middle.) Under this arrangement, a boy and a girl would lie on the bed without undressing. Second was the use of "bundling bags." Under this system, the female got into a large sack with a wax seal at the neck. Obviously, this seal was supposed to remain unbroken. Third, there were also instances recorded where the female's ankles were tied together.

To understand bundling, it must be seen in the context in which it occurred. Among New England families and among the Amish, wood and candles were commodities that required much time and labor. To use these commodities throughout the evening hours would be a waste of materials. Also, where winters were cold and distances of travel were sometimes great, bundling provided an opportunity for the male and female to visit alone without disturbing the rest of the family or using the heat and light commodities. One should also recognize that within the household were likely to be parents, six to fourteen children, and often grandparents and other relatives. Thus, the sexual connotations that many people associate with bundling today were perhaps minimal. Add to this the rigid sexual codes that existed, and one should get a relatively accurate picture of bundling in its social context. This subject has been widely exploited by the popular press; however, it is not known whether bundling exists today among the Amish.

Value theory helps explain findings about homogamy, endogamy, propinquity, parental image, and ideal-mate conception. Sharing values brings people together, both spatially and psychologically. A person may want to marry a member of the same religious denomination, for example, because this might be a very important value in and of itself. Persons who share similar social backgrounds have likely been socialized under similar conditions and have consequently developed similar value systems.

The same holds true for other explanations, such as parental image. Since parents are the major socializing agents for most children, it can be expected that one's personal values, those of one's parents, as well as those desired in a mate will all be similar or related. Thus, it is perhaps not parent image that influences marital choice but rather parent-image influence via the internalization of a set of values.

Role theory

Role theory, like value theory, appears to be conceptually more justifiable as an overall explanation of marital choice than any of the previous individualistic explanations. All social humans—or, more specifically, all marriageable persons—have expectations regarding their own behavior and also that of their respective partners. One perception of *role* (as described in Chapter 2) refers to a set of social expectations appropriate to a given status: husband, wife, male, female, single, and the like. These expectations, implicit or explicit, have been internalized and serve to direct and influence personal behavior as well as the behavior desired in a prospective marriage partner. Basically, people tend to desire (internalize) the roles defined by the society, subculture, and family in which they live.

Roles and personality needs differ in a very important respect. With roles, the focus of attention is on behaviors and attitudes appropriate to situations, irrespective of the individual, whereas with personality needs, the focus is on behaviors and attitudes that are characteristic of the individual, irrespective of the situation. The difference is crucial. Roles focus on definitions, meanings, and social expectations. In regard to mate selection, individuals select one another on the basis of role consensus (compatibility) or on the basis of courtship, marital, and family-role agreement.

Role consensus, widely used as an indicator of marital success or adjustment, has been applied relatively infrequently to partner selection. However, similar processes in partner selection are likely operative prior to marriage as they also are during marriage. When role discrepancies exist, marriage is unlikely to occur in the first place. Would a man who expects a wife to care for children, cook meals, and clean the house marry a woman who despises these activities? Or reciprocally, would this woman want to marry this man if that is what he expects?

Disparity in role agreement can be obtained by listing a series of expectations associated with various statuses and comparing the responses of the couple. The expectations of the couple can be used: decision making, recreation, sex, church attendance, care of children, employment, and the like. A given role expectation is less crucial than the agreement of the persons involved. For example, if one spouse expects to sleep in on the Sabbath, believing this is more important than church attendance, no conflict will exist if the other spouse holds a similar expectation or attaches little importance to the expectation. The role itself is not as important as the consensus of the partners in regard to the role. Also, the role expectation itself may change as the situation changes. Maybe one spouse thinks the other should attend church on the Sabbath but does not expect him or her to do so when out of town or on vacation.

In brief, the couple likely to marry are the male and female who share similar role definitions and expectations. This assumes, of course, that other forces—such as an existing marriage, age, parents, money, schooling, or other sociocultural factors—do not hinder or prevent it.

Exchange theory

Exchange theory was described briefly in Chapter 2. Also, as mentioned in several instances in the previous and current chapters, the idea of some type of exchange is basic to the mate-selection process. Whether it is an exchange of athletic prowess for beauty or an exchange of sex for money, the central idea is that some type of transaction and bargaining is involved in the selection of an intimate partner.

Prior to 1940, a major contribution of Willard Waller's treatise on the family was his analysis of courtship conduct as bargaining and/or exploiting behavior. In his words, "When one marries he makes a number of different bargains. Everyone knows this and this knowledge affects the sentiment of love and the process of falling in love."[6]

Today, it is doubtful that only *he* makes bargains or that "everyone knows this." But it is well established that bargaining or some type of social exchange takes place in partner selection and affects the process of falling in love. The difference between *bargaining* and *exchange* is that bargaining implies a certain purposive awareness of the exchange of awards. Bargaining entails knowing what one has to offer and what the other person can get, whereas in a simple exchange, this awareness is not always readily apparent. What is apparent is that few people get something for nothing; thus, articles tend to support mate selection as a process of social exchange.[7]

Exchange theorists argue that the behavior of socialized persons is purposive, or goal-oriented, and not random. Implicitly, this indicates that people repeat behaviors that are rewarded and avoid those that go unrewarded. Also, each party in a transaction will attempt to maximize gains and minimize costs. Over the long run, however, in view of the principle of reciprocity, actual exchanges tend to become equalized. If reciprocity does not exist—that is, nothing is given in return—the relationship will likely terminate. A key factor in exchange theory that may deter or delay termination of an inequitable exchange is the lack of an alternative to the current relationship. But if an alternative to the current relationship is perceived as superior to the present relationship, one of the partners will terminate the present relationship in favor of pursuing the more attractive alternative.

There are perhaps few areas where social exchange appears more evident than in research on dating and mate selection. In dating, for example, the male may consider sexual intercourse as a desired goal and a highly valued reward. To achieve this reward, he may have to offer in exchange flattery ("My, how beautiful you look tonight"), commitment ("You are the only one I love"), goods ("I thought you might enjoy these flowers"), and services ("Let me get you a drink").

The social exchange approach to partner selection neither explains how interaction arises nor describes the larger social environment. Rather, it seeks to explain why certain behavioral outcomes take place.

---

[6] Willard Waller, *The Family: A Dynamic Interpretation* (New York: Cordon, 1938): 239.

[7] James W. Michaels, Alan C. Acock, and John N. Edwards, "Social Exchange and Equity Determinants of Relationship Commitment," *Journal of Social and Personal Relationships* 3 (1986): 161–175; and Rodney M. Cate, Sally A. Lloyd, and Edgar Long, "The Role of Rewards and Fairness in Developing Marital Relationships," *Journal of Marriage and the Family* 50 (May 1988): 443–452.

Sequential theories

Up to this point, it should be evident that, although single factors were stressed as significant in the process of selecting an intimate partner, most explanations take into account factors implied in other explanations. Several writers have consciously and intentionally combined or placed in sequence selected single factors: roles, values, needs, exchanges, and the like. An example of this is seen in the SVR idea of Bernard Murstein.[8]

Murstein described dyadic pairing as a three-stage sequence, involving *stimulus-value-role* (SVR). These three stages denote the chronological sequence in the development of a relationship. Social exchange theory is used within each stage to explain the dynamics of interaction and attraction.

SVR theory holds that, in a relatively free-choice situation, as exists in the United States, most couples pass through three stages before deciding to marry. In the *stimulus* stage, individuals may be drawn to one another based on the perception of qualities that might be attractive to the other person (physical attributes, voice, dress, reputation, social standing). Because initial movement is due primarily to noninteractional cues not dependent on interpersonal interaction, these are categorized as stimulus criteria.

If mutual stimulus attraction occurs between a man and a woman and they are both satisfied, they enter the second stage, *value comparison.* This stage involves the appraisal of value compatibility through verbal interaction. The couple may compare their attitudes toward life, politics, religion, abortion, nuclear energy, or the roles of men and women in society and in marriage. If, as they discuss these and other areas, the couple find that they have very similar value orientations, their feelings for one another are likely to develop. Murstein suggested that couples may decide to marry on the basis of stimulus attraction and verbalized value similarity. But for most persons, it is important to be able to function in compatible roles, an ability that is not as readily observable as verbalized expressions of views on religion, politics, and the like. For this reason, Murstein placed the role stage last in the sequence leading to marital choice.

The *role* stage requires the fulfillment of many tasks before the couple is ready to move into marriage. It is not enough to have similar values if each partner is dissatisfied with how the other is perceived in such roles as lover, companion, parent, and housekeeper. The partners must increasingly confide in each other and become more aware of each other's behavior. They must measure their own personal inadequacies and those of their partner. If the partners navigate the three stages successfully, they are likely to become a permanent pair (marry or cohabit), subject to such influences as parents, friends, job transfers, competition from more attractive partners, and so forth.

Other sequential theories exist. For example, Bert N. Adams established a series of propositions in summarizing mate selection that include:

---

[8] Bernard I. Murstein, "A Clarification and Extension of the SVR Theory of Dyadic Pairing," *Journal of Marriage and the Family* 49 (November 1987): 929–933.

1. Conditions or barriers, such as proximity

2. Early attractions, such as physical qualities, similar interests, disclosure, and rapport

3. Deeper attractions, such as the development of consensus, personality similarity, lack of unfavorable parental intrusion, empathy, and role compatibility

4. A final series of escalators or perpetuators that move the persons toward marriage, that is, defining the other as "right" or "the best I can get"[9]

All sequential theories of relationship development or partner selection tend to view the movement toward marriage or cohabitation as a series of changing criteria, stages, or patterned regularities. However, the progression to marriage may not be quite so orderly or simplistic. Many alternative pathways may exist that involve other partners, may involve getting into and out of a relationship with the same partner several times, or may involve factors totally separate from the personal and interactional exchanges generally involved in relationship developmental processes. Factors external to the person or couple (family/kin influence, socioeconomic conditions, community heterogeneity, technological changes) are likely, from a sociological perspective at least, to be important factors or dimensions in understanding the process of changing status from single to married.

PROCESSES OF STATUS CHANGE: SINGLE TO MARRIED

The mate-selection process is the manner in which an individual selects a partner or changes status from single to married (or a married-like relationship) or from divorced or widowed to remarried. All human societies have some socially approved and structured procedures to follow in getting married, particularly for the first time. Remarriage, an increasingly common event in industrialized societies, involves less established norms and procedures for partner selection, and what norms exist may or may not parallel those of first marriage. A selection process that involves the individuals themselves only exists where there is some degree of personal choice in marital partners. As described earlier, where marriages are arranged, the process generally occurs between kin groups. In any case, it is rare for mate-selection processes to exist independently of other institutions, such as schools, churches, and businesses.

In the United States, the partner-selection process, particularly for first marriages, is highly youth-centered and competitive. It encompasses a wide range of social relationships prior to marriage, involving increasing degrees of commitment. Writers have used different terminology to describe this process, but gener-

---

[9] Bert N. Adams, "Mate Selection in the United States: A Theoretical Summarization," in *Contemporary Theories About the Family*, vol. 1, ed. by Wesley R. Burr et al. (New York: The Free Press, 1979): 259–267.

ally, it entails a series of stages that may include group activities, casual dating, going steady, being pinned, being engaged, cohabiting, or some other type of classification indicating a more binding relationship or even a marriage commitment. The flexibility of the process provides that it can be followed once or many times prior to marriage, covering a time span of days to years and including or omitting one or several stages.

Perhaps the partner-selection process in the United States can be compared to a male/female game, which has rules, goals, strategies, and counterstrategies.[10] Even though playing the game is voluntary, it is probably more difficult to avoid playing than to play. In elementary school (or before), parents inquire about boyfriends or girlfriends. As children mature, parents, peers, and an internalized self-concept all encourage getting involved. The goals of the game may range from simple enjoyment to affection and group approval and then learning to play more congenially to getting a mate. Since a double standard exists, females play by a different set of rules and set different goals than males.

Traditionally at least, the social norm for the male in the United States implied that his basic goal in this game was to move the relationship toward sexual intimacy. Even before the first meeting or date, the key question was, Will she or won't she? The extent to which direct or rapid approaches were used to answer the question depended on a wide range of social and interpersonal factors: previous marriage, age, social class, income, religion, beauty, and friends. Factors of social exchange were also relevant: what he had to offer relative to what he wanted.

The traditional social norm for the female in the United States implied that her basic goal in the male/female game was to move the relationship toward commitment. Even before the first date, key questions were, Will he ask me out again? or Is he a potential husband? To get the commitment, the female had the responsibility to regulate the progression of the intimacy goal of the male. To get intimacy (*sex* is a more accurate term, at this point), the male had to convince the female that she was not like all other women but was different, unique, and special.

These two norms worked reciprocally. Progress toward one called for progress toward the other. As commitment increased, intimacy increased and vice versa. Much of the communication in this game was likely to be in the form of nonverbal cues, signs, gestures, and other symbolic movements.

Suppose the rules were not followed: The male made no move toward intimacy or the female made no move to halt the intimacy or to get a commitment. The female, after one date, may have said to herself or others, What a nice guy; he really is a gentleman, or the like. Suppose after two, four, or eight dates, the male still made no move toward intimacy. Now the female was likely to ask questions such as, What's wrong with him? or What's wrong with me? Suppose the female made no move to stop or slow down the intimacy moves of the male, or suppose

---

[10] This idea is an expansion of Waller and Hill's "courtship bargains" and "courtship barter." See Willard Waller (revised by Reuben Hill), *The Family: A Dynamic Interpretation* (New York: Holt, Rinehart and Winston, 1951): 160–164.

Interaction among unmarried intimates may include a variety of activities such as bike riding, taking walks, attending concerts, or watching a rented video. Ultimately, these activities may lead to selecting an exclusive partner for a live-in relationship or marriage.

she made the initial move. The game may have continued but under a new set of less traditional rules and conditions.

Traditionally, and even today, a major part of the game has involved dating. The following discussion will briefly consider dating and stages of greater commitment in the process of mate selection.

Dating

Dating has been called a curious institution.[11] By definition, it is an activity that is supposed to be separate from selecting a spouse yet is expected to provide valuable experience in choosing a partner. Dating is experienced by most persons in the United States, young and old, seeking intimate or close relationships, marriage, or remarriage. Of all the stages of the mate-selection process, dating is the one that carries the least commitment in continuing the relationship.

Dating is a U.S. invention that emerged after World War I among college students and other young adults. In most of the world, where parents have extensive involvement in selecting marriage partners for their children, dating is not relevant. However, as shifts occur, away from family control over selection of a marriage partner, an increasing amount of emphasis is placed on establishing social

---

[11] Martin King Whyte, "Choosing Mates—The American Way," *Society* 29 (March/April 1992): 71–77.

structures that permit the persons themselves to interact and get to know one another. In the United States, dating is one of these structural patterns, although certainly not the only one established for purposes of male/female interaction.

The traditional date followed this scenario: The male called the female several days or a week ahead and verbally contracted a time and activity, picked her up at her house, wined and dined her at his expense, took in a movie or social activity, and returned her to her residence prior to the time established by her parents. This type of date may be a dying or dead event. Today, dating more likely involves students or young people congregating in groups, evolving into pairs while retaining allegiance to the group, sharing food or entertainment expenses, and engaging in less structured and predetermined behaviors. Today, dating also continues beyond the student scene. One consequence of the older age at marriage has been the emergence of new forms of partner selection for dating, including computer matchups, videotape selections, singles clubs and groups, newspaper advertisements, singles bars, and other informal opportunities for meeting.[12]

What are people looking for in dating partners? Two analyses of published advertisements yielded highly similar results.[13] Men, more than women, tended to focus on physical appearance, more casual relationships, and youth. Women, more than men, tended to focus on financial security and longer-term relationships.

Steven Nock cautions us to be aware of different "marriage markets" and to note that partner selection preferences are patterned according to men's and women's prior experience with marriage, divorce, and cohabitation.[14] Divorced persons, for example, are more accepting of other divorced people or of those who already have children, and those who have cohabited and/or divorced are less traditional in their views.

The fact that partner-selection preferences vary by sex, age, or marital status, and that dating is not what it used to be does not mean that dating is unimportant. Dating has, however, changed structure. Sheila Korman, in looking at nontraditional dating behavior, found that, while feminists tended to initiate dates and share dating expenses more than nonfeminists, even nonfeminists who held traditional beliefs ventured into nontraditional forms of heterosexual dating.[15] Among feminists and nonfeminists, males and females, writers agree that dating fulfills various functions for the individual. Dating may be:

---

[12] Note, for example: Aaron C. Ahuvia and Mara B. Adelman, "Formal Intermediaries in the Marriage Market: A Typology and Review," *Journal of Marriage and the Family* 54 (May 1992): 452–463; and Stanley B. Woll and Peter Young, "Looking for Mr. or Ms. Right: Self-presentation in Videodating," *Journal of Marriage and the Family* 51 (May 1989): 483–488.

[13] I. A. Greenlees and W. C. McGrew, "Sex and Age Differences in Preferences and Tactics of Mate Attraction: Analysis of Published Advertisements," *Ethnology and Sociobiology* 15 (1994): 59–72; and Frank N. Willis and Roger A. Carlson, "Singles Ads: Gender, Social Class, and Time," *Sex Roles* 29 (1993): 387–404.

[14] Steven L. Nock, "Spouse Preferences of Never-Married, Divorced, and Cohabiting Americans," *Journal of Divorce and Remarriage* 22 (1995): 91–107.

[15] Sheila K. Korman, "Nontraditional Dating Behavior: Date-Initiation and Date Expense Sharing Among Feminists and Nonfeminists," *Family Relations* 32 (October 1983): 575–581.

News Item: Dateline—Please Reply to ur4me

SBM, 23. Intelligent, handsome, fit, enjoys hiking and outdoor fun. Seeks SF 18–25 who is intelligent and attractive for good times and possible long-term relationship.

SWF, 35. I know you're there, Mr. Right. Must be nonsmoker. I'm down to earth, open-minded, with good values and morals. I love dogs.

SBF, 31. Voluptuous and sexy. Enjoys movies, walks, cooking, music, dancing. Seeks male who is sensual and caring, honest, open-minded, and loves to be pampered.

SWM, 26. This bud's for you. You must be very good looking, physically fit, with great personality. Me? You'll be pleasantly surprised.

GWF, 21. BiCurious, in search of an experienced bifemale to have hot fun and explore the world of bi-activities. I'm just like honey: sweet, thick, slow, and tasty.

GBM, 39. Corporate professional, emotionally and financially secure with a good sense of humor. I'm attracted to African, Latin, or Italian men who are clean, hard-bodied, masculine bull studs for monogamous safe encounters.

1. *A form of recreation*—Dating provides entertainment for the individuals and is a source of immediate enjoyment. Since dating per se is fun, it carries no future obligations or commitments.

2. *A form of socialization*—Dating provides an opportunity for individuals to get to know each other, to learn to adjust to each other, and to develop appropriate techniques of interaction.

3. *A means of status grading and status achievement*—By dating and being seen with persons who are rated highly desirable by one's peer group, individuals may raise their status and prestige within the group.

4. *A form of partner selection*—Dating provides an opportunity for unmarried individuals to associate with each other for the purpose of selecting a person whom they may eventually marry or define as an exclusive live-in partner.

The primary reasons for dating and the functions dating fulfills influence dating roles. In other words, it could be expected that persons who date for recreation will behave differently from those who date for socialization, status achievement, or partner selection. For example, emotional involvement, sexual intimacy, exclusivity of the relationship, paying patterns, and discussions of future plans will likely differ depending on the motive for dating—whether to have fun, be seen with a prestigious person, or find a husband or wife. It follows that the person who is more emotionally involved and more committed to the relationship will likely be hurt the most if the relationship ends. Finally, it will be likely that the person with the lower status or prestige will have less say (power) in what interactions and activities occur.

This idea parallels that of Waller more than fifty years ago, in what he termed the **principle of least interest**.[16] He observed that seldom are both persons in a dating relationship equally interested in continuing the relationship. In cases where both parties are not equally emotionally involved, if dating should terminate, it will be more traumatic for one than for the other. Essentially, the principle of least interest says that the person who is less interested in continuing the dating relationship is in a position to dominate and possibly exploit the other party. Conversely, the person most interested is in a position to be dominated and used. Felmlee, for example, found research support for the idea that individuals who were less invested emotionally had more say (power) in their romantic relationships.[17]

Traditional norms have given men more power to dominate women. But when either individual rejects these traditional norms, the principle may suggest that inequality is a key factor involved in the breakup of relationships. If an imbalance or unequal interest exists, it may be difficult to continue and further develop the relationship. Consistent with exchange theory, when there is no perception of equity between what one receives relative to what one gives, the relationship is likely to end or result in a power imbalance, where one person can dominate the other. (This principle, by the way, may not only apply to dating interactions but to friendships and marriages, as well.)

Steady dating: narrowing the "field of eligibles"

In the process of selecting a partner or mate, most adolescents make the move from an uncommitted relationship to a premarital relationship that involves some commitment to one another and an exclusion of others. Irrespective of the term used—*going steady, steady dating, going with someone, being serious,* or *being pinned*—societies that permit individuals to choose their spouses need some device for individuals to lessen the competition with others and at the same time provide anticipatory socialization for the marital or living-together role. Opportunities are needed to focus on the "field of eligibles," to get to know what is expected of oneself and others, and to get to know someone better without making a major commitment or attaching a norm of permanence to the relationship. Steady dating, or "going with someone," fills the gap between recreational or dalliance dating and engagement or marriage.

The functions filled by this form of interaction are highly similar to those described under dating: recreation, socialization, status achievement, and selection of a partner. The specific patterns of activity or meanings attached to the relationship may vary considerably from one context to another.

---

[16] Waller, "The Family: A Dynamic Interpretation," p. 275.

[17] Diane H. Felmlee, "Who's on Top? Power in Romantic Relationships," *Sex Roles* 31 (1994): 275–295.

On college campuses, over the past few decades, a series of terms and meanings was available to categorize relationships as perhaps more serious than dating but less committed than engagement. Perhaps the best known of these arrangements was *pinning*. The custom involved a gift of the male's fraternity or dormitory pin to the female. The pin was considered a temporary gift and was returned to the male when the pair broke up. Pinning was one means of publicly announcing to the campus community that the couple had a commitment to one another. In many instances, the commitment may have been a little more serious than steady dating, whereas in others, the commitment may have been similar to engagement.

Engagement

Engagement, in some form, has existed in almost every society in the world. Since marriage is seldom taken lightly, most societies have provided some social structure to instill an awareness in the couple and the community that the relationship is a serious one and that marriage will likely occur. In many societies, engagement is considered extremely important and much more binding than it is in the Western world today. Because engagement implies the final transition in the process of changing status from single to married and involves a transfer from dating availability to dating exclusiveness, various rituals are conducted and gifts are given to reinforce publicly and privately the importance of the relationship.

Engagement serves a variety of functions for both the couple and society. For the couple, it provides a clear indication that marriage is about to occur. Due to the exclusive nature of the relationship, personal and interpersonal testing can continue with less threat from competitive forces. A more thorough awareness of value consensus or dissensus, marital-role expectations, and future aspirations can be examined. Engagement provides the final opportunity prior to the legal union for each person to understand himself or herself in relation to the other. It is likely that many couples view an engagement as a kind of trial marriage, including total sexual intimacy, the sharing of certain financial obligations, and, in some instances, living together. (A discussion of nonmarital cohabitation follows.)

Engagement also provides the function of making the couple's plans public. In colonial days, the announcement was accomplished by the posting of **banns.** A number of days or weeks prior to the marriage, a public notice of intent to marry would be published, posted at key locations in the community, and announced in the churches. In the smaller folk- or gemeinschaft-like communities, characterized by a sense of solidarity and a common identity, the word traveled quickly and the community served as a key force in the binding of the relationship. The practice of publishing banns also exists today in Catholic and most Protestant churches. In modern urbanized societies, it is questionable how significant a formal newspaper announcement is in publicizing the plans and applying community pressures upon the couple.

An engagement ring, like a public announcement, serves the purpose of enabling the female to publicly and continuously display her symbol of commitment. The ring, which involves a financial commitment on the part of the male (and sometimes on the part of the female), symbolizes the seriousness of the relationship and the intent of a forthcoming marriage. To provide equality between the sexes, perhaps the time is near when the male will expect an engagement ring, as well.

NONMARITAL COHABITATION

Is it possible that selecting an intimate partner in the 1990s is not necessarily marriage oriented, is not limited to a single partner, is not always heterosexual, and does not stress permanence? That a decrease in the sexual double standard will totally eliminate the male/female game described earlier? That the premarital structures of dating, going steady, and engagement are significant only as historical phenomena? Or are the traditional mate-selection and marriage processes simply adapting and reconfiguring?

An alternative to marriage and an increasingly prevalent nonmarital arrangement is **nonmarital cohabitation**, also termed *unmarried-couple households, living together,* and *consensual unions.* This pattern is a situation where two adults of the same or opposite sexes who are not married to each other, either by ceremony or by common law, occupy the same dwelling. The arrangement, among the young or the old, may or may not be marriage oriented; may be a long-range life-style or a short-term convenience; may or may not involve an intimate, unrestricted sexual union; and may or may not be made known to parents by young people or perhaps to children by older people.

One could question the extent to which nonmarital cohabitants are, for all practical purposes, married couples minus legal sanction. One way to explore this question is to note if living together, as does dating, serves functions such as recreation, socialization, status grading, and partner selection or if living together serves functions of marriage, such as procreation, exclusive sexual intimacy, extension of a kin network, economic partnership, tension management, and socialization of children. Maybe what exists today is a large number of nonmarried marrieds.

In order to understand these couples, a number of characteristics will be considered: their prevalence, how they differ from noncohabitants, consequences of their cohabitation, patterns among people who are elderly, and legal factors related to cohabitation.

Prevalence of cohabitation

How prevalent is the living together of persons who are not married to one another? Recent U.S. census reports have provided some interesting data. The United States has witnessed a dramatic increase in the number of unmarried couples who live together. In 1994, there were about 3.7 million unmarried opposite-sex couple households and an additional 1.7 million same-sex couple households. The

Figure 10-1
Unmarried-couple households, by presence of children under 15 years old:
1960–1994

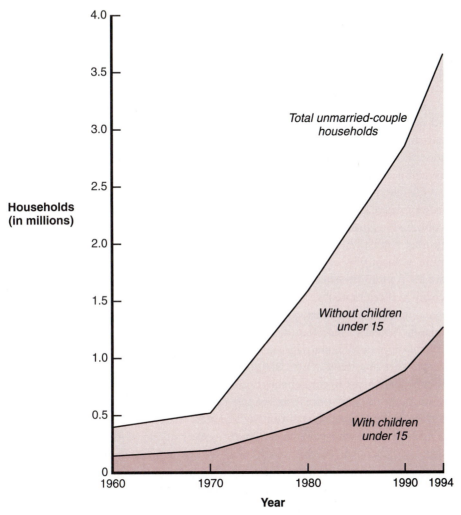

Source: U.S. Bureau of the Census, *Statistical Abstract of the United States: 1995.* 115th ed.
(Washington, DC: U.S. Government Printing Office, 1995), no. 60, p. 55.

unmarried heterosexual-couple households represent a 131 percent increase since
1980, when there were an estimated 1.6 million, and a 700 percent increase since
1970, when there were an estimated 523,000 households of this type (see Figure
10–1). Two-thirds (65 percent) of the unmarried-couple opposite sex households
in 1994 consisted solely of the two partners, and more than one-third (35 percent)
of these couples had one or more children living with them.

Of all households with two unrelated adults of the same or opposite sexes, one-fifth (20 percent of the men and 24 percent of the women) were under age twenty-five. Thirty-none percent were ages twenty-five to thirty-four, 34.0 percent were ages thirty-five to sixty-four, and 45.2 percent (4.5 percent of the men and 6.1 percent of the women) were ages sixty-five and over. More than half of the adults in unmarried-couple opposite-sex households had never been married (54 percent), one-third were divorced (33 percent), and the others were married but separated (about 6 percent), currently married with the spouse absent (less than 2 percent), or widowed (5 percent).[18]

That 54 percent of the 3.7 million unmarried-couple heterosexual households had never been married signals the likely emergence of a normative pattern of courtship and marriage-like relationships. Cohabitation in the United States may indeed become institutionalized as a new step between dating and marriage, or it may serve as a permanent alternative to legal marriage for many couples.

The latter already appears to be the case in Sweden (note Chapter 5) and in Norway where nonmarital cohabitation is a civil status accepted by all and is an established institution.[19] The concept of in- or out-of-wedlock has lost most of its meaning for children because the government has taken steps to secure their future. Cohabiting couples have the same rights to subsidized housing as married couples. And homosexual unions have been granted the right to register their partnership and celebrate it in a civil ceremony.

Unmarried cohabitation is increasing in most Western nations (Sweden, Finland, Norway, Netherlands, France, Great Britain, Canada, Australia), while first marriage and remarriage rates are declining. Larry Bumpass and others claimed that one trend offsets the other; that is, a decline in the marriage rate is offset by an increase in the cohabitation rate. The authors asserted that the increase in the proportion of unmarried young people should not be interpreted as an increase in singlehood, as traditionally regarded. Instead, young people are setting up housekeeping with partners at almost as early an age as they did before marriage rates declined. In this study, even though most cohabitants expected to marry, many disagreed about marriage. The picture that emerged was one of cohabitation as a family status but one in which levels of certainty about the relationship are lower than in marriage.[20]

Cohabitation, given its increasing frequency, obviously provides functions that are viewed as positive and of value. For many couples, cohabitation provides a financially practical condition; a warm, home-like atmosphere; more privacy

---

[18] U.S. Bureau of the Census, *Current Population Reports,* Series P20-484, Arlene F. Saluter, "Marital Status and Living Arrangements, March 1994" (Washington, DC: U.S. Government Printing Office, 1994), Table 8, pp. 71–73.

[19] Natalie Rogoff Ramsoy, "Non-marital Cohabitation and Change in Norms: The Case of Norway," *Acta Sociologica* 36 (1994): 23–37.

[20] Larry L. Bumpass, James A. Sweet, and Andrew Cherlin, "The Role of Cohabitation in Declining Rates of Marriage," *Journal of Marriage and the Family* 53 (November 1991): 913–927; and Fjalar Finnas, "Entry into Consensual Unions and Marriages Among Finnish Women Born Between 1938 and 1967," *Population Studies* 49 (1995): 57–70.

than a dormitory or cooperative housing arrangement; easy access to a sexual partner; an intimate interpersonal relationship; a nonlegal, nonpermanent, nonbinding union; and, for some, a form of trial marriage.

Comparing cohabiting and noncohabiting couples

Reviews of the cohabitation literature that compare cohabiting couples with married couples and noncohabiting-engaged or going-steady couples suggest various similarities and differences. In regard to housework, irrespective of marital status, women spend more time than men doing housework but the gender gap is widest among married persons. National data show that married women spend more time doing housework than do female cohabitants who spend more time than never-married females.[21] Men's housework time is very similar for cohabitants, those in a marriage relationship, and those never-married. Divorced and widowed men, however, do substantially more household work (such as cooking, cleaning and laundry) than any other group of men. This study suggested that the division of labor between cohabitants may be closer to that of married persons than single ones, but in other areas such as number of children, employment, school enrollment, and home ownership, cohabitants more closely resemble single persons.

It appears that cohabiting couples tend to mirror the society around them and engage in gender-role behavior characteristic of other couples their age. The same is true for exclusivity. While most believe in sexual freedom within the relationship, most voluntarily restrict their sexual activity as evidence of their commitment to the relationship.

Differences between cohabiting and noncohabiting couples exist on a wide range of issues. For example, Nock found that cohabitants expressed lower levels of commitment to their relationships, reported lower levels of happiness with their relationship, and had poorer relationships with parents than comparable married persons.[22] He argues that the poorer quality of cohabiting relationships stems largely from the absence of institutional norms related to cohabitation. Based on the institutionalization of cohabitation in the Scandinavian countries where few differences exist, he is probably correct.

Cohabitants in the United States indicate a lower desire to marry than engaged couples. Cohabitants are more likely than married couples to keep their financial affairs separate and not to engage in home ownership. Unmarried cohabitants have intercourse significantly more frequently than either married women or unmarried noncohabitants. In a study of nearly eight thousand women conducted by the National Center for Health Statistics, slightly over 60 percent of all unmarried cohabitants had intercourse either daily or several times a week,

---

[21] Scott J. South and Glenna Spitze, "Housework in Marital and Nonmarital Households," *American Sociological Review* 59 (June 1994): 327–347.

[22] Steven L. Nock, "A Comparison of Marriages and Cohabiting Relationships," *Journal of Family Issues* 16 (January 1995): 53–76.

Case Example:
Josie Recommends Nonmarital Cohabitation

Josie was a thirty-year-old undergraduate student at Wayne State University. She was raised in a devout Catholic family, got married at age twenty, divorced at age twenty-seven, moved back to her parents' home for two years, and then moved in with Joe. Was that a good idea for her, and would she recommend it to others? In Josie's words:

"Cohabitation is definitely a good idea before you get married. You get a clearer idea about someone when you see them morning, noon, and night rather than on an occasional evening and weekend. In many ways I'm very traditional. I do all the housework and cooking but I want to work full time when I finish school. Joe accepts that but he'd be just as happy with me in the traditional housewife role.

"I guess I'm very traditional in my commitment to Joe. I wouldn't even consider going out with or sleeping with anyone else, although I did go to bed with several men after my divorce. But now I'm really committed to Joe and would be badly hurt if he went out with someone else. I know he feels the same. I love him and know he loves me.

"We have thought about marriage but I don't believe that would change much. The only reason I can think of for marrying is that it might be a statement on the part of each of us of the trust we really have for each other. Sometimes I feel that my life is secondary to his, less important, since he's earning all the money. But I saved quite a bit from when I worked full time before I went back to school. Since I have a merit scholarship and he pays all the groceries, I don't see anything changing with marriage. I don't ask him for money now and don't think I would even if we were married.

"Joe's really a great guy. Unlike my ex-husband, we can talk openly about anything. For example, my ex-husband would never talk about sex—what I liked or how I felt—and he never seemed to hear me or give any expression of hearing. Now it's so different. For me, physical pleasure isn't enough. I must feel strongly about someone and be able to communicate and share openly with them.

"I really believe God led me to Joe. He's all I ever could want in a guy—warm, affectionate, expressive, willing to talk, caring. We might marry someday but he brings it up more than I do. I like living with him and don't see how marriage would improve anything. So for now, I'm happy with things as they are."

compared with 47 percent of married women and about 23 percent of unmarried noncohabitants. However, cohabitants were considerably more likely than noncohabitants to practice contraception, particularly if they had never been married.[23]

Many other factors differentiate cohabitants and noncohabitants. Individuals whose mothers married young and were pregnant at marriage enter into cohabitational unions (and marriage) at a substantially higher rate than other individuals.[24] Background factors that increase the propensity to cohabit include not com-

---

[23] Christine A. Bachrach, "Cohabitation and Reproductive Behavior in the United States," *Demography* 24 (November 1987): 623–637.

[24] Arland Thornton, "Influence of the Marital History of Parents on the Marital and Cohabitational Experiences of Children," *American Journal of Sociology* 96 (January 1991): 868–894; and William G. Axinn and Arland Thornton, "Mothers, Children, and Cohabitation: The Intergenerational Effects of Attitudes and Behavior," *American Sociological Review* 58 (April 1993): 233–246.

pleting high school, growing up in a family that received welfare, and coming from a single-parent family.[25] And of particular interest in the research literature is the difference in quality and stability of married versus cohabiting relationships.

Cohabitation and marital stability

Does establishing an unmarried-couple household provide a basis for a successful long-term relationship or even make for a better marriage? Does cohabitation increase, decrease, or have no effect on the chance for marital stability? Data from the National Survey of Families and Households showed that couples who cohabited before marriage reported lower-quality marriages, lower commitment to the institution of marriage, more individualistic views of marriage, and greater likelihood of divorce than couples who did not cohabit.[26]

Similar results came from other studies of national samples in the United States, Canada, and Sweden. Alan Booth and David Johnson, in a national sample of over two thousand married persons in the United States, rejected the idea that cohabitation improves mate selection and marital training.[27] They stated that cohabitation is negatively related to marital interaction and positively related to marital disagreement and proneness to divorce. Some support was found for the notion that some people who cohabit are poorer risks before they marry.

In Canada, it was found that the parallel increases in cohabitation and divorce are more than coincidental.[28] Contrary to popular expectations, cohabiting with one's first spouse did not enhance marital stability but rather was linked to a higher risk of first-marriage dissolution. Another Canadian study suggested that the presence of children had a strong and positive impact on stabilizing cohabitation relationships.[29]

In Sweden, a national sample of nearly five thousand women found that those who cohabited premaritally had almost 80 percent higher marital dissolution rates than those who did not.[30] With an increase in marital duration came a decrease in the difference of dissolution rates between premarital cohabitants and noncohab-

[25] Larry L. Bumpass and James A. Sweet, "National Estimates of Cohabitation," *Demography* 26 (November 1989): 615–625.

[26] Elizabeth Thompson and Ugo Colella, "Cohabitation and Marital Stability: Quality or Commitment?" *Journal of Marriage and the Family* 54 (May 1992): 259–267. Note also: Alfred DeMaris and K. Vaninadha Rao, "Premarital Cohabitation and Subsequent Marital Stability in the United States: A Reassessment," *Journal of Marriage and the Family* 54 (February 1992): 178–190.

[27] Alan Booth and David Johnson, "Premarital Cohabitation and Marital Success," *Journal of Family Issues* 9 (June 1988): 255–272.

[28] David R. Hall and John Z. Zhao, "Cohabitation and Divorce in Canada: Testing the Selectivity Hypothesis," *Journal of Marriage and the Family* 57 (May 1995): 421–427.

[29] Zheng Wu, "The Stability of Cohabitation Relationships: The Role of Children," *Journal of Marriage and the Family* 57 (February 1995): 231–236.

[30] Neal G. Bennett, Ann Klimas Blanc, and David E. Bloom, "Commitment and the Modern Union: Assessing the Link between Premarital Cohabitation and Subsequent Marital Stability," *American Sociological Review* 53 (February 1988): 127–138.

itants, with no differences found among those whose marriages remained intact for eight years. The conclusion strongly suggests a weaker commitment to the institution of marriage on the part of those who cohabit premaritally.

Robert Schoen[31] noted that the association between cohabitation and marital dissolution may largely disappear as cohabitation becomes more common. When comparing earlier cohabitants to more recent cohabitants (rather than to noncohabitants), Schoen found the earlier cohabitants were at a greater risk. Thus, as the probability of cohabiting increases and becomes more acceptable, so may the negative aspects associated with cohabitation decrease.

Why is cohabitation related to less marital stability and higher rates of marital dissolution? Explanations vary widely, but Thompson and Colella provided three major ones:

1. Those who cohabit rather than marry perceive themselves or the relationship as a poor risk in terms of long-term happiness and commitment.

2. Cohabiters are less committed to the institution of marriage than noncohabiters and therefore more likely to dissolve a problematic marriage.

3. Cohabiters define marriage in more individual than couple terms, so that cohabiters view marital quality as more central to the relationship's stability than noncohabiters.[32]

Whatever the reasons, existing data do not support the contentions that cohabitation serves as an effective training ground for marriage or that it results in improved marital quality or stability.

Cohabitation among people who are elderly

In 1994, 101,000 men and 81,000 women (182,000 persons) over the age of sixty-five admitted to living in unmarried-couple heterosexual households. Since 1970, the proportion and number of unmarried couples involving persons age sixty-five and over has declined significantly. In 1970, such couples numbered 115,000, representing 22 percent of the total. By 1994, they numbered about 91,000 couples but represented only about 5 percent of all unmarried-couple households.

The significant changes in number and proportion of cohabiting older persons is noteworthy, given the significant increase in the elderly population in the United States. This may be explained by changes in Social Security regulations, which make remarriage more practical for elderly people, and also by the large increase in younger unmarried couples who choose to live together.

---

[31] Robert Schoen, "First Unions and the Stability of First Marriages," *Journal of Marriage and the Family* 54 (May 1990): 281–284.

[32] Thompson and Colella, op. cit., pp. 259–260.

The advantages of nonmarital cohabitation for older persons are likely to be similar to those for college-age and younger persons: companionship, financial savings, sexual gratification, and the like. Two areas in which people who are older may differ from those who are younger might include (1) greater disapproval from their age cohort, in general, and their friends and associates, in particular, and (2) interference in their relationships by their children and grandchildren. This may be a fruitful area for research.

Cohabitation and the law

Family law may be undergoing more change in substance and procedure than any other area of law. Contemporary legal concerns include male alimony, test-tube babies, surrogate motherhood, embryo transplants, abortion, contraceptives for minors, rights of children born out of wedlock, joint custody, spousal immunity, and divorce kits for "do-it-yourselfers." Beyond these are various issues related to unmarried cohabitation.

The legal controversy over cohabitation becomes acute when one partner dies or the couple separates. At this point, problems arise regarding real estate and personal property, insurance, wills, estates, and child custody. The legal rights, particularly for women and children, are unclear. Traditionally, an unmarried woman who intentionally lived with an unmarried man acquired no property rights. If she contributed any service, she was not entitled to recover an interest in resulting property. Similar situations existed for children of unmarried partners. They were considered illegitimate and, on the death of the father, received no financial or property benefits.

Within the past two decades, a trend has emerged toward granting increased legal protection for the "spouse" and children of cohabitants. In the 1970s, a California appellate court held that a meretricious spouse (one who is intentionally living with a person of the opposite sex and is unmarried) had the same property rights as a married person. A few years later, in the much publicized case of Michelle and Lee Marvin, who had an alleged oral contract at the beginning of their nonmarital relationship, the California Supreme Court set a precedent by defining the value of the woman's services for the purpose of property settlement. This decision also recognized the validity of an oral contract between cohabitants by making it legally binding upon both parties.

A similar trend seems evident for children born of cohabiting nonmarried parents. A U.S. Supreme Court decision found that the Social Security Act discriminated against children of unmarried parents by failing to pay death benefits to those children. Another court held a father responsible for child support.

Decisions such as these have reduced but not eliminated the negative legal consequences of cohabitation for adults and children. There is wide variation in state law, and most states have not defined the rights of cohabitants and their children.

SUMMARY

1. The processes followed in partner or mate selection vary widely from one society to another—from totally arranged marriages to limited freedom of choice. The difference lies in who makes the choice of partner.

2. A range of explanations addresses who selects whom and why. At one extreme are individualistic explanations, which are rooted in instinct, genetic similarity, needs, drives, parental images, and complementary needs. In contrast are sociocultural explanations, which are rooted in norms, values, roles, and social exchanges.

3. Sociocultural explanations operate at a more conscious level, are more readily testable, and have greater research support than individualistic explanations. One sociocultural theory suggests that interpersonal attraction is facilitated when persons share or perceive themselves as sharing similar value orientations. This sharing of values, in effect, validates oneself, promotes emotional satisfaction, and enhances the means of communication.

4. Related to sharing values is sharing roles—the internalized, learned, social expectations as to what attitudes and behaviors are appropriate or inappropriate in the selection of a partner. In brief, the couple likely to cohabit or marry are the male and female who share similar role definitions and expectations.

5. Exchange theorists view partner selection as a bargaining or social exchange process. The choice of partner is based on the selection of persons who share equivalent resources; namely, each has something to offer that is desired by the other. A relationship characterized by an unequal exchange may continue if no better alternative to that relationship is perceived.

6. Some writers see the selection of a partner as the result of several of the above processes operating simultaneously or sequentially. One explanation involves a three-stage chronological sequence of stimulus, value, and role (SVR).

7. The partner-selection process is the means by which an individual changes status from single to married. The process involves all sorts of rules and roles applicable to male/female interaction. Generally, various types of dating fulfill a variety of functions and lead to increasing degrees of intimacy and commitment, such as steady dating and engagement.

8. Unmarried cohabitation is an increasingly popular life-style choice in the United States and much of the Western world. Among people who are elderly, the proportion and number of cohabiting couples has dropped significantly.

9. Even though unmarried people who cohabit enjoy many of the same positive relationship functions that married people enjoy, unmarried people are less committed to their relationships, in general. Cohabitation does not

serve as a successful trial for marriage. In fact, there is a positive correlation between cohabitation and later marital dissolution.

10. Family law is changing at a rapid rate, due in part to issues regarding cohabitation. Traditionally, women and children from cohabiting households had little or no legal protection. Recent court cases have set precedents in which unmarried "spouses" and children of cohabitants are entitled to the same rights as married spouses and their children.

11. Although the male/female sexual relationship is generally an important dimension in understanding partner selection, only minimal attention was given to it in this and the previous chapter. Sexual relationships, of significance to marital and family systems throughout the world, are analyzed and described in Chapter 11.

KEY TERMS AND TOPICS

Arranged marriage versus free choice
    of mate p. 288
Individualistic explanations of
    partner selection p. 290
Oedipus complex p.291
Electra complex p. 291
Complementary needs theory p. 292
Sociocultural explanations of
    partner selection p. 293
Value theory p. 293
Role theory p. 295
Exchange theory p. 296
Sequential theories p. 298
Processes of status change:
    single to married p. 299

Dating p. 301
Principle of least interest p. 304
Steady dating p. 304
Engagement p. 305
Banns p. 305
Nonmarital cohabitation p. 306
Prevalence of cohabitation p. 306
Comparing cohabiting and
    noncohabiting couples p. 309
Cohabitation and marital
    stability p. 311
Cohabitation among people
    who are elderly p. 312
Cohabitation and the law p. 313

DISCUSSION QUESTIONS

1. Would there be any advantages for young people to have their live-in partners or marriages arranged for them? Would their relationships or the consequences of them be different? How?

2. To what extent is partner selection likely to be a result of instincts, innate drives, parental images, and complementary needs? Consider your personal experience.

3. In spite of the logical and rational basis of the theory of complementary needs, why is there so little empirical support for it?

4. What values are most important to you? Could you marry someone who did not share these values? Why?

5 List a number of role expectations that you hold for yourself and your partner. Have a dating partner do the same. (Examples: "I expect the male to do the laundry." "Both the husband and wife should be employed full time.") On a rating scale of 1 to 5, indicate whether you agree or disagree with one another's expectations. Compare and discuss the results.

6. Discuss with your peers the process of changing your status from single to married or cohabiting. Is dating, going steady, and an engagement necessary? Contrast your ideas with those of your parents.

7. To what extent is the portrayal of the male/female game in the mate-selection process an accurate one? Has the game changed over the years? If so, how and why?

8. Recall your own past love affairs or those of your friends. Is the principle of least interest applicable? How was it manifested?

9. What explains the increase in cohabitation as well as its seemingly negative relationship to marital satisfaction and stability? How is cohabiting similar to and different from marriage?

10. What are the advantages and disadvantages of cohabitation for males in contrast to females, for youth in contrast to the elderly, or in verbal contracts in contrast to legal, written ones? Review some of the legal implications of cohabitation.

FURTHER READINGS

Buss, David M. *The Evolution of Desire: Strategies of Human Mating.* New York: Basic Books, 1994. An evolutionary psychological approach to understanding why conflict, competition, and manipulation pervade human mating.

Cate, Rodney M., and Lloyd, Sally A. *Courtship.* Newbury Park, CA: Sage, 1992. An exploration of courtship, including its importance, history, interpersonal models, and future perspectives.

Douglas, Jack D., and Atwell, Freda Cruse. *Love, Intimacy and Sex.* Newbury Park, CA: Sage, 1988. An effort at establishing a systematic, scientific model of love, including its major dimensions and their interdependencies.

Hendrick, Susan S., and Hendrick, Clyde. *Romantic Love.* Newbury Park, CA: Sage, 1992. An interdisciplinary overview of the complexity as well as the elusiveness of love.

Murstein, Bernard I. *Paths to Marriage.* Newbury Park, CA: Sage, 1986. A concise theoretical and research-oriented work on marital choice, including historical, sociocultural, developmental, and tactical determinants.

Rubin, Lillian B. *Just Friends: The Role of Friendship in Our Lives.* New York: Harper and Row, 1985. While not a book on mate selection, a clear expression of friendship relationships among women, men, women and men, couples, families, and kin.

Tzeng, Oliver C. S. (ed.). *Theories of Love Development, Maintenance, and Dissolution: Octagonal Cycle and Differential Perspectives.* New York: Praeger, 1992. A compilation of major theorizations of love development, maintenance, and dissolution. Dr. Tzeng followed this work by a publication in 1993 titled *Measurement of Love and Intimate Relations: Theories, Scales, and Applications for Love Development, Maintenance, and Dissolution.*

Whyte, Martin King. *Dating, Mating, and Marriage.* New York: Aldine, 1990. Survey data of women from the Detroit metropolitan area are used to report on mate choice and marriage experiences.

Chapter 11

Sexual Relationships in Social and Marital Contexts

- Social Regulation of Sexual Relationships
- Biological Versus Sociological Approaches to Sexual Behavior
- Sexualization and Sexual Scripts
    - Consistency between attitudes and behavior
- Nonmarital Sexual Behavior
    - Family antecedents of sexual behavior
    - Relevance of formal sex education
- Premarital Sexual Intercourse
    - The incidence and prevalence of premarital intercourse
    - Changes in premarital sexual activity
    - High-risk sexual behavior and AIDS
- Sex and Marriage
    - Changes in marital sexual activity
    - Factors related to marital sexuality
    - Sexual adjustment in marriage
- Extramarital Coitus
    - Incidence of and attitudes toward extramarital sex
- Summary
- Key Terms and Topics
- Discussion Questions
- Further Readings

Few topics draw as much widespread attention and occupy as much thought as matters relating to sex, as both a social and a personal phenomenon. The significance of sex in modern life is evidenced by the recent controversies centering around AIDS, abortion, gays in the military and in particular professions, sex education in the public schools, pornography, distribution of contraceptives to adolescents, and general concern over gender identity and male/female roles, to mention a few.

Many distinctions can be made in classifying sexual relationships. A sexual relationship may involve persons of the same sex (homosexuality) or of opposite sexes (heterosexuality). It may involve persons who are not married but whose relationship is marriage oriented (premarital) or persons who are not married and to whom marriage is not a factor (nonmarital). It may involve a husband and wife (marital). Married persons may have a sexual relationship with partners other than their spouses (extramarital), perhaps involving a sexual exchange of married partners ("swinging"). A sexual relationship may involve divorced or widowed persons who were once married but are currently socially and legally single (postmarital).

Ira Reiss, in a sociological analysis of **human sexuality** defined *sexuality* as erotic and genital responses produced by the cultural scripts of a society.[1] He suggested that sexuality is universal in that, in all societies, it is viewed as important and in need of societal regulation of some sort. The basic reason for the importance of sex is that it encompasses the elements of physical pleasure and self-disclosure. These are crucial elements in forming relationships in a society, sexual or otherwise.

SOCIAL REGULATION OF SEXUAL RELATIONSHIPS

All societies have social norms that grant approval to certain sexual behaviors and disapproval to others. Perhaps the most universal *taboo* on sexual behavior relates to incest; the most universal *approval* is granted to sexual behavior in marriage. Clearly, no society grants unrestricted sexual liberties; all societies control sexuality. How is this done?

First, basic social institutions are key components in controlling human sexual expression.

- The *family* plays a primary role in the regulation and control of sexual conduct through the socialization process, controlling who marries whom and providing negative sanctions when sexual norms are violated.
- Around the world, *religion* mandates what persons are legitimate sexual partners and what behaviors are acceptable. In the United States, for example, the Judeo-Christian doctrine embodies a procreational orientation toward sex.

---

[1] Ira L. Reiss, *Journey into Sexuality: An Exploratory Voyage* (Englewood Cliffs, NJ: Prentice-Hall, 1986), p. 37.

Global Diversity: Dutch Tax Prostitutes but Permit Write-Offs

Prostitution is legal in the Netherlands. But until 1992, freelance prostitutes enjoyed an unfair advantage over brothels. After that, the self-employed prostitute has to charge clients a sales tax as well as pay an 18.5 percent tax (which admittedly will consistently be underreported and under-paid). In turn, however, the government permits prostitutes to write off business expense items, such as condoms and beds.

Source: Charlotte Observer, 4 January 1992.

Acts that have no reproductive value—such as masturbation, sodomy (anal, oral, bestiality), and homosexuality—are taboo and sinful, as are activities that threaten the family unit, such as incest and adultery.

- *Education* is often assigned a regulatory role in defining, clarifying, and teaching what sexual conduct is appropriate.
- Even the *workplace* establishes boundaries and restrictions on sexual expression through dress and behavioral codes, such as sexual harassment rules.

Beyond the role of institutions, sexual expression is regulated and controlled through social norms, social statuses and roles, and social sanctions. Sexual expectations, as well as rights and privileges, differ for males and females; in public and private places; for married people and single ones; for grandparents and grandchildren; or for heterosexuals and homosexuals. Laws may be established that punish the prostitute, the distributor of child pornography, or the rapist. Violators of approved behavior may face public shame, ridicule, fines, imprisonment, physical and/or mental torture, and even death. In brief, sexual expression is highly regulated in a variety of ways in every society in the world.

BIOLOGICAL VERSUS SOCIOLOGICAL APPROACHES TO SEXUAL BEHAVIOR

The arguments usually given to explain differing sexual attitudes and behaviors, particularly between men and women, have, among most sociologists, been credited to socialization and social control factors. **Socialization theories** explain how sexual attitudes and values are learned. The argument that men and women develop differing sexual scripts explains, in large part, the different standards for and behaviors of males and females. (See the section on sexualization that follows.) **Social control theories** assume that "everyone wants to do it" and that, without societal restraints or controls, everyone would engage in socially undesirable (deviant) sexual activity. Social controls clearly exist to regulate sexual activity, as described at the beginning of this chapter.

But how much of sexual behavior, in general, and male/female differences, specifically, can be credited to **biological theories**? Do behaviors differ because of genetics, hormone levels, anatomical factors, or innate physiological predispositions? Considerable data have demonstrated that men and women appear to be very similar in their needs, drives, and responses. Research findings of Masters and Johnson, nearly thirty years ago, indicated that women have as definite an orgasm as do men and that, in general, women have a greater potential for sexual responsiveness than do men, since women tend to respond faster, more intensely, and longer to sexual stimulation. Aside from obvious anatomical variants, men and women are homogeneous in their physiologic responses to sexual stimuli.[2]

Kinsey came to the same conclusion almost fifteen years earlier when he reported:

> The anatomic structures which are most essential to sexual response and orgasm are nearly identical in the human male and female. The differences are relatively few. They are associated with the different functions of the sexes in reproductive processes but they are of no great significance in the origins and development of sexual response and orgasm. If females and males differ sexually in any basic way, those differences must originate in some other aspect of the biology or psychology of the two sexes.[3]

Ideas such as these led most social scientists to ignore or overlook biological explanations of sexual behavior. Biological components, while necessary, were not sufficient to explain or predict values and behaviors. And besides, are not biological factors believed to be the business of the biologist, whose theories will not affect the sociologist? J. Richard Udry, a sociologist at the University of North Carolina, did not believe so. With colleagues, he explored the interplay between biological predispositions and sociological models of adolescent sexuality and argued that biological components could not be ignored.[4]

Udry examined the hormonal changes of puberty, commonly regarded as the foundation for sexual behavior, for evidence of their role in adolescent sexual behavior. He stated that, since adolescents mature at different rates and at different ages, some will be more predisposed to sexual activity than others. The inclusion of a hormone measure with the social control measures would not make the sociological

---

[2] William H. Masters and Virginia E. Johnson, *Human Sexual Response* (Boston: Little, Brown, 1966), Chapter 17 and p. 285.

[3] Alfred C. Kinsey, Wardell B. Pomeroy, Clyde E. Martin, and Paul H. Gebhard, *Sexual Behavior in the Human Female* (Philadelphia: W. B. Saunders, 1953): 593.

[4] J. Richard Udry, "Biological Predispositions and Social Control in Adolescent Sexual Behavior," *American Sociological Review* 53 (October 1988): 709–722. See also: Carolyn Tucker Halpern, J. Richard Udry, Benjamin Campbell, Chirayath Suchindran, and George A. Mason, "Testosterone and Religiosity as Predictors of Sexual Attitudes and Activity Among Adolescent Males: A Biosocial Model," *Journal of Biosocial Science* 26 (1994): 217–234.

models wrong but rather more complete. Udry tested a biosocial theory that combines elements of social science with a biological model of hormonal dispositions.

What Udry found was evidence of strong biological as well as sociological effects on coitus with more balanced effects on subjective (thoughts and feelings) sexual variables. Social controls acted to suppress the effects of hormones on behavior. Udry concluded that a biosocial model of sexual behavior produces results that are more convincing than either a sociological or biological model alone. He urged caution, however, in applying his results only to early adolescence and not to coital transitions occurring earlier or later.

Male and female sexual behaviors in adolescence or adulthood go beyond hormonal and biological factors to include social and technological ones. For example, male/female differences are thought to have been weakened by the feminist movement (which sought gender equality), the development of contraception (which eliminated much of the fear of pregnancy), and the Industrial Revolution (which gave women greater economic opportunities). But behavior differences by gender are still very evident in U.S. society.

SEXUALIZATION AND SEXUAL SCRIPTS

Sexualization, that is, sexual socialization, is the process by which persons learn of and internalize their sexual self-concepts, values, attitudes, and behaviors. It is a process that begins at birth and continues into adulthood and old age. Details of the socialization process, with regard to sexuality, gender, violence, and other factors, are described in Chapter 14. At this point, attention will focus specifically on the learning and development of sexual knowledge, attitudes, and values. These aspects of sexualization are vital to understanding sexual behavior.

Symbolic interaction theory posits that people become sexual beings through social interaction. Even though there is an important biological and hormonal basis to sexual development, simply having female or male genitals does not guarantee that one's gender identity or preferences will follow anatomical makeup. This is evidenced in transvestism (dressing in the clothing of the opposite sex), transsexualism (feeling trapped in the body of the wrong sex), and homosexuality (preference for same-sex relationships). That behaviors differ in spite of genetic similarities is evidenced as well in the wide range of acceptable or nonacceptable attitudes and behaviors that exist among persons in general: sexual abstinence, fellatio, masturbation, sodomy, voyeurism, rape, experimentation with sexual positions, and so forth.

Symbolic interaction theory posits as well that sexual behavior can be understood only in terms of internalized symbolic meanings. This suggests that the definition of the situation and the meaning given to a certain behavior are basic to understanding that behavior or lack of behavior. If premarital coitus is defined as sinful, if masturbation is believed to cause insanity, and if homosexuality is perceived as perverted, these meanings will have a major but not absolute influence on whether the behavior occurs and also how. That is, definitions, attitudes, meanings, values, and other internalized mental processes predispose behavior.

These ideas, basic to a symbolic interaction frame of reference, parallel the ideas of William Simon and John Gagnon. They conceptualized the outcome of what is here termed *sexualization* in terms of **sexual scripts.**[5] Like a script for a play or movie, a sexual script provides an overall blueprint of what sexuality is and how it is practiced. The sexual script designates the *who, what, when, where,* and *why* of sexuality.

Scripts are the plans that people have in their heads. The sexual script defines *whom* one has sex with. Sex is not allowed with certain categories of people, but others are on the "approved" list. The script defines *what* sexual behaviors are right or wrong, appropriate or inappropriate. While kissing or masturbation may be on the approved list, oral or anal sex may not. The script includes the *when* and *where* of sex. Is it appropriate only at night in a bedroom? Is it also appropriate at noon in an automobile? And finally, the script includes the *why* issue. Is sex for fun, intimacy, reducing tension, procreation, or some other reason?

One's sexual script is the internalized notions of these who, what, when, where, and *why* questions. It is learned in interaction with others and contains notions of the society, subculture, reference groups, and significant others in which one is a member and with whom one interacts. In interaction with others, individuals build their scripts, those cognitive schemes that affect their actual conduct.

The process by which one's sexual script is formulated tends to illustrate the importance of adult socialization in contrast to the Freudian emphasis on the early years (see Chapter 14). At puberty, a young person may be largely ignorant of adult sexuality. Adolescence is a period when adult sexual scripts become formulated, experienced, and modified. Scripts are devices for organizing, guiding, and understanding behavior. They justify actions that are in accord with them and cause people to question those actions that are not. Simon and Gagnon argued that, for behavior to occur, something resembling scripting must occur on three distinct levels: cultural scenarios, interpersonal scripts, and intrapsychic scripts.[6]

Cultural scenarios are the instructional guides that exist at the level of collective life. The enactment of virtually any role reflects the institutions, groups, and social context in which one was born and raised and currently functions. *Interpersonal scripts* transform the person trained in cultural scenarios and general social roles to context-specific behavior. What one does is influenced by the responses of others. These cultural scenarios and interpersonal scripts result in *intrapsychic scripting,* an internal dialogue, a world of fantasy, or in interaction terms—a personal self that is in reality a social self. The private world of individual wishes and desires is bound to social life. All sexual behavior includes these three levels of scripting.

---

[5] William Simon and John H. Gagnon, "Sexual Scripts: Permanence and Change," *Archives of Sexual Behavior* 15 (1986): 97–120. For a more detailed discussion of sexual scripts see William Simon and John H. Gagnon, "A Sexual Script Approach," in James H. Geer and William T. O'Donohue, *Theories of Human Sexuality* (New York: Plenum Press, 1987), Chapter 13, pp. 363–383.

[6] Simon and Gagnon, "Sexual Scripts," 98–104.

News Item: If You Can't Talk of Rock, How Can You Discuss Sex?

This column is about sex. Parental discretion is advised.

[Politicians seem] to be going ahead with a rule requiring that any organization receiving federal funds for dispensing contraceptives to a minor must notify the parents within 10 days of the request.

[Their] heart is in the right place. But trying to put such a rule into effect presents problems. Many parents can't talk with their teenagers about rock music, much less discuss with them the subject of sex.

Let's assume that the Wallingfords have just received a letter from Planned Parenthood, noting that their daughter Sue Anne has requested a prescription for the Pill.

Both are waiting for her when she comes home from school.

"And what were you doing in school?"

"I don't know. I just went to class, and stuff."

"What kind of stuff?" Wallingford yells.

"You know, just stuff. What are you guys all excited about?"

"Are you sure you didn't sneak off in a clothes closet and do it with some boy?"

"Do what? And with what boy?"

"Any boy. We know everything," she says, waving the letter from Planned Parenthood. "So what do you have to say for yourself?"

"I knew if I asked you for permission to buy the Pill you wouldn't give it to me."

"You're damn right we wouldn't give it to you. What kind of parents do you think we are?" Wallingford says.

"I know what kind of parents you are. That's why I went somewhere else to protect myself."

"To protect yourself from what?"

"Having a baby."

"What do you know about having babies?" Mrs. Wallingford says.

"Well, when the male's sperm fertilizes the woman's ovum ..."

"That's enough of that kind of dirty talk," Wallingford shouts.

"Relax, Daddy-O. I haven't done it. But if I ever decide to, I want to be protected. They told us at the clinic, it's the woman and not the man who has to take precautions. Men couldn't care less about the consequences."

"You seem to know a lot about sex, young lady," Wallingford says. "You certainly didn't learn any of this at home."

"I know. That's why I went to the clinic. Every time I brought up the subject you said it was none of my business."

"It isn't any of your business," Mrs. Wallingford says. "You're 17 years old and nice girls don't discuss such things with their parents."

"Where are you going?"

"To the basketball game with Jack."

"So that's where you're going to do it," Wallingford cries.

"How am I going to do it at a basketball game?"

"In the parking lot," Wallingford says. "That's where I used to do it."

"I can't take any more of this. Goodby."

After Sue Anne leaves, Mrs. Wallingford wipes the tears from her eyes. "You know, George, I think we both would be happier today if Planned Parenthood had never let us know."

Source: Art Buchwald, *Detroit Free Press,* 10 February 1983, p. 13-B. Reprinted with permission of the author.

Sexual socialization is a process that begins at birth and continues into adulthood and old age. Social responses to nudity or child sexual play influence the meanings internalized—the sexual scripts—about what is appropriate sexual behavior.

One illustration of *scripting theory* is seen in an attempt to understand female topless behavior on Australian public beaches.[7] Female students at a university in Sydney, half of whom had gone topless on the beach, were asked a series of questions about their behavior. There was universal agreement about toplessness not being appropriate when walking off the beach area. Scripts differed considerably between the women who had gone topless and those who had not. Those who had gone topless focused on the natural aspect of sunbathing and the sense of personal freedom, believed the behavior was not sexual or exhibitionist, believed that the community as well as their peers and significant others approved of the behavior, and had higher self-esteem and higher body image. Those who had not gone topless perceived it as being too embarrassing and had a more negative body image.

Sexual scripting, like the general process of sexual socialization, follows the life cycle. Until recently, infancy, childhood, and old age were periods in which sex-seeking behavior was viewed as pathological; namely, these people were either too young or too old to be capable of comprehending or experiencing the full meaning of sexual behavior. In the context of this and most family texts, sexual life cycles tend to be subsumed under headings of *premarital, marital,* and *extramarital* experiences. Each of these labels carries specific requirements and meanings for

---

[7] Edward Herold, Bruna Corbesi, and John Collins, "Psychosocial Aspects of Female Topless Behavior on Australian Beaches, *The Journal of Sex Research* 31 (1994): 133–142.

appropriate sexual behavior. Thus, a traditional premarital sexual script says that "nice girls don't" whereas a marital sexual script says that "nice girls do."

This section on sexualization and sexual scripts has focused on the processes by which sexual definitions and meanings become internalized; they are part of the basic process of socialization, in general, which will be discussed more fully in Chapter 14. At this point, a brief discussion will examine the consistency between the attitudinal and behavioral aspects of sexual scripts.

Consistency between attitudes and behavior

Sexual scripts include both attitudinal and behavioral components. How consistent are sexual beliefs, values, and attitudes with sexual behavior?

One could assume that, for the most part, attitudes and behavior are highly related. That is, people tend to behave, for the most part, in ways consistent with their beliefs. Research over the years has provided strong evidence that where sexual norms are restrictive (such as with certain religious groups such as the Amish or Mormons) conservative behavior will result. Where sexual norms are more permissive (such as in Scandinavian countries or among certain college groups in the United States), behaviors will be more free and less restrictive. The result is a high correlation between beliefs and behaviors. On the other hand, many people experience interests, desires, and fantasies that may greatly exceed any possibility (or opportunity) of carrying them out. Here beliefs will be more permissive than actual behaviors.

It is important to recognize that attitudes, behaviors, and the relationship between them must be viewed in a cultural/social context. Socialization practices in Judeo-Christian cultures have led to the internalization of sexual attitudes and beliefs that tend to be highly restrictive (don't masturbate, engage in oral/genital sex, have premarital intercourse, and the like). During adolescence, as young people court and develop committed relationships, behaviors will probably go beyond the boundaries of what is believed to be proper. After engaging in a certain behavior, the belief toward that behavior will likely change in the direction of greater permissiveness. An interaction process is at work. More permissive behavior further modifies the belief.

There are several reasons for greater permissiveness of actual behavior than of beliefs about proper behavior. Traditional values will likely continue to be applied even after the behavior has been changed. Also, it is possible that sexual behavior is subject to more rapid social change than are attitudes. When behavior exceeds the belief limits, this conflict may produce guilt.[8] Even though guilt is likely to be

---

[8] For the impact of guilt on sexual responsiveness, see Kenneth Davidson and Carol A. Darling, "Masturbatory Guilt and Sexual Responsiveness Among Adult Women: Sexual Satisfaction Revisited," *Journal of Sex and Marital Therapy* 19 (1993): 289–300; and J. Kenneth Davidson and Nelwyn B. Moore, "Guilt and Lack of Orgasm During Sexual Intercourse: Myth Versus Reality Among College Women," *Journal of Sex Education and Therapy* 20 (1994): 153–174.

a common component of the sexualization process, the tendency is to continue the behavior until it is accepted. Once accepted, the feelings of guilt will be reduced or totally eliminated and the behavioral opportunities may not meet the attitudinal desires.

There is considerable support for the ideas just presented, including findings from a study of about 3,500 high school students.[9] Eighty-three percent of sexually experienced adolescents cited a best age for first intercourse that was older than the age at which they themselves experienced that event. A much higher proportion of virgins believed premarital sex is wrong than did nonvirgins, and even among the nonvirgins, about one-fourth of both genders said they believe sex before marriage is wrong. In other words, the study found that attitudes were more restrictive or conservative than behavior, whether the adolescents were sexually active or virgins.

This relationship of behavior exceeding the belief is likely to be reversed among adolescents and adults whose scripts have become more permissive while the social/cultural context does not provide the avenue or opportunity to carry them out. With a permissive sexual script comes permissive behaviors. But if opportunities are not available (for orgies, oral/anal sex, intercourse with famous people, or whatever) the belief will exceed the behaviors.

NONMARITAL SEXUAL BEHAVIOR

Family antecedents of sexual behavior

Antecedents of sexual behavior are factors that precede or occur prior to a given sexual activity. These include biological antecedents, such as age and sexual maturation; psychological antecedents, such as cognitive and emotional development; and social antecedents, such as family, peers, religion, and cultural norms. Although we tend to assume sexual behavior is private and personal, it is shaped by social/cultural factors. Even the community context of racially segregated neighborhood environments, labor force participation of women, population composition, and family planning service availability were found to affect the likelihood of sexual activity.[10] The primary focus in this section, however, will be on family and parental actions.

Families and parents are considered central in forming sexual attitudes and behaviors, in providing role models, in promoting a healthy social and economic environment, and in teaching appropriate standards of sexual conduct. Social structural dimensions such as ethnicity, age or education of the parents, employ-

[9] Laurie S. Zabin, Marilyn B. Hirsch, Edward A. Smith, and Janet B. Hardy, "Adolescent Sexual Attitudes and Behavior: Are They Consistent?" *Family Planning Perspectives* 16 (July/August 1984): 181–185.

[10] John O. G. Billy, Karin L. Brewster, and William R. Grady, "Contextual Effects on the Sexual Behavior of Adolescent Women," *Journal of Marriage and the Family* 56 (May 1994): 387–404; and Karin L. Brewster, "Race Differences in Sexual Activity Among Adolescent Women: The Role of Neighborhood Characteristics," *American Sociological Review* 59 (June 1994): 408–424.

ment of one or both parents, presence or absence of siblings and the number of them, religious affiliation and commitment, and a never-married/divorced/remarried parental status may all influence the likelihood of intercourse and/or pregnancy occurring prior to or separate from marriage.[11] In Great Britain, for example, family environments characterized by parent-child arguing, parental divorce or separation, and a family history of nonmarital fertility were all found to be related to premarital conception.[12]

Simple logic would seem to indicate that a major antecedent factor in explaining premarital sexual behavior is parental influence in the sexual socialization process. For example, is it not logical to assume that individuals brought up in sexually conservative homes will have less premarital heterosexual involvement than those from more liberal home environments? In other words, children who grow up in homes in which parents do not openly display affection, have a rigid and concerned attitude toward nudity, never discuss sex openly, and never have books or pamphlets available on sexual subjects will demonstrate conservative behavior and have little sexual involvement.

Data from two independent studies that included teenagers and their mothers showed that neither parental attitudes toward premarital sex nor parent/child communication about sex and contraception affected teenagers' subsequent sexual and contraception behavior.[13] Teens who communicated little with their mothers were as likely to use effective birth control as were those who communicated well. Authors of both studies suggested that family communication does not count for very much in terms of either sexual behavior or contraceptive use. One reason may be that parental communication about sex and contraception is generally too vague or too limited to have an impact.

What about the related issue of parental discipline? Are adolescents from homes with very strict discipline and rules about dating sexually conservative, and are those from homes with few rules and lenient discipline sexually permissive?

Survey data from several thousand adolescents (ages fifteen to eighteen) and their parents were analyzed to determine how parental discipline was related to the sexual permissiveness of their children.[14] As just hypothesized, sexual permissive-

---

[11] See for example Robert L. Flewelling and Karl E. Bauman, "Family Structure as a Predictor of Initial Substance Use and Sexual Intercourse in Early Adolescence," *Journal of Marriage and the Family* 52 (February 1990): 171–181; and Ellie Wright Young, Larry Cyril Jensen, Joseph A. Olsen, and Bert P. Cundick, "The Effects of Family Structure on the Sexual Behavior of Adolescents," *Adolescence* 26 (Winter 1991): 977–986.

[12] Stephen T. Russell, "Life Course Antecedents of Premarital Conception in Great Britain," *Journal of Marriage and the Family* 56 (May 1994): 480–492.

[13] Susan F. Newcomer and J. Richard Udry, "Parent-Child Communication and Adolescent Sexual Behavior," *Family Planning Perspectives* 17 (July/August 1985): 169–174; and Frank F. Furstenberg, Jr., Roberta Herceg-Baron, Judy Shea, and David Webb, "Family Communication and Teenagers' Contraceptive Use," *Family Planning Perspectives* 16 (July/August 1984): 163–170. See also Kristin A. Moore, James L. Peterson, and Frank F. Furstenberg, "Parental Attitudes and the Occurrence of Early Sexual Activity," *Journal of Marriage and the Family* 48 (November 1986): 777–782.

[14] Brent C. Miller, J. Kelly McCoy, Terrance D. Olson, and Christopher M. Wallace, "Parental Discipline and Control Attempts in Relation to Adolescent Sexual Attitudes and Behavior," *Journal of Marriage and the Family* 18 (August 1986): 503–512.

ness was highest among adolescents who viewed their parents as not being strict or not having rules about dating. But interestingly, adolescents who experienced very strict parental discipline and many dating rules were more permissive than those with moderate parental strictness and rules. In other words, a curvilinear relationship was found showing that both strict and lenient disciplinary patterns resulted in higher levels of sexual permissiveness. The lowest level of permissiveness was among adolescents with moderately strict parents.

How might the preceding findings be explained? First, perhaps children do not interpret the presence or absence of sexual behavior on the part of parents as being particularly relevant to their own sexual needs and experiences. Second, perhaps parental disciplinary behavior is a consequence of adolescent permissiveness. That is, if parents suspect their teenager is engaging in sexual intercourse, they may impose more dating rules. Third, while parents may be extremely influential in general socialization, they may be less influential in sexual socialization than significant others outside the home, particularly peers.

Support for this idea comes from a study of Hispanic adolescents.[15] Family measures of parent-child communication and parental warmth were not related to Hispanic adolescent sexual involvement. However, peer influences were. Perceived peer sexual behavior was a significant predictor of adolescent sexual expression for both males and females but strongest for males. Attitude toward premarital sex was also found to be significantly related to young Hispanic teens' sexual behavior when controlled for age. Consistent with reference group theory, peers were chosen ahead of parents as referents for judging the correctness of sexual involvement for Hispanic youth.

While this section has focused on family and parental antecedents, a word must be added on drug involvement as an antecedent to sexual behavior. A nationally representative sample of young Americans revealed that, even when controlling for important risk factors (family intactness, school context, biological maturity, and sociodemographic characteristics), the reported prior use of cigarettes, alcohol, marijuana, and illicit drugs greatly increases the risk of early sexual activity for adolescent males and females.[16] The higher the stage of drug involvement and the earlier the reported onset of drug use, the greater the probability of early sex.

Relevance of formal sex education

Formal sex education—that is, education dealing with the general area of sexuality in a structured context of classes, seminars, workshops, clinics, and the like—is, in general, supported by the public. Disagreement exists over what is appropriate content, who should teach it, whether to include moral values, and so forth.

---

[15] F. Scott Christopher, Diane C. Johnson, and Mark W. Roosa, "Family, Individual, and Social Correlates of Early Hispanic Adolescent Sexual Expression," *The Journal of Sex Research* 30 (February 1993): 54–61.

[16] Emily Rosenbaum and Denise B. Kandel, "Early Onset of Adolescent Sexual Behavior and Drug Involvement," *Journal of Marriage and the Family* 52 (August 1990): 783–798.

Consider, for example, the topic of abortion, currently an emotionally charged issue in the United States. Should objective information on the prevalence, techniques, safety, and psychological consequences of abortion be taught to adolescents? Should it be taught by physicians, nurses, clergy, sex educators, social scientists, or others? Should this information be presented, regardless of whether it contradicts the moral and religious values and beliefs of adolescents or their parents?

While some will argue that the need for services and information related to pregnancy prevention and safe abortion cannot be denied, others will argue that to teach or demand abstinence—or at the most, safe sex—eliminates any need for abortion or abortion education in the first place. A study of adolescent knowledge and attitudes about abortion revealed a lack of accurate knowledge. Most adolescents described abortion as medically dangerous, emotionally damaging, and widely illegal, despite much published evidence to the contrary.[17]

One might say, So what? Should information be presented that contradicts value and belief systems? Is ignorance better than knowledge? Or is false information that fits one's value system better than truth that contradicts it?

One argument against formal sex education, irrespective of topic, asserts that it should be taught in the home. However, many parents find it difficult to communicate openly and freely about sexuality and birth control with their children. Even when parents have accurate knowledge and make conscientious efforts to encourage sexual discussion and effective contraceptive behavior, emotional factors in the parent/child relationship may make such discussion difficult. Sexually active teenagers, who are likely to think their parents want them to be sexually inactive, are not likely to discuss experiences such as masturbation, oral/genital sex, and intercourse with their parents. Neither are they likely to go to their parents for contraceptive information or devices. Numerous legislative efforts to require clinics and agencies to inform parents of their adolescents' inquiries about contraception and abortion may make matters worse. Specifically, such efforts may have the unintended consequence of more unwanted pregnancies and sexually transmitted diseases rather than the intended consequence of improving parent/child communication.

Several key questions concerning formal sex education programs and clinics include: Does sex education lead the sexually inactive to become active? Does adolescents' knowledge increase? Are diseases and pregnancies prevented? In short, does sex education make any difference at all?

The results of formal programs are mixed, at best. Few lead to the negative consequences feared or the positive consequences hoped for. In general, sex knowledge gained through school classes, programs, and clinics has little, if any, influence on hastening the onset of sexual activity or in increasing or decreasing its frequency. Data have provided overwhelming support for the claim that the decision to engage in sexual activity is seldom influenced by school-based clinics or sex

---

[17] Rebecca Stone and Cynthia Waszak, "Adolescent Knowledge and Attitudes about Abortion," *Family Planning Perspectives* 24 (March/April 1992): 52–57.

education programs.[18] In fact, a large proportion of teenagers initiate coitus before they have entered high school or participated in any sex education programs.

Sex education does, however, influence knowledge and behavior regarding contraceptives. Sexually active teenagers who had formal instruction reported knowing how to use more methods of contraception and using them more effectively than adolescents who had no instruction.[19] Also, sexually active women who had sex education were less likely to become pregnant than those who did not. The availability of contraceptives per se and taking sex education does not appear, however, to have much influence on premarital sexual behavior.

Although most research has shown that formal sex education programs have mixed results in achieving their intended purposes, research has not discounted the merit of offering such programs to provide young people with a greater understanding of human physiology, interpersonal relationships, and social values. It is clear, however, that a sex education program that focuses exclusively on a single topic or approach—abstinence, pregnancy prevention, a "just say no" theme—is likely to be ineffective.[20]

PREMARITAL SEXUAL INTERCOURSE

Premarital sexual intercourse is defined as coitus involving at least one partner who is single and has not been previously married. Premarital denotes that the person has never been married, not that the relationship is confined to the person one will marry.

First sexual intercourse in the United States most often occurs within a dating relationship, is a spontaneous and unplanned event, and seldom includes the use of contraceptives. It is often looked upon as a major life transition and an event that most people remember. However, it is not always a pleasurable experience, especially for females. Data from over 1,600 college students who had had sexual intercourse revealed that men reported experiencing more pleasure and less guilt than did women.[21] Both sexes reported more pleasure and less guilt when sex occurred in a close relationship than in a casual one. A pleasurable reaction for women was associated with a continuing involvement in the relationship.

---

[18] Douglas Kirby, Cynthia Waszak, and Julie Ziegler, "Six School-Based Clinics: Their Reproductive Health Services and Impact on Sexual Behavior," *Family Planning Perspectives* 23 (January/February 1991): 6–16.

[19] Marvin Eisen, Gail L. Zellman, and Alfred L. McAlister, "Evaluating the Impact of a Theory-Based Sexuality and Contraceptive Education Program," *Family Planning Perspectives* 22 (November/December 1990): 261–271; and William Marsiglio and Frank L. Mott, "The Impact of Sex Education on Sexual Activity, Contraceptive Use and Premarital Pregnancy Among American Teenagers," *Family Planning Perspectives* 18 (July/August 1986): 151–162.

[20] F. Scott Christopher and Mark W. Roosa, "An Evaluation of an Adolescent Pregnancy Prevention Program: Is Just Say No Enough?" *Family Relations* 39 (January 1990): 68–72; and Mark W. Roosa and F. Scott Christopher, "Evaluation of an Abstinence-Only Adolescent Pregnancy Prevention Program: A Replication," *Family Relations* 39 (October 1990): 363–367.

[21] Susan Sprecher, Anita Barbee, and Pepper Schwartz, "Was It Good for You Too?: Gender Differences in First Sexual Intercourse Experiences," *The Journal of Sex Research* 32 (1995): 3–15.

U.S. Diversity: Substitute for Overeating and Drinking

Dr. Sol Gordon, professor emeritus at Syracuse University and the author of many books on sexuality, suggested that if one must have a compulsion, he or she should choose masturbation rather than overeating or overdrinking. Nobody has ever died from overmasturbating.

While writing somewhat in jest, Gordon argued that the issue is more important than it appears. Masturbation is one of the biggest concerns of young people, and they need to know that it is a normal expression of sexuality. While few take seriously the myths that masturbation causes acne, tired blood, mental illness, or blindness (Gordon questioned if that's why he wears glasses), most parents don't give outright approval to their children to masturbate. Some people suggest it may be all right if done in private and if not done too much. But Gordon questioned how much is too much? After every meal, twice a week, once a year?

Since teenagers and adults have strong sexual urges, Gordon asked why dumb solutions are offered, such as taking cold showers. He questioned the value of how people deal with anxieties—by eating when not hungry or drinking when not thirsty. Why not encourage people to masturbate, which is a much more effective solution to coping with high levels of anxiety, tension, and sexual needs. In his thirty years of clinical work, Gordon had yet to hear about a rapist, child molester, or chronically sexually dysfunctional person who grew up feeling comfortable about masturbation. In response to researchers who have suggested that masturbation itself provides a powerful stimulus for sexual abuse, Gordon argued that this was true only if the molester despises masturbation, feels guilty about it, or both.

Source: Sol Gordon, "What Kids Need to Know," *Psychology Today* 20 (October 1986): 22–26.

Cross-culturally, it appears that many societies permit or even encourage premarital sexual relationships, particularly for males. The taboo that falls primarily on females is more a precaution against childbearing out of wedlock than a moral sanction. Using a global perspective, the crucial question, particularly for females, may not be whether premarital intercourse is permitted but whether unmarried motherhood is allowed. It is likely that a female's commitment to norms of chastity lessens as a separation of premarital intercourse from pregnancy becomes possible. Thus, if contraceptives, sterilization, abortion, and other social arrangements exist to prevent or terminate a pregnancy, premarital sexual permissiveness will increase.

Premarital **sexual permissiveness** will also increase as a couple approaches marriage or even a commitment to the relationship. The most conservative behaviors can be expected on a first meeting or date; behavior becomes increasingly permissive as the couple moves from casual dating to a more serious commitment, both to the relationship and to each other, and eventually toward marriage or a marriage-like relationship. Since marriage is the context of the greatest approval or legitimization of coitus, it can be expected that, the more exclusive the relationship (the more marriage-like), the more permissive the sexual behavior.

Evidence for an increase in permissiveness with an increase in commitment has existed for decades. More recently, evidence from undergraduate college students revealed that, whether the behavior was heavy petting, sexual intercourse, or oral/genital sex, the percentage of people who agreed each behavior was acceptable increased with each relationship stage.[22] That is, each behavior had the lowest level of acceptability when the relationship constituted dating with no particular affection; acceptability increased with dating and being in love, dating one person only, and engagement. While practically no females and only 1–3 percent of males agreed that any of the three behaviors were acceptable in dating where there was no particular affection, more than three-fourths of all respondents agreed that all three behaviors were acceptable during engagement.

Arland Thornton also noted the relationship between the courtship process and sexual intimacy. In his words:

> Very few people experience sexual intercourse before they begin to date, but as they initiate dating, the transition to sexual experience begins. However, it is only after young people develop a "steady" dating relationship that the transition to sexual experience becomes rapid. And, as young people begin to think about the possibility of marriage, sexual intercourse often becomes a frequent element of the relationship.[23]

The incidence and prevalence of premarital intercourse

The **occurrence of premarital intercourse** can be viewed in a number of ways. One way is to look at the incidence, that is, the occurrence or nonoccurrence of an experience. Generally, one has or has not had intercourse, is or is not a virgin, has or has not experienced orgasm. Since few people have sex only once, another way to view frequency is to deal with prevalence, that is, how often the experience has occurred or occurs. Premarital intercourse may have occurred once or a thousand times; it may occur infrequently or on a regular basis. Thus, the *incidence* of premarital sex (number who have or have not) differs considerably from the *prevalence* (frequency). Both incidence and prevalence appear to have increased significantly over the past several decades.

Changes in premarital sexual activity

Many social forces in the contemporary United States have led to behavioral changes regarding premarital coitus and have the potential for producing further

---

[22] John P. Roche and Thomas W. Ramsbey, "Premarital Sexuality: A Five-Year Follow-Up Study of Attitudes and Behavior by Dating Stage," *Adolescence* 28 (Spring 1993): 67–80.

[23] Arland Thornton, "The Courtship Process and Adolescent Sexuality," *Journal of Family Issues* 11 (September 1990): 239–273.

changes. In the 1960s, a large proportion of college students were deeply involved in the civil rights movement and later in protest over the Vietnam War. On most university campuses, the birth control pill became available and acceptable for personal use among a large number of unmarried college women. In addition, sexual candor became increasingly legitimized in the mass media, even by one of the most conservative media: television. Over the past several decades, social forces such as these have led to increased rejection of many traditional values, resulting in many changes in the sexual behavior of never-married people.

An analysis of premarital sexual behavior and attitudes over an extensive range of years—1965, 1970, 1975, 1980, and 1985—revealed a continued but asymptotic increase in reported premarital sexual behavior among both men and women.[24] Namely, the increase continued but at a slower rate over time; the rate of premarital coitus was much greater before 1980 than after. The reported change in the percentage of college males engaging in premarital sexual activity increased by 12.3 percent between 1965 and 1980; the increase for college females over the same period was 35 percent. Between 1980 and 1985, however, the rate of increase was a mere 2 percent for males, while for females the rate actually decreased a half percent.

The authors cited above concluded that the determination as to whether a sexual conservatism has returned depends upon the nature of premarital sex considered. If premarital sex refers to intercourse and heavy petting, there has been no return to conservatism. That is, steady increases in both have occurred over a twenty-year period (albeit at diminishing rates) along with a steady decline in negative attitudes toward premarital sex. When promiscuity (casual sexual relationships with numerous partners) is considered, a more conservative pattern emerges. Compared to the 1970s and 1980s, a greater percentage of both males and females now consider promiscuity immoral or sinful. The offense is still considerably more serious for the female: the double standard has not disappeared (let alone "returned").

A review of thirty-five studies conducted over the past eighty years noted two major trends:

1. A major increase in the proportion of young people reporting coital involvement
2. A more rapid increase in the proportion of females reporting coital involvement than males, although the initial base for males was greater[25]

The so-called sexual revolution in the United States over the past two or three decades was real, but it was restricted to premarital heterosexual relations.

---

[24] Ira E. Robinson, Ken Ziss, Bill Ganza, and Edward Robinson, "Twenty Years of the Sexual Revolution, 1965–1985: An Update," *Journal of Marriage and the Family* 53 (February 1991): 216–220.

[25] Carol A. Darling, David J. Kallan, and Joyce E. VanDusen, "Sex in Transition, 1900–1980," *Journal of Youth and Adolescence* 13 (1984): 385–399. Note also: Sandra L. Hofferth, Joan R. Rahn, and Wendy Baldwin, "Premarital Sexual Activity Among U.S. Teenage Women over the Past Three Decades," *Family Planning Perspectives* 19 (March/April 1987): 46–53.

Attitudes toward extramarital and homosexual relations and, as noted above, promiscuity, have remained distinctly restrictive.

In contrast to the social forces supporting increased sexual permissiveness in the 1960s and 1970s, the 1980s and 1990s saw the arrival of conservative political and religious movements. In addition, a new and serious health epidemic, involving an STD now widely known as AIDS, appeared on the world scene. Forces such as these can be expected to restrict or modify the sexual activities of people of all ages.

High-risk sexual behavior and AIDS

As reported in Chapter 1, as of June 1995, nearly 500,000 AIDS cases and 300,000 deaths resulting from AIDS have been reported in the United States alone. What's more, 12 million Americans are infected with some type of STD each year.[26] Two-thirds of these persons are under age twenty-five, yet young people continue to engage in **high-risk sexual behavior.** High-risk sexual behavior basically refers to sex with multiple partners and a failure to protect themselves or their partners against sexually transmitted diseases and/or unwanted pregnancies. These behaviors are most common among men, younger people, and the unmarried.[27]

A sample of college students at a midwestern university revealed that 80 percent of heterosexual males and 73 percent of heterosexual females were sexually experienced, defined as having had either penile/vaginal or penile/anal intercourse at some time in their lives.[28] About one-fifth of both the men and the women had engaged in anal intercourse. Males reported more sexual partners than did females (an average of 8.0 for males and 6.1 for females). Over one-third of the respondents who had engaged in vaginal or anal intercourse during the previous year used no form of protection from STDs or no method of contraception for pregnancy protection. These high levels of sexual activity, the tendency toward multiple partners, and the nonuse or inconsistent use of condoms and contraception are well-documented antecedents to unplanned pregnancy and contraction of STDs.

Why do young people in the United States and around the world engage in these high-risk behaviors? Susan Moore and Doreen Rosenthal, after studying one thousand nonvirgin adolescents in Australia, found that young people gave many reasons for not using condoms: they defined their current relationships as monogamous, with promises to be long term.[29] Risk among the young with both regular

---

[26] Division of STD/HIV Prevention. *Sexually Transmitted Disease Surveillance, 1990,* Centers for Disease Control, Atlanta, GA: July 1991.

[27] M. Margaret Dolcini, Joseph A. Catania, Thomas J. Coates, Ron Stall, Esther S. Hudes, John H. Gagnon, and Lance M. Pollack, "Demographic Characteristics of Heterosexuals with Multiple Partners: The National AIDS Behavioral Surveys," *Family Planning Perspectives* 25 (September/October 1993): 208–214.

[28] June M. Reinisch, Craig A. Hill, Stephanie A. Sanders, and Mary Ziemba-Davis, "High-Risk Sexual Behavior at a Midwestern University: A Confirmatory Survey," *Family Planning Perspectives* 27 (March/April 1995): 79–82.

[29] Susan M. Moore and Doreen A. Rosenthal, "Condoms and Coitus: Adolescents' Attitudes toward AIDS and Safe Sex Behavior," *Journal of Adolescence* 14 (1991): 211–227.

and multiple partners was associated with negative attitudes toward taking precautions: "Condoms are a nuisance," "Precautions are a hassle," and so forth. Many denied the existence of risk: "None of my friends are the kind of people who would be AIDS carriers" or "Self-control is the answer, not condoms." Abrogation of responsibility was another key reason for high-risk behavior: "If I talk about AIDS with a sex partner, they might be insulted" or "My partner should be responsible for initiating the use of condoms." A fourth and final reason for not using condoms was termed *fatalism* by the authors: "Life is full of risks, and AIDS is just one example," "It's hard to know what to think about AIDS—even the experts don't agree," or "There's a chance I could get AIDS, I suppose, but that's life."

What kinds of factors are associated with sexual risk-taking among adolescents? A sample of several thousand midwestern sexually active teenagers comparing high-risk takers (multiple partners with rare or no use of contraception) with low-risk takers (one partner and regular use of contraceptives) revealed significant differences between the two groups.[30] For females and males, the high-risk takers had lower GPAs, more frequent alcohol consumption, lower levels of parental monitoring, a lack of communication with mothers about birth control, more frequent contemplation of suicide, a much greater history of sexual and physical abuse, and more troubled relationships with their parents.

In contrast to the large proportion of adolescents and people in general who refuse to practice safe sex, many others do. Nationally representative data from over 3,000 men revealed that overall, a very small proportion of the male population is engaging in sexual conduct that involves a high risk of AIDS transmission.[31] Only two percent of sexually active men age 20–39 had had any same-gender sexual activity during the last 10 years, about one-fifth of never-married and formerly married men had four or more partners over an eighteen-month period, and two-thirds of the never-married and one-third of the formerly married did not have any coitus in the four weeks preceding the interview.

Nationally representative data from some 8,500 American women revealed that nearly one-third of sexually experienced unmarried women changed their sexual behavior in response to the threat of AIDS.[32] The most common change was to limit their number of sexual partners to one. This may explain as well why most women perceived their risk of developing AIDS to be low; 80 percent claimed they have little or no chance of becoming infected with the human immunodeficiency virus (HIV) that causes AIDS. The same report revealed that, although American women in general are well informed about AIDS, misinformation persists, especially among African American, Hispanic American, and low-income women.

---

[30] Tom Luster and Stephen A. Small, "Factors Associated with Sexual Risk-Taking Behaviors Among Adolescents," *Journal of Marriage and the Family* 56 (August 1994): 622–632.

[31] John O. G. Billy, Koray Tanfer, William R. Grady, and Daniel H. Klepinger, "The Sexual Behavior of Men in the United States," *Family Planning Perspectives* 25 (March/April 1993): 52–60.

[32] J. W. McNally and W. D. Mosher, "Digest" *Family Planning Perspectives* 23 (September/October 1991): 234–235.

Case Example:
High-Risk Behavior—One Rape, Eight Pregnancies, and Two Children

Andrea is a 29-year-old mother of two young children, ages 4 and 3. She has a Master's degree in social science and is employed full time. She is currently married but separated from her husband. Prior to the birth of her two children, she had experienced a rape, five abortions, and a miscarriage.

The rape, a very traumatic experience, occurred at age 12. She was walking home from school with a boyfriend who was one year older. He wanted to kiss her, but she refused. So, behind a church, he held a broken glass pop bottle to her neck, removed her clothes and forcibly raped her. She recalls how he called her black and ugly and how no one would ever want to marry her. Arriving home badly battered, she told her mother that two high school girls jumped her. Not until age 21 did she reveal the rape experience to anyone.

At age 15, Andrea began having intercourse on a regular basis. Her first pregnancy occurred at age 16 by an older boy she was "sleeping with" regularly and felt she loved. She had the pregnancy terminated at a local clinic. The same year, she got pregnant again by another boyfriend and miscarried. Then she met Eugene whom she dated for two years. She got pregnant again and wanted to keep the child but Eugene insisted she get an abortion. In her words, "I really loved him and felt sex was the way to keep him. I wanted him so badly I even let him sodomize me, which was worse than the rape. I was so humiliated. He became more abusive and violent, so four months later, I had no choice but to break off our relationship.

"At age 18, I became involved with the man (let's call him Vic) who is now my husband. With him, I had three abortions, two at his insistence. I really wanted a child but knew I couldn't make it as a single mother and continue my schooling. Vic offered no support at all and wasn't willing to marry me. Several times we broke off our relationship but would get back together.

"At age 25, I got pregnant again. I was extremely depressed and wanted to commit suicide. I had earlier made a promise to God that I would never have another abortion. Vic wanted me back so I said only if he married me. So, five months into my pregnancy, I married him. Three months after my son was born, I was pregnant again and, following a very difficult pregnancy, gave birth to my daughter. Again, my worst nightmares were being realized. We were in trouble financially since I wasn't working. I didn't want to accept food stamps (but had to) and our marriage declined even more. For a long time, Vic had been sleeping on the couch. Recently, when my three-year-old daughter told me how daddy rubbed himself against her, I knew we had to separate.

"Looking back over all my sexual experiences, I can say that until my marriage, I never really enjoyed sex. It was something you do to please (and keep) a man. I didn't even know girls could have an orgasm until I was 18 and read about it in a magazine. Now I can really enjoy sex. I'm currently seeing a 67-year-old married attorney who really is kind to me. He buys me things, pays for my day care, and tells me he loves me. I never had that happen before. I know that I was adequate as a student, and am adequate as an employee, and as a mother. Now, for the first time, I am beginning to feel adequate as a woman: pretty, wanted, and loved."

Misinformation, combined with high-risk behaviors among low-income groups, may explain the high number of blacks and Hispanics with AIDS. According to the *HIV/AIDS Surveillance Report* published by the Centers for Disease Control and Prevention, African Americans accounted for 33.6 percent and Hispanic Americans accounted for 17.4 percent of the 476,000 reported cases of AIDS in the United States through June 1995.[33] These numbers are far in excess of their proportion to the total population (12.7 percent black, 9.0 percent Hispanic). Data have shown that significantly more African American and selected Hispanic American women have unplanned pregnancies, currently use no contraceptives, have intercourse at an early age, have multiple partners, and engage in the high-risk behaviors associated with the transmission of sexual diseases, including AIDS. These findings are consistent with the large numbers of unmarried and single mothers reported previously in this text.

SEX AND MARRIAGE

Social norms regarding sex make coitus between husbands and wives the one totally approved type of heterosexual activity in every society in the world. Few would deny the importance of sexual intercourse in marriage. It is the one factor that, normatively at least, differentiates the marital relationship from any other social relationship.

Human sexuality, within and outside of marriage, was brought into the public arena with the publication of the *Kinsey studies* in 1948 and 1953.[34] This landmark research set the stage for making sexuality a legitimate area of research and also provided a wealth of information, making sexuality a legitimate subject for popular discussion as well.

According to Kinsey, the frequency of marital coitus decreased with age, dropping from an average of 3.7 times per week during the teens to about 2.7 at the age of thirty, 1.4 at the age of forty, and 0.8 at the age of sixty.[35] Male and female estimates were highly comparable, although females tended to estimate the frequency of marital coitus higher than males did. The incidence and frequency of marital coitus reached their maximums in the first year or two after marriage. From that point, levels steadily dropped into minimum frequencies in the oldest age groups. No other activity among females showed such a steady decline with advancing age.

Kinsey found one common pattern in a number of marriages: Many husbands reported that, early in marriage, they wanted coitus more often than their wives, and young married females reported that they would be satisfied with lower coital rates than their husbands wanted. But in the later years of marriage, many of the older females expressed the wish to have coitus more frequently than their husbands desired. Over the years, most females became less inhibited and developed

---

[33] U.S. Department of Health and Human Services, *HIV/AIDS Surveillance Report* (Atlanta: Centers for Disease Control and Prevention 7 (mid-year edition 1995): Table 8.

[34] Alfred C. Kinsey, Wardell B. Pomeroy, Clyde E. Martin, and Paul H. Gebhard, *Sexual Behavior in the Human Female* (Philadelphia: W. B. Saunders, 1953); and Alfred C. Kinsey, Wardell B. Pomeroy, and Clyde E Martin, *Sexual Behavior in the Human Male* (Philadelphia: W. B. Saunders, 1948).

[35] Kinsey, *Sexual Behavior in the Human Female*, 77.

an interest in sexual relations that they might then maintain until they were in their fifties or sixties.[36]

How do Kinsey's findings compare with research done since then? This may be a difficult question to answer, since recent research in the area of human sexuality has been limited. One of the consequences of the political and religious atmosphere of the 1980s and 1990s was to severely restrict funds as well as to define investigations into sexuality as off limits. Even an 18-million-dollar project that had been peer-reviewed, approved, and funded by the National Institutes of Health (NIH) was retracted when a few conservative legislators (Congressman Dannemeyer and Senator Helms) objected to sex research as part of a "conspiracy of the liberal left and the organized homosexual community."[37]

Changes in marital sexual activity

Data reported earlier in the chapter showed an increase in nonmarital sexual permissiveness, so might one expect an increase in sexual activity in marriage, both in frequency and in the type of behaviors that occur? Why?

For one, the availability of reliable contraception and abortion may decrease anxiety over an unintended pregnancy and, therefore, relax some of the constraints on sexual expression. In addition, the portrayal of sex in the mass media, the availability of sex videos to be viewed in the privacy of one's home, the developing emphasis on women's rights to personal fulfillment, the shift from the traditional passive sexual role to more assertive behavior among women, and the viewing of sex itself as a natural, less taboo topic may all serve to decrease inhibitions and modify sexual frequencies and acceptable behaviors.

Some evidence has supported these contentions. The first year of marriage is clearly the time of most frequent marital coitus. After the first year, everything that happens to a couple—children, jobs, commuting, housework, financial worries, fatigue, familiarity—combines to reduce intercourse frequency while nothing leads to increasing it.

Data from a national U.S. sample of 7,463 adults shows a decline in marital sexual incidence and frequency over the life course.[38] On average, the frequency of marital sex by the respondents was 6.3 times a month. Couples under age 30 had intercourse two to three times a week. By age 65, marital sex among those sexually active was limited to three times a month. Note that the frequency of marital sex of those over age 65 is among the sexually active. The authors point out that the incidence (those having sex at all) drops sharply after age 65. By age 75, only one-fourth of the respondents reported having sex with their spouse at least once during the preceding month.

---

[36] Ibid., 353.

[37] J. Richard Udry, "The Politics of Sex Research," *The Journal of Sex Research* 30 (May 1993): 103–110.

[38] Vaughn Call, Susan Sprecher, and Pepper Schwartz, "The Incidence and Frequency of Marital Sex in a National Sample," *Journal of Marriage and the Family* 57 (August 1995): 639–652.

Figure 11-1

Frequency of sex last month by age and marital status

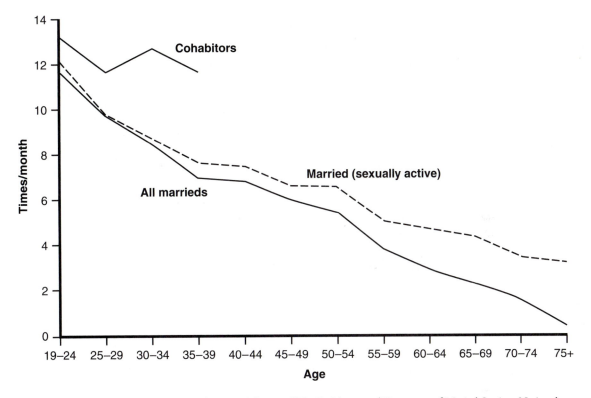

Source: Vaughn Call, Susan Sprecher, and Pepper Schwartz, "The Incidence and Frequency of Marital Sex in a National Sample," *Journal of Marriage and the Family* 57 (August 1995): 646. Copyrighted 1995 by the National Council on Family Relations, 3989 Central Ave. NE, Suite 550, Minneapolis, MN 55421. Reprinted by permission.

Figure 11–1 shows the frequency of sexual intercourse by age for all marrieds, the sexually active marrieds, and cohabitants. For all married couples, the frequency has a steady decline with age. More specifically, the average times a young married couple ages 19 to 24 had sex was 11.7 times a month. This drops to 8.5 times for those ages 30 to 34, 5.5 times at ages 50 to 54, and 2.4 times for those 65 to 69. Cohabiting relationships, according to the authors, are definitely "sexy relationships."[39] They reported having sex an average of 11 to 13 times a month, but sample sizes were too small to provide estimates for those over age 35. This higher rate of sexual intercourse was explained, at least in part, by their more permissive values, including the justification of sex without marriage.

---

[39] Ibid., p. 646.

Coitus, or sexual intercourse—while not confined to married, cohabiting, or sexually exclusive partners—is an expected behavior between people in such relationships. The frequency of intercourse among couples tends to decrease with age and duration of the relationship; nonetheless, sex remains important throughout the life course.

Several factors were said to contribute to the decline in sexual intercourse over time, including biological aging, diminished health, and habituation to sex. Age was the single most important factor associated with a declining sexual frequency. The second most important predictor was marital happiness. The higher the overall happiness, the more sex the couple had. The writers say that unfortunately, their results don't reveal whether couples became unhappy with the marriage and then had less sex or whether their reduced sex had consequences for marital happiness. This issue will be discussed later.

Other factors were found to have a modest effect on sexual intercourse frequency: a pregnancy, the presence of children, and sterilization (which increased frequency). Those who had cohabited before marriage or those in their second or later marriage had intercourse more frequently than those who had not experienced these events.

The discussion of declining coital frequency with age should not be interpreted to mean that sex becomes unimportant in marriage after ages forty, or seventy. The study just cited gave no information on less genital-focused sex or the quality and length of lovemaking. In fact, results from more than fifteen hundred randomly chosen men and women in Sweden, who were between sixty and eighty years old, revealed that 61 percent of the total group expressed their sexuality through intercourse, mutual sexual stimulation (other than intercourse), and masturbation.[40]

The fact that a definite decrease in intercourse frequency occurs with increasing age may call for a redefinition of sexual behavior among aging couples and for the development of values that maximize the sexual relationships of these couples.[41] One appropriate values change would be elimination of the stereotype that links sex with youth and the early years of marriage. Other appropriate values changes may include viewing sexual activity as being more than performance-oriented, more than genitally or intercourse-oriented, and more than orgasm-oriented. Sexual activity may also include nongenital sexual pleasuring and oral and digital manipulations, which may or may not result in actual physiological orgasm.

Factors related to marital sexuality

Many factors other than age have been found to be highly related to marital sexuality. For example, it is known that intercourse is less frequent during menstruation. Pregnancy as well influences sexual activity for both the married and the nonmarried.[42] Evidence has suggested that, during pregnancy, particularly during the first and third trimesters, women experience diminished sexual desire, frequency, and satisfaction. For men, diminished sexual desire and decrease in sexual satisfaction seem to exist only during the third trimester of the partner's pregnancy.

Earlier studies support the hypothesis that intercourse is related to stress within the marriage. The more severe the marital strain, the lower the frequency of marital coitus. Other earlier research has suggested that coital frequency increases with the amount of education of the wife, is higher among women who work in paid employment (highest among career-motivated women), and is positively associated with the effectiveness of contraception.

Regarding contraception, it is of interest to note that a national survey of women, ages fifteen to forty-four, showed a long-term trend in the United States toward convergence of **contraceptive usage** among the major religious groups.[43] About 77 percent of married Protestant women and 75 percent of married Catholic women used some type of contraception or practiced some type of pregnancy control. Among women who used contraceptives, Protestants were the most likely to use female sterilization (30 percent, compared to 18 percent Catholic and 12 percent Jewish). Catholic women were the most likely to use the pill (34 percent, compared to 28 percent Protestant and 14 percent Jewish). Jewish women

---

[40] Maj-Briht Bergstrom-Walan and Helle H. Nielsen, "Sexual Expression among 60- to 80-Year-Old Men and Women: A Sample from Stockholm, Sweden," *The Journal of Sex Research* 27 (May 1990): 289–295.

[41] Richard A. Kaye, "Sexuality in the Later Years," *Ageing and Society* 13 (1993): 415–426.

[42] Lennart Y. Bogren, "Changes in Sexuality to Women and Men During Pregnancy," *Archives of Sexual Behavior* 20 (1991): 35–45.

[43] Calvin Goldscheider and William D. Mosher, "Patterns of Contraceptive Use in the United States: The Importance of Religious Factors," *Studies in Family Planning* 22 (March/April 1991): 102–115.

were most likely to use a diaphragm (26 percent, compared to 5 percent Protestant and 7 percent Catholic) or a condom (23 percent, compared to 13 percent Protestant and 18 percent Catholic).

While certain female/male and Catholic/non-Catholic differences appear to be decreasing, marital sexual activities still vary considerably in numerous respects, such as social class. Contrary to the notion that people of the lower social classes are less sexually inhibited, people from the middle and upper classes are more likely to have intercourse in total nudity, use a variety of positions in intercourse, and engage in oral/genital contact. Although social stratification literature has suggested that working-class people have increasingly adopted middle-class values and behaviors, Martin Weinberg and Colin Williams found that social class is still an important determinant of sexual behavior.[44] Compared to the lower and working classes, middle-class men and women start their sexual activities at a later age, are more likely to enjoy their first sexual experiences, and are more likely to react positively to masturbation.

One key reason for these differences may be related to gender roles. Generally, the lower the social class, the greater the division between traditional male and female roles. Where there exists a high degree of role segregation between husbands and wives, the couple will tend not to develop as close or as gratifying an interpersonal sexual relationship. Where husbands and wives are likely to segregate work, recreational, and domestic activities into male or female roles, so, too, are they likely to clearly differentiate sexual roles. The result? Different sexual expectations and behaviors by social class.

Sexual adjustment in marriage

Sexual adjustment has been highlighted by certain writers as the keystone to marital adjustment. However, it is highly unlikely that adjustment of any sort is a dichotomous, either/or phenomenon. Within any marriage, sex is better or worse at certain times or in various situations. Also, to assume that frequency of intercourse, attainment of female orgasm, or lack of inhibition is equal to sexual adjustment is both misleading and false. It is very difficult to separate sex from the complex interaction of variables that constitute married life. Sexual adjustment may be one indicator of general marital adjustment, but it is doubtful that having a good sex life alone will maintain an otherwise poor relationship. Dissatisfaction in marriage is likely to be reflected in the frequency and performance of marital coitus, and conflict in sexual coitus may be symptomatic of other tensions within the marital relationship.

In a national sample of over 6,000 married couples, Donnelly wanted to determine if sexually inactive marriages were less happy and stable than those with

---

[44] Martin S. Weinberg and Colin J. Williams, "Sexual Embourgeoisment? Social Class and Sexual Activity: 1938–1970," *American Sociological Review* 45 (February 1980): 33–48.

sexual activity.[45] It was determined that 16 percent of the marriages had been sexually inactive during the month prior to the interview, indicating that such marriages are not uncommon. It was also determined that these couples were not happy, stable marriages in which the partners simply did not have sex. The lack of sexual activity appeared to be associated with the existence of other problems in the relationship and may indeed be a danger signal for many marriages.

Blumstein and Schwartz, too, find support for a linkage between sexual adjustment and the quality of the relationship.[46] Their findings led to the overwhelming conclusion that a good sex life is central to a good overall relationship. In their study, the married couples felt so strongly about having sex often that those who said they have it with the partner infrequently tended to be less satisfied with the entire relationship. What is not known definitively is whether an unsatisfactory relationship leads to less frequent sexual activity or whether the problems begin in the bedroom and eventually corrode the entire relationship. The former notion— that when nonsexual parts of a marital relationship are going poorly, the quality and frequency of the sexual relationship will decline as well—seems to have real merit.

EXTRAMARITAL COITUS

A chapter on sexual relationships would be incomplete without a look at sexual relationships among married persons with persons, married or single, other than their spouses. Extramarital sex is a behavior that, in the United States, at least, is seldom looked upon favorably. In fact, in 1990, when one national opinion survey asked about a married person having sexual relations with someone other than the marriage partner, 78 percent said it was "always wrong" (up from 70 percent in 1980) and an additional 13 percent said it was "almost always wrong." Only 2 percent said it was "not wrong at all."[47]

The terms **extramarital coitus** and *adultery* are defined as nonmarital sexual intercourse between a man and a woman, at least one of whom is married at the time to someone else. Almost without exception in the United States, adultery is legally punishable. And although actual prosecution is rare, the moral condemnation that accompanies extramarital coitus is, in general, much stronger than that directed at coitus among nonmarrieds. It is widely held that adultery is condemned in practically all Western cultures because of the threat it poses to the family unit. Secondly, it is assumed (sometimes falsely so) that marriage provides a socially approved legitimate sexual partner; thus, sexual deprivation is minimized.

Lynn Atwater argued that several myths contribute to an unrealistic faith in sexual exclusivity in the United States.[48] One myth is that one person can and will

---

[45] Denise A. Donnelly, "Sexually Inactive Marriages," *The Journal of Sex Research* 30 (May 1993): 171–179.

[46] Philip Blumstein and Pepper Schwartz, *American Couples* (New York: Pocket Books, 1983): 201–206.

[47] Floris W. Wood (ed.), *An American Profile—Opinions and Behavior 1972–1989* (Detroit: Gale Research, Inc., 1990), p. 603.

[48] Lynn Atwater, *The Extramarital Connection* (New York: Irvington Publishers, 1982): 18.

supply all of another's emotional, social, and sexual needs. That people grow to love each other more as years go by is another common myth. A third is that sexual exclusivity comes easily and naturally. These myths lead people blindly to believe that, if only their partners will be faithful, all their emotional needs will be satisfied. Yet the extent of extramarital relations suggests otherwise.

Today, there is much greater concern for the extramarital behavior of the wife than that of the husband. Kinsey noted that most societies permit or condone extramarital coitus for the male if he is reasonably circumspect about it and if he does not carry it to extremes that would break up his home, lead to the neglect of his family, outrage his in-laws, stir up public scandal, or start difficulties with the husband or other relatives of the women with whom he has relationships.[49] Such extramarital activity is much less frequently permitted or condoned for the female.

Even though a **double standard** exists in the United States, it is far less pronounced than in many countries, which permit considerable freedom for the male yet place harsh restrictions on the female. For example, prior to World War II, Japan was considered a "man's world." Japanese husbands were permitted to engage in sexual contact outside of marriage. In contrast, infidelity by wives was condemned as a crime both legally and morally. Since World War II, social and economic conditions for Japanese women have improved, radically changing the situation. However, the sexual freedom of women has not approached that of men. Even today, Japanese men openly seem to enjoy more sexual freedom than do U.S. and probably European men.

Incidence of and attitudes toward extramarital sex

What factors account for, or are highly related to, extramarital coitus? Of all the factors that Kinsey examined, religious devoutness, more than any other, affected the incidence of extramarital coitus, particularly for females. The lowest incidence of extramarital coitus occurred among people who were most devoutly religious, and the highest incidence occurred among those who were least closely connected with any church activity. This was true of all Protestant, Jewish, and Catholic groups in the sample.[50]

Justification for extramarital relationships were found to relate to a number of dimensions, including sexual, emotional, and extrinsic.[51] *Sexual dimensions,* more common justifications for men, included sexual excitement, sexual curiosity, novelty or variety, and sexual enjoyment. *Emotional dimensions,* more common justifications for women, included romantic love, getting love and affection, intellectual sharing, understanding, companionship, ego-bolstering, aspects of enhancing self-esteem, and respect. *Extrinsic dimensions* included career advancement and

---

[49] Kinsey, *Sexual Behavior in the Human Female,* p. 414.

[50] Ibid., p. 424

[51] Shirley P. Glass and Thomas L. Wright, "Justifications for Extramarital Relationships: The Association between Attitudes, Behaviors, and Gender," *The Journal of Sex Research* 29 (August 1992): 361–387.

getting even with spouse. Consistent with arguments presented earlier in the chapter on attitude/behavior differences, the actual incidence of extramarital involvement (behavior) exceeded the approval (attitude) given to it. The incidence figures range from 30 to 60 percent for men and 20 to 50 percent for women while survey reports suggest that 75 to 90 percent disapprove of it.

Atwater, in studying fifty feminist-oriented women, suggested that extramarital coitus for these women was a direct response to the women's movement. They were breaking out of a traditional scene that demanded faithfulness for them but not for their husbands. Extramarital behavior for these women was an arena where they were free to establish the kinds of sexual patterns they preferred, with no social pressure to maintain less-than-satisfactory relationships, no deep investment of love and romance, and no long-term institutional pattern that defined sex as having a purpose other than personal pleasure. For these women, participation in extramarital sex signaled continued liberation from traditional sexuality and, in Atwater's words, was "the final assault on the double standard."[52]

Another partial assault on the double standard is a specific type of extramarital coitus referred to as *swinging, consensual adultery, mate swapping, wife swapping, comarital sexual behavior,* or *group sexual activities.* While these involve a single standard of sexual permissiveness, it is doubtful they will find widespread acceptance or will ever approach the frequency of extramarital sexual relationships. These extramarital encounters, however, differ from adultery in their nonsecrecy, openness, and greater degree of honesty between partners.

SUMMARY

1. Human sexual activity is regulated through social institutions, social norms, and a wide range of social sanctions.

2. Male/female differences in premarital sexual attitudes and behaviors have generally been attributed by sociologists to socialization and social control factors. However, a number of researchers have explored the interplay between biological predispositions and sociological models of human sexuality.

3. Sexualization is the process by which people acquire their sexual self-concepts, values, attitudes, and behaviors. These meanings and definitions make up individuals' sexual scripts, designating the *who, what, when, where,* and *why* of sexuality.

4. Sexual attitudes and behavior are highly interrelated. When they differ, attitudes and beliefs will be more conservative and restrictive than will actual behavior. During adolescence, permissive behavior in dating, love, and interpersonal relationships will tend to modify beliefs.

---

[52] Atwater, *The Extramarital Connection*, pp. 190–191.

5. Family antecedents to sexual behavior include parenting behaviors. However, neither parental attitudes nor parent/child communication appear to affect teenagers' subsequent sexual and contraceptive behavior. Parental discipline appears to have a curvilinear effect; both the most restrictive and permissive disciplinary patterns result in greater permissiveness.

6. Formal means of sex education seldom result in the type of positive consequences desired or the negative consequences feared. The decision to engage in sexual activity is not influenced by sex education classes but appears to have some effect on contraceptive knowledge and effective use.

7. Premarital heterosexual intercourse has attracted widespread research attention. Major changes have taken place in the sexual behavior of never-married individuals. These changes have been most pronounced for females, moving toward increased permissiveness; male/female differences have lessened, but the double standard has not been eliminated.

8. Data have suggested that many people continue to engage in high-risk behaviors, while others have moved toward increased selectivity of sexual partners and greater condom use (but not abstention from sexual activity).

9. Marriage legitimizes the sexual relationship. The social norms that surround sex and marriage are the key factors in differentiating marital sex from nonmarital sex, extramarital sex, and any other encounters outside the marital relationship.

10. Studies have indicated that the incidence and frequency of marital coitus reach their maximums in the first year or two after marriage, with a steady decline from that time on. As with nonmarital coitus, marital coitus rates have shown an increase over the past several decades.

11. Not all heterosexual coitus of married persons occurs among spouses. Extramarital coitus appears to be widespread, with major differences between males and females and across cultures.

12. This chapter examined sexual relationships in a variety of contexts. Whether the context is nonmarital, marital, or extramarital, each is significant to interaction among intimate partners. Continuing within a partner selection and marital life course sequence, attention is directed in Chapter 12 to marital structures and processes.

KEY TERMS AND TOPICS

Human sexuality p. 320

Social regulation of sexual
relationships p. 320

Biological versus social approaches
to sexual behavior p. 321

Socialization theories p.321

DISCUSSION QUESTIONS

1. All societies control sexual activities. Why? How?

2. Which is more important to understanding sexual behavior: (a) biological needs, drives, hormones, and the like; (b) social norms, values, attitudes, and so on; or (c) social controls and sanctions? Explain.

3. Are males and females inherently different in sexual socialization? If so, in what ways does society contribute to the difference?

4. Consider your own sexual script—with whom, what, where, when, why, and so forth. What factors are most influential in your script?

5. Examine the relationship between attitudes and behavior: what you believe versus what you do or have done. For you, how accurate is the idea that behavior often exceeds the acceptable belief/value script, which in turn modifies the belief of value?

6. What explains the finding that parental attitudes and parent/child communication seem to have little effect on adolescent sexual behavior and contraceptive usage?

7. Discuss the impact, if any, of sex education on adolescents' sexual attitudes, sexual behavior, and contraceptive usage. Should topics be taught (nonmarital sexuality, abortion, homosexuality) that may run counter to individuals' religious or moral values? Why?

8. What changes in sexual behavior have occurred over the past few decades? What accounts for these changes? Why have the changes been greater for females than males?

9. What explains the continuation of high-risk behaviors? Discuss the impact of AIDS on sexual behavior.

10. In what ways is marital coitus likely to be influenced by length of time married, age, the media, employment of husband and/or wife, religion, number and/or presence of children, and the like? What explains changes that have taken place?

11. What constitutes good sexual adjustment in marriage? Is it possible to have good sexual adjustment and poor marital adjustment? Is the opposite possible? Why?

12. What are the arguments for and against extramarital sex and "swinging"? Are these activities inherently disruptive to marriage? Can they ever benefit or improve marriage? Why?

FURTHER READINGS

Bullough, Vern L., and Bullough, Bonnie. *Sexual Attitudes: Myths and Realities.* Amherst, NY: Prometheus Books, 1995. An attempt to explore and come to terms with cultural and historical traditions on sexual attitudes in the United States.

Irvine, Janice M. (ed.). *Sexual Cultures and the Construction of Adolescence.* Philadelphia: Temple University Press, 1994. A collection of 14 articles focusing on cultural differences in adolescent sexuality and development.

Janus, Samuel S., and Janus, Cynthia L. *The Janus Report on Sexual Behavior.* New York: Wiley, 1993. Research results providing a comprehensive overview of a wide variety of sexual behaviors in numerous contexts within the United States.

Laumann, Edward O.; Gagnon, John H.; Michael, Robert T.; and Michaels, Stuart. *The Social Organization of Sexuality: Sexual Practices in the United States.* Chicago: University of Chicago Press, 1994. A comprehensive survey of sexual behavior based on a probability sample of 3,432 American women and men age 18–59.

Martinson, Floyd M. *The Sexual Life of Children.* Westport, CT: Bergin and Garvey, 1994. The author explores a range of issues dealing with children and sex such as their early experiences, sex play, encounters with other children and adults, and education.

Reibstein, Janet, and Richards, Martin. *Sexual Arrangements: Marriage and Affairs.* London: Heinemann, 1992. An examination of extramarital affairs, including who, why, and what and also the impact these affairs have on marriage.

Reiss, Ira L. *An End to Shame: Shaping Our Next Sexual Revolution.* Buffalo, NY: Prometheus Books, 1990. A sociologist who devoted his life to the study of sexuality suggests ways of alleviating the major sexual crisis that U.S. society is facing.

Rossi, Alice S. (ed.). *Sexuality Across the Life Course.* Chicago: University of Chicago Press, 1994. A multidisciplinary team presents 14 articles dealing with the biopsychosocial perspective, sexual diversity in history and life-style, sexuality at different phases of the life course, and health issues.

Sprecher, Susan, and McKinney, Kathleen. *Sexuality.* Newbury Park, CA: Sage, 1993. A focus on same- and opposite-sex close relationships and the attitudes, behaviors, and satisfaction with these relationships.

Voydanoff, Patricia, and Donnelly, Brenda W. *Adolescent Sexuality and Pregnancy.* Newbury Park, CA: Sage, 1990. An overview of adolescent sexual activity and pregnancy: determinants of, correlates of pregnancy resolutions, consequences of childbearing, and intervention strategies.

Weinberg, Martin S.; Williams, Colin J.; and Pryor, Douglass W. *Dual Attraction: Understanding Bisexuality.* New York: Oxford University Press, 1994. Readers are introduced to a group of people who define themselves as bisexual and to their struggles in putting together satisfying relationships.

Wyatt, Gail Elizabeth; Newcomb, Michael D.; and Riederle, Monika H. *Sexual Abuse and Consensual Sex: Women's Developmental Patterns and Outcomes.* Newbury Park, CA: Sage, 1993. A developmental approach to the impact of both voluntary and involuntary sexual experiences in childhood and adolescence and the impact of adolescent experiences on adult behavior.

Chapter 12

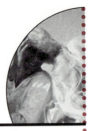

The Marital System

- Functions of Marriage and Marriage-Like Relationships
    Marital status and well-being
- Marriage Trends and Characteristics
    Reasons people marry
    Variations in marriage rates
- Power in Conjugal and Intimate Relationships
    Characteristics of power
    Power and decision making in conjugal
        and intimate relationships
    Theory of resources issue
    Egalitarian ethic
- Marital Quality
    Dimensions of marital quality
    Evaluating marital quality
    Marital conflict
    Marital quality over the life course
- Summary
- Key Terms and Topics
- Discussion Questions
- Further Readings

Although this chapter concentrates exclusively on marriage, with particular emphasis on the dominant husband/wife patterns and roles in the United States, each previous chapter has discussed selected aspects of the marital system. The first chapter included census data on marriage and issues within U.S. marriages. Subsequent chapters differentiated marriages from families; presented a wide range of nontraditional marital life-styles, including those with multiple spouses and dual careers; examined Chinese, Swedish, African American, Hispanic American, Asian American, and Native American marital practices; and provided information on social-class differences, interfaith and interracial situations, structures and processes in mate selection, and sexual relationships in marital contexts. This chapter will consider the functions of marriage, marriage trends and characteristics, conjugal power, and factors associated with marital quality.

FUNCTIONS OF MARRIAGE AND MARRIAGE-LIKE RELATIONSHIPS

Today, marriage and marriage-like relationships are popular. Despite conflict, divorce, and a changing marital scene, most Americans marry or choose to live in monogamous, sexually based, or primary opposite-sex or same-sex relationships. Around the world normative expectations include marriage as an appropriate and desirable state, and norms are changing in many countries to include cohabitation. Most persons and groups fulfill these expectations. Despite the complex tasks of mastering partner-selection interactions, celebrating the rituals and ceremonies that accompany the act of marriage, and fulfilling the requirements of domestic life, many people achieve these goals throughout their lifetimes. Obviously, marriage and marriage-like relationships fulfill various functions for individuals and society.

Marriage and sexually bonded relationships, operating within the context of the family system, fulfill many functions attributed to the family in general. These family functions include basic personality formation, status ascription, nurturant socialization, tension management, replacement of members, economic cooperation, reproduction, stabilization of adults, and the like. Even though many of these functions do not require marriage or sexual exclusivity to be fulfilled, they are enhanced by the marital system. Note, for example, the impact that marriage has on personal well-being.

Marital status and well-being

Robert Coombs, in reviewing more than 130 empirical studies on a number of well-being indices, found that married men and women are generally happier and less stressed than unmarried men and women.[1] The pattern was highly consistent.

---

[1] Robert H. Coombs, "Marital Status and Personal Well-Being: A Literature Review," *Family Relations* 40 (January 1991): 97–102. See also Walter R. Gove, Carolyn Briggs Style, and Michael Hughes, "The Effect of Marriage on the Well-Being of Adults," *Journal of Family Issues* 11 (March 1990): 4–35.

Studies of alcoholism, suicide, mortality (death) and morbidity (diseased or unhealthy); schizophrenia and other psychiatric problems; and self-reported happiness have supported the hypothesis that married individuals experience fewer emotional and health problems than their unmarried counterparts.

It has been suggested that marital and intimately bonded partners provide companionship, interpersonal closeness, emotional gratification, and support that serve to buffer individuals against physical and emotional pathology (a **marriage-protection hypothesis**). Married individuals are more likely to abstain from smoking, drink moderately, avoid risk-taking behavior, and lead more stable, secure, and scheduled life-styles.

One explanation as to why married women are healthier than single women (including those separated, divorced, or widowed) is because of greater economic resources.[2] This economic "safety net" provides access to better housing, food, and services than she would have otherwise, resulting in a lower level of stress and a higher level of health. For both men and women, income was found to be a mediating effect on the lower mortality rate of married individuals than single ones. For example, nonmarried individuals with high incomes experienced lower mortality than married ones with low incomes. The highest mortality was experienced by those who were both poor and single.[3]

Marriage and these marriage-like relationships have been shown to be particularly rewarding for men. Research has clearly rejected the popular folklore that marriage is a blessed state for women and a burdensome trap for men. In reality, men, more than women, receive mental-health benefits from marriage. Women, more than men, provide emotional aid and other support in marriage. Even public opinion polls have shown that more married men are satisfied with their marriages than are women. When asked, "Would you say that your marriage is very happy, pretty happy, or not too happy," about two-thirds of the men said "very happy" compared to 57 percent of the women.[4] Very few said "not too happy" (1 percent men and 4 percent women), but these figures must be considered carefully. Perhaps many of those people who responded "not too happy" have been divorced, ending an unhappy situation.

The differences among married and unmarried people may be declining, however. Norval Glenn, using national survey data, demonstrated a substantial decline in marital stability and quality of the positive relationship between being married and marital happiness.[5] The changes occurred primarily through an increase in the reported happiness of never-married males and a decrease in the reported happiness of married females.

---

[2] Beth A. Hahn, "Marital Status and Women's Health: The Effect of Economic Marital Acquisitions," *Journal of Marriage and the Family* 55 (May 1993): 495–504.

[3] Richard G. Rogers, "Marriage, Sex, and Mortality," *Journal of Marriage and the Family* 57 (May 1995): 515–526.

[4] Floris W. Wood (ed.), *An American Profile—Opinions and Behavior, 1972–1989.* (Detroit: Gale Research, Inc., 1990), p. 239.

[5] Norval D. Glenn, "The Recent Trend in Marital Success in the United States," *Journal of Marriage and the Family* 53 (May 1991): 261–270.

Global Diversity: Marital Status and Mortality in Developing Countries

Two researchers at the Office of Population Research at Princeton University reported on several consistent and striking patterns that emerged from an exploration of marital status differentials in mortality across sixteen developing countries. They found that:

1. In all countries, the excess mortality of unmarried men relative to married men greatly exceeded that of unmarried women.

2. In most countries, divorced men had the highest rates of mortality among the three unmarried groups (single, divorced, widowed). This finding also held true for females in more than half of the countries.

3. Age-specific effects indicated that widowed and divorced persons in their twenties and early thirties experienced the highest mortality risks, sometimes ten times as high as those for married persons of the same age. Among single persons, the highest risks were associated with men and women between the late twenties and early forties.

4. In the majority of countries, the relative mortality ratios of the three unmarried groups increased over the past two to three decades. Japan emerged as the most apparent exception to these generalizations.

This consistency of findings across countries strengthened previous speculations about the importance of marriage in maintaining health and reducing the risk of dying and also about the increased stresses associated with both single and formerly married life-styles.

Source: Yuanreng Hu and Noreen Goldman, "Mortality Differentials by Marital Status: An International Comparison," *Demography* 27 (May 1990): 233–50.

It was suggested that these changes may relate to the increasingly similar circumstances of being married and unmarried. A substantial proportion of unmarried persons, for example, have regular sexual relations without stigma. Also, given the ease with which divorce can be obtained by either spouse who wants it, marriage no longer provides the security it once did, financial or otherwise. In other words, the functions that marriage has traditionally fulfilled may be increasingly found in contexts other than marriage. Evidence has shown that Americans are becoming increasingly individualistic and less committed to social groups of all kinds; thus, calling for a reassessment of the belief that the institution of marriage in the United States is as strong as ever.

Perhaps the early 1980s was a unique time period. Whether the trend toward similarity between married and unmarried life-styles has reversed is uncertain, but more recent data suggest that the "happiness gap" increased again in the late 1980s.[6] That is, data since 1986 have reflected more distinct differences in happi-

---

[6] Gary R. Lee, Karen Seccombe, and Constance L. Shehan, "Marital Status and Personal Happiness: An Analysis of Trend Data," *Journal of Marriage and the Family* 53 (November 1991): 839–844; and Arne Mastekaasa, "Marital Status and Subjective Well-Being: A Changing Relationship," *Social Indicators Research* 29 (1993): 249–276.

ness and subjective well-being between married and never-married people than demonstrated in the early part of the decade.

When examined cross-culturally, the consequences of marriage differ as the structure of marriage differs. For example, when marriage is specifically an extension of the kin- and extended-family system, then procreation, passing on the family name, and continuation of property become basic functions. Consequently, not having a child (or more specifically, not having a male child) is sufficient reason to replace a present wife or add a new wife. In the United States, even though most children are born to married couples (and many married couples want children), not having children is rarely sufficient reason to divorce and remarry. Conversely, not wanting or being unable to have children—an issue faced by women who are career-oriented, infertile, or older—is not sufficient reason for not marrying. Thus, why marriage?

Chapter 10 on partner selection mentioned that, for arranged marriages, important factors include the bride's price, the reputation of the potential spouse's kin group, levirate and sororate arrangements, and traditions of prescribed marriage. When marriage is based on free choice, individualistic forces are accorded greater significance. In the United States, marriage has many functions and involves many positive as well as negative personal factors: a family of one's own, children, companionship, happiness, love, ego support, economic security, an approved sexual outlet, affection, escape, elimination of loneliness, pregnancy, and so on. The greater the extent to which the perceived needs of marriage are met and the fewer the alternatives to replacing unmet needs, the greater the likelihood of marriage and the continuation of marriage. Still, why marriage?

At a personal level, any perceived reason may explain marriage, but at a social level, all societies sanction certain reasons and renounce others. Thus, personal factors operate within the confines of social boundaries; the functions that marriage performs are determined and qualified by the social and cultural context.

The social and cultural context for marriage in the United States demonstrates a variety of forms other than the traditional monogamous, sexually exclusive marriage pattern for the fulfillment of individuals' perceived needs. A familiar pattern is *sequential* or *serial monogamy:* the marriage, divorce, remarriage, divorce pattern. Another familiar pattern is *adultery,* the maintenance of the marriage with a secret satisfaction of sexual and emotional needs outside the conjugal relationship. *Nonmarital cohabitation,* a relatively common practice today, involves two unmarried adults of the same or opposite sex sharing a common residence in a marriage-like relationship. These and other nontraditional patterns have been examined previously. In the United States, as around the world, marriage or some alternative exists to fulfill basic functions generally attributed to the husband/wife relationship.

MARRIAGE TRENDS AND CHARACTERISTICS

As just discussed, the reasons for marriage and the functions it performs vary extensively when viewed from a global perspective. There is also variation in

marriage rates: the proportion of people who marry in a given population. For example, one investigation of 111 countries showed that high sex ratios (a relative undersupply of women) were positively associated with the proportion of women who married and inversely associated with women's average age at marriage.[7] That is, the fewer the number of women relative to that of men, the higher the proportion who marry and the younger the age at which they do so. The number and proportion of people who marry are influenced by other factors as well: economic conditions, wars, male/female roles, and so forth. What are the specific marriage trends in the United States?

In 1994, of the 190.0 million persons ages eighteen and over in the United States, 115.1 million, or 60.6 percent, were married.[8] As shown in Figure 12-1, the percentages of persons married differed considerably by sex, race, and Spanish origin. About 65 percent of white males but only 36 percent of black females ages eighteen and over were married.

Reasons people marry

Why the extreme differences? Broadly viewed, marriage results from two factors: composition and propensity to marry. *Composition* refers to the availability of potential marriage partners with certain characteristics, and *propensity to marry* refers to the mutual attraction for marriage between males and females with specific characteristics, independent of the composition of the population. A review of black and white marriage rates suggested that propensity plays a major role in accounting for black/white differences and for change over time in black marriage rates.[9] The suggestion is that, irrespective of population composition, the marriage relationship is less significant to African Americans, as exemplified by the greater likelihood of consensual unions, ties outside the nuclear family, and children born out of wedlock and reared in single-parent households. Blacks, especially women, are more skeptical of the value of marriage than are whites. Black women hold lower expectations for realizing a stable, monogamous marriage where husbands provide much financial support, and they have negative expectations about relationships that they see as exploitative. Again, irrespective of composition, rather than enter marriages from which little is expected and that hold the promise of exploitation, many lower-income black women prefer to remain unmarried.

In spite of the increase in age at marriage, a divorce rate perceived as very high, a dramatic increase in cohabitation, and the talk of a declining popularity of and

---

[7] Scott J. South, "Sex Ratios, Economic Power, and Women's Roles: A Theoretical Extension and Empirical Test," *Journal of Marriage and the Family* 50 (February 1988): 19–31.

[8] U.S. Bureau of the Census, *Statistical Abstract of the United States: 1995,* 115th edition. (Washington, DC: U.S. Government Printing Office, 1995), No. 58, p. 54.

[9] Robert Schoen and James R. Kluegle, "The Widening Gap in Black and White Marriage Rates: The Impact of Population Composition and Differential Marriage Propensities," *American Sociological Review* 53 (December 1988): 895–907.

Figure 12-1

Marital status of persons eighteen years old and over by sex, race, and Spanish origin, 1994

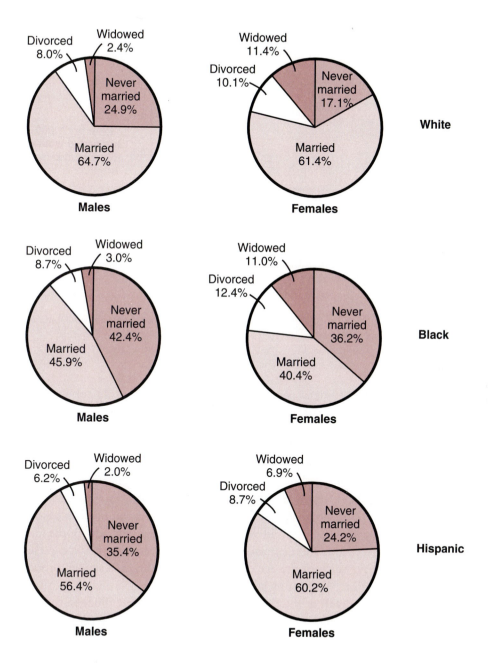

Males / **Females** — **White**

Divorced 8.0%
Widowed 2.4%
Never married 24.9%
Married 64.7%

Widowed 11.4%
Divorced 10.1%
Never married 17.1%
Married 61.4%

Males / **Females** — **Black**

Divorced 8.7%
Widowed 3.0%
Never married 42.4%
Married 45.9%

Widowed 11.0%
Divorced 12.4%
Never married 36.2%
Married 40.4%

Males / **Females** — **Hispanic**

Divorced 6.2%
Widowed 2.0%
Never married 35.4%
Married 56.4%

Widowed 6.9%
Divorced 8.7%
Never married 24.2%
Married 60.2%

Source: U.S. Bureau of the Census, *Statistical Abstract of the United States: 1995,* 115th ed. (Washington, DC: U.S. Government Printing Office, 1995), no. 58, p. 54.

Figure 12-2
U.S. marriage rates: 1940–1994

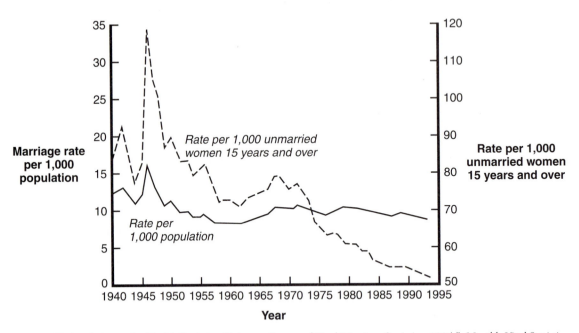

Source: National Center for Health Statistics, "Advance Report of Final Marriage Statistics, 1994," *Monthly Vital Statistics Report,* Vol. 43, No. 12 (Hyattsville, Maryland: Public Health Service, 14 July 1995), Figure 1, p. 2, and *Statistical Abstract of the United States: 1995,* 115th ed. (Washington, DC: U.S. Government Printing Office, 1995).

propensity for marriage, many people still choose marriage. For the population as a whole, 2.36 million marriages occurred in 1994, a marriage rate (number of marriages per 1,000 population) of 9.1.[10] This rate has varied widely over the past fifty-five years (see Figure 12-2), fluctuating because of the influence of wars, changing economic conditions, the sex ratio of the marriageable population, and the number of potential brides and grooms in the general population. Characteristically, the marriage rate has risen at the outset of a major war, declined during the course of the conflict, and increased sharply in the immediate postwar years. This was the pattern for World Wars I and II and probably also for the Civil War. Economic recessions and depressions generally have had an inhibiting effect on marriage, as have shifts in the age distribution, resulting in a smaller proportion of the population being young adults.

In 1932, at the depth of the Depression, the marriage rate plunged to a low of 7.9, probably unprecedented in the United States except during the Civil War. The increase in the marriage rate during the World War II era remains unparal-

---

[10] National Center for Health Statistics, "Annual Summary of Births, Marriages, Divorces, and Deaths: United States, 1994," *Monthly Vital Statistics Report,* Vol. 43, No. 13 (Hyattsville, Maryland: Public Health Service, 23 October 1995), Table D, p. 4.

leled in the history of the United States. Just before and immediately after the United States' entry into the war, the rate rose sharply as young men sought to avail themselves of the deferred status granted to married men or simply wanted to marry before going overseas. The end of the war and the return of millions of men to civilian life precipitated another upsurge in the marriage rate. In 1946, the marriage rate reached 16.4, an unprecedented and yet unsurpassed peak. By 1949, the rate had returned to the pre–World War II level, dropping as rapidly as it had climbed. This marked the end of twenty years of the most frequent and pronounced fluctuations in the history of the U.S. marriage rate.

The marriage rate declined below 9.0 in the late 1950s and then increased again through the 1960s to a level between 10.0 and 11.0. The rate fluctuated between these levels for nearly twenty years. The 1994 rate of 9.1 approaches the lowest rate since 1967.

A number of recent changes in family life have been attributed to the decline and delay in marriage:

- Increases in sexuality among people who are unmarried and an accompanied increase in out-of-wedlock births
- Increases in the independence of young people, nonmarital cohabitation, and labor force participation of women
- A reduction in fertility
- A temporary shortage of eligible males in the marriage market (a "marriage squeeze")
- An increase in divorce (the trend over the past few decades)[11]

Although these represent dramatic changes from the past that could suggest further declines in marriage, strong evidence has shown that people in the United States continue to value marriage. Marriage is viewed as a popular choice for most Americans.

Variations in marriage rates

In the United States, marriage rates have a distinct seasonal pattern: More marriages typically occur in June, July, and August than in any other months. The seasonal low for marriage tends to occur in January, February, and March. Seasonal variations are also greatly affected by holidays, the beginning and ending of the school year, climatic conditions, and religious holy periods such as Lent.

Marriage rates also vary widely by day of the week. Over half of all marriages take place on Saturday, three times as many as are performed on Friday, the next

---

[11] Willard L. Rodgers and Arland Thornton, "Changing Patterns of First Marriage in the United States," *Demography* 22 (May 1985): 265–279; Thomas J. Espenshade, "Marriage Trends in America: Estimates, Implications, and Underlying Causes," *Population and Development Review* 11 (June 1985): 193–245.

most popular day. Less than one-tenth as many marriages occur on Tuesdays, Wednesdays, and Thursdays—the least popular days—as on Saturdays.

Marriage rates in the United States (per 1,000 population) have consistently shown distinct differences by state. In 1994, the highest marriage rates were in Nevada (96.3), Arkansas (15.6), Tennessee (15.5), Hawaii (15.2), South Carolina (13.9), and Idaho (13.4), all favored states for nonresidents who wish to marry. The lowest marriage rates were in West Virginia (6.0), Pennsylvania (6.3), California (6.5), Connecticut (6.7), and New Jersey (6.7). Other states with low rates (under 7.5 per 1,000 population) were Delaware, Minnesota, New Mexico, North Carolina, Rhode Island, and Wisconsin.[12]

Marriages are reported by and subject to laws of the state in which the ceremony is performed. Lenient marriage laws attract couples from out of state, particularly if the adjoining states have more restrictive laws. The major attractions are (1) laws that do not require a waiting period between the date of application and issuance of the license or between license issuance and the ceremony, and (2) laws that do not require a medical examination or blood test. These factors have a two-pronged effect: They lower the rates of the states from which the couples are drawn and raise the rates of the states to which the couples are attracted.

POWER IN CONJUGAL AND INTIMATE RELATIONSHIPS

One important aspect of the marital system (a conjugal relationship) and of other intimate relationships is the power positions of the partners—as individuals and in relation to each other. There is considerable agreement that *power* is the ability to influence others and affect their behavior. Power is often measured by determining who makes certain decisions or who performs certain tasks.

Power involves the crucial dimensions of authority and influence. Social norms determine who has **authority** in that the culture designates the positions that have the legitimate and prescribed power (authority). In some societies, authority is invested in the husband; in others, it rests with the oldest male in an extended-family situation; and in others, authority goes to the mother-in-law. Other family members can **influence**—that is, exert pressure on—the person with authority. For example, the president of the United States has the prescribed authority to make a wide range of decisions, but he can be influenced by the press, the public, and his own family, none of whom are given the authority to make political decisions. Similarly, the husband may have authority over his wife and children, but he can be greatly influenced by them.

Throughout this text are frequent references to patriarchy, male dominance, male authoritarianism, and the like. Yet it is clear that, in spite of cultural norms proclaiming patriarchy and male rule, females, in or out of marriage, influence

---

[12] *Monthly Vital Statistics Report,* Vol. 42, No. 13, Table 2, p. 12.

U.S. Diversity: Gender and Power

> The Woman who will not be ruled
> must live without marriage.
> —*Susan B. Anthony, 1877*

other people, affect their behavior, and get them to do what they want. (In other words, they have power.) The domestic arena is one in which women, wives, and mothers are not likely to be as passive and powerless as is often described or believed. Domestic power—the ability to impose one's will in decisions concerning sexual relations, household tasks, and the lives of children—frequently departs from male ideals. In a study of domestic power in Southern Spain, for example, an anthropologist showed that working-class women often united with their mothers to prevail in domestic decision making, despite opposition from their husbands.[13] In fact, the statement has been made that male dominance in the lower classes is mythical.

How can this be explained or understood? Where and how do women get power in contexts of male dominance and patriarchal norms? The following section will examine some characteristics of conjugal power and the key theories that explain it.

Characteristics of power

Several decades ago, Mary Rogers made several key points about power:[14]

1. Power is a capacity or an ability to influence others, *not* the exercise of that ability. Ability does not denote social action. The perceived or real ability to influence can affect outcomes even when the exercise of that ability is not undertaken.

2. An individual's power must be viewed relative to specific social systems and the positions (statuses) a person occupies within a given social system. Note that power is not inherent within a person. Power must be viewed in dynamic terms; one must note that the power of individuals to influence others is linked to the social statuses and social roles they occupy and perform within special social systems.

---

[13] David D. Gilmore, "Men and Women in Southern Spain: 'Domestic Power' Revisited," *American Anthropologist* 92 (December 1990): 953–970.

[14] Mary F. Rogers, "Instrumental and Infra-Resources: The Base of Power," *American Journal of Sociology* 79 (May 1974): 1418–1433.

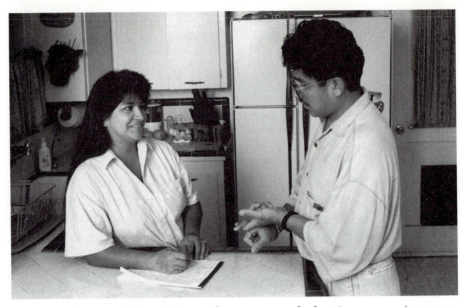

The issues of power, including decision-making processes and role assignments, are important in all relationships. Egalitarianism may be the norm or goal of many couples, but the reality is that male activities and control are pervasive in most societies.

3. If power is an ability to influence others, resources are the primary determinants of that ability. A *resource* is "any attribute, circumstance, or possession that increases the ability of its holder to influence a person or group."[15] Attributes might include age, sex, race, health, and level of energy; circumstances might include location, friendships or acquaintances, flexibility, and access to information; possessions might include money, land, property, goods, and so on.

The contention is that persons with greater resources have an advantage over those without those resources. In a social exchange perspective, they can bargain with others from a position of strength.

Rebecca Warner and others made a strong case for broadening the conceptualization of resources to include selected features of family and kinship structures (family organization).[16] For example, wives will have more power in marriages in societies with nuclear- rather than extended-family structures and in societies with matrilateral rather than patrilateral customs of residence and descent. Ethnographic data on over one hundred nonindustrial societies provided support for these propositions, highlighting the fact that *organizational resources* may be as important as material and personal resources in understanding conjugal power.

[15] Ibid., p. 1425.

[16] Rebecca L. Warner, Gary R. Lee, and Janet Lee, "Social Organization, Spousal Resources, and Marital Power: A Cross-Cultural Study," *Journal of Marriage and the Family* 48 (February 1986): 121–128.

Power and decision making in conjugal and intimate relationships

One of the ways in which power has traditionally been measured is to determine which spouse or partner makes the major decisions and how decision-making patterns vary by area of concern. One of the most widely cited studies and one that served to stimulate many others was done in the late 1950s by Robert Blood and Donald Wolfe.[17] In an attempt to measure the balance of power between husbands and wives, they interviewed 731 city wives in metropolitan Detroit.

Blood and Wolfe selected eight situations that they felt would include both masculine as well as feminine decisions about the family as a whole:

1. What job the husband should take
2. What kind of car to get
3. Whether or not to buy life insurance
4. Where to go on vacation
5. What house or apartment to take
6. Whether or not the wife should go to work or quit work
7. What doctor to have when someone is sick
8. How much money the family can afford to spend per week on food

The wives' answers to the eight situations revealed that two decisions were primarily the husband's province (his job and car), two were primarily the wife's province (her work and food), and all the others were joint decisions in the sense of having more same responses. Even the wife's working turned out to be a middling decision from the standpoint of the mean score, leaving only decisions about food expenditures predominantly to the wife.

Even though the results of this study were published more than thirty-five years ago, perhaps the responses of the wives to these eight decision-making questions would not be surprising even today. In the United States, it is expected that the male is responsible for the economic support of his wife and children. His job is his primary responsibility and consumes both time and energy. Factors related to automobiles might also be expected to be primarily the concern of the husband or male partner; although most wives and female partners in U.S. society have drivers' licenses, the male most likely does the driving when the couple travel together. Traditionally, it has also been the husband or male partner who repairs and cares for the automobile.

Whether or not to buy life insurance, where to go on vacation, and what house or apartment to take are decisions that are more apt to be shared equally by spouses or partners than made by either person separately. It could be assumed that both partners have equal competencies in these choices. Furthermore, these areas affect both partners more equally than do the other decision-making areas.

[17] Robert O. Blood, Jr., and Donald M. Wolfe, *Husbands and Wives: The Dynamics of Marital Living* (Glencoe, IL: The Free Press, 1960): 20.

Blood and Wolfe's theoretical explanation of why husbands and wives make certain decisions individually rather than together is based on *resource availability.* That is, the source of authority and power lies in the comparative resources each spouse has available. The balance of power is weighted toward the partner who has the greatest resources, as perceived by the other partner.

A number of writers have questioned the theoretical accuracy of explaining power based on resources. The theory of resources (in reality, a proposition rather than a theory) contends that the more partners control resources of value to themselves and their mates, the greater the relative power. Data on this subject have shown some mixed and inconsistent results. To understand why requires examining the theory of resources issue more intensely.

Theory of resources issue

The **theory of resources** provides the conceptual core around which many of the later studies have been built. Over the past several decades, a number of authors have stressed that power is not merely based on an individual's resources but on the comparative contributions (resources) and exchange processes of the husband and wife relative to each other. Hyman Rodman, for example, developed a theory of resources in a cultural context that takes into account the theory of resources, the theory of exchange, the comparative contributions of both husband and wife, and the cultural context in which the interaction occurs.[18] Rodman argued that one must not only be aware of resources in attempting to explain conjugal power but must consider as well the cultural context in which decision making takes place. Thus, in certain societies, it is the upper- and middle-status groups (the highest income, educational, and occupational groups) that first accept norms of marital egalitarianism. This, in effect, diminishes the impact of resources upon power in marital settings.

This differentiation of a basic resource theory from a **cultural resource theory** sheds some light on understanding variations in power between men and women and between social classes, various groups, and even countries. One example that focused on this differentiation was a study of dual-career couples where half the wives earned at least one-third more than their husbands and half the husbands earned at least one-third more than their wives.[19] Consistent with *resource theory,* spouses who earned more viewed their careers as more important and had more say at home than spouses who earned less. Consistent with *cultural resource theory,* men overall had more say in financial matters, took less responsibility for the children

---

[18] Hyman Rodman, "Marital Power in France, Greece, Yugoslavia, and the United States: A Cross-National Discussion," *Journal of Marriage and the Family* 29 (May 1967): 320–324; Hyman Rodman, "Marital Power and the Theory of Resources in Cultural Context," *Journal of Comparative Family Studies* 3 (Spring 1972): 50–69.

[19] Janice M. Steil and Karen Weltman, "Marital Inequality: The Importance of Resources, Personal Attributes, and Social Norms on Career Valuing and the Allocation of Domestic Responsibilities," *Sex Roles* 24 (1991): 161–179.

and the household, and saw their own careers as more important than their wives' careers. Thus, even though resources had significant effects on the wives who had them (those who earned more than their husbands), these women were still more likely to say they would move to another location on their husbands' behalf.

Other studies have drawn similar conclusions. Mark Rank found that increments in wives' resources correlated positively with wives' influence, supporting the theory of resources argument.[20] But increments in husbands' resources correlated negatively with husbands' influence, thus not supporting the argument that greater resources lead to greater influence and power. The explanation is that as husbands gain higher levels of income, education, and occupational prestige, they come in contact with egalitarian norms regarding spousal relations. In brief, as both husbands and wives gain resources, women become less economically dependent on their spouses while men become socialized into an egalitarian ethic.

Another cautionary note on accepting the theory of resources per se or without qualifications comes from Karen Pyke.[21] It is her contention that women's market work (employment) is not considered a resource in some marriages and hence does not have a positive effect on marital power. Why? Consistent with a symbolic interaction perspective, it is necessary to examine the meanings couples give to the material and structural conditions of their lives. Thus a woman married to a man who views her employment as a threat rather than as a gift will derive less power from her employment. Likewise, the extent to which a woman views her own paid or unpaid labor as a gift or a burden will also affect her marital power.

Pyke's research gave support to these ideas in that men who were denied a sense of occupational success were less likely to view their wives' market work as a gift and some wives, sensitive to their husbands' feelings of failure, responded by not resisting their husbands' dominance to "balance" the husband's low self-esteem. Pyke's research suggests that any explanation of marital power must reflect the gender of the actors and the gendered meanings these actors give to the powering process.

Egalitarian ethic

Joint decision making, sharing marital power, perceptions of both self and partner doing a fair share of family work, and a feeling of equity appear to be positively related to marital and relationship satisfaction. This is particularly true of husbands who hold less traditional gender-role attitudes.[22] Husbands who were more

---

20 Mark R. Rank, "Determinants of Conjugal Influence in Wives' Employment Decision Making," *Journal of Marriage and the Family* 44 (August 1982): 591–604.

21 Karen D. Pyke, "Women's Employment as a Gift or Burden? Marital Power Across Marriage, Divorce, and Remarriage," *Gender and Society* 8 (March 1994): 73–91.

22 Paul R. Amato and Alan Booth, "Changes in Gender Role Attitudes and Perceived Marital Quality," *American Sociological Review* 60 (February 1995): 58–66.

progressive (less traditional) were found to show increases in reported positive marital quality. Increases in egalitarianism were found to be associated with declines in reports of negative aspects of the marriage (problems, disagreements, divorce proneness). The pattern was different, however, for women. Wives who held nontraditional gender-role attitudes reported increases in negative aspects of the marriage (less happiness, more disagreements, more problems). In contemporary marriages, stress is lessened when husbands, with their wives, have attitudes that support role sharing and gender equality.

Perhaps feminists lead the way in stressing an egalitarian ethic. Feminists have demonstrated the problematic nature of marital and family life for women and have provided an awareness of how traditionally structured marriage has an overwhelming cost to women in financial, emotional, and physical dimensions. Given the incongruence between the ideology and practice of marital equality, a key question may be whether a feminist ideology of full equality is compatible with marriage.

A partial answer comes from a study of feminist heterosexual marriages.[23] Assessed was the possibility of establishing marital equality through a series of processes that involves the partners critiquing the gender injustices (an ongoing dialogue of gender expectations); engaging in public acts of equality (different names, common financial decisions); the husband's support of the wife's activity (her career, his children); reflective assessment (monitoring of the contributions of each); and emotional involvement (openness about feelings). Rather than rejecting marriage, these feminist couples considered revitalizing the relationship by promoting a vigilance to equality. The study suggests that feminist women need not forgo relationships with men but can expect men to assume feminist beliefs and, with women, strive to enact them.

Findings such as these have lent support to social exchange theories and equity models suggesting that personal happiness, the highest levels of marital satisfaction, and the lowest levels of depression occur when individuals, men and women, believe their partners contribute a fair share to housework and child care and perceive equity in the exchange. For many married persons, particularly wives, an inequitable balance of marital power is a serious problem.

This pattern of personal happiness and marital satisfaction appears to be true even among successful women in dual-career couples, who manage successfully to carry out the demands of two occupations while maintaining a quality relationship in their marriage. This study, like those reported previously, found that wives in the labor force experienced higher marital quality if their husbands' expectations were less traditional.[24] Marital quality suffered when wives felt competitive with their spouses. The more balance the husband perceived in role behaviors, the higher the wife's perceived marital quality, especially among women in the labor

---

[23] Karen R. Blaisure and Katherine R. Allen, "Feminists and the Ideology and Practice of Marital Equality," *Journal of Marriage and the Family* 57 (February 1995): 5–19.

[24] Dana Vannoy-Hiller and William W. Philliber, *Equal Partners: Successful Women in Marriage* (Newbury Park, CA: Sage, 1989).

force and especially among those whose achievements equaled or surpassed those of their husbands. The perceived balance of costs and rewards in a marriage is relevant to success. In fact, this felt or perceived balance, the element of equity, matters more than any objective reality.[25]

MARITAL QUALITY

While the term **marital quality** is used throughout this section, *marital* is meant to incorporate the quality of any marriage-like relationship. What may be more significant than a legal status of being married is the degree of social attachment. Catherine Ross, for example, specified four levels of marital status on a continuum of social attachment: no partner, partner outside the household, living with partner in the household, and living with a married partner.[26] She discovered that the higher the level of social attachment, the lower the level of psychological distress. There were no significant differences in those living with a partner and those being married. Social attachments were stronger predictors of well-being than marital status.

    The literature on marital quality and the quality of marriage-like relationships is prolific.[27] Many attempts have been made to assess the quality of relationships, using such concepts as *adjustment, success, satisfaction, stability, happiness, well-being, consensus, cohesion, adaptation, integration, role strain,* and the like. Sometimes these terms are used interchangeably; at other times, each denotes something different. The terms are also used in a psychological sense, describing the state of one of the partners, or they are used in a social/psychological sense, referring to the state of the relationship. They are used also in a sociological sense, referring to the state of the group or system. In addition, the terms refer to the achievement of a goal or a dynamic process of making changes. All the concepts emphasize a dimension that contrasts with maladjustment, dissatisfaction, instability, and unhappiness.

Dimensions of marital quality

From the introductory statement, it should be clear that marital quality, marital adjustment, and marital well-being are varied concepts that lack a general consensus of definition. *Marital quality* or *adjustment* is essentially a relative agreement by husband and wife as to what issues are important, the sharing of similar tasks

---

[25] Ibid., p. 143.

[26] Catherine E. Ross, "Reconceptualizing Marital Status as a Continuum of Social Attachment," *Journal of Marriage and the Family* 57 (February 1995): 129–140.

[27] See Norval D. Glenn, "Quantitative Research on Marital Quality in the 1980s: A Critical Review," *Journal of Marriage and the Family* 52 (November 1990): 818–831.

and activities, and the demonstration of affection for one another. *Marital success,* as distinguished from *marital quality,* generally refers to the achievement of one or more goals: permanence, companionship, fulfilling expectations of the community, and so forth. *Marital happiness,* distinguished from both *adjustment* and *success,* is an individual emotional response. Although marital happiness is an individual phenomenon, marital quality, success, and adjustment are dyadic achievements or states of the marriage or the relationship.

One study asked newlyweds to evaluate the quality (well-being) of their marriage.[28] Four dimensions of marital well-being emerged from a factor analysis of responses: happiness, equity, competence, and control. Happiness was more clearly associated with all aspects of well-being than any other, but feelings of equity in the relationship, feelings of competence in the marital role, and feelings of control over marital outcomes were important and separate dimensions of marital well-being.

Feelings of equity were addressed earlier. In regard to feelings of control, Catherine Ross suggested that, for women, marriage has a price and represents a trade-off.[29] On the one hand, marriage increases women's household incomes, thus giving them more control over their lives. On the other hand, since women do most of the housework and child care, marriage decreases their sense of control, independence, and autonomy. For men, marriage has little effect on their sense of control.

About thirty years ago, Jessie Bernard included the quality of the relationship as one of three major dimensions of marital adjustment. Namely, marital adjustment is determined by:

1. The degree or nature of the *differences* between or among the parties involved

2. The degree or nature of the *communication* between or among the parties

3. As just noted, the *quality of the relationship* between or among the parties (positive or negative, friendly or hostile)[30]

Differences may be a matter of degree, or they may be categorical (no flexibility, no leeway). Often, matters of principle are categorical and thus the most difficult to resolve. Statements such as "We will never miss Mass" and beliefs such as "Oral sex is wrong," if taken categorically, do not permit flexibility in dealing with a mate or spouse who feels differently. On the other hand, differences of degree permit give and take, bargaining, and negotiation. The point is that differences as well as the nature and extent of those differences affect dyadic or interpersonal adjustment.

---

[28] Susan E. Crohan and Joseph Veroff, "Dimensions of Marital Well-being among White and Black Newlyweds," *Journal of Marriage and the Family* 51 (May 1989): 373–383.

[29] Catherine E. Ross, "Marriage and the Sense of Control," *Journal of Marriage and the Family* 53 (November 1991): 831–838.

[30] Jessie Bernard, "The Adjustment of Married Mates," in *Handbook of Marriage and the Family,* ed. by Harold T. Christensen (Chicago: Rand McNally, 1964): 690.

The quality of a marriage is based on a wide variety of factors. These include satisfaction with the relationship, agreement on issues such as finances and friends, enjoying doing things together and exchanging ideas, and affectionate expressions of love and support.

The second dimension, communication, necessitates interaction. Few people would doubt or question the importance of communication to successful relationships of any kind. Yet communication is an extremely complex factor in marital relationships: It may be verbal or nonverbal, it may be explicit or tacit, it may clarify or mislead, or it may draw relationships closer together or tear them apart. To not talk at all, to talk constantly, to order, to nag, to scold, to praise—each may convey a certain message.

A review of research over the past twenty years revealed strong support for the relationship between communication and marital satisfaction.[31] This relationship held true for both the content and the process of communication. Findings consistently replicated were that couples with higher rates of self-disclosure and

31 Patricia Noller and Mary Anne Fitzpatrick, "Marital Communication in the Eighties," *Journal of Marriage and the Family* 52 (November 1990): 832–843; and W. Kim Halford, Kurt Hahlweg, and Michael Dunne, "The Cross-Cultural Consistency of Marital Communication Associated with Marital Distress," *Journal of Marriage and the Family* 52 (May 1990): 487–500.

News Item: Meaningful Conversation and Marriage Don't Mix

At a party the other evening, people were discussing marriage. Marilyn turned and looked at her husband lovingly (as if she had just popped a Geritol tablet) and said, "Dan and I have a good marriage because we have meaningful conversations with one another."

I couldn't get it off my mind. On the way home I asked my husband, "Have we ever had a meaningful conversation?"

"I don't think so," he said.

"That's hard to believe," I persisted. "In 26 years we've never had one?"

"Not that I can remember."

We drove along in silence for about 20 minutes. Finally I said, "What is a meaningful conversation?"

"You're kidding! You actually don't know?"

"No. What is it?"

"Well," he said, "it's a conversation with meaning."

"Like the oil embargo and Paul Harvey?"

"Exactly."

"What about them?" I asked.

"What about who?"

"The oil embargo and Paul Harvey."

"It doesn't have to be a conversation about the oil embargo and Paul Harvey," he said. "It could be a discussion on anything in your daily schedule that is pertinent."

"I shaved my legs yesterday."

"That is not pertinent to anyone but you."

"Not really. I was using your razor."

"If you read the paper more," he said, "your conversations would be more stimulating."

"Okay, here's something meaningful I read just yesterday. In Naples—that's in Italy—police were searching for a woman who tried to cut off a man's nose with a pair of scissors while he was sleeping. What do you think of that?"

"That's not meaningful," he said.

A few minutes later I offered, "Suppose it was the American Embassy and the woman was a spy, and the nose belonged to Henry Kissinger which held secret documents about an oil embargo between Saudi Arabia and Paul Harvey?"

He drove in silence. "How long have Dan and Marilyn been married?"

"Twelve years," I said.

"They must pace their meaningful conversations."

Source: From *At Wit's End* by Erma Bombeck. Reproduced through the courtesy of Field Newspaper Syndicate.

expressions of love, support, and affection tended also to experience greater satisfaction. Research on process variables suggested that positive forms of nonverbal communication—such as laughter, voice tone, touching spouse, and body position—were found more frequently in happy couples. Nondistressed couples were more likely to show good listening skills and clarity of speech and to positively interpret their partners' behavior.

The quality of the relationship was Bernard's third major dimension of adjustment. Spouses who are friendly and loving are not necessarily well adjusted to marriage, but such qualities make accommodation easier. Making sacrifices or changing plans is easier when spouses have love and genuine concern for one another. If the relationship is affectionate, results will be far different than if it is hateful or hostile.

The dynamics of marital quality were assessed in a recent national sample of married persons interviewed three times over an eight-year period.[32] It was found that marital quality, regardless of how it is measured, is a remarkably stable phenomenon, unaffected by gender and marital duration. Even among those couples who eventually divorced, the relationship, from formation to dissolution, did not fluctuate appreciably. Marital quality was said to be a dyadic property, not something that individuals carry from one marriage to another.

Alan Booth and others ask the question: Does religion matter in today's marriage?[33] Using longitudinal data from a large sample of married persons, little support was found for the idea that an increase in religious activity leads to improved marital relations. Decreases in religiosity do, however, decrease slightly the probability of thinking about divorce but were not found to enhance marital happiness or interaction nor decrease the conflicts and problems thought to cause divorce.

Evaluating marital quality

Assessment of the quality of marriage and intimate relationships began in earnest in the late 1920s. Each decade since then, an extensive body of literature has been accumulated in an effort to predict marital success and determine factors, psychological and social, associated with marital quality or adjustment.

It is likely that the most widely used measurement of marital quality or interpersonal adjustment has been the Dyadic Adjustment Scale developed by Graham Spanier.[34] The scale consists of thirty-two items centering around four basic components: dyadic satisfaction, dyadic cohesion, dyadic consensus, and affectional expression.

- *Satisfaction* is measured by asking questions (Do you confide in your mate? Do you regret that you married?) and inquiring into the degree of happiness in the relationship.

- *Cohesion* focuses on whether the couple does things together and exchanges ideas.

- *Consensus* measures the extent of agreement on issues such as finances, friends, religious matters, and household tasks.

32 David R. Johnson, Teodora O. Amoloza, and Alan Booth, "Stability and Development Change in Marital Quality: A Three-Wave Panel Analysis," *Journal of Marriage and the Family* 54 (August 1992): 582–594.

33 Alan Booth, David R. Johnson, Ann Branaman, and Alan Sica, "Belief and Behavior: Does Religion Matter in Today's Marriage?" *Journal of Marriage and the Family* 57 (August 1995): 661–671.

34 Graham B. Spanier, "Measuring Dyadic Adjustment: New Scales for Assessing the Quality of Marriage and Similar Dyads," *Journal of Marriage and the Family* 38 (February 1976): 15–28; and Graham B. Spanier and Linda Thompson, "A Confirmatory Analysis of the Dyadic Adjustment Scale," *Journal of Marriage and the Family* 44 (August 1982): 731–738.

• *Affectional expression* refers to the extent of agreement regarding demonstrations of affection, sexual relations, and showing love.

Other measures of marital quality or relationship adjustment, satisfaction, or well-being focus on related issues. Susan Hendrick developed a seven-item relationship assessment scale that asks each partner the following questions:

• How well does your partner meet your needs?
• What is your level of satisfaction with the relationship?
• How good is your relationship compared to most?
• How often do you wish you hadn't gotten into it?
• What is the extent to which the relationship meets your original expectations?
• How much do you love your partner?
• What are the problems in the relationship?[35]

Hendrick claimed that her seven-item scale is easily administered, is highly correlated with the longer Dyadic Adjustment Scale, and effectively discriminates between partners (married couples, cohabitors, gay couples, friends) who stay together versus those who split.

Jessie Bernard made a different point for evaluating marital relationships. She suggested that a criterion be set up in terms not of the best *imaginable* relationship but of the best *possible* one.[36] Thus, a marriage may be successful to the extent that it provides the highest satisfaction possible, not imaginable. However unsatisfactory the relationship may be in terms of happiness, it may still be judged better than the alternatives.

From this exchange and relativistic (viewed in context) point of view, a marital relationship is successful (1) if the satisfaction is positive (the rewards to both partners are greater than the costs) and (2) if the relationship is preferable to other alternatives. The following two examples illustrate exchange and relativistic perspectives:

A and B do not like one another; they get on one another's nerves; the costs of remaining married are great in frustration and loneliness. But the rewards are great also; together they can afford a lovely home; they have high status in the community; the children are protected from scandal; the church approves of them; etc. This relationship is "successful" or "good," not because it is the best imaginable, but only because it is the best possible in the sense that the satisfactions are greater than the costs…

---

[35] Susan S. Hendrick, "A Generic Measure of Relationship Satisfaction." *Journal of Marriage and the Family* 50 (February 1988): 93–98.

[36] Bernard, "The Adjustment of Married Mates," p. 732.

An example in which a marital relationship is successful only because it is better than any alternative would be the marriage of a dependent woman to, let us say, an alcoholic, in which the costs in misery were much greater than the rewards in security or status; but the spread between costs and satisfactions would be much greater if she left him. She would then be alone; she would not have the protection of the status of marriage; she would not even have the occasional sober companionship of a husband, etc. Bad as it is, therefore, her marriage seems better to her than any alternative she has.[37]

Richard Udry suggested that the dimension of **marital alternatives** appears to be a better predictor of marital disruption than are measures of satisfaction.[38] Using longitudinal data of married couples from sixteen U.S. urban areas, he measured the respondents' perceptions of marital alternatives: that is, how much better or worse they would be without their present spouse and how easily that spouse could be replaced with one of comparable quality. In the ensuing year or two after these resources were measured, couples in which spouses were rated high in marital alternatives had several times the disruption rate of those rated low in alternatives.

This observation perhaps gives a clearer idea of why many unhappy marriages remain intact: The spouses have no or few alternatives, or, as suggested by exchange theory, the existing alternatives have costs that exceed their benefits. Recent data have shown that about 7 percent of intact marriages are stable but unhappy. Age, lack of prior marital experience, commitment to marriage as an institution, low social activity, lack of control over one's life, dependency, and belief that divorce would detract from happiness are all factors that predict stability in unhappy marriages.[39]

What about marital conflict? Is it a sure sign of low marital quality?

Marital conflict

A social conflict frame of reference, as described in Chapter 2, is rooted in the basic assumption that conflict is natural and inevitable in all human interaction. This is true of marital interaction, as well.

As couples interact, as they define and redefine their relationship with one another, and as they perform daily activities and fulfill role expectations, conflict is inevitable: over work, over children, over criticism, over in-laws, over expenditures, over sex, over politics, over drinking or smoking, and, as stressed in popular literature, even over matters such as how one should squeeze the toothpaste. These conflicts, when ongoing and unresolved, are likely to be linked to dissatisfaction

---

[37] Ibid., pp. 732–733.

[38] J. Richard Udry, "Marital Alternatives and Marital Disruption," *Journal of Marriage and the Family* 43 (November 1981): 889–897.

[39] Tim B. Heaton and Stan L. Albrecht, "Stable Unhappy Marriages," *Journal of Marriage and the Family* 53 (August 1991): 747–758.

with or even the ending of the relationship. But if conflicts are inevitable, the question now focuses on how conflict is managed in a way mutually satisfactory to both marital partners.

In a chapter entitled "Marital Conflict as a Positive Force," John Scanzoni argued that, in order to understand the dynamics of husband/wife interaction, the first step is to throw out the notion that equilibrium or stability is a necessary ideal, and the second step is to throw out the idea that conflict is by nature bad or unhealthy within marriage.[40]

Conflict brings into the open the issues that one or both partners consider unjust or inequitable. When such issues are presented, negotiated, and resolved in a way that is satisfactory to both partners, the outcome may be a new, more positive level of marital adjustment or solidarity. In contrast, failure to engage in conflict when injustice is perceived may result in a less beneficial, less rewarding situation for both marital partners and may actually increase the chances for dissolution of the marriage.

Conflict, when viewed from this perspective of injustice, should not be confused with difficulties and discord brought about by economic hardships or constraints. These, too, produce conflict and change in marital relations. Longitudinal data of couples who suffered income loss during the major depression (1929–1933) showed marked decline in marital quality and an increase in marital discord.[41] Men who lacked adaptive resources became more difficult to live with and more tense, irritable, and explosive. More recently, economic distress induced by a downturn in agriculture was found to have clear effects on the marital quality of farm couples. Increased depression and contemplation of divorce were two of the strongest effects of economic hardship.[42] These behaviors in themselves may produce conflict but seem related less to interpersonal inequities than to disrupted patterns of social interaction and adverse psychological changes brought about by economic loss.

Marital quality over the life course

Developmental models and life-course models have been used effectively to study family change. These approaches, which deal with changes over time, have been used to test a number of issues: satisfaction with the division of household labor (with wives' satisfaction starting high, decreasing dramatically, then increasing again, following a pronounced U-shaped curve across the life cycle),[43] variations

---

[40] John Scanzoni, *Sexual Bargaining: Power Politics in the American Marriage,* 2d ed. (Chicago: The University of Chicago Press, 1982): 61–102. Note also: Suzanne M. Retzinger, *Violent Emotions: Shame and Rage in Marital Quarrels.* (Newbury Park, CA: Sage, 1991).

[41] Jeffrey K. Liker and Glen H. Elder, Jr., "Economic Hardship and Marital Relations in the 1930s," *American Sociological Review* 48 (June 1983): 343–359.

[42] David R. Johnson and Alan Booth, "Rural Economic Decline and Marital Quality: A Panel Study of Farm Marriages," *Family Relations* 39 (April 1990): 159–165.

[43] J. Jill Suitor, "Marital Quality and Satisfaction with the Division of Household Labor across the Life Cycle," *Journal of Marriage and the Family* 53 (February 1991): 221–230.

in the life course of U.S. women (with blacks having greater variation than whites in factors such as having more children and having them sooner),[44] and perceived marital quality (again, supporting a curvilinear, U-shaped trend).[45]

What happens to marriages and marital quality over long periods of time? Most studies have sought answers to this question by comparing groups at different points in the life course or at different stages of the family life cycle. That is, newlyweds have been compared with families which have preschool children who have in turn been compared with families which have adolescents in the home and so forth.

One unique exception to this approach took place at the Institute of Human Development at the University of California in Berkeley.[46] Seventeen couples, who had been married for fifty to sixty-nine years, were the survivors of an original study of 250 couples, who were first studied in 1928 and 1929 and then interviewed again from time to time over the following years. In all of the surviving marriages, partners had both shared and separate interests and had both a commitment to the marriage and an acceptance of each other. Husbands tended to be more satisfied with their marriages than were wives. Of the authors' model of six types of very long-term marriages,[47] the greatest number exhibited a U-shaped or a curvilinear pattern, that is, starting at a high level of affect and satisfaction, dipping during the years when having young children until the children left, and increasing in the later years to a point as high as at the beginning. All of the other couples were categorized as stable (positive, neutral, or negative), and no couples showed a continuous increase or a continuous decline in marital satisfaction. (Any such couples may have previously divorced.)

Numerous other studies have attempted to discover how families manage their lives, what explains their relative successes and failures, and how their relationships change over time. One study asked 1,140 families, "What makes families work?" and analyzed results, using a seven-stage, family life-cycle model.[48] This study confirmed the findings of other studies,[49] namely, that satisfaction with marriage and family life tends to decrease over the early stages of the life cycle and

---

[44] Graham B. Spanier, "Marital Trajectories of American Women: Variations in the Life Course," *Journal of Marriage and the Family* 47 (November 1985): 993–1003.

[45] Stephen A. Anderson, Candyce S. Russell, and Walter R. Schumm. "Perceived Marital Quality and Family Life-Cycle Categories: A Further Analysis," *Journal of Marriage and the Family* 45 (February 1983): 127–139; Walter R. Schumm and Margaret A. Bugaighis. "Marital Quality over the Marital Career: Alternative Explanations." *Journal of Marriage and the Family* 48 (February 1986): 165–168.

[46] Sylvia Weishaus and Dorothy Field, "A Half Century of Marriage: Continuity or Change?" *Journal of Marriage and the Family* 50 (August 1988): 763–774.

[47] These six types were classified as stable/positive (5 couples); stable/neutral (3 couples); stable/negative (2 couples); curvilinear (7 couples); continuous decline (no couples); and continuous increase (no couples).

[48] David H. Olson, Hamilton I. McCubbin, and Associates, *Families: What Makes Them Work* (Beverly Hills: Sage, 1983).

[49] David M. Lawson, "Love Attitude and Marital Adjustment in the Family Life Cycle," *Sociological Spectrum* 8 (1988): 391–406. Canadian data as well show a curvilinear relationship. See Eugene Lupri and James Frideres, "The Quality of Marriage and the Passage of Time: Marital Satisfaction Over the Family Life Cycle," *Canadian Journal of Sociology* 6 (1981): 283–305.

Case Example:
Fifty Years of Marriage and Family Life

Jim and Effie have experienced fifty years of married life. They, more than any couple I have ever known, fit my image of a model marriage/family. Much to my pleasure, they consented to be interviewed.

Jim is a husband, father, grandfather, retired farmer, retired postal worker, and part-time Amish tour guide in Lancaster County, Pennsylvania. Effie is a wife, mother, grandmother, homemaker, and quilter. Together, they raised three children and today have five grandchildren. In addition, from birth until three months, they took in the daughter whose mother had cancer. For eight summers, they took in fresh-air inner-city children from New York City. Literally hundreds of friends of their children, family members, church and community people, and guests from throughout the world can testify to delicious home-cooked meals by Effie and visits or assistance of every kind from Jim.

Jim and Effie went to different high schools but were active in the same youth groups and church/community choral groups. She married at age 19, he at age 21. Effie had completed one year of college and had planned to major in home economics. She dropped out to get married, commenting that in the 1940s, it would have been unheard of for a farmer's wife to get a college degree. Jim, being the only son, was expected to take over the family farm. His home became their home for the next 50 years and is where they live today.

And their marriage? What did they find so special in each other? Jim spoke of the sparkle that Effie had in her eyes, her neatness, her devotion to their children, and her homemaker skills. He spoke with pride of her quilting accomplishments (at this writing she had completed 88 quilts by herself—many of which she has given away. She has won many honors, and is a recognized quilting authority in Eastern Pennsylvania). Effie spoke of Jim's tolerance and understanding, his compassion, his sense of humor, and how they enjoy doing things together, such as gardening, singing, community concerts, and spending time with their children and grandchildren.

Neither Jim nor Effie ever doubted or questioned their love for one another. They mentioned some very difficult times, both financially and in trying to fulfill professional obligations that put tremendous pressure on their marriage and on their children. They spoke of some of their differences, such as how he enjoyed travel and she didn't and how he liked baseball and she tolerated it. Effie felt she was always the one more focused on saving money while Jim was more willing to spend and, if need be, borrow. They mentioned times when they got upset with one another and raised their voices but never lost their tempers.

When I asked them if they ever struck one another or contemplated separation, I immediately recognized what a foolish question it was. The immediate response was "Oh my, no." Both took their marriage vows to love until death as a sacred oath and commitment. Both viewed the other as understanding, tolerant, compassionate, and forgiving. Both spoke of their Christian values and their attempt to exhibit daily these values toward each other and everyone else with whom they came in contact. The church family, as they call it, has always been a priority in their lives and this was and is expressed through their kind words, hospital visits, providing meals and assistance as needed, and literally loving their neighbors as themselves.

Figure 12-3
Family satisfaction by stage of family life cycle

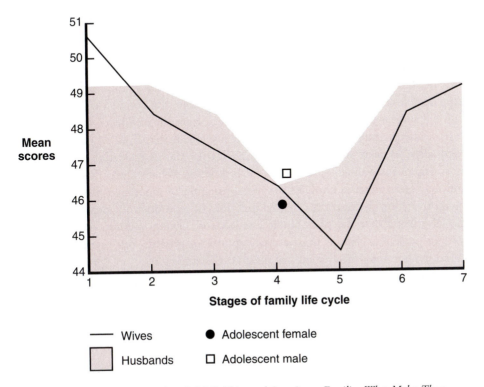

Source: David H. Olson, Hamilton I. McCubbin, and Associates, *Families: What Makes Them Work* (Beverly Hills: Sage, 1983), Figure 10.5, p. 181. Reprinted by permission of Sage Publications, Inc., and David H. Olson.

then increase over later stages. The data, when plotted, form a U-shaped curve (see Figure 12-3). Specifically, from young couples without children (stage 1) to families with preschool-age children (stage 2) to families with school-age children (stage 3) to families with adolescents in the home (stage 4), there was a decline in family satisfaction for both husbands and wives. The decline continued for wives through the launching period (stage 5), but satisfaction increased slightly for husbands at this time. A sharp increase in family satisfaction occurred at the "empty nest" stage (stage 6), and satisfaction increased more or remained high through retirement (stage 7).

Some explanations for the dramatic increase in satisfaction found following the launching stage and into the later years may result from the relaxation of sex roles, the time couples have to spend together, and the sense of belonging. After the children leave home, women feel freer to look for work and organizational roles outside the home, and men find themselves with decreased financial responsibility and more ability to be passive and dependent. Russell Ward suggests that the quality of marital relationships in the later years is quite high, that time spent together and perceived fairness in the relationship is enhanced while arguments are relatively infrequent.[50] For both men and women, the quality of the longer-term marriages is said to revolve around intimacy, interdependence, and a sense of companionship.

Results of studies showing what effect having children has on the marital happiness of parents are highly consistent. Overwhelming evidence has documented that, in American society, the presence of children in the family lowers marital happiness for the parents. Glenn and McLanahan, in conducting their own national surveys and in reviewing many others, found no evidence for distinctly positive effects and strong evidence for negative effects that children have on marital quality.[51] Given this highly consistent evidence, they suggested it is ironic that most Americans want to have and do have children. What's more, this phenomenon may serve as an example of the social function of ignorance; that is, people are motivated to perform the essential functions of reproduction and child care by the false belief that the psychological rewards of having children outweigh the costs or penalties. Perhaps there are perceptions of rewards, but research has not found them among the elements of marital satisfaction.

This negative effect of children on marital adjustment seems to appear very early in parenthood. Immediately following the birth, there seems to be a happy, loving phase, but within six months, a decline in marital adjustment occurs that is significantly lower than that during the pregnancy.[52] The authors concluded that lowered marital adjustment during pregnancy would not be solved or improved by the birth of a child.

The Olson-McCubbin study *Families* as well as other research has provided some precautionary notes to the life-cycle data presented. First, while consistent variation from stage to stage is found, the amount of change may be neither as great nor as significant as is often implied in textbooks such as this. For example, adding data from those marriages that had dissolved would reduce the increase in satisfaction reported by most studies. Second, while male/female, husband/wife differences are found in most studies, these differences tend to be overplayed. Often, the sex differences were even less pronounced than were differences across the life cycle. Third, reliance on cross-sectional data for the study of trends can be very misleading. That is, comparing groups who are at different stages in the life cycle (cross-sectional comparisons) rather than following the same group over time and through stages (longitudinal) does not adequately account for cohort effects, social desirability, or the tendency found in longitudinal studies to report as happy those marriages that have survived.

---

[50] Russell A. Ward, "Marital Happiness and Household Equity in Later Life," *Journal of Marriage and the Family* 55 (May 1993): 427–438.

[51] Norval D. Glenn and Sara McLanahan, "Children and Marital Happiness: A Further Specification of the Relationship," *Journal of Marriage and the Family* 44 (February 1982): 63–72.

[52] Pamela M. Wallace and Ian H. Gotlib, "Marital Adjustment during the Transition to Parenthood: Stability and Predictors of Change," *Journal of Marriage and the Family* 52 (February 1990): 21–29.

SUMMARY

1. Marital and marital-like systems fulfill many functions. For whatever reasons, married people are generally happier and experience fewer emotional and health problems than their unmarried counterparts. When the sexes are compared, men in particular benefit from marriage.

2. In the United States, marriage rates have fluctuated because of war, changing economic conditions, the sex ratio of the marriageable population, and the number of potential brides and grooms present in the general population. Marriage rates also vary by season, day of the week, and region of the country.

3. An important and widely researched area of marriage has addressed the power positions of husband and wife or intimate partners as individuals and in relation to each other. *Power* is the ability to influence others and affect their behavior. Power includes the crucial dimensions of authority (legitimized power) and influence.

4. Studies of decision-making outcomes have indicated that certain decisions are made primarily by the husband, others primarily by the wife, and others jointly. Who makes which decision has been widely explained by a theory of resources: The person with the most resources—information, education, income, and so forth—makes the decision.

5. Resource theory per se has been viewed as inadequate. Thus, a theory of comparative resources or a cultural resource theory has been developed and tested. It recognizes that resources are important but only understood in the context of the dominant values of a society or culture.

6. As with conjugal power, many attempts have been made to measure marital quality. Although there is no general consensus as to what *quality* means, definitions generally include characteristics such as high levels of husband/wife agreement and sharing of activities, tasks, and affection.

7. A number of writers have suggested that marital alternatives may be a better predictor of marital disruption than are measures of adjustment or satisfaction. As suggested by exchange theory, when alternatives are perceived as having greater costs than benefits, many unhappy marriages are likely to remain intact.

8. When marital quality, adjustment, and satisfaction are examined throughout the life cycle or life course, satisfaction appears to be highest at the beginning of marriage and lowest when the family has teenagers. Studies have indicated a curvilinear (U-shaped) relationship throughout the marital life course; the beginning and the end of marriage are the points of highest satisfaction.

9. Chapter 12 examined selected aspects of the marital system, including trends, characteristics, power, and quality. Chapter 13 will return to an

early stage of the marital life course and investigate the parental system, including the transition to parenthood, young and unwed parenthood, family size, and birth order.

KEY TERMS AND TOPICS

DISCUSSION QUESTIONS

1. Why do people marry or choose not to marry? What explains the "happiness gap"—that the well-being of people who are married exceeds that of people who are unmarried?

2. Check marriage rates of a given state or community. How do they compare with rates of other states or communities and with national data? What may explain the differences?

3. Differentiate among the terms *power, authority,* and *influence.* How can women and other groups in subordinate positions obtain power?

4. Make a list of ten topics common in family decision making. Take a brief survey among friends to determine who—father, mother, or both—makes what decisions. Are certain decisions consistently made by one or the other? Give examples.

5. What is your theory of conjugal power? In what (if any) instances does the person with the greatest resources not have the most power? In what (if any) instances does the person with few resources still have a high degree of power?

6. Define the *egalitarian ethic,* and discuss its relationship to satisfaction in marriage. What might this suggest about the quality of relationships in highly patriarchal countries?

7. Discuss the concept of *marital quality.* What is it? Can it be measured or determined? How? Why do some couples rated low on marital quality remain together?

8. From the couples you know, select two or three who seem to have the most ideal marriages or relationships. What factors tend to make those relationships ideal? Do the same features exist in each? Give examples.

9. What is the significance of conflict in a marriage or other relationship? Is conflict always destructive, or can it be beneficial, as well? Explain.

10. What explains the curvilinear relationship between marital adjustment and the family life cycle or family life course?

FURTHER READINGS

Blumstein, Philip, and Schwartz, Pepper. *American Couples.* New York: Pocket Books, 1983. An intensive look at money, work, sex, and the lives of couples in the United States: married, cohabitors, gays, and lesbians.

Fitzpatrick, Mary Anne. *Between Husbands and Wives: Communication in Marriage.* Newbury Park, CA: Sage, 1988. A book that establishes typologies of different types of marriage, styles of communication, and patterns of happiness.

Kayser, Karen. *When Love Dies: The Process of Marital Disaffection.* New York: Guilford Press, 1993. Both clinical data and a random sample of spouses who no longer love their partner were used to understand the factors associated with disaffection.

Olson, David H.; McCubbin, Hamilton I.; and Associates. *Families: What Makes Them Work.* Beverly Hills: Sage, 1983. A study of more than eleven hundred couples and nearly twenty-seven hundred individuals in intact marriages and families from thirty-one states considered at seven stages of the family life cycle on five dimensions: family types, family resources, family stress and changes, family coping, and family satisfaction.

Retzinger, Suzanne M. *Violent Emotions: Shame and Rage in Marital Quarrels.* Newbury Park, CA: Sage, 1991. With primary emphasis placed on the social bond, a theory (conflict) and method (case study) is proposed to deal with alienation, shame, and anger.

Scanzoni, John; Polonko, Karen; Teachman, Jay; and Thompson, Linda. *The Sexual Bond: Rethinking Families and Close Relationships.* Newbury Park, CA: Sage, 1989. A stimulating and innovative process approach to examining close, primary, sexually based relationships that extend beyond marriage and family to characterize the reality of relationships in the United States today.

Schwartz, Pepper. *Peer Marriage: How Love Between Equals Really Works.* New York: The Free Press, 1994. In-depth interviews with egalitarian marriages reveals how true equality is possible but only by a radical departure from traditional marriage patterns.

Ucko, Lenora Greenbaum. *Endangered Spouses: The Legacy of Marital Inequality.* Lanham, MD: University Press of America, 1995. Folk stories are used to focus graphically on the interaction of wives and husbands as they illustrate the central issues of family life.

Vannoy-Hiller, Dana, and Philliber, William W. *Equal Partners: Successful Women in Marriage.* Newbury Park, CA: Sage, 1989. An investigation of couples who manage successfully to carry out the demands of two occupations while maintaining a quality relationship in their marriage.

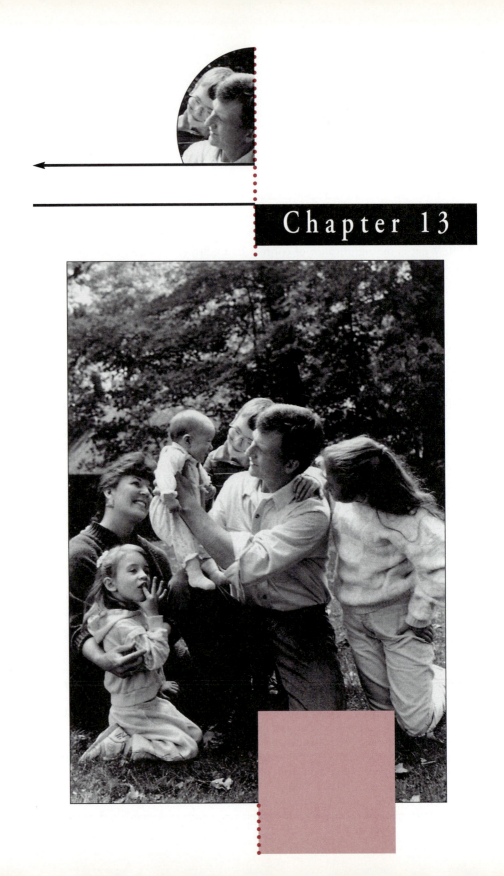

Chapter 13

The Parental System

The parental system centers on the interrelated statuses of parents and children. All societies have normative restrictions on appropriate and inappropriate behavior for both as well as sets of role expectations accorded to the parent and child statuses. Some parent/child norms are nearly universal; others are relatively unique to a particular society or subculture. For example, no society is known to place the primary responsibility for childrearing on men; no society is known in which young children customarily are dominant over the parents; and almost all societies place restrictions and taboos on pregnant women eating certain foods.

Wide variations occur from one society to another in family size, methods of childrearing, extended family sharing in child-related tasks, rates of out-of-wedlock births, and the like. On the other hand, certain similarities exist in the norms and consequences of particular structural patterns within the parental system. Parents from the lower classes rear children differently than do parents from the upper classes. Children born to single mothers begin life at a disadvantage when compared with children born in two-parent contexts. First-born children differ from other children in a wide variety of personal characteristics and activities.

The parental system and selected structural patterns are the focus of description and analysis in this chapter. The next chapter, while dealing with some organizational characteristics, will focus more on interactional and social/psychological dimensions of the parent/child relationship.

TRANSITION TO PARENTHOOD

According to family development theorists, becoming a parent is one of the most significant family life-course transitions. Many such theorists do not consider a person or couple a *family* until they have children. Others consider parenthood to be the final recognition of reaching adulthood or the culmination of the adult socialization process.

What is involved in the transition to parenthood? What must be learned and what readjustments of roles must be made in order to move smoothly from a childless state to parenthood? What is the effect of parenthood on the adult? What distinct roles and responsibilities do fathers and mothers have toward infants and young children?

There is little doubt that, when a dyad (two persons, such as a husband and wife) becomes a triad (parents and child) or when a single person becomes a parent, a major reorganization of statuses, roles, and relationships takes place. The effect that having children and caring for them during the preschool years has on the parent or parents seems fairly well established. As noted in Chapter 12, general marital satisfaction tends to decrease after the birth of children through the preschool and school years until the children are getting ready to leave home.

Ralph LaRossa found that when parents were asked how their lives changed after their babies were born (rather than asked whether they were bothered or gratified), the one consistent response was *time*.[1] Both parents reported that sleep time, television time, communication time, sex time, and even bathroom time were in short supply as the result of having a child. Many of the difficulties in making the transition to parenthood may be resolved by adjusting to the additional time it takes to do all the tasks associated with children.

Mothers' roles

Many theories of childrearing and socialization in the United States (note Chapter 14) stress that the wife and mother is the primary caretaker. Parenting tends to be viewed as primarily a maternal duty. In fact, it is often referred to as *mothering* because of the assumption that the birth, the nurturing, and the primary responsibility of rearing children belongs to women.

Mothers in the Detroit metropolitan area, when asked about ideal caregivers for preschool-age children, gave clear priority to the maternal role.[2] In their own lives, this maternal role held priority over the worker role. Although substantial numbers of mothers regarded nursery schools and day-care centers as ideal for older preschool children, the majority of mothers of preschool-age children believed that "mother is best" until a child enters first grade.

Fathers' roles

What about fathers? In the previously mentioned study, many working mothers cited fathers as the ideal daytime caregivers. In fact, the mothers often arranged their work schedules so that the fathers could take care of their children. But generally, when compared to the role of mothers, the role of fathers in parenting is deemphasized. The implied message is that fathers are not important in the parenting process, or if they are important, they tend to be too busy, indifferent, or incompetent to be good parents.

This supposed neglect and indifference of fathers does not seem to be empirically supported. Data from ninety nonindustrialized societies indicated that, in many of these societies, men assumed substantial responsibility for childrearing, with a majority of these men classified as having close father/child relationships.

Studies of fathers in the United States indicate that fathers are important figures in the lives of children and young adults.[3] Closeness of children to fathers has been found to make a significant contribution to offspring happiness, life satis-

---

[1] Ralph LaRossa, "The Transition to Parenthood and the Social Reality of Time," *Journal of Marriage and the Family* 45 (August 1983): 579–589.

[2] Karen Oppenheim Mason and Karen Kuhlthau, "Determinants of Child Care Ideals among Mothers of Preschool-Aged Children," *Journal of Marriage and the Family* 51 (August 1989): 593–603.

[3] Paul R. Amato, "Father-Child Relations, Mother-Child Relations, and Offspring Psychological Well-Being in Early Adulthood," *Journal of Marriage and the Family* 56 (November 1994): 1031–1042; and J. Snarey, *How Fathers Care for the Next Generation* (Cambridge, MA: Harvard University Press, 1993).

··

U.S. Diversity: Remember Mother's Day with Cards and Flowers

One to the mother who donated the egg

One to the mother who housed the egg for insemination

One to the mother who hosted the embryo and gave birth to the child

One to the mother who raised the child at day care on weekdays from eight to five

One to the mother who raised the child evenings and weekends

One to the mother (grandmother) who raised any of the above mothers

One to the mother (godmother) who provided support and assistance as needed

One to the mother with legal custody

faction, psychological well-being, intellectual development, and educational and occupational mobility. Likewise, the important role that fathers play in the lives of children is demonstrated in studies of father absence, showing lower levels of academic achievement, a heightened risk of delinquency and deviant behavior, and a greater likelihood of dropping out of school.

Parents' roles

One report, using an international perspective, suggests that parenting is becoming more difficult around the world. Social changes such as high unemployment and poverty; high rates of divorce and single parenting; parents and children sharing fewer activities and engaging in less face-to-face interaction; more emphasis on children's independence and autonomy accompanied by less tolerance of parental supervision; and the loss of traditional family structures and value conformity, all contribute to difficulties in parenting.[4]

Nevertheless, a wealth of data exists showing that parenting patterns and disciplinary practices of parents continue to make a difference in children's behavior. Take the use of tobacco by young adolescents, for example. Parents of seventh-graders were interviewed about parenting practices that were either harsh and inconsistent or nurturant and involved.[5]

Harsh/inconsistent parenting practices included interacting with the adolescent in an angry, irritable way; inconsistent discipline in response to rule violations; and punitive discipline, such as yelling, threatening, and physical punish-

---

[4] Anne-Marie Ambert, "An International Perspective on Parenting: Social Change and Social Constructs," *Journal of Marriage and the Family* 56 (August 1994): 529–543.

[5] Janet N. Melby, Rand D. Conger, Katherine J. Conger, and Frederick O. Lorenz, "Effects of Parental Behavior on Tobacco Use by Young Male Adolescents," *Journal of Marriage and the Family* 55 (May 1993): 439–454. Note also: Grace M. Barnes and Michael P. Farrell, "Parental Support and Control as Predictors of Adolescent Drinking, Delinquency, and Related Problem Behaviors," *Journal of Marriage and the Family* 54 (November 1992): 763–776.

ment. Nurturant/involved parenting practices included interacting with the adolescent in an affectionate and responsive manner; using praise, approval, and special privileges when a good job was done; and setting standards and encouraging adolescent input regarding the reasons for rules and expectations.

As their model of social development predicted, harsh/inconsistent parenting behaviors were found to be directly related to adolescent tobacco use, while nurturant/involved parenting behaviors were related to a lower level of adolescent tobacco use. In addition, nurturant/involved parenting reduced the risk of children associating with peers who model or encourage substance use.

Other research shows that parental roles and the quality of parenting are influenced by many factors, including marital satisfaction, the emotional well-being of parents, parental satisfaction with children's behavior, the parents' own exposure to harsh parenting during childhood, economic resources, social support from grandparents, and so forth.[6] Parenting roles and disciplinary practices, assumed under the topic of parent-child interaction and socialization, are addressed more comprehensively in the next chapter.

Value of parenthood

In most countries, married couples in general and women in particular face considerable social pressures to become parents. In the United States and other highly industrialized countries, these cultural and social pressures appear to have decreased over recent years, as evidenced by the delay in first pregnancies; the increased ability to control conceptions and births; the decline in birthrates; the movement of increasing numbers of women into the labor force; and the emphasis on two-child or childless families. Of course, many unplanned conceptions result from sexual acts that were recreative rather than procreative or from rape. These unplanned and often undesired pregnancies lead to personal and social concerns over terminating the pregnancy or having the child and raising it alone or placing it for adoption.

In spite of unplanned pregnancies, a decreasing birthrate, a decrease in the average family size, and an increase in childless marriages (all discussed later in this chapter), women continue to want and voluntarily have children. In fact, over 2 million women of reproductive age are estimated as having sought to adopt and about 200,000 are estimated to be currently seeking to adopt.[7] Given the number of both married and single persons who want to adopt; the legal battles of child custody following divorce; and even the numerous incidents of child snatching (the abduction of a child by one parent from another), it must be assumed that children are valued. Children satisfy certain needs for individuals and couples and fulfill basic functions for society as defined in the following paragraph.

---

[6] Ronald L. Simons, Jay Beaman, Rand D. Conger, and Wei Chao, "Childhood Experience, Conceptions of Parenting, and Attitudes of Spouse as Determinants of Parental Behavior," *Journal of Marriage and the Family* 55 (February 1993): 91–106.

[7] Christine A. Bachrach, Kathryn A. London, and Penelope L. Maza, "On the Path to Adoption: Adoption Seeking in the United States, 1988," *Journal of Marriage and the Family* 53 (August 1991): 705–718.

A random sample of six hundred couples in the early years of marriage revealed that they felt the primary advantages of children were (1) that they were necessary for "having a real family life" and (2) that they were "sources of love and affection."[8] Children were also seen as buffers against loneliness and impersonality. Only a few couples regarded children as very important for the fulfillment of sexual love, for establishing oneself as a mature person, or for spiritual fulfillment. By only a small margin, couples rated children as more valuable than having extra money to save, invest, or spend; having a neat and orderly household; and finding new interests and hobbies. Values such as freedom of movement, leisure time, and employment opportunities of the wife were rated by nearly half of the couples as equally or more valuable than having children. For both husbands and wives, "being alone with my spouse" clearly took precedence over childrearing.

While children are significant to men and women around the world, the number of children and their value is changing. One explanation of these changes is based on an **uncertainty reduction theory** of parenthood.[9] The assumption of this theory states that throughout the world, people seek to reduce uncertainty. Children are of value in providing security (increasing certainty) when parents face divorce, widowhood, and financial insecurity. In many developing countries it is desirable to produce as many sons as possible to pass on the family name and provide assistance in old age. In more developed countries, fewer children (but some children) are needed to fulfill these uncertainties. The number of wanted children could continue to diminish but not to zero.

SOCIAL CONSEQUENCES OF PARENTHOOD

Parenthood and its consequences cannot be evaluated apart from the society in which the family functions. In the United States, for example, selected politicians, religious leaders, and journalists suggest that the quality of parent/child relationships are at an all-time low. Divorce, single-parenthood, maternal employment, and a general erosion of parental support have been cited as *causes* for increases in children's delinquency, alcohol and drug use, sexual activity, and other negative outcomes.

This book, among others, has documented the many profound changes that have taken place for both parents and children. But David Demo, in assessing recent changes, has argued that the consequences of maternal employment, divorce, and single-parent family structure have been greatly exaggerated.[10] He has pointed to persuasive evidence that factors such as single-parenthood cannot be equated with lack of parental commitment or as *causes* of distress and maladjust-

---

[8] Arthur G. Neal, H. Theodore Croat, and Jerry W. Wicks, "Attitudes about Having Children: A Study of 600 Couples in the Early Years of Marriage," *Journal of Marriage and the Family* 51 (May 1989): 313–328.

[9] Debra Friedman, Michael Hechter, and Satoshi Kanazawa, "A Theory of the Value of Children," *Demography* 31 (August 1994): 375–401.

[10] David H. Demo, "Parent-Child Relations: Assessing Recent Changes," *Journal of Marriage and the Family* 54 (February 1992): 104–117.

ment in children. In spite of widespread parent/child conflict, delinquency, unwed parenthood, drug use, and so forth, most parents are deeply concerned about their children's welfare. In addition, adolescents generally report close and satisfying relationships with parents to whom they routinely turn for advice and guidance on important decisions. In sum, although work and family expectations have changed and expanded, there has been no corresponding delimitation of the parental role.

What types of social consequences of parenthood have been documented? For one, parenthood changes the employment patterns of women. The majority of ever-married women have jobs prior to pregnancy, but most leave these jobs as the pregnancy progresses. In studies by Linda Waite and others, only one in five women remained employed in the month that her child was born.[11] Many of these mothers returned to work, but by two years after the birth, their rate of employment was only about 60 percent of what it was prior to childbirth. Thus, one major social consequence of parenthood in the United States is the withdrawal of women from employment. In contrast, in the same study, fathers showed higher levels of work activity than would be expected at the time of the first birth.

Another consequence of parenthood, at least in the short run, relates to marital stability. In Chapter 12, data were presented that showed how marital satisfaction drops with the presence of children. Data will be presented later in this chapter that show how couples without children have higher levels of marital adjustment than couples with children. In contrast, studies from both New Zealand and the United States have shown the strong, positive effects of the first-born and preschool children on the marital stability of young adults. It was estimated that, by the time the first child reached age two, more than 20 percent of the parents would have been divorced or separated if the child had not been born compared with actual disruption rates of 5 to 8 percent.[12] The presence of preschool children in the family acts as a protective factor that reduces risk of family breakdown.

Lynn White and Alan Booth referred to this factor as the **braking hypothesis.** They suggested that although having children does not prevent divorce, doing so may cause couples to approach the divorce decision more slowly.[13] These researchers also found that new parents were significantly less likely to divorce over a three-year period than those who remained childless, again in contrast to the persistent negative correlation between the presence of children and marital happiness. The explanation for these seemingly inconsistent findings was not that persons in

---

[11] Linda J. Waite, Gus W. Haggstrom, and David E. Kanouse, "Changes in the Employment Activities of New Parents," *American Sociological Review* 50 (April 1985): 263–272; and Young-Hee Yoon and Linda J. Waite, "Converging Employment Patterns of Black, White, and Hispanic Women: Return to Work After First Birth," *Journal of Marriage and the Family* 56 (February 1994): 209–217.

[12] David M. Fergusson, L. John Horwood, and Michael Lloyd, "The Effect of Preschool Children on Family Stability," *Journal of Marriage and the Family* 52 (May 1990): 531–538; and Linda J. Waite, Gus Haggstrom, and David E. Kanouse, "The Consequences of Parenthood for the Marital Stability of Young Adults," *American Sociological Review* 50 (December 1985): 850–857.

[13] Lynn K. White and Alan Booth, "The Transition to Parenthood and Marital Quality," *Journal of Family Issues* 6 (December 1985): 435–449.

more stable marriages have children (a selectivity argument) and was only partially based on the argument that a new baby causes major negative changes in marital structure. Rather, White and Booth focused on a differential propensity to divorce. Childless couples, they suggested, value marital happiness more than parents. The result is a greater willingness of childless couples to divorce when unhappy.

Whatever the reason, fewer divorces seem to occur among couples with very young children. Studies reported in Chapter 17 will indicate how older children do not provide the same deterrent to divorce.

The social consequences of parenthood may be either positive or negative and, of course, affect far more than female employment, marital stability, and divorce. Discussion of young and unwed parenthood, for example, often centers around its negative consequences.

Concern about young parenthood

The concern about young parenthood is closely linked to the discussion in Chapter 9 entitled "Concern About Young Marriages," which greatly overlaps with the following section, "Concern About Unwed Parenthood." To be married young (generally in one's adolescence or teens), to be a young parent (to have a child as a teenager), and to be an unwed parent (to have a child apart from marriage, irrespective of age) are three interrelated social structural patterns that involve processes often perceived as not planned, desired, or preferred. All three result in social consequences defined as difficult and negative. Yet for some people, any of the three may result from consciously planned and preferred decisions, and under certain conditions, each may have positive outcomes.

Why do teenagers get pregnant and become young parents? One source reported that, of teenagers who do become pregnant, 26 percent obtain abortions, 22 percent marry before childbirth, and 52 percent have out-of-wedlock births.[14] The choice of what to do with an unplanned pregnancy is seldom easy for anyone but particularly difficult for a female who is young and unmarried. White teens are more likely than black teens to end a pregnancy through abortion.[15] Placing a child for adoption, traditionally an uncommon choice for young black women, seems to be less popular for white teens as well (see Figure 13-1). Marriage is also declining as an option for both black and white teenagers, but blacks are still more likely to become single mothers. Family members and other significant adults are very important to teens in the decision-making process. The input parents have is strongly affected by their level of education; for example, highly educated parents are more likely to recommend abortion for their teens.

---

[14] Elizabeth C. Cooksey, "Factors in the Resolution of Adolescent Premarital Pregnancies," *Demography* 27 (May 1990): 207–218.

[15] Naomi B. Farber, "The Process of Pregnancy Resolution Among Adolescent Mothers," *Adolescence* 26 (Fall 1991): 697–716; and Christine A. Bachrach, Kathy Shepherd Stolley, and Kathryn A. London, "Relinquishment of Premarital Births: Evidence from National Survey Data," *Family Planning Perspectives* 24 (January/February 1992): 27–32.

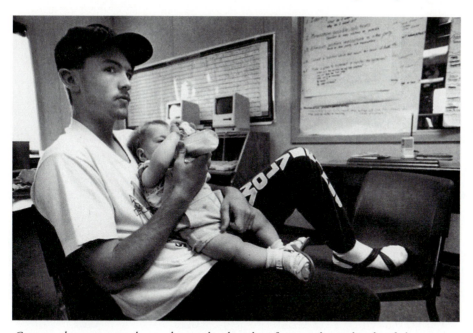

Concern about young and unwed parenthood tends to focus on the mother, but fathers are affected as well. Some father's assume responsibility for supporting and caring for both mother and child while others ignore any responsibility to either.

One study of teenage pregnancies found that 92 percent of those conceived premaritally (unwed) and half of those conceived in marriage (by teenagers) were unintended.[16] Startling evidence explained this high incidence of unplanned teenage pregnancies: Only one in three sexually active young women used contraceptives and only one in two of these relied on the most effective methods. The two most common reasons for not using contraceptives were the failure to anticipate intercourse and the belief that pregnancy risk was small.

An intergenerational pattern appears to exist for both teenage marriage and childbearing. One study found that the daughters of both white and black teen mothers faced significantly higher risks of teen childbearing than the daughters of older mothers.[17] This propensity for early childbearing is not inherited biologically, at least not through factors related to the timing of puberty. Rather, teenage childbearing, particularly for whites, is related to the socioeconomic and family context in which these teenagers grow up. For black teenage mothers, other variables, such as peer environments and less traditional attitudes regarding family formation, may account for the repetition of premarital motherhood across generations.

---

[16] James Trussell, "Teenage Pregnancy in the United States," *Family Planning Perspectives* 20 (November/December 1988): 262–272. For determinants of adolescent pregnancy, see: Patricia Voydanoff and Brenda W. Donnelly, *Adolescent Sexuality and Pregnancy* (Newbury Park, CA.: Sage, 1990), Chapter 3.

[17] Joan R. Kahn and Kay E. Anderson, "Intergenerational Patterns of Teenage Fertility," *Demography* 29 (February 1992): 39–57.

Figure 13-1
Children placed for adoption by unwed mothers: before 1973, 1973–1981, and 1982–1988

Source: Christine A. Bachrach, Kathy Shepherd Stoley, and Kathryn A. London, "Relinquishment of Premarital Births: Evidence from National Survey Data," *Family Planning Perspectives* 24 (January/February 1992): Table 1, p. 29.

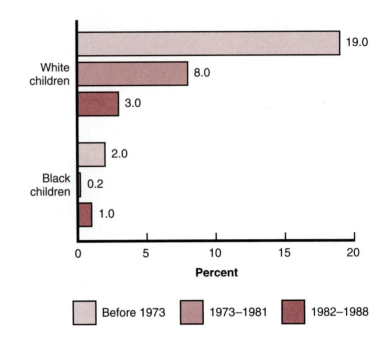

It is clear that U.S. teenagers are far more likely to become pregnant than are comparable women in other developed countries. Charles Westoff found that the teenage pregnancy rates in six other Western countries—Canada, England and Wales, Finland, the Netherlands, Norway, and Sweden—ranged from only 13 to 53 percent of the U.S. rate.[18] Teenagers in the United States appeared to be no more likely than their Canadian or European contemporaries to marry or engage in intercourse, but they seemed less likely to practice contraception.

Why are U.S. teenagers so different, even when compared to teens from countries very similar to the United States, such as Canada and Great Britain? Westoff, just cited, suggested that U.S. teenagers may not have the same access to contraceptives that other teens have, may face different costs in family-planning services than teens from countries with national health care systems, may comprise a large underclass of ethnic diversity and unequal income distribution that alienates them from middle-class values, may be greater risk takers (even teenage auto accident rates are two to eight times as high), and may have an ambivalence toward sexuality. That is, although sex saturates American television programs, movies, and advertisements, the media fail to communicate responsible attitudes about it; for the most part, birth control for teenagers is a taboo subject.

High rates of teenage pregnancy and young parenthood have tremendous costs: educational, social, and economic consequences for the individuals involved and for society at large. One way to determine the impact or cost of being a young parent is to compare adolescents who relinquish (place for adoption) their children to those who raise them. One source showed that, when background and other

[18] Charles F. Westoff, "Unintended Pregnancy in America and Abroad," *Family Planning Perspectives* 20 (November/December 1988): 254–261.

characteristics were controlled, young people who relinquished their babies were more likely to complete vocational training and to have higher educational aspirations.[19] They were more likely to delay marriage, be employed six and twelve months after the birth, and live in higher-income households. Young parents who chose to raise their children were more likely to become pregnant again sooner and to resolve subsequent pregnancies by abortion. It was noted that adolescents who relinquished their children did not suffer more negative consequences than those who raised their children.

Young parenthood magnifies the general issues surrounding parenthood that have been discussed thus far. When compared to women in the twenty- to thirty-five-year-old age group, teenage mothers are most likely to postpone prenatal care, have children of low birthweight, and experience a higher rate of infant mortality.[20] Even when controlling for family background by comparing teenage mothers with sisters who were not mothers, teen mothers were less likely to finish high school, attend college, or be married. They were more likely to be poor and on public assistance.[21] Ahn indicates that having a teenage birth leads to a 50 percent reduction in the likelihood of high school completion compared to not having a teenage birth. She suggests that this negative association between early childbearing and high school completion is attributable partly to childbirth itself, partly to individual differences, and partly to family background differences such as maternal education and marital stability (both of which have positive aspects on school completion).[22] Evidence has strongly suggested that many, but not all, of the adverse consequences of teenage childbearing may be of social and economic origin (particularly poverty), rather than attributable to the effects of young age per se.

Although young (teenage) parenthood is often associated in the public's mind with single-parent, female-headed families, the vast majority of mothers 15 to 19 years of age do not live alone with their children. Rather, over 90 percent live with their husbands or other relatives.[23] Whites are more likely than African Americans or Asian Americans to marry and establish their own nuclear households (although they are at high risk of divorcing and later forming single-parent households). African Americans and Mexican Americans are more likely than whites to "double up" in extended households. These extended households serve as a major resource both financially and emotionally. Support is often given in the form of

---

[19] Steven D. McLaughlin, Diane L. Minninen, and Linda D. Wingers, "Do Adolescents Who Relinquish Their Children Fare Better or Worse Than Those Who Raise Them" *Family Planning Perspectives* 20 (January/February 1988): 25–32.

[20] H. A. Hein, L.F. Burmeister, and K. A. Papke, "The Relationship of Unwed Status to Infant Mortality," *Obstetrics and Gynecology* 76 (1990): 763; and Richard A. Davis, "Adolescent Pregnancy and Infant Mortality: Isolating the Effects of Race," *Adolescence* 92 (Winter 1988): 899–908.

[21] Saul D. Hoffman, E. Michael Foster, and Frank F. Furstenberg, Jr., "Reevaluating the Costs of Teenage Childbearing," *Demography* 30 (February 1993): 1–13.

[22] Namkee Ahn, "Teenage Childbearing and High School Completion: Accounting for Individual Heterogeneity," *Family Planning Perspectives* 26 (January/February 1994): 17–21.

[23] Katherine Trent and Sharon L. Harlan, "Teenage Mothers in Nuclear and Extended Households," *Journal of Family Issues* 15 (June 1994): 309–337.

Global Diversity: Perinatal Outcomes and Marital Status: Results from Finland

Is marital status related in any way to perinatal death, low birthweight, and preterm infants? Apparently it is. The perinatal outcomes of more than 56,000 births were examined in Finland. After adjusting for the mother's age and education, the geographical area, and the degree of urbanization, it was found that perinatal death, low birthweight, and preterm infants were more common among single mothers than among married mothers.

Results for cohabiting mothers were more similar to those of married mothers than to those of single mothers. Cohabiting women gave birth to somewhat more infants with low birthweight than did married women, but there were hardly any differences in the numbers of preterm infants or deaths.

Why did infants of single mothers have poorer outcomes? The authors suggested that marital status may include causal factors such as social support and working conditions, which have a direct impact on the outcome of the birth. Other causal factors, such as parity, social class, and smoking, may also be associated with marital status. Likewise, partner selection may be an issue, with healthier people marrying and those with more severe health problems having greater difficulty in finding and keeping marriage partners.

Reviews of other studies presented two basic explanations for the advantage of marriage on health: social support and economic well-being. Single mothers may have less support, and marriage and cohabitation may be associated with higher levels of economic well-being.

Source: Kristina Manderbacka, Jouni Merilainen, Elina Hemminki, Ossi Rahkonen, and Juha Teperi, "Marital Status as a Predictor of Perinatal Outcome in Finland," *Journal of Marriage and the Family* 54 (August 1992): 508–515.

free room and board and partly or wholly subsidized child care. This assistance can significantly alter the life chances of the young mother, enhancing her prospects of educational achievement and economic advancement.

Concern about unwed parenthood

Closely related to and often simultaneous with the concern over young parenthood is the issue of unwed parenthood, including the attached label of illegitimacy placed upon the child. It is the marital and family system that universally fulfills the function of giving legal status and social approval to a birth. Legal changes granting equal rights to children born in or out of parental wedlock are in process, but the unwed parent and her child still do not, in large part, enjoy the approval and congratulations granted to the married parent and the child born into a conjugal family unit.

It appears that marriage bestows legitimacy on parenthood more than on sex. That is, most societies are more concerned with illegitimacy than with sexual intercourse outside marriage. This greater concern for unwed parenthood than for unwed intercourse may be the key to understanding the emphasis and attention given to the mother and the relative lack of attention given to the father. Despite his obvious involvement in the pregnancy, the male is studied far less frequently and is assigned a less deviant label than the female.

Data from a nationally representative survey showed that 7 percent of young males ages twenty to twenty-seven had fathered a child while teenagers.[24] One-third of those who were responsible for a nonmarital conception married within twelve months of conception, and half the young men lived with their children shortly after the birth. Young black men were more likely to have been responsible for a nonmarital first birth than were males of other racial and ethnic backgrounds, but only 15 percent of black teenagers lived with their first children, compared with 48 percent of Hispanics, 58 percent of disadvantaged whites, and 77 percent of nondisadvantaged whites. Teenage fathers, compared to other male teenagers, were more likely to be high school dropouts, to be from low-income families, and to face distinct disadvantages in the labor market. These factors clearly hamper young fathers' abilities to contribute financially to the support of their partners and children and also provide low incentives for either mothers or fathers to marry. In sum, all information on unwed parenthood has suggested that a double standard, while operative for sexual behavior, is much more obvious for the consequences of pregnancy that result from sexual behavior.

Should young parenthood be of concern? To answer this question, let us first examine how prevalent it is (the rates of birth outside marriage), followed by an examination of a "so what" or "who cares" question (the consequences of birth outside marriage).

Rates of birth outside marriage

At the very time that birthrates in general are steadily declining or leveling off (to be discussed later in this chapter), the birthrates outside marriage are showing a dramatic increase. The *number* of births to unmarried women exceeded 1.2 million in 1992 (see Table 13-1), which represented an 884 percent increase since 1950. Equally dramatic was the change in the *percentage* of all births to unmarried women. In 1950, the rate was 4.0 percent, or one in twenty-five births. By 1970, the same figure was 10.7 percent, or one in ten births. By 1980, it was approaching one in five births (18.4 percent). By 1990 it exceeded one in four (28 percent) and by 1992 it was approaching one birth in three (30.1 percent) to an unmarried mother.

---

[24] William Marsiglio, "Adolescent Fathers in the United States: Their Initial Living Arrangements, Marital Experience and Educational Outcomes," *Family Planning Perspectives* 19 (November/December 1987): 240–251; and William Marsiglio, "Young Nonresident Biological Fathers," *Marriage and Family Review* 20 (1995): 325–348.

Table 13-1

Births to unmarried women, by race and age of mother: 1950–1992

Race and age	Year					
	1950	1960	1970	1980	1990	1992
Total live births	142	224	399	666	1165	1225
(in thousands)						
White	54	83	175	320	647	722
Black and other	88	142	224	346	473	459
Percent of all births	4.0%	5.3%	10.7%	18.4%	28.0%	30.1%
Total rate	14.1	21.6	26.4	29.4	43.8	45.2
(number per 1,000)						
White	6.1	9.2	13.9	17.6	31.8	35.2
Black and other	71.2	98.3	95.5	82.9	93.9	86.5
Number by age of mother						
(in thousands)						
Under 15 years	3	5	10	9	11	11
15–19 years	56	87	190	263	350	354
20–24 years	43	68	127	237	404	436
25–29 years	21	32	41	100	230	233
30–34 years	11	19	19	41	118	128
35 years and over	8	14	12	16	53	63
Percent 19 years and under	41.8	40.9	50.2	40.9	30.9	28.9

Source: U.S. Bureau of the Census, *Statistical Abstract of the United States: 1995,* 115th ed. (Washington, DC: U.S. Government Printing Office, 1995), no. 94, p. 77, and earlier editions.

The rate of births to unmarried mothers varies dramatically by racial and ethnic category. For example, the rate of all births to unmarried white women was 22.6 percent. For African American women it was 68.1 percent; Native American women, 55.3 percent; Hispanic American women, 39.1 percent; Japanese American women, 9.8 percent; and Chinese American women, 6.1 percent.[25] How does one explain that two of three births to African American women but only about one in seventeen births to Chinese American women were born outside of a marital context?

A key factor in understanding the wide variation in births among racial and ethnic groups lies in differential social norms pertaining to sex, pregnancy and

---

[25] U.S. Bureau of the Census, *Statistical Abstract of the United States: 1995,* 115th ed. (Washington, DC: U.S. Government Printing Office, 1995), no. 88, p. 73.

cohabitation. For example, among many Asian American groups, sexual norms are very restrictive, leading to few unwed parents. Religious norms play a major role for groups such as the Amish, Mormon, and selected Hispanic subcultures. Cohabitation norms, such as exist in Scandinavian countries, show that many children are born outside of a marriage but often in a two-parent household. Other norms relating to the acceptability and availability of contraception or abortion enter the picture. Many of these factors are closely linked to the socioeconomic and class status of the child, family, and community.

In fact, one study claimed that 81 percent of the variance in predicting state teenage birthrates could be explained by state poverty rates, low school completion rates, low state-per-capita expenditures for public welfare, and high unemployment rates.[26] These class-related issues illustrate how economic factors and educational and occupational opportunity structures influence the prevalence of both teenage and unwed parenthood.

In addition, it might be predicted that unwed parenthood among the lower classes would be of less concern to society than would unwed parenthood among the higher classes. Among the lower classes, there is less property to protect and inherit and lineage and family honor are less a focus of attention; therefore, lower-class families have less to lose if a birth out of wedlock occurs. The expected result of this would be more unwed births among the lower classes.

Among the higher classes, where property control and family name are at stake to a greater degree, unwed parenthood would likely bring different results, including pressure on the couple to marry, to place the child for adoption, or to leave home to bear the child. Or the birth could be avoided altogether via abortion, which is more accessible to people who are educated and financially able.

The incidence of live births by age of mother has shown a profound change. Namely, unwed mothers are getting older. In 1970, 50.2 percent of births were to teenage mothers, compared to 40.9 percent in 1980, 30.9 percent in 1990 and 28.9 in 1992 (see Table 13-1). While the *number* of teenage unwed mothers ages fifteen to nineteen increased by 164,000, or 86 percent, between 1970 and 1992, the increase in the number of unwed mothers ages twenty to twenty-four was 309,000, or 243 percent. Even greater increases occurred among the twenty-five to twenty-nine and thirty to thirty-four age categories (up 468 and 574 percent, respectively).

Unwed parenthood is no longer most prevalent among teenagers. In 1992 most unwed births (436,000) were to mothers in the twenty to twenty-four age category with another 361,000 between the ages of 25 and 34. Why do these older single women become mothers? In a comparison of single women who became mothers with married women who became mothers (all of whom were at least 25 years old), it was revealed that both groups accepted motherhood as a fundamental part of their own womanhood. Single mothers, however, had a greater ambivalence

---

[26] Shirley Zimmerman, "State Level Pubic Policy Choices as Predictors of State Teen Birthrates," *Family Relations* 37 (July 1988): 315–321.

toward marriage and how they viewed relationships with men. The composite picture that emerged was a combination of an idealized image of what marriage should be with an unwillingness to accept compromise as an essential relationship strategy.[27] This trend among older single women toward separating marriage and childbearing may suggest fewer problems than among teenagers who lack emotional maturity, drop out of school, and have no childrearing skills.

Consequences of birth outside marriage

Now the questions "so what?" or "who cares?" Does it really make a difference that more than 1.2 million births each year occur outside of wedlock? Do these children have more social, economic, and health problems than children born in wedlock? Is the presence of both male and female parents essential to the growth and development of a child? Does the unmarried mother face increased emotional and economic difficulties that seriously affect both her and her child?

Some of these specific questions are discussed in the section on the single parent in Chapter 8 (social class), the section in Chapter 6 on the African American family, and Chapter 14 on parent-child socialization. However, several research studies are worthy of consideration here.

Being born outside of wedlock does have an impact on the child, the parent, and society, as evidenced in studies completed in California and elsewhere.[28] Information from a sample of two-year-old children born within marriage and outside marriage indicated that, despite significant social changes, children born to unwed mothers were more likely to be unsuccessful than those born to married mothers. Children born to unwed mothers had a higher infant mortality rate, and the unadopted children of such mothers did not fare well on a number of measures, including school performance. Unmarried mothers were less likely to marry within three years after the birth than the general population of unmarried women and were more likely to separate from their husbands if they did marry later.

Adopted children born to unwed mothers do as well or better than children born to wed mothers. Despite a decrease in the degree of stigma attached to birth out of wedlock and the proliferation of services and programs for these children and their mothers, children born to unwed mothers do not begin life on equal footing with legitimate children, and their disadvantages persist beyond infancy.[29]

Other data clearly supported negative and long-lasting repercussions of teenage and/or unwed childbearing. Young parents are less educated than their contemporaries; they are also often limited to less prestigious jobs and, in the case

---

[27] Judith M. Siegel, "Looking for Mr. Right? Older Single Women Who Become Mothers," *Journal of Family Issues* 16 (March 1995): 194–211.

[28] Beth Berkov and June Sklar, "Does Illegitimacy Make a Difference? A Study of the Life Chances of Illegitimate Children in California," *Population and Development Review* 2 (June 1976): 201–217; and Ronald R. Rindfuss and Jo Ann Jones, "One Parent or Two? The Intertwining of American Marriage and Fertility Patterns," *Sociological Forum* 6 (1991): 311–326.

[29] Ibid. "Does Illegitimacy Make a Difference?" p. 215. Also see Wendy Baldwin and Virginia S. Cain, "The Children of Teenage Parents," *Family Planning Perspectives* 12 (January/February 1980): 34–43.

of women, to more dead-end jobs. From the moment they become aware of pregnancy, young parents and unwed mothers, in particular, have difficult decisions and adjustments to make. Society, in general, may offer little toleration to the young unwed mother who wishes to keep her child as her own, but among lower-class strata, where the commitment to the norm of legal marriage is less stringent, greater toleration is likely.

In 1935, the U.S. Congress established a national policy of providing financial aid to a mother and her children when they did not have financial support. The Aid to Families with Dependent Children (AFDC) program enabled a mother to keep her children with her. Programs such as these receive constant protests from taxpayers who argue (perhaps falsely) that mothers have more children to increase their aid. Gregory Acs, an Urban Institute researcher, noted that AFDC generosity has, at best, a very modest impact on a woman's childbearing decision and virtually no effect on subsequent births.[30]

FAMILY SIZE AND RELATED FACTORS

Birthrates and birth expectations

Most married couples want, have, or expect to have children. In 1993, there were 4.04 million births in the United States, a rate of 15.7 births per thousand population.[31] That same year, 18 percent of all ever-married women ages fifteen to forty-four, either by choice or circumstance, were childless.[32]

Birthrates are one of the best-documented series of descriptive social data available today. Census data reveal that in the United States, rates of birth vary widely by state (see Table 13-2). In 1992, Utah and Alaska had the highest rate (about 20) while West Virginia had the lowest rate (about 12).

These rates vary widely over time as well. For example, in 1910, the birthrate was 30.1 per one thousand population. This rate decreased to 18.7 during the Depression years of the mid-1930s, increased to 25.0 in 1955, and steadily decreased until the mid-1970s, when it reached a low of 14.6. The birthrate varied between 15.5 and 15.9 through most of the 1980s and increased to 16.7 by the start of the 1990s. This late-1980s "baby boomlet" cannot be attributed solely to births among older persons or couples who delayed childbearing because birthrates increased in all age groups.[33]

---

[30] Gregory Acs, "Does AFDC Encourage Childbearing?" *The Urban Institute: Policy and Research Report* (Fall 1993): 19–20.

[31] U.S. Bureau of the Census, *Statistical Abstract of the United States: 1995,* 115th ed. (Washington, DC: U.S. Government Printing Office, 1995), no. 87, p. 73.

[32] Ibid., Table 102, p. 80. (Comparable figures for 1940 were 26.5; 1950, 22.8; 1960, 15.0; 1970, 16.4; and 1980, 18.8 percent.)

[33] C. Haub, "The Late 1980s Baby Boomlet: Delayed Childbearing or Not?" *Population Today* 20 (February 1992): 3.

Table 13-2
States ranked by rates of live births, 1992
Birthrates in the United States vary widely by region and state. In 1992, birthrates were below the national average in the Northeast and Midwest and above the national average in the South and West. Utah (at 20.5 births per 1,000 population) led the nation, Alaska (at 20.0) and California (at 19.5) followed in second and third places, respectively. West Virginia had the lowest birthrate in the nation (at 12.3 per 1,000 people). The bottom one-fourth of the ranking was comprised primarily of states in the Northeast and Middle Atlantic regions of the country.

Ranking/state	Live births (per 1,000 pop.)	Ranking/state	Live births (per 1,000 pop.)
1. Utah	20.5	26. Alabama	15.0
2. Alaska	20.0	27. Indiana	14.9
3. California	19.5	28. Oklahoma	14.8
4. Texas	18.1	29. Minnesota	14.7
5. Arizona	18.0	30. Missouri	14.7
6. New Mexico	17.7	31. Ohio	14.7
7. Hawaii	17.2	32. Massachusetts	14.6
8. Nevada	16.7	33. Nebraska	14.6
9. Illinois	16.5	34. Tennessee	14.6
10. Louisiana	16.5	35. Arkansas	14.5
11. Georgia	16.4	36. Connecticut	14.5
12. Idaho	16.3	37. Rhode Island	14.5
13. Mississippi	16.3	38. Wyoming	14.5
14. New York	15.9	39. Kentucky	14.3
15. Maryland	15.8	40. New Hampshire	14.3
16. Colorado	15.7	41. Florida	14.2
17. South Carolina	15.6	42. Wisconsin	14.2
18. South Dakota	15.6	43. Oregon	14.1
19. Delaware	15.4	44. Montana	14.0
20. Washington	15.4	45. North Dakota	13.9
21. Michigan	15.3	46. Pennsylvania	13.7
22. New Jersey	15.3	47. Iowa	13.7
23. North Carolina	15.2	48. Vermont	13.5
24. Virginia	15.2	49. Maine	13.0
25. Kansas	15.1	50. West Virginia	12.3

Source: National Center for Health Statistics, *Monthly Vital Statistics Report,* vol. 43, no. 5 "Advance Report of Final Natality Statistics, 1992" (Hyattsville, MD: Public Health Service, 25 October 1994), Table 8, p. 43.

Figure 13-2
Rates of live births and fertility: 1930–1993

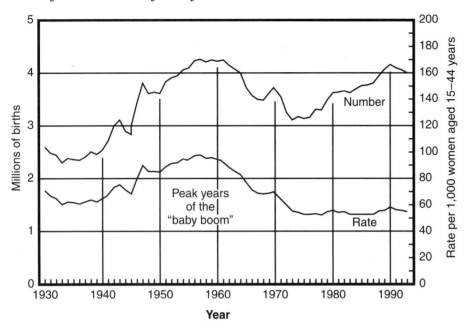

Source: National Center for Health Statistics, *Monthly Vital Statistics Report,* Vol. 44, no. 3, "Advance Report of Final Natality Statistics, 1993" Hyattsville, MD: Public Health Service, 21 September 1995), Figure 1, p. 3.

What do demographers and journalists mean when they talk about the **"baby boom"**? Simply stated, the baby boom was a postWorld War II event that upset what had been a century-long decline in the U.S. fertility rate. The baby boom was an unanticipated, pronounced, and consequential rise in the United States birthrate during the late 1940s and 1950s (see Figure 13-2). Theories as to its cause include increases in normative pressure on women to have children, the disruption and dislocation brought about by the war, postwar economic prosperity, and the long-term psychological effects of growing up during the Depression.

This postwar spurt in annual births did not represent a return to the large families of the nineteenth century. Rather, the boom was a movement away from singlehood, childless marriage, and one-child families, and a compilation of births. Only a minor part of the baby boom can be attributed to an increase in the number of families having three or more births.[34]

In 1992, the average number of lifetime births *expected* by currently married women ages eighteen to thirty-four was 2.25, a slight increase from the 2.19 average of twelve years earlier in 1980 but well below the 3.05 average reported in

---

[34] Leon F. Bouvier, "America's Baby Boom Generation: The Fateful Bulge," *Population Bulletin* 35 (1980): 4. Published by The Population Reference Bureau, Inc., Washington, DC.

1967. About 5 percent of currently married women (age 18-34) said they expected to be childless, 12 percent expected to have one child, 50 percent expected to have two children, and 33 percent expected to have three or more. Of never-married women (age 18-34), about 16 percent expected to be childless, 14 percent expected to have one child, 47 percent expected to have two children, and 23 percent expected to have three or more.

A comparison of the average number of lifetime births expected by currently married women versus never-married women indicated that never-married women expected a lower average number of births than married women (1.88 versus 2.25 in the eighteen- to thirty-four age group).[35] The difference in lifetime birth expectations between married and single women decreases with age, indicating decreases both in the remaining number of reproductive years and the marriage prospects for single women. If women currently in their late teens and twenties live up to their expectations for the future, the number of persons who come from large families will be small.

There seems to be some disagreement as to whether the fertility rate and average family size will exhibit a downward trend, an upward trend, or level off at no more than two children. Due to factors such as improved methods of birth control, availability of abortion, various sterilization procedures, and an older age at marriage, a decrease in the number of unplanned and unwanted births might be likely. It is clear that over the past few decades there has been a trend to delay first births. Around the world, women who delay childbearing have fewer children and are significantly better off economically than average-age childbearers. In Japan, for example, which has one of the lowest fertility rates in the world, the decline over the past two decades has been attributed not to contraceptive use, but to the postponement of marriage.[36] The mean age at which Japanese women marry—about 27 years—is among the highest in the world and the proportion who likely will never marry has tripled in the past 20 years. Both delayed marriage and nonmarriage reduce fertility rates.

Related to the delay in first births is the spacing of births. Patterns of **child spacing** have not received the research attention given to number of births and family size, but this is an important issue for consideration. Particular child-spacing factors are likely to influence the labor force participation and education of women as well as the health of the child. For example, low birthweight, a condition strongly associated with morbidity (sickness and disease) and mortality (death) among infants, is highest among children born very shortly after the end of their mothers' last pregnancies. In countries such as Bangladesh and the Philippines, for example, it was demonstrated that children who were born with-

---

[35] U.S. Bureau of the Census, *Current Population Reports,* Series P20-470, Amara Bachu, "Fertility of American Women: June 1992" (Washington, DC: U.S. Government Printing Office, 1993), Table 5, p. 16; Table 9, p. 31; and Table 10, p. 34.

[36] Naohiro Ogawa and Robert D. Retherford, "The Resumption of Fertility Decline in Japan: 1973–1992," *Population and Development Review* 19 (December 1993): 703–741.

in fifteen months of a preceding child were 60 to 80 percent more likely than other children to die in the first two years of life.[37]

In spite of trends toward delayed childbirth, greater control of spacing, and fewer births, many variables are related to marital fertility: socioeconomic status, multiple marriages, religion, race/ethnicity, education, urbanization, female income, child-care arrangements, gender roles, age at marriage, age at first birth, interval since last birth, age of women, and others.[38] Even the size of the family of origin (number of brothers and sisters) appears to influence marital fertility. And, of course, many couples make a conscious choice to have no children or, for some reason, fail to have them. The next section will briefly examine childless marriages.

Childless marriages

For many years, the myth existed that, because of a so-called maternal instinct, all women wanted children. This instinct even went one step further and assumed that, once children were born, the mother would instinctively love and care for them.

These assumptions were quickly disproved when statistics, research reports, newspaper accounts, and gossip networks revealed the widespread termination of pregnancies through legal and illegal abortions, the commonality of mothers abusing and even killing their children, the discovery that some women didn't want children, and those who never had children—in or out of marriage—did not suffer physical or emotional damage. These and other factors tended to dispel the notion of the biological linkage between being female and having a natural desire for and love of children.

There is little doubt that children place enormous demands on parents in terms of emotional and financial costs. Yet most married couples, either voluntarily or involuntarily, want and have children. As shown in Figure 13-3, in the United States, Britain, and Australia, few people believe that no children or even one child is an ideal family size. It is possible that many of these individuals or couples want or have children because they were never socialized to believe that *not* having children is a viable alternative.

For whatever reasons, actual childless rates are low. Among those people who can have children, temporary childlessness or delayed childbearing is more likely than permanent childlessness. This is a result of factors such as divergent value orientations that include both a desire for work or career and a desire for parenthood.

U.S. census data showed that, in 1992, 10.8 percent of ever-married women ages forty to forty-four were childless. This figure increased to 17.0 percent among

---

[37] Jane E. Miller, James Trussell, Anne R. Pebley, and Barbara Vaughan, "Birth Spacing and Child Mortality in Bangladesh and the Philippines," *Demography* 29 (May 1992): 305–318.

[38] Howard Wineberg, "Variations in Fertility by Marital Status and Marriage Order," *Family Planning Perspectives* 22 (November/December 1990): 256–260; and William D. Mosher, Linda B. Williams, and David P. Johnson, "Religion and Fertility in the United States: New Patterns," *Demography* 29 (May 1992): 199–214.

Figure 13-3

Ideal family size, as reported in Australia, Britain, and the United States

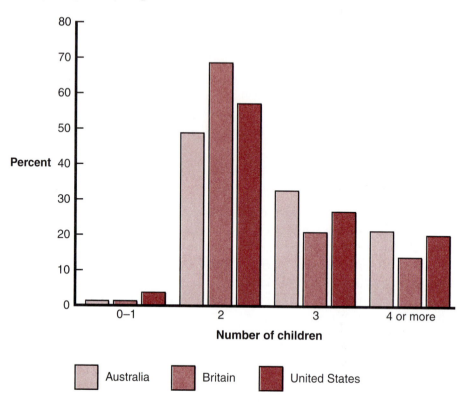

Number of children

Australia   Britain   United States

Source: Audrey Vandenheuvel, "In a Class of Our Own?" *Family Matters* 29 (August 1991): 20.

thirty- to thirty-four-year-old married women and to 38.2 percent among those twenty to twenty-four years of age.[39] These younger age groups had not, however, completed their childbearing years, and most of these women expected to have children at some time in their lives. Only 5.0 percent of currently married women ages eighteen to thirty-four did not expect to have any children in their lifetimes (compared to 15.8 percent of never married women).

The rate of childlessness has increased over the past few decades. The most important demographic predictors of childlessness were found to be:

- *Fecundity* — Some people are unable to have children.
- *Marital status* — Never-married people are more likely to be childless than people who are or have been married.
- *Age* — As people grow older, they are less likely to have children.

---

[39] U.S. Bureau of the Census, *Current Population Reports,* Series P20-482. Amara Bachu, "Fertility of American Women, June 1994" (Washington, DC: U.S. Government Printing Office, 1995), Table 1, p. 1.

- *Labor force participation* — People who are working or temporarily unemployed are less likely to have children.
- *Education* — The higher the level of education attained, the greater the likelihood of childlessness.
- *Race/ethnicity* — Asian Americans and American Indians are less likely to be childless than members of other racial/ethnic groups.[40]

Voluntarily childless women, married or single, rate the costs of having a child higher and the satisfactions lower than other groups of women (such as parents or those who desire to become parents).[41] Victor Callan found that educated professional women, who had lived and enjoyed an adult-centered life-style, gave high ratings to the restrictions and disruptions of children and to general life-style costs and low ratings to the emotional satisfaction and personal fulfillment a child might give them. These women also felt that their current life-style choices—especially their careers—did meet such needs.

Parenthood not only seems to interfere with personal happiness and freedoms, it seems also to interfere with marriage and family life. As noted previously in several chapters, children impose a strain on marriage. Does this suggest that couples without children have higher levels of health and marital adjustment and satisfaction than do couples with children?

Apparently it does. When voluntarily childless wives, undecided wives, and postponing wives were compared with mothers, the results from one study were that all three groups of childless wives had higher mean levels of marital satisfaction than did mothers.[42] Most available evidence shows that the consequences of voluntary childlessness to persons or marriages is more positive than negative.

Is this satisfaction true among **involuntarily childless women** too? In other words, what about women or couples who want children but can't have them? Infertility has been estimated to affect approximately 15 percent, or one in seven couples, in the United States. Studies of infertile couples with a desire for children have revealed high levels of stress.[43] Infertility is a major negative life event that has deleterious effects on both women's and men's subjective well-being. Infertility would seem to be especially relevant for sexual and marriage issues, but its strongest impact may be on global well-being. That is, frustrations over infertility

---

[40] Cardell K. Jacobsen, Tim B. Heaton, and Karen M. Taylor, "Childlessness Among American Women," *Social Biology* 35 (1988): 186–197.

[41] Victor J. Callan, "The Impact of the First Birth: Married and Single Women Preferring Childlessness, One Child, or Two Children," *Journal of Marriage and the Family* 48 (May 1986): 261–269.

[42] Karen A. Polenko, John Scanzoni, and Jay D. Teachman, "Childlessness and Marital Satisfaction," *Journal of Family Issues* 3 (December 1982): 545–573.

[43] Margaret V. Pepe and T. Jean Byrne, "Women's Perceptions of Immediate and Long-Term Effects of Failed Infertility Treatment on Marital and Sexual Satisfaction," *Family Relations* 40 (July 1991): 303–309; and Antonia Abbey, Frank M. Andrews, and L. Jill Halman, "Infertility and Subjective Well-Being: The Mediating Roles of Self-Esteem, Internal Control, and Interpersonal Conflict," *Journal of Marriage and the Family* 54 (May 1992): 408–417.

spill over into other domains, including work, finances, and social life, producing strained relationships with co-workers, friends, and family.

It would appear that, for couples of childbearing age, the choice to have or not to have children and the ability to carry out that choice may be one of the most significant factors in the satisfaction or dissatisfaction that results from being childless. In other words, there's a big difference between being able to have children but choosing not to and wanting to have children but not being able to. People who remain childless by choice are more likely to be satisfied with that result than are people who remain childless by fate.

What about older persons who, either by choice or necessity, have no children? As will be evident in later chapters, children serve as an important source of gratification and support to older persons. Surveys by the National Opinion Research Center of the University of Chicago asked males and females ages sixty-five and over how much satisfaction they got from family life.[44] The findings indicated that childlessness had an overall significant negative effect on family satisfaction; the effect was most pronounced among the oldest age cohort and more pronounced for females than for males. Whether the current cohorts of voluntary childless women under ages forty and thirty will be negatively affected by the absence of children when they reach ages sixty-five and seventy-five remains to be seen.

The reproductive technology available today can decrease the number of people who are involuntarily childless. Until recently, women and couples who were involuntarily childless and wished to comply with societal norms would resort to adoption. But the decline in the availability of infants for adoption has led many infertile women to seek alternative solutions, such as artificial insemination with the sperm of the husband (AIH); artificial insemination with the sperm of an anonymous donor (AID); in vitro fertilization, where an artificial environment outside the living organism is used; and surrogate motherhood, in which another woman is used to conceive, carry, and give birth to a child. These alternative methods of reproduction have led to heated debates over their social, legal, and moral implications.

Effects of family size on members

There is little doubt that the number of people in a group influences the interaction and behavior of the members of that group. For instance, when there are two roommates and they happen to agree, a decision is unanimous. When there are three roommates, only two of whom agree, the third person has the unhappy choice of accepting their decision, trying to change the decision of at least one roommate, or going his or her own way.

---

[44] B. Krishna Singh and J. Sherwood Williams, "Childlessness and Family Satisfaction," *Research on Aging* 3 (June 1981): 218–227. See also Arthur L. Greil, Thomas A. Leitke, and Karen L. Porter, "Infertility: His and Hers," *Gender and Society* 2 (June 1988): 172–199; and Victor J. Callan, "The Personal and Marital Adjustment of Mothers and of Voluntary and Involuntary Childless Wives," *Journal of Marriage and the Family* 49 (November 1987): 847–856.

Clearly, the number of interactions, the probability of disagreement, and the attention given to any one person are influenced by the number of members in the group. The same factors hold true within a family system. One-child families are conducive to certain patterns of life that differ from two-, three-, and four-child families.

One-child families

One-child families have, in general, not been viewed in positive terms for either parents or children. The only child has been described as spoiled, selfish, overly dependent, maladjusted, and lonely. Parents of an only child have been described as selfish, self-centered, immature, cold, and abnormal. National surveys over the past thirty years have consistently showed a majority of respondents indicating that being an only child is a disadvantage. Very few people say they want to have just one child or that the ideal number of children for a family is one (review Figure 13-3). The popular stereotype of the unhappy, maladjusted only child and the view that a one-child family is neither a preferred nor desirable family size calls for an empirical look at this small family.

In looking at only children as adults, data from seven U.S. national surveys were used to establish the effects of having a number of siblings on eight dimensions of well-being.[45] Without exception, all the effects of having siblings were negative, or, stated differently, all the effects of being an only child were positive. Only children were more likely to say they were very happy, find life exciting, see their health as excellent, and get satisfaction from where they live, from their non-working activities, from their family life, from their friendships, and from their physical condition. The evidence most clearly contradicted the popular stereotype of the unhappy, maladjusted only child.

Research on adult Canadian women who were only children indicated that, when compared with women who grew up with siblings, only children were less likely to have large families, more likely to marry and have their first children at older ages, more likely to attain high levels of education, and, among the younger cohort, more likely to cohabit at younger ages.[46] This study demonstrated that being an only child has an important impact on life-course events and transitions.

Similar results came from Judith Blake, who concluded that research findings on the only child do not support the negative stereotypes that still persist about singletons.[47] She claimed that only children are intellectually superior, have no obvious personality defects, tend to count themselves happy, and are satisfied with important aspects of life, notably jobs and health. Single children have increased problems with health and achievement only when they come from a broken fam-

---

[45] Norval D. Glenn and Sue Keir Hoppe, "Only Children as Adults," *Journal of Family Issues* 5 (September 1984): 363–382.

[46] Ellen M. Gee, "Only Children as Adult Women: Life Course Events and Timing," *Social Indicators Research* 26 (1992): 183–197.

[47] Judith Blake, "Number of Siblings and Personality," *Family Planning Perspectives* 23 (November/December 1991): 272–274; and *Family Size and Achievement* (Berkeley: University of California Press, 1989).

ily with its attendant loss of income or when mothers were young enough at birth to continue childbearing but, due to difficulties of their own, failed to do so. When parental background is controlled, only children do better than children from any other family size.

Additional siblings and achievement levels

Is bigger better? Does increasing the number of siblings improve school performance and achievement? Precise answers to these questions come from Judith Blake who analyzed numerous national data sets, all of which showed that an increased number of siblings had negative effects on both child and adult achievement outcomes. For example, the larger the family, the fewer the years of completed schooling. Even after controlling for major parental background differences such as race and age, there was approximately a two-year difference in educational attainment of children between small and large families.

Other national data, noting the negative relationship between size of the family of origin and sibship size, indicate that for each additional sibling, the odds of graduating from high school are reduced by 13 percent in traditional male-breadwinner families and by 19 percent in dual-career families. These differences suggest that time constraints play a larger role in the educational socialization of children if the mother is working outside the home.[48]

Why does increased family size negatively affect educational performance and graduation rates? Both Blake and Downey propose a **resource dilution hypothesis** that, in effect, suggests a dilution of familial resources available to children in large families and a concentration of such resources in small ones.[49] Downey, for example, in analyzing data from a national sample of nearly 25,000 eighth-graders, found that parental *interpersonal resources* (frequency of talk, educational expectations, knowing their children's friends, and knowing their parents) were all negatively affected by additional children. Parental *economic resources* (having a computer, having other educational objects—a place to study, newspapers and magazines, an encyclopedia and atlas, more than fifty books, calculators—money saved for college, cultural classes in art, music, dance, and cultural activities of art, science, and history museums) were all negatively related to additional children.

While the availability of parental resources was found to decrease as sibship size increased, so did school performance (grades as well as standardized math and reading test scores) decrease as sibship size increased. And surprisingly, even when children in large families had the same level of parental resources available as their counterparts in smaller families, they accrued less benefit from them. Having more children comes at a price, even if you can afford them. And according to

---

[48] Matthijs Kalmijn, "Mother's Occupational Status and Children's Schooling," *American Sociological Review* 59 (April 1994): 257–275.

[49] Blake, *Family Size and Achievement*, pp. 10–12; and Douglas B. Downey, "When Bigger Is Not Better: Family Size, Parental Resources, and Children's Educational Performance," *American Sociological Review* 60 (October 1995): 746–761.

Blake, the idea that the older children in large families function as parents to the younger ones assumes too much about sibling goodwill and maturity. Youngsters are not adults and are seldom the emotional and intellectual equivalent of parents.

Large families

Perception of a family as large or small is relative. Today in the United States, the family with four or more children will likely be viewed as large. But in many other countries and perhaps in the United States at the turn of the century, having four children would lead to a reaction such as "only four?" Family size is certainly relative to cultural context.

Regardless of what is considered a large or small family, a small family is small for one of two primary reasons: either the parents wanted a small family and achieved their desired size, or they wanted a large family but were unable to attain it. In both cases, there is a low probability of having unwanted children. In contrast, a large family is such because the parents achieved the size they desired or because they had more children than they in fact wanted. The probability is therefore greater that large families include unplanned, unwanted, or unloved children; last-born children are more likely to be unwanted than first- or middle-born children.

A substantial body of evidence has been compiled concerning the relationship between family size or number of children and factors such as discipline, child abuse and neglect, delinquency, and health. One review of family size effects showed that, in large families, childrearing was more rule ridden and less individualized, corporal punishment was more prevalent, and resources such as time and money were more limited.[50] Persons from small families tended to have higher IQs and greater levels of academic achievement and occupational performance. Large families also produced more delinquents and alcoholics. In regard to health, in large families, perinatal (surrounding birth) morbidity and mortality rates were higher, and mothers were at greater risk of several physical diseases.

In the words of the authors:

> Women who have many children more frequently develop hypertension, stress symptoms, gall bladder disease, diabetes, and postpartum depression. Women with many children are at higher risk for cancer to the cervix, digestion organs, and peritoneum, but are at less risk for breast cancer… Fathers of large families are at greater risk of hypertension and peptic ulcers.[51]

Are there no positive effects of having many siblings or coming from a large family? For example, are not children from large families more sociable, personable, friendly, warm, affiliative, and less aloof?

Apparently not. Several national surveys found no relationship between sibling number and sociability or being affiliative as an adult (or perhaps at any

---

[50] Mazie Earle Wagner, Herman J. P. Schubert, and Daniel S. P. Schubert, "Family Size Effects: A Review," *The Journal of Genetic Psychology* 146 (March 1985): 65–78.

[51] Ibid., p. 72.

Traditionally, families with eight or ten children were a common occurrence among rural farm families in the United States. Today, few positive effects appear to result from large families, and, except for selected subcultures such as the Amish or Mormons, families of that size are infrequent.

age).[52] While a number of studies found no effects, positive or negative, associated with family size, very few studies substantiated positive effects associated with large families. The consequences of large family size, as with most social structural variables, will tend to vary by factors such as educational level, social class, and religious subculture.

It should be emphasized that family size per se does not create varied systems of family living. Rather, the life factors and personal values that arise in relation to a certain size of group create variety. Large families heighten the complexity of intragroup relations, pose additional problems in the fulfillment of family needs, and are likely to influence the amount of parental comfort or praise available per child.

Birth order and sibling relationships

Birth order (sibling position) has a major influence on a wide variety of behavioral and attitudinal phenomena. Research has shown that, in general, first-borns tend to be intellectual achievers and have high levels of self-esteem. Female first-borns, in particular, tend to be more religious, more sexually conservative, more traditionally oriented toward feminine roles, and more likely to associate with adults.

---

[52] Judith Blake, Barbra Richardson, and Jennifer Bhattacharya, "Number of Siblings and Sociability," *Journal of Marriage and the Family* 53 (May 1991): 271–283.

News Item: Fallout from Excess Kids

There has been a dramatic decrease in big families. Today 48 percent say 2.1 children is the ideal family.

Where does that leave me? Somewhere between the propagation of the faith, the population explosion and 1.1 surplus kid at my dinner table.

And don't think I haven't paid dearly for my 1.1 overflow. To begin with, he fouled up the family vote. We used to vote even, at two-all, which left some room for persuasion. Since he arrived, my husband and I haven't won a decision in 15 years. Whether it is a vote on a vacation site, what TV show we are going to watch, or whether or not parents are to be impeached, the vote is always the same: Kids, 3—Parents, 2.

I am not being dramatic when I say this is a two-child-geared society. If the Good Lord had meant for people to have more than two children, he would put more than two windows in the back seat of the car. We once threatened to put one on the front fender and the other two cried because they each wanted one.

A popsicle can only be divided two ways. There are two pairs of shoelaces in a package, so that one child always goes around with gym shoes that flop off his feet when he walks. There are only four chairs to a dinette set (so that one never matches) and four breakfast sweet rolls to a package.

We always had one too many for a rowboat, and when we rode the Ferris wheel, it was two to a seat and the odd one always rode alone like an only child.

Few people realize this, but did you know that a No. 2 can of fruit cocktail contains only two maraschino cherries? This means when you divide two maraschino cherries between three children, two are happy and the other one runs right out and retains F. Lee Bailey to fight a cherry custody suit.

Chores are geared toward twos—one washes dishes and the other dries, but what does the third child do? He becomes a useless bum and grows up to steal hubcaps.

Bunk beds come in twos. There are two sinks to a bathroom, two Hostess Twinkees to a package and free circus tickets come in pairs.

I mentioned this to the kids the other night and half-kiddingly said, "You know what this means, don't you? One of you has to go. Just for kicks, let's take a vote on it."

When the votes were counted, it was 4–1.

I had been phased out of the family.

Somehow, I expected more from a full-grown man who has his own car window.

Source: From *At Wit's End* by Erma Bombeck. Reproduced through the courtesy of Field Newspaper Syndicate.

Last-born or youngest children, like only children, tend to be more sexually permissive, more likely to engage in social activities, more likely to visit with friends frequently, more likely to make use of the media, and consistently less traditional. Explanations for these differences have often focused on the older child being a role model for the younger, having more responsibility for other children, and receiving less attention as siblings enter the scene.[53]

Even middle-born children appear to differ from first-borns and last-borns. An analysis of a national sample of several thousand adolescent males found middle-borns to have significantly lower levels of self-esteem than first- or last-borns.[54]

---

[53] Note for example: Joseph Lee Rodgers, David C. Rowe, and David F. Harris, "Sibling Differences in Adolescent Sexual Behavior: Inferring Process Models from Family Composition Patterns," *Journal of Marriage and the Family* 54 (February 1992): 142–152.

[54] Thomas Ewin Smith, "Sex and Sibling Structure: Interaction Effects Upon the Accuracy of Adolescent Perceptions of Parental Orientations," *Journal of Marriage and the Family* 46 (November 1984): 901–907.

Case Example: Growing Up in Large Families

Stewart and Joyce have been married 39 years. They have two adult children, both graduates of North Carolina State University, married, and successful in their careers. Stewart was the twelfth of fourteen children and Joyce was the youngest of twelve children. What was it like for them to grow up in large families?

Stewart and Joyce expressed many similar childhood experiences. Both lived on farms and each had their specific tasks or chores to perform, including carrying wood and coal and helping with farm chores. Both indicated they didn't have much but always had plenty to eat and felt they were very similar to other families in the community. Neither home had electricity and none of the parents owned or drove an automobile. Both had mothers who would discipline the children but fathers who would perform any needed spankings. Both had mothers who would serve three meals a day and families that would eat meals together, sitting on benches around one long table. Both, being younger siblings, felt closer, and even today feel closer, to their younger brothers and sisters than the older ones.

Joyce, being the youngest, felt she got more privileges than the others. She liked having lots of brothers and sisters because there was always someone around to help her. She had special memories of how her older brothers, who had jobs away from home, would come home weekends and give her money or how her mother would make her new dresses from colorfully designed cotton feed sacks. She shared how she had wanted a hair permanent but not having any money, picked blackberries to pay for it. What she missed most was not having a grandmother like the other kids had.

Stewart, too, felt he got some special privileges but not like his kid brother who lived like a king and got whatever he wanted. He, too, has special memories of working beside and learning from his dad who was a skilled carpenter. Since his grandpa gave the land his school was built on, he and his brothers and sisters only had to walk one-fourth of a mile to school and would walk home each day for lunch.

Today, both Stewart and Joyce keep in close touch with their siblings. Joyce remembers all their birthdays, and Stewart says he remembers certain ones. Joyce's siblings, their spouses, and her nephews and nieces get together twice a year, once in June and again in December at which time they give a Christmas present to the person whose name they had drawn earlier. Stewart's family gets together every May. Does either have any regrets in having so many siblings? None whatsoever. Neither would have wanted it any other way.

A one- or three-year spacing between siblings was more positive for children's self-esteem than a two-year spacing, as was having female siblings as opposed to male or both male and female siblings. The explanation of a lower self-assessment of middle-born children may be based on a theory that first- and last-born children have a uniqueness that facilitates recognition and attention by parents and siblings. Middle children lack this inherent uniqueness.

Judith Blake found no birth-order effects for small families, but in large families, middle-born children early in the sequence of offspring had their problems.[55]

---

[55] Blake, *Family Size and Achievement*, pp. 300–301.

These children experience the full negative force of large *sibsize* (size of sibling group). Specifically, they have older siblings close in age, with whom they have to compete for resources, and they also have to endure a long period during which younger siblings are born and are dependent.

The roles played by and significance of having siblings are often underrepresented in family textbooks. Yet it is clear that siblings have a major impact on one's socialization (described in Chapter 14), on each other as friends and companions, and on parents. Based on a review of research, Ann Goetting illustrated how the sibling bond typically persists over the life cycle.[56] Some aspects of sibling relationships are relatively constant, such as companionship and emotional support, while others, such as specific types of caretaking and sibling rivalry, stand out as unique to specific stages in the life cycle. Sibling relationships are unique in their duration, their common genetic and social heritage, and their common early experiences with the family.

In an era of frequent remarriages and the formation of many stepsibling and halfsibling relationships, one might question if these relationships differ from full sibling relationships in adulthood. National survey data have revealed that they do.[57] On the one hand, individuals define *stepsiblings* as real kin and maintain these relationships into adulthood. On the other hand, sibling relationships are prioritized, with full siblings reporting significantly more contact with one another than with stepsiblings. Contact with both full and stepsiblings was facilitated by factors such as geographical proximity and being young and female. Having no full siblings also encouraged contact with step- and halfsiblings.

Sex control

What will be the consequences for parents when they can increasingly control whether to have a boy or a girl (sex control)?

The day is at hand when parents can choose the sex of their child using either of two basic procedures: (1) by controlling the type of sperm that will fertilize the egg or (2) by prenatally determining the sex of an embryo and then aborting it if it is of the undesired sex.[58] Amniocentesis and ultrasound photography are becoming low-risk, routine ways to both diagnose the health of fetuses already conceived and confirming their sex months before birth occurs. In brief, it is no longer unrealistic to foresee the ability to guarantee the reproduction of offspring of the chosen sex.

---

[56] Ann Goetting, "The Developmental Tasks of Siblingship Over the Life Cycle," *Journal of Marriage and the Family* 48 (November 1986): 703–714.

[57] Lynn K. White and Agnes Riedmann, "When the Brady Bunch Grows Up: Step/Half- and Fullsibling," *Journal of Marriage and the Family* 54 (February 1992): 197–208; and Lawrence Ganong and Marilyn Coleman, "An Exploratory Study of Stepsibling Subsystems," *Journal of Divorce and Remarriage* 19 (1993): 125–141.

[58] See Elizabeth Moen, "Sex Selective Eugenic Abortions: Prospects in China and India," *Issues in Reproductive and Genetic Engineering* 4 (1991): 231–249; and Alison Dundes Renteln, "Sex Selection and Reproductive Freedom," *Women's Studies International Forum* 15 (1992): 405–426.

Of course, there is more to this issue than technology. Debate surrounds the general issue of controlling life, as evidenced by the controversy over abortion and surrogate motherhood as well as various types of genetic research and engineering. Traditional views hold that life is God given and should not be manipulated by humans, for any purpose. Other views hold that knowledge about and abilities to control life should be used to improve and sustain the human condition. The controversy is likely to increase as techniques such as sex control become more prevalent. But the fact is, the technology exists.

Will techniques such as sex control result in an unbalanced sex ratio as appears to have occurred under the one-child policy in China where males are preferred (review Chapter 5)? It has been estimated that choosing the sex of the child will increase the proportion of male births by 7 to 10 percent. If this excess of males were to occur, would it increase the number of males who never marry due to a "marriage squeeze," would it delay their age at marriage, would it force an increase in homosexuality and prostitution, or would it even force the introduction of polyandry?

Would a consequence of choosing the sex of a child be a reduction in the birthrate? Parents would not have to bear additional children in order to have one or another of a particular sex. Studies have indicated that the desire for more children is closely correlated with the number of sons.

Finally, would a consequence of choosing a boy or a girl be improved family relationships because births of the undesired sex were avoided? Would there be fewer resented or rejected children, or would gender-role confusion be eliminated? Irrespective of choice, having female children does seem to affect support for feminism and more egalitarian views. In studies in both the United States and Canada, women in both countries and men in Canada were more likely to recognize gender inequality, to support a more feminist ideology, and to hold more egalitarian views if they had female children.[59] Family structure, in terms of the sexes of children, affects attitudes and behaviors of parents and children.

People today are living in a biological revolution of which sex control is one aspect. Clearly, this and other biological advancements could have a far-reaching social impact on parental and family systems in the United States and around the world.

SUMMARY

1. The transition to parenthood and parenting requires a major reorganization of statuses, roles, and relationships. Shortage of time appears to be the major problem for most parents. Parenting tends to be viewed primarily as a maternal duty and is often referred to as *mothering*, but fathers have been found to assume substantial responsibility as well.

2. Although children are valued as necessary for a "real family life," as buffers against loneliness, and as sources of self-esteem and self-fulfillment, many

---

[59] Rebecca L. Warner, "Does the Sex of Your Child Matter? Support for Feminism among Women and Men in the United States and Canada," *Journal of Marriage and the Family* 53 (November 1991): 1051–1056.

couples in the United States place a greater emphasis on personal freedom, leisure time, and employment opportunities, all of which become more restricted with the arrival of children.

3. The consequences of parenthood can only be understood in a social context. Many negative aspects in the lives of children have been attributed to family changes such as divorce, single-parenthood, and maternal employment. However, to suggest that the family *causes* these negative aspects would be to exaggerate. Without doubt, parenthood does have significant consequences for employment patterns and marital satisfaction.

4. Young parenthood and unwed parenthood are issues of specific concern, both for parents and children. The number of births outside of marriage is increasing sharply. The greatest increases are not among teenagers but among women in their early twenties. These young parents are often at a disadvantage in terms of marriage, education, income, employment, and training in general. Being born to unwed parents also hinders the child's ability to get started on an equal footing with children born in wedlock and to avoid disadvantages after infancy, as well.

5. Most couples want, have, or expect to have children. Birthrates vary during wars and periods of economic depression and prosperity. Over the past few decades, women have delayed their first births; the consequences of this delay are having fewer children and being better off economically.

6. Some couples have no children by choice; for instance, some women choose career paths and marital styles that reject mothering and parenthood. Childless couples appear to have higher levels of health and marital satisfaction than do couples with children. However, involuntarily childless couples experience negative effects on their well-being. Many infertile couples turn to adoption or alternative means of conceiving and/or having children, such as surrogate motherhood and artificial insemination.

7. Family size influences development of children. Research has supported the *dilution hypothesis,* which suggests a dilution of familial resources available to children in large families and a concentration of such resources in small families. Most of the negative stereotypes about small families and only children have little, if any, research support.

8. As with family size, order of birth also influences children's development. First-borns appear to be more traditionally oriented, less sexually permissive, and more achievement oriented. Later-born children also differ in a variety of ways. Sibling and half-/stepsibling relationships are unique in their duration and social heritage.

9. Some evidence has suggested that gender preferences exist within the population of many countries for male children. Perhaps within the near future, parents will be able to choose to have a child of one sex or the other. This ability in sex control could result in dramatic changes in the sex ratio, in birthrates, and in family relationships in general.

10. This chapter covered a range of topics dealing with parents and parenthood: its value, young and unwed parenthood, birthrates, family size, birth order, and so forth. Chapter 14 will continue with the parenthood issue but focus more specifically on parent/child interaction, socialization patterns, and gender-role differences.

KEY TERMS AND TOPICS

Transition to parenthood p. 386

Mothers' and fathers' roles p. 387

Parents' roles p. 388

Value of parenthood p. 389

Uncertainty reduction theory p. 390

Social consequences of
    parenthood p. 390

Braking hypothesis p. 391

Young parenthood p. 392

Unwed parenthood p. 396

Rates of birth outside marriage p. 397

Consequences of birth outside
    marriage p. 400

Family size p. 401

Birthrates and birth expectations p. 401

"Baby boom" p. 403

Child spacing p. 404

Childless marriages p. 405

Voluntary childlessness p. 407

Involuntary childlessness p. 407

Effects of family size on members p. 408

One-child families p. 409

Resource dilution hypothesis p. 410

Birth order and sibling
    relationships p. 412

Sex control p. 415

DISCUSSION QUESTIONS

1. What is involved in the transition to parenthood? How does the presence of a child affect one's time, finances, marital adjustment, and household responsibilities?

2. To what extent are family changes—such as single-parenthood, divorce, and employment of mothers—responsible for teenage drug and alcohol use, juvenile delinquency, and adolescent sexual activity? Explain.

3. Why are young parenthood and unwed parenthood considered social problems? To alleviate these problems, why doesn't society enforce the use of birth control, abortion, sterilization, and the like on unwed teenage males or females?

4. A number of states have passed legislation that requires Planned Parenthood and similar clinics to notify parents when their teenage children have requested contraceptive or abortion information. What will likely be some of the consequences of this type of action?

5. Discuss the myth of maternal instinct. What explains the widespread acceptance of this myth? What evidence disproves its existence?

6. Why are childless marriages not likely to become the norm in U.S. society? Are there advantages to marriage without children? Explain.

7. Discuss the implications of the slogan "stop at two" in regard to family size. Why two? What if everyone had two children? What means should be used to accomplish this goal, if it is perceived as desirable?

8. Itemize advantages and disadvantages of growing up in large and small families. What are the consequences of being an only child? What types of factors are likely to influence the size of a family?

9. Discuss the implications of being an oldest, middle, or youngest child. Does child spacing affect the impact of birth order on an individual? How?

10. If the sex of the fetus could be determined accurately within a few weeks following pregnancy, what effect, if any, would this have on birthrates? Would most parents in the United States choose to have boys or girls or have no preference? What about in other countrie?

FURTHER READINGS

Blake, Judith. *Family Size and Achievement.* Berkeley: University of California Press, 1989. An examination of what the author calls the "sibsize revolution," with a focus on the cognitive and educational consequences of coming from families of different sizes.

Blankenhorn, David. *Fatherless America: Confronting Our Most Urgent Social Problem.* New York: Basic Books, 1995. The founder and president of the Institute for Family Values argues for reinstituting marriage, which would in turn reestablish fathers as responsible husbands and providers.

Debner, Charlene E., and Bray, James H. (eds.). *Nonresidential Parenting: New Vistas in Family Living.* Newbury Park, CA: Sage, 1993. Nine chapters are presented on a variety of aspects related to nonresidential parents such as marital disruption, parental role reversal, parent-child relationships, and approaches in research policy and practice.

Freeman, Ellen W., and Rickels, Karl. *Early Childbearing: Perspectives of Black Adolescents on Pregnancy, Abortion, and Contraception.* Newbury Park, CA: Sage, 1993. A study of urban, poor, African American adolescents who described their decisions about having or not having babies in the context of their goals and the attitudes of their families and peers.

Hetherington, E. Mavis, Reiss, David, and Plomin, Robert (eds.). *Separate Social Worlds of Siblings: The Impact of Nonshared Environment on Development.* Hillsdale, NJ: Lawrence Erlbaum Associates, 1994. An investigation of both shared experiences and individual differences in growing up in the same family.

Marsiglio, William (ed.). *Fatherhood: Contemporary Theory, Research and Social Policy.* Thousand Oaks, CA: Sage Publications, 1995. A volume of empirical and theoretical research on fathers in families, examining differences in culture, class, nationality, and custodial status.

Ribbens, Jane. *Mothers and Their Children: A Feminist Sociology of Childrearing.* Thousand Oaks, CA: Sage Publications, 1995. The author considers the impact of social constraints on the development of mothers' approaches to childrearing.

Rossi, Alice S., and Rossi, Peter H. *Of Human Bonding: Parent-Child Relations Across the Life Course.* New York: Aldine, 1990. A major research effort exploring the parent/child relationship as it varies by stage of the life course and by gender.

Zabin, Laurie Schwab, and Hayward, Sarah C. *Adolescent Sexual Behavior and Childrearing.* Newbury Park, CA: Sage, 1993. Empirical research is presented from diverse perspectives related to adolescent pregnancy.

Chapter 14

Parent/Child Interaction and Socialization

Chapter 13 examined selected structural arrangements of the family system: norms and values surrounding parenthood, young parenthood, unwed parenthood, birthrates and birth expectations, effects of large or small families, birth order, and the like. This chapter, as well, will look at selected social structural patterns such as gender (male/female) differences, but it will focus on interactional and social psychological patterns in parent/child relationships. Of central concern are various theoretical frames of reference that explain the child-rearing/socialization process.

SOCIALIZATION OF PARENTS AND CHILDREN

The helplessness of human infants is perhaps unequaled among newborns. Human infants cannot walk, feed themselves, recognize danger, seek food or shelter, or even roll over. Infants may grow up to be criminals, teachers, or athletic superstars, but first they must learn to care for basic needs, learn to interact with other humans, and learn what behavior is expected and accepted. In short, they must learn to be human.

The process of acquiring the physical and social skills needed to become a social being and a member of society is called *socialization*. Socialization, the central concept of this chapter, is a never-ending process of developing the self and of learning the ways of a given society and culture. While the focus of socialization literature is generally on the newborn and the young child, people in their teens, middle years, and even older are also in a continual process of learning skills, developing the self, and participating in the groups and social systems of society. Parents, too, need to be socialized to parenthood. Parents influence and shape not only the behavior of children, but children do the same to parents.

Socialization, particularly of young infants, appears to be one function of the family found in every society in the world. There may be other functions, such as social placement, but every society appears to link people by affinity (marriage) or consanguineous (blood) ties to the nurturant socialization of persons. This does not imply that families do not fulfill other functions, that socialization only occurs among infants, or that the family is the only socializing agent. Rather, the key implication is that a basic function of the family in all societies is nurturant socialization.

Preconditions for socialization

Frederick Elkin and Gerald Handel stated that there are two preconditions for adequate socialization:

1. Children must have the requisite biological inheritance.
2. There must be an ongoing society.[1]

---

[1] Frederick Elkin and Gerald Handel, *The Child and Society: The Process of Socialization*, 5th ed. (New York: Random House, 1989): 8–25.

The first precondition for socialization is a biological inheritance that permits learning processes to occur. Therefore, a brain, a digestive system, and a beating heart are clearly prerequisites for socialization. These prerequisites, while necessary, are not sufficient. A perfect biological system, which may influence the socialization process, will not be the determinant of what is internalized mentally. Factors such as brain damage, deafness, extreme tallness or shortness, shape of nose and chin, and a wide variety of other physical conditions may hinder or influence interaction and socializing processes.

But it should be made extremely clear that biological inheritance, while influencing learning processes and necessary for their occurrence, is never sufficient for socialization. Certain needs, such as food, drink, and sleep, are basic to survival, but they can be satisfied in a wide variety of ways. And even though temperaments and intelligence may be basically biological, the development or direction that they take is influenced and modified by the society in which the infant exists. In brief, biological requisites are necessary for adequate socialization, but they alone are not determinants of socialization.

The second precondition for socialization is an existing society that has values, norms, statuses, roles, institutions, and a wide variety of social structures that are highly regular and patterned but in constant change. The unsocialized infant has no knowledge of these changes, structures, and processes. The patterns of thinking, feeling, and acting in that society are what the socializing agents must pass on to the newcomer. This is the task of socialization.

THEORIES OF SOCIALIZATION PROCESSES

As previously defined, *socialization* refers to the process by which the infant and adult learn the ways of a given society and culture and develop into participants capable of operating in that society. A number of relatively comprehensive theories have been developed to explain various aspects of this process.

Learning/behaviorist frame of reference

Learning theory—also recognized as reinforcement theory, stimulus/response theory, and behaviorism—assumes that the same concepts and principles that apply to lower animals apply to humans. Thus, it is logical and rational to spend time in the laboratory experimenting with rats, cats, dogs, pigeons, monkeys, and other animals to learn more about humans. Although there are many variations of learning theory, as with the theories that follow, basic assumptions and common lines of agreement do exist.

Learning, or socialization, as applied to the newborn infant, involves changes in behavior that result from experience. (This is opposed to changes in behavior that result from physiological maturation or biological conditions.) Learning

News Item: Sect Parents Who Don't "Spare the Rod"

The Northeast Community Church, a 400-member religious sect group in Vermont, was under investigation by state officials in the mid-1980s because of allegations of child beating. A public meeting was called after the state seized 112 children of church members to have them examined for signs of physical and psychological abuse. The children were released within hours after a judge ruled there was not enough evidence to warrant the emergency detention.

Newspaper accounts of the public meeting gave comments of the seven church elders in attendance. One told the angry townspeople that a lost generation would result unless youngsters, even babies, were "properly spanked." When asked at what age children should be spanked, someone responded that if one waited until a child were able to reason, that would be too long. Another said that even little babies have a fallen nature and needed strict discipline.

A Mr. Wiseman, who faced charges that he beat a thirteen-year-old for seven hours, quoted the Book of Psalms, saying, "Serve the Lord with fear." Wiseman argued that strict discipline is part of the standard of God. Strict discipline included the use of slender wooden rods for reasons ranging from lying to asking for second helpings at meals.

involves conditioning that may include classical conditioning or instrumental (operant) conditioning.

Classical conditioning links a response to a known stimulus. Many people are familiar with Pavlov's dog experiment, which provides a good example of classical conditioning. The hungry dog, placed in a soundproof room, heard a tuning fork prior to receiving meat. When repeated on several occasions, the dog salivated upon hearing the tuning fork prior to receiving and even without receiving the meat. The tuning fork, a conditioned stimulus, produced the response, salivation. In the classical conditioning experiment, the focus of attention is largely on the stimulus. If conditioning works with dogs, the same principle should hold true with infants upon hearing their mothers' voices or approaching footsteps. The voice or footstep stimulus, with repeated occurrences, should elicit a response from the child.

Instrumental conditioning, or what Skinner called **operant conditioning**, places the focus of attention on the response. The response is not related to any known stimuli; rather, it functions in an instrumental fashion. One learns to make a certain response on the basis of the consequences that response produces. It is the response, rather than the stimulus, that correlates with reinforcement. Return to the example of the hungry dog. Under classical conditioning, the dog salivated upon hearing the tuning fork, the stimulus. Under operant conditioning, the hungry dog would sniff, paw, and chew whatever was around. If, upon pawing, the dog opened a door, behind which was food, the sniffing and chewing would soon decrease and the pawing on the door would occur whenever food was desired. Thus, instrumental conditioning is a response followed by a reward (reinforcement).

How does this apply to an infant? Suppose the infant utters sounds such as "da-da-da." Father, who is convinced the child is saying "Daddy," rewards him or her by picking up, feeding, or rocking the child. As a result, the infant uses the response ("da-da-da") all day long. The infant has learned to make a certain response on the basis of the consequence or result the response has produced; hence, the response is correlated with reinforcement.

These same general principles—refined by behaviorists with reference to intermittent reinforcement, partial reinforcement, negative and positive reinforcement, discrimination of stimuli, differentiation of response, behavior modification, and the like—apply in learning any kind of behavior. Socialization results from stimulus/response conditioning and from positive and negative reinforcements. The conditioning stimuli (classical conditioning) and the consequences of responses (operant conditioning) are both *external* to the animal or human.

Many of these processes are most readily observed in early childhood, when parents use rewards and punishments as deliberate techniques for teaching the child-approved forms of behavior. As individuals mature, sanctioning becomes increasingly complex. Candy, weekly allowances, spanking, and other forms of rewards and punishments lose their ability to either eliminate undesirable behavior or increase desirable behavior.

Within the learning theory/behaviorist framework, symbols, language, reasoning, internalized meanings, and other internal processes play a minimal role. This is in sharp contrast to the symbolic interaction framework (described in Chapter 2 and later in this section), in which socialized beings can create their own stimuli and responses, can define and categorize, can distinguish between self and others, can separate inner and outer sensations, and can take the role of the other. As a result, the behavioristic approach to socialization is rejected by most sociologists to whom the self, roles, reference groups, symbolic processes, and meanings *internal* to the individual are viewed as central to understanding human behavior. Although learning theory has been extremely illuminating in research with animals and infants, it has been less successful in explaining social situations, group norms, and the learning of language itself.

From the biased perspective of this author, it is largely a waste of time, effort, and expense to attempt to understand the behavior of socialized humanity (capable as we are of dealing with symbolic processes, reasoning, shared meanings, and the like) by studying nonhuman forms. Behaviorism does, however, add greatly to understanding the human (1) who has not learned to share meanings (the infant, people who are isolated or severely retarded) or (2) who once learned but no longer has the capacity to share meanings (people with severe cases of aphasia or schizophrenia, where words may exist but the meanings are not shared with others).

This brief, minimal treatment of learning theory may seem unfair to the disciples of behaviorism. The same can be said for the minimal treatment of psychoanalytic theory, which follows. Both discussions are intended to illustrate contrasting views on the nature of socialization.

Psychoanalytic frame of reference

Classic psychoanalytic theory, developed by Sigmund Freud and his adherents, stresses the importance of biological drives and unconscious processes.[2] This theory is in sharp contrast to the behaviorist theory just described.

The process of socialization, according to this framework, consists of a number of precise though overlapping stages of development. What happens at these stages, from birth to age five or six, although unconscious, becomes relatively fixed and permanent. These stages are referred to as the *oral, anal,* and *phallic* stages, followed later by a period of *latency* and then a *genital* phase. Attention is focused around three principal erogenous zones—the mouth, the anus, and the genitals—which are the regions of the body where excitatory processes tend to become focalized and where tensions can be removed by some action such as stroking or sucking. These regions are of extreme importance in the socialization process because they are the first important sources of irritating excitations with which the baby has to contend and upon which the first pleasurable experiences occur.

The first stage of development, the **oral stage,** occurs during the first year of the child's life. The earliest erotic gratifications come from the mouth, and as a result, the child forms strong emotional attachments to the mother, who supplies the source of food, warmth, and sucking. During the first year, the child is narcissistic; self-gratification is derived via the oral source, namely, the mouth. The mouth's functions include taking in, holding on, biting, spitting out, and closing, all prototypes for ways of adjusting to painful or disturbing states. These functions serve as models for adaptations in later life.

The **anal stage** of development follows and overlaps with the oral stage. This phase is so called because the child experiences pleasure in excretion and because toilet training may become a major problem. At this point, two functions become central: retention and elimination. Since the mother is still the predominant figure in the child's life, her methods of training the child and her attitudes about such matters as defecation, cleanliness, and control are said to determine the impact that toilet training will have upon the development of the person. Carried to the extreme, the mother who praises the child for a large bowel movement may produce adolescents or adults who will be motivated to produce or create things to please others or to please themselves, as they once made feces to please their mothers. On the other hand, if the mother is very strict and punitive, the child may intentionally soil himself or herself and, as an adolescent or adult, be messy, irresponsible, disorderly, wasteful, and extravagant.

The **phallic stage** is the period of growth during which the child is preoccupied with the genitals. Prior to this stage, the first love object of both the boy and girl is the mother. But in the phallic stage, the sexual urge increases, the boy's love for his mother becomes more intense, and the result is jealousy of the father, who

---

[2] For a recent application of psychoanalytic theory with the chronically emotionally ill, see Alexander Grainick, "Psychoanalytic Principles and Long-Term Hospital Practice," *Psychoanalysis and Psychotherapy* 8 (Fall/Winter 1990): 169–179. For an excellent treatment of feminism, see Nancy J. Chodorow, *Feminism and Psychoanalytic Theory* (New Haven, CT: Yale University Press, 1989).

is seen as the boy's rival. The boy's attachment to his mother is widely known as the *Oedipus complex.* Concurrently, the boy becomes fearful that his father will remove his (the boy's) genitals and develops a fear known as *castration anxiety.* This anxiety increases upon observation of the female, who has, in his unconscious mind, already been castrated. A similar or reverse process is in operation for the female. She forms an attachment to her father, the *Electra complex,* but has mixed feelings for him because he possesses something that she does not have. The result is *penis envy.* According to traditional Freudian psychology, penis envy is the key to feminine psychology. Located in this phenomenon are the roots of male dominance and female submissiveness, male superiority and female inferiority.

The oral, anal, and phallic stages taken together are called the *pregenital period* and occur in the first five or six years of one's life. These are the important years, during which basic personality patterns are established and fixed. Following this time, for the next five or six years until the onset of puberty, the male and female egos go through a **latency phase,** during which the erotic desires of children are repressed and they form attachments to the parent of the same sex.

Finally, with the arrival of puberty, the **genital phase** of development begins. This period is less a stage than the final working out of the previous stages, particularly the oral, anal, and phallic stages that occurred during the pregenital period. During the genital phase, group activities, marriage, establishing a home, developing vocational responsibilities, and adult interests become the focus of attention. Given the importance of the early years, one can readily understand why factors such as bottle or breastfeeding, nursing on a regular or self-demand time schedule, weaning abruptly or gradually, bowel training early or late, bladder training early or late, punishment or nonpunishment for toilet accidents, and sleeping alone or with one's mother serve as crucial developments to the psychoanalyst.

Freudian claims regarding the importance of infant training to personality adjustment have received mixed empirical support. What support exists has, in general, been derived from clinical studies of emotionally disturbed individuals. Other studies have shown different results.

For example, one attempt to test empirically the crucial role of infant discipline in character formation and personality adjustment was published about forty-five years ago and has since become a somewhat classic article on the subject.[3] That study set up a series of null hypotheses concerning the relationship of specific infant disciplines to subsequent personality adjustments. The general hypothesis was that the personality adjustment and traits of children who had undergone varying infant-training experiences would not differ significantly from each other. These infant-training experiences included the self-demand feeding schedule, gradual weaning, late bowel training, and similar factors. The results supported the *null hypothesis;* that is, there were no significant differences in the personality adjustments of children who had undergone varying infant-training

---

[3] William H. Sewall, "Infant Training and the Personality of the Child," *The American Journal Sociology* 58 (September 1952): 150–159.

experiences. Of 460 statistical tests, only 18 were significant at or beyond the 0.05 level.[4] Of these, 11 were in support of basic psychoanalytic writings, and 7 were not in support. Such practices as breastfeeding, gradual weaning, demand schedule, bowel training, and bladder training, which have been so emphasized in the psychoanalytic literature, were almost completely insignificant in terms of their relationship to personality adjustment.

Child development frames of reference: Erikson and Piaget

The ideas of Erik Erikson and Jean Piaget are also of interest in dealing with the socialization issue. Like Freud, both focused primarily on stages of development. Unlike Freud, both extended their stages beyond the early years and placed more importance on social structure and reasoning.

Erik Erikson, one of Freud's students, was a psychoanalyst who saw socialization as a lifelong process, beginning at birth and continuing into old age. Erikson developed and is well known for his eight stages of human development.[5] Each stage constitutes a crisis brought on by physiological changes and the constantly changing social situation.

In infancy (the first year), the crisis centers around *trust versus mistrust.* In early childhood (the first two to three years), the issue centers around *autonomy versus shame and doubt.* The play stage (age four or five) involves the issue of *initiative versus guilt.* From school age up to adolescence, the issue is *industry versus inferiority.*

In adolescence, the issue is *identity versus role confusion. Identity,* the focal concern of Erikson, is defined as being able to achieve a sense of continuity about one's past, present, and future. Young adulthood, another major turning point in life, involves the issue of *intimacy versus isolation.* In young adulthood and middle age, the issue is *generativity versus stagnation.* Old age, the last stage of development, is a time of reflection and evaluation and focuses on the issue of *integrity versus despair.*

In sum, Erikson sees the social order as resulting from and being in harmony with these eight stages of development. As people work out solutions to these developmental concerns, those solutions become institutionalized in the culture.

Jean Piaget, a Swiss social psychologist, spent more than thirty years observing and studying the development of intellectual functions and logic in children.[6] His work has stimulated an interest in maturational stages of development and in the importance of cognition in human development. Differing dramatically from supporters of the learning and psychoanalytic frames of reference, Piaget characterized development as an ability to reason abstractly, to think about hypothetical

---

[4] The 0.05 level means that these relationships would occur simply by chance less than 5 times in 100.

[5] Erik K. Erikson, *Childhood and Society,* 2d ed. (New York: Norton, 1963), Chapter 7.

[6] Jean Piaget and Barbara Inhelder, *The Psychology of the Child* (New York: Basic, 1969); and Jean Piaget, *The Construction of Reality in the Child* (New York: Basic, 1954).

situations in a logical way, and to organize rules (which he calls *operations*) into complex, higher-order structures. For instance, children are able to invent ideas and behaviors that they have never witnessed or had reinforced.

Piaget asserted that there are four major stages of intellectual development:

1. *Sensorimotor* — zero to eighteen months old
2. *Preoperational* — eighteen months to seven years old
3. *Concrete operational* — seven to twelve years old
4. *Formal operational* — twelve years old and up

The stages are continuous; each is built upon and is derived from the earlier one.

The *sensorimotor stage* is characterized by children's physical understanding of themselves and the world. Unlearned responses, such as sucking and closing one's fist, become repetitive, but the child performs them with no intent, purpose, or interest in the effect this behavior has on the environment. Later in this first stage, activities become more intentional. The *preoperational stage* involves language and its acquisition. Objects are treated as symbolic of things other than themselves. For example, a doll may be treated as a baby, or a stick may be treated as a candle. At this stage, overt actions and the meanings of objects and events are manipulated, but the child has difficulty seeing the point of view of another child or adult.

During the *concrete operational stage,* children learn to manipulate the tools of their culture and also learn that mass remains constant in spite of changes in form. They learn to understand cause and effect, to classify objects, to consider the viewpoints of others, and to differentiate between dreams and reality. By approximately age twelve, the child enters the adult world and the stage of formal operations. The *formal operational stage* is characterized by the ability to think in terms of abstract concepts, theories, and general principles. Alternate solutions to problems can be formulated, and hypothetical propositions can be formulated and answered. Preoccupation with thought is the principal component of this stage of development.

Piaget's insights into cognitive development are unsurpassed. His stages take into account both social and psychological phenomena. Like Freud, Piaget had a specific conception of the goals of maturity and adulthood. Also like Freud, Piaget believed that the child passes through stages. But whereas Freud emphasized emotional maturity and the unconscious as extremely important, Piaget emphasized reasoning and consciousness. And whereas Freud focused on bodily zones, Piaget focused on the quality of reasoning.

Overview

The frames of reference covered up to this point can be summarized by suggesting that the learning theorists are concerned with overt behavior, the Freudians with motives and emotions (often unconscious and rooted early in childhood), and the child developmentalists with motor skills, thought, reasoning processes, and conflicts. The symbolic interaction frame of reference, discussed next, shares many assumptions of Erikson and Piaget in the importance given to language, reasoning, and societal influences.

Symbolic interaction frame of reference

Contrasting considerably with the learning and psychoanalytic frames of reference is the symbolic interaction frame of reference. Within this framework, the first five years of life are considered important, but it is not believed that personality becomes fixed; rather, socialization is a lifelong process. Although mothers are important figures, so too are fathers, siblings, grandparents, teachers, and many others who are perceived as significant to the child or adult.

Internal needs and drives are important energy sources and motivating devices, but greater significance comes from interactions with others and the internalized definitions and meanings of the world in which one interacts. For instance, erogenous zones may be sources of pleasure and gratification, but the significance of these zones depends on the learned internalized meanings attached to them. Unconscious processes may be at the core of socialization (purely speculative), but conscious processes relating to perceptions of self and others have prime importance. Although rewards and punishments influence behavior, even these can only be understood in light of the meanings attached to them. Thus, while conditioning (classical or operant) is significant and basic to learning, internal processes cannot be ignored.

To understand socialization, as explained within a symbolic interaction frame of reference (see Chapter 2), it is necessary to review in more detail the basic assumptions and meanings of key concepts such as *social self, significant others,* and *reference group.*

Basic assumptions

As summarized in Chapter 2, the interactionist frame of reference, when applied to the study of the family and to an understanding of socialization, is based on several basic assumptions. Four of these were delineated by Sheldon Stryker several decades ago.[7]

- *Humans must be studied on their own level.* Symbolic interactionism is antireductionistic. If one wants to understand socialization, infant development, and parent/child relationships among humans, then one must study humans and not infer their behavior from the study of nonhuman or infrahuman forms of life.

---

[7] Sheldon Stryker, "The International and Situational Approaches," in *Handbook of Marriage and the Family,* edited by Harold T. Christensen (Chicago: Rand McNally, 1964): 134–136; and Sheldon Stryker, "Symbolic Interaction Theory: A Review and Some Suggestions for Comparative Family Research," *Journal of Comparative Family Studies* 3 (Spring 1972): 17–32.

Global Diversity: Traditional Childrearing in the Kibbutz

The kibbutz has been and continues to be extremely child centered. Children represent the future. Traditionally, childrearing followed a collective pattern from infancy to adulthood. In that context, the infant was born of a kibbutz couple who generally married just before or soon after the first child was born. This was done in accordance with the laws of Israel and gave the child legal rights. Upon return from the hospital, the infant was placed in the infant house. During the first year of the infant's life, his or her mother came to this house to breastfeed the infant as long as she physically could. Young fathers participated at this period in bottle feeding and diapering. In a radical departure from childrearing in most of the world, neither infants nor any older children lived with or were directly supported by biological fathers and mothers. The socialization and education of kibbutz children were functions of nurses and teachers.

During the first year, the general pattern of child care emerged. Most of the child's time was spent with peers in the children's house. In the afternoon, two or three hours could be spent with parents in their flat or room, meeting with other families or engaging in some joint activity. On the Sabbath, only the essential chores were performed, and children of all ages spent much time with their parents. In addition to these hourly and Sabbath visits, the child frequently saw the parents while they worked or by attending this weekly assembly of the kibbutz. Thus, parents were extremely important in the life of the child but were, in a sense, junior partners.

Training occurred, for the most part, separate from the residence of the parents. For the first year, the infant was in the nursery. The child was then moved to a toddler's house, each of which had approximately two nurses and eight children. This was where toilet training, learning to feed oneself, and learning to interact with agemates occurred. When the children reached the age of two or three, a nursery teacher replaced one of the nurses. By the fourth or fifth birthday, the children moved into the kindergarten. This involved a different building, sometimes a new nurse and teacher, and an enlargement of the original group to approximately sixteen members. This enlarged group remained together as a unit until age twelve and the completion of sixth grade. At this point, they entered high schools, where for the first time they encountered male educational teachers and began to work directly in the kibbutz economy. Their work varied from one to three hours per day, depending on age, and was done in one of the economic branches under the supervision of adults (not parents). Upon completion of high school, the students were expected to live outside the kibbutz for approximately one year. Membership in the kibbutz followed this experience.

Even though the children did not sleep with; did not have their physical needs cared for; were not taught social, book, or economic skills by; and were not—for the most part—disciplined or socialized by their parents, most writers stress the importance of parents in the development of the child. Parents serve as the object of identification and provide a certain security and love not obtained from others.

The basic difference between *human* and *infrahuman* is not simply a matter of *degree* but one of *kind*. The evolutionary process involves quantitative differences among species, not merely qualitative ones. Human/nonhuman differences include language, symbols, meanings, gestures, and related processes. Thus, to understand a person's social development and behavior, relatively little can be gained by observing chimpanzees, dogs, pigeons, or rats.

Social life—unlike biological, physiological life or any nonhuman form—involves sharing meanings and communicating symbolically. Using language and gestures, human beings can correspond with one another, relaying intentions and meanings.

This assumption is in direct contrast with the behaviorist assumption, which suggests that humans can best be understood by studying forms of life other than human. Psychologists who assume that the difference between humans and animals is one of degree can explain and control those who do not share meanings or communicate with one another at a symbolic level: infants, isolated children, and people who are extremely psychotic, severely retarded, brain damaged, or aphasic. To the interactionist, the possession of language enables humans alone to deal with events in terms of the past, present, or future and to imagine objects or events that may be remote in space or entirely nonexistent.

The differences between socialized human beings and the lower animals (or between human families and nonhuman families) may be summarized by saying that the lower animals do not have culture. They have no system of beliefs, values, and ideas that is shared and symbolically transmitted among the group. Animals have no familial, educational, religious, political, or economic institutions. They have no sets of moral codes, norms, or ideologies.

Similarities between the animal and human worlds are often stressed, but equal emphasis should be given to understanding and focusing on the differences. Recognizing these differences, symbolic interactionists assume that one must study humans to understand humans. Thus, very little can be learned about socialization—of any people in any life-style or social class—by studying nonhuman forms.

• *The most fruitful approach to social behavior is through analysis of society.* One can best understand the behavior of a husband, wife, or child through a study and an analysis of the society and subculture of which they are a part. Personal behavior is not exclusively or even primarily an individual phenomenon but is predominantly a social one. The assumption is not made that society is the ultimate reality, that society has some metaphysical priority over the individual, or that cultural determinism explains all behavior. Neither biogenic nor psychogenic factors are excluded as important in explaining or understanding behavior. However, these factors are not salient variables. They are viewed as constants in a social setting and as random variables in a personality system.

Being born into a given society means that the language one speaks, how one defines situations, and the appropriateness or inappropriateness one assigns to any activity are those learned within that social and cultural context. Thus, the behavior of a couple from the rural Philippines, who would not be seen holding hands in public, versus the behavior of a U.S. couple, kissing and caressing in a public park, can only be understood by analyzing the society in which each of these behaviors takes place.

- *The human infant at birth is asocial.* Original nature lacks organization. Thus, the infant is neither social nor antisocial (as with original sin in certain religious organizations or the id within the psychoanalytic scheme). The "equipment" with which newborns enter life does, however, give them the potential for social development.

  Society and the specific social context in which a behavior occurs determine whether that behavior is social or antisocial. A newborn infant does not cry all night to punish or displease parents nor does he or she sleep all night to please them. Only after these expectations become internalized do social and antisocial acts take on meaning. Although the newborn infant has impulses, as does any biological organism, these impulses are not channeled or directed toward any specific ends. But, having the potential for social development, the human infant can, with time and training, organize these impulses and channel them in specific directions. This process, by which the newborn infant becomes a social being, is the main concern of social psychologists, who are interested in the process of socialization, and of family sociologists, who are interested in childrearing.

- *A socialized human being (meaning one who can communicate symbolically and share meanings) is an actor as well as a reactor.* This does not simply mean that one person acts and another reacts. Socialized human beings do not simply respond to stimuli from the external environment. Rather, humans respond to a symbolic environment that involves responses to interpreted and anticipated stimuli. Humans can talk to themselves, think through alternative courses of action, feel guilty over past behaviors, and dream of future possibilities.

  That humans are actors as well as reactors suggests that investigators cannot understand behavior simply by studying the external environment and external forces; they must see the world from the viewpoint of the subject of their investigation. Humans not only respond to stimuli but select and interpret them. As a result, it becomes crucial and essential that this interpretation and meaning be known. It is this assumption that most precisely differentiates symbolic interactionists from positivists in sociology and behaviorists in psychology.

  The assumption that humans are both actors and reactors suggests that humans alone can take the roles of others; that is, they can view the world from perspectives of other people. Thus, one can put oneself "in someone else's shoes," feeling sad over the misfortune of a friend or sharing the joys of one's children. A professor can take the role of the student and anticipate his or her response to a three-hour lecture or a certain type of exam without giving either the lecture or the exam. A wife can anticipate the response of her husband to an embrace or to inviting friends to dinner. The responses of the professor and the wife may be inaccurate, but the perception and meaning or definition attached to the situation will influence and direct behavior. In short, a person's behavior is not simply a response to others but is a self-stimulating response: a response to internal symbolic productions.

Like father, like son. Mead postulated that, in the process of socialization to adulthood, children go through a play stage in which they imitate people whom they observe. Children are particularly likely to model their behavior after that of their parents.

Development of a social self

Self is the key concept in understanding socialization and personality. Self, although often defined in psychological and personal terms, is a social phenomenon. Self is developed in interaction with others. The process of socialization, a primary concern of childrearing and that which makes humans social beings, is the development of a social self: the organization of internalized roles.

A woman may occupy the statuses of wife, mother, sister, student, executive, Methodist, and many others. Each status has expectations (roles) assigned to it. A person must know how each role is related to the others, and all these roles must be organized and integrated into some reasonable, consistent unity. This organization of internalized roles is the **social self.**

This organization and internalization of roles occurs in interaction with others; the social self is never fixed, static, or in a final state. George Herbert Mead used the term *self* to mean simply that persons are the object of their own activities; they can act toward themselves as they act toward others.[8] Thus, one can talk to oneself or feel proud, ashamed, or guilty of oneself.

Who one is, how he feels, what he wants, and so on constitute his social self. One's social self consists of self-concepts, self-perceptions, and definitions of self-worth and self-esteem. Personality then, consists of these definitions of self with the predisposition to act and behave consistently. The person who is convinced

[8] George Herbert Mead, *Mind, Self and Society* (Chicago: University of Chicago Press, 1934).

that she is not capable of passing the exam, not attractive enough to meet that special person, or not able to fulfill the expectations of a job may position herself for failure. A *self-fulfilling prophecy* may become operative. That is, the person will fail at the very thing she knew would bring failure. The opposite is equally true. Knowing one can do something increases the probability that she will do it.

These self-concepts and senses of self-worth develop in interaction with others. Such feelings and values do not exist at birth but must be internalized; that is, they must be learned. It does not take much imagination to assess the central role a spouse, sibling, parent, or grandparent—that is, family members—may each play in the development of the social self. Research has shown that parent support and behavior affect the self-esteem of children and adolescents, and reciprocally, the self-esteem of children affects how much support their parents give them.[9]

In another study, perceived parental rejection was found to be a potent cause of depressive symptoms and low self-esteem among young people.[10] Mothers with high self-esteem were more likely to provide their children with greater decision-making freedom, to communicate better with them, and to be less concerned about their children's behavior. Fathers with high self-esteem were less likely to report using a physical form of punishment.[11]

An interactionist frame of reference cautions against assuming that specific parental acts will always produce identical outcomes or results. Take spanking or the physical punishment of children, for example. Spanking (corporal punishment) is deeply rooted in the legal and religious traditions of American culture. Although it varies by sex (boys more than girls), age of children (pre-school more than older), marital status (unmarried mothers more than married ones), social class (higher among the lower classes), and region of the country (highest in the south), most parents (90–95 percent) claim to have spanked their children and most parents (75-85 percent) approve of spanking and believe it is necessary to discipline a child.[12]

But with what effects? Does it improve the mental health and well-being of children and adolescents or lead to aggression and psychological disorders? Does it lead to conformity and tolerance of others or result in adolescent delinquency and adult abusiveness? A literature review can perhaps find evidence for any or all

---

[9] Viktor Gecas and Michael L. Schwalbe, "Parental Behavior and Adolescent Self-Esteem," *Journal of Marriage and the Family* 48 (February 1986): 37–46; and Richard B. Felson and Mary Z. Zielinski, "Children's Self-Esteem and Parental Support," *Journal of Marriage and the Family* 51 (August 1989): 727–735.

[10] Joan F. Robertson and Ronald L. Simons, "Family Factors, Self-Esteem, and Adolescent Depression," *Journal of Marriage and the Family* 51 (February 1989): 125–138.

[11] Stephen A. Small, "Parental Self-Esteem and Its Relationship to Childrearing Practices, Parent-Adolescent Interaction, and Adolescent Behavior," *Journal of Marriage and the Family* 50 (November 1988): 1063–1072; and Ronald P. Rohner, Kevin J. Kean, and David E. Cournoyer, " Effects of Corporal Punishment, Perceived Caretaker Warmth, and Cultural Beliefs on the Psychological Adjustment of Children in St. Kitts, West Indies," *Journal of Marriage and the Family* 53 (August 1991): 681–693.

[12] Jean Giles-Sims, Murray A. Straus, and David B. Sugarman, "Child, Maternal, and Family Characteristics Associated with Spanking," *Family Relations* 44 (April 1995): 170–176; and Clifton P. Flynn, "Regional Differences in Attitudes Toward Corporal Punishment," *Journal of Marriage and the Family* 56 (May 1994): 314–324.

of the above. Is it corporal punishment per se that produces (causes) specific outcomes or do parental intents and social contexts modify the results?

Support for the latter position was revealed in a study that examined the impact of harsh corporal punishment and quality of parental involvement on adolescent aggressiveness, delinquency, and psychological well-being.[13] Basically the results indicated that it was not corporal punishment per se that predicted negative adolescent outcomes but the disregard, inconsistency, and uninvolvement of parents that increases a child's risk for problem behaviors. Spanking in a context of parental support and involvement did not have a detrimental impact. Spanking in different contexts, however, often results in physical injury to the child, feelings of anger, defiance, and rejection, psychological disturbances, aggressive action, and delinquent behaviors. In fact, given the high prevalence of spanking per se, much of which is outside a context of love and parental involvement, led Straus to recommend that spanking elimination should become a public health agenda because it presents a serious threat to the well-being of American children.[14]

In brief, the development of self-esteem, sound mental health or well-being, or any other aspect of internalizing definitions of the self must be viewed in a sociocultural context. Since everyone learns in interaction with others, attention must be paid to *culturally prescribed meanings* of socialization behaviors as well as to *social structural variations* in which the socialization occurs.[15]

Note again the futility of studying nonhumans in dealing with issues such as these. Animals and other forms of life (including newborn infants) who have neither language nor internalized role definitions (senses of self-worth) have no social selves. They cannot take the positions of others and cannot view themselves as objects. Neither can they judge past, present, or prospective behavior. Only humans, who have the potential to share meanings, can develop social selves.

Importance of significant others and reference groups

Significant others and reference groups are of central importance in understanding the development of the child and modification of the social self. Not all persons or groups are of equal importance to individuals. Certain persons and groups—again, in processes of interaction—come to be perceived as more important, as more significant, and as sources of reference. These persons and groups with which one psychologically identifies are termed, respectively, **significant others** and **reference groups**.

To most infants and young children, Mother is a significant person, that is, an object of emotional involvement, especially in the child's development. Note that

---

[13] Ronald L. Simons, Christine Johnson, and Rand D. Conger, "Harsh Corporal Punishment Versus Quality of Parental Involvement as an Explanation of Adolescent Maladjustment," *Journal of Marriage and the Family* 56 (August 1994): 591–607.

[14] Murray A. Straus, *Beating the Devil Out of Them; Corporal Punishment by Parents and Its Effects on Children* (Boston: Lexington/Macmillan, 1994); and Murray A. Straus, "Discipline and Deviance: Physical Punishment of Children and Violence and Other Crime in Adulthood," *Social Problems* 38 (1991): 101–123.

[15] Note for example: Elizabeth Thomson, Sara S. McLanahan, and Roberta Braun Curtin, "Family Structure, Gender, and Parental Socialization," *Journal of Marriage and the Family* 54 (May 1992): 368–378.

Case Example:
Resocializing a Child Who Has Been Severely Deprived

I could write volumes about this foster child we've raised. When he came to us, he was two years and four months old and was really a basket case. I had read about children from deprived backgrounds, but I had never seen one. It was really a cultural shock for all of us.

The child didn't seem to know what people were for. He could ignore a person like he ignored a piece of furniture. He apparently had never had any interpersonal relations with another human. He did not want anybody near him and he was only two years old. Our way was to hold our children, cuddle them, tell them bedtime stories, and carry them around. The older children played with him, but he had no idea what they were doing. Everything terrified him. It was a lot more than "I miss my mother." In fact, he did not know the words *mama, daddy*. He didn't miss anybody 'cause he didn't know what anybody was for. He had no language in that he didn't understand like our two-year-olds understood everything. He had no understanding of the difference between *yes, go ahead and do it* and *no, you can't do that. No* was a concept he never heard.

Apparently, he never sat at a table and ate a meal. He was more like an animal. I really hate using that word when we are talking about humans. But you could not sit him at a table; he didn't know what it was for. I recall the first breakfast we had—that he had with us. He drank orange juice for as long as I gave it to him. Like he had four or five glasses of orange juice. He gobbled up toast and ate huge bowls of cereal. First I thought, "Gee, the kid is starved." But then I realized that he ate like that probably because that's his pattern. You eat all you could get when you could get it because you didn't know where the next meal was coming from. But we ate three times a day. It was years, and I mean years, before he could really sit at the table with us, eat a meal, and then leave without creating a major disturbance. By major, I mean he thought he could get his jollies by just sweeping everything off the table or grabbing the table and making things spill or taking his own food and throwing it around. You

would think that in a few weeks this will all go away. But it didn't, and we started bringing him around to psychologists and the agency was very helpful. He was seen by neurologists and psychologists and he had EEGs, intelligence tests, and all of the support that seemed to be available in the community. They would all just say that, as far as they could see, he had no brain damage; his intelligence was maybe below normal.

For a long time, he was as rigid as a door. He would not bend an inch. Like here's an example of what I mean. At our house, the children play outside in the summer. We have playground equipment in the backyard, and the children have bikes. I raised a bunch of kids who really love the outdoors. But I don't think he had ever been outside his little apartment or whatever it was they lived in. So, I would put him outside in the morning, and his hands would go up to his eyes like he couldn't stand the light. I'd stay out there with him, but unless I was holding his hand, he would spin right around and go into the house again. So I'd take him out and put him outside again. We actually had to physically hold him out there. You could not walk him. You couldn't put him in the sandbox. He didn't know what a sandbox was for. He didn't know what toys were for. He had no idea what you did with a toy. We had to very patiently teach him all of this.

Eventually, he began to show that it became important to him that he start pleasing us. But now, this didn't happen until he was almost school age. Prior to that, he couldn't care less whether he pleased us or pleased anybody else. He had not been socialized that way, and I think that kind of socialization happens really early. I'm even more aware of it with my own grandchildren. They're sensitive. They cry if they are corrected. He never cried. We still laugh about the time I broke the pingpong paddle on him and he got up and said, "That didn't hurt." He went back and started doing exactly the same thing he was spanked for. I just had to take a deep breath and sit back and let him do it. Or I would have killed him that day. I'm sure I would have.

Mother, in terms of interaction and involvement, is a social, not a biological, concept. As a result, an adoptive parent, foster parent, grandparent, or other person—male or female—can fulfill the expectations (roles) of Mother. And Mother (socially or biologically) is not the only significant other. Fathers, siblings, peers, teachers, athletes, and movie stars are all important people with whom one psychologically identifies. To do so is to attempt to conform to the expectations one perceives these people have of oneself. An attempt is made to please and receive approval from those others who are significant.

Significant others present themselves in two essential ways: (1) by what they do and (2) by what they say and how they say it. Doing and saying are organized in terms of roles. Mothers (traditionally, at least) change diapers, cook meals, clean house, offer tenderness, and the like. Fathers read newspapers, complain about bills, watch football games, and so on.

As a children or adults interact with other people, they will become interested in some and attached to others; it follows that they will share certain expectations and behaviors with those people. Significant others are perceived as role models. Personal behavior and thinking are patterned on the conduct of these persons. Uncle Pete the pilot or Marcia the teacher, as a significant other, may each play a decisive part in the socialization and development of one's social self. A sister or brother, a boyfriend or girlfriend, or a television figure may become a role model, a significant other, and thus a person with whom one psychologically identifies.

In addition to persons who are viewed as significant, groups (real or imaginary) are used as frames of reference with which a person psychologically identifies. These groups, generally termed *reference groups,* are any from which individuals seek acceptance or that they use as a source of comparison. A church, a club, or a company may serve as a point of reference in making comparisons or contrasts, especially in forming judgments about oneself. In some instances, a person may attempt to gain membership or acceptance in the group, although this is not always the case. These groups, like significant others, serve as standards for conduct, as bases for self-evaluation, and as sources of attitude formation.

To most adolescents, peers rather than parents are key reference groups. As such, peers cannot be ignored in theories of child development and socialization. Central themes in peer culture include:

1. The importance of sharing and social participation
2. An attempt to deal with confusions, concerns, fears, and conflicts in their daily lives
3. A resistance to and challenging of adult rules and authority[16]

Thus, peers—who understand the adolescent and share his or her world—become a reference point for sizing up problems, strivings, and ambitions.

---

[16] William A. Corsaro and Donna Eder, "Children's Peer Cultures," *Annual Review of Sociology* 16 (1990): 197–220.

Including peers as a source of reference may help one understand why the values of adolescents appear to be more like those of similar-age youth than those of parents.

Peers as a source of reference may also help one understand that behavior defined as deviant by parents may be given social approval by peers. Using drugs or alcohol, engaging in sexual intercourse, dating interracially, espousing political liberalism, and the like may be conforming behavior to peers. The antisocial behavior of adolescents, as viewed by parents, may simply mean that the adolescent is "in step with a different drummer" (peers).

Socialization stages and interaction processes

The importance of the early years cannot be denied. Very early experiences provide infants with their first sense of self, other people, and social relationships. The mother usually becomes the first, primary, and most significant other. The significant dimensions in the socialization process become attention, love, and warmth (or their absence), rather than specific priorities such as breast- or bottle feeding or toilet training early or late.

More important, the nature of the social relationships with the mother and others influences the image that the infant or child has of himself or herself. Scolding, slapping, pampering, or praising may not be crucial per se, but their repetitive nature leads to internalization of a sense of self-worth and an image of oneself. Although the mother is crucial in the development of these images, so are the father, siblings, other kin, and friends. Although the mother may carry out most infant care, the socialization experiences of many infants include interaction with members of the nuclear family, extended family, and others. Since relationships with different persons signify statuses and roles in relation to kin, each provides a unique and different contribution to socialization.

In the development of the self, Mead postulated that children go through three continuous **stages of observation:** preparatory, play, and game.[17] In the *preparatory stage,* children do not have the ability to view their own behavior. Actions of others are imitated. As described under the learning frame of reference and also under the interaction frame of reference, certain sounds, such as "da-da-da," bring attention and response from others. This operant conditioning leads the child to repeat and learn the sounds.

The second stage, overlapping with and continuing the preparatory stage, is the *play stage.* At this point, children take roles of others; that is, they play at being whom they observe. A child may sweep the floor, put on a hat, or pretend to read a book. Elkin and Handel described a four-year-old "playing Daddy" who put on his hat and coat, said "goodbye," and walked out the front door, only to return a few minutes later because he did not know what to do next.[18]

---

[17] Mead, *Mind, Self and Society,* p. 150. For a comparison of Piaget and Mead regarding play and games, see Norma K. Denzin, "Play, Games and Interaction: the Contexts of Childhood Socialization," *The Sociological Quarterly* 16 (Autumn 1975): 458–478.

[18] Elkin and Handel, *The Child and Society,* p. 57.

Later, children enter the *game stage*. At this point, they do not merely play or take the roles of others; they now participate in games involving an organization of roles and the development of self. At this point, they have to recognize the expected behaviors of everyone else, which involves responding to the expectations of several other people at the same time. This is termed the **generalized other.** In Mead's famous example of the baseball game,

> the child must have the responses of each position involved in his own position. He must know what everyone else is going to do in order to carry out his own play. He has to take all of these roles. They do not all have to be present in consciousness at the same time, but at some moments he has to have three or four individuals present in his own attitude, such as the one who is going to throw the ball, the one who is going to catch it, and so on. These responses must be, in some degree, present in his own makeup.[19]

The concept of generalized other enables one to understand how given individuals may be consistent in their behavior even though they move in varying social environments. People learn to see themselves from the standpoints of multiple others who are either physically or symbolically present.

In light of this perspective of socialization, it should be recognized that any behavior results less from drives and needs, unconscious processes, and biological characteristics than from interaction processes and internalized meanings of self and others. As a result, the behavior appropriate to whites or blacks, royalty or outcasts, Jews or gentiles, or males or females is dependent less on skin color, genital makeup, and other biological facts than upon the internalized meanings and definitions that result from interaction with others. These interactions, viewed in their broadest context, include schools, peers, the mass media, and all involvement of daily living.

Given this, the concern over latchkey children, day-care centers, neglected and abused children, foster children, and the extensive violence portrayed on television can be viewed in a different light and be more fully understood. Traditional norms continue to relegate child-care responsibility and childrearing to women and mothers.[20] But with the changes taking place in society regarding the roles of men and women, the increasing proportion of mothers in the paid labor force, and so on, there seems to be a weakening link between marriage and the care of children.[21]

Perhaps research is more important now than at any time in history in assessing the impact of parental substitutes and nontraditional patterns of interaction on the development of children. For these interactions and socializing influences,

---

[19] Mead, *Mind, Self and Society,* p. 151.

[20] For an overview of child care and children's development, see: Jay Belsky, "Parental and Nonparental Child Care and Children's Socioemotional Development: A Decade in Review," *Journal of Marriage and the Family* 52 (November 1990): 885–903.

[21] Andrew J. Cherlin, "The Weakening Link Between Marriage and the Care of Children," *Family Planning Perspectives* 20 (November/December 1988): 302–306.

both within families and external to them, are not only important to infants and preschool children; they also continue beyond early childhood, through adolescence and middle age, into old age.

SOCIALIZATION IN ADOLESCENCE AND BEYOND

Most books on socialization, most chapters on childrearing, and the greatest public interest in both topics generally focus on the young child. Perhaps this is readily understandable, since, to the newborn child, the entire world is new. Even the most common and routine events must be learned. But if socialization involves learning roles and the ways of a given society and culture and ultimately develops members who are capable of operating in society, then how can anyone argue that socialization is complete after five or six years of life? Particularly in a rapidly changing society, such as exists in the United States, persons are newcomers to unfamiliar events almost daily. Without a doubt, early socialization experiences will have a major influence and impact on the types of events and experiences that are acceptable or unacceptable. But socialization is a continuous process. What's more, learning experiences after the early years not only mean incorporating the new but discarding much of the old.

It is a rare society in which individuals can be prepared during childhood for the complex roles they will undertake later in life. This in no way denies the fundamental importance of socialization experiences in the childhood years but only asserts that role learning is a continuous process. The emphasis placed on education at the junior high, senior high, and college levels represents formalized attempts at changing adolescents' perceptions about the world in which they live.

Many studies and reviews have clearly indicated the significance of socialization during the adolescent years.[22] During the teen years, in addition to the family, the peer group, the school, the media, and the community are powerful and pervading socializing forces. Learning processes similar to those in early childhood are in operation. The adolescent is actively engaging in sex-role identification, learning the norms and expectations of the opposite sex, participating in new and different types of social activities, gaining insights and skills for the future occupational world, attempting to become emancipated from parents, and developing a new sense of self-reliance.

Even though socialization does not end at adolescence, research interest apparently does. In regard to persons ages twenty through sixty, a mythical assumption seems to exist, namely, that socialization to new roles, tasks, and activities either does not exist or is unnecessary. The social self, it seems, is believed to

---

[22] Viktor Gecas and Monica A. Seff, "Families and Adolescents: A Review of the 1980s," *Journal of Marriage and the Family* 52 (November 1990): 941–958; and Jeffrey Jensen Arnett, "Broad and Narrow Socialization: The Family in the Context of a Cultural Theory," *Journal of Marriage and the Family* 57 (August 1995) 617–628.

be relatively stable or even fixed in these adult years; thus, adult socialization is not an exciting or vital area for research. The only exception is the topic of people at retirement; some literature has made reference to the need for resocialization to new life-styles associated with aging and people who are aged (see Chapter 15).

Socialization—of young children, adolescents, midlife adults, or people who are aged—is rooted in basic interaction processes. The same is true in terms of content: socialization to violence (Chapter 16); socialization to parenthood (Chapter 13); sexual socialization (Chapter 11); and socialization to gender/sex roles. This issue of sex-role socialization will be addressed for the rest of this chapter.

GENDER IDENTITY AND SEX-ROLE SOCIALIZATION

Confusion often exists over concepts such as *sex, sex roles, gender roles,* and *gender identity.* Precisely, one's **sex**, irrespective of behavior, refers to the biological condition of being male or female. **Sex roles**, therefore, refer to the expectations associated with being biologically of one sex or the other. **Gender,** in contrast to *sex,* is the umbrella term that refers to the totality of being male or female, masculine or feminine. **Gender roles** are thus the expectations associated with being masculine or feminine, which may or may not correspond precisely with one's sex. Doesn't *he* (biological male) act *feminine* (gender expectation)? is one example of how sex and gender can be differentiated. **Gender identity** refers to the way one defines or perceives oneself in terms of his or her sex, as male or female, as masculine or feminine, or as heterosexual, bisexual, or homosexual.

Sexual or gender identity formation is a developmental process but one that does not always move through stages in an orderly sequence. For example, one study of more than 400 lesbians and bisexual women noted that these women experienced periods of ambivalence during which they wondered about their sexual identities and periods during which they had no particular sexual identity. Bisexual-identified women became aware of their homosexual feelings and questioned their heterosexual identities at older ages than lesbian-identified women. Identities changed as a result of available social constructs, the sociopolitical landscape, and their own positions on that landscape.[23]

Roles, differentiated both by sex and gender, are discussed frequently throughout this book, particularly those of male/female and husband/wife. Chapter 1 included a discussion of the issue of marital- and gender-role differentiation, including the psychological concept of androgyny. Chapter 2 described various approaches to roles consistent with structural-functional and interactional theoretical orientations. Chapter 3 examined differential treatment given to male and female members of kin groups. The entire fourth chapter focused on family and work, particularly the employment of women and male/female roles in the home.

---

[23] Paula C. Rust, "'Coming Out' in the Age of Social Constructionism: Sexual Identity Formation Among Lesbian and Bisexual Women," *Gender and Society* 7 (March 1993): 50–77.

Other chapters have looked at gender-role differences among families from other countries and racial/ethnic groups, in mate selection, in sexual behavior, in marriage, in childrearing, and throughout the life cycle, with a particular focus on sexual differences in midlife and old age, in crisis, and in remarriage.

Female/male differences

There is no denying that normatively, attitudinally, behaviorally, and physically, males and females differ. Anthropologists have provided clear evidence that, from a worldwide perspective, certain activities—such as hunting, trapping, herding, and fishing—are predominantly the province of men. Other activities—such as care of infants and children, grinding grain, carrying water, gathering herbs, and preserving food—are predominantly the province of women.

These divisions are found both in the most primitive as well as the most egalitarian societies. Even in Finland and Sweden, where sex roles are deemphasized and a parental leave policy has been designed to eliminate the traditional gender-based division of labor, wives and mothers in the majority of families feed the family, shop for and wash the clothes, and serve as primary caretakers for the children.[24] Likewise, in the Israeli kibbutz, which was founded on sex-egalitarian terms, most of the men are in agricultural and industrial roles and most of the women are in service and educational roles. Similar household and child-care patterns exist today in mainland China (see Chapter 5), even though the overwhelming majority of women are employed outside the home.

Not only do females and males differ in behaviors but gender differences exist as well in value orientations. A national representative sample of U.S. adolescents found support for females being (1) more likely than males to express concern and responsibility for the well-being of others, (2) less likely than males to accept materialism and competition, and (3) more likely than males to indicate that finding purpose and meaning in life is extremely important.[25] In spite of major changes in gender-role attitudes and young women's occupational aspirations between the mid-1970s and early 1990s, these value differences persisted.

Beyond these male/female task and value differences, who would deny that physical differences exist between males and females? Probably no one. But who would argue that differences in the behavior of males and females are innate, biological, or anatomical? Probably some people would, others wouldn't be so sure, and still others would deny it forcefully. Maybe all three groups are partially correct.

For centuries, it was assumed that male/female differences in behavior were inborn or natural. Females had maternal instincts and were submissive; males were aggressive and dominant. More recently, certain social scientists—particularly anthropologists, who discovered societies in which men are passive and women are

---

24 Linda Haas, "Gender Equality and Social Policy," *Journal of Family Issues* 11 (December 1990): 401–423.

25 Ann M. Beutel and Margaret Mooney Marini, "Gender and Values," *American Sociological Review* 60 (June 1995): 436–448.

domineering—have questioned any relevance of biological factors in behavior. They have argued that all behavior is learned. While this author tends to lean more toward the latter position, the most accurate answer probably lies between the two positions and is far more complex than suggested by a nature/nurture, biology/ culture argument.[26]

It had been argued (and tested) that, irrespective of the extent of actual inborn differences between the sexes, the *belief* that they are innate provides a major ideological justification for a system of stratification by sex. Since men/husbands are in the advantageous power position, it could be expected that they would believe in innate, inborn sex roles more than women/wives. Research has found this to be true. Within a marriage, however, disagreement about the origin of sex roles was reduced by the mutual influence that husband's and wife's beliefs had on each other, resulting in more similar beliefs.[27]

The biological argument is deeply rooted in a number of theories of socialization, including the psychoanalytic frame of reference discussed earlier in this chapter. This view is further enhanced by research into hormones (such as progesterone and estrogen secreted by the ovaries in females and testosterone and the androgens secreted by the testes in males) that initiate sexual differentiation in the fetus and later, at puberty, activate the reproductive system and the development of secondary sex characteristics. Research has shown that if a female fetus is given testosterone, she will develop male-like genitalia. If a male is castrated (testes removed) prior to puberty, he will not develop secondary sex characteristics such as a beard. But do these chemical substances, known generally as *hormones,* determine or predict behavior?

The strength of cultural factors is overwhelming in understanding gender identity and sex-role socialization. One prime example comes from cross-cultural data that have shown great diversity in the attitudes, values, and behavior of both men and women. Margaret Mead's classic study of three primitive tribes in New Guinea found both men and women among the Arapesh to be cooperative, mild-mannered, gentle, and unaggressive (sex-typed feminine behavior). Among the Mundugumor, both men and women were hostile, aggressive, combative, individualistic, and unresponsive (sex-typed masculine behavior). Among the Tchambuli, the typical sex roles found in the Western cultures were reversed: Women were dominant, powerful, and impersonal; men were emotionally dependent and less responsible.[28]

If it can be assumed that the biological makeups and hormonal balances of men and women in these tribes and men and women in the Western world are similar, then how can these differences be explained? It is not necessary to go to

---

[26] See, for example, Lois Wladis Hoffman, "The Changing Genetics/Socialization Balance," *Journal of Social Issues* 41 (1985): 127–148.

[27] John Mirowsky and Catherine E. Ross, "Belief in Innate Sex Roles: Sex Stratification versus Interpersonal Influence in Marriage," *Journal of Marriage and the Family* 49 (August 1987): 527–540.

[28] Margaret Mead, *Sex and Temperament in Three Primitive Societies* (New York: Mentor, 1950). Originally published in 1935 by Morrow.

New Guinea in the 1930s to note the strength of cultural factors in gender differences and sex-role socialization. Data from students in the 1990s, for example, showed that the attitudes toward appropriate roles for men and women were strongly affected by fraternity and sorority membership, by race and ethnicity, and by religious affiliation.[29]

Another and even more convincing line of research came from studies of *hermaphrodites* (persons who possess complete sets of both male and female genitalia and reproductive organs). Infants who were assigned one sex at birth and were later found to belong biologically to the opposite sex behaved as they were assigned and taught to behave. For instance, biological females, defined and reared as males, had fantasies typical of males, enjoyed sports assigned generally to males, and fell in love with girls. Biological males, defined and reared as females, had an interest in mothering, preferred marriage over career, and were oriented toward dolls and domestic tasks.[30] Thus, when socialization contradicts biological, hormonal, or genetic factors, learned and interactional experiences prove to be powerful determinants of current gender roles. (See the box "Brother Becomes Sister".)

Sex-role socialization

Socialization to sex (female/male) and gender (masculine/feminine) roles follows the basic socialization processes described earlier in this chapter. Socialization to anything, including sex roles, begins at birth and continues throughout one's lifetime. Following the moment of sex determination in the hospital, different colored blankets are assigned to girls and boys, and they are treated differently from then on. From birth, socialization as to appropriate roles for males and females constitutes one of life's most important learning experiences. In interaction with others as well as in words, deeds, films, and books, the child is taught what behavior is appropriate for each sex.

Even as adolescents, the home continues as a key source of sex-role socialization.[31] His and her tasks are evident in who does inside chores and who does outside chores. Daughters perform more labor than sons, and their greater labor contributions are disproportionately allocated to those tasks traditionally defined as "women's work." Intergenerational continuity of stereotypical gender roles are being perpetuated in North American home life.

---

[29] Ilsa L. Lottes and Peter J. Kuriloff, "Sexual Socialization Differences by Gender, Greek Membership, Ethnicity, and Religious Background," *Psychology of Women Quarterly* 18 (1994): 203–219.

[30] John Money, *Sex Research: New Developments* (New York: Holt, Rinehart and Winston, 1965). See also John Money, "Sex Assignment in Anatomically Intersexed Infants," in M. A. Watson (ed.), *Readings in Sociology* (Dubuque, IA: Kendall/Hunt, 1984.

[31] John F. Peters, "Gender Socialization of Adolescents in the Home: Research and Discussion," *Adolescence* 29 (Winter 1994): 913–934; and Sampson Lee Blair, "The Sex-Typing of Children's Household Labor: Parental Influence on Daughters' and Sons' Housework," *Youth and Society* 24 (December 1992): 178–203.

U.S. Diversity: Brother Becomes Sister: Alteration of Masculine/Feminine Behaviors

A young rural couple took their identical twin boys to a physician to be circumcised. During the first operation, performed with an electric cauterizing needle, a surge of current burned off the baby's penis. Desperate for a way to cope with this tragedy, the parents took the advice of sex experts: "Bring the baby up as a girl." The experiment has apparently succeeded. Aided by plastic surgery and reared as a daughter, the once normal baby boy has grown into a nine-year-old child who is psychologically, at least, a girl.

This dramatic case, cited by Medical Psychologist John Money at an annual meeting of the American Association for the Advancement of Science and reported in *Time* magazine, provides strong support for a major contention of women's liberationists: that conventional patterns of masculine and feminine behavior can be altered. It also casts doubt on the theory that major sexual differences, psychological as well as anatomical, are immutably set by the genes at conception. In fact, said Money, there are only four imperative differences: women menstruate, gestate, and lactate; men impregnate. Many scientists believe that crucial psychological imperatives

follow from these biological facts, limiting the flexibility of sexual roles. Money, however, is convinced that almost all differences are culturally determined and therefore optional. The Johns Hopkins psychologist further spelled out his views on sex-role learning in a book titled *Man & Woman, Boy & Girl.*

In the normal process of sexual differentiation, Money explained, if the genes order the gonads to become testes and to produce androgen, the embryo develops as a boy; otherwise, it becomes a girl. Androgen not only shapes the external genitals but also programs parts of the brain, so that some types of behavior may come more naturally to one sex than to the other. For instance, both men and women can mother children—the necessary circuits are there in every brain—but the threshold for releasing this behavior is higher in males than in females. The same phenomenon is demonstrated by laboratory animals. If a mature female rat is put into a cage with newborn rats, she begins mothering them at once. In a similar situation, a male rat does nothing at first, but after a few days, he, too, begins to display maternal behavior.

continued

Sex-typed behaviors are taught so effectively that, by adulthood, even within the same occupation, employed men more than employed women (1) are concerned about income, job security, and advancement into administration; (2) want to avoid being supervised; (3) are more likely to seek self-employment and/or autonomy in the work setting; and (4) value the opportunity to exercise leadership. Women more than men (1) want to work with and help people; (2) prefer part-time and employee status; and (3) emphasize the use of special occupational skills.[32]

If it is assumed that the workplace, parents, and others are influential in sex-role socialization, one can predict a continuation of sex-role stereotyping in this and future decades. For example, throughout the school years, the educational system continues to stereotype males and females. Textbooks, achievement tests, athletic emphases, vocational counseling, and parental and peer pressures all tend to

---

[32] Michael Betz and Lenahan O'Connell, "Work Orientations of Males and Females: Exploring the Gender Socialization Approach," *Sociological Inquiry* 59 (August 1989): 318–329.

Money believed that hormones secreted before and after birth have less effect on brain and behavior in human beings than the sex assignment that takes place at birth with the announcement "It's a boy!" or "It's a girl!" This exultant cry tells everyone how to treat the newborn baby and sets off a chain of events, beginning with the choice of a male or female name, that largely determines whether the child will behave in traditionally masculine or feminine ways.

Money's evidence for this familiar thesis came largely from cases in which accidents before or after birth made it impossible to raise children according to their genetically determined sex. In each of his examples, youngsters learned to feel, look, and act like members of the opposite sex.

For the little boy who lost his penis, the change began at seventeen months with a girl's name and frilly clothes. An operation to make the child's genitals look more feminine was done, and plans were made to build a vagina and administer estrogen at a later age. The parents, counseled at the Johns Hopkins psychohormonal research unit, began to treat the child as if he were a girl. The effects of the parents' changed attitude and behavior were marked. "She doesn't like to be dirty," the mother told the clinic in one of her periodic reports. "My son is quite different. I can't wash his face for anything. She seems to be daintier. Maybe it's because I encourage it. She is very proud of herself when she puts on a new dress, and she just loves to have her hair set."

The experience of two hermaphrodites, from different families, further bolstered Money's view. Each was born with the female chromosome pattern, and each had internal female organs but a penis and empty scrotum outside. One set of parents believed they had a boy and raised their child accordingly; the other set raised their offspring as a girl. (Surgery and hormones made the youngsters' appearance conform to the chosen sex.) According to Money, the children's "antithetical experiences signified to one that he was a boy and to the other that she was a girl." The girl therefore reached preadolescence expecting to marry a man; in fact, she already had a steady boyfriend. The boy, by contrast, had a girlfriend and "fitted easily into the stereotype of the male role in marriage," even though "he and his partner would both have two X chromosomes."

reinforce stereotypical expectations and behaviors. Beyond school, the mass media, governmental policies, religious and work worlds, and most social institutions tend quite consistently to stress appropriate and clearly different behaviors for women and men.

In the socialization of males and females, empirical evidence has documented a continuation of sex-role stereotyping and gender segregation in spite of tremendous shifts in sex-role attitudes.[33] Current conceptions of femaleness and maleness have marked similarities to earlier conceptions. A contemporary view of men as aggressive, work-minded, and capable of leadership is remarkably similar to that presented in earlier research. Current conceptions of femaleness, stressing sensitivity, affection, and consciousness of appearance, are also similar to earlier stereotypes of women. In spite of shifts in attitudes, socialization to sex/gender roles continues to emphasize differentiation between males and females, concentrating on the perpetuation of traditional expectations and behaviors for each sex.

---

[33] Barrie Thorne and Zella Luria, "Sexuality and Gender in Children's Daily Worlds," *Social Problems* 33 (February 1986): 176–190.

From birth, girls are taught to be and act feminine and boys, masculine. But children must be "carefully taught" or boys, like girls, will shed tears and engage in mothering behaviors and girls, like boys, will withhold their feelings and enjoy activities such as football and fixing cars.

SUMMARY

1. The central concept in dealing with parent/child relationships is socialization: the process by which the infant and adult learn the ways of a given society and culture and develop into participants capable of operating in that society. Socialization of the young infant, believed to be a function of the family, is found in every society in the world. Preconditions for socialization include biological inheritance and an ongoing society.

2. Several frames of reference were examined to explain various aspects of socialization: a learning/behaviorist theory, a psychoanalytic theory, two theories of child development, and a symbolic interaction theory.

3. Learning (reinforcement) theory assumes that the same concepts and principles that apply to lower animal forms apply to humans. The conditioning processes may be classical or operant. Childrearing and socialization processes result from conditioning and positive or negative reinforcements.

4. Classic psychoanalytic theory contrasts sharply with behaviorist theory. Internal drives and unconscious processes are of central importance. Socialization takes place according to precise though overlapping stages of development. These include the oral, anal, and phallic stages, followed later by a period of latency and a genital phase. What happens in these early stages, from birth to age five or six, although unconscious, becomes relatively fixed and permanent, serving as the basis for responses in later life.

5. Child development theories focus on the individual and the manner in which motor skills, thought, and reasoning develop. Erikson described eight stages of human development, each constituting a crisis brought on by changing social situations as the individual moves from infancy through old age. Piaget focused more on the cognitive development of the child and described four major stages of intellectual development.

6. Symbolic interaction theory contrasts greatly with the theories already described. Infants are not born social; they develop through interaction with other persons. As interaction occurs, meanings are internalized and organized and the self develops. The social self enables a person to consciously and purposively represent to himself what he wishes to represent to others.

7. A social being can take the role of others, can interpret and define, and can have and use symbols. In interaction with others, the child learns to define herself and the world in certain ways. These definitions and meanings in turn predispose her to behave in ways consistent with these self-concepts. Interaction, the social self, significant others, reference groups, and the generalized other are concepts basic to the socialization process.

8. Socialization does not end at any given age; it is a lifelong process. For teens, school and peer groups serve as important sources of reference, interaction, and identity.

9. *Sex/gender identity* and *sex/gender roles* refer to one's identity and the expectations associated with being male or female. Male/female differences are universal. Debate continues over the extent to which sex and gender roles have their roots in biology, culture, or a combination of the two.

10. Sex-role socialization follows the principles of any type of socialization. In interaction with others, children learn about gender/sex roles very early in their lives. These roles are heavily reinforced in schools, the media, the workplace, and the home. While some change in attitudes toward sex roles has taken place, current conceptions of femaleness and maleness fit earlier stereotypes and highly traditional expectations.

11. Chapter 13 on the parental system and this chapter on parent/child interaction follow a life-course sequence that generally but not always follows marriage. Chapter 15 will continue this time sequence by turning to families in the middle and later years.

KEY TERMS AND TOPICS

Socialization of parents and
  children p. 422
Preconditions for socialization p. 422
Learning/behaviorist frame of
  reference p. 423

Classical conditioning p. 424
Operant conditioning p. 426
Psychoanalytic frame of
  reference p. 426

DISCUSSION QUESTIONS

1. Discuss ways in which parents need to be socialized. What role does the infant, young child, and adolescent play throughout this process?

2. Review the two preconditions for adequate socialization. What would happen if either of them were absent? Would socialization be possible? Why or why not?

3. What factors are most important in the development of stable, healthy adults? Why?

4. Contrast the learning/behaviorist, psychoanalytic, child development, and symbolic interaction frames of reference in regard to how each defines *socialization*. What contributions does each theory make? What drawbacks does each have?

5. Interview three mothers or fathers of preschool children. Find out whether they toilet-trained their child early, breastfed or bottle fed him and whether they believe it made any difference; what means of punishment they have used; what role the father plays in childrearing; how other children assist or hinder the socialization process; and so forth. What similarities link the parents' answers?

6. In what ways and areas are you being socialized? To what extent are you a victim of early childhood experiences, perhaps a father-absent family, a lower-class background, or a home with marital conflict? When will you be fully socialized? Why?

7. What influence did early adolescence, dating, friendship relationships, siblings, and teenage experiences have on your personality? To what extent is your personality today a product of your early (as opposed to more recent) socialization experiences?

8. Is a marriage with no sex- or gender-role differentiation (androgyny) possible? Explain and give examples.

9. To what extent does one's biological sex determine her behavior? Could you be socialized to think and act like someone of the opposite sex? Why?

10. In spite of the women's movement, the increasing number of women entering the paid work force, decreasing family size, and so forth, why do school materials, the mass media, and the work world continue to differentiate and segregate people by sex?

FURTHER READINGS

Ambert, Anne-Marie. *The Effect of Children on Parents.* Binghamton, NY: Haworth Press, 1992. An interdisciplinary approach with a feminist orientation to various aspects of how children affect their parents.

Brettell, Carolyn B., and Sargent, Carolyn F. *Gender in Cross-Cultural Perspective.* Englewood Cliffs, NJ: Prentice-Hall, 1993. A reader including more than 45 articles that focus on anthropological and cross-cultural aspects of gender.

Chodorow, Nancy J. *Feminism and Psychoanalytic Theory.* New Haven, CT: Yale University Press, 1989. A fascinating application of psychoanalytic theory as a basis for feminist theory, with a recognition of the significance of the unconscious and emotional in gender relations.

Elkin, Frederick, and Handel, Gerald. *The Child and Society: The Process of Socialization.* 5th ed. New York: Random House, 1989. A coherent treatment, from a sociological standpoint, of how children are socialized in modern society.

Lorber, Judith. *Paradoxes of Gender.* New Haven, CT: Yale University Press, 1994. An extensive analysis of gender as a social institution that establishes patterns of expectations for individuals, orders the social processes of everyday life, and is built into the major social organizations of society.

Nsamenang, Bame A. *Human Development in Cultural Context: A Third World Perspective.* Newbury Park, CA: Sage, 1992. A challenging look at the roles played by the physical and cultural context in delimiting the nature of the opportunities available to children and the goals of their parents.

Rowe, David C. *The Limits of Family Influence: Genes, Experience, and Behavior.* New York: Guilford Press, 1994. A book on socialization proposing the radical theme that family environments may exert little influence on child outcomes such as intelligence, personality, and psychopathology.

Sollie, Donna L., and Leigh, Leslie A. *Gender, Families, and Close Relationships: Feminist Research Journeys.* Thousand Oaks, CA: Sage Publications, 1994. A feminist analysis of close relationships, including intimacy, the role of work, and the experience of violence.

Stafford, Laura, and Bayer, Cherie L. *Interaction Between Parents and Children.* Newbury Park, CA: Sage, 1993. A focus on the interpersonal communication of parents and children organized thematically by unidirectional, bidirectional, and systemic perspectives on theory and research.

Straus, Murray A., with Donnelly, Denise A. *Beating the Devil Out of Them: Corporal Punishment in American Families.* New York: Lexington Books, 1994. Straus makes the argument that corporal punishment is violence, is a major social problem, and that the ending of it is one of the most important steps to achieving a less violent world.

Weitzman, Lenore J. *Sex Role Socialization.* Palo Alto, CA: Mayfield, 1979. A brief, easy-reading paperback covering socialization to sex roles from early childhood through the school and college years, with a concluding chapter on where socialization fails to help women to achieve.

Chapter 15

Marriages and Families in the Middle and Later Years

- Postparental Period: The Middle Years
  Marital status and coresidence in the
  middle years
  Significance of the middle years

- Grandparent Status

- Families of Later Life and People Who Are Aged
  Growth of the elderly population
  Marital status in the later years
  Intergenerational relationships
  Living arrangements among the elderly

- Common Problems of People Who Are Aged
  Health and care
  Children's problems
  Income and standard of living
  Abuse and neglect

- Socialization in Later Life

- Retirement

- Dying and Death

- Widows and Widowers

- Summary

- Key Terms and Topics

- Discussion Questions

- Further Readings

Chapters 13 and 14 examined selected aspects of families with children. But marriage and family life do not end when children enter adolescence or in later adolescence, when the children leave home for marriage, employment, school, or some other reason. Family structure, interactions, and life-styles change considerably at this period of the family life cycle: the second half. A prime example of this change was shown in Chapter 12, regarding marital satisfaction over the life cycle. Studies indicated increasing disenchantment and decreasing satisfaction throughout the years of parenting, followed by increasing satisfaction in the later years, after the children have left home.

This chapter will examine two major periods in the life course: the middle years, from approximately age forty to retirement, and the later years, from approximately age sixty or sixty-five. This examination will include general descriptions of families at these periods; specific consideration will be given to grandparents, retirement, socialization of people who are aged, and social conditions and problems faced by this group.

POSTPARENTAL PERIOD: THE MIDDLE YEARS

In order to describe the experience of the period after children leave home, a number of phrases have been used. Among these are the *empty-nest* period, the *launching stage,* the period of *contracting family size,* and the term used here, the **postparental period.**

Technically, the term *postparental* is a misnomer, for parents do not stop being parents or become ex-parents after their children leave home. Postparental suggests that, at this time, the children are now legally and socially recognized as adults and assume greater independence from their parents as well as greater personal autonomy and responsibility. They are, in effect, ready to be "launched" from the family. For many families, the postparental period may include episodes of child "reentry" into the parental home. But essentially, this period is characterized by the return of the conjugal family to a two-person, married-couple household and of many nuclear one-parent families to a one-person household. The periods of family life from this point until the death of one or both parents can be classified as:

1. Families launching their oldest children — parents ages forty-five to fifty-four
2. Families of preretirement — parents ages fifty-five to sixty-four
3. "Young/old" retired families — parents ages sixty-five to seventy-four
4. "Old/old" families in the later years — parents ages seventy-five and older

The following section examines families in the middle years, as they launch their children and approach retirement, when the parents are approximately forty-five to sixty-four years old.

Table 15-1

Marital status of men and women, ages forty-five to sixty-four: March 1994, (percent distribution)

Marital Status	Age of men		Age of women	
	45–54	55–64	45–54	55-64
Never married	8.2%	5.4%	5.9%	4.1%
Married, spouse present	75.5	77.9	68.3	66.1
Married, spouse absent	3.2	3.0	4.5	3.3
Widowed	0.9	3.3	4.7	13.9
Divorced	12.2	10.4	16.6	12.6
Total	100.0	100.0	100.0	100.0

Source: U.S. Bureau of the Census, *Current Population Reports,* Series P20-484, Arlene F. Saluter, "Marital Status and Living Arrangements, March 1994" (Washington, DC: U.S. Government Printing Office, 1996), Table 1, p. 1.

Marital status and coresidence in the middle years

In 1994, of those persons ages forty-five to sixty-four, about 75.5 percent of the men and 68.3 percent of the women were married with a spouse present (see Table 15-1). Compared with other age categories, the percentage of people married was high, and the percentages of people never married, separated, widowed, and divorced were relatively low. For women, the percentage who were widowed climbed sharply at ten-year intervals after age fifty-four. The figures changed from 4.7 percent for ages forty-five to fifty-four, to 13.9 percent for ages fifty-five to sixty-four, to 34.2 percent for ages sixty-five to seventy-four, and to 63.3 percent for ages seventy-five and over (see Tables 15-1 and 15-3 presented later in the chapter).

The period after the children leave home lasts longer than any other in the marital life cycle. Interestingly, this phenomenon is unique to families of the twentieth century. In 1900, a man married at age twenty-six, had his last child at age thirty-six, saw his last child marry at age fifty-nine, and lost his spouse at age fifty-seven. A woman married at age twenty-two, had her last child at thirty-two, saw her last child married at fifty-five, and lost her spouse at fifty-three.[1] The result for both sexes was no postparental period, since the average couple died two years before their last child (which, on average, was their fifth) was expected to marry.

In contrast today both sexes marry in their midtwenties, have their last child in their early thirties, see their last child launched in their mid- to late forties, but

---

[1] Figures are taken from Paul C. Glick, "The Life Cycle of the Family" *Marriage and Family Living* 17 (1955): 3–9.

do not lose their spouse until the early or midseventies. The result is a postparental period of twenty to twenty-five years. Although couples still marry at a similar age, they have fewer children and thus gain an earlier release from childrearing. These factors, combined with longer life expectancies for both sexes, give the average couple several decades together prior to retirement or the death of one spouse.

There are, of course, many exceptions to parents gaining an early release from childrearing. Demographic indicators show that more young adults reside with their parents now than they did a few years ago. Although more than four-fifths of young adults leave home by age 23, the parental home is nevertheless the primary residence for most of the transition to adulthood. Even during the ages 21 to 23, parental living accounts for more than 40 percent of all residential experience.[2]

Women tend to leave home earlier than men, but for men in particular, the trend toward earlier leaving has been reversed with more cohorts leaving later. Compared to the past, young people in both the United States and Canada are more likely to leave to achieve independent living and less likely to leave for reasons of marriage. Both single-parent families and stepparent families increase the probability of both men and women leaving to achieve independent living. The same is true for household density: crowding is a positive incentive to leave home. Nest leaving and the process of the transition to adult and independent status involve not merely the children but parental/home conditions as well.[3]

Some who have left the home return for a variety of reasons: following a job loss or divorce or separation; unwed motherhood; or when other hardships, particularly economic, arise. Both nonfamily living and cohabitation lead to much higher return rates than does marriage. The parents' characteristics—such as health, marital, and employment status—have little bearing on whether their children return in either middle or later life. Rather, the child's needs and situations are more important predictors of **coresidence**.[4]

Even after launching all children, some postparental families become extended households when they take in aged parents.[5] Traditionally, the common pattern was adult children moving into the homes of parents. The situation today is often reversed, with aged parents moving into the homes of adult children.

The effect of either children or parents returning to the family in the middle years is to modify the nature of the postparental period. Namely, either event will delay return of the family to the single-householder or two-person-household unit.

---

[2] Arland Thornton, Linda Young-DeMarco, and Frances Goldscheider, "Leaving the Parental Nest: The Experience of a Young White Cohort in the 1980s," *Journal of Marriage and the Family* 55 (February 1993): 216–229.

[3] Nicholas Buck and Jacqueline Scott, "She's Leaving Home: But Why? An Analysis of Young People Leaving the Parental Home," *Journal of Marriage and the Family* 55 (November 1993): 863–874; and Barbara A. Mitchell, "Family Structure and Leaving the Nest: A Social Resource Perspective," *Sociological Perspectives* 37 (1994): 651–671.

[4] Russell Ward, John Logan, and Glenna Spitze, "The Influence of Parent and Child Needs on Coresidence in Middle and Later Life," *Journal of Marriage and the Family* 54 (February 1992): 209–221.

[5] Scott H. Beck and Rubye W. Beck, "The Formation of Extended Households During Middle Age," *Journal of Marriage and the Family* 46 (May 1984): 227–287.

Significance of the middle years

What is the significance of being a *quadragenarian* (ages forty through forty-nine)? To many couples, the middle years are the "prime of life." Business and professional men, in particular, are likely to hold their top positions, women are likely to be in the paid labor force, and total family income is at its peak. For example, in 1993, the mean income of married-couple families, where the householder was between the ages of forty-five and fifty-four, was $63,190 compared to $34,156 for those sixty-five and over and $24,795 for those ages fifteen to twenty-four.[6]

Debate exists over whether the middle years are, in fact, the prime of life, as family income data suggest, or a period of great stress and even depression. The middle years bring many physical and emotional changes, which may create confusion and anxiety. The man who saw himself as a "ladies' man" at twenty or thirty may, at forty, need to convince himself of his virility. The woman who loses her ability to "make men look twice" may have similar doubts about her attractiveness and sexuality. What's more, menopause brings on the loss of reproductive capacity and other emotional changes, which may challenge the woman's self-perception. Children growing up, leaving home, and getting married will likely stir emotions of both parents, who see their families changing and themselves aging.

The middle years are also filled with pressures to be successful and get ahead. For many people, "it's now or never." During this time, the prestigious position one wants to attain, the book he or she wants to write, the children he or she wants to have, or the stardom he or she yearns for may become a reality or simply remain a dream, never to be fulfilled. Supporting a comfortable life-style, paying for things such as college tuition and weddings, and planning for retirement add to economic pressures. Thus, the argument can be made that the middle years are rough—physically, socially, emotionally, and economically.

The opposite argument suggests that the middle years are a period of life when things are brightest. Income is highest, leisure time is greatest, childbearing responsibility is past, and opportunities exist as never before. Which view is correct—or is it possible that both are?

Michael Farrell and Stanley Rosenberg addressed this issue, comparing three hundred men entering middle age to men in their late twenties. Contrary to their expectations, they did not find evidence of a universal midlife crisis or signs of increased alienation or social disconnection.[7] The exception was among men in the lowest socioeconomic class. Men who were unskilled laborers gave evidence of personal disorganization and psychopathology as they approached middle age. Lower-middle-class men (skilled workers, clerical workers, small businessmen) showed a remarkable ability to ignore, distort, or deny information that chal-

[6] U.S. Bureau of the Census, *Current Population Reports,* Series P60-184, "Money Income of Households, Families and Persons in the United States: 1992," (Washington, DC: U.S. Government Printing Office, 1993), Table 17, pp. 50–51.

[7] Michael P. Farrell and Stanley D. Rosenberg, *Men at Midlife* (Boston: Auburn House, 1981).

lenged their world views. Professionals and middle-class executives exhibited neither denial patterns nor identity problems but reported satisfaction with work, family, and position in the community.

Some social scientists have referred to a **midlife transition** for men around age forty. This transition may go relatively smoothly or may involve considerable turmoil. The transition to an "empty nest" may or may not be an important factor for men. For example, the vast majority of fathers do not report distress or unhappiness when their children leave home. Some research has, however, suggested greater distress and unhappiness among fathers when the youngest child leaves home, particularly among farm families.[8] But most research has documented that the majority of families, farm or nonfarm, are not affected negatively when their children leave home. A greater stressor may be the unexpected return home of a young adult child.

What about women? Is the empty-nest (postparental) period of the family life course traumatic and unhappy? Not according to two psychologists who studied seven hundred women between young adulthood and old age.[9] Women in their early fifties rated their quality of life as higher than did younger or older women. This was their prime of life, a time of good health combined with greater autonomy and relational security.

The notion of the **empty-nest syndrome** as a period of depression, identity crisis, role loss, and lowered sense of well-being for females has little research support. The extent to which it occurs at all may vary by factors such as socioeconomic level and employment status. Dolores Borland hypothesized that, if an empty-nest syndrome does occur, it may occur to a greater degree in a particular cohort of white middle-class women because of the unique set of social circumstances in which they live and the unique set of family values and social norms concerning women's so-called proper roles.[10] Specifically, these women dedicate their lives selflessly to their families' needs and believe that to be feminine and happy is to be married and a mother. Lower- and upper-socioeconomic status women, Borland argued, are less likely to experience this syndrome. The former have had to work throughout their lives to help support their families, and the latter have developed other community roles, have the resources to find parental-role substitutes, and have smaller families, which lead them to the empty-nest stage at a younger age.

A study of the passage of U.S. women through thirteen years of midlife demonstrated a significant diversity in the occurrence of life events as well as in

---

[8] Robert A. Lewis, Robert J. Volk, and Stephen F. Duncan, "Stresses on Fathers and Family Relationships Related to Rural Youth Leaving and Returning Home," *Family Relations* 38 (April 1989): 174–181; and Pauline Boss, Debra Pearce-McCall, and Jan Greenberg, "Normative Loss in Mid-Life Families: Rural, Urban, and Gender Differences," *Family Relations* 36 (October 1987): 437–443.

[9] Valory Mitchell and Ravenna Helson, "Woman's Prime of Life," *Psychology of Women Quarterly* 14 (1990): 451–470.

[10] Dolores Cabic Borland, "A Cohort Analysis Approach to the Empty-Nest Syndrome Among Three Ethnic Groups of Women: A Theoretical Position," *Journal of Marriage and the Family* 44 (February 1982): 117–129.

their sequencing and spacing.[11] A large portion of these women experienced no transitions, at least with respect to marriage and the presence of children in the home. Two events, however, had detectable and important effects on their employment patterns and economic well-being: the launching of the last child and marital dissolution.

These two events were found to have opposite effects. The empty-nest transition (launching the last child) increased both labor market involvement and economic well-being, while marital dissolution (divorce and widowhood) decreased well-being. The sequence of these events made a difference, as well. If marital dissolution occurred first, the woman suffered a reduction in income while maintaining custody of the child. Recovery from this situation was difficult, even when benefits of an empty-nest transition were forthcoming. If the empty nest occurred first, the woman benefited economically as long as her marriage was kept intact.

The absence of children symbolizes the mother's new independence. Once the children are gone, many mothers form new nonfamilial relationships to fill the void. Many women in this age category become more active in civic and religious affairs, and an increasing number of wives and mothers become employed (see Chapter 4). This is also the time period when parents become grandparents.

GRANDPARENT STATUS

Grandparenting has become a middle-age as well as an old-age phenomenon, given the potential of being a grandparent for three or four decades of life. With the majority of men and women in U.S. society marrying in their mid-twenties and with many of them having children within the first year or two of marriage, parents may become grandparents in their forties. The rocking chair and the cane-carrying grandfather images seem grossly inappropriate. The reduction in family size, closer spacing of children, and women having their last children at a younger age have made the transition into grandparenthood a distinct status of the middle years, separate from one's own parenting years.

Two key demographic changes have shaped modern grandparenthood in U.S. society: increased life expectancy and changed fertility patterns. Because more people reach old age, more people experience grandparenthood as well as great- and great-great-grandparenthood. Consistent with grandparents, great-grandparents revealed in interviews that most found the role to be significant and emotionally fulfilling, providing a sense of personal and familial renewal, a diversion to their lives, and served a mark of longevity.[12]

---

[11] Ken R. Smith and Phyllis Moen, "Passage Through Midlife: Women's Changing Family Roles and Economic Well-Being," *The Sociological Quarterly* 29 (1988): 503–524. Note also Phyllis Moen, "Transition in Mid-Life: Women's Work and Family Roles in the 1970s," *Journal of Marriage and the Family* 53 (February 1991): 135–150.

[12] Kenneth J. Doka and Mary Ellen Mertz, "The Meaning and Significance of Great-Grandparenthood," *The Gerontologist* 28 (1988): 192–197.

U.S. Diversity: Farm, Rural Nonfarm, and Urban Adolescents' Relationships with Grandparents

Does living on a rural farm, living in a rural area but not on a farm, or living in an urban area affect how adolescents interact with their grandparents? Research has suggested that in urban areas, maternal grandparents are more prominent than paternal grandparents. This favored status of the mother's parents has been attributed to women's roles as "kin keepers."

What about grandparent relationships in rural areas? Researchers examined differences between rural farm and nonfarm families on the extent and quality of relationships between adolescents and their grandparents. They found that grandchildren in farm families live closer to their grandparents and have more contact with them when compared with nonfarm rural adolescents. This was particularly the case for paternal grandparents. Contact was mediated by proximity but proximity had little direct effect on the quality of their relationship.

Quality of the farm family grandchildren/grandparent relationships was higher with paternal grandparents than in nonfarm families. This greater prominence of paternal grandparents was said to reflect the more interdependent nature of farm family life which is male-centered with residence, work, and inheritance patterns acting together to promote a patrilineal bias. These paternal grandparent ties serve as a striking contrast to the prominence of the maternal grandmother in urban areas.

Source: Valerie King and Glen H. Elder, Jr., "American Children View Their Grandparents: Linked Lives Across Three Rural Generations," *Journal of Marriage and the Family* 57 (February 1995): 165–178.

It has been suggested that the grandparent role represents a double bind.[13] On the one hand, grandparents are helpful and supportive, act warmly toward their grandchildren, and serve as resources for knowledge of family heritage and affective bonds. On the other hand, grandparents often interfere in childrearing and provide children and grandchildren with unwelcomed advice.

Perhaps this double bind illustrates the "roleless role" idea and the confusion that centers around the appropriate expectations for grandparents. The kinship status of the grandparent includes role expectations to provide nurturance, assistance, and support to children and grandchildren. At the same time, no clear normative expectations exist as to specific rights, duties, and obligations or at what point assistance becomes interference. Perhaps grandparents, particularly middle-class ones, must construct roles for themselves as babysitters, surrogate parents, gift givers, crisis interveners, and the like. In contrast to middle-class grandparents, lower-class grandparents appear to be far more integrated into daily family life. The lower-class maternal grandmother frequently parents (socializes and nurtures)

---

[13] Jeanne L. Thomas, "The Grandparent Role: A Double Bind," *International Journal of Aging and Human Development* 31 (1990): 169–177.

Throughout most of the world, grandparents serve as a valuable family resource to their children and grandchildren. Grandparents can fulfill many roles: custodians of family history, mediators in family conflicts, friends, gift givers, child care providers, and significant others.

her grandchildren, engages in regular interaction, and feels a sense of obligation far more than simple contact between generations.

Grandparenthood appears to have different meanings for grandmothers and grandfathers. Sometimes, the grandparent role is depicted as maternal, with women, rather than men, feeling greater responsibility to their grandchildren. One study, for example, concluded that the grandfather role was more affectionate than functional.[14] For both black and white older men, levels of association with grandchildren and help exchanged were low; expressions of closeness and getting along were more characteristic of the relationship than interaction. The same study found greater centrality of the grandfather role among black than white men, as demonstrated by association with grandchildren, help given, feelings of closeness, and perceptions of getting along with grandchildren. These racial differences were said to be based on cultural distinctiveness and not a function of economic or structural factors.

14 Vira R. Kivett, "Centrality of the Grandfather Role Among Older Rural Black and White Men," *Journal of Gerontology* 46 (1991): S250–S258.

In contrast to grandfathers, grandmothers are likely to have high levels of interaction with and provide mutual assistance to grandchildren. Grandmothers are more likely than grandfathers to be regular providers of day care. National data of a youth cohort, for example, showed that over one-half of young mothers with children relied upon relatives for child care when they were employed, and the primary relative was the grandmother.[15] The number of hours of child care provided per week by grandmothers was substantial, even though one-third of these middle-age grandmothers were also employed. Like employed husbands and wives, who juggled their work schedules to care for children, so also grandmothers and their children juggled their work schedules to provide child care.

One underlying assumption of these patterns is that a relative, particularly the grandmother, is more emotionally committed to the child and will provide more loving care than nonrelatives. This assumption continues to be made, even today, when the availability of grandmother care seems to be declining while the need for infant and toddler care is increasing.

Given the frequency of divorce and remarriage, **stepgrandparents** are taking on new significance. Grandparenthood has been described as a "roleless role," but that description is even more apt for the grandparent by marriage rather than birth. Unlike grandparents, stepgrandparents have no biological tie and a shorter relationship time with newly acquired grandchildren. Thus, children have greater contact, more social involvement in personal and social roles, and stronger relationships with grandparents than stepgrandparents.[16]

Divorce/remarriage patterns not only affect stepgrandparents; they also have a major impact on grandparents. Many grandparents experience frustration in having infrequent interaction and even maintaining contact with their grandchildren. This is particularly true when the grandchildren reside with the son- or daughter-in-law rather than the son or daughter.

These frustrations have prompted a relatively new and increasingly frequent phenomenon, specifically, legal cases involving **grandparent/grandchild visitation rights.**[17] All fifty states now statutorily provide an avenue by which grandparents can petition the courts for visitation with their grandchildren over a parent's objections. Such visitation laws allow grandparents to petition for the opportunity to visit with a grandchild following the child's adoption by a stepparent, to visit with a grandchild who has been adopted by strangers, to visit with a child who has been

---

[15] Harriet B. Presser, "Some Economic Complexities of Child Care Provided by Grandmothers," *Journal of Marriage and the Family* 51 (August 1989): 581–591. Note also Margaret Platt Jendrik, "Grandparents Who Parent Their Grandchildren: Effects on Lifestyle," *Journal of Marriage and the Family* 55 (August 1993): 609–621.

[16] Carolyn S. Henry, Cindi Penor Ceglian, and Diane L. Ostrander, "The Transition to Stepgrandparenthood," *Journal of Divorce and Remarriage* 19 (1993): 25–44; and Carolyn S. Henry, Cindi Penor Ceglian, and D. Wayne Matthews, "The Role Behaviors, Role Meanings, and Grandmothering Styles of Grandmothers and Stepgrandmothers: Perceptions of the Middle Generation," *Journal of Divorce and Remarriage* 17 (1992): 1–22.

[17] Edward M. Burns, "Grandparent Visitation Rights: Is It Time for the Pendulum to Fall?" *Family Law Quarterly* 25 (Spring 1991): 59–81.

surrendered to an agency for adoption, and to force visitation with a grandchild living with his married parents in an intact home over the objection of those parents.

With the changes that take place over the life course, great-grandparenthood, rather than grandparenthood, is emerging as the familial status associated with old age. It is likely that this status is even more roleless than the described middle-class grandparent status. Great-grandparents must construct the types of roles and determine the behaviors they wish to perform in their ascribed great-grandparent status.

FAMILIES OF LATER LIFE AND PEOPLE WHO ARE AGED

Growth of the elderly population

Since the turn of the century, one of the more significant changes in family and marital relationships has been **life expectancy.** People are living longer and more people are living, both of which have increased the number of older persons in the United States today (see Figure 15-1). An early marriage age, the absence of divorce, and a longer life have combined to increase the length of marriage, the number of generations of family living, and the kin network.

A person born in 1992 could expect to live 75.8 years. For white males, the life expectancy was 73.2 years and for white females, 79.8 years (see Table 15-2). Life expectancies for black males and females—65.0 and 73.9, respectively—were considerably lower than those for whites. Those individuals who reach age sixty-five can expect to live an average of 17.5 more years (15.5 for white men; 19.3 for white women; 13.5 for black men; and 17.4 for black women).

There has been relatively little increase in the life expectancy of older persons since the turn of the century. In 1900, the person who reached age sixty-five could expect to live until age 76.9. In 1992, the person who reached age sixty-five could expect to live until age 82.5, or slightly more than five years longer than his or her counterpart of ninety-two years earlier. What is significant is that more people are living longer, as fewer die in infancy and childhood. In 1992, approximately 75 percent of the men and 86 percent of the women in the sixty-five-year-old cohort actually reached age sixty-five.[18] In 1900, only 39 percent of the men and 44 percent of the women actually reached age sixty-five. Thus, there has only been a relatively small increase in life expectancy, but more people are living longer.

In 1994, approximately 33.2 million U.S. citizens were ages sixty-five and over.[19] This group comprises about 12.7 percent of the population of the United States, and its size has been expanding far more rapidly than the nation's popula-

---

[18] U.S. Bureau of the Census, *Statistical Abstract of the United States, 1995,* 115th ed. (Washington, DC: U.S. Government Printing Office, 1995), no. 115, p. 86.

[19] Ibid., no. 14, p. 15.

Figure 15-1

Growth of population, ages sixty-five and older, by sex: 1900–2020

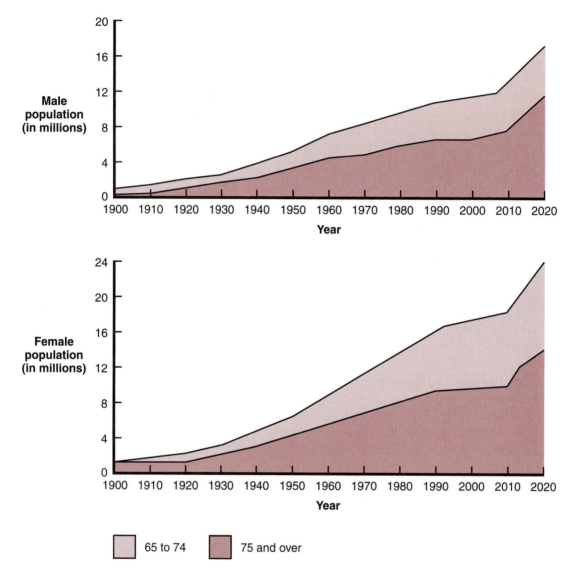

Source: U.S. Bureau of the Census, *Current Population Reports*

tion as a whole. While the number of U.S. citizens has increased by 28.1 percent since 1970 (203.2 million to 260.3 million), the number of people ages sixty-five and over has increased by 66.0 percent (20 million to 33.2 million). The continual increase in the over-sixty-five age group has not been due to an increase in the **life span** (the biological age limit) but rather to an increase in the number of people living. If birthrates decline or remain stable, people over sixty-five will likely constitute an even larger proportion of the U.S. population for decades to come.

Table 15-2

Life expectancy, by race, age, and sex: 1992

Age	Total	White		Black	
		Male	Female	Male	Female
At birth	75.8	73.2	79.8	65.0	73.9
5	71.6	68.9	75.4	61.4	70.3
10	66.6	64.0	70.4	56.5	65.4
15	61.7	59.1	65.5	51.7	60.4
20	56.9	54.3	60.6	47.2	55.6
25	52.2	49.7	55.7	42.9	50.8
30	47.5	45.1	50.9	38.7	46.1
35	42.9	40.5	46.0	34.5	41.5
40	38.3	36.0	41.2	30.5	37.1
45	33.8	31.5	36.5	26.7	32.7
50	29.3	27.1	31.9	23.0	28.5
55	25.1	22.9	27.5	19.5	24.5
60	21.1	19.1	23.2	16.3	20.8
65	17.5	15.5	19.3	13.5	17.4
70	14.2	12.4	15.6	11.0	14.3
75	11.2	9.6	12.2	8.9	11.4
80	8.5	7.2	9.2	6.8	8.6
85 and over	6.2	5.3	6.6	5.1	6.3

Source: U.S. Bureau of the Census, *Statistical Abstract of the United States, 1995,* 115th ed.
(Washington, DC: U.S. Government Printing Office, 1995), no. 116, p. 87.

Throughout history, older persons have played significant roles. Men, in particular, have often received increased status, prestige, and deference with age. In the United States and apparently in modernized societies, in general, old age does not bring increased prestige and status but rather negative perceptions and definitions. Frequently, old age is defined as a time of dependency and declining productivity and vitality. Elderly persons' socioeconomic status is generally determined by their achievements earlier in life; if the achievements were limited and provisions for these later years were inadequate, opportunities for a full, meaningful life will be limited.

It is not difficult to be sensitive to the aging process and the people experiencing it. Community newspapers are filled with pictures of couples celebrating their fiftieth wedding anniversaries, announcements of community and business leaders retiring, polls showing attitudinal differences between the old and the young, and of course, obituary notices. All these serve as reminders of the social dimension of aging and of the position of the older person in society.

Global Diversity: The "Long Living" Abkhasians of Southern Russia

The Abkhasians, who live in a rough mountainous region in southern Russia, are said to have a disproportionate number of people who live to be over 100 years old and some who live to be 120. Many scientists, however, have questioned the authenticity of these ages. Nevertheless, whether they are 70 or 107, how does one account for their good eyesight, having their own teeth, little loss of hearing, few, if any, cases of mental illness or cancer, rare hospitalization, and their longevity?

Some accounts attribute these factors to their work habits and their physical daily labor as herders and farmers, to their taking walks of more than two miles a day, and to swimming in the mountain streams. Others claim they are due to their diet and the value they attach to staying slim, eating lots of fruits and vegetables, and consuming few fatty substances.

Explanations of longevity related to family life focus on (1) the family status accorded to them, and (2) their sex practices. As to family status, Abkhasians are said to gain status throughout the life course with no self-devaluation and few abrupt changes in their lives. The old are granted certain rights and privileges not accorded to the young. They feel needed by their children and grandchildren and enjoy secure roles and statuses in extended families.

As to their sexual practices, the norms of the culture call for sexual relations to be postponed until after 30, the traditional age at marriage. Writings suggest it was even considered unmanly for a new husband to exercise his sexual rights on his wedding night. Sex was a pleasure to be regulated for the sake of one's health, and like a good wine, to get better with age. Reports exist of Abkhasian men fathering children at the age of 100.

Adapted from: Harold G. Cox, *Later Life: The Realities of Aging* (Saddle River, NJ: Prentice-Hall), 4th ed., 1996, pp. 70–74.

Social gerontology, the study of older persons and the aging process, as well as the closely related field, the sociology of aging, have both been concerned with the social definition of who is thought to be old; their interaction patterns and behaviors; the expectations that are imposed upon them; their age, sex, place of residence, and other demographic factors; as well as the problems and needs that they have living in society. Within this framework, the family of later life has taken on particular significance when one studies these and other factors of concern to people who are aged.

Marital status in the later years

Later-life families are characterized by continuity and change as they experience marriage, divorce, widowhood, remarriage, childlessness, grandparenthood, sibling relationships, and family caregiving. In 1994, there were an estimated 12.7

Table 15-3

Marital status of men and women, ages 65 and over, March 1994
(percent distribution)

Marital Status	Age of men		Age of women	
	65–74	75 and over	65–74	75 and over
Never married	4.9%	4.4%	3.8%	5.0%
Married, spouse present	77.9	70.4	52.4	26.2
Married, spouse absent	2.3	1.7	1.9	1.7
Widowed	8.8	20.4	34.2	63.3
Divorced	6.1	3.1	7.7	3.8
Total	100.0	100.0	100.0	100.0

Source: U.S. Bureau of the Census, *Current Population Reports,* Series P20-484, Arlene F. Saluter, "Marital Status and Living Arrangements: March 1994" (Washington, DC: U.S. Government Printing Office, 1996), Table 1, p. 1.

million men and 18.0 million women in the United States who were sixty-five years old and over. Eighty percent of the men and 54 percent of the women ages sixty-five to seventy-four were married. Of those ages seventy-five and over, 72 percent of the men and 28 percent of the women were married (see Table 15-3).

A relatively small percentage of men and women in these age categories were never married or divorced (see Figure 15-2). However, among these age groups, widowed status becomes increasingly frequent. Less than one in ten men ages sixty-five to seventy-four and one in five ages seventy-five and over were widowers, but more than one in three women ages sixty-five to seventy-four and nearly two-thirds ages seventy-five and over were widows. (Widows and widowers will be discussed later in this chapter.)

Married couples comprise a high proportion of this over-sixty-five group. Of those couples in first marriages, most had previously celebrated silver wedding anniversaries (25 years), and many had celebrated or would soon celebrate golden anniversaries (50 years). Over the years, these couples have shared many joys and weathered many crises. One rarely reads about divorce or incompatibility among these couples, but such problems do exist. Even when unhappy in their marriages, the experiences of their years, the lives and activities of their children, and perhaps the lack of realistic alternatives to the marriage keep the older couple together.

Marital and family relationships are often proclaimed to be the primary sources of social involvement, companionship, fulfillment, and happiness for people who are elderly. Existing studies have suggested that marriage has a positive effect on psychological well-being among people who are elderly (particularly

Figure 15-2

Percentage of persons ages sixty-five and older, by marital status and sex: 1994

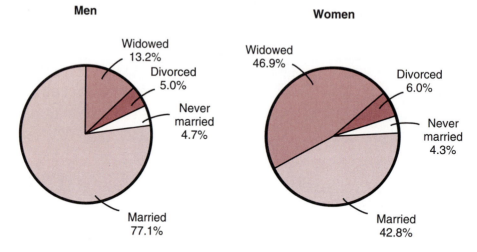

Source: Adapted from U.S. Bureau of the Census, *Statistical Abstract of the United States: 1995.* 115th ed. (Washington, DC: U.S. Government Printing Office, 1995), no. 59, p. 55.

when compared to people who are divorced and widowed)[20]and, as shown earlier, that marital satisfaction may be higher for married elderly people than for married people in the intermediate stages of the family life course.

What about the approximately 10 percent of the elderly who never married or are divorced? How important are families to them? Studies have shown that geographic proximity to siblings, particularly same-sex siblings, exerts a positive influence on life satisfaction and well-being.[21] Another study, based on two national samples, concluded that unmarried men and women were more isolated from neighbors and friends than from family. Men were somewhat more likely to be isolated from family than were women.[22] Women were more likely than men to see relatives and maintain contacts with them by phone.

Interestingly, one hedge against loneliness for the unmarried was found to be dating.[23] Older women derived increased prestige and status rewards from dating,

---

[20] Walter R. Gove and Hee-Choon Shin, "The Psychological Well-Being of Divorced and Widowed Men and Women," *Journal of Family Issues* 10 (March 1989): 122–144.

[21] Jerrie L. McGhee, "The Effects of Siblings on the Life Satisfaction of the Rural Elderly," *Journal of Marriage and the Family* 47 (February 1985): 85–91; and Shirley L. O'Bryant, "Sibling Support and Older Widows' Well-Being," *Journal of Marriage and the Family* 50 (February 1988): 173–183.

[22] Pat M. Keith, "Isolation of the Unmarried in Later Life," *Family Relations* 35 (July 1986): 389–395.

[23] Kris Bulcroft and Margaret O'Connor, "The Importance of Dating Relationships on Quality of Life for Older Persons," *Family Relations* 35 (July 1986): 397–401; and Richard A. Bulcroft and Kris A. Bulcroft, "The Nature and Functions of Dating in Later Life," *Research on Aging* 13 (June 1991): 244–260.

and older men stressed the importance of dating as a means for self-disclosure. For most persons, greater emphasis was placed on the compassionate nature of such relationships than as a means for marriage. As one seventy-three-year-old woman stated:

> It was a lot harder when my boyfriend, Ted, died than when my husband of 40 years passed away. I needed Ted in a way I never needed my husband. Ted and I spent so much time together; he was all I had. And at my age I know it will be hard to find someone else… but, well, let's face it; how many men want a 73-year-old woman?[24]

Intergenerational relationships

Intergenerational relationships encompass a wide variety of interaction patterns between family members of different generations. Chapters 13 and 14 focused primarily on the generations of young children and their parents. This chapter focuses more on parents (adult children) and their parents. Parents in these middle years have sometimes been referred to as the "sandwich generation," squeezed between the demands and needs of their children and those of their aging parents.

An overview of the dominant themes between these adult children and their parents concluded that, after years of investigation, there is no evidence that older people are alienated from their children.[25] Relationships between adult children and their older/aging parents are characterized by reciprocal support. These family members have frequent face-to-face contacts, keep in touch by phone and correspondence, exchange care during illnesses, give money and gifts, run errands, prepare meals, give emotional support and affection, and, in general, promote one another's well-being (happiness, satisfaction, morale). Again, note that the exchange patterns are mutually supportive. Contact, support, and so forth are seldom one way but are instead reciprocal interactions.

In spite of older people not being alienated from their children and mutually supportive relationships between adult children and their parents exist, national data indicates that one-half of Americans do not *routinely* engage in giving or receiving relationships with their parents, and only one in ten are engaged in extensive exchange relationships.[26] This general pattern varied considerably, however, by demographic characteristics and the needs and resources of each generation. Aging parents are likely to be involved in giving and/or receiving aid with at

---

[24] Ibid., p. 401.

[25] Jay A. Mancini and Rosemary Blieszner, "Aging Parents and Adult Children: Research Themes in Intergenerational Relations," *Journal of Marriage and the Family* 51 (May 1989): 275–290. Note also Teresa M. Cooney and Peter Uhlenberg, "Support from Parents over the Life Course: The Adult Child's Perspective," *Social Forces* 71 (September 1992): 63–84.

[26] Dennis P. Hogan, David J. Eggebeen, and Clifford C. Clogg, "The Structure of Intergenerational Exchanges in American Families," *American Journal of Sociology* 98 (May 1993): 1428–1458.

Members of the "sandwich generation" may find themselves caring for their young grandchildren as well as their elderly parents. Family members—particularly wives, mothers, and daughters—serve as caregivers and primary sources of support and affection for both the young and the old.

least one of their adult children, and elderly parents are assisted more often in situations of poor health. Black and Mexican American parents receive less assistance than white parents from grandparents, largely because they have, on average, more siblings competing for this support. On the other hand, more adult children can mean higher levels of support for the minority grandparents. Family support does provide an important security net for family members (old and young) during periods of high need (the presence of preschool children or when disability occurs).

Who is likely to provide a disproportionate amount of this support, particularly to older parents? As one might guess, significant differences exist by gender. Daughters, far more than daughters-in-law, not only provide more support, but do so for different reasons, than do sons.[27] Daughters are most motivated to provide support by intergenerational affection and altruism. Sons, on the other hand, are more motivated by principles of obligation, familiarity, and self-interest. They contribute to the support of their parents more out of an expectation of financial reward implicit in the endorsement of intergenerational inheritance than out of sentiment. Affection is a stronger predictor of support when mothers are the recipients, and inheritance is a more salient predictor when fathers are the recipients of

[27] Merril Silverstein, Tonya M. Parrott, and Vern L. Bengston, "Factors That Predispose Middle-Aged Sons and Daughters to Provide Social Support to Older Persons," *Journal of Marriage and the Family* 57 (May 1995): 465–475; and Deborah M. Merrill, "Daughters-in-Law as Caregivers to the Elderly," *Research on Aging* 15 (March 1993): 70–91.

care. Irrespective of motives, the notion that adult children abandon their elderly relatives or fail to meet their needs is basically a myth.

Another myth appears to be that high levels of conflict exist among generations who live together. Certain circumstances, such as financial dependency and unemployment, seem to increase parent/child conflict, but episodes of open disagreement and arguing occur much less often than episodes of enjoyable leisure time. Coresidency results in surprisingly low levels of conflict between parents and their resident adult children.[28] Even the parents' health and dependency are not related to parent/child conflict. Most parents and adult children, including those who live together, get along quite harmoniously.

What about people who are elderly and childless? The value of children to their elderly parents in providing emotional, material, financial, and other support has been widely asserted and empirically supported. However, one study of childless elderly people demonstrated levels of well-being that matched and sometimes exceeded those of elderly parents.[29] The childless group was more financially secure (see Chapter 13 on childless couples, as well) and in better health; parents, however, tended to be surrounded by a greater number of friends and have more general satisfaction with life. By and large, this study and others showed that people who are elderly, whether parents or childless, are very satisfied with family, friendships, and life. They are less satisfied with health and income, two problems that will be discussed later in this chapter.

Living arrangements among the elderly

As persons reach and pass the age of sixty-five, an increasing number retire, suffer decreases in income, and experience the loss by death of spouses and siblings. Where do people of this age category live? Are they institutionalized? Do they live with children? Do they live alone? Living arrangements depend greatly on the sex to which one is referring.

In 1994, three-fourths of the men ages sixty-five and over lived with their spouses compared to 41 percent of the women (see Table 15-4). More women than men lived alone (40 percent versus 16 percent) or lived with someone other than a spouse (19 percent versus 9 percent).

Many older people who do not live with spouses live with children or other relatives. A situation of this nature may be a matter of choice or of necessity. Where parents and children elect to live together, the arrangements frequently work out to the satisfaction of both. If a woman is employed, her mother or moth-

---

28 William S. Aquilino and Khalil R. Supple, "Parent-Child Relations and Parent's Satisfaction with Living Arrangements When Adult Children Live at Home," *Journal of Marriage and the Family* 53 (February 1991): 13–27; and J. Jill Suitor and Karl Pillemer, "Explaining Intergenerational Conflict When Adult Children and Elderly Parents Live Together," *Journal of Marriage and the Family* 50 (November 1988): 1037–1047.

29 Judith Rempel, "Childless Elderly: What Are They Missing?" *Journal of Marriage and the Family* 47 (May 1985): 343–348.

Table 15-4

Characteristics of persons ages sixty-five years and over, by sex: 1970 and 1994

Characteristics	1970		1994	
	Male	Female	Male	Female
Total (in millions)	8.3	11.5	13.5	19.7
Percent of population	8.5%	11.1%	10.6%	14.8%
Percent below poverty level	20.2%	29.2%	7.9%	15.2%
Family status (by percent)				
In families	79.2%	58.5%	81.3%	57.8%
Non-family householders	14.9	35.2	17.1	41.1
Secondary individuals	2.4	1.9	1.6	1.1
Residents of institutions	3.6	4.4	(n/a)	(n/a)
Years of school completed				
8 years or less	61.5%	56.1%	23.3%	21.5%
1–4 years of high school	25.0	32.0	43.7	53.6
1 or more years of college	13.5	11.9	33.0	24.9
Labor-force participation (by percent)				
Employed	25.9%	9.4%	16.2%	8.8%
Not in labor force	74.1	90.6	83.8	91.2
Living arrangements (by percent)				
Living in household	95.5%	95.0%	99.9	99.8%
Living alone	14.1	33.8	16.0	40.2
Spouse present	69.9	33.9	75.1	41.0
Living with someone else	11.5	27.4	8.8	18.6
Not in household	4.5	5.0	0.1	0.2

Source: U.S. Bureau of the Census, *Statistical Abstract of the United States, 1995,* 115th ed. (Washington, DC: U.S. Government Printing Office, 1995, nos. 14 and 48, pp. 15 and 47.

er-in-law is likely to assume much of the responsibility of the household. Babysitting, lawn care, cooking, and other daily tasks are often functions that an older person can satisfactorily perform. If, however, the arrangement is not one of choice but of necessity, difficulty may arise. Frequently, the relationship is unsatisfactory both for the aging parents and for the children, and in some instances, the problems extend to the grandchildren.

The pattern of the elderly living with children or other relatives was found to vary by ethnicity.[30] Chinese and Japanese Americans are more likely than their

[30] Yoshinori Kamo and Min Zhou, "Living Arrangements of Elderly Chinese and Japanese in the United States," *Journal of Marriage and the Family* 56 (August 1994): 544–558.

white counterparts to live in extended-family households, particularly in their *ever-married* children's homes. This appears to be greatly influenced by the traditional value of filial responsibility. Living with *never-married* children or other relatives is attributed more to specific adaptive strategies of old age than to the continuation of a cultural tradition. While the impact of immigrant culture on elderly living arrangements is significantly reduced through acculturation, even those born in the United States adhere to the cultural traditions of children having an obligation to assist and care for their aging parents.

Another living arrangement that is frequently satisfactory is for the aging parents and the married children to have separate but geographically close residences, which supports maintaining close relationships. Many parents prefer to be independent and want their children to allow them to remain so. This arrangement permits both generations to give favors or suggestions with fewer threatening feelings. In addition, parents and children can share interests and life-styles without having the constant physical presence of one another. Unfortunately, census data are not available on the number or percentage of persons in the later years who maintain residences separate from but close to their children.

An estimated 5 percent of the population of men and women sixty-five years of age and over live in long-term care institutions, primarily nursing homes. About 20 percent of all persons eighty-five years of age and older live in institutions, and over a lifetime, about one in four persons will spend some time in an institution. As a result of differing mortality rates between the sexes, women not only greatly outnumber men among the older population, in general, but among the population living in institutions.

Figures such as these have supported the idea that (1) most people who are elderly are not in nursing homes or long-term care institutions, and (2) most elderly are not abandoned by their families. Even those people who are institutionalized are disproportionately drawn from those who are childless, widowed, and living alone.

COMMON PROBLEMS OF PEOPLE WHO ARE AGED

Health and care

As already suggested, people who are aged have definite problems, one of which is health and care. During these later years, a disproportionate number of people are isolated, disabled, sick, or in poor health. Some type of health problem almost invariably accompanies old age. Sometimes, hospitalization is required, which raises a range of issues: medical payments, visiting patterns, care for the residence of the hospitalized, and, on occasion, legal matters.

Research confirmed the preference for and the importance of family members and adult children, particularly daughters, as caregivers for noninstitutionalized elderly people. Daughters serve as caregivers to dependent mothers and self-sufficient elderly mothers, as well. One study found that caregiving was an intensification of a preexisting pattern of aid giving, which is evident in female intergenerational relationships.[31]

Findings such as these have led many to question the popular notion that families today are less willing than those of the past to care for their elderly and perhaps impaired family members. This notion, referred to as the *myth of abandonment,* has received little scientific support; indeed, there is much evidence to the contrary. National surveys showed that informal caregiving by families was the dominant mode, by far, of providing care to people who are aged, in general, and to people who are functionally disabled, more specifically.[32] People who are functionally disabled may require assistance with personal care (bathing, eating, toileting), mobility (from room to room or in and out of chairs or beds), and daily living tasks (shopping, cleaning, cooking).

Are caregiving tasks such as these defined as a burden and does it produce stress? Common logic would suggest it is and does and an abundance of literature documents the physical, emotional, financial, and interpersonal costs experienced by family members caring for parents with a disability. Exchange theory, too, suggests that if an elderly infirmed parent requires much and can return little, stress will be high. Support was found to exist for this idea in that reciprocity by impaired mothers significantly reduced the stress and burden experienced by caregiving daughters.[33] The greater the number of reciprocal tasks the elder was able to perform, the lower the reported stress and burden of the primary caregiver. When tasks performed by the primary caregiver increased, both stress and burden were greater. Interestingly, reciprocity did not affect the satisfaction of the elderly parent. Explanations given were that the investments that elderly mothers made in their children over the life course may have been perceived as compensation and that mothers may feel they are reciprocating to the best of their abilities even though these abilities may be limited.

Family caregiving does not seem to extend to multigenerational families. A study of four-generational families found that ties extended only to aging parents who cared for their now adult children.[34] Consistent with other studies, the closest relationships were between mothers and daughters. In some families, such ties extended to three generations, but beyond two generations was a rarity. Ties weaken as the family line lengthens. Three- and four-generation families often have large numbers of members, but close ties among them are few. In most cases, the arrangement could not be called an extended-family caregiving system.

---

[31] Alexis J. Walker and Clara C. Pratt, "Daughters' Help to Mothers: Intergenerational Aid versus Caregiving," *Journal of Marriage and the Family* 53 (February 1991): 3–12.

[32] Pamela Doty, "Family Care of the Elderly: The Role of Public Policy," *The Milbank Quarterly* 64 (1986): 34–75.

[33] Jeffrey W. Dwyer, Gary R. Lee, and Thomas B. Jankowski, "Reciprocity, Elder Satisfaction, and Caregiver Stress and Burden: The Exchange of Aid in the Family Caregiving Relationship," *Journal of Marriage and the Family* 56 (February 1994): 35–43.

[34] Martha Baum and Mary Page, "Caregiving and Multigenerational Families," *The Gerontologist* 31 (1991): 762–769.

Children's problems

A second difficulty is a reversal of the common theme that elderly parents place stress and burden on their adult offspring. That is, do adult children's problems affect the well-being of their elderly parents?

Evidence has suggested that they do. A national survey of elderly people in Canada demonstrated that parents whose adult children have mental, physical, or stress-related problems experience greater depression than parents whose children do not have these problems.[35] While health status, described earlier, appears to be the most powerful predictor of distress in the elderly, their children's major problems have a direct and profound effect, as well.

Income and standard of living

In economic terms, people who are aged remain a sizable segment of the U.S. poor, particularly people who do not live in family households. Yet in 1993, the percentage of elderly people living below the poverty level was about half of what it was in 1970 (see Table 15-4). Social Security, retirement plans, tax allowances, and other benefits have succeeded in reducing poverty for the segment of the population over age sixty-five.

For those elderly people who do not enjoy improved economic status, the poverty rate varies dramatically by race, sex, and marital status. As of 1993, African Americans (black females, in particular) had a poverty rate nearly three times and Hispanic Americans more than two times that of white males and females in the sixty-and-over age category (10.7 percent white; 21.4 percent Hispanic; 28.0 percent black).[36] Marriage generally protects elderly people from poverty; thus, elderly people who were widowed or divorced all had poverty rates significantly higher than those of married people. And among this age group, non-married categories included women predominantly.

Madonna Mayer showed how the supposedly gender-neutral eligibility and benefit structures of Social Security, private pensions, and personal pensions such as Individual Retirement Accounts (IRAs)—three major retirement income programs—all are structured around gender.[37] How?

1. Retirement income is linked to waged labor, which is itself gender based.

2. Nonwaged reproductive labor, performed predominantly by women, is not recognized as labor.

---

[35] Karl Pillemer and J. Jill Suitor, "Will I Ever Escape My Child's Problems? Effects of Adult Children's Problems on Elderly Parents," *Journal of Marriage and the Family* 53 (August 1991): 585–594.

[36] U.S. Bureau of the Census, *Statistical Abstract of the United States, 1995,* 115th ed. (Washington, DC: U.S. Government Printing Office, 1995), no. 747, p. 481; and U.S. Bureau of the Census, *Current Population Reports, Special Studies,* P23-178, "Sixty-Five Plus in America" (Washington, DC: U.S. Government Printing Office, 1992), Table 4-4, p. 4–13.

[37] Madonna Harrington Mayer, "Family Status and Poverty among Older Women: The Gender Distribution of Retirement Income in the United States," *Social Problems* 37 (November 1990): 551–563.

News Item: "Casserole Women"

In South Florida's retirement communities, women in pursuit of husbands are called "casserole women" because they descend on newly eligible men bearing food and sympathy. Men who live to an old age and want to date have little trouble finding partners.

One seventy-five-year-old retired speechwriter said he has lots of fun and to prove it, pulled from his wallet photographs of a woman leaning on his shoulder and another of a blond woman talking on the telephone. A seventy-eight-year-old ex-chef spurned women his own age and said he doesn't take to the old because they have no pep, no sex life.

Yet the intense shortage of unmarried older men is not without its difficulties. Unattached men report periods of intense loneliness while women often find a supportive community of other women in similar situations. The chairman of a governing board of one of the retirement communities said that there are two basic social units in retirement communities—couples and widows. Single men aren't a viable entity as a group. Widowers are so scarce that the single man becomes the "odd man out" in retired life.

An attorney who often draws up prenuptial agreements to preserve the separation of assets said that older people date and marry with few illusions. They come in holding hands, saying, "Dearie this" and "Dolly that"—but "Don't touch my money."

Source: Wall Street Journal, 22 April 1986.

3. Old-age pension schemes are grounded in a conceptualization of family status as permanent—having a male breadwinner—despite insurmountable evidence that family status is transient. That is, with age, women are increasingly likely to become single.

All three factors contribute to disproportionate impoverishment among older women.

Despite gender inequality, overall, the quality of life of elderly people in the United States has improved dramatically, particularly when compared to children. A growing number of elderly are demanding and getting what they want, whereas the needs of many children are being ignored. As of 1993, whereas 12.2 percent of all persons age 65 and over in the United States were below the poverty level, nearly one in four children under age eighteen (23 percent) were so listed. By race/ethnicity, this included 17.8 percent of white children, 40.9 percent of Hispanic children, and 46.1 percent of black children.[38] For mother-only families, figures for children under age six living below the poverty level increased to 46.2 for white children, 68.6 for Hispanic children, and 69.2 for black children (review section in Chapter 8 under single parents and poverty). This contrast in econom-

---

[38] *Statistical Abstract of the United States,* 1995, no. 747, p. 481.

ic well-being between the elderly and preschool age children and those under age eighteen can be partly attributed to the expansion of Social Security and noncash benefits, such as Medicare. The politics of this contrast reveals the power of special interest groups, as determined by wealth and size. Children don't vote nor do they have much financial clout.

An argument could be made that elderly people in the United States are overall not as deficient in economic resources as the image generally presented suggests. While average income declines sharply with age, so do average expenditures. The ownership of domestic assets such as a family home, Social Security, retirement plans, savings, and the coverage of major health care costs through Medicare, makes it possible for most people who are elderly to enjoy a "comfortable" standard of living.

Abuse and neglect

A fourth problem facing the elderly is abuse and neglect. This may be one of the newest social problems in the United States in that little or no information prior to the late 1970s was published about domestic mistreatment of the elderly in their homes by relatives or other domestic caregivers. (This issue will be examined more thoroughly in Chapter 16.)

Extreme caution must be taken in categorizing people who are aged as a homogeneous population. To be sure, dependency, sickness, isolation, and abuse occur frequently among elderly people. Nonetheless, a sizable proportion of these people have few health problems, carry on active lives with families and friends, and continue to make major economic and social contributions to their communities and society.

SOCIALIZATION IN LATER LIFE

Tremendous emphasis has been given to children and youth in socialization literature, and consequently the resocialization needs of the aged have largely been ignored and overshadowed. In contrast to people who are aged, children receive much of their socialization within the family and from peers, schools, jobs, and the community. But what socializing agents direct the aged? Where is the training for retirement? Where is the training for widowhood? Where is the training to prepare for illness and death? Where is the training regarding the narrowing of social relationships?

In many ways, U.S. society overlooks the fact that persons over sixty-five are social beings, that their world is maintained and meaning is found through interaction with others. The previous chapter clarifies the primary importance of the socialization process and defines and redefines the self, the extent and nature of friendship ties, association with significant others, involvement in groups of reference, and social interaction, in general. Why should these factors be less important to persons over age sixty-five than to those under age twenty? In fact, one could argue that social relationships take on increased importance as persons move outside of their occupational spheres and as they experience the deaths of their peers.

Intimacy and familiarity characterize the family system and make it highly suitable for fulfilling many of the needs, services, and interaction patterns of the individual members. Even when the family system is absent or when persons have no living kin, older people tend to substitute for missing relatives by converting close friends into quasi-kin.[39] *Fictive kin* for the elderly serve in much the same way as the fictive kin described in Chapter 8 among families in poverty. These nonrelatives serve as meaningful kin components of their social networks and as a valuable resource in meeting specific needs of elderly people.

It should be noted that family factors do not operate independently of the culture in which families exist. To avoid having people who are aged become "socially disabled," there must be congruence between the cultural goals and structural opportunities that society provides. The effectiveness of the family as a resource is largely contingent on the values and services of the larger society: job opportunities, leisure-time activities, health care, clarity of roles, perception of the aged as fulfilling valuable functions, and socializing and resocializing opportunities appropriate to the later stage of the life cycle.

RETIREMENT

One major issue in retirement involves resocializing men and women to new roles and life-styles. Traditionally, men assumed the major economic responsibility for their families, and their lives revolved around work/employment roles. Thus, it followed that the literature on retirement focused heavily on men. Women's retirement was less studied because it was not perceived to constitute a salient social issue. With the dramatic increase in the labor force employment of women and the growing proportion of women retirees, studies of the preparation for and effects of retirement on both sexes are appearing with increasing frequency.[40]

Robert Atchley views retirement as an event, as a role, and as a series of phases.[41] As an *event,* retirement occurs at a specific time and may involve a ceremonial rite of passage. As a *role,* it involves the right to economic support without holding a job and duties associated with managing one's own life and living within one's income. As a *series of phases,* it involves ways in which retirement is approached, taken on, and relinquished. Among others, these phases include pre-

---

[39] Hazel MacRae, "Fictive Kin as a Component of the Social Networks of Older People," *Research on Aging* 14 (June 1992): 226–247.

[40] Kathleen F. Slevin and C. Ray Wingrove, "Women in Retirement: A Review and Critique of Empirical Research Since 1976," *Sociological Quarterly* 65 (February 1995): 1–21.

[41] Robert C. Atchley, *Social Forces and Aging,* 7th ed. (Belmont, CA: Wadsworth, 1994), Chapter 9, pp. 297–302.

retirement (gearing up for job separation), honeymoon (an active euphoric period), disenchantment (a letdown period), reorientation (taking stock and pulling oneself together), retirement routine (mastering available time and managing one's affairs), and termination of retirement (return to a job, illness, and disability).

Most family-related studies of retired men and women have paralleled the findings of a study done in rural Iowa.[42] There, elderly people were well integrated into kinship networks. Satisfaction with family life was high for both sexes. Retired elderly people were neither abandoned nor neglected by their families; in fact, these elderly turned to family members rather than to formal support services. Children and siblings played a special role in support. Retired females had significantly more contact with siblings and children than did males. Overall, personal background characteristics of health, financial status, age, length of retirement, and marital status affected both the quantity and quality of kinship relations.

Retirement appears neither to threaten nor benefit marital quality. Both retired husbands and employed husbands were found to be comparable in levels of marital complaints.[43]

As indicated previously, with the increased employment of women, their retirement is likely to take on increased significance and, in many ways, parallel the experiences and issues traditionally faced by men. One study of 1,530 retired residents of Washington state found that retirement was not materially different for women than for men.[44] The idea that retirement is less stressful for women was not supported. In fact, women reported somewhat lower levels of satisfaction with retirement than men. Reasons given include their lower incomes and, if they were widows or divorced, their lower probability of getting married. Regardless of gender, people in good health and those with high incomes were most likely to express satisfaction with retirement.

Irrespective of the reasons for retirement, it seems likely it will require major role readjustments for both sexes. Health, income, status, and feelings of self-worth often tend to decrease at the time of retirement, and the problems are compounded upon the death of a spouse.

DYING AND DEATH

Death is an inescapable event, one that will occur within all family and kin networks. Certainly, the loss of those one loves most intensely—parent, spouse, child, or other family member—causes tremendous pain. Few relationships are more intimate and few groups more primary than those of marriages and families.

---

[42] Lorraine T. Dorfman and Carol E. Mertens, "Kinship Relations in Retired Rural Men and Women," *Family Relations* 39 (April 1990): 166–173.

[43] David J. Ekerdt and Barbara H. Vinick, "Marital Complaints in Husband-Working and Husband-Retired Couples," *Research on Aging* 13 (September 1991): 364–382.

[44] Karen Seccombe and Gary L. Lee, "Gender Differences in Retirement Satisfaction and Its Antecedents," *Research on Aging* 8 (September 1986): 426–440.

Case Example:
An African American Widow and Grandmother

After 38 years of married life, Phyllis has been a widow for four years. She and her husband had five children and today at age 60, she is the proud grandmother of eight grandchildren. She is currently employed as a special education teacher. Following are thoughts she shared.

"It was very hard for me around the time of my husband's death. He had been making some visits to the doctor but one day when he asked me to take off work to go with him, I feared something serious. The doctor explained he had leukemia and estimated he had six months to a year to live. Eight months later he died. At that same time, I was providing care to my mother who had Alzheimer's disease. Thank goodness for the support and help from my children. With work and all that was happening at home, the time was very stressful.

"Adjusting to his absence has been difficult. What I miss most are the little things he'd do for me—fix breakfast, warm my car, or surprise me with small gifts. I miss the walks we'd take together, his companionship, and would you believe even the squabbles we'd have over things in the news. Of course we had our differences but these don't appear so important now.

"I enjoy being a grandmother. Three of them are staying with me now and I see all eight of them at least three times a week. You ask, what is my role or responsibility as a grandmother? I guess to just give them love and do what your heart tells you to. I only give advice when asked. Four of my five children are boys, and I'm fortunate that I'm close to my daughters-in-law. We do lots of things together as a family like going on outings. I like when the grandchildren call and I always try to find time for them, even with helping with their homework.

"I think about retirement in a few years but wonder if I'll be ready. I know that when I retire I'll do volunteer work. Even now, I'm very active in church. For me, life is good. I believe life is what you make it. If you want happiness, you can find it in the smallest things. If you carry a smile, cheer will follow. I've known for a long time that if you treat people the way you want to be treated, and if you try to make someone happy, what you put out comes back."

The death of a parent adversely affects marital relationships as well as the physical and psychological well-being of adult children.[45] Beraved children suffer a decline in social support from their partners and an increase in the partner's negative behaviors. They and their partners may also experience a significant increase in psychological distress, alcohol consumption, and a decline in physical health status. These individuals for whom relationships with parents were salient and positive prior to the parents' death were more adversely affected. The loss of a parental relationship characterized by negativity (a difficult family history) sometimes led to an improvement in an adult child's well-being. But for most, psychological distress was very apparent in the first few months following the death of a parent with healing effects apparent later.

---

[45] Debra Umberson, "Marriage as Support or Strain? Marital Quality Following the Death of a Parent," *Journal of Marriage and the Family* 57 (August 1995): 709–723; and Debra Umberson and Meichu D. Chen, "Effects of a Parent's Death on Adult Children: Relationship Salience and Reaction to Loss," *American Sociological Review* 59 (February 1994): 152–168.

Terminal illness, dying, and death are separate but interrelated events and processes. The application of interaction theory to these events would suggest that definitions and meanings attached to illness and death greatly influence one's ability to accept, cope, or adjust to them. This theory may help explain why, from a life-course perspective, middle-age adults seem to be the most adversely affected by the death of a spouse or sibling.[46] Recognizing significant others may help explain why many persons choose to endure illness and death at home rather than in a hospital or institutional setting. Understanding reference groups may help explain the relevance of religion, friends, and kin networks as support systems in facing these circumstances. While death may be a physical process, cultural, social, and interpersonal processes all influence and affect it. To mourn, to wear black, to commit suicide by burning following the death of a spouse, to build mausoleums, or to bury in airtight vaults are all responses dependent on cultural, class, and other social conditions.

The circumstances surrounding the death of a friend, child, or spouse frequently require major decisions by family members.

- Should dying family members be assured the right to die with dignity and to determine the time, place, and manner of their death?
- Should euthanasia (the deliberate ending of a loved one's life to spare that person from the suffering that goes with an incurable and agonizing disease) be permitted?
- If permitted, should euthanasia be **passive** (not preventing death through means of life-support systems) or **active** (causing death by poisoning, strangling, shooting)?
- What about funeral and burial decisions—how, where, payment, and so forth?
- What about the disbursement of personal effects, the carrying out of a will, and the settlement of an estate?
- If a long-term illness preceded the death, is care and its cost the sole responsibility of the family?
- If the family cannot care for or pay, does the church, community, state, or someone else bear the responsibility?

The list of questions that surround dying and death could go on and on.

In the United States as well as in most cultures, the immediate family and the immediate kin network are the major sources of decision making and social support. With the help of relatives, bedridden persons can live outside institutions. Elderly people turn first to their families for help, then to friends and neighbors, and, as a last resort, to bureaucratic organizations. It is not surprising that surveys indicate that most people would prefer to die at home.

---

[46] H. Wesley Perkins and Lynne B. Harris, "Family Bereavement and Health in Adult Life Course Perspective," *Journal of Marriage and the Family* 52 (February 1990): 233–241.

Movements are underway in health care to make family/kin interaction with the terminally ill or dying patient more possible. One plan, called **hospice,** is a therapeutic environment for the terminally ill, designed from the patient's point of view. Unlike a regular hospital, which stresses privacy, a hospice program emphasizes space for interaction with staff, family, and friends. Instead of subordinating the patient to the needs of the institution, leaving families waiting in the hall, a hospice program is designed to provide as much care in the patient's home as possible; when medical facilities are needed, they involve a team of medical, nursing, psychiatric, and religious people plus social workers and family members, as appropriate. The concern in a hospice is on increasing the quality of the last days of life and on making humane care synonymous with good medical practice. As a result, the family of the home-institutionalized patient is encouraged to be involved, perhaps by bringing in home cooking, bathing the patient, supplying medication, or bringing along the family dog. Hours of visits are unlimited, and interaction is permitted with young children and grandchildren.

The significance of family ties takes on an added dimension when one looks at the relationship between marital status and mortality.[47] Mortality is lower for married persons than unmarried ones and lower for people with children than for those without children. These findings suggest that protection against death itself may be afforded by different kinds of social ties, particularly marital, parental, and kin ties. Losing these ties is likely behind some of the difficulties of the widow or widower.

WIDOWS AND WIDOWERS

Being a widow or widower is not unique to older people but they are disproportionately represented among people older than age sixty-five (see Figure 15-3). In 1994, there were 11.1 million widows and 2.2 million widowers in the United States; 76.3 percent of them were ages sixty-five and over.[48] Facing the loss of a spouse and making the shift from a married to a widowed status may present extreme emotional and financial difficulties.

Society compounds the difficulty of adjusting to the widowed status by placing an unstated taboo on the discussion of death between husband and wife or parents and children while they are alive. As a result, the widow or widower is often unprepared for the decisions that need to be made following the death of a spouse.

Even if discussions preceded the death, the likelihood is great that loneliness, social isolation, and a need for major readjustments in living patterns will result. Readjustment may be less difficult if widowhood follows a major illness or some type of major role change on the part of the spouse. Adjustment to widowhood is

---

[47] Cathleen D. Zick and Ken R. Smith, "Marital Transitions, Poverty, and Gender Differences in Mortality," *Journal of Marriage and the Family* 53 (May 1991): 327–336; and Richard G. Rogers, "Marriage, Sex, and Mortality," *Journal of Marriage and the Family* 57 (May 1995): 515–526.

[48] U.S. Bureau of the Census, *Statistical Abstract of the United States: 1995,* 115th ed. (Washington DC: U.S. Government Printing Office, 1995), no. 59, p. 55.

Figure 15-3

Number of persons ages sixty-five and older, by marital status and sex: 1994

Source: Adapted from U.S. Bureau of the Census, *Statistical Abstract of the United States: 1995,* 115th ed. (Washington, DC: U.S. Government Printing Office, 1995), no. 59, p. 55.

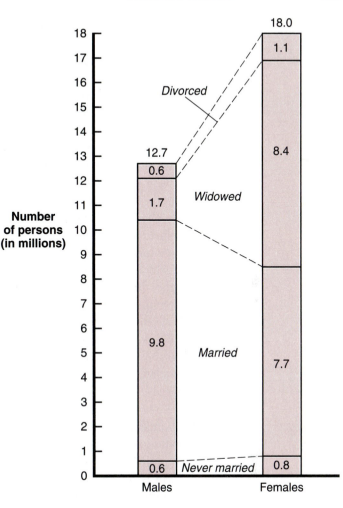

often best when a person has already established some personal autonomy, close continuing friendships, a realistic philosophy of life, economic security, and meaningful personal interests.

One problem, believed to be widespread among elderly persons in general but particularly among the widowed, is that of social isolation and loneliness.[49] *Social isolation* is the objective condition of having few contacts with family, friends, or both. *Loneliness* is a subjective condition that includes feelings of emptiness, aimlessness, and lack of companionship. It also involves dissatisfaction with one's present level of social interaction. Social norms of the United States and numerous other countries stress independence, but independence apart from frequent social

---

[49] Marilyn J. Essex and Sunghee Nam, "Marital Status and Loneliness Among Older Women: The Differentiated Importance of Close Family and Friends," *Journal of Marriage and the Family* 49 (February 1987): 93–106; and Larry C. Mullins and Mary Mushel, "The Existence and Emotional Closeness of Relationships with Children, Friends, and Spouses: The Effect on Loneliness Among Older Persons," *Research on Aging* 14 (December 1992): 448–470.

interaction, marriage, employment, and adequate income leads to an increased vulnerability for loneliness and to low levels of mental and physical health.

The extreme outcome of such conditions is demonstrated by the frequency of suicide. Suicide rates of people who are widowed are consistently higher than those of people who are married, at any age group; the rate of completed suicides is significantly higher for males than for females.

Rosemary Blieszner, in viewing widowhood from a socialist-feminist perspective, writes, that in some respects, women who have been dependent upon and subordinate to men over the life course have an edge over men in bereavement.[50] Widowed women are adept at housekeeping and kinkeeping, whereas widowed men are inexperienced at these tasks and are more susceptible to dependence on others. On the other hand, widows are less likely to have adequate financial resources since they have neither the savings, pension benefits, skills or work experiences more common to men.

Some widows and widowers remarry, but the chances of remarriage are, of course, higher for widowers than for widows. In one study, age was found to be the single most important factor in the remarriage of widows; the younger the age, the greater the likelihood of remarriage. For widowers, age was not significant. Older widowers did not have higher remarriage rates than younger widowers, despite the greater availability of potential marriage partners.[51] The sex ratio of unmarried men per one hundred unmarried women (about 84 for all age groups) becomes extremely unbalanced in the later years. In 1994, the ratio of unmarried males ages sixty-five and over to unmarried females ages sixty-five and over was 28 (see Figure 15-3; note 2.9 million unmarried men versus 10.3 million unmarried women).

Programs to encourage remarriage among widows and widowers would not be successful, given the unbalanced sex ratio, at least not in a monogamous system. The problem is further compounded in U.S. society by the norm that suggests that women should marry men of their own age or older. The remarriage problem for widowers is less severe, since there are both an excess of women their own age and social approval for marriage to women younger than themselves.

SUMMARY

1. This chapter examined two major periods of the life cycle: the middle years, from approximately age forty to retirement, and the later years, from approximately age sixty or sixty-five until the end of the life span.

2. The postparental period—those middle years after the departure of children and prior to retirement—is one in which most men and women are still married, with small percentages of single, widowed, and divorced

---

50 Rosemary Blieszner, "A Socialist-Feminist Perspective on Widowhood," *Journal of Aging Studies* 7 (1993): 171–182.

51 Ken R. Smith, Cathleen D. Zick, and Greg J. Duncan, "Remarriage Patterns Among Recent Widows and Widowers," *Demography* 28 (August 1991): 361–374.

people. This is one of the longest periods of the marital life cycle, covering a span of twenty to twenty-five years.

3. The significance of the middle years appears to differ somewhat for both men and women. While family income approaches its peak, there is mixed evidence as to the extent to which this period of life is bright or difficult. Researchers talk of a midlife crisis or transition for men and an "empty-nest" syndrome for women. The idea of a crisis in midlife seems to have little research support.

4. Grandparenting has become a middle-age and an old-age phenomenon. Grandparent appears to be a positive status for most respondents, although the roles are seldom clearly defined and tend to vary considerably by social class and cultural context.

5. In the United States, about 77 percent of the men but only about 42 percent of the women over age 65 are married. Marriage in the later years is perceived as favorable when compared to marriage in preceding periods of the life course. Most of the men and women of this age are living in families or in geographical proximity to their children. Relatively few older people are in long-term care institutions, such as nursing homes.

6. The problems facing elderly people are many, but this chapter focused briefly on four: health and care, children's problems, income and standard of living, and abuse and neglect. Most health problems are handled in the home rather than hospitals, with primary care coming from spouses or children. Income drops in old age, but most families cope quite well. Abuse and neglect, a relatively new social problem, is covered in the next chapter.

7. Retirement, widowhood, changing relationships, and the like create a need for resocialization of people who are elderly to new roles and definitions of self in relation to society.

8. Dying and death are processes and events of major importance and significance to family members. Family members offer support systems both to the dying person as well as to one another following death. Recognition of this support seems to be encouraging movements in treating terminally ill and dying patients in home settings and in family-focused medical settings.

9. The widow or widower is not unique to the aged family but is disproportionately represented among persons over age sixty-five. More women occupy a widow status than any other marital status. With the unbalanced sex ratio, remarriage is unlikely for a large number of women.

10. This chapter examined selected factors relating to the postparental periods: middle years, retirement, and old age. Conflict, crisis, and marital disorganization, although present at these periods of the life course, are not confined to these periods. Chapter 16 will explore social patterns surrounding crisis and disorganization, with a particular focus on abuse and violence among intimates.

KEY TERMS AND TOPICS

Postparental period p. 454

Marital status and coresidence
   in the middle years p. 455

Parent/adult child coresidence p. 456

Significance of the middle years p. 457

Midlife transition p. 458

"Empty-nest" syndrome p. 458

Grandparent status p. 459

Stepgrandparents p. 462

Grandparent/grandchild
   visitation rights p. 462

Families in later life and people
   who are aged p. 463

Growth of the elderly population p. 463

Life expectancy p. 463

Life span p. 464

Social gerontology p. 466

Marital status in the later years p. 466

Intergenerational relationships p. 469

Living arrangements among the
   elderly p. 471

Common problems of people
   who are aged p. 473

Socialization in later life p. 477

Retirement p. 478

Dying and death p. 479

Passive and active euthanasia p. 481

Hospice p. 482

Widows and widowers p. 482

DISCUSSION QUESTIONS

1. What is unique about the middle years, or the postparental period? How is the period of adjustment different for women and men?

2. Discuss the midlife transition and the "empty-nest" syndrome. Do they exist, and if so how serious are they? How might sex-role socialization patterns affect the middle years for men versus women?

3. Discuss changes in the grandparent role over the last thirty years. How might the grandparent status differ by class and subculture? What roles do stepparents and great-grandparents play?

4. How true is the argument "You can't teach an old dog new tricks" when applied to the socialization or resocialization of the middle-aged or aged couple?

5. Health, children's problems, money, and abuse are problems facing people who are aged. What other problems exist? What types of social programs, tax structures, and social policies might lessen the negative impact of these problems?

6. Discuss changes in husband/wife roles that are likely to accompany illness, retirement, grandparenthood, remarriage, and so forth. How can resocialization be facilitated?

7. What are the implications of retirement at age seventy, sixty, or fifty? Note marital status and male/female differences in adjustment patterns after retirement.

8. Should dying family members be assured the right to die with dignity and be allowed to determine the time, place, and manner of their death? Should active or passive euthanasia be supported? Why?

9. What advantages or disadvantages does the widow or widower have if living alone, if living with kin, if living in a private home with other than kin, or if living in an institution? What types of conditions make one situation more favorable than another?

10. Invite several persons over age seventy-five to your class or to a discussion group to address such topics as the "empty-nest" syndrome, grandparenthood, retirement, widowhood, and facing death. Examine the significance of having children and their importance as systems of support.

FURTHER READINGS

Anderson, Carol M., Stewart, Susan, and Dimidjian, Sona. *Flying Solo: Single Women in Midlife.* New York: W. W. Norton, 1994. Stories are told of the lives of single women in midlife based on interviews with about 90 women who were never married, divorced, or widowed.

Barusch, Amanda S. *Older Women in Poverty: Private Lives and Public Policies.* New York: Springer Publishing Co., 1994. Based on interviews with 62 low-income women, the book deals with a range of issues of older women in poverty, including chapters covering marriage, divorce, death, and remarriage.

Brown, Arnold S. *The Social Processes of Aging and Old Age.* Saddle River, NJ: Prentice-Hall, 2nd ed., 1996. A paperback focusing on many aspects of aging covered in this chapter, including demographics, the elderly in the family, economic dependency, retirement, health, and death and dying.

Brubaker, Timothy H. *Families' Relationships in Later Life,* 2d ed. Newbury Park, CA: Sage, 1990. An excellent collection of research-based articles on family relations and issues facing older persons in later life.

Cox, Harold G. *Later Life: The Realities of Aging.* Saddle River, NJ: Prentice-Hall, 4th ed., 1996. A textbook on aging with specific chapters dealing with family patterns, minority groups, cross-cultural comparisons, and death and dying.

Lopata, Helena Znaniecka. *Current Widowhood: Myths and Realities.* Thousand Oaks, CA: Sage Publications, 1995. An examination of two major themes of widowhood: how changes in society influence it and myths and assumptions surrounding it.

Norris, Joan E., and Tindale, Joseph E. *Among Generations: The Cycle of Adult Relationships.* New York: W. H. Freeman, 1994. A successful attempt at answering questions of how couples become involved in intergenerational relationships, how parents parent their adult children, how interactions occur with grandparents, siblings, and friends, and the results.

Szinovacz, Maximiliane; Ekerdt, David J.; and Vinick, Barbara H. (eds.). *Families and Retirement.* Newbury Park, CA: Sage, 1992. Leading researchers in family studies and gerontology present information on retirement, marital, and extended-kin relationships and selected issues focusing on gender, ethnicity, and changes brought on by retirement.

Zal, H. Michael. *The Sandwich Generation.* New York: Plenum Press, 1992. An examination of the unique problem facing middle-age Americans who have to cope with maturing children as well as increasingly dependent parents.

Chapter 16

Family Crisis and Violence Among Intimates

- Social Stresses on Families
    - ABCX model of stress
    - Variations on the ABCX model

- Violence in Families and Among Intimates
    - Myths of family violence
    - Causes of family violence
    - Child abuse and violence
    - Parent abuse and violence
    - Wife and female-partner abuse and violence
    - Husband and male-partner abuse and violence
    - Mutual abuse and violence between couples
    - Sibling abuse and violence
    - Elderly abuse and violence
    - Violence among other intimates
    - Treating and preventing family violence

- Summary

- Key Terms and Topics

- Discussion Questions

- Further Readings

In the preceding chapters, marriages and families have been examined through-out the life course. Clearly, no period in life is without the potential for **marital and interpersonal stress and crisis.** Earlier chapters addressed social conflict, lower levels of marital satisfaction ten to fifteen years into marriage, role conflicts, and the like. Each chapter referred to some event or process that produces strain, stress, and various degrees of crisis.

If observations about the American family are to be believed, this institution and the interpersonal relationships within it have been in a state of decline for the past several hundred years. Preachers, teachers, philosophers, political leaders, commentators, and others—irrespective of the generation in which they lived—have recorded their beliefs that parental authority was becoming more lax, that sexual taboos were weakening, that spouses were rebelling against one another, and so forth. These beliefs were usually contrasted to values and behaviors of the "old days," when authority was respected, when sexual taboos were observed, and when spouses were more understanding and tolerant.

That each generation makes reference to weakness and decline may indicate dissatisfaction with present events, whatever those events may be, or it may indicate that actual conditions are never equal to the ideal. In either case, intimate relationships and family life are seldom perfect, for couples, families, or the marital and family system. At any given time over the life course within every society, stressful events produce crises and the need for family reorganization. The first section will examine social stresses on the family.

SOCIAL STRESSES ON FAMILIES

In a widely quoted article, now about forty years old, Reuben Hill spoke of **stressor,** or crisis-provoking, **events.**[1] These are *sources* of stress and situations for which families have little or no preparation. Stressor events are never the same for different families but vary in the power with which they strike and the hardships that accompany them. *Hardships* are those complications in a crisis-precipitating event that demand competencies from the family that the event itself may have temporarily paralyzed or made unavailable.

Stress as used by Pauline Boss means "pressure or tension in the family system."[2] Stress is an *outcome,* or the degree of family disruption that results from particular events. With change comes disturbance and pressure—*stress.* It is normal, inevitable, and even desirable at times. The family's level of stress results from events or situations that have potential to cause change.

Why do different families respond so differently to particular events or circumstances? For example, why is a pregnancy a blessing to some and a curse to others? Why is a geographical move a thrilling event to some family members and

---

[1] Reuben Hill, "Social Stresses on the Family," *Social Casework* 39 (February/March 1958): 139–150.

[2] Pauline Boss, *Family Stress Management* (Newbury Park, CA: Sage, 1988).

a severe disruption to others? Why do unemployment, divorce, or death severely cripple some persons while others seem to take them in stride? A key to answering questions such as these is to look at mediating factors between the *source* (event) and the *outcome* (level of stress).

ABCX model of stress

A simple but powerful model was provided by Hill in what today is widely referred to as the **ABCX model of stress.** According to this model, A (the event) interacts with B (the family's crisis-meeting resources), which interacts with C (the meaning or definition the family gives to the event) to produce X (the crisis).[3] This sequence may be stated as a formula:

$$A + (B + C) = X$$

The two key dimensions in the formula are B and C. If both are adequate, the level of stress will be low or nonexistent. If one or both are inadequate, the level of stress will be high. Consider this ABCX formulation more closely.

Stressor events (A) may come from a wide variety of sources, both within and outside the family. The consequences of the events are likely to differ considerably depending on their source. For example, a general principle in sociology is that certain events outside a group, such as a war, flood, or depression, tend to solidify the group. Thus, although stressful, certain external events may tend to unify the family into a more cohesive unit, rather than leading or contributing to its breakdown. Also, the same events may not be defined as critically stressful when other persons are in the same situation or worse. For example, it is disappointing to professional researchers to have their writings rejected by editors of journals. The pain may be less severe if the researchers recognize that a given publication has a 90 percent rejection rate. To know that many others submitted articles and were rejected, did not get their research funded, lost their homes, had premature births, or were unemployed often makes events appear less critical. It helps to know that others share similar misfortunes.

Events within the family that are defined as stressful may be more disruptive because they arise from troubles that reflect poorly on the family's internal adequacy. These events may be nonsupport, mental breakdown, violence, suicide, or alcoholism, among others. The range of events, either within or outside the family, that disturb the family's role patterns is numerous. These events involve losses of persons, jobs, or incomes and additions, as well. The arrival of a child, grandmother, or mother-in-law may be as disruptive as the loss of any of the three. Gaining sudden fame or fortune may be as disruptive as losing either. Any sudden change in family status or conflict among family members in the conceptions of their roles may produce further family crisis.

---

[3] Hill, "Social Stresses on the Family," 141.

The dimensions that characterize any given stressor or crisis-provoking event extend far beyond whether it occurs internally or externally to the family. A crisis-producing event may affect the entire system or only a limited part, may occur gradually or suddenly, may be intense or mild, may be a short- or long-term problem, may be expected and predicted or random, may arise from natural conditions or artificial and technological effects, may represent a shortage or an overabundance of vital commodities, may be perceived to be solvable or unsolvable, and may vary in substantive content. The nature of the crisis event will influence the specific response of an individual or family system.

It should be noted that not all events or changes, irrespective of whether they come from within the family or outside it, are stressor events. For example, research has shown that major life changes and role transitions (job loss, divorce, retirement, widowhood, first marriage, first child, and so forth), often assumed to be stressor events, actually relieve stress when prior role stress is very high.[4] That is, life-transition events were found to be nonproblematic or even beneficial to mental health when preceded by chronic role problems—a case where more stress is actually relief from existing stress.

What factors make for crisis proneness and freedom-from-crisis proneness? The explanation lies in B and C in the formula presented earlier. That is, to what extent do families have resources to meet the event (factor B) and to what extent do families define the event as a crisis (factor C)? Crisis-meeting resources (factor B) may include family adaptability, family roles, kin-support systems, money income, insurance, friends, religious beliefs, education, good health, and the like. Problem families often do not have adequate resources with which to handle stressor events.

The extent to which the family defines the event as a crisis (factor C) reflects their value system and previous experience in meeting crisis. This definition of the event refers to the meaning attached to it, the appraisal or the interpretation as to its seriousness, and the perception of the event as **enabling** (making other things possible) or **disabling** (weakening or destroying possibilities).

Crisis proneness (X)—that is, the level or degree of stress—is therefore a function of both a deficiency in family organization resources (factor B) and the tendency to define hardships as crisis-producing (factor C). These two factors combine into one concept: family inadequacy or family adequacy.

Variations on the ABCX model

Hamilton McCubbin and others, in an attempt to build on Hill's ABCX model, proposed a **double-ABCX model,** which differentiates the precrisis and postcrisis

---

[4] Blair Wheaton, "Life Transitions, Role Histories, and Mental Health," *American Sociological Review* 55 (April 1990): 209–223.

variables and adds the idea of a *pile-up of demands.*[5] This pile-up of demands acknowledges that other life stressors and strains affect the family prior to and following a crisis-producing event. The model becomes a longitudinal one, and the factors of time plus the accumulation of demands differentiates the precrisis from the postcrisis situation. The initial stressor event becomes a double-A by separating the changes that occur irrespective of the initial stressor from those changes that are consequences of the family's efforts to cope with the hardships of the situation. The resources become a double-B by differentiating those resources already available to the family from those coping resources strengthened or developed in response to the crisis situation. The perception and meaning become a double-C by likewise differentiating the definition prior to the event of how stressful it may be from the postcrisis perceptions of the level of stress. Combining the pre- and postcrisis ABC factors leads to family adaptation (or maladaptation) as a possible outcome.

Many attempts have been made to test this double ABCX model of family stress and adaptation, two of which will be mentioned here.[6] One model, dealing with relocation stress among clergy husbands and wives, found that wives reported significantly higher stress, more negative perceptions of their most recent relocation, lower coping resources, and lower well-being than did their clergy husbands. The other model, dealing with women who had severe physical disabilities, found that a perceived high level of stress and strain and a low level of individual resources contribute to a low level of personal and family adaptation.

Alexis Walker made a case for expanding the ABCX model of stress and crisis to incorporate new dimensions, recognizing that:

1. All levels of the social system are interdependent.
2. Stress occurs in a unique and influential sociocultural context.[7]

The interdependence of levels incorporates individual factors with dyadic, family, nonfamily, and community levels. That is, levels more macro than individuals and families need to be incorporated into the model. Individual resources may be very different from family, community, and societal resources. Definitions or perceptions may vary among members of a family. Whose definition or perception is most important? If members don't agree, will the crisis be unresolvable?

The sociohistorical context recognizes how perceptions of stressful circumstances and resources available vary considerably over time. Different contexts and

5 Hamilton I. McCubbin and Joan M. Patterson, "Family Adaptation to Crisis," *Family Stress, Coping, and Social Support,* edited by Hamilton I. McCubbin et al. (Springfield, IL: Charles C Thomas, 1982): 44–46.

6 Marsha Wiggins Frame and Constance L. Shehan, "Relocation Stress and Coping Among Clergy Husbands and Wives," *Family Relations* 43 (April 1994): 196–205; and Victor Florian and Nira Dangoor, "Personal and Familial Adaptation of Women with Severe Physical Disabilities: A Further Validation of the Double ABCX Model," *Journal of Marriage and the Family* 56 (August 1994): 735–746.

7 Alexis J. Walker, "Reconceptualizing Family Stress," *Journal of Marriage and the Family* 47 (November 1985): 827–837.

the unique perspectives and resources related to a given context need to be recognized. In brief, in examining the process of adjustment to stress, it becomes necessary to focus, over time, on individual changes, dyadic changes, social network changes, and developments in the wider society that influence the ability of an individual, dyad, or family to respond effectively.

Another factor to consider is how stress in one area or from one source spills over into other areas. An article on the contagion of stress across multiple roles documented that home-to-work stress occurs more strongly among men than women and that both men and women reduce their involvements in stressful home situations following a stressful day at work.[8] Wives, in particular, modified their housework efforts to compensate for the work stresses of their spouses. Stresses in one area, such as work, affect stresses in other areas, such as home. What's more, stresses experienced by one spouse or partner affect stresses in the other.

While the list of stressor events, family problems, and conflict situations in relationships and families may seem infinite, this chapter will focus on only one: violence. A number of other potentially stressful events were discussed in some detail in prior chapters, including AIDS, abortion, homelessness, incest, mobility, commuter marriages, dual-career situations, sexual and racial inequality, poverty, intermarriage, conjugal decision making, parenthood, father/mother absence, midlife crisis, widowhood, death, and aging. Other issues—including separation, divorce, and stepchildren—will be discussed in Chapter 17.

VIOLENCE IN FAMILIES AND AMONG INTIMATES

Since 1970, research on family violence has grown exponentially, despite the fact that evidence has not indicated an increase in levels of family violence.[9] The terms **family violence** and **violence among intimates** are used to refer to any act that is carried out with the intention of causing physical harm to legally related individuals or those in close primary relationships. This broad definition includes acts such as spanking a disobedient child, raping a lover, and murdering a spouse. Many people (readers included) are not aware that they are more likely to be physically assaulted, beaten, raped, or killed in their own homes at the hands of loved ones than they are in any other place or by anyone else in society.[10]

Consider the following:

• Pictures of missing children on cards and milk cartons seldom document that children are more likely to be kidnapped by their own parents than by strangers.

---

[8] Niall Bolger, Anita DeLongis, Ronald C. Kessler, and Elaine Wethington, "The Contagion of Stress Across Multiple Roles," *Journal of Marriage and the Family* 51 (February 1989): 175–183.

[9] Murray A. Straus, "Sociological Research and Social Policy: The Case of Family Violence," *Sociological Forum* 7 (1992): 211–237.

[10] Richard J. Gelles and Murray A. Straus, *Intimate Violence* (New York: Simon and Schuster, 1988): 18.

- Most people believe that marriage is based on love and respect, yet more than half of all couples report physical violence by a partner at some time during their marriage.

- Sensational headlines report "Woman raped in public park," "Child beaten in day-care center," and "Elderly person mugged in parking lot," but in reality, these events occur most frequently in homes and are perpetrated by persons close to the victims.

- Nearly one out of every four murder victims in the United States is killed by a member of his or her own family; this is also the case in Africa, Great Britain, and Denmark.[11]

It should be noted that violence, while frequent in most societies, is not an inevitable consequence of family life. David Levinson, for example, after examining violence cross-culturally, found that sixteen societies of the ninety in his sample were relatively free of family violence.[12] Hunter-gatherers (Ona, Andamans, Siriono, Bushman), for example, rarely mistreated their children and were overrepresented among the societies without family violence.

According to Levinson:

> In general, in societies without family violence, husbands and wives share all domestic decision making, wives have some control over the fruits of family labor, wives can divorce their husbands as easily as their husbands can divorce them, marriage is monogamous, there is no premarital sex double standard, divorce is relatively infrequent, husbands and wives sleep together, men resolve disputes with other men peacefully, and intervention in wife beating incidents tends to be immediate.[13]

The central conclusion reached from these findings is that family violence does not occur in societies in which family life is characterized by cooperation, commitment, sharing, and equality. In contrast, family violence is more common in societies in which men control women's lives, violent resolution to conflicts is acceptable, and mothers bear the major responsibility for childrearing.

Precise data on conjugal and parental abuse and violence in the United States and other world societies are difficult to obtain. Not only do violence and abuse occur behind closed doors, hidden from public view, but they also may not be perceived as improper. Spouse shoving, child spanking, and sibling fighting may be defined as normative, appropriate, and even necessary marital and family behaviors.

Given the lack of exact data, one can only infer how much intrafamily violence and abuse exist. One need not doubt, however, that violence is a pervasive and common feature between intimate partners or spouses and among family members in most societies of the world.

---

[11] Richard J. Gelles, *Family Violence* (Beverly Hills: Sage, 1979): 11.

[12] David Levinson, *Family Violence in Cross-Cultural Perspective* (Newbury Park: Sage, 1989): 102–107.

[13] Ibid., 103.

Global Diversity: Worldwide Perspective of Family Violence Over the Life Course

Infants
Killing babies at birth or when very young
Harsh disciplinary practices, such as hitting, pinching, burning, overly hot baths
Deprivational feeding, punitive bladder/bowel training behaviors
Selling or offering for sacrifice
Binding head, feet, or other body parts

Early Childhood
Fights between siblings
Child prostitution, slavery, marriage
Harsh disciplinary practices, including spanking, hitting, beating, burning, pinching
Forced labor
Ridicule, threats, teasing
Mutilating, selling, killing for money or ritual

Adolescence
Physical punishment as with infants and children

Sibling fighting and abuse
Rape, forced sexual relations with same or opposite sex, between children, or adults and children
Initiation ceremonies that may involve scarring, circumcision, clitoridectomy, bloodletting, or other painful activities
Killing or forced suicide

Adulthood
Wife/husband beating and abuse
Co-wife beating and abuse
Marital and nonmarital rape
Physical and mental torture
Killing and forced suicide

Old Age
Physical and mental abuse
Abandonment and neglect
Beating, killing, forced suicide

Myths of family violence

In a chapter entitled "People Other Than Us: Public Perceptions of Family Violence," Richard Gelles and Murray Straus revealed a number of stereotypes about abusive partners and families.[14] Stereotypes about the nature and causes of domestic violence are often more pieces of conventional wisdom than facts or truths. In effect, they are myths. The perpetuation of these myths serves a very significant function: Violence is attributed to "other people" (namely, mentally disturbed, unbalanced people) rather than acknowledged as an outgrowth of the very structures of society and family.

Consider the following seven myths:

• *Myth 1 — The family is nonviolent.* This double-sided myth relates to the one just cited above. One view is that family violence is rare, and the other view

---

[14] Gelles and Straus, *Intimate Violence,* Chapter 2, 37–51.

is that an increase in violence is of epidemic proportions. The range of estimates, from thousands to millions, suggests that no one really knows how much violence there is in families. The conclusion drawn is that the problem is not a problem at all.

- *Myth 2 — Abusers are aliens, and victims are innocents.* The stereotype is that the abuser is mentally disturbed, psychologically unbalanced, or even psychotic, whereas the victim is a defenseless innocent. Not wanting to see their own behavior or that of friends or relatives as improper, people envision family violence as being committed by horrible persons against innocent people. Gelles and Straus suggested that, in fact, only about 10 percent of abusive incidents are caused by mental illness.

- *Myth 3 — Abuse is confined to poor, minority families.* Research has found that intimate violence is more likely to occur in lower-income and minority households, but it is not confined to them. Violence cuts across all classes and races; the poor have a greater likelihood of being violent and also run the risk of being overrepresented in official statistics. Attributing violence to poor and minority families is another way of seeing others as violent and one's own behavior as normal.

- *Myth 4 — Alcohol and drugs are the real causes of violence in the home.* A high association has been shown between violence and alcohol and drug use. But does it follow that violence will end when the drinking/drug problem is eliminated? Are alcohol or drugs actually the cause of the violence? Evidence has disputed the claim that alcohol causes violence and supported the claim that certain drugs are rarely associated with violence; in fact, some drugs produce a euphoric effect, reducing the level of violence. In short, curing or eliminating an alcohol or drug problem will not eliminate domestic violence.

- *Myth 5 — Children who are abused grow up to be abusers.* Again, this myth has some truth in that abused children *tend* to be abusive adults, but *all* abused children do not grow up to be abusive. The claim that people who are abused are preprogrammed to be abusers has not been supported.

- *Myth 6 — Battered women like being hit.* This myth is rooted in misunderstanding as to why abused women stay in abusive situations and whether battered women provoke the abuse and thus desire to be beaten. The dynamics of family violence and the social position of women in U.S. society destroy this myth. The reality is that abused women do not have the resources (including healthy self-esteem) to get out of abusive situations. And the longer they stay, the harder it is to leave.

- *Myth 7 — Violence and love are incompatible.* Many battered spouses have strong loving feelings for their partners, and most battered children continue to love their parents. Unlike violence in the streets, violence in the home includes bonds of love, attachment, and affection.

Gelles and Straus concluded the discussion of myths by stating:

> It is not only the myths that have to be abandoned, but the social function that they serve. The greatest function served by the seven myths we have discussed is that collectively they serve as a smoke screen that blinds us to our own potential for violence. Moreover, when our explanations focus on "kinds of people" (mentally disturbed, poor, alcoholics, drug abusers, etc.) we blind ourselves to the structural properties of the family as a social institution that makes it our most violent institution with the exception of the military in time of war.[15]

Causes of family violence

Why is there so much violence in the family? Many theories have been advanced to explain interpersonal violence in general, and family violence more specifically. Some theories, as noted, place the cause within the individual, attributing violent behavior to psychopathologies and alcohol and drug use. Other theories are social/psychological in nature and attribute violence to social learning, exchange, and interaction. A third group of theories is sociocultural and attributes violence to societal resources, conflict systems, and the larger culture.

This third group of theories helps us understand, for example, why there is a higher incidence of black-on-black violence as well as more violence toward black women than white women.[16] A structural-cultural theory looks at structurally induced economic problems (including unemployment and underemployment) as an important variable affecting black men's ability to enact traditional male roles in the family.

Murray Straus and Christine Smith presented five social factors that converge to cause the high rates of intrafamily violence:

1. *Intrafamily conflict* — An irony of family life is that many of the same characteristics that contribute to intimacy and love among family members also contribute to conflict.

2. *Male dominance in family and society* — Given the concept of the male/husband as head of the family and the domination of men in U.S. society, force is a key resource in resolving conflict.

3. *Cultural norms permitting family violence* — Parents have a legal right and often a moral obligation to spank or slap their children.

---

[15] Ibid., 51.

[16] Robert L. Hampton and Richard J. Gelles, "Violence Toward Black Women in a Nationally Representative Sample of Black Families," *Journal of Comparative Family Studies* 25 (Spring 1994): 105–119.

4. *Family socialization in violence* — Children's early and continuing experience with violence between parents or by parents provides role models and a specific script in training for future violence.

5. *Pervasiveness of violence in society* — In American society, socially legitimate violence includes physical punishment by teachers, force by police, widespread ownership of guns, the death penalty, military force against governments, violent acts on television and in the movies, and so forth. Violence in one area of life spills over into other spheres of life.[17]

There is abundant data to support the above factors and all are incorporated throughout this chapter. In factor number 4 above, *Family socialization in violence,* the general processes of socialization described in Chapter 14 are equally applicable to this factor. It is clear that violence begets violence and that aggression is transmitted across generations. Parents who yell frequently are the ones most likely to hit frequently, and both verbal and physical violence appear to be transgenerational.[18] Fortunately, most people are able to break out of this intergenerational cycle of abuse, but this does not negate the increased probability of yelling at children, spanking children, or hitting a partner if family violence was a pattern in one's childhood.

Child abuse and violence

Throughout the history of the world, children have been subject to a range of abuses and cruelties, including sexual abuse, beatings, and abandonment (infants left to die). Today, only isolated incidents of abandonment are reported, but cases of physical and sexual abuse are quite common.

Hitting children to punish them is legal in every state in the United States; in contrast, in Sweden, a parent can be imprisoned for striking a child. Parents in the United States tend to view corporal punishment (striking and spanking) as an acceptable and appropriate means of discipline. Traditionally, this "privilege" of spanking was even extended to schoolteachers and administrators as a means of inflicting punishment and maintaining discipline. The guideline commonly followed was "Spare the rod and spoil the child."

In most nations, including the United States, **physical punishment** is central to the discipline of children and the socialization process. Almost all parents and the majority of teachers believe that physical punishment is an appropriate and effective form of discipline. Straus found that over 90 percent of parents of chil-

[17] Murray A. Straus and Christine Smith, "Family Patterns and Primary Prevention of Family Violence," in Murray A. Straus and Richard J. Gelles, *Physical Violence in American Families* (New Brunswick, NJ: Transaction, 1990), 512–521.

[18] David Hemenway, Sara Solnick, and Jennifer Carter, "Child-Rearing Violence," *Child Abuse and Neglect* 18 (1994): 1011–1020; and Diana Doumas, Galya Margolin, and Richard S. John, "The Intergenerational Transmission of Aggression Across Three Generations," *Journal of Family Violence* 9 (1994): 157–175.

In contrast to Sweden, where it is illegal to spank children or treat them in a humiliating way, in the United States, many parents view corporal punishment as an acceptable and appropriate means of discipline. Since physical punishment usually occurs "behind closed doors" most cases of child abuse are never discovered.

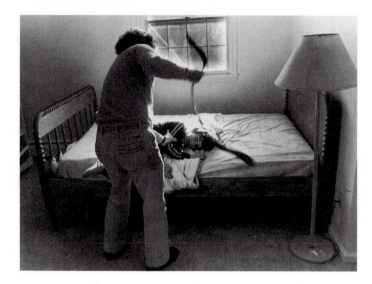

dren ages three and four in the United States used physical punishment to correct behavior.[19] The most common forms include spanking, slapping, and grabbing and shoving a child with more force than is needed. Hitting a child with an object is also legally permissible and widespread if done by someone in a custodial relationship to the child.

What are the effects of physical punishment? Straus hypothesized that physical punishment by parents and teachers may produce conformity in the immediate situation, but in the long run, it increases the probability of deviance, including delinquency in adolescence and wife beating, child abuse, and crime outside the family (robbery, assault, and homicide) in adulthood.[20] Studies have not proven that physical punishment causes these problems but that there is a *spillover effect.*

A **cultural spillover theory** suggests that violence in one sphere of life tends to engender violence in other spheres. The more a society uses force to attain socially desired ends (maintaining order in schools, deferring criminals, defending itself from foreign enemies), the greater the tendency is for those engaged in illegitimate behavior to also use force in attaining their ends. Straus conceded that he could not prove the theory but that empirical findings were almost entirely consistent with it: There is a linkage between physical punishment of children and crime in society and support for Straus' assertion that physical punishment may produce conformity in the short term but creates or exacerbates deviance in the long term.

Violence toward children is found in all U.S. social classes and among families across the full spectrum of income. However, violence toward children, especially severe violence, is more likely to occur in households at or below the poverty line. Based on a national probability sample of over 6,000 households, Gelles

---

[19] Murray A. Straus, "Discipline and Deviance: Physical Punishment of Children and Violence and Other Crime in Adulthood," *Social Problems* 38 (May 1991): 136.

[20] Ibid., 133–152.

reported that the incidence of overall violence was 4 percent higher among households with poverty-level incomes than among households with higher incomes. Severe violence (high probability of causing an injury) was 46 percent higher and very severe violence (such as burning, threatening with or using a knife or gun) was 100 percent higher among the poverty-level households.[21] Child abuse tends to increase as unemployment increases.[22] Factors such as poverty and unemployment are stressor events that influence family functioning, as exhibited in the greater abuse of children.

The child abuser, the victim, and the type of abuse all vary by gender and by the type of biological relationship. This seems to be particularly true with **child sexual abuse.**[23] Children are assumed to be incapable of consenting to sex with an adult because they lack the power to decline involvement and often do not understand to what they are consenting. Sexual abuse generally includes elements of force, manipulation, or coercion.

In a national survey of adults and their history of childhood sexual abuse, 27 percent of the women and 16 percent of the men reported being abused.[24] The median age of abuse was slightly under ten. Boys were more likely to have been abused by strangers, whereas girls were more likely to have been abused by family members.

Another source, representing several thousand cases of child sexual abuse, revealed that nonbiologically related caretakers (stepparents, adoptive parents, foster parents, babysitters, institutions) were substantially overrepresented, and biologically related caretakers (parents, siblings, grandparents) were substantially underrepresented in reports of child sexual abuse.[25] The numbers of male perpetrators greatly surpassed those of female perpetrators in all situations: three times as many biological fathers as mothers, nearly five times as many male babysitters as female, and more than twenty times as many males as females in other caretaker roles (stepparents, parents' paramours or lovers, institutional staff).

The consequences of child sexual abuse appear to be severe and long lasting. In another study, both females and males who were sexually abused as children showed greater evidence than those not abused of sexual disturbance or dysfunction, homosexual experiences in adolescence or adulthood, depression, and even

---

21 Richard J. Gelles, "Poverty and Violence Toward Children," *American Behavioral Scientist* 35 (January/February 1992): 258–274.

22 Loring Jones, "Unemployment and Child Abuse," *Families in Society: The Journal of Contemporary Human Services* 71 (December 1990): 579–586.

23 For a review of research in the 1980s see Richard J. Gelles and Jon R. Conte, "Domestic Violence and Sexual Abuse of Children: A Review of Research in the Eighties," *Journal of Marriage and the Family* 52 (November 1990): 1045–1058.

24 David Finkelhor, Gerald Hotaling, I. A. Lewis, and Christine Smith, "Sexual Abuse in a National Survey of Adult Men and Women: Prevalence, Characteristics, and Risk Factors," *Child Abuse and Neglect* 14 (1990): 19–28.

25 Leslie Margolin and John L. Craft, "Child Sexual Abuse by Caretakers," *Family Relations* 38 (October 1989): 450–455.

suicidal ideas.[26] Sexual maladjustment among abused females has been documented in several studies. Research on over five hundred young women from the state
of Washington found that two-thirds of those who became pregnant as adolescents
had been sexually abused.[27] Childhood sexual abuse was also found to be a precursor to prostitution and victimization among adolescent and adult homeless
women.[28] The evidence showing both the severity and the long-term negative
effects of child sexual abuse appears to be clear and highly consistent among most
studies.

Is there an epidemic of child abuse in the United States? Does the number of
children who are abused increase each year? Apparently, no. Straus and Gelles compared the rate of physical abuse of children from a 1975 study with the rates from
a 1985 replication.[29] Both studies showed extremely high incidences of severe physical violence against children; however, the 1985 rate of physical child abuse (as
measured by the number of children who were kicked, punched, bitten, beaten up,
or attacked with a knife or gun) was 47 percent lower than the 1975 rate.

How could this dramatic drop in violence toward children be explained?
Critics argued that the change may have been due to methodological artifacts (differences resulting from gathering data by telephone rather than in home interviews). Straus and Gelles discounted that argument and even suggested that the
anonymity provided by telephone would have led to more rather than less reporting of violence. A second explanation for the drop focused on people's greater
reluctance to report severe violence following the massive amount of public and
media attention paid to abuse over the decade. Again, the authors discounted the
argument, suggesting that, if anything, the increase in public attention should
have made abused wives and children more likely to report their abuse. Despite
the critics, Straus and Gelles remained convinced that a decline took place in violence toward children and (as reported later) toward women as well.

These declines in levels of child abuse are reported to be consistent with other
changes that have occurred in the family and society over the past decade and these
changes most likely served to reduce violence in the home. Changes in *family
structure*—such as increased age at marriage and the birth of the first child, the
decline in the number of children per family, and the decreased number of
unwanted children—are all related to lower rates of child abuse. Changes in the
economy—for instance, lower rates of unemployment and inflation in 1985 than
in 1975—also likely reduced the frequency of child abuse. The growth of new and

---

[26] Joseph H. Beitchman, Kenneth J. Zucker, Jane E. Hood, Granville A. DaCosta, Donna Akman, and Erika
Cassavia, "A Review of the Long-Term Effects of Child Sexual Abuse," *Child Abuse and Neglect* 16 (1992):
101–118.

[27] Debra Boyer and David Fine, "Sexual Abuse as a Factor in Adolescent Pregnancy and Child Maltreatment,"
Family Planning Perspectives 24 (January/February 1992): 4–11.

[28] Ronald L. Simons and Les B. Whitbeck, "Sexual Abuse as a Precursor to Prostitution and Victimization
Among Adolescent and Adult Homeless Women," *Journal of Family Issues* 12 (September 1991): 361–379.

[29] Murray A. Straus and Richard J. Gelles, "Societal Change and Change in Family Violence from 1975 to 1985
as Revealed by Two National Surveys," *Journal of Marriage and the Family* 48 (August 1986): 465–479; and
Richard J. Gelles and Murray A. Straus, *Intimate Violence,* 109–114.

News Item: Mother Guilty of Murdering Her Sons

In July 1995, newspapers and magazines around the United States focused on Susan Smith, a mother who drowned her two boys. Mrs. Smith, the mother of two sons (Michael, age 3, and Alex, 14 months), strapped them into their car seats and allowed the automobile to slide down the boat ramp into John D. Long Lake in South Carolina. There the boys remained for nine days.

No dispute existed over what happened that night at the lake. The dispute centered around a just punishment for a mother who would kill her sons. The prosecution argued for the death penalty using words such as murderer, evil, and wicked. The defense wanted a verdict of involuntary manslaughter and countered with words focusing on mental illness, mental disorder, a depressed woman, and a sexually abused woman.

A psychiatrist who had extensive interviews with Mrs. Smith described her as a woman scarred by the suicide of her father when she was a child, molested by her stepfather when she was a teenager, and separated from her husband as a young mother. Suicide had long been on her mind and she had attempted it twice previously. The psychiatrist reported that just weeks before the drownings, she was so desperate not to be alone and to be loved that she had intercourse with her stepfather, her estranged husband, the son of the owner of the textile plant where she worked as a secretary and whose affection she was seeking, and the father himself—the owner of the textile plant.

In what seemed like a break for Mrs. Smith, the judge granted a defense request to consider a verdict of involuntary manslaughter, permitting the jury to decide whether she should be executed or imprisoned for life. After only two-and-one-half hours, the jury reached a unanimous decision: life imprisonment.

innovative *treatment programs,* social services, and therapy approaches has probably helped to reduce intrafamily violence, as well. And finally, deterrence in the form of legal *sanctions* and the perceived high probability of getting caught and punished serve as reminders that abusive behavior is inappropriate behavior.

The issue of child abuse and violence is extremely complex. Concerns relate not merely to the frequency and types of abuse but extend to child neglect, to the availability of services, and to the forms of legal intervention (custody and placement), decision making, and program coordination. Case identification lags considerably behind the actual rates of abuse, and increased levels of reporting place strains on the limited services available.

Parent abuse and violence

Violence between parents and children is reciprocal. That is, children not only are victims of violence but are perpetrators as well. Many cases of parental abuse of children go unnoticed and unreported, but assaulted parents, who are generally more powerful than their children, may go to great lengths to conceal being abused by them. Acts of severe violence, such as a child killing a parent, may get publicity, but cases of hitting and biting or making threats are likely to remain unnoticed by outsiders.

Parent assault is common but rarely studied. More attention has been focused on adolescents who abuse parents than on younger children. Data from a national survey of adolescents showed that roughly 5 percent of these adolescents had hit one of their parents in the past year.[30] Both males and females assaulted parents; males were less likely to hit mothers and more likely to hit fathers as they got older, and females became more likely to hit either parent as they aged. The study reported that adolescents who assaulted parents were more likely to (1) have friends who assaulted parents; (2) approve of delinquency, including violence; (3) perceive the probability of official sanction to be low; (4) hold weak attachments to parents; and (5) be white. More traditional violence factors—such as social isolation, drug use, stress, and power differentials—were largely unrelated to parent assault.

Wife and female-partner abuse and violence

Michael Johnson argues that there are two distinct forms of violence against women.[31] One he calls *common couple violence.* This involves conflict between couples with an occasional outburst of violence from either husbands or wives. The other he calls **patriarchal terrorism.** From a feminist perspective this is a product of patriarchal traditions of men's right to control "their" women (wives), not only by a systematic use of violence but by economic subordination, threats, isolation, and other control factors. This pattern of violence is often referred to as wife beating, wife battery, and battered women. Johnson notes that patriarchal terrorism escalates (increases in frequency and intensity over time) while common couple violence does not. Common violence is an intermittent response to the occasional conflicts of everyday life, motivated by a need to control in the specific situation, but not a more general need to be in charge of the relationship.

Much research has focused on wives, but interestingly, findings have consistently shown that physical aggression is at least twice as common among cohabiting couples as it is among married couples. During a given year, about thirty-five out of every one hundred cohabiting couples experience physical aggression compared to fifteen out of every one hundred married couples.[32] And much of this physical aggression is directed at women, many of whom believe that their husbands or partners have the right to slap them or shove them under certain condi-

---

[30] Robert Agnew and Sandra Huguley, "Adolescent Violence toward Parents," *Journal of Marriage and the Family* 51 (August 1989): 699–711.

[31] Michael P. Johnson, "Patriarchal Terrorism and Common Couple Violence: Two Forms of Violence Against Women," *Journal of Marriage and the Family* 57 (May 1995): 283–294.

[32] Jan E. Stets, "Cohabiting and Marital Aggression: The Role of Social Isolation," *Journal of Marriage and the Family* 53 (August 1991): 669–680.

Case Example:
Twenty Years of Domestic Abuse

Delores, age 46, was married for 21 years until she divorced her husband several years ago. She has three adult children and in her words, two-and-one-half grandchildren. Except for the first year of married life, she suffered from verbal, emotional, and physical abuse by her husband.

"When we got married, I really loved my husband. He had a good job with an auto company so money was not an issue. I looked forward to starting a family and having a home we could call our own. As for having a family, I found myself pregnant one month after our wedding. After five years of marriage, we purchased a home.

"Six months after our son was born, I experienced being hit for the first time. He came home and made a comment about the floor not being mopped. An argument escalated until, in anger, he struck me. I was shocked, went and picked up the baby and headed for my mother's home. Only when I got to her place did I start crying. I guess I was very naive because at that time I didn't perceive it as abuse.

"As was the case on numerous occasions over the years, I'd leave him and, for a variety of reasons, go back with him. The abuse wasn't regular but I could never predict when it was coming. My husband, who never was very affectionate, needed to be in complete control. He drank but his hitting me was seldom due to his drinking. I could never please him. Over time, after hearing how stupid I was, how I wasn't worth anything, and that no one would want me, I lost a sense of who I was. I came to believe that maybe his womanizing, drinking, hitting me, and so forth was really my fault.

"The final blow, literally, came in 1984. The children and I had left him for seven months. He convinced me that he was a changed person, was going to church, and would operate under a budget. That was important because even with a good paycheck, more and more of it was going for alcohol and other women. So, I returned to him. I knew he was under tremendous pressure at work so I tried to do the best I could. But one day dinner wasn't ready or fixed properly or something. In the kitchen he threw a pot, which was followed by him hitting me in the eye with his fist. I bled profusely and was rushed to a hospital with broken bones in my face and a fear of losing my eyesight. They asked if I had been in a car accident. When told that my husband did it, they called the police who wanted to know if I wanted to press charges. I knew that if I did, he would be put in jail and lose his job which meant no income or food for the children. So I refused to file charges. That experience convinced me I had to get out or he would eventually kill me. I prayed like I never prayed before and with the help of Legal Aid, got a divorce. The church and my parents were my primary means of support and the source of me keeping my sanity.

"If it was only me, I think I might have done things differently. Today, when I see how the effects of domestic abuse have carried over to my children, it really hurts. My son has not married and my youngest daughter says she fears any kind of commitment. My oldest daughter, who has two children, postponed marriage. My ex-husband has remarried and I understand he beats her too. For the past six years, I've been with a wonderful man but we have been burned so badly over our lifetime, both of us are hesitant about getting into another marriage."

Some violence against women is an intermittent response to the occasional conflicts of everyday life. However, patriarchal traditions of men's superiority over women lends support to men using any means to maintain their dominant position, including partner abuse and wife beating.

tions. And as women learn that their male partners have this right, so do men learn that violence against their female partners is acceptable.

According to feminists and as noted above, this acceptability is based on societal norms supporting patriarchy. Male dominance and superiority is viewed as the root cause of violence against women. Within relationships, men are generally observed to exercise more power than women. One way of expressing such power is through the roles in violent marriages, in which the man is usually the more powerful, violent person and the woman is the less powerful, abused person. Patriarchy reinforces the appropriateness of male dominance, power, aggression, and violence, whether they be exhibited in international conflicts or in interpersonal ones.

That violence against women, as is much family violence, is not always viewed as improper or deviant has historical precedence. As recently as the late nineteenth century in Great Britain and the United States, it was considered a necessary aspect of a husband's marital obligation to control and chastise his wife through the use of physical force. Violence against wives and intimate partners, as suggested earlier, is a logical extension of the patriarchal family system, in which the husband, as the dominant ruler and head, uses whatever means necessary to obtain obedience and control. And considerable evidence has shown that, irrespective of whether violence toward wives is a historical pattern, a logical extension of a patriarchal system, or acceptable for some other reason, violence against women is common, both in the United States and around the world.[33]

Most physical abuse and violence toward wives and female partners does not take the form of beating; rather, throwing things, shoving, pushing, grabbing, slapping, and hitting are more common. To be sure, however, many women are seriously hurt by their partners. Nursing research reported that at least 8 percent of women in prenatal and primary care settings and approximately 20 percent of women in emergency room settings were abused by male intimate partners.[34] Approximately 8 percent of women were physically abused while pregnant and an additional 15 percent were beaten prior to the pregnancy.

Female physical abuse is not uniformly distributed in all major social and demographic groups. Sociodemographic risk factors associated with wife abuse include low income, unemployment, and race; wife abuse is particularly common among blacks who have low incomes and high levels of unemployment. Wife abuse is also more prevalent among people who are nonreligious, divorced or separated, and under age thirty.[35]

The questions raised about changes in rates of child abuse must also be raised about wife or spouse abuse: Is there an epidemic of wife abuse in the United States? Are more women abused each year? And again, the answer is apparently no. The same Straus/Gelles studies mentioned earlier, comparing violence rates in 1975 and 1985, showed that wife beating (as measured by the number who were kicked, punched, hit with an object, bitten, beaten up, or attacked with a knife or gun) decreased by 27 percent over these ten years.[36] Interestingly, similar severe assaults by wives on husbands decreased only 4.3 percent. Even if these rates indicated actual reductions, the number of wives beaten each year in the United States is staggering: 1.5 million. Quite often, these women stay in their abusive situations. The logical question is, Why?

Some answers to this question are offered in the panel on abused wives. Most answers suggest that wives who are highly dependent on marriage are less able to discourage, avoid, leave, or put an end to abuse than women in marriages where the balance of resources between husband and wife is more nearly equal. Dependent wives lack both alternatives to marriage and resources within marriage to negotiate change. Other answers focus on the psychological strategies women use to help them perceive their relationship in a positive light or convince themselves of their obligation to stay. In sum, these two variables—no resources or

33 Kristi L. Hoffman, David H. Demo, and John N. Edwards, "Physical Wife Abuse in a Non-Western Society: An Integrated Theoretical Approach," *Journal of Marriage and the Family* 56 (February 1994): 131–146.

34 Jacquelyn C. Campbell, "A Review of Nursing Research on Battering," in Carolyn M. Sampselle, *Violence Against Women: Nursing Research, Education, and Practice Issues* (New York: Hemisphere Publishing Corp., 1992), 69–81.

35 Michael D. Smith, "Sociodemographic Risk Factors in Wife Abuse: Results from a Survey on Toronto Women," *Canadian Journal of Sociology* 15 (1990): 39–58.

36 Straus and Gelles, "Societal Change and Change in Family Violence," pp. 465–479; and Gelles and Straus, *Intimate Violence,* 109.

U.S. Diversity: Abused Women and Wives: Why Do They Stay?

Gelles and Straus reported a number of factors that distinguish battered or abused wives who stay in the home or relationship from those who leave abusive relationships. They found that:

1. Women who left seemed to have experienced more severe violence.
2. Women who grew up in violent homes were more likely to stay with abusive husbands.
3. Women who stayed in violent marriages were less educated, had fewer job skills, and were more likely to be unemployed than women who sought help, called the police, or left their violent partners.
4. Women with young children were more likely to stay.

What this suggests is that:

1. The more severe the violence the greater the likelihood of leaving.
2. Experience with or exposure to violence seems to make women more tolerant of domestic violence or more lacking in hope of really escaping.
3. Women who have few resources are more entrapped in violent homes.
4. As children get older and perhaps less dependent on them, women are more likely to leave.

Other studies suggested, as well, that limited educational resources and occupational skills result in wives who are economically dependent and more "forced" to remain with abusive husbands. These studies suggested that other reasons for staying in an abusive relationship included a commitment to the spouse, a belief their husbands will reform, low self-concept, a belief that divorcees are stigmatized, and the difficulty for women with children to get work. These factors all point to social factors entrapping women in violent marriages and disprove the myth that wives who remain with violent men are masochistic—seeking or deriving pleasure from mistreatment.

Source: Richard J. Gelles and Murray A. Straus, *Intimate Partners* (New York: Simon & Schuster, 1988), 143–146.

alternatives and perception of and meaning attached to the relationship—seem to fit the B and C in the ABCX model and explain why many abused women remain with their partners.

Of those abused wives who leave, a number turn to shelters, which are short-term refuges from violent relationships. Again, within the context of the ABCX model, shelters represent an important community resource for many abused wives.

Rape among intimates

Sexual abuse and rape by a spouse or by intimate partners is another common form of violence inflicted on women. The husband who forces sexual intercourse (technically, marital rape, although legally not usually recognized as such) is seldom viewed as a rapist by his wife, who may blame herself for the incident. That women blame themselves or learn to accept forced sexual intercourse by someone they know and have loved may be why so little attention has been devoted to this issue.

Rape, simply defined, is forced sex without consent. Legal definitions generally involve three separate factors: (1) sexual intercourse, involving vaginal, anal, or oral penetration; (2) force or threat of force; and (3) nonconsent of the victim. Until recently, marital rape and rape among intimates has been ignored in the marital/family literature. It has been brought to light as a feminist issue: Rape is a mechanism for maintaining male control and domination and a violent means of inducing fear in women and reinforcing their subordination to men.[37]

In the colonial period, it was a man's personal privilege to have access to a woman's body. He was dominant, and she was subordinate. This subordination meant that, sexually, she was a receptacle, the answer to his sexual needs. Sexuality was channeled into marriage for the procreation of legitimate offspring, while nonmarital sexual intercourse was immoral and an offense against both the family and the community. Since the entire community was responsible for upholding morality, sexual crimes were severely punished. The punishment was often directed most harshly against women because they bore the primary responsibility for regulating sexual contact. Female virginity, meaning purity, was held in high esteem and vital to a woman's successful future. For instance, a woman who was raped could not expect to marry into a respectable family.

Do any of these ideas have a ring of truth today? Are women still often blamed for their own victimization? Do some people believe that women ask to be assaulted or harassed by how they dress and act, perhaps even that they enjoy being raped? And within an intimate relationship, is the woman subordinate to the man, sexually and otherwise? Does the state, through legislation, have any right to intrude into bedrooms and protect a woman from sexual mistreatment or violence of any type, rape included?

Diana Russell indicated that the 1980s was a decade of tremendous achievement in changing state laws regarding rape.[38] In 1980, only three states had completely abolished the marital rape exception and three others had partially stricken it. As of 1990, sixteen states allow the prosecution of husbands for raping their wives, without exception. In another twenty-six states, husbands can be prosecuted for raping their wives in some circumstances but are totally exempt in others. Some examples of exemptions include: if a rape is imposed by force but without additional violence, such as being threatened with a weapon; if nonforceful rape is

---

[37] Patricia L. N. Donat and John D'Emilio, "A Feminist Redefinition of Rape and Sexual Assault: Historical Foundations and Change," *Journal of Social Issues* 48 (1992): 9–22.

[38] Diana E. H. Russell, *Rape in Marriage* (Bloomington: Indiana University Press, 1990), 23.

imposed when a wife is mentally or physically helpless and cannot give her consent; and if the victim does not report the rape within a specified time period. In the remaining eight states (Kentucky, Missouri, New Mexico, North Carolina, Oklahoma, South Carolina, South Dakota, and Utah), a husband cannot be prosecuted for raping his wife unless the couple is living apart, is legally separated, or have filed for divorce. Yet Russell reported that one out of every seven women in her study who had ever been married reported at least one and sometimes many experiences of rape by her husband.[39]

Lee Bowker, in reviewing studies of marital rape, made several points:[40]

1. Marital rape may be more common than all other kinds of rape combined.
2. Marital rape is common among battered wives.
3. Motivating factors for marital rape include anger, the need to dominate, and occasionally, sexual obsession.
4. Marital rape may be as psychologically disturbing as nonmarital rape and may have severe, long-term effects.
5. Marital rape within violent marriages seems to have a negative effect on women's self-esteem and on their attitudes toward men and heterosexual behavior.
6. Husbands who rape their wives are likely to have problems with alcohol, to have had serious dysfunctions in their families of orientation, and to totally dominate their marriages.

Today, few women deny that rape among marital or intimate partners is a serious matter, that women undergo severe emotional and behavioral reactions, or that rape among intimates is abusive and unwarranted behavior.

Husband and male-partner abuse and violence

The abuse of husbands and male partners by women has received far less attention than the abuse of females. One writer noted the following:

1. Less empirical data exist on relationship violence committed by women.
2. Feminists, in particular, fear that drawing attention to battered husbands will impede attempts to battle the more serious problem of wife abuse.
3. Men are reluctant to acknowledge that they have been beaten by their wives, given traditional social values about male/female relationships.

---

[39] Ibid., 57.

[40] Lee H. Bowker, "Marital Rape: A Distinct Syndrome?" *Social Casework* (June 1983): 347–348.

4. Women's abuse is more visible, given the greater severity of physical damage that they suffer.[41]

Yet research has consistently shown that men and women engage in comparable amounts of violence; Straus and Gelles found this to be true. They state that "assaults by women on their male partners occur at about the same rate as assaults by men on their female partners, and women initiate such violence about as often as men."[42] Straus and Gelles estimated that one out of six (about 16 percent), or 8.7 million, couples experienced an incident of physical assault in 1985, the year of their second national study. Most of these assaults were relatively minor—pushing, slapping, shoving, or throwing things—but a substantial number were serious—kicking, punching, biting, or choking.

The fact that the rates for violence by wives were so similar to the rates for violence by husbands is quite surprising, given the extremely low rate of assault by women outside the family. The high rate within marriage may be explained by recognizing that many assaults by wives are acts of retaliation or self-defense, that implicit cultural norms tolerate or even accept marital violence, and that marriages involve a high degree of frustration. Wives, in comparison to husbands, are relatively powerless, yet some women have learned through training since childhood that violence within the family is appropriate.

Mutual abuse and violence between couples

Wife/female abuse and husband/male abuse have been treated separately here, yet it needs to be emphasized that *mutual* abuse is more common than either form alone. This is true not only for physical abuse but for verbal/symbolic aggression, as well. Again, men and women engage in about equal amounts of verbal/symbolic aggression against their partners.[43]

Disparity between husbands and wives in recall of violence is evident. Women typically report more violence in intimate relationships than do men.[44] Spouses report more violence by their partners than they are willing to acknowledge by themselves. Also, spouses are more likely to report their own victimization rather than their use of violence.

The effects of family structure on both spouse and child abuse are evident from data on stepfamilies and remarriages. Findings showed that spouse and child

---

[41] Clifton P. Flynn, "Relationship Violence by Women: Issues and Implications," *Family Relations* 39 (April 1990): 194–198.

[42] Murray A. Straus and Richard J. Gelles, *Physical Violence in American Families* (New Brunswick, NJ: Transaction, 1990), 110.

[43] Murray A. Straus and Stephen Sweet, "Verbal/Symbolic Aggression in Couples: Incidence Rates and Relationships to Personal Characteristics," *Journal of Marriage and the Family* 54 (May 1992): 346–357.

[44] Alfred DeMaris, Meredith D. Pugh, and Erika Harman, "Sex Differences in the Accuracy of Recall of Witnesses of Portrayed Dyadic Violence," *Journal of Marriage and the Family* 54 (May 1992): 335–345.

abuse are more likely in stepfamilies and families in which one or both spouses have been divorced (remarried and reconstituted) than in never-divorced (intact) families.[45] Explanations for this occurrence may relate to carrying on previously learned behavior patterns, to stepparents not having strong bonding and blood ties to children, to selecting spouses who dominate or can be dominated, and to higher levels of stress in remarried families. In any case, there is a continuity of abuse in reconstituted families.

Violence between spouses or intimate partners affects persons other than those who are directly abused. Specifically, children who witness parents being abused may be vulnerable to a variety of behavioral and emotional difficulties, including psychosomatic disorders and aggression.[46] In one study, students who viewed parental violence were significantly more anxious than those from satisfactory parental relationships. Females, in addition, showed elevated levels of depression and aggression. This finding is consistent with a *learned helplessness* model of wife abuse, which suggests that seeing one's mother in a helpless situation transmits the message that women are helpless to control their own lives. This message promotes depression in women, who are most likely to identify with the victim/mother. In contrast, men who witness parental violence might be more likely to identify with the aggressor/father and thus avoid depression. These men, in turn, are more likely to be abusive husbands themselves.

Sibling abuse and violence

The most frequent and accepted form of violence within families occurs between siblings. Parent interviews from the Straus and Gelles studies, mentioned previously, revealed that 40 percent of children had hit a brother or sister with an object during the preceding year and 82 percent had engaged in some form of violence against a sibling.

Sibling violence is granted a high degree of tolerance. Identical acts between parent and child or husband and wife might well result in criminal charges and social service intervention. It appears that, although male sibling pairs outdo female sibling pairs in throwing things and pushing and hitting one another, the greatest amount of physical violence occurs between boy/girl pairs.

Sibling violence is usually explained in terms of sibling rivalry or jealousy. Supposedly, one sibling resents something the other has: parental attention, privileges, clothes, objects, and the like. Differences may also center around limited resources: use of the bathroom or telephone, what TV show to watch, or who gets the remaining candy bar. These resentments and differences may become aggra-

---

[45] Debra Kalmuss and Judith A. Seltzer, "Continuity of Marital Behavior in Remarriage: The Case of Spouse Abuse," *Journal of Marriage and the Family* 48 (February 1986): 113–120; and Jean Giles-Sims and David Finkelhor, "Child Abuse in Stepfamilies," *Family Relations* 33 (July 1984): 403–413.

[46] Barbara Forsstrom-Cohen and Alan Rosenbaum, "The Effects of Parental Marital Violence on Young Adults: An Exploratory Investigation," *Journal of Marriage and the Family* 47 (May 1985): 467–472.

vated when parents intervene and insist that the children share or make a decision that favors one over the other. Reacting abusively toward a sibling, who is more one's equal in terms of size and age, is both more equitable and more acceptable than reacting abusively toward one's parents. (Although as noted later in this chapter, parent abuse occurs, as well.)

Sometimes sibling discord revolves around the division of labor in the family. Siblings normally compete in avoiding undesirable tasks or chores, such as doing dishes, cleaning rooms, sweeping walks, and so on. Age differences may aggravate the situation if younger children are assigned fewer chores. In short, exchange theory is operative, and perceived inequalities lead to conflict. Obviously, not all inequity leads to abuse or violence, but fighting or throwing objects is a common reaction of many children. When one child is outmatched, parental intervention may be warranted in stopping the fight, protecting the younger sibling, and perhaps punishing the older sibling. Unfortunately, doing so may exacerbate the general problem of competition among siblings.

It is factors such as these that help to explain the common occurrence and perhaps cyclical nature of sibling abuse and violence. Recognizing the importance of socialization experiences and social contexts, one could expect that, even among siblings, differences in abuse would exist by sex, ethnicity, and social class.

Elderly abuse and violence

The battered elderly parent (as noted in Chapter 15) is increasingly prevalent in the literature of aging with a consensus among these writers that a substantial problem exists. The variety and severity of mistreatment ranges from passive neglect (being unintentionally ignored, forgotten) to active neglect (financial exploitation; withholding medicine, food, assistance) and from verbal or emotional abuse (name-calling, threatening, humiliating) to physical abuse (slapping, pushing, injuring). Abuse may take the form of tying the elderly parent to a bed or chair, excessive use of medication or other drugs to keep the parent more manageable, battering with fists or objects to enforce particular behaviors, and nearly any conceivable activity.

Elderly persons who are abused are generally frail, mentally or physically disabled, female, and living with the person responsible for mistreatment. A commonly cited cause of the abuse is the caregiver becoming overtaxed by the requirements of caring for the elderly adult, which often leads to despair, anger, resentment, or violence in the caretaker. In some instances, the abuse is clearly malicious and intentional; in other instances, caretakers have serious emotional and dependency problems and do not deliberately intend to abuse but are unable to control their behavior.

Other research found that the typical abused elder, rather than being a dependent, may be an older woman supporting a dependent child or, to a lesser extent, a physically or mentally disabled spouse.[47] In this scenario, the powerlessness of the *abuser* who is dependent on an elderly parent may be a critical factor in understanding the abuse. This clearly contradicts the common notion that the dependency of the elderly *victim* on the abuser is a primary cause of abuse. From an exchange perspective, the victims perceive themselves as being on the losing end, or giving much and receiving little. In the study, most abused elders did not leave the situation but felt trapped by a sense of family obligation.

Violence among other intimates

Abuse and violence may be part of a relationship long before people marry and have children. One key example centers around friendships and intimates involved in the mate-selection process. Most studies of the courtship processes of dating, going steady, and becoming engaged have portrayed these events in a context of love, attraction, affection, mutual disclosure, and increasing closeness and commitment as the relationship moves toward increasing exclusivity and marriage. Other recent studies, however, have suggested that violence and sexual exploitation are the dark side of courtship,[48] and that dating violence is very prevalent.[49]

A number of studies have been completed in an attempt to estimate the incidence of **courtship violence** and gender differences in abuse. In a study of college students, at least one-third of those who dated had experienced physical aggression at some point in their dating history.[50] As expected, the incidence of courtship violence "known of" by students greatly exceeded what had been directly experienced. Also, as expected, extreme forms of violence, such as assault with an object or weapon, were less common than milder forms, such as pushing and slapping. Nearly two-fifths of the students knew of instances of threats, pushing, or slapping. Overall, males and females were about equal in initiating, committing, and sustaining violence. Females, the principal reported victims, more frequently related serious forms of violence done to them; they also reported more often sustaining sexual assault, physical injury, and emotional trauma. Males rarely reported that sexual assault was attempted or occurred and did not perceive that females sustained greater physical or emotional harm. Attempts to explain these disparities were rooted in denial by the males, as shown by the nonrecognition or recall of details of experiences and the minimization of the frequency and intensity of the males' abuse.

---

[47] Karl Pillemer, "The Dangers of Dependency: New Findings on Domestic Violence Against the Elderly," *Social Problems* 33 (December 1985): 146–158.

[48] Sally A. Lloyd, "The Darkside of Courtship: Violence and Sexual Exploitation," *Family Relations* 40 (January 1991): 14–20.

[49] David B. Sugarman and Gerald T. Hotaling, "Dating Violence: Prevalence, Context, and Risk Markers," in Maureen A. Pirog-Good and Jan E. Stets (eds.), *Violence in Dating Relationships* (New York: Praeger, 1989), 3–32.

[50] Gordon E. Barnes, Leonard Greenwood, and Reena Sommer, "Courtship Violence in a Canadian Sample of Male College Students," *Family Relations* 40 (January 1991): 37–44; and James M. Makepeace, "Gender Differences in Courtship Victimization," *Family Relations* 35 (July 1986): 383–388.

Consistent with studies of college students, a national representative sample of never-married persons between the ages of eighteen and thirty found that women were at least as likely, if not more likely, to be physically aggressive than men.[51] This finding led the authors to note that, when developing a theory of dating aggression, the mechanisms that bring about both male and female aggression must be considered. Thus, patriarchy may help explain dating aggression among men, but it does not explain why women are aggressive. The same source noted that people who are young, from the lower class, and who drink before a conflict are more prone to physical aggression. Thus, once again, it seems that verbal aggression may be the seed of physical aggression and that both verbal and physical aggressive behavior are reciprocated in kind.

Date rape and sexual aggression and coercion

This type of forced sexual contact constitutes a particular kind of violence among intimates. Estimates of unwanted sexual assaults against female students, committed by acquaintances as well as by strangers, have been in the range of 20 to 25 percent. A study at the University of New Hampshire revealed that 39 percent of the women had experienced some forced contact, 20 percent had experienced forced attempted intercourse, and 10 percent had experienced forced completed intercourse (rape).[52]

Another study found that fraternity members were more likely than non-members to commit forced sexual contact. It was suggested that fraternity members associate with many other men who engage in coercive or violent sexual activities. These men are therefore more likely to be reinforced by their friends for engaging in sexual coercion and aggression. These men are also more likely to use drugs and alcohol as a sexual strategy to control women.[53]

The occurrence of violence during childhood or adolescence, whether exhibited toward parents or during courtship, seems to be a foundation for marital and parental violence. Unfortunately, the experience of violence between spouses and between parents and children is seldom the perpetrator's first experience.

Treating and preventing family violence

Application of the ABCX model (described at the beginning of this chapter) to violence in families and among intimate partners suggests that the various types of

---

[51] Jan E. Stets and Debra A. Henderson, "Contextual Factors Surrounding Conflict Resolution While Dating: Results from a National Study," *Family Relations* 40 (January 1991): 29–36; and Jan E. Stets, "Interactive Processes in Dating Aggression: A National Study," *Journal of Marriage and the Family* 54 (February 1992): 165–177.

[52] Sally K. Ward, Kathy Chapman, Ellen Cohn, Susan White, and Kirk Williams, "Acquaintance Rape and the College Social Scene," *Family Relations* 40 (January 1991): 65–71.

[53] Scot B. Boeringer, Constance L. Shehan, and Ronald L. Akers, "Social Contexts and Social Learning in Sexual Coercion and Aggression: Assessing the Contribution of Fraternity Membership," *Family Relations* 40 (January 1991): 58–64.

violence that take place may or may not represent crisis events. A crisis event depends on (B) the resources available to members and (C) the meanings or definitions attached to the acts.

It has been clearly shown in previous discussions that many acts between siblings, parents and children, and partners are perceived as expected and normal behaviors. Even a Gallup Poll in 1994 indicated that almost one person in four (23 percent) said they could imagine a situation in which they would approve of a wife slapping her husband.[54] People were more cautious about the opposite situation, however, as only 10 percent said they would ever approve of a husband slapping a wife.

The response of the abused persons—to endure, to fight back, or to escape—will depend on the meanings and perceptions of the event as well as the resources available to those abused: strength, peer support, friends and kin, money or services, police and crisis intervention centers, and particularly, self-esteem.

When Gelles and Straus asked women who had experienced violence how they reacted to the most recent incidence, more than half said they cried. Other responses, in order of frequency, were to run to another room, hit back, run out of the house, and call a friend or relative; the response in last place was to call the police.[55] The first few responses are all immediate and personal reactions to being hurt: crying, yelling, and running to get away. Longer-term responses are more closely related to personal and social resources—friends and relatives as well as community services, such as the police.

Gelles and Straus suggested that an important and beneficial way of helping battered women would be to empower them to negotiate with their husbands to end the violence. A particularly important intervention service (resource) would be education in mediation or conflict-resolution techniques. Other important resources for battered women include sources of help, such as police, social workers, shelters, medical services, and so forth.

Providing these resources is important, certainly, a step in the right direction. But how can family violence be prevented in the first place? Specifically, how can assumptions that violence is a legitimate solution to conflict be modified?

Gelles and Straus argued that prevention policies and programs must be directed at the two factors that make it possible for people to abuse and maltreat those whom they love.[56] First, eliminate cultural norms and values that accept violence as a means of resolving conflict and problems in families. Second, develop programs and policies that support families and reduce internal and external stresses and inequalities. How can these goals be accomplished?

The first goal—to eliminate cultural norms and values that support violence—necessitates establishing a moral code that loved ones are not to be hit.

---

[54] David W. Moore, "Approval of Husband Slapping Wife Continues to Decline," *The Gallup Poll Monthly* 341 (February 1994): 2.

[55] Gelles and Straus, *Intimate Violence,* Figure 10, p. 258.

[56] Ibid., 194.

This means banning spanking and corporal punishment. Sweden and all other Scandinavian countries, for example, have taken the lead in this regard by banning capital punishment, outlawing corporal punishment of children in schools, and passing legislation prohibiting spanking. Firearm ownership is also rigorously controlled. Violent programming on Swedish television is severely restricted.

In contrast, most people in the United States are aware of the controversies over capital punishment; corporal punishment; spanking; control over sale and registration of firearms; and violence on TV, in movies, in sports, and in children's games. A review of 217 studies dating back to 1957 revealed a positive and significant correlation between television violence and aggressive behavior.[57] This held true regardless of age, suggesting that the influence of violent television portrayals is not confined to young children or adolescents. Violence, in general, including family, marital, parental, and sibling violence, will remain prevalent as long as the society in which it occurs glorifies killing, shooting, beating, hitting, and abusing.

The second goal of developing programs and policies that support families is closely related to the first goal of changing norms and values. Policies and programs have been enacted in many states to address child abuse, spouse abuse, and marital rape. Additional efforts to eliminate poverty and unemployment; to provide adequate medical and hospital care to all families; to support effective planned parenthood; to reduce sexual, class, and racial inequality, both in the home and community; and to promote kin and community linkages and support networks would likely result in lowering levels of family violence.

SUMMARY

1. The central issues of this chapter—stress, crises, and violence—are not unique to any given point of the family life course or any particular family structure. A stressor, or crisis-provoking, event includes any situation that threatens the status quo and well-being of the system or its members. These events may come from sources both within and outside the family. Certain events may solidify the unit, while others may be very disruptive.

2. The ABCX model refers to some event (A) interacting with the family's crisis-meeting resources (B) and the definition or meaning given to the event (C), resulting in the level or degree of crisis (X). When and if B and C are adequate, the levels of stress and crisis will be minimal. If they are inadequate, the levels of stress and crisis will be high.

3. A common stressor event in many marriages and intimate relationships is that of abuse and violence. Various myths about violence tend to attribute it to others rather than to acknowledge it as an outgrowth of and component of a given society.

[57] Haejung Paik and George Comstock, "The Effects of Television Violence on Antisocial Behavior: A Meta-Analysis," *Communication Research* 21 (August 1994): 516–546.

4. Considerable research attention has been focused on the abuse of children. Traditional modes of discipline grant legitimacy to spanking and other forms of physical punishment of children. Since most of such punishment occurs behind closed doors, most abuse never comes to the attention of the public.

5. Violence is sometimes directed by children, particularly adolescents, toward parents. Research has shown that parental assault is extensive, occurring among both males and females and being directed at both mothers and fathers.

6. Wife and female partner abuse may involve common couple violence or patriarchal terrorism. Like child abuse, abuse toward women is not always viewed as inappropriate, particularly in contexts of male authority and dominance. As with child abuse, abuse of female intimates may have actually decreased in recent years. Many female partners do not or cannot leave their violent male partners due to economic dependency and lack of alternatives and sometimes due to positive perceptions of the relationship.

7. Rape, or forced coitus without consent, is another form of violence against wives and women. Many states have changed their laws concerning rape but the issue remains a point of controversy when occurring between spouses or intimate partners.

8. Husband and male-partner abuse is granted far less attention than the abuse of children and wives; however, physical violence seems to be one aspect of intimate relationships that approaches equality between spouses.

9. Sibling abuse is the most frequent and accepted form of violence within families, often centering around sibling rivalry and jealousy. Supposedly, one sibling resents something the other has, or tensions center around differences over availability of limited resources.

10. Abuse of people who are elderly frequently involves aging parents, particularly mothers. The mistreatment of elders ranges from positive or active neglect to verbal and physical abuse.

11. Other forms of violence among intimates include adolescents and young adults in the dating/courtship process. Such violence may take the form of threats or physical injury or may frequently involve sexual aggression, coercion, or date rape.

12. This chapter focused on marital and family stress and violence. Chapter 17 will turn to terminating marriages, particularly via divorce, and the subsequent pattern of remarriage.

KEY TERMS AND TOPICS

Marital and interpersonal stress
   and crisis p. 490

Stressor events p. 490

ABCX model of stress p. 491

Enabling and disabling events p. 492

Double-ABCX model p. 492

Family violence p. 494

Violence among intimates p. 494

Myths of family violence p. 496

Causes of family violence p. 498

Child abuse p. 499

Physical punishment p. 499

Cultural spillover theory p. 500

Child sexual abuse p. 501

Parent abuse p. 503

Wife and female-partner abuse p. 504

Patriarchal terrorism p. 504

Rape among intimates p. 509

Husband and male-partner abuse p. 510

Mutual abuse and violence
   between couples p. 511

Sibling abuse p. 512

Elderly abuse p. 513

Violence among other intimates p. 514

Courtship violence p. 514

Date rape and sexual aggression
   and coercion p. 515

Treating and preventing family
   violence p. 515

DISCUSSION QUESTIONS

1. List five stressor events for families. How could families prepare for events such as these? How is it possible that certain events strengthen families whereas others tear them apart?

2. What factors enhance crisis proneness and crisis preparedness? Using the ABCX formula given in the chapter, show how *resources* and *meanings* lead to family adequacy or inadequacy in facing potential crisis situations.

3. Select any personal or family problem. How could or does the availability of resources affect one's ability to address the problem? What types of resources are significant to families or individuals? How does one's definition of the problem affect the level of stress experienced?

4. Examine the seven myths of family violence. How many seem to be partially true? With which ones do you agree or disagree? Why?

5. What family and social circumstances put children at greater risk for abuse, physical and sexual? What long-term effects does being abused have on individuals?

6. Consider the position that marital and intimate relationships (including abuse and rape) are private and personal matters. If so, should the community or state get involved in what lovers, couples, and families do to each other? Why or why not?

7. Why don't many abused wives or female partners leave abusive situations? What factors make a difference in women's decision making?

8. Is it necessary to be concerned about or do research on violence toward husbands or between siblings? Can't husbands take care of themselves? Aren't fights among children natural? Explain.

9. Think of personal childhood experiences of violence. What experiences do you recall? With whom? For what reasons?

10. Discuss various forms of abuse within families toward elderly parents. What types of action or programs might lessen the severity of or even resolve the problem?

11. Are you aware of abuse or violence in dating and nonmarital interactions? What forms does it take? Is sexual aggression or coercion actually violence? Why or why not?

12. What is the relationship of factors such as alcoholism, drug addiction, unemployment, and lack of money to violence and abuse? How might a pregnancy, birthday, or holiday affect the likelihood of violence?

FURTHER READINGS

Allison, Julie A., and Wrightsman, Lawrence S. *Rape, The Misunderstood Crime.* Newbury Park, CA: Sage, 1993. An extensive overview of available literature on the topic of rape, including information about the rapist, date rape, spousal rape, the law, as well as treatment of and preventive approaches to rape.

Burr, Wesley R., Klein, Shirley R., and Associates. *Reexamining Family Stress: New Theory and Research.* Thousand Oaks, CA: Sage, 1994. Building upon recent methodological developments, the writers introduce several systemic concepts into the family stress literature that contribute to theory, research, and practice.

Gelles, Richard J., and Loseke, Donileen R. (eds.). *Current Controversies on Family Violence.* Newbury Park, CA: Sage, 1993. Key professionals take varying perspectives on issues in conceptualization, definition and measurement, causes, and social intervention of family violence.

Hampton, Robert L.; Gullotta, Thomas P.; Adams, Gerald R.; Potter, Earl H.; and Weissberg, Roger (eds.). *Family Violence: Prevention and Treatment.* Newbury Park, CA: Sage, 1993. A multidisciplinary focus on family violence from a variety of abusive contexts, including children, marriage, elderly, families of color, and how it can be prevented and treated.

Kaplan, Lisa, and Girard, Judith L. *Strengthening High-Risk Families: A Handbook for Practitioners.* New York: Lexington Books, 1994. A book written for practitioners with a focus on family preservation, agencies, and treatment strategies but including as well valuable information on high-risk family issues.

Kirkwood, Catherine. *Leaving Abusive Partners: From the Scars of Survival to the Wisdom for Change.* Newbury Park, CA: Sage, 1993. A feminist analysis of formerly abused women's experiences after leaving their partners.

Levinson, David. *Family Violence in Cross-Cultural Perspective.* Newbury Park, CA: Sage, 1989. An anthropological look at family violence in its various forms and frequencies in societies around the world.

McHenry, Patrick C., and Price, Sharon J. (eds.). *Families and Change: Coping with Stressful Events.* Thousand Oaks, CA: Sage, 1994. Eight chapters deal with stress and change over the family life cycle, such as gender issues, work/family, and aging. Five chapters deal with situational stressors such as divorce, drug and alcohol abuse, and violence.

Mendel, Matthew Parynik. *The Male Survivor: The Impact of Sexual Abuse.* Thousand Oaks, CA: Sage, 1995. An original study of 124 men, including nine extensive clinical interviews, of male survivors of childhood sexual abuse.

Stacey, William A.; Hazlewood, Lonnie R.; and Shupe, Anson. *The Violent Couple.* Westport, CT: Praeger, 1994. A sample of violent partners is drawn from a counseling program to analyze the forms, pathways, and healing strategies for mutual abuse.

Straus, Murray A., and Gelles, Richard J. *Physical Violence in American Families.* New Brunswick, NJ: Transaction, 1990. An informative and extensive report of violence in American families, based on two national surveys conducted a decade apart.

Tifft, Larry. *Battering of Women: The Failure of Intervention and the Case for Prevention.* Boulder: Westview Press, 1993. An attempt to understand the battering of women as a social phenomenon, exploring battering from both social structural and interpersonal perspectives.

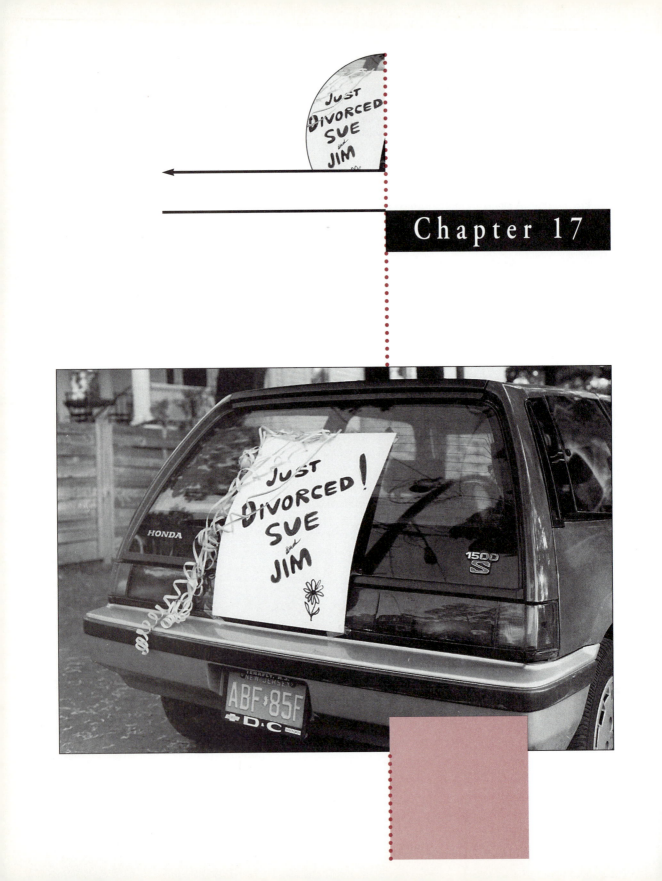

Chapter 17

Divorce and Remarriage

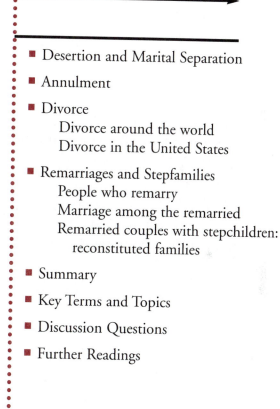

- Desertion and Marital Separation
- Annulment
- Divorce
  Divorce around the world
  Divorce in the United States
- Remarriages and Stepfamilies
  People who remarry
  Marriage among the remarried
  Remarried couples with stepchildren:
    reconstituted families
- Summary
- Key Terms and Topics
- Discussion Questions
- Further Readings

All societies provide one or more ways for husbands, wives, or both to deal with unsatisfactory marital relationships. Highly patriarchal, male-dominant societies are likely to permit men to have mistresses or concubines while they are married. In many societies, including the United States, marriage may be regarded as a civil contract, in which the state specifies how old people have to be to get married, how many spouses they may have, and the conditions under which marriages can be dissolved.

In some countries, often in conformity with the Canon Law of the Roman Catholic Church, marriage was, until recently, indissolvable except by death. This was true in countries such as Argentina, Brazil, Chile, and Colombia in Latin America; the Philippines in Southeast Asia; and Italy, Ireland, and Spain in Western Europe. In some countries, such as the United States, France, Switzerland, Russia, Poland, and the Scandinavian countries, a divorce is granted if one or both parties have been guilty of a grave violation of marital obligations or if it is shown that the marriage has completely broken down. Finally, the official laws of Islam and of Judaism grant free power of the husband to terminate his marriage by repudiating his wife. In reality, this occurs infrequently, and movements exist to provide power to wives to bring about dissolution of their marriages as well.

In the United States, divorce is the best-known and most common means of ending an unsatisfactory marital relationship; thus, most attention in this chapter will be devoted to divorce. Desertions, legal separations, informally agreed upon separations, and annulments are other means that people use to get out of a marriage, at least temporarily, if not permanently.

DESERTION AND MARITAL SEPARATION

Desertion is the willful abandonment, without legal justification, of one's spouse, children, or both. Little is known about desertion, and few studies have considered this issue.

Traditionally, it has been assumed that desertion applied only to men. Today, there are reports on "runaway wives," as well. Unlike men, who may want out of a marriage, women who desert are more likely to seek escape from childrearing and home responsibilities that have become unbearable. For both sexes, it appears that desertion is a response to one issue or many that seem unsolvable: children, marital conflicts, alcoholism, infidelity, inability to support a family, and the like.

Unlike divorce, desertion is not institutionalized. No registration takes place with the courts or any other official body, and the deserting and nondeserting spouses cannot remarry. Exactly what constitutes desertion and what roles are appropriate in legal, economic, and social situations are not very clear. For example, how many days' absence constitutes desertion? When a spouse leaves and returns on multiple occasions, do marital and parental role patterns resemble those of the one- or two-parent family? Is one spouse legally responsible for the expenses and activities of the other? Because of the lack of institutionalized norms and the ambiguity of events surrounding desertion, it is believed that desertion has far more negative effects than divorce.

What about **marital separation**? A widely held assumption is that marital separation is a stepping-stone to divorce, sometimes soon followed by another marriage. While divorce follows separation for many couples, others use separation as a time to work out a reconciliation, ending marital difficulties. Still other couples remain married but live in long-term, unresolved separations.

The U.S. census distinguishes people who are *married, spouse present* from those who are *married, spouse absent.* The married, spouse-absent persons are further categorized as *separated* or *other.* The *separated* category includes those people with legal separations, those living apart with intentions of obtaining a divorce, and other persons permanently or temporarily separated because of marital discord. The *other* group of married, spouse-absent people includes those married but living apart due to employment or serving away from home in the armed forces or residing apart for any reason except separation, as just described. In 1994, 6.7 million persons, or 3.4 percent of the U.S. population, were classified as married, spouse absent. More than 4.7 million of these people were separated.[1]

In cases of **legal separation,** the husband and wife are authorized to live apart, and formal agreements specify visiting patterns, support, and so forth. These separations are sometimes referred to as *limited divorce, partial dissolution,* or *divorce from bed and board.*

The majority of separations are not legalized. An **informal separation** is often an arrangement between husband and wife, where one or both decide to live separately. Unlike cases of desertion, each knows the whereabouts of the other, and unlike cases of divorce, the couple is legally married and cannot remarry. These couples seem to be overrepresented among low-income families; thus, informal separation has been referred to in the literature as the "poor man's divorce."

One of the few studies of marital separations was done in the metropolitan Cleveland area with a random sample of over eleven hundred residents.[2] It was found that one in six couples was likely to separate for at least forty-eight hours at some point in their relationship because of arguments or disagreements. Some separations were a step on the way to permanent separation or divorce. Other separations were used as a conflict-resolution technique or a dramatic gesture to force some action on the part of the spouse. Those most likely to separate were blacks, women, and those with low incomes and minor children. For most people, separations were associated with a high sense of emotional distress.

---

[1] U.S. Bureau of the Census, *Current Population Reports,* Series P20-484, Arlene F. Saluter, "Marital Status and Living Arrangements, March 1994" (Washington, DC: U.S. Government Printing Office, 1996), Table 1, p. 1.

[2] Gay C. Kitson, "Marital Discord and Marital Separation: A County Survey," *Journal of Marriage and the Family* 47 (August 1985): 693–700. Note also: Stephen B. Kincaid and Robert A. Caldwell, "Marital Separation: Causes, Coping, and Consequences," *Journal of Divorce and Remarriage* 22 (1995): 109–128.

What about separations, temporary or permanent, for reasons other than marital discord? One source concluded that marital noncohabitation does not make the heart grow fonder.[3] Couples living in separate households—most often because of military service or incarceration (confined in prison) were nearly twice as likely to divorce within three years compared to persons cohabiting with their spouses.

ANNULMENT

The word *annul,* legally defined, means to reduce to nothing, to obliterate, to make void and of no effect, to abolish, to do away with, to eradicate. When a marriage has been annulled, a court, acting under the law of the state, has found that causes existed *prior* to the marriage that render the marriage contract void. The court concludes that the marriage, when performed, was in fact no marriage at all. By annulling the marriage, the court, in effect, says that it never existed.

Generally, the distinction between divorce and annulment lies in the time in which certain actions occurred. Divorce generally involves an action that occurred *after* the date of marriage—adultery, incompatibility, cruelty, desertion, nonsupport, alcoholism, and the like. Annulment generally involves an action that occurred *before* the date of marriage—being underage, already being married, insanity, incurable impotence, incestuous relationship, and the like.

It may seem odd that, while the marriage was a social and psychological reality, legally, it never existed. If there are children from the annulled marriage, the husband who "never existed" may be required by the court to support minor children. Socially, relatives and friends are well aware of the once-existing marriage. And psychologically, both the male and female involved are well aware of once being married and the mate-selection process that preceded it.

DIVORCE

Divorce around the world

In the Western world, divorce has traditionally been viewed as an unfortunate event for the persons involved and as a clear index of failure of the family system. But over the past few decades, in the United States and other Western countries, attitudes toward separation and divorce have changed. An examination of divorce laws in the United States, England and Wales, France, and Sweden revealed that divorce has become increasingly easy to obtain, spousal support has become less common, efforts have been made to increase child-support awards and improve payment compliance, and shared parental decision-making authority has become increasingly encouraged.[4]

---

[3] Ronald R. Rindfuss and Elizabeth Hervey Stephen, "Marital Noncohabitation: Separation Does Not Make the Heart Grow Fonder," *Journal of Marriage and the Family* 52 (February 1990): 259–270.

[4] Mark A. Fine and David R. Fine, "An Examination and Evaluation of Recent Changes in Divorce Laws in Five Western Countries: The Critical Role of Values," *Journal of Marriage and the Family* 56 (May 1994): 249–263.

Global Diversity: Divorce in Japan

The Japanese divorce rate is about one-third that of the United States and about half that of Western Europe. Japan is the only one among developed countries (except Italy) that has a low divorce rate. Suggested explanations for this include that the family is still powerful and that many men and women do not divorce for the sake of the children.

Yasuhiko Yuzawa described three common kinds of divorce in Japan:

1. *Divorce by consent* is effected simply by notifying the registration office of the divorce, so long as both husband and wife agree. This is recognized as the simplest mode of divorce procedure in the world, with no conditions or checks imposed. About 91 percent of Japanese divorces are of this kind.

2. *Divorce by conciliation* is for those who cannot reach an agreement. These couples go to family court and get a divorce through mediation of a conciliation committee. About 8 percent of the divorces in Japan are of this type.

3. *Divorce by judgment* most closely parallels the common procedure for divorce in Western countries. When divorce cannot be settled by any of the above two methods, it is brought to the general court. Reasons for divorce must meet conditions of adultery, abandonment, an unknown fate of the spouse, a severe mental disorder with no hope of recovery, or other reasons that make continuation of the marriage impossible. Only about 1 percent of Japanese divorces are by judgment.

Source: Journal of Divorce 13 (1990): 129–141.

Divorce is not unique to Western countries, however, but is a factor in nearly all the world's nations and has traditionally been common in most tribal societies. In addition, in the past, a few nations have had higher divorce rates than the United States has now, such as Japan in the period 1887–1919, Algeria in 1887–1940, and Egypt in 1935–1945.

At present, the United States may have the highest divorce rate in the world. Based on the latest figures available from United Nations sources, the U.S. rate of divorce per 1,000 persons in the population was 4.6 compared to 4.2 in Cuba, 3.0 in Canada, 2.6 in Australia, 2.5 in Sweden, 2.2 in Switzerland, 1.4 in Japan, 1.3 in Israel and Singapore, 0.7 in Poland, 0.6 in Mexico, and 0.4 in Italy.[5] Divorce rates are not available (or perhaps not even computed) for a number of strongly Catholic countries (Philippines, Spain, Colombia, and others).

How are variations in the rate or frequency of divorce explained? One study sampled sixty-six countries to investigate societal-level correlates of divorce.[6] Four variables were shown to bear a significant relationship to the likelihood of divorce.

[5] United Nations, *Demographic Yearbook,* 1993 (New York, 1995), Table 25, pp. 557–559.

[6] Katherine Trent and Scott J. South, "Structural Determinants of the Divorce Rate: A Cross-societal Analysis," *Journal of Marriage and the Family* 51 (May 1989): 391–404.

Associated with lower divorce rates were (1) a high sex ratio, indicating a relative undersupply of women, and (2) a late average age at marriage for women. Significantly but nonlinearly related to divorce were (3) level of socioeconomic development and (4) female labor force participation rate. Both of these variables exhibited U-shaped associations with divorce. This suggests that socioeconomic development and increased female labor force participation in the early stages of industrialization tend to reduce the rate of divorce, but at later stages of industrialization and modernization, they tend to increase the incidence of divorce.

Many societies in the Western world, including the United States, rate high in socioeconomic development and female labor force participation. Thus, with an erosion of traditional patriarchal patterns and a heavy emphasis on the individual and small nuclear family in contrast to an emphasis on extended kin, one could expect high rates of divorce. The following sections will examine how divorce rates are determined and consider trends in the United States.

Divorce in the United States

Divorce rates

Divorce rates are likely to be calculated in one of three ways:

1. By the number of divorces that take place per 1,000 persons in the total population

2. By the number of divorces per 1,000 married females, ages fifteen and over

3. By the ratio of divorces granted in a given year to the number of marriages contracted in that same year

Note the differences in rate, depending on which figure is used. For instance, the number of divorces that took place *per 1,000 persons in the total population* in the United States in 1994 was 4.6. This means that for every 1,000 persons in the population (men, women, children, adults, married, single), 9.2 *persons* became divorced, or 4.6 *marriages* ended in divorce (or annulment). Or said another way, in a city of 100,000 population, if 460 divorces were granted in 1994, the divorce rate was 4.6. Since the American system is monogamous (two persons per divorce), 920 individuals in a city of 100,000 persons were divorced last year. Note how this divorce rate can be influenced by factors such as the age distribution or the proportion of the married to the single population. In a country or city with a large family size, a low life expectancy, a late age at marriage, a sizable proportion of the population being children or single teenagers, or a disproportionate number of the population unmarried, a sizable percentage of those married could get divorced, yet the country or city would have a seemingly low divorce rate.

The number of divorces (again, including annulments) that took place *per 1,000 married women, ages fifteen and over,* in the United States in 1994 was approximately 20.5. This means that there were about 21 divorces per 1,000 (205 per 10,000) married females, ages fifteen and over. Of the three rates mentioned, this one is probably the most accurate. Unlike the first rate described, in this calculation, men, single persons, children, and so on are excluded. It is based on the number of legally married women, who constitute the group that is susceptible to divorce. This figure could be used to compare divorce rates cross-culturally without being influenced by the number, age, or marital status of the total population.

The ratio of *divorces granted in a given year to the number of marriages in that year* was about 46 in 1994. This is the rate used to best illustrate the "breakdown in the U.S. family." Nearly one out of two marriages ends in divorce—or does it?

Assume that a city of 100,000 population issued 1,000 marriage licenses in 1996. In the same year, 500 divorces were granted. This would result in a divorce/marriage ratio of 1 to 2, or 50 divorces per 100 marriages. Thus, there was one divorce for every two marriages in the community in 1996. Suppose, however, that the state modified its divorce law that year, and instead of 500 divorces, 2,000 divorces took place; the number of marriages remained constant at 1,000. Now, according to this rate, there are two divorces for every marriage, or a divorce rate of 200.

While it may be accurate to speak of twice as many divorces as marriages occurring in a given year, it is not accurate to say that, of those marriages that occurred, one-half will end in divorce. The inaccuracy is due to at least three reasons:

1. The marriages that occurred that year are not the ones that ended in divorce; those marriages began perhaps one, eight, or thirty years ago. There is no relevant link between the number of marriages begun and ended in 1993.

2. Approximately 40 percent of all marriages are remarriages for one or both spouses, which is not taken into account. Persons who divorce and remarry in the same year contribute to both the number of marriages and the number of divorces, producing a ratio of 1 to 1: as many divorces as marriages. To redivorce in the same year would produce the impossible result of having more divorces than marriages.

3. As in the example just shown, it is possible to calculate a number of marriages that is smaller than the number of divorces. Note an example using 1994 census figures. In 1994, there were 2.36 million marriages; in the same year, there were 1.19 million marriages that ended in divorce (50 percent). Also in that year, there were approximately 2.29 million deaths, giving a ratio of deaths to marriages of 2.29 million to 2.36 million, or .97 (97 percent). Since the majority of these deaths occurred among married persons, the sum of marriages that ended in death or divorce was 147 percent (47 percent more marriages ending in 1994 than were formulated that year).

Irrespective of the manner of calculation, one should be aware that statistics on divorce are not perfect. Even national data reported by the National Office of Vital Statistics are based on estimates obtained from states participating in the divorce-registration area (DRA). As of 1995, thirty-one states and the Virgin Islands participated in the DRA.[7] Thus, actual data from all fifty states are not available. What's more, sampling rates vary among the DRA states, depending on the sizes of their annual divorce totals. All statistics estimated from probability samples have a sampling error. Completeness of reporting individual demographic items on divorce records also varies considerably among DRA states. For example, some states do not require the reporting of race, and others do not require the reporting of the number of these marriages. Finally, many items on divorce records are often left blank, particularly personal characteristics of husband and wife (age, race, and number of marriages).

Although the accuracy of divorce rates and statistics is improving, divorce data are not perfect. The best available information is presented with the recognition that the figures are based on estimates from selected available data.

U.S. trends

The number of divorces and annulments granted in the United States increased from the pre–World War II figure of 264,000 in 1940 to the post–World War II figure of 379,000 in 1954 to 708,000 in 1970 to a peak of 1,213,000 in 1981. The number of divorces and annulments has declined since then; in 1994, the figure was 1,191,000. The divorce rate per 1,000 population increased from 2.0 in 1940 to 2.4 in 1954 to 3.5 in 1970 to 5.3 in 1981; the rate declined to 4.6 in 1994. The increase was not as steady as it appears from the selected figures given (see Table 17-1 and Figure 17-1).

The 1981 figure of 1,213,000 divorces—that is, more than 2.42 million divorced persons—was the highest national total ever observed for the United States. During the 1970s and until 1981, the number of divorces increased more rapidly than the total population and the married population of the United States. The 1982 figures, however, showed the first annual decrease in several decades. In 1994, an estimated 1.19 million couples divorced, 2 percent fewer than in 1981.

Numerous factors have been cited to explain changes in divorce rates over time. Many have focused on social characteristics such as social structural variables rather than on individual characteristics. One structural explanation of the changing divorce rate included variables such as increasing industrialization, increasing urbanization, increasing female labor force participation, decreasing fertility rate, changing gender-role norms, religious diversity, and legal diversity.[8] Another explanation looked at the impact of wars, in particular, World War II.[9] And still another focused on economic conditions, as follows.

---

[7] U.S. Bureau of the Census, *Statistical Abstract of the United States: 1995,* 115th ed. (Washington, DC: U.S. Government Printing Office, 1995), p. 72.

[8] Leonard Beeghley and Jeffrey W. Dwyer, "Social Structure and the Divorce Rate," *Perspectives on Social Problems* 1 (1989): 147–170.

[9] Eliza K. Pavalko and Glen H. Elder, Jr., "World War II and Divorce: A Life-Course Perspective," *American Journal of Sociology* 5 (March 1990): 1213–1234.

Table 17-1
Number of divorces and divorce rates: United States, 1945–1994

Year	Number of divorces	Divorce Rate per 1,000 Total population	Married women
1994	1,191,000	4.6	20.5
1993	1,187,000	4.6	20.5
1992	1,215,000	4.8	21.2
1991	1,187,000	4.7	20.9
1990	1,175,000	4.7	20.9
1988	1,183,000	4.8	21.0
1986	1,178,000	4.9	21.2
1984	1,169,000	5.0	21.5
1982	1,170,000	5.0	21.7
1980	1,189,000	5.2	22.6
1978	1,130,000	5.1	21.9
1976	1,083,000	5.0	21.1
1974	977,000	4.6	19.3
1972	845,000	4.1	17.0
1970	708,000	3.5	14.9
1968	584,000	2.9	12.4
1966	499,000	2.5	10.9
1964	450,000	2.4	10.0
1962	413,000	2.2	9.4
1960	393,000	2.2	9.2
1958	368,000	2.1	8.9
1956	382,000	2.3	9.4
1954	379,000	2.4	9.5
1952	392,000	2.5	10.1
1950	385,000	2.6	10.3
1948	408,000	2.8	11.2
1946	610,000	4.3	17.9
1945	485,000	3.5	14.4

Source: National Center for Health Statistics, *Monthly Vital Statistics Reports,* vol. 43, no. 12 "Births, Marriages, Divorces, and Deaths for 1994" (Hyattsville, MD: Public Health Service, 13 June 1995); and *Statistical Abstract of the United States: 1995,* 115th ed. (Washington, DC: Government Printing Office, 1995), no. 87, p. 73.

Figure 17-1
Divorce rates: 1925–1994

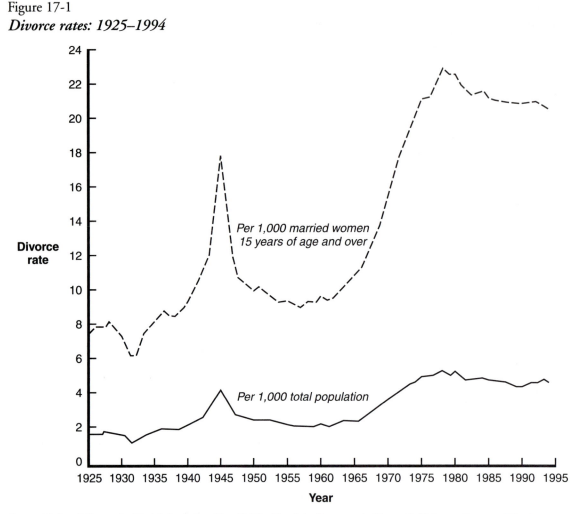

Source: National Center for Health Statistics, *Monthly Vital Statistics Reports,* vol. 43, no. 9, "Advance Report of Final Divorce Statistics, 1989 and 1990" (Hyattsville, MD: Public Health Service, 22 March 1995), Table 1, p. 9; and U.S. Bureau of the Census, *Current Population Reports,* Series P23-189, "Population Profile of the United States: 1995" (Washington, DC: Government Printing Office, 1995), Appendix A, pp. 58–59.

Generally, divorce rates have declined in times of economic depression and risen during times of prosperity (see Figure 17-1). During the Depression years, 1932–1933, the rate of divorce per one thousand married women was the lowest in the last sixty-five years. Following the Depression, the rate of divorce moved upward almost steadily until the first postwar year, 1946. After 1946, the rate dropped sharply until 1950. For about fifteen years, until 1965, the divorce rate showed considerable stability, increasing slightly some years and decreasing during the minirecession years of 1954 and 1958. Since 1965, the divorce trend has climbed relatively sharply, reaching the highest rate in the history of the United States in 1981. Since then, modest variations have been exhibited, with a slight overall decline in the number and rate of divorces.

Variations in divorce

Divorce is permitted in every state in the United States. Each state has its own divorce code, so it could be expected that the probability of divorce would vary widely by geographic, demographic, and social characteristics. The following sections will examine several variations and seek explanations for higher or lower likelihoods of divorce according to selected characteristics.

Geographic distribution Since the nineteenth century, the geographic distribution of divorce in the United States has followed a general trend, increasing as one moves from east to west. The divorce rate is highest in the West, followed closely by the South, with a considerable drop in the Midwest, followed by the Northeast.

Major variations exist among individual states as well. In 1990, the divorce rate per 1,000 population was lowest in Massachusetts (2.7) and highest in Nevada (10.8). States with rates of 3.5 or less per 1,000 population included Connecticut, Maryland, Massachusetts, New Jersey, New York, and Pennsylvania. States with rates of 6.0 or more included Alabama, Arizona, Arkansas, Florida, Idaho, New Mexico, Nevada, Oklahoma, Tennessee, and Wyoming.[10] Note that the lowest rates generally occurred in the Northeast and the highest rates in the South and West.

How can these geographical variations be explained? Different factors likely operate in different areas, but in general, the probability of divorce is believed to be lower in culturally homogeneous rather than heterogeneous communities and in communities with primary, face-to-face interactions in contrast to communities with anonymous relationships, segmentalized relationships, or both. In traditional Durkheimian social structural terms, this pattern can be explained by a social integration hypothesis of fewer divorces in areas of high consensus on rules of behavior (norms) and effective social controls to ensure conformity. Communities or areas (regions, states) that are highly integrated socially would tend to exert stronger social pressures against nontraditional behaviors (which divorce is generally perceived to be) and exert both formal and informal pressures for conformity to community norms.

The levels of social integration and pressure toward conformity are likely to be influenced by residential mobility as well. High levels of residential movement are related both to higher levels of divorce and lower levels of social integration. Norval Glenn and Beth Anne Shelton stated that the very high level of marital dissolution in the U.S. "divorce belt" (the West, South Central, Mountain, and Pacific census divisions) can be accounted for by the very high level of residential

---

[10] National Center for Health Statistics, *Monthly Vital Statistics Reports,* vol. 43, no. 9, "Advance Report of Final Divorce Statistics, 1989 and 1990" (Hyattsville, MD: Public Health Service, 22 March 1995) Table 2, p. 10.

mobility in that region.[11] Residential mobility and other variables associated with lower levels of social integration would affect variations in divorce rates not only by region and by state but would result in lower levels of divorce in rural than in urban areas, as well.

Unique circumstances such as those that exist in Nevada are greatly influenced by legal requirements. Even though Nevada may produce a small fraction of the total divorces granted nationally (about 1.1 percent), the divorce rate per 1,000 population within that state can be affected significantly by a relatively small number of couples who come there from other states to get divorced. Except for Nevada and a few other states, it is unlikely that migratory divorce has a major effect on divorce rates.

Ages of husbands and wives Divorce is very common among young couples. Census data reveal that for women, divorce rates are at their peak for teenagers ages 15–19 and decline with increasing age. For men, divorce rates are highest in the 20–24 age category and then decline with increasing age.[12] Overall, women who marry as teenagers are two to four times as likely to divorce as those who marry later and men who marry below age 25 are twice as likely to divorce as those who marry later.

Explanations for these high rates may include emotional immaturity, inability to assume marital responsibilities, greater incidences of early marriage in lower socioeconomic statuses (where divorce is more likely), more premarital pregnancies (also related to higher incidences of divorce), and similar factors.

Young marriages are not, however, responsible for the dramatic increases in family dissolution witnessed in the United States. While young couples have higher rates of marital disruption, the typical age at divorce after the first marriage is between twenty-five and thirty-four. Age at divorce has shifted upward over the past several decades, reflecting the steady rise in the age at first marriage.

Although divorce rates are highest in young marriages and occur most frequently in the first few years following a marriage, these factors should not obscure the reality that divorce may occur at any age or point in the life course, including the middle and later years. Results from Peter Uhlenberg et al.'s study of midlife women showed that the socioeconomic well-being of divorcees of this age group was significantly below that of widowed or married women.[13] The increasing number of persons who are older, the changes in the perceptions of the roles of women, and a shifting social acceptability of divorce present a realistic potential for dramatic increases in the number of divorced older persons.

---

[11] Norval D. Glenn and Beth Anne Shelton, "Regional Differences in Divorce in the United States," *Journal of Marriage and the Family* 47 (August 1985): 641–652; and Beth Anne Shelton, "Variations in Divorce Rates by Community Size: A Test of the Social Integration Explanation," *Journal of Marriage and the Family* 49 (November 1987): 827–832.

[12] *Monthly Vital Statistics Reports*, vol. 43, no. 9, March 22, 1995, p. 3.

[13] Peter R. Uhlenberg, Teresa M. Cooney, and Robert L. Boyd, "Divorce for Women After Midlife, *Journal of Gerontology* 45 (1990): S3–S11.

Duration of marriage The largest number of divorce decrees are granted one to four years after marriage, and that number declines relatively consistently with increased duration (see Figure 17-2). The second, third, and fourth years of marriage appear to be the modal (most common) years for divorce. Few divorces (3.3 percent in 1990) occurred within the first year of marriage, due partly to requirements by many states that couples be separated for at least one year before obtaining a divorce. One-third of divorcing couples (31.7 percent) had been married one to four years, and about one-fourth (28.3 percent) had been married five to nine years. The remaining one-third of divorcing couples had been married ten years or more, including 6.2 percent who had been married twenty-five years or more.[14]

Divorce occurs irrespective of age or length of marriage; there is no evidence showing an increase in midlife divorce. A divorce that occurs late in the marriage may simply be the legal end of a marriage severely disrupted years earlier.

Figure 17-2

Percent distribution of divorces by duration of marriage

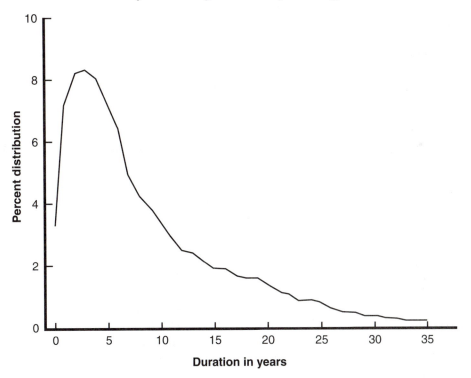

Source: National Center for Health Statistics, "Advance Report of Final Divorce Statistics, 1989 and 1990," *Monthly Vital Statistics Reports,* vol. 43, no. 9 (Hyattsville, MD: Public Health Service, 22 March 1995), Figure 3, p. 4.

---

[14] National Center for Health Statistics, *Monthly Vital Statistics Report,* vol. 43, no. 9, March 22, 1995, Table 11, p. 20.

In 1990, the median interval between the first marriage and divorce was 8.2 years. For those who remarried and got another divorce, the median interval between the second marriage and divorce was 6.2 years. For the third marriage or more, the median interval was 4.3 years.[15] It would appear that the median length of each succeeding marriage that ends in divorce is shorter than the previous one. Most likely, the first divorce experience is the most difficult one. Having been through a divorce, accepting divorced status, and later remarrying may tend to make divorce a more acceptable solution to an unsuccessful second, third, or fourth marital relationship.

The duration of remarriages is influenced by many factors not at issue in first marriages: ex-spouses, ex-in-laws, stepchildren, and so on. For example, national data suggest that bringing stepchildren into a second marriage appears to weaken the marital unit, childbearing prior to remarriage increases the risk of marital dissolution but having a child in the second marriage reduces the probability of dissolution.[16] In addition, perhaps, remarriages are composed disproportionately of people who have problems that make having stable marriages difficult: alcoholic, abusive, or unstable persons. Whatever the reason, the time span of remarriages that end in divorce is shorter than in first marriages.

Many marriages that never end in divorce are seriously disrupted in all but the legal sense. This observation leads to a point made at various times throughout the book: Length of marriage is not necessarily an index of marital success or adjustment, and divorce is not necessarily a good index of marital breakdown. Divorce may simply indicate a couple's willingness to provide a legal ending to their marital relationship.

Race, religion, and socioeconomic status   The success levels of interracial and interfaith marriages were discussed in Chapter 9. The discussion turns now to how rates differ by race, religion, and socioeconomic level in nonmixed (endogamous) marriages. Is the probability of divorce different for blacks and whites, Protestants and Catholics, and people of lower and higher socioeconomic levels?

The likelihood of divorce by race usually differs within a state as well as within the same racial group among different states. For example, in 1991, for the United States as a whole, white males had a divorce rate per 1,000 married persons with a spouse present of 11.7 compared to 23.9 for black males. The rate for white females was 15.9 compared to 37.0 for black females.[17] These striking racial differences may be partly explained by urban residence, mobility patterns, social-class differences, and differing accessibility to various types of social and economic resources. Generally, the greater the accessibility to such resources, the lower the incidence of divorce.

---

[15] Ibid., Table 10, p. 19.

[16] Howard Weinberg, "Childbearing and Dissolution of the Second Marriage," *Journal of Marriage and the Family* 54 (November 1992): 879–887.

[17] U.S. Bureau of the Census, *Statistical Abstract of the United States: 1992*, no. 50, p. 44.

What about religion? Do divorce rates differ by major religious affiliation? Data from seven U.S. national surveys by Norval Glenn and Michael Supancic showed that marital dissolution is moderately higher for Protestants, considered as a whole, than for Catholics and lower for Jews than for Catholics.[18] The highest divorce rates are among persons with no religious affiliation. This finding is consistent with the data on frequency of attendance at religious services; religiosity is an important deterrent to divorce and separation.

Contrary to what one might expect, the Glenn and Supancic study, as well as others, showed that Protestant fundamentalists—the most conservative Protestant denominations (Nazarene, Pentecostal, Baptist)—have relatively high dissolution rates, in spite of their strong disapproval of divorce. Factors associated with conversion to these fundamentalist denominations were found to be important in producing the high dissolution rates.[19] Conversion may signify the cultural conflict that results from the radical transition from one context to another. It may also indicate a lack of normative integration in the antiseparation/divorce doctrine, on the one hand, while urging acceptance and tolerance of the converted "sinner," on the other. The higher divorce/separation rate may also reflect the lower than average socioeconomic status of persons in these denominations; the strong demands these groups make on the time, energy, and money of their adherents (which may negatively affect marriages); the inflexibility or rigidity of their theological position; or even the focus and emphasis on the next life rather than the current one.

What about socioeconomic level? The divorce rate has increased at all socioeconomic levels, yet the proportion of persons ever divorced remains highest among relatively disadvantaged groups. When education, occupation, or income is used as an index of socioeconomic level, the divorce rate goes up as the socioeconomic level goes down. One exception to this relationship exists among professional women who have five or more years of college education. Generally, compared to women of similar age groups, professional women were more likely never to have married, were more likely to divorce if they had married, and were less likely to remarry if they divorced. Female lawyers, in particular, were found to have a markedly higher rate of divorce and a lower rate of remarriage than women in other professions, such as teachers and physicians.[20] Marital disruption is high among professional women, in general, due perhaps to their lessened dependence on men, to the viable alternatives they have to marriage, and to the strain resulting from their efforts to balance both work and family roles.

18 Norval D. Glenn and Michael Supancic, "The Social and Demographic Correlates of Divorce and Separation in the United States: An Update and Reconsideration," *Journal of Marriage and the Family* 46 (August 1984): 563–575.

19 S. Kenneth Chi and Sharon K. Houseknecht, "Protestant Fundamentalism and Marital Success: A Comparative Approach," *Sociology and Social Research* 69 (April 1985): 351–375.

20 Teresa M. Cooney and Peter Uhlenberg, "Family-Building Patterns of Professional Women: A Comparison of Lawyers, Physicians, and Postsecondary Teachers," *Journal of Marriage and the Family* 51 (August 1989): 749–758; and Sharon K. Houseknecht, Suzanne Vaughn, and Anne S. Macke, "Marital Disruption Among Professional Women: The Timing of Career and Family Events," *Social Problems* 31 (February 1984): 273–284.

The greater marital instability and higher divorce rates at low socioeconomic levels may stem from a number of factors:

1. The frustrations that come from having difficulty meeting expenses and having too little income may affect other areas of marital life.

2. At higher social strata, satisfaction in work and sexual spheres may alleviate the need to escape from marriage.

3. People in the upper strata are more tied to long-term investment expenditures that are less easily stopped or ended in contrast to the immediate, daily-need expenditures of the lower strata.

4. Although income among people of lower strata is insufficient for the type of car, house, or fur coat enjoyed by the higher strata, the desire for these things remains.

5. Kin and friend networks of the upper strata are larger and more tightly knit, making divorce more difficult.

The alert reader may note what appears to be a contradiction in the data. For example, it was shown in Figure 17-1 and mentioned in the text that divorce rates tend to decrease during times of economic depression and rise during times of prosperity. And it was just mentioned that the incidence of divorce increases as the socioeconomic level goes down. How is it possible that divorce rates decrease during Depression, when times are hard, and also increase among the lower strata, when times are also difficult?

Several factors are involved. During economic depression, divorce rates drop at all class levels. During the Great Depression of the 1930s, the lower classes still had the highest divorce rate. Many of the marriages that survived the 1930s ended in divorce in the 1940s. Also, general life-style, sense of loyalty, linkages with kin, occupational and income security, and group support, all affect rates of divorce. These factors were different in the 1930s for Depression families than they are now for lower-class families. Once again, the powerful influence of the social network is evident in something perceived to be as individualistic and personal as divorce.

There are other social factors beyond geographic, demographic, and socioeconomic variations that may contribute to the likelihood of divorce. For example, couples who have siblings or friends who have divorced are themselves more likely to divorce.[21] Having divorced peers may release inhibitions and reduce pressure to remain in an unhappy marriage, or it may actually encourage individuals to seek out more attractive partners.

[21] Alan Booth, John N. Edwards, and David R. Johnson, "Social Integration and Divorce," *Social Forces* 70 (September 1991): 207–224.

U.S. Diversity: How About Divorce Insurance?

In the United States, people are encouraged to protect themselves against future difficulties through insurance. They buy automobile insurance to protect themselves from the economic loss of the automobile and the possibility of suit against loss of life and property. They buy health insurance to protect themselves from the possibility of major medical bills. They buy dental insurance to protect themselves from major costs associated with tooth decay, removal, or correction. They buy property insurance to protect themselves from destruction or loss of their homes. They buy disability insurance to protect themselves from an inability to work and maintain an income. They pay dues or taxes to cover unemployment compensation as protection against the loss of a job. They pay into a Social Security system to (hopefully) provide income for their retirement years. Should people not be covered by divorce insurance?

As shown in this chapter, more than one million divorces occur annually. An overwhelming number of female-headed households and some male-headed households face the serious problem of not having adequate income. Welfare and child-support payments are available to many persons, but it can be argued that a welfare dollar is different from an insurance dollar and child-support payments are different from Social Security payments. Divorce insurance, involving largely the private sector of the economy, may provide many parents with the freedom and autonomy to plan for their own lives and those of their children with assurance and certainty.

Consider how such a system might work: Divorce insurance premiums, contrary to most health and life insurance premiums, could be large during the early years of the policy and decrease with the length of time married. Benefits could work inversely: small benefits for brief marriages and increasingly larger benefits for longer-term marriages. If the benefits were paid over time rather than in one lump sum, divorce for the purpose of insurance collection could be minimized.

The basic principle behind this type of insurance, as with any other insurance, would be to provide guaranteed financial resources to single parents, particularly those with children. Would newly married couples be motivated to invest in such insurance? If not, how would the insurance be funded?

What do you think?

Legal and social grounds for divorce

The legal grounds for divorce vary somewhat for each state.[22] Apart from "no-fault" divorce, the most widely accepted legal grounds for divorce are breakdown of marriage, incompatibility, cruelty, and desertion. In all states, adultery is either grounds for divorce or evidence of incompatibility, irreconcilable differences, or breakdown of the marriage. Other legal grounds in at least one state include non-support, alcohol or drug addiction, felony conviction or imprisonment, impotence, insanity, disbelieving in marriage, treatment that injures health or endan-

---

[22] See *World Almanac and Book of Facts* (Mahwah, NJ: Funk and Wagnalls Corp., 1995): 728.

gers reason, pregnancy at marriage, fraudulent contract, gross neglect of duty, bigamy, attempted homicide, and the like. California, Colorado, and Oregon have procedures whereby a couple can obtain a divorce without an attorney and without appearing in court, provided certain requirements (such as being married less than two years, having no children, no real estate, and few debts) are met.

The adversary divorce system in the United States, in which one party must be innocent and the other guilty, has been replaced in all fifty states with **no-fault divorce.** Traditional fault grounds were abolished in favor of dissolution of marriage based on **irreconcilable differences,** defined as any grounds that are determined by the court to be substantial reasons for not continuing the marriage and that conclude that the marriage should be dissolved.

Under no-fault divorce law, consent of both spouses is not required. The law is gender-neutral in that both spouses are responsible for alimony and child support and both spouses are eligible for child custody. Financial rewards such as child support and property distribution are not linked to "fault" but rather to the spouses' current financial needs and resources. The basic goals of no-fault divorce were intended (1) to make divorce less restrictive by reducing the legal and economic obstacles to divorce, and (2) to improve the social-psychological and communication climate of divorce by abolishing the concept of fault. Some states have even replaced the term *divorce* with *dissolution of marriage.*

What have been the consequences of no-fault divorce laws? Have fewer restrictions resulted in increased divorce rates? Do mothers and women fare better under the no-fault system? The answer to the first question appears to be yes and to the second appears to be no. An analysis of pre–no-fault and post–no-fault divorce rates of all fifty states revealed that all but six states had an increase in the rate of divorce following the enactment of the law.[23] Nevada, for example, had a large decrease that may be attributed to divorce being less restrictive and more accessible in other states. This reduced the need for couples to travel to Nevada for a quick and expedient divorce.

In response to the second question, studies of property settlements have suggested consistently that divorcing mothers are faring more poorly under the no-fault system than they did under the former adversary system. The no-fault system reduced the bargaining power of spouses who did not want to divorce, which led to substantial declines in the financial settlements received by women. One writer suggested that no-fault divorce probably reduced the quality of family life.[24] And a law review article expressed concern about the increased impoverishment of custodial mothers and their children and the extent to which no-fault statutes foster a casual commitment to marriage.[25]

---

[23] Paul A. Nakonezny, Robert D. Shull, and Joseph Lee Rodgers, "The Effect of No-Fault Divorce Law on the Divorce Rate Across the 50 States and Its Relation to Income, Education, and Religiosity," *Journal of Marriage and the Family* 57 (May 1995): 477–488.

[24] Allen M. Parkman, *No-Fault Divorce: What Went Wrong?* Boulder, CO: Westview Press, 1992, Chapter 5, pp. 71–109.

[25] Lynn D. Wardle, "No-Fault Divorce and the Divorce Conundrum," *Brigham Young University Law Review* 1 (1991): 79–142.

Over the past few decades, divorce has changed considerably in the United States from an adversarial system in which fault had to be determined, to a "no-fault" system, in which irreconcilable differences are recognized. Divorcing mothers fare more poorly under the "no-fault" system. Movements are under way in some states to return to a fault system and to make divorce more difficult to obtain.

Divorce proceedings under the no-fault system are relatively routine. Where cases are contested, they can become drawn-out affairs, resulting in much bitterness and expense. Attempts to decrease such conflict have led to **divorce mediation.** Mediation is a conflict resolution process in which the divorcing couple meets with a neutral third-party intervenor (mediator), who helps them negotiate an agreement about property distribution, support, and child custody. The emphasis is on direct communication, openness, attention to emotional issues and the underlying causes of the disputes, and avoidance of blame. Proponents of mediation stress that it relieves court dockets clogged with matrimonial actions, reduces the alienation couples experience in court, inspires durable consensual agreements, helps couples resume workable relationships to jointly rear their children, and translates into savings in time and money. The mediation process works on building and strengthening relationships, whereas the adversary process tends to weaken and destroy them.

Most divorce settlements are the result of a negotiation process in which parents make decisions concerning child support, custody, visitation, and marital property without bringing any contested issue into court for adjudication (judicial settlement). The modal or standard divorce package is one in which the mother has custody of the children and is awarded child support, and the father pays child support and has visitation rights.[26]

Generally, the reasons why marriages dissolve, forcing settlement and custody issues, focus on "push" factors that drive persons apart, such as adultery, abusiveness, drunkenness, or interpersonal conflict. However, a more open systems perspective on marital dissolution looks as well at "pull" factors: conditions in the environment that pull persons away from their current spouses or partners. These, as described in Chapter 12, can be referred to as **marital alternatives.** Consciously or not, people compare their current relationships with alternative ones. If internal attractions and forces that keep a couple together become weaker than those from a viable alternative, the consequence is likely to be breakup.

Support for this idea comes from various sources. Scott and Kim, for example, found that the risk of dissolution is highest where either partner encounters alternatives to the existing relationship.[27] They note that a sizable percentage of recently divorced persons had been romantically involved with someone other than their spouse prior to the divorce. This suggests that many married persons continue to be open to the possibility of an intimate (extramarital) relationship. Thus, a married man who works in an environment where a substantial percentage of unmarried women are employed is more likely to find an attractive alternative to his current wife or partner. Esterberg and others found that the increase in women's options outside of marriage such as returning to school and consequent increased self-esteem are more important than attitudinal factors in hastening the transition to divorce.[28]

This approach is highly similar to that adopted by exchange theorists; the decision to divorce clearly contains important reward/cost considerations. The rewards (attractions) may include love, goods, services, security, joint possessions, children, sexual enjoyment, and so forth, and the costs (barriers) may include feelings of obligation or inadequacy, fears of family/friend reactions, religious prohibitions, financial costs, and the like. The probability for divorce increases as alternatives are perceived that provide greater rewards or lower costs than exist in marriage.

Consequences of divorce for adults

Consequences of divorce are evident at both the individual and interpersonal (micro) levels as well as at the organizational and societal (macro) levels.[29] Most

---

[26] Jay D. Teachman and Karen Polonko, "Negotiating Divorce Outcomes: Can We Identify Patterns in Divorce Settlements?" *Journal of Marriage and the Family* 52 (February 1990): 129–139.

[27] Scott J. South and Kim M. Lloyd, "Spousal Alternatives and Marital Dissolution," *American Sociological Review* 60 (February 1995): 21–35.

[28] Kristin G. Esterberg, Phyllis Moen, and Donna Dempster-McCain, "Transition to Divorce: A Life Course Approach to Women's Marital Duration and Dissolution," *The Sociological Quarterly* 35 (1994): 289–307.

[29] See Gay C. Kitson and Leslie A. Morgan, "The Multiple Consequences of Divorce: A Decade Review," *Journal of Marriage and the Family* 52 (November 1990): 913–924; and Frank F. Furstenberg, Jr., "Divorce and the American Family," *Annual Review of Sociology* 16 (1990): 379–403.

research has focused on the micro levels. But one macrolevel finding from several countries—including the United States, Finland, Norway, and Canada—supported the proposition of a direct relationship between divorce and suicide.[30] This proposition is consistent with the work on suicide originally published in 1897 by Emile Durkheim, who theorized that societies with low degrees of social integration typically share high rates of suicide.

Apart from suicide, one clearly defined consequence of divorce is its influence on adult well-being. Data from over thirty-seven studies revealed that having one's parents divorce (or permanently separate) has broad negative consequences for that individual's quality of life in adulthood.[31] Outcomes associated with parental divorce included psychological well-being (depression, low life satisfaction), family well-being (low marital quality, divorce), socioeconomic well-being (low educational attainment, income, and occupational prestige), and physical health. These highly negative findings are somewhat tempered when community samples rather than clinical samples are used, when more recent studies rather than earlier studies are used, and when statistical controls (such as parental education and occupational status) are used rather than simple zero-order differences.

Divorce also impacts the separating spouses in several ways. For example, in one study, persons with a history of serial divorces reported less happiness and more frequent depression than persons with a history of one divorce, and persons with a history of one divorce reported more frequent depression than those with a history of no divorce. Divorced women reported more frequent depression than divorced men.[32] Newly divorced people, in particular, were significantly more depressed, reflecting greater economic problems, the perception that one's standard of living had deteriorated, and the lesser availability of close, confiding relationships.

The economic consequences of divorce differ dramatically by gender. In short, the economic situation improves for men and declines for women. California data in the 1970s showed a radical change in the standard of living just one year after a legal divorce. Men experienced a 42 percent improvement in their postdivorce standard of living, while women experienced a 73 percent loss.[33] This situation has not changed much over the past two decades. Even though more women are employed and having fewer children, Pamela Smock notes that the economic cost

---

[30] Steven Stack, "The Effect of Divorce on Suicide in Finland: A Time Series Analysis," *Journal of Marriage and the Family* 54 (August 1992): 636–642; Steven Stack, "The Impact of Divorce on Suicide in Norway, 1951–1980," *Journal of Marriage and the Family* 51 (February 1989): 229–238; and Frank Trovato, "The Relationship Between Marital Dissolution and Suicide: The Canadian Case," *Journal of Marriage and the Family* 48 (May 1986): 341–348.

[31] Paul R. Amato and Bruce Keith, "Parental Divorce and Adult Well-Being: A Meta–analysis," *Journal of Marriage and the Family* 53 (February 1991): 43–58.

[32] Lawrence A. Kurdek, "The Relations Between Reported Well-being and Divorce History, Availability of a Proximate Adult, and Gender," *Journal of Marriage and the Family* 53 (February 1991): 71–78.

[33] Lenore J. Weitzman, "The Economics of Divorce: Social and Economic Consequences of Property, Alimony, and Child Support Awards," *UCLA Law Review* 28 (August 1981): 1251.

of marital disruption for women is as severe today as in the 1960s and 1970s.[34] Similarly, men continue to experience substantial increases in per capita income when they separate or divorce.

Apparently, this is not merely a United States phenomenon but holds true in other countries as well. In Germany, women experienced an even bigger drop in economic status following divorce than their U.S. female counterparts. German men fared about as well as their U.S. male counterparts.[35] In both countries, men were more likely than women to work and to earn more in the labor market both before and after a divorce. In both countries, mothers were more likely than fathers to care for children after a divorce. These and other factors pose a greater economic hardship for divorced women than for divorced men.

National longitudinal surveys showed that 40 percent of widows and over 25 percent of divorced women fall into poverty for at least some time during the first five years after being single.[36] It is little wonder that more divorced women report that they are in constant financial crisis, are perpetually worried about not being able to pay their bills, have more stress, and feel less satisfied with their lives than any other group in the United States. In contrast, men who divorce or separate are immediately better off. They retain most of their labor incomes, typically do not pay large amounts of alimony and child support to their ex-wives, and no longer have to provide for their former families. While writers frequently refer to *his* and *her* marriages, those differences appear minor when comparing *his* and *her* divorces.

Children of divorced parents

Children of divorced parents are a rapidly growing group in the United States. Data from a national survey discovered that nearly one-third of all children have experienced family disruption by the time they reach the age of fifteen. When children of never-married parents and those not currently living with a biological parent are included in this group, the authors expect "that close to half of all children living in the United States today will reach age eighteen without having lived continuously with both biological parents."[37]

The number of children affected by divorce has exceeded 1 million every year since 1971 (see Figure 17-3). The average number of children per decree granted

---

[34] Pamela J. Smock, "The Economic Costs of Marital Disruption for Young Women over the Past Two Decades," *Demography* 30 (August 1993): 353–371; and Pamela J. Smock, "Gender and the Short-Run Economic Consequences of Marital Disruption," *Social Forces* 73 (September 1994): 243–262.

[35] Richard V. Burkhauser, Greg J. Duncan, Richard Hauser, and Roland Berntsen, "Wife or Frau, Women Do Worse: A Comparison of Men and Women in the United States and Germany After Marital Dissolution," *Demography* 28 (August 1991): 353–360.

[36] Leslie A. Morgan, "Economic Well-Being Following Marital Termination," *Journal of Family Issues* 10 (March 1989): 86–101.

[37] Frank F. Furstenberg, Jr., Christine Winquist Nord, James L. Peterson, and Nicholas Zill, "The Life Course of Children of Divorce: Marital Disruption and Parental Contact," *American Sociological Review* 48 (0ctober 1983): 667.

Case Example:
A Divorce for a Marriage That Never Was

Dee is a 37-year-old mother of three children, ages 16, 10, and 8. She was legally married at age 27 and officially divorced at age 33. But she claims she never had a husband or a marriage. Permit her to explain.

"I honestly don't know why I married him. Perhaps it was because he was the first and only man I was ever involved with sexually. Perhaps it was because I had one child with him, was pregnant again and gave him an ultimatum. Maybe at the time I believed I loved him and if we got married he'd be a father to his children and assume some financial responsibility. But he was a total deadbeat dad and never voluntarily helped out financially.

"We drove to a neighboring state to get married. We both said the vows but they meant nothing to him. We had no honeymoon and within the week he was gone. He'd come back occasionally to see the kids or to have sex with me, but he never stayed more than two days at a time. Only because the Friend of the Court forced money to be withheld from his paycheck did we ever get anything from him. He would never play ball with the kids, take them anywhere, or buy them things. Would

you believe that when he got in trouble with the IRS, he wanted me to write them a letter saying the kids lived with him more than six months of the year? Of course, I wouldn't do it. Once when he really got mad at me, he mentioned to my daughter that he's leaving for good so he probably wouldn't see her for a couple of years. I was really surprised when my daughter told him that if that's the case, you don't need to see me then, either.

"Because of my kids and being married, I didn't see other men. And I waited so long to get a divorce because somehow I believed he might change. He constantly made promises that he would never keep. I threatened to divorce him several times but he didn't take me seriously. But finally, I could take no more of his mental abuse and unfulfilled promises and with the help of free legal aid, had divorce papers served and made it official. The reason was based on irreconcilable differences rather than adultery. That would have been easy to prove since he has about nine or ten kids, including my three. As I look back on those years, I can say I was married, but you know, I guess I never was."

has generally been falling since 1964, when it peaked at 1.36. By 1993, there were about 0.90 children per decree, meaning that today there are more divorces than children involved. One reason for the decline is the drop in the birthrate. Other reasons include a slight increase in the proportion of childlessness at divorce and a decline in the estimated interval between marriage and divorce.

Are children a deterrent to divorce? The answer appears to be both yes and no. Data have shown that firstborn and other children increase the stability of marriage through their preschool years.[38] At least in the short run, young preschool children tend to keep couples together who would otherwise divorce. (Consider the braking hypothesis from Chapter 13.) However, older children and children born before marriage significantly increase chances of marital disruption. It is pos-

---

[38] Linda J. Waite and Lee A. Lillard, "Children and Marital Disruption," *American Journal of Sociology* 96 (January 1991): 930–953.

Figure 17-3
Numbers of divorces and divorces with children involved: 1950–1993

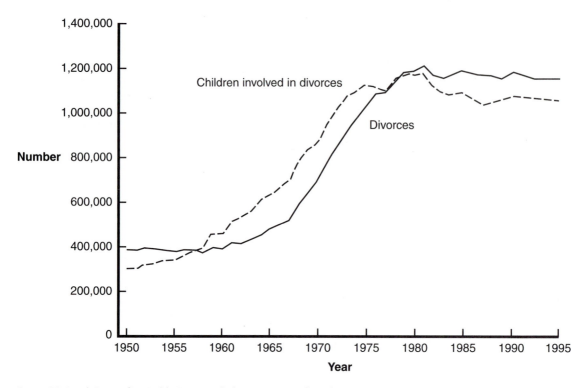

Source: National Center for Health Statistics, "Advance Report of Final Divorce Statistics, 1989 and 1990," *Monthly Vital Statistics Reports,* vol. 43, no. 9 (Hyattsville, MD: Public Health Service, 22 March 1995); and "Annual Summary of Births, Marriages, Divorces, and Deaths: United States, 1994," *Monthly Vital Statistics Reports,* vol. 43, no. 13 (Hyattsville, MD: Public Health Service, 23 October 1995), p. 5.

sible that the inhibiting effect of children on keeping couples together fades and that, as children get older, the strains of parenthood augment the strains of marriage, leading to increased risks of disruption.

Data from over eleven thousand divorcing families in northern California clearly supported the relationship between the duration of marriage and the presence of children.[39] Explanations for children delaying (not preventing) divorce included the following: children make divorce more costly than continuation of the marriage; the cost of having the wife confined to the home and less free to take employment; the articulation of older children about their feelings; people who have children may be more secure in the marriage than their childless counterparts;

---

[39] Robert M. Rankin and Jerry S. Maneker, "The Duration of Marriage in a Divorcing Population: The Impact of Children," *Journal of Marriage and the Family* 47 (February 1985): 43–52.

the stigma couples may feel toward parents who divorce; and anticipated complications attending divorce action (child custody, co-parenting, single-parent problems). Note that all the couples in this study got divorced; thus, it provided no support for the myth that children prevent divorce. The study did support the notion of a longer duration of marriage before divorce when children were present.

Consequences of divorce for children Each year, more than one million children are the victims of divorce. Therefore, the question of greatest concern is, What are the consequences of divorce for children? Should couples, although unhappily married, stay together for the sake of the children?

Laypeople assume that the psychological, economic, and social effects of divorce on children are predominantly negative, and these negative assumptions influence how people think about particular children. Research found that this negative prototype of children of divorce leads people to recall unfavorable information and fail to recall favorable information about such children.[40] This may lead to a self-fulfilling prophecy when teachers, counselors, social workers, and parents expect children from divorced families to have more than their share of problems and treat them in ways that exacerbate or even generate these very problems.

Few people would argue that children are better off in happy, stable families than in divorced or unhappy, unstable families. Evidence has shown that divorce diminishes the economic and social resources available to children, which has negative consequences for educational attainment, marital timing, marital probability, and divorce probability.[41] Adolescent children of divorced parents are less likely to graduate from high school, tend to marry at an earlier age, have a lower probability of ever marrying, and have a higher probability of getting divorced. Other evidence has shown that adolescents from divorced homes are more prone to commit delinquent acts, experience problems in peer relations, and are highly associated with family-related offenses, such as running away and truancy.[42] These findings confirm the popular notion that divorce is bad for children.

But are the findings just presented the result of a divorce or separation as the central event in shaping the lives of children? Furstenberg and Teitler note that to focus on the impact of divorce itself makes it easy to overlook the circumstances leading up to the separation, some of which may begin even before the birth of the children.[43] These circumstances and processes that often end in divorce may

---

[40] Paul R. Amato, "The 'Child of Divorce' as a Person Prototype: Bias in the Recall of Information about Children in Divorced Families," *Journal of Marriage and the Family* 53 (February 1991): 59–69.

[41] Gary D. Sandefur, Sara McLanahan, and Roger A. Wojtkiewicz, "The Effects of Parental Marital Status During Adolescence on High School Graduation," *Social Forces* 71 (September 1992): 103–121; Norval D. Glenn and Kathryn B. Kramer, "The Marriages and Divorces of the Children of Divorce," *Journal of Marriage and the Family* 49 (November 1987): 811–825; and William R. Catton, Jr., "Family Divorce Heritage and Its Intergenerational Transmission," *Sociological Perspectives* 31 (October 1988): 398–419.

[42] L. Edward Wells and Joseph H. Ranken, "Families and Delinquency: A Meta-Analysis of the Impact of Broken Homes," *Social Problems* 38 (February 1991): 71–93; and David H. Demo and Alan C. Acock, "The Impact of Divorce on Children," *Journal of Marriage and the Family* 50 (August 1988): 619–648.

[43] Frank F. Furstenberg, Jr., and Julien O. Teitler, "Reconsidering the Effects of Marital Disruption: What Happens to Children of Divorce in Early Adulthood," *Journal of Family Issues* 15 (June 1994): 173–190.

News Item: Children Divorcing Parents

When most people think of divorce, they think of adults terminating a marital relationship. But what about *children* divorcing their parents?

In September 1992, for the first time in the United States, family rights were ended based on legal action brought by a Florida child. Gregory Kingsley, a twelve-year-old boy, went to court for the right to divorce his parents. He realized his goal when a juvenile court judge ended the parental rights held by his birthmother and allowed the boy's foster parents to adopt him.

In making his decision in favor of Gregory, the judge said, "By clear and convincing evidence, almost beyond a reasonable doubt, the child has been abandoned and neglected by his mother" and that "it was in his best interest" that Gregory's mother's rights be terminated so that he could be adopted.

However, in August 1993, a Florida appeals court reviewed the original decision and, while agreeing with the basic outcome, decided the case on different legal grounds. Namely, the court ruled that, as a minor, Gregory could not take legal action to terminate his relationship with his parents; he could only do so upon turning eighteen. But because Gregory's foster parents (i.e., adults) were also parties to the action, the decision stood to end Gregory's mother's parental rights. The appeals court also confirmed that Gregory could be adopted but overturned the original adoption on a technicality, requiring Gregory's foster parents to repeat the adoption process.

Additional legal action on this case may be pending, as the courts decide this and other issues involving children's versus parents' rights.

be harmful to children whether the parents stay together or separate. High levels of marital conflict, poor parenting practices, or persistent economic stress may compromise children's economic, social, and psychological well-being in later life irrespective of a divorce or separation. Thus it may make little sense to argue that, for the sake of the children, partners in unhappy marriages should stay together. Unhappy families have two choices, neither of which are ideal or highly favorable for children. Both the intact home with persistent conflict and the divorced home are likely to cause varying degrees of stress, pain, and difficulty.

Amato suggests focusing on two concepts: *resources* and *stressors*.[44] Children's development can be facilitated by resources such as parental emotional support, practical help, guidance, supervision, and role models, as well as economic resources. Stressors include interpersonal conflict that may follow divorce and subsequent disruptive life changes. Amato argues that rather than looking at single factors such as parental conflict or economic hardships, one must look at the total configuration of resources and stressors. Thus economic hardship may be less problematic for children who have a close relationship with a warm and compe-

---

[44] Paul R. Amato, "Children's Adjustment to Divorce: Theories, Hypotheses, and Empirical Support," *Journal of Marriage and the Family* 55 (February 1993): 23–38.

tent parent. Likewise, a severe stressor may negate a particular resource, such as contact with the noncustodial parent when there is continuing conflict between the parents. This type of perspective may highlight more clearly the variations that exist in children's reaction and adjustment to divorce.

The impact of divorce on children varies considerably according to the age of the children as well as age of the parents. If the children are adults, custody is not necessary but divorce still has an impact. As with young children, young adults had less contact with their fathers.[45] Even parental divorce in later life after the children are grown was shown to lower relationship quality and contact between adult children and parents.[46] The effects were stronger for father-child than for mother-child relations.

Child custody If children are minors, **child custody** and *economic support* become issues of major concern. As of 1992, 11.5 million women and men were custodial parents of children under 21 years of age with the other parent not living in the household.[47] A majority of these (9.9 million, or 86.2 percent, were women. Mothers living with children from an absent father had a poverty rate of 35 percent, approximately two-and-one-half times the poverty rate of their male counterparts (13 percent) and more than four times the rate for all married-couple families with children (8 percent).

Although mothers are far more likely to get custody and be in poverty, a number of factors were found to influence final child-custody arrangements. An analysis of more than 500 cases of divorce in Michigan involving minor children revealed that the odds of father custody are improved when children are older, especially when the oldest child is male, when the father is the plaintiff, and when a court investigation has occurred during divorce proceedings. Odds of mother custody are enhanced by higher educational level for mothers, higher income for fathers, paternal unemployment, and support arrearages prior to final divorce judgments.[48]

Joint custody appears to be on the increase but about only one in six decisions are of this type. This arrangement is generally perceived to be the most ideal from the perspective of parent-child relationships. Yet, a nationally representative sample of children whose parents were divorced, separated, or unmarried found no evidence that children in shared custody had less conflictual or better relationships

---

[45] Teresa Cooney, "Young Adults' Relations With Parents: The Influence of Recent Parental Divorce," *Journal of Marriage and the Family* 56 (February 1994): 45–56; and Teresa M. Cooney, M. Katherine Hutchinson, and Diane M. Leather, "Surviving the Breakup? Predictors of Parent-Adult Child Relations After Parental Divorce," *Family Relations* 44 (April 1995): 153–161.

[46] William S. Aquilino, "Later Life Parental Divorce and Widowhood: Impact on Young Adults' Assessment of Parent-Child Relations," *Journal of Marriage and the Family* 56 (November 1994): 908–922.

[47] U.S. Bureau of the Census, *Current Population Reports,* Series P60-187, "Child Support for Custodial Mothers and Fathers: 1991" (Washington, DC: U.S. Government Printing Office, 1995): 1.

[48] Greer Litton Fox and Robert F. Kelly, "Determinants of Child Custody Arrangements at Divorce," *Journal of Marriage and the Family* 57 (August 1995): 693–708.

with their parents.[49] Children in sole-custody households actually gave their parents more support and affection than those in shared custody. The authors suggest the relationships between the types of custody and their outcomes for children is not a simple one and the simplistic idea that joint custody is better because it leads to improved parent-child relations should be abandoned. On the other hand, research does exist that shows joint-custody fathers to be more in compliance with financial child-support obligations, to be more involved in making parental decisions, to share responsibilities, and to make contact and participate in activities with their children than noncustodial fathers.[50]

Custodial fathers, representing about one case in seven, are, like joint custody cases, increasing at a rapid rate. An analysis of custodial fathers indicated that single fathers are more likely to be black, younger than 30, and less educated than custodial fathers who are more likely to be white, older, and more highly educated.[51] Custodial fathers had much higher incomes than single fathers or custodial mothers (but less than married fathers). Consistent with their higher incomes, only about 20 percent of custodial fathers received assistance from at least one welfare program. About 30 percent of these fathers obtained a child-support award through the courts. Compare these figures with those of mother-only families, 45 percent of whom received welfare assistance and 80 percent who received child-support awards. Even among the fathers who got a child-support award, about half of the noncustodial mothers paid nothing.

Custodial mothers represent about 86 percent of reported cases. As was shown in Chapter 8, the impact of being a female-headed household and single parent and the likelihood of being at poverty level are very great. The figures of about 50 percent of Hispanic and African American single parents below the poverty level included the never-married, widowed, married-but-absent husband, as well as the divorced. But even among the divorced, more than one-third of single-parent women are below the poverty level. One primary reason for this poverty status following divorce is the father's noncompliance with child-support awards. The severity of this problem has been well documented by U.S. census and other reports, which have shown that only about one-half (51.5 percent) of all children for whom child support has been decreed actually receive the full amount. Another one-fourth (23.7 percent) of the children receive less than the specified amount, and the remaining one-fourth (24.8 percent) receive no support at all.[52]

[49] Denise Donnelly and David Finkelhor, "Does Equality in Custody Arrangement Improve the Parent-Child Relationship?" *Journal of Marriage and the Family* 54 (November 1992): 837–845.

[50] Judith A. Seltzer, "Relationships Between Fathers and Children Who Live Apart: The Father's Role after Separation," *Journal of Marriage and the Family* 53 (February 1991): 79–101; and William N. Bender, "Joint Custody: The Option of Choice," *Journal of Divorce and Remarriage* 21 (1994): 115–131.

[51] Daniel R. Meyer and Steven Garasky, "Custodial Fathers: Myths, Realities, and Child Support Policy," *Journal of Marriage and the Family* 55 (February 1993): 73–89.

[52] U.S. Bureau of the Census, *Current Population Reports,* Series P60-187, "Child Support for Custodial Mothers and Fathers: 1991" (Washington, DC: U.S. Government Printing Office, 1995): Table B, p. 7.

Reasons for nonsupport or insufficient support extend well beyond court enforcement and even ability to pay. Interpersonal reasons are likely issues, such as the level of attachment between former spouses, the quality of their relationship, and the frequency of visits by noncustodial parents to their children. It has been clearly documented that divorced noncustodial fathers have little contact with their children. Fathers are particularly unlikely to provide assistance that requires direct participation, such as helping their children with homework or attending school events.[53] One article cautions us, however, against "father bashing" in our descriptions of noncustodial fathers.[54] They are men faced with issues and tasks that are most difficult for them to handle effectively because of the gender-typed socialization in our culture. The more traditionally "feminine" roles and behaviors they may be attempting to assume are devalued.

Two key determinants of economic well-being for divorced custodial mothers are **child support** and *remarriage*. It has already been noted how few mothers get regular or full child support. Research found that about 50 percent of all non-black, ever-divorced mothers eligible for child support remarried within the first five to six years after divorce. Mothers who received child support and mothers who received above-average amounts of child support were less likely to have remarried within five or more years after divorce. Receiving child support may be a negative factor in the remarriage of divorced mothers.[55]

REMARRIAGES AND STEPFAMILIES

The United States is recognized as a monogamous society. Yet it is likely that a greater number as well as a larger proportion of people in the United States have more spouses than in many countries recognized as polygamous. This is especially true for women, since polyandry occurs rarely. The marriage of one man to several women is common; however, the marriage of one woman to several men is infrequent. Thus, it is possible that, in the United States, more than anywhere in the world, women are likely to experience multiple husbands—albeit only one at a time.

Couples who remarry are likely to do so for reasons of love, to be monogamous, and to expect the marriage to last until death—just as they did the first time. Yet remarried couples face life experiences and engage in life-styles that, in many ways, differentiate them from couples in first marriages. People who remarry are older, on average, than those who marry for the first time; are presumably more mature; and are more likely to have children.

---

[53] Jay D. Teachman, "Contributions to Children by Divorced Fathers," *Social Problems* 38 (August 1991): 358–371.

[54] Greer Litton Fox and Priscilla White Blanton, "Noncustodial Fathers Following Divorce," *Marriage and Family Review* 20 (1995): 257–282.

[55] Karen Fox Folk, John W. Graham, and Andrea H. Beller, "Child Support and Remarriage," *Journal of Family Issues* 13 (June 1992): 142–157.

The majority of people who divorce or end an intimate relationship eventually enter another marriage or exclusive relationship. Those people who have children create stepfamilies, in which multiple sets of parents interact with and assume responsibility for multiple sets of children. The step-, or binuclear family may include the children of one or both partners.

People who remarry

The United States has the highest remarriage rate in the world: Over 40 percent of marriages are remarriages for one or both partners.[56] An estimated two-thirds of all divorced persons in the United States remarry, but the rate of remarriage has declined over the past two decades not only in the United States but in Canada and Western Europe as well. One explanation for this decline is the rising rate of nonmarital cohabitation after divorce.[57] And although women are less likely than men to remarry, they are just as prone to cohabit as men. As one might expect, younger people remarry and cohabit more quickly than older people.

---

[56] For a review of this topic, see Larry Bumpass, James Sweet, and Teresa Castro Martin, "Changing Patterns of Remarriage," *Journal of Marriage and the Family* 52 (August 1990): 747–756; and Marilyn Coleman and Lawrence H. Ganong, "Remarriage and Stepfamily Research in the 1980s: Increased Interest in an Old Family Form," *Journal of Marriage and the Family* 52 (November 1990): 925–940.

[57] Zheng Wu and T. R. Balakrishnan, "Cohabitation After Marital Disruption in Canada," *Journal of Marriage and the Family* 56 (August 1994): 723–734.

Today, there are over 11 million remarried families in the United States, including more than 4.3 million stepfamilies.[58] In one in five households maintained by a married couple, one or both spouses have been divorced, and one-sixth of all U.S. children under age eighteen live in these households.

Census data have shown the median age at divorce after the first marriage to be 35.6 for males and 33.2 for females. The median age at remarriage was about 37.0 for divorced males (63.0 for widowed males) and 33.6 for divorced females (53.9 for widowed females).[59] Accordingly, the time lapse between the median age at divorce for first marriage and the median age at remarriage was 1.4 years for males and 0.4 years for females. Thus, while remarriage rates are higher for men than for women, the women who do remarry do so more quickly than the men.

Obviously, since widowhood increases with age, the median age of widows who do remarry is more than twenty years greater than the remarriage age of those divorced. Interestingly, the mean age at remarriage after widowhood for women was ten years less than the mean age at widowhood. This paradox suggests that, even though the probability of remarriage following widowhood is small for females, the youngest widows are most likely to remarry. Remarriage among older widows is compounded by the declining supply of potential husbands due to higher male mortality rates.

It is assumed that, in all countries in which remarriage occurs at all, the likelihood of remarriage varies, depending on social and demographic characteristics.[60] In the United States:

- *By race and ethnicity* — Remarriage is both more likely and more timely for white than for black women; however, both are more likely to remarry than women of Hispanic origin.

- *By age* — Remarriage is more likely for those who married at a relatively young age and who are under age thirty at the time of divorce.

- *By children* — Remarriage is more likely for those who have no children or who have only a small number of children in their first marriage.

- *By education* — Remarriage is greater for those who have less than a college education.

- *By employment* — Remarriage is more likely if the woman is not in the labor force.

- *By income* — Remarriage is more likely for men with higher incomes and for women with lower incomes.

---

[58] Paul C. Glick, "Remarried Families, Stepfamilies, and Stepchildren: A Brief Demographic Profile," *Family Relations* 38 (January 1989): 24–27.

[59] U.S. Bureau of the Census, *Statistical Abstract of the United States, 1995*, nos. 145 and 146, p. 103.

[60] Paul C. Glick and Sung-Ling Lin, "Recent Changes in Divorce and Remarriage," *Journal of Marriage and the Family* 48 (November 1986): 737–747.

In analyzing remarriage according to the financial condition of women, Anne-Marie Ambert suggested that financially secure women display behavior that is considered dysfunctional on the "remarriage market."[61] While these women have more opportunities to meet men, have more dates, and have more steady relationships, they are also more likely to break up relationships that do not suit them, less likely to tolerate abusive male behavior toward them, and less likely to flatter a man's ego. In brief, consistent with an exchange-theory model, high-status women have less to gain from remarriage than low-status women.

Similar patterns of remarriage were found in Japan but with some interesting differences. As in the United States, Japanese men were more likely to remarry than were women (although in far greater proportions), and the supply of available husbands decreased with age (a declining sex ratio). But inconsistent with women in the United States, the percentage of Japanese women who said they "do not want to remarry" was high, even among young women, and it increased with age. A result is that Japanese women are actually much less likely to remarry than are their American peers.[62] This was explained by suggesting that, in a society where there is little divorce and where marriage is treated more as a practical relationship than as a romantic one, divorced women are more likely to be completely unenamored with both their partners and the institution of marriage itself. When asked why they have not remarried, Japanese widows and divorcees both frequently responded, "I'm fed up with it."

Marriage among the remarried

Remarriage offers many benefits to those who experienced the ending of a previous marriage. It offers those involved a second or third chance. Remarriage is likely to involve older persons, which implies greater maturity, improved finances, and prior experiences from which to benefit. Yet, earlier in this chapter, it was stated that the length of the typical remarriage that ends in divorce is less than that of the average first marriage. In addition, single men and women who marry divorced partners generally have higher divorce rates than primary marriages contracted at the same ages. Why? Is there a difference in marital satisfaction for those in first marriages compared with those in remarriages? The answer from a review of sixteen studies that addressed this question was yes.

Alan Booth and John Edwards addressed the issue of why remarriages are more unstable.[63] From a national sample of married persons, they found that those in remarriages were more likely to be poorly integrated with parents and in-laws, more willing to leave the marriage, more likely to be poor marriage materi-

---

61 Anne-Marie Ambert, "Separated Women and Remarriage Behavior: A Comparison of Financially Secure Women and Financially Insecure Women," *Journal of Divorce* 6 (Spring 1983): 43–54.

62 Laurel L. Cornell, "Gender Differences in Remarriage after Divorce in Japan and the United States," *Journal of Marriage and the Family* 51 (May 1989): 457–463.

63 Alan Booth and John N. Edwards, "Starting Over: Why Remarriages Are More Unstable," *Journal of Family Issues* 13 (June 1992): 179–194.

al, have lower socioeconomic status, and be in age-heterogamous marriages. All factors but socioeconomic status were found to explain a decline in marital quality and a higher probability of marital instability.

In Canada, a study comparing first-married and remarried couples demonstrated that the remarried group reported elevated levels of tension and disagreement.[64] The remarried group more frequently experienced financial difficulties that made the spousal relationship more difficult. They also reported disagreement more often over the rearing and discipline of children but less disagreement over relationships with in-laws. Marital adjustment scores were not significantly different for the first-married and remarried groups, but the remarried husbands gave in to their wives with greater frequency than their first-married fellows, as reported by both husbands and wives. This might imply that wives have more leverage in remarried than in first-married situations, that husbands have greater needs in remarriages than in first marriages, or both.

Remarriages alone show tremendous variations, as well. Considerable research over the past decade has noted the special problems of remarriage when adolescent children from prior marriages are present. These children appear to have a destabilizing effect on the husband/wife relationship. Remarried couples with adolescent stepchildren experience higher rates of divorce than other remarriages. These stepfamilies also move teenagers out of the home faster than first-married families.[65] Adolescents living in stepfamilies also report difficulties. Divided loyalty and discipline are particularly stressful problems for these youth. The nature and problems of remarried couples with stepchildren will be considered more closely in the following section.

Remarried couples with stepchildren: reconstituted families

Most children who experience their parents' divorce also experience their custodial parent's remarriage and thus, the creation of a **stepfamily**. Traditionally, remarriages and stepfamilies were formed primarily when a spouse died; today, their formation results primarily from divorce. Terms including *remarried, reconstituted, binuclear, blended,* and *stepparent families* have been used to describe what constitutes significant nontraditional marital and family arrangements that present unique circumstances and relationships. A stepfamily may include a stepfather plus a mother and her children; a stepmother plus a father and his children; or a mother and father joining two sets of children.

Stepfamilies differ structurally from first families in a number of ways. First, one biological parent does not presently live in the household. Second, the parent-and-child relationship predates the new marriage. And third, even though a legal relationship binds the remarriage, none binds the stepchildren and stepparents.

---

[64] Charles Hobart, "Conflict in Remarriages," *Journal of Divorce and Remarriage* 15 (1991): 69–86.

[65] Lynn K. White and Alan Booth, "The Quality and Stability of Remarriages: The Role of Stepchildren," *American Sociological Review* 50 (October 1985): 689–698.

These structural elements of stepfamilies have altered parenting practices in major ways. One national sample of children between the ages of seven and eleven found that, in a majority of families, marital disruption effectively destroyed the relationship between the children and the biological parent living outside the home.[66] Nearly half of all children had not seen their nonresident fathers in the past year. Contrary to the picture painted by the media, children of divorce rarely have two homes, and only a minority ever sleep over at their fathers' houses. It was suggested that perhaps a majority have never set foot in the houses of their nonresident fathers.

When contact does exist with the outside parent, it tends to be a social rather than an instrumental exchange. That is, the nonresident parent may take the children to dinner or on trips but rarely helps with schoolwork and daily projects. Nonresident fathers are often characterized by similar circumstances: Some are still embroiled in conflicts with their former spouses, some have personal problems or barriers, some are long-distance fathers, and some have teenage children with busy lives.[67]

Research shows that parents who cohabit before marriage have less negative parent/child relationships after marriage.[68] Cohabitation may provide a more gentle transition to remarriage, gradually incorporating the future stepfather into family routines. It was also found that the earlier the courtship for remarriage was introduced after divorce, the less the disruption of family and individual functioning. It seems that, with a more rapid transition to a new marriage, there is less time for children to adjust to living in a custodial-mother household. In any case, these findings have called into question the idea that considerable time between divorce and remarriage is desirable or beneficial for the adjustment of children.

Many structural variations of remarriage have the potential to create **boundary ambiguity:** the uncertainty of family members as to who is part of the family and performs or is responsible for certain roles and responsibilities within the family system. This uncertainty of boundaries is likely to increase both family stress and the risk of behavior problems in children.[69] This is true not only in cases with alcoholic parents or missing husbands but also in cases where it is not clear who *really* is a member of the family and what roles or tasks should be performed (such as between a stepmother and her nonresidential children or grandparents with the children of their stepson).

Ambiguity and difficulty with children may be heightened when children visit rather than live with a stepparent. In her research, Ambert found the stepparent-

66 Frank F. Furstenberg, Jr., and Christine Winquist Nord, "Parenting Apart: Patterns of Childrearing After Marital Disruption," *Journal of Marriage and the Family* 47 (November 1985): 893–904.

67 James R. Dudley, "Increasing Our Understanding of Divorced Fathers Who Have Infrequent Contact With Their Children," *Family Relations* 40 (July 1991): 279–285.

68 Marilyn J. Montgomery, Edward R. Anderson, E. Mavis Hetherington, and W. Glenn Clingempeel, "Patterns of Courtship for Remarriage: Implications for Child Adjustment and Parent-Child Relationships," *Journal of Marriage and the Family* 54 (August 1992): 686–698.

69 B. Kay Pasley and Marilyn Ihinger-Tallman, "Boundary Ambiguity in Remarriage: Does Ambiguity Differentiate Degree of Marital Adjustment and Integration," *Family Relations* 38 (January 1989): 46–52. Note also: Pauline Boss, *Family Stress Management* (Newbury Park, CA: Sage, 1989): Chapter 4.

ing experience, particularly for stepmothers, to be more positive with live-in stepchildren.[70] Most research has suggested that the role of stepmother is more difficult than that of stepfather, in large part because most stepmothers do not have live-in stepchildren. In contrast, most stepfathers do. When stepchildren visit, it is usually the stepmother and not the children's father who has to do the extra housecleaning, shopping for food, and cooking. Women often perceive this work as a burden because they receive little emotional benefit from the visits. Similarly, stepsiblings' relations were found to be more positive when the children lived together rather than just visited.

Stepmothers are often viewed with trepidation in remarried families with children. Most of us have experienced the "Cinderella" story of the evil, uncaring stepmother or read fairy tales about witches and stepmothers. Yet, why are step-mothers expected to immediately assimilate into a family and instantly love the children as if they were their own? Statements about the "evil stepmother" and "instant love" represent myths (falsehoods) that show no signs of losing strength and that negatively affect the experiences of stepmothers.[71] Empirical evidence does support some of the cultural stereotypes. Stepmothers are less satisfied with their relationships with stepchildren and display more negative behaviors toward them than do stepfathers. A point of particular difficulty for stepmothers often centers around accepting the attachment between the stepchild and the stepchild's biological mother. Becoming "another" mother (stepmother) is often difficult.

What happens to parent/child relationships when stepfamilies include children from both parents (**complex stepfamilies**) rather than from just one parent (**simple stepfamilies**)? A study of Australian couples discovered that the complex stepfamily had lower agreement scores on areas dealing with financial management, communication, personality scores, adjustments, and parenting.[72] In general, persons in complex stepfamilies experienced greater dissatisfaction and stress than did those in simple stepfamilies. Perhaps complex stepfamilies are well named in that they must deal with more complexities in discipline and external relationships than simple stepfamilies.

In general, the stepfamily has been classified as a high-risk setting for children.[73] In comparison to first families, stepfamilies are characterized by more pathological behaviors and higher rates of child sexual abuse. Sexual abuse, in particular, is likely more common because of issues of boundary ambiguity, as discussed before. Stepfathers, for instance, are not blood kin to their stepdaughters, which may weaken the taboo on incest. In addition, the simple fact that more people are around children in stepfamilies—including parents' boyfriends and girl-

[70] Anne-Marie Ambert, "Being a Stepparent: Live-in and Visiting Stepchildren," *Journal of Marriage and the Family* 48 (November 1986): 795–804.

[71] Marianne Dainton, "The Myths and Misconceptions of the Stepmother Identity," *Family Relations* 42 (January 1993): 93–98.

[72] Noel C. Schultz, Cynthia L. Schultz, and David H. Olson, "Couple Strengths and Stressors in Complex and Simple Stepfamilies in Australia," *Journal of Marriage and the Family* 53 (August 1991): 555–564.

[73] For a good overview of research on stepfamilies see Marilyn Ihinger-Tallman, "Research on Stepfamilies," *Annual Review of Sociology* 14 (1988): 25–48.

friends as well as *their* children, relatives, and friends—increases the potential for child sexual abuse.

The unique structural elements of stepfamilies clearly raise a variety of questions not likely relevant to the traditional nuclear unit: How does the ex-spouse affect the children's relationship with the new spouse? Which parent gets the child for birthdays, holidays, and special events? Do parents compete in giving the children expensive gifts? Do gifts come equally from parents and stepparents? Is discipline likely to be equal and consistent coming from a mother and stepfather or a father and stepmother? Are incestuous and other types of sexual abuse issues of concern, particularly between stepfathers and stepdaughters? Are children the messengers or communication links between the mother and father, who may or may not be on cordial terms? Are children living in homes with stepparents at risk for increased emotional and behavioral problems? What socialization difficulties occur in the process of stepparenting?

These and other questions will likely be the subject of future research, given the predominance of stepfamilies in U.S. society today.

SUMMARY

1. In the United States, divorce is the best-known and most common means of ending an unsatisfactory marital relationship. Desertion, marital separation, and annulment are other means of escaping a marriage, even if only temporarily.

2. When viewed cross-culturally, lower divorce rates are associated with a high sex ratio and a late average age at marriage. A curvilinear relationship exists between the level of socioeconomic development and the rate of participation of females in the paid labor force.

3. The rate of divorce may be calculated in a number of ways such as (a) per 1,000 persons in the total population, (b) per 1,000 women ages fifteen and over, or (c) the ratio of divorces to the number of marriages in a given year.

4. Within the United States, divorce varies according to a wide range of geographic, demographic, and social characteristics. Divorce rates are higher for young couples than for those who marry when in their late twenties and older. By race, divorce rates are higher for blacks than for whites; by religion, divorce rates are higher for Protestants than for Jews and Catholics; and by socioeconomic level, divorce rates tend to go up as educational level, income, and occupational position go down. One exception to this relationship exists among educated, professional women.

5. The legal grounds for divorce vary somewhat for each state; the most widely accepted grounds are marital incompatibility and evidence of irreconcilable differences. In the past decade, "no-fault" divorce has been adopted in most states to resolve many of the difficulties traditionally associated with

proving "fault." Studies have suggested, however, that economically, women fare more poorly under no-fault than under the former adversary system.

6. Social grounds for divorce often differ considerably from legal grounds. Divorce mediation, as a conflict-resolution process, has grown rapidly as a means of diminishing the bitterness and divisiveness that usually accompany divorce. Reasons for staying in or ending a marriage constitute attractions (rewards) and barriers (costs). The decision whether to divorce is made in light of the alternatives available.

7. The consequences of divorce for adults are evident at both macro- and microlevels, as reflected by factors such as higher rates of suicide and depression. The economic consequences differ dramatically for males and females; men usually do much better and women much worse following divorce.

8. Children are a primary concern in considering divorce. Research does not support the idea that unhappy or unsuccessful marriages should remain intact for the sake of the children; however, research does acknowledge that children of divorced parents go through periods of stress and major readjustment. Mothers tend to get custody of children; the underpayment or nonpayment of child support by fathers creates hardships for many women and children.

9. Most persons who end one marriage eventually enter another. The remarriage rate climbs with the divorce rate. Remarriage is, in general, more likely for men than for women, for divorcees than for widows, for younger persons than for older persons, for whites than blacks or those of Hispanic origin, for the childless than those with children, for those with less education and lower incomes than those with higher levels, and for women not in the paid labor force.

10. Remarriages appear to be more unstable than first marriages. Compared to first-married people, remarried people have poorer integration with parents and in-laws, are more willing to leave the marriage, and report more difficult events.

11. The complexities of remarriage are compounded by the presence of children. Stepfamilies are structurally different from traditional nuclear families. Elements such as one biological parent not living in the home, the child predating the new marriage, and the lack of legal, binding relationships between stepchildren and stepparents alter parenting in dramatic ways.

12. This chapter focused on divorce and remarriage and addressed issues relevant to the contemporary American family. As such, these issues are also relevant to society. To offer programs and establish policies that support marriages and families is, at least in terms of rhetoric, the goal of government and community units. Chapter 18 will consider this issue of the family and social policy.

KEY TERMS AND TOPICS

DISCUSSION QUESTIONS

1. What are some of the reasons for desertion, separation, and annulment versus divorce? How does each situation affect husbands, wives, and children?

2. How are divorce rates determined? In this chapter, three different divorce rates were calculated for the same year. What does each mean? What factors influence each rate even when the number of divorces remains constant?

3. Divorce rates were found to differ by duration of marriage and by race, religion, socioeconomic status, and the like. What differences have been supported, and how can these variations be explained?

4. Research has shown that conservative and fundamentalist Protestant religious groups that oppose divorce tend to have high divorce rates. Why?

5. Visit a local court that handles divorce cases. Arrange to meet with a judge to discuss the legal process, the legal grounds for divorce compared to the nonlegal reasons for divorce, and his views on divorce mediators, joint custody, grandparents' rights, and other legal issues. What legal changes does he view as necessary? Why?

6. Discuss the implications and consequences of "no-fault" divorce. What are its pros and cons? What effect is it likely to have on divorce rates, long-term trends, and the like?

7. Examine some of the consequences of divorce for adults. Why are the consequences so different for males and females?

8. What are the consequences of divorce for children? What are the consequences for children who live in unbroken but unhappy homes?

9. How do remarriages differ from first marriages? Address duration of marriage, likelihood of divorce, roles and boundaries, and common problems.

10. How do stepchildren affect a marriage? Discuss some of the advantages and problems that characterize reconstituted families or stepfamilies.

FURTHER READINGS

Arendell, Terry. *Fathers & Divorce.* Thousand Oaks, CA: Sage Publications, 1995. Based on interviews with 75 divorced fathers, the author examines the masculine discourse of divorce, relationships with former wives, and parenting behaviors.

Booth, Alan, and Dunn, Judy. *Stepfamilies: Who Benefits? Who Does Not?* Hillsdale, NJ: Lawrence Erlbaum Associates, 1994. Seventeen chapters cover marriages that create stepfamilies, how they function as childrearing organizations and as sources of support, and also detail needed research and policy agendas.

Cherlin, Andrew J. *Marriage, Divorce, Remarriage.* Rev. ed. Cambridge, MA: Harvard University Press, 1992. A brief paperback that the author suggests should be titled *Cohabitation, Marriage, Divorce, More Cohabitation, and Probably Remarriage.*

Emery, Robert E. *Renegotiating Family Relationships: Divorce, Child Custody, and Mediation.* New York: Guilford Press, 1994. A discussion of how families renegotiate their relationships as a result of divorce and the conflicts that accompany divorce.

Funder, Kathleen; Harrison, Margaret; and Weston, Ruth. *Settling Down: Pathways of Parents After Divorce.* Melbourne: Australian Institute of Family Studies, 1993. A follow-up to an earlier study, *Settling Up,* tracing how five hundred parents in Australia fared five to eight years after separation and divorce.

Ganong, Lawrence, and Coleman, Marilyn, *Remarried Family Relationships.* Thousand Oaks, CA: Sage Publications, 1994. A comprehensive look at remarried families, including pathways from divorce to remarriage and key relationships in remarried families, including stepparent-stepchild relationships.

Gottman, John Mordechai. *What Predicts Divorce?: The Relationship Between Marital Processes and Marital Outcomes.* Hillsdale, NJ: Lawrence Erlbaum Associates, 1994. A clinical psychologist examines marital processes that predict dissolution with a heavy focus on observing physiological arousal and its association with patterns of marital interaction.

Kitson, Gay C. *Portrait of Divorce.* New York: Guilford Press, 1992. Data are presented from four studies of marital instability and divorce; an excellent comprehensive portrait of the divorce process.

Parkman, Allen M. *No-Fault Divorce: What Went Wrong?* Boulder, CO: Westview Press, 1992. The repercussions of "no-fault" divorce are addressed, followed by a proposed program for divorce law reform.

Pasley, Kay, and Ihinger-Tallman, Marilyn (eds.). *Stepparenting: Issues in Theory, Research, and Practice.* New York: Praeger, 1994. An analysis of the current literature on stepparenting and a summary of the progress made in research, theory, and practice related to stepfamilies.

Chapter 18

Family and Social Policy

Most persons, married and single, recognize that intimate relationships and families are significant and important in their own lives and the lives of others. In fact, one could argue the value-laden position that, across cultures and throughout history, no single institution has had greater influence in shaping the lives of persons, in affecting interpersonal relationships, and even in determining national stature than the family.

Why then, one must ask, doesn't the United States have an explicit national policy (or policies) for families? Among all the agencies overseeing education, health, commerce, labor, energy, transportation, defense, agriculture, and the like, no U.S. agency is devoted specifically to the family. Recent administrations, while professing the importance of the family and even campaigning on the issue of family values, vetoed family-leave bills, cut funding for family-planning programs, and punished persons or groups who didn't conform to a particular marital and family life-style. President Clinton made efforts to establish governmental policies that would support a range of individual and family needs and interests: gay rights, pro-choice, parental leave, health care, and child protection. It remains to be seen, however, whether governmental policies will change the course followed for so many years, when family policy was not considered relevant.

Perhaps a national family policy is both unnecessary and unwanted. United States citizens have survived without an explicit family policy for centuries. Why is one needed now? Perhaps establishing a family policy is an unrealistic goal, since no single policy could meet the needs of the many family life-styles in the United States (see Chapters 6 through 8). Moreover, no single policy would be able to deal with the range of nonmarital and marital interactions, from partner selection to sexual relationships (see Chapters 9 through 11). Nor could one policy be made equally relevant to families at all stages of the marital and family life cycle (see Chapters 12 through 15). Thus, no one policy could answer questions that affect everything from violence to divorce and stepparenting (see Chapters 16 and 17). To address these issues, this chapter will begin with an examination of what is meant by *family policy.*

MEANING AND USE OF FAMILY POLICY

Many illustrations of family policy—from a one-child-only policy in China to policies establishing a legal age for marriage or grounds for divorce—have been presented throughout the text. But what is meant by **family policy**?

It is clear that family policy can mean very different things to different people. **Implicit family policy** is not specifically addressed to families but has significant consequences for them. This type of policy can be defined broadly enough to incorporate everything that touches the lives of family members, or it can be defined so narrowly that it includes very little or nothing because specific policies can be subsumed under policy headings such as health, taxation, employment, and education. **Explicit family policy** is directed specifically at families with an intent to achieve precise family goals. In terms of government action, explicit family policy seems minimal.

Phyllis Moen and Alvin Schorr, two leading family policy scholars, used the term *family policy* to mean a widely agreed on set of objectives for families, which the state and other major social institutions try to realize through deliberately structured programs and policies.[1] This definition incorporates the notion that family policy is coherent and more or less deliberate or intended.

Shirley Zimmerman noted that *family policy* constitutes a collection of separate but interrelated policy choices that aim to address problems that families are perceived as experiencing in society.[2] These problems are likely to include many of the topics covered in this text: intimate violence, family breakup, AIDS, abortion, child care, unwed parenthood, poverty, homelessness, minority families, home/work demands, later life families, and the like.

Zimmerman's goal of family policy is to maximize the well-being of families.[3] She defines family well-being as a value that includes the state of being healthy, happy, and free from want as well as achieving satisfaction with marriage, work, leisure, housing, and so forth. The goal of her family policy is to assist families in attaining these values.

One immediate difficulty in family policy is determining who and what constitutes a *family*. Must members be related economically, morally, or socially/psychologically rather than by birth or law? Moen and Schorr suggested that, rather than settling for one particular definition, it seems more appropriate to define families according to the particular issues involved. For example, if the issue is the socialization of children, define the family to include households with children. If the issue involves a property settlement with cohabiting adults, define the family to include intimate primary relationships. The definition should not become so rigid and sacred that it defeats the program or action.

The range of programs and policies affecting families is very broad. Some support a *nurturance* function: child care, health care, and services to people who are elderly or disabled. Other programs support the *economic* functions of the family by providing welfare benefits or stimulating employment. *Social* functions are served by programs that promote helping arrangements, social networks, and the exchange of services.

The approach in this book is to deal with family policy in general terms, particularly in defining both *family* and *policy*. Families will refer both to traditional forms as well as intimately bonded relationships and life-styles that may not conform to traditional norms. Policies will refer to any laws, programs, or activities that affect families and influence their activities.

---

[1] Phyllis Moen and Alvin L. Schorr, "Families and Social Policy," in *Handbook of Marriage and the Family*, by Marvin B. Sussman and Suzanne K. Steinmetz (eds.) (New York: Plenum Press, 1987): Chapter 28, p. 795.

[2] Shirley L. Zimmerman, *Understanding Family Policy: Theories and Applications*. (Thousand Oaks, CA: Sage Publications, 1995): 3.

[3] Ibid., p. 8.

RESEARCH ON FAMILY POLICY

Within the social sciences, an issue frequently contested is the extent to which social research can or should be value free. This issue becomes particularly acute when dealing with **family-policy research.** One side of the issue argues for value neutrality, objectivity, and basic research apart from any policy objective. The opposite side of the issue argues that value-free research is impossible, even if desired, and that trained social researchers need to apply their expertise to constructive ends.

One solution to this debate is to acknowledge both positions by "wearing two hats": one of researcher and one of citizen/advocate. The researcher provides empirical evidence of what exists, and the citizen/advocate works for goals she deems important. The *researcher* attempts to maintain objectivity throughout the research endeavor and ideally is open to all sides of an issue. This includes a willingness to accept findings that may contradict one's personal positions. The **advocate/citizen** endorses and actively works for a course of action that improves family life and hopefully enhances the well-being of its members. The advocate takes one side of an issue, usually consistent with her own value system, with the intent of influencing an action or decision viewed as beneficial to families and their members.

In the early 1980s, John Scanzoni made a case for both positions.[4] His research and theory in *Shaping Tomorrow's Family* was basically positivistic because it described and analyzed *what is,* yet it was stimulated by policy and normative considerations of *what should be.* According to Scanzoni, research itself should be conducted under the strictest positivist procedural canons possible. Yet researchers should not be deluded into thinking they have no vested interest in the outcome of the investigation any less than a medical researcher has an interest in finding some cure or solution to a sickness or disease. Scanzoni recognized the difficulty in ensuring that empirical research was simultaneously distinct from, yet connected with, practical applications. This sort of "balancing act" is required because family *research* has often been devoid of practical application and family *policy* has been devoid of basic research and organizing principles.

Research with a policy focus can take a number of directions: (1) to establish family policy, (2) to do family evaluation, and (3) to analyze family impact. Bogenschneider includes these three research positions (described in the sections that follow) as models of professional roles for building family policy. In addition, she views family policy advocacy as an appropriate professional role when considered within the context of a new role of family policy **alternative education.**[5]

Unlike the advocacy approach, the alternative educator does not lobby for a particular policy but rather clarifies the potential consequences of various policy alternatives. This position is based on the premise that when individuals have suf-

---

[4] John Scanzoni, *Shaping Tomorrow's Family: Theory and Policy for the 21st Century* (Beverly Hills, CA: Sage Publications, 1983).

[5] Karen Bogenschneider, "Roles for Professionals in Building Family Policy," *Family Relations* 44 (January 1995): 5–12.

··

U.S. Diversity: Policy Research: State Welfare Expenditures and Rates of Teen Births, Poverty, Divorce, and Suicide

Spending for public welfare is a frequent issue in political campaigns. The popular message is that spending for such worthless causes is a waste of taxpayers' money, a public dole, and an antiwork incentive. But what has research shown about state welfare expenditures?

Shirley Zimmerman looked at state per capita expenditures for public welfare and a range of other variables. Examining all fifty states, the following inverse relationships were found. Lower state per capita expenditure for public welfare was related to:

1. Higher state teen birthrates

2. Higher state poverty rates

3. Higher state divorce rates

4. Higher state suicide rates

For those persons with political interests, each of these relationships is directly opposite what is typically implied by conservatives, who argue that welfare is the culprit that causes teen parenthood, poverty resulting from a desire not to work, and family breakup. The added belief that welfare is a key cause of high state taxes led many states to reduce their welfare budgets sharply in the 1980s. Thus, these views about the effects of welfare persist. What do you think?

Source: Shirley L. Zimmerman, *Understanding Family Policy* (Newbury Park, CA: Sage, 1988).

ficient knowledge, they can make judgments for themselves better than others can make judgments for them. This knowledge of the consequences of policy alternatives is based on an objective integration and dissemination of research findings. Three selected directions that research with a policy focus can take follow.

Research to establish family policy

There are various ways to establish family policy. Steven Wisensale noted that four "think tanks," in particular, are actively involved in both family research and advocacy: The Brookings Institution, The American Enterprise Institute, The Urban Institute, and The Heritage Foundation.[6] Members of these institutes and foundations publish books, special reports, and position papers; testify before congressional committees; and hold seminars and conferences to disseminate their information. Some, such as The Heritage Foundation, spend less than half of their total

---

[6] Steven K. Wisensale, "The Family in the Think Tank," *Family Relations* 40 (April 1991): 199–207.

Family policy and formal legislation take place at local, state, and national levels. The United States has no national family policy per se; traditionally, the federal government has allocated funds to state governments, who set specific policies and provide services for families, often through local agencies.

expense budget on research but rather define their primary role as providing conservative policymakers with arguments to bolster their views. Others, such as The Urban Institute, have guidelines that direct them to sharpen thinking about society's problems, improve government decisions, and increase citizens' awareness about important public issues.

Much of the research done in think tanks is focused on the first purpose mentioned: that is, **research to establish family policy**. Typically, research to establish policy starts with a general hypothesis that some kind of social action may be desirable. Such research does not necessarily assume a problem exists, does not evaluate an existing policy or program, and does not assess the consequences of a policy or program. Rather, given some nontraditional life-style (cohabitation, dual-career marriage, female-headed household, reconstituted family, never-married parents, and so forth), research for family policy examines that life-style and seeks to discover the outcome of that way of life for the individuals involved as well as for society as a whole. The research may find that all is well and nothing needs to be done, or it may recommend that laws need to be changed, programs developed, or action taken to fulfill specific needs.

An example of research to establish family policy is a study aimed at discovering the socioeconomic processes that determine the use of welfare and its accompanying dependency and the impact of labor market conditions on the determinants of dependency.[7] The life-style at issue was low-income female-headed households dependent on welfare. Data were gathered from more than three hundred such women in New Jersey at three different time periods. One of the hypotheses of the study was that the most immediate economic trade-off faced by low-income, single-female parents was between the expected return from labor supplied to the formal labor market and the need for the parent at home. Findings provided basic support to the idea that welfare could be reduced by making the expected value of work outside the home greater than that of home-related work. The policy implication is not merely to expand jobs or provide work of any kind (known as "workfare") but to provide jobs that maximize the potential for financial independence. In other words, producing fewer but relatively better jobs may be a more useful strategy than producing poor jobs for a broad cross-section of the low-income population.

The research suggested that welfare dependency among low-income women could be reduced by providing jobs with internal job ladders, the possibility of advancement, on-the-job training, and the job protection afforded by unionization. Unfortunately, federal support has largely been withdrawn for these types of training and job experiences. And as this research found, workfare is unlikely to have a long-term positive impact if it is only an administrative requirement that some job be found, regardless of quality.

Research on family evaluation

A second type of policy research is done to evaluate existing policy. Family-evaluation research is conducted at a programmatic level to determine the degree to which social programs have achieved or are achieving the stated goals of a public policy or resultant program.

The need for family-evaluation research is evident on an issue such as parental leave. In 1992, President Bush vetoed a family-leave bill, primarily on the rationale that it would be an added financial cost to business. Others argued that such a bill is unnecessary because many firms already provide parental leave and that what parents want and need is child care, not parental leave.

Connecticut passed a law (effective July 1, 1988) that provides up to twenty-four weeks of unpaid parental/family leave within any two-year period with a guaranteed return to the same or comparable job. Thus, it was possible to check Connecticut businesses to see if any of the arguments stated against family leave have empirical support. A task force reviewed the research pertaining to issues of parental leave and conducted a survey of a randomly drawn sample of two thousand firms with ten or more employees. In brief, the survey indicated that less than

---

[7] Robert F. Kelly, "Welfare Dependency Under Depressed Labor Market Conditions: Lessons from the 1970s for the 1980s," *Journal of Urban Affairs* 5 (Fall 1983): 331–348.

15 percent of Connecticut firms provided job-guaranteed parental leave. Where it did exist, excessive leave-taking was not a problem and most firms exhibited the resourcefulness and flexibility to deal with leaves without incurring substantial direct costs.[8]

Shirley Zimmerman, using a family perspective, examined research findings and other data dealing with government policies and programs to determine their effectiveness or lack thereof.[9] *Effectiveness* was viewed as a fit between the goals or objectives of a program and their actual outcomes. Drawing upon other studies as the source of her evaluation attempts, she assessed the effectiveness of income guarantee experiments, Aid to Families with Dependent Children (AFDC), Supplementary Security Income (SSI), and Social Security, deinstitutionalization policies in relation to family members who are mentally ill or retarded, compensatory preschool education, and abortion services. Zimmerman claimed that, from a family perspective, government programs seem to have promoted family well-being under conditions that take family variables into account. When programs do run counter to family interests, the negative effects of such policies and programs on affected families tend to reflect the absence rather than the presence of supportive service policies and programs.

Research to analyze family impact

A third type of policy research is family-impact analysis. Here, the attempt is to assess the intended and unintended consequences of public policy and social programs. For example, what is the impact of mortgage interest deductions on those who cannot afford to purchase homes? What are the effects of a program such as Head Start on mothers as well as children? What are the employment and income consequences of a policy that prohibits a woman from terminating a pregnancy?

Unlike evaluation research, which is focused on whether the goals or objectives are being met, family-impact analysis looks at how families are affected beyond the explicit intentions or goals of the policy or program. As a result, evaluation research may show the intended goals are being met, but impact analysis may show the goals are counterproductive, producing unintended but negative consequences for families.

For example, in Chapter 17, it was mentioned that two key determinants of economic well-being for divorced mothers are remarriage and child support. Evaluation research of child support showed that those mothers who get support are better off economically than those who do not. This is an obvious result. But what other consequences (impact analysis) does child support have? For one, child

---

[8] Elizabeth Trzcinski and Matia Finn-Stevenson, "A Response to Arguments against Mandated Parental Leave: Findings from the Connecticut Survey of Parental Leave Policies," *Journal of Marriage and the Family* 53 (May 1991): 445–460.

[9] Shirley L. Zimmerman, "Public Policies and Family Outcomes: Empirical Evidence or Ideology?" *Social Casework* 64 (March 1983): 138–146.

support was shown to negatively affect the remarriage of divorced mothers, the other key determinant of economic well-being.[10]

Another example that assessed the impact of an existing policy, in this case, welfare, came from Zimmerman. Drawing on Durkheim's theory of social integration, an analysis was done on states' spending for public welfare and their divorce rates.[11] Zimmerman wanted to test the assumption that state welfare activity serves as a destabilizing influence on family life, thus contributing to family breakup. She found that states that spent more for public welfare had lower rates of divorce as well as lower rates of population change and unemployment. She concluded that the connection that critics have drawn between the welfare state and family breakup is mythical, at best. In other words, irrespective of whether welfare accomplishes its intended goals (as would be determined in evaluation research), it does not increase the likelihood of divorce.

Overview of research

Effective family policy is highly dependent on all three types of research: research to determine what type of policy is needed, research to evaluate an existing program or policy, and research to assess the impact or consequences of a program or policy beyond its specific intent. The formulation and enforcement of policies affecting families will be addressed in the next section, where some key issues are presented again in ideal-type terms.

ISSUES SURROUNDING FAMILY POLICY

Policy matters are usually characterized by a divergence of ideas, conflicts over positions, and opposing recommendations. When policy is made, it seldom satisfies all interest groups or gets the endorsement of all social and political organizations. At times, policy differences relate to basic philosophies of life, perceptions of the role of government, and images of what the family is or should be.

In the following sections, several of these differences will be examined. While each is presented in dichotomous terms, remember that both views exist simultaneously. Rarely can an issue be resolved into an "either/or" position.

Goals and objectives of family policy

The first issue addresses questions of goals and objectives: namely, the type of family or families desired. Should policy be directed toward the traditional family or toward a diversity of life-styles, relationships, and families? Also, should policy be

---

[10] Karen Fox Folk, John W. Graham, and Andrea H. Beller, "Child Support and Remarriage," *Journal of Family Issues* 13 (June 1992): 142–157.

[11] Shirley L. Zimmerman, "The Welfare State and Family Breakup: The Mythical Connection," *Family Relations* 40 (April 1991): 139–147.

News Item: Punishment Policy Justice?

The *Detroit Free Press* (10 September 1995) published a series of examples of "News of the Weird." Three of these examples included the case of:

... a man in California who was charged with beating his girlfriend and strangling her pet rabbit. As reported, for beating his girlfriend, the maximum fine in California is $1,000 but for strangling the rabbit the maximum fine is $20,000.

... two Oklahoma police officers. One officer abused his girlfriend so badly she suffered a ruptured eardrum. The other officer kicked a cat at the airport in Oklahoma City. The first officer faced the possibility of a maximum jail time of 90 days. The second officer faced the possibility of a maximum prison time of five years.

... a dead woman in Florida. Sheriff's deputies charged a man with killing his mother and were set to charge his friend with having sex with her corpse. The latter charge failed when they discovered there is no law in Florida against having sex with a corpse.

directed at preventing the family from change and maintaining the status quo or at supporting change, flexibility, and creativity? This issue is at the heart of Scanzoni's differentiation of conventionals from progressives.[12]

Conventionals are those who believe the normal family is conjugal. A male, as husband and father, is head of the household and the sole economic provider. A female, as wife and mother, is a helpmate to her husband and a homemaker who is responsible for household duties, domestic care, and the socialization of the children. Children are helpless and dependent.

Conventionals, represented by political and religious conservatives, want to save this traditional image of what families should be. Groups representing this perspective view family change as a breakdown of morality and disintegration of *the* family. They have demonstrated substantial political power in crippling sex-education programs, halting the Equal Rights Amendment, and electing persons who oppose abortion. They have influenced legislation such as the Family Protection Act, which provides that parents be notified when an unmarried minor receives contraceptive devices or abortion services from a federally supported organization. They have restricted the federal government from interfering with state statutes pertaining to child abuse and changed the definition of *abuse* to exclude corporal punishment (spanking). They have opposed legal services for groups such as homosexuals or the poor and also opposed educational materials that do not espouse traditional and conservative values. The function of policy, from the perspective of conventionals, is to maintain the status quo or return to some idealized image of what the family once was and should be.

---

[12] Scanzoni, *Shaping Tomorrow's Family;* and John Scanzoni, "Reconsidering Family Policy: Status Quo or Force for Change?" *Journal of Family Issues* 3 (September 1982): 277–300.

Progressives are those who believe a normal family can take many forms. The view is not of *the* family but of a *variety* of families and close relationships. A progressive model is a pluralistic one that allows many options. At the core of this model is the notion that involved adults should strive to become equal partners and to achieve equity among family members. Scanzoni stated that, given their pluralistic view of society, progressives accept the notion that alternative views of family should be allowed to compete in the marketplace, allowing nonaligned persons to gravitate toward those patterns suiting them best. Conservatives cannot accept this notion.[13]

Theoretically, Scanzoni linked the functionalist approach with conventionals. The emphasis is on structure and stability. Thus, couples who stay together are successful and represent stability, and those who divorce are failures and represent breakdown. Out-of-wedlock births and female-headed households represent disorganization. In contrast, progressives are linked more closely with the conflict approach, where the emphasis is on process and change. A wide variety of goals are legitimate and result from complex negotiations between interest groups, each with preferred patterns and relationships. From this view, any number of life-styles are acceptable: childless marriages; egalitarian relationships; divorce; marriage in middle or old age; diverse family forms among people who are minorities or poor; cohabitation without marriage; homosexual relationships; access to abortion; women, wives, and mothers in the employed labor force; and males as housekeepers and childrearers.

Scanzoni noted that, in spite of the unified and influential efforts of conventionals, the major weakness of their model is that it is out of sync with the times. Their theory does not conform to reality—what is actually happening. Society is not static, families are not uniform, and goals are not unanimous.

From the progressive perspective, the purpose of intimate relationships, including marriage, is not to carry out predictable, predetermined duties, where males do certain things and females do others; rather, such relationships are to provide a context for the facilitation of interests held by both persons. For instance, children are not helpless and dependent but can be effectively trained in the dynamics of equitable decision making. Individuals may choose not to marry, to cohabit, not to have children, and to find employment that was traditionally defined as inconsistent with their particular gender.

Policy is aimed not at maintaining past traditions of the status quo that the majority of citizens have already discarded but at looking ahead and coming up with fresh ideas molded around an equal-partner framework. The functions of policy are (1) to recognize and accept the reality of changes already apparent in Western society and (2) to implement further change in a fashion that is responsive both to the question of social order and to the preferences of the persons involved. Other related issues surround this task.

---

[13] Scanzoni, *Shaping Tomorrow's Family*, 153.

Levels of policy control

A second issue is at what level—federal, state, or local—family policy should be formulated and enforced. Under the Reagan and Bush administrations as well as the Republican-controlled Congress of the Clinton administration, this issue was central to funding activities. Traditionally, the federal government position has been that states, upon receiving block grants from the federal government, should determine how and for what purposes the money should be spent. Opponents of this position have argued that family-related concerns will be ignored and that policies that are established will reflect the views of the most conservative segments of the population. Evidence has suggested that the thrust of state family laws continues to support the conventional family model, described in the preceding section on functions of policy.

As indicated earlier, the United States has no federal family policy as such. Discussions in previous chapters noted that the legal control of marriage and divorce in the United States currently resides with the states rather than the federal government. Even though no state permits polygamy per se, states differ considerably as to grounds for divorce and ease of remarriage. Even though all states have a welfare reform program, states set different standards as to the conditions of eligibility and the amounts of payment. Similarly, even though no state permits the marriage of pre-teenage children, states vary as to the age that youth may legally marry.

Involvement at the federal level becomes evident when one notes how certain restrictions set at the state level—such as the prohibition of miscegenation (marriage between members of different races), abortion, and the distribution of contraceptives—were ruled unconstitutional by the Supreme Court. So even though marriage laws are formulated and enforced by the states, federal courts have, at times, declared various practices to be unconstitutional. Also at the federal level, the United States Congress has established both explicit and implicit civil rights policies that impact every facet of marriage and family life.

This issue, like all others, is not an "either/or" question. There are both advantages and disadvantages to the establishment of family policies at either a national or a state level. Some advantages of family policies at the federal level include:

- Making the family and family-related issues visible nationally, not simply in a given state or community
- Giving family issues a national priority, as is done with defense, labor, and agriculture, for example
- Setting uniform standards for a nation that minimize local prejudices and indifferences
- Providing large-scale funding of programs and research that local or state units cannot do

In contrast to the distinct advantages of family policy at the federal level, there are inherent problems also. One problem is having national-level policies that impact negatively on select groups of the population. For example, one writer assessed the impact of so-called supply-side economics of the Reagan administration on family-support services, food-related programs, employment, education, and housing.[14] The policies of the Reagan administration were shown to have affected people who are poor (many of whom are African American) more negatively than people who are in a better economic position. The philosophy stressing hard work, independence, thrift, minimum government intervention in the lives of citizens, tax cuts and the like have hurt the poor.

A second problem centers around how policies can be maximally adapted to the special needs of racial, ethnic, regional, and cultural groups and the assessing of the adequacy of monitoring services provided, which requires local control. According to this view of more local-level policy and control, neither money alone nor one level of government can do the job.

Public versus private positions

A third issue revolves around the extent to which intimate relationships and families are *public* or *private*. Many times, the family is seen, even reverenced, as a private institution, separate from and closed to public scrutiny. Family policy, in contrast, demands that the family be open to public view and subject to public scrutiny.

The privacy position argues that the family or an intimate relationship is a matter of personal concern; a haven for privacy; a place of unconditional affection and love; a network for sharing fears, anxieties, and joys; and a source of protection and security free from "Big Brother" and public dominance. Cannot husbands and wives decide for themselves when, where, and how they desire to make love; the number of children they want or do not want to have; the manner in which they control that number; and how they discipline, educate, clothe, and feed these children?

The public position argues that the state and community have the right (and even the obligation) to establish boundaries on what happens in private. If children are hungry, wives are raped, or families are homeless, should not state or public agencies intervene? If so, when and to what extent? What about issues such as minimum income, day care, discipline and corporal punishment, abortion, alcohol and drug dependency, health care, and housing?

Advocates of the privacy position argue for minimal intervention of the state into family and intimacy matters. Advocates of the public position argue that laws

---

[14] Maurice A. St. Pierre, "Reaganomics and Its Implications for African-American Family Life," *Journal of Black Studies* 21 (March 1991): 325–340.

Case Example:
Family Preservation Programs

Over the past two decades, Wayne State University has conducted two highly-related family reunification programs: "Parents and Children Together" and "Families First." While Families First is a more intensive, shorter-term, crisis-intervention program, Parents and Children Together has similar goals but with a longer-term approach and a different type of staffing. Today, both programs, contracted by the Department of Social Services through the University, is commonly referred to as PACT.

The PACT In-Home Services Program is one of the early family-based service programs that send trained persons into the home to help them organize their family life. Efforts were directed toward parenting skills, home management, nutrition, informing about community services, improving self-esteem, or assisting with whatever was needed. One part of the program involves training of graduate students who are the in-home providers. They have a year-long paid internship during which they carry four hours of required, relevant coursework for each of three semesters. With the emphasis on training human service providers, close quality supervision is provided in all case management. In the 18 years of the program's existence, more than 200 master's-level students have served approximately 3,000 families. In the mid-1980s, as many as 22 students participated in a given year but due to funding cuts and increased costs, this year's program has eight regular PACT students working 29 hours a week and four MSW graduate students doing their field placement work three days a week for a year.

The clients of PACT are usually African American, inner-city, single-parent families living below the poverty level. Unlike Families First, which sends one full-time employee into the home for eight hours each week over four to six weeks, the PACT in-home program sends trained students into the home just a few hours in any given week but over a nine- to twelve-month period. Each student works with about eight families. Both programs get referrals from the Department of Social Services that usually involve cases of child abuse and neglect, often involving parental drug use. The immediate goal is to get the families through the current crisis with the longer-term goal of keeping the family together. In addition to working with parents in the home, PACT provides group-parenting classes on campus two hours a week for ten weeks for the clients of In-Home Services. Transportation is provided as is child care. Groups can be found meeting nearly every day of the week.

The cost of the In-Home Services Program, calculated at a per-family rate, is far less expensive than the cost of foster care. PACT and Families First have similar philosophies of assisting both parent and child: training and assisting the parent and keeping parents and children together.

must be written and enforced to protect all group members and enhance equal rights and opportunities for all citizens. Interestingly, advocates of the privacy position on certain issues such as child care and a minimum family income often take a public position on governmental intervention in sex-role behavior or the prohibition of abortion. For example, right-wing religious and political groups have led organized efforts in the past two decades against passage of the Equal Rights Amendment but for the passage of antiabortion and antigay laws.

The fact that no explicit U.S. national family policy exists should not lead one to believe that the government is totally uninvolved in or neutral to issues pertaining to families. A wide range of public policies deals with Social Security, health and medical care, child welfare, education, day care, and most areas of interest to family members. The lack of a coherent plan, set of services, or national policy may be testimony to the fact that families have no organized or powerful lobby groups to influence legislation and oversee the impact of legislative matters on marriages and families. In contrast, business, religious, and medical groups have made strong, organized efforts to protect their vested interests.

Preventive or ameliorative policy

Assuming certain policies are necessary, a fourth issue is whether these policies should be directed toward (1) all families and intimate relationships in an attempt to prevent abuse, divorce, or any family-type problem or toward (2) only those that already have problems. That is, is policy directed toward all families irrespective of their life-style or toward marriages, families, or groups with pathologies that need help.

A preventive policy for *all* families or intimate relationships focuses on issues that affect everyone: employment, health, minimum wages, housing, sexual and racial/ethnic equality, tax equity, and the like. The ameliorative, or *need* position, focuses on select groups or behaviors that are defined as problems: unwed parenthood, abortion, child and spouse abuse, single parenthood, divorce, and the like.

Perhaps a medical analogy is relevant. Traditionally, medical care in the United States was directed toward people who were sick. Physicians were seen only when colds, diseases, or broken bones created the need for medical care. An emerging view is directed at prevention, at a holistic orientation to care, and toward maintaining a high level of health for everyone.

The ameliorative problem or need position includes an added dimension of *deserving* or *undeserving*. Poor children and elderly persons who are ill have special needs. But in addition, they deserve help. Why? Because their condition or circumstances exist through no fault of their own. Thus, child support and Medicare are legitimate programs because there is a need for them and the recipients deserve help. Likewise, Social Security is a worthwhile income-support program, without stigma, because the benefits were earned; working people paid into the program and deserve the payback. That many people have other income and do not really need Social Security or that most people get back what they paid in the first few years becomes irrelevant, according to this view. Certainly, Social Security is not labeled or stigmatized as welfare because people deserve and are entitled to it. In contrast, welfare and AFDC carry connotations of disrepute. Why? Although these people may need the support, they are considered undeserving. They should be able to work, be thrifty, be independent, and support themselves, and they should not have had those children out of wedlock in the first place. What's more, they never paid into any plan that would make them worthy recipients.

It is of interest to note that labeling specific types of relationships or structures as *problematic, pathological,* or *ill* may, in itself, affect the types of policies directed toward them. Consider single parenthood as an example. If this form of structure—one parent with children—is pathological, then policy will likely focus on preventing the formation of single-parent family structures and providing services designed to facilitate reconstitution of these "less than complete" families. On the other hand, if single-parent families are simply considered one of many accepted family life-styles, the policy will likely focus on what is necessary for all families: minimum incomes, adequate housing, inexpensive child care, employment opportunities, support services, and the like.

Micro- versus macrolevel policy

A fifth issue is whether policy should operate at primarily the *microlevel* or *macrolevel.* Microlevel policy focuses on persons and patterns of personal interactions that characterize everyday life. Macrolevel policy focuses on the social patterns and forms of social organization that shape an entire society, which are beyond the control of any individual yet play a powerful role in affecting families and influencing personal lives.

At the microlevel, the individual or set of individuals in interaction is the unit of analysis and focus of attention. To deal with a marital problem, counsel the husband or wife. To deal with unwed mothers, delinquent youth, abused children, or people who are elderly, ill, or mentally retarded, provide housing (or institutionalization), personal counseling, and individual attention. This microlevel position is well understood and highly emphasized in terms of social policy and specific courses of action. The unwed mother or the person who is sick or mentally retarded is the one with the problem and in need of treatment or attention.

In contrast, at the macrolevel, the organization, system, or society is the unit of analysis and focus of attention. At this level, individuals or relationships are affected by how society is structured and by the nature of social systems within that society. Policies related to areas such as taxation, health care, employment, housing, education, and leisure all affect persons and families, but the focus of such policies is not on a given person or family with a specific problem.

For instance, if poverty status is characterized by lower levels of commitment to marriage and if high rates of marital dissolution are related to frequency of unwed parenthood, child abuse, and low levels of mental and marital health, then it seems imperative that social policy be directed not merely at counseling the mother or the abused wife or child but at the conditions maintaining poverty. If welfare policies force men to live separately from their spouses and children, or if federal tax laws or Social Security requirements impose penalties on marriage, then these policies, operating at a macrolevel, need to be reexamined. If sexual or racial inequality in society prevents wives from establishing credit or owning property and prevents African American families from living in certain neighborhoods or

Global Diversity: Parental Leave in Sweden

Calls for equal parenthood in Sweden began in the early 1960s. In 1974, Sweden became the first country to institute parental leave for both mothers and fathers. What are some of the features of the contemporary parental-leave policy in Sweden?

A married or unmarried Swedish father has fifteen months of paid leave; return to his original job is guaranteed. He can share this with his partner so that one parent can stay home with a newborn or adopted child. An additional six months' leave is available for parents of twins. As of 1990, the first twelve months of the leave are paid at the level of 90 to 100 percent of regular pay. The last three months are paid at a minimum level (about ten dollars a day).

Even maternal care practices have changed to encourage participation of fathers in prenatal care, parental education, and delivery. In employment, fathers get two weeks off with pay at the time of childbirth, sixty days off per year with pay (shared with mothers) to care for sick children, two days off to visit day-care centers and schools (again, with pay), and the right to reduce the workday to six hours for child-care purposes.

Benefits are paid out directly from social insurance offices rather than from employers. The leave program, however, is paid for mainly by employers, through payroll taxes on all employees.

The Swedish parental leave policy developed in response to three social concerns. One was a concern over the low birthrate. Swedes have a high regard for children and view having children as something that should be encouraged. Parental leave is believed to improve a couple's chance of having children by helping them combine parental and employment roles. A second concern was the need for women's labor power. A low birthrate and a booming economy led to the employment of women in numbers that today make the female labor force participation rate among the highest in the world. Third was a concern over changing both men's and women's traditional roles. Extending maternity leave to fathers was intended to liberate men from traditional gender stereotypes. Today, while men are not fully liberated, they do share more in child care than fathers elsewhere in the world.

Source: Linda Haas, *Equal Parenthood and Social Policy: A Study of Parental Leave in Sweden* (Albany: State University of New York Press, 1992).

attending certain schools, then these practices and conditions need to be addressed at a level beyond any given individual or family.

One example of this was provided by a paper dealing with the consequences of unemployment for families in the 1980s.[15] Phyllis Moen, using data from several Depression periods, noted the following:

---

[15] Phyllis Moen, "Unemployment, Public Policy, and Families: Forecasts for the 1980s," *Journal of Marriage and the Family* 45 (November 1983): 751–760.

1. Most families of unemployed people who suffered financial hardship received no government income support.

2. Unemployment benefits were an important coping mechanism for families of the long-term unemployed.

3. Limiting the duration of unemployment appeared to be as important a strategy for preventing financial hardship as was the availability of income support.

4. Families with more than a single wage earner were much more able to avoid economic privation.

The differential distribution and unequal sharing of the costs of unemployment across families highlights the plight of African American families, single parents, and parents of young children as well as how unemployment and its financial repercussions are shaped by broad social, economic, and political forces operating at the macrolevel. Even with a healthy economy with "full employment," some portion of the labor force remains jobless. Given major cutbacks in social programs plus the lag in governmental response, the financial toll on families experiencing unemployment can be traumatic. Note how events at the macrolevel increase or decrease the level of unemployment and how macrolevel policies lessen or heighten the negative impact of being unemployed.

Moen suggested as well that public policies facilitating the employment of women (flexible work patterning, day care, nondiscriminatory hiring and wage practices) could help both two-earner families and single-parent women make ends meet.[16] The policies are, however, being developed and implemented slowly.

Scanzoni presented the argument that macrolevel family-related objectives have rarely addressed fundamental issues, since it is impossible to define a family in concrete terms and not exclude many of the nontraditional forms, as described throughout this text.[17] Likewise, he suggested that microlevel responses have been inadequate because a gap often exists between the demands of contemporary society and the capabilities of conventional families and individuals to grapple with those demands. Thus, he argued for policy at a **mesolevel,** an alternative between the macro- and microlevels.

The mesolevel involves *mediating structures,* that is, groups and organizations that extend beyond the person or family but don't encompass an entire state or nation. These include community groups and agencies; churches and temples; local chapters of national organizations, such as the National Organization for Women (NOW), the American Civil Liberties Union (ACLU), Planned Parenthood, and Family Service Associations; veterans associations; unions and

---

[16] Ibid., 758.

[17] Scanzoni, *Shaping Tomorrow's Family,* pp. 97–118 and 225–227. Note also: Frances G. Pestello and Patricia Voydanoff, "In Search of Mesostructure in the Family: An Interactionist Approach to Division of Labor," *Symbolic Interaction* 14 (1991): 105–128.

political action groups; and so forth. These groups could mediate, train, and support the diverse range of family structures and concerns found in the pluralistic U.S. society.

FUTURE OF THE FAMILY SYSTEM

The underlying issue in this chapter on family policy–related issues is that of the future of the family system. Will it survive? What types of sexually bonded relationships, families, and societies will exist in the next ten, fifty, or one hundred years? How can people prepare for them? What types of training do people need to provide for their children and grandchildren (assuming they will be "their" children)? What types of structures will exist in the family realm? What functions will be expected of this institution? Will families be necessary? Will marriages exist? Will women have equal status with men? Will marriage and children be allowed only for heterosexual partners?

In reviewing the current status and future prospects of families in the United States, Mark Fine summarizes a number of strengths and weaknesses.[18] *Strengths* of families include their durability, their diversity, and their resilience. Families remain the basic institution in which individuals aggregate socially and family life remains as important to individuals as it ever was. Diverse family forms have achieved a greater level of acceptance with a recognition that they do not necessarily impact negatively on the members' well-being. In spite of problems, most families are resilient and tend to function relatively well. *Weaknesses* of families include being less potent as socializing agents than they once were, the decreasing level of role clarity, the intensive value placed on individualism, the declining status of some aspects of children's well-being, and a lack of involvement by some fathers in several areas of family life.

But what about the future of the family system? Can it be predicted? The following observations are made in predicting its future:

- Changes that take place (and will take place) in society at large or among people in intimate relationships are not necessarily pleasing or regrettable, good or bad, or constructive or destructive per se. Changes are likely to be welcomed or rejected depending largely on one's own frame of reference, the groups with which one identifies, and the value orientations to which one adheres. For example, rising divorce rates may be viewed either as a problem or as a solution to other problems. Homosexuality may be viewed as an illness or as a right to love whomever one chooses. War may be viewed as vital to national defense or as an immoral destruction of life and property. This is not meant to imply that changes are never disruptive to the social order; rather, the point is that social matters must be seen in the context in which they occur.

---

[18] Mark A. Fine, "Families in the United States: Their Current Status and Future Prospects," *Family Relations* 41 (October 1992): 430–435.

What does the future hold for marriages and families? Clearly what form they take and what functions they serve will be greatly impacted by what happens in other systems of the larger society. For example, given advances in computer technology, the home may increasingly become the center for education, employment, shopping, and entertainment.

- Although many people see the family as the core of society and as the most basic of all institutions, it must be clear that (as has been stated time and again) the family cannot be understood as an isolated phenomenon. The family must be viewed in relation to economic, educational, religious, and political institutions. In addition, factors such as population density, mobility patterns, and stratification divisions must be taken into account. It is not by chance that agricultural societies tend to emphasize extended families, parental involvement in partner selection, and often plural marriage. Neither is it by chance that the United States places an emphasis on romantic love, separate households, and monogamous marriages. The central point is that, if accurate predictions are to be made, it is essential to understand what is going to take place in other social systems. A change in any element of a social system will likely lead to changes in other elements, including the family.

- The family is not a uniform entity. Change will occur, almost without question. But to speak of the changing family as if it were a uniform entity or that only one particular form or structure is appropriate is both misleading and unrelated to the real world. From the very beginning of U.S. society, the cultural base of the population was diverse and varied. Then, as today, one could expect to find variations in intimate relationships and family patterns when considering such factors as rural/urban residence, region of the country, religious affiliation, racial and ethnic identity, social-class background, and age. One could also expect to find variations in number of spouses, number of children, and size of the kinship network. Finally, there will be variations in employment patterns of both men and women, in the household tasks they perform, and in how they rear and disciplin their children. One must recognize the tremendous differences that exist in family structures and interpersonal relationships. At the same time, it must be realized that, within this diversity, strands of unity belie heterogeneous origins.

Having provided these qualifications, permit the author to state, unequivocally, that, as long as society exists, some form of family system will exist. I agree with DaVanzo et al.,[19] that over the next few decades, certain demographic trends will continue, including:

- Women, including those who are mothers of young children, will likely continue to work outside their homes. Policies that would increase the compatibility of working and caring for children, or reduce the costs of child care, are likely to lead to even higher rates of labor force participation by mothers of young children.
- Economic opportunities for women will reduce the incentive to marry and have children, or at least delay marriage and childbearing, and may keep divorce rates fairly high. It is unlikely we will see important reversals in the trend toward cohabitation.
- There will be continued shifts in the proportions of children and older people in the population, with fewer of the former and more of the latter.

The passing of the traditional family has caused a great deal of trauma and left a good number of loose ends. But the rebuilt family will include many variations of sexually bonded, primary, intimate, close relationships that will fulfill family-type functions. Most Americans will continue to find marriage and family interactions as basic sources of emotional and psychic stability. Families will continue to be the primary sources of socialization, security, affection, and meaning. Families are likely to remain the largest collective social service agency in the nation and world—responsible for the care of children and people who are sick, disabled, and elderly; and responsible for the economic welfare of their members. The nature of partners who comprise a relationship or marriage may change, the expectations of men and women may change, sexual codes and practices may change, and general family life-styles may be vastly different.

But change by itself does not necessarily bring decay, immorality, and general deterioration of families. Rather, destruction of society and the family are more likely to result because of an inability to change.

---

[19] Julie DaVanzo, M. Omar Rahman, and Kul T. Wadhwa, "Current Items: American Families: Policy Issues," *Population Index* 59 (Winter 1993): 547–566.

SUMMARY

1. All areas of marriage and family life are affected by certain economic, political, and social policies. It seems safe to assume that, while most social policies have an effect on families, few were developed or formulated with marriages and families in mind.

2. As used in this chapter, *family policy* refers to objectives concerning family well-being that are met through specific courses of action. The intent of social policy is to guide, influence, or determine the structure, functions, behavior, ideas, and values of its members.

3. Three types of family policy research were discussed in this chapter. Research to establish family policy examines some particular family structure or life-style to determine if certain policies or programs are necessary and to make recommendations as to what they should be. Family-evaluation research attempts to determine the degree to which social programs achieve their stated goals. Family-impact analysis assesses the intended and unintended consequences of public policy and social programs.

4. Policy matters are usually characterized by a divergence of ideas, conflicts over positions, and opposing recommendations. At a general level of analysis, five of these issues or differences were examined in this chapter:

    a. *Goals and objectives* — the extent to which policies are aimed at maintaining the status quo or serve as forces for change. Conventionals seek the status quo, as idealized in the traditional conjugal family, whereas progressives seek change and multiple family forms more consistent with a pluralistic society.

    b. *Levels of control* — the extent to which policies should be established and enforced at the federal, state, or local level.

    c. *Public versus private positions* — the extent to which families and intimate relationships are public or private institutions, meaning basically the extent to which there should be a separation of family and governmental or legal intervention.

    d. *Preventive or ameliorative policy* — the extent to which policies should be directed toward all close relationships and aimed at prevention or toward families with problems that need help.

    e. *Micro- versus macrolevel* — the extent to which policies should operate at primarily the microlevel or macrolevel, that is, focusing on small-group or interpersonal relationships or focusing on social patterns or forms of social organization that shape entire societies.

5. What is the future of the family? Social policies will, without doubt, affect the future patterns of intimate and family relationships. The family is changing and will continue to change. In sum:

    a. These changes are not good or bad, per se.

b. The future of the family cannot be understood separate from other institutions and systems.

c. The family of the future will not be a uniform entity.

d. Any type of social projection must be made cautiously.

6. Given qualifications such as these, it is predicted, unequivocally, that, as long as a society exists, some form of family system will survive. It will include many differing structural arrangements, perform a variety of functions, and fulfill a range of personal and social needs. Whether one's interest in the family is at a professional level of teaching, research, or social action or at a personal level of dating, childrearing, or caring for aged parents, it will be impossible not to affect and be affected by the family.

KEY TERMS AND TOPICS

Family policy p. 564

Implicit family policy p. 564

Explicit family policy p. 565

Family policy research p. 566

Family policy advocate p. 566

Alternative education p. 566

Research to establish family policy p. 567

Research on family evaluation p. 569

Research to analyze family impact p. 570

Issues surrounding family policy p. 571

Goals and objectives of family policy p. 571

Conventionals p. 572

Progressives p. 573

Levels of policy control p. 574

Public versus private positions p. 575

Preventive or ameliorative policy p. 577

Micro- versus macrolevel policy p. 578

Mesolevel policy p. 580

Future of the family system p. 581

DISCUSSION QUESTIONS

1. Differentiate among the terms *policy, social policy,* and *family policy.* Can social policy exist independently of and have no impact on families? Why or why not?

2. Can or should family policy research be value free? Can or should policy *research* be separated from policy *advocacy*? How can family policy researchers integrate knowledge of *what is* with concern over *what should be*?

3. Describe the different goals of (a) research to establish family policy, (b) family-evaluation research, and (c) family-impact analysis.

4. What arguments can be made for establishing policy to maintain the status quo as opposed to policy that permits or forces change and diversity? Is it possible to talk about *the* family in the Western world? Why or why not?

5. Contrast the stances taken by conventionals and progressives. How do these stances translate into policy directives on issues such as teenage sexual behavior and contraceptive usage, sex education, abortion, day-care facili-

ties, cohabitation, divorce, remarriage, the employment of mothers of young children, and so forth? (Select three issues.)

6. What arguments can be made for establishing family policy at a federal as opposed to a state or local level? What arguments can be made against this idea? Is a national U.S. family policy possible or realistic? Why or why not?

7. What arguments can be made for and against the separation of family and state. In which areas does the government clearly have no right to get involved? In which areas is government involvement mandatory?

8. What arguments can be made for directing policy toward prevention for all intimate relationships versus only at helping families with problems? What are some effects of labeling certain life-styles or structural arrangements "problems"?

9. Is effective family change more likely to occur within society by directing programs and policies at individuals and interpersonal relationships (at a microlevel) or at social patterns and organizations (at a macrolevel)? Explain.

10. What predictions can be made about families and marital life-styles in the twenty-first century? Describe their structures and functions, the impact made on them by new technologies, changing parent/child relationships, the division of marital roles and tasks, the status of women, and sexual norms. Are any areas likely to remain static, stable, and relatively unchanged? Why or why not?

FURTHER READINGS

Anderson, Elaine A., and Hula, Richard C. (eds.). *The Reconstruction of Family Policy.* New York: Greenwood Press, 1991. Sixteen essays examine three major subject areas: the normative context of family policy, the link between theory and action, and the impact of specific policies.

Haveman, Robert H., and Wolfe, Barbara. *Succeeding Generations: On the Effects of Investments in Children.* New York: Russell Sage Foundation, 1994. Based on an ongoing longitudinal national survey, the authors present evidence on numerous fronts showing that American children do not fare well. The final chapter focuses on some policy implications.

Jacobs, Francine H., and Davies, Margery W. (eds.). *More Than Kissing Babies: Current and Family Policy in the United States.* Westport, CT: Auburn House, 1994. A case study approach is used to illustrate basic issues and themes of child and family policy in the United States.

Kagan, Sharon L., and Weissbourd, Bernice (eds.). *Putting Families First: America's Family Support Movement and the Challenge of Change.* San Francisco: Jossey-Bass, 1994. Twenty chapters that deal with family support in terms of change, social institutions, programs, and policies.

Lechner, Viola, and Creedon, Michael A. *Managing Work and Family Life.* New York: Springer, 1994. Two doctorates of social work provide a review of work and family dilemmas and recommend ways/policies to improve them.

Scanzoni, John. *Shaping Tomorrow's Family: Theory and Policy for the 21st Century.* Beverly Hills: Sage, 1983. An insightful analysis of the struggle between *conventionals* and *progressives* in determining the type of family or families appropriate for U.S. society.

Zimmerman, Shirley L. *Understanding Family Policy: Theories and Applications.* Thousand Oaks, CA: Sage Publications, 2nd edition, 1995. An examination of what family policy is and the putting together of policy frameworks with family frameworks to enhance family well-being.

Glossary

ABCX model A model of family crisis in which A (an event or situation) interacts with B and C (the resources available and the definition or meaning of the event) to produce X (the level or degree of crisis).

Abortion The termination of a pregnancy, either spontaneously (miscarriage) or by induced means.

Achieved status A social position obtained through one's own efforts, such as husband or teacher.

Adoption The process of legally becoming the parent of a child not biologically one's own.

Affiliated families A variation of an extended family in which a nonrelative (often an older person) becomes recognized as a part of the nuclear-family network.

Affinity A relationship by marriage or a very close relationship.

African American An American of African ancestry; a black American.

AIDS (Acquired Immune Deficiency Syndrome) A sexually transmitted disease in which white blood cells, which hinder resistance to viruses and bacteria, are broken down.

Androgyny The condition of no sex-role differentiation; androgynous individuals are those who are capable of expressing both or either masculine or feminine behavior.

Annulment The process of ending a marriage because of conditions that existed prior to it, in effect, making the marriage nonexistent.

Arranged marriage The pattern in which marital partners are selected by persons other than the couple themselves (parents, matchmakers, etc.).

Ascribed status A social position that is assigned to persons by society or by birth, such as age, race, or sex.

Asian American The diverse collection of Americans with ethnic ties to Asia such as the Chinese, Japanese, Filipinos, Asian Indians, Koreans, and others.

Assortive marrying The idea that people marry those like themselves more often than could be due to chance.

Authority Legitimate power.

"Baby boom" The dramatic rise in the number of births following World War II until about 1960.

Behaviorism A theory of learning that focuses on actual behavior believed to be the result of conditioning through rewards and punishments.

Bigamy The marriage of one person to two persons of the opposite sex; similar to polygamy but restricted to two spouses.

587

Bilateral system A family system that traces descent and inheritance through both the male and the female lines.

Bilocal residence A family system in which a newly married couple lives near the parents of either spouse.

Biological predispositions The idea that certain biological or genetic characteristics predispose people toward certain kinds of behavior.

Birth order Sibling position based on order of birth.

Birthrate The number of births per one thousand population in a given year.

Bisexual The lack of sexual preference; that is, sexual involvement with both sexes.

Blue-collar families The working class, or the upper-lower class of semiskilled, service, and other workers with various sorts of manual skills.

Boundary ambiguity The uncertainty of family members as to who is part of the family and performs or is responsible for certain roles and responsibilities within the family system; a common issue in stepfamilies.

Bourgeoisie The class, or social group, of people who control the means of production and use capital, natural resources, and labor to generate profit.

Braking hypothesis The notion that spouses may delay getting divorced or approach the decision to divorce more cautiously when they have children.

Bride price The goods, services, or money a family receives in exchange for giving their daughter in marriage.

Chicano A Mexican American.

Child abuse Overt acts of physical, sexual, or verbal aggression against a child.

Child custody The legal arrangement (usually following divorce) providing parental responsibility for the care of a child. Under *sole custody*, one parent has this responsibility; under *joint custody*, both parents share this responsibility; and under *split custody*, each parent assumes responsibility for certain children.

Childless marriage A marriage in which the couple has no children, either voluntarily or involuntarily.

Child neglect The failure to provide for adequate physical and/or emotional care of a child.

Child snatching Stealing one's own child in a custody dispute.

Cohabitation An arrangement in which an unmarried male and female share a common dwelling.

Cohort A category of people who are born within a specific time period, such as five or ten years.

Coitus Sexual intercourse.

Common-law marriage A marriage in which cohabitating couples are recognized as legally married if they meet certain requirements (such as time living together or recognition of each other as husband and wife), as specified by the state in which they reside.

Commune A group of people holding collective ownership and use of property.

Commuter marriage A marriage in which the couple desire to live together but maintain separate residences to enhance pursuit of their own goals.

Complementary marriage A traditional marriage in which the husband and wife perform interdependent but different tasks; for instance, he is employed outside the home, and she performs the domestic tasks.

Complementary needs A theory of mate selection based on the idea that people marry those providing maximum need gratification; needs tend to be complementary rather than similar.

Concept A miniature system of meaning; a symbol that enables a meaning to be shared and a phenomenon to be perceived in certain ways.

Conceptual framework A cluster of interrelated concepts used to describe and classify phenomena.

Conjugal family A nuclear family that always has a husband and wife (the conjugal unit) and may or may not include children (see *Nuclear family*).

Conjugal power The ability of husbands and wives to control or influence the behavior of one another.

Consanguine families Extended families based on blood relationships, namely, descent from the same ancestors.

Conventional Denoting groups and persons who want to maintain the status quo and adhere to a traditional image of what the family should be.

Courtship The process that couples go through in developing a close relationship or commitment to marriage.

Crisis A disturbance in the state of the family that leads to tension or pressure (see *ABCX model*).

Dependent variable A variable that is changed or influenced by the effect of another variable (termed *independent variable*).

Developmental frame of reference A perspective that emphasizes the life cycle and various stages of transition, with specific tasks to be accomplished at each stage.

Dilution hypothesis The notion that less resources (material, physical, and emotional) are available to children in large families than to children in small families.

Displaced homemaker A full-time homemaker who, through widowhood or divorce, loses her means of economic support.

Divorce The legal dissolution of a marriage.

Double-standard The use of one set of norms and values for females and a different set for males.

Dowry The sum of money, property, and possessions brought to marriage by a female.

Dual-career marriage A marriage in which both husband and wife have careers requiring high levels of commitment and offering continuous developmental sequences.

Dual-earner marriage A marriage in which both the husband and wife are in the paid labor force.

Ecology The relationship between the physical environment and the human population that lives in that environment.

Egalitarian family One in which the husband and wife have equal authority in family matters.

Electra complex The unconscious desire of the female to marry her father.

"Empty nest" syndrome A postparental stage of family life when children leave the "nest" and the family household contracts in size to the couple or individual member.

Endogamy A marriage pattern in which persons marry others within their own social groups.

Ethnic group A group distinguished by their national origin or distinctive cultural patterns, such as religion, language or region of the country.

Evaluation research As applied to families and family policy, research conducted at a pragmatic level to determine the extent to which stated goals are being achieved.

Exogamy A marriage pattern in which individuals marry outside their own group.

Extended family A family in which two or more generations of the same kin group live together; extension beyond the nuclear family.

Extramarital coitus Nonmarital sexual intercourse between a man and a woman, at least one of whom is married to someone else.

Familism Philosophy under which the needs or interests of the family take precedence over those of the individual.

Family A kinship/structural group of persons related by blood, marriage, or adoption; usually related to the marital unit and including the rights and duties of parenthood.

Family life cycle The social sequence of events (such as marriage, children, "empty nest," retirement, and death) that are repeated by successive generations of families.

Family of orientation The nuclear family into which one was born and reared; consists of self, siblings, and parents.

Family of procreation The nuclear family formed by marriage; consists of self, spouse, and children.

Family policy A definite course or method of action with the intent of influencing or determining present and future forms of family organization, behaviors, and decisions; may be implemented and enforced at local, state, and national levels.

Fecundity The biological potential of a woman to bear children (in contrast to *fertility*, the actual number of births).

Fertility The actual number of births to women of childbearing age.

Fertility rate The number of live births per one thousand women ages fifteen to forty-four.

Fictive kinship Exchange patterns resembling those of kin in which nonrelated friends offer services, support, and goods.

Fraternal polyandry The marriage of one woman to two or more men, all of whom are brothers.

Function As related to a structural-functional frame of reference, what a system does (the functions it performs) or the consequences of a given form of structure.

Gender The umbrella term that refers to the totality of being male or female, which may or may not correspond precisely with one's sex.

Gender identity The way one defines or perceives oneself in terms of his or her sex, male or female; sexual identity.

Gender role The expected behaviors appropriate to one's gender that are assigned by a given culture.

Group marriage The marriage of two or more women to two or more men at the same time.

Heterosexuality Sexual preference for members of the opposite sex.

Hispanic American An American of any race who has a Spanish or Latin American origin or background.

Homelessness The condition of individuals and families who do not have dwellings in which to live and thus no stable place of residence within a community.

Homogamy A marriage pattern in which people marry others with similar social characteristics.

Homosexuality Sexual acts or feelings directed toward members of the same sex.

Homosexual marriage A couple of the same sex who share a common residence, who have made a sexual and emotional commitment, and who recognize one another as united in marriage.

Horizontal mobility A change from one social status to another that is roughly equivalent.

Household The group of persons who occupy a housing unit.

Househusband A husband who stays at home and performs the domestic tasks and takes care of the children while his wife is engaged in full-time employment.

Hypergamy A marriage pattern in which the female marries upward into a higher social stratum (male marries downward).

Hypogamy A marriage pattern in which the female marries downward into a lower social stratum (male marries upward).

Hypothesis A statement of a relationship between variables that can be put to an empirical test.

Ideal-type constructs Hypothetical models of opposite extremes that provide contrasting (polar) qualities with which to characterize any social phenomenon.

Illegitimate birth The birth of a child to an unmarried woman.

Impact analysis Research aimed at assessing the intended and unintended consequences of family policy and programs.

Incest Socially forbidden sexual relationships or marriage with certain close relatives.

Independent variable A variable that causes a change or variation in another variable (termed the *dependent variable*).

Infertility The inability to conceive or give birth to a child.

Influence The ability to model the thinking and behavior of persons who hold authority.

Institution A stable cluster of values, norms, statuses, and roles that develop around a basic social need.

Intergenerational mobility A change in the social status of family members from one generation to the next.

Intermarriage A marriage between persons of different groups; exogamy.

Internalization The process by which one makes society's values part of one's personality.

In vitro fertilization The conception of a baby outside a woman's body (as in a laboratory dish); the fertilized egg is then placed within the woman's uterus for development.

Joint family One type of extended family in which brothers share property but do not always live in a single household.

Kin A network of persons who are related by common ancestry (birth), adoption, or marriage.

Latchkey children Children who are unsupervised for part of the day, often the time between the end of the school day and the time a parent gets home from work.

Legal separation The state in which legally married couples maintain separate residences but have established legal responsibilities of support, rights of visitation, and so on.

Legitimate birth The birth of a child to parents who are married to each other.

Lesbian A female who is sexually oriented toward other females.

Levirate The marriage of a widow to the brother of her deceased husband.

Life course A developmental perspective of change that focuses on an individual's own life span, social time and transitions, or the historical time in which a person lives.

Life expectancy The average number of years that a person in a given population cohort can expect to live.

Lifespan The maximum length of life possible in a given society.

Life-style As related to families, the shared patterns of marital and family relationships, childbearing, dress, eating, recreation, and so on.

Macho or **Machismo** As used popularly in the United States, *macho* means to be very masculine; as used in traditional Spanish or Latin America, *machismo* is an ideal of manliness, characterized by strength, daring, virility, and authoritarianism.

Macrolevel policy A policy that focuses on large-scale units, such as social categories, systems, and forms of social organization that affect families (taxation, medical care, employment, housing, education, laws, and so forth).

Marital separation The state in which individuals are legally married but do not share a common household or residence.

Marriage A socially approved sexual union of some permanence between two or more persons.

"Marriage squeeze" The effects of an imbalance between the number of males and females in the prime marriage ages due to rising or falling birthrates and the median age difference at marriage.

Masturbation A form of autoeroticism; manual or mechanical stimulation of the genitalia by self or partner.

Mating gradient The tendency for women to seek men of similar or higher status and men to seek women of similar or lower status; the result is that high-status women and low-status men are less likely to date and marry.

Matriarchal family A family in which the wife rules or has dominance over the husband.

Matrilineal system A family system that traces descent and inheritance through the mother's line.

Matrilocal residence A family system in which a newly married couple is expected to live with the wife's family.

Mediation A conflict resolution process where a divorcing couple meets with a third party who helps them negotiate an agreement on property settlement, child support and custody, and other important matters.

Mesalliance Marriage with a person of a lower social position.

Mesolevel policy A policy that focuses on groups and organizations as mediating structures between the large-scale macro units and the small-scale micro units.

Mexican American A U.S. citizen of Mexican ancestry.

Microlevel policy A policy that focuses on small-scale units, such as individuals and small-group interaction.

Midlife transition The changes that take place in men and women at about age forty or forty-five as they reassess where they have been and what lies ahead; traditionally referred to as *midlife crisis.*

Minority group Any group that is subordinate to another group.

Miscegenation Marriage and interbreeding between members of different races, as in the United States between blacks and whites.

Modified-nuclear and modified-extended families Nuclear families that retain considerable autonomy yet maintain a coalition with other nuclear families with whom they exchange goods and services.

Monogamy A marriage pattern in which one male is married to one female at a time.

Native American The native or indigenous people to North America, sometimes referred to as American Indians.

Neolocal residence A family system in which a newly married couple is expected to establish a new place of residence, separate from their parents.

No-fault divorce The legal dissolution of marriage based on irreconcilable differences where neither party is at fault.

Norm A rule that tells members of a society how to behave in a particular situation.

Nuclear family Any two or more persons of the same or adjoining generation, related by blood, marriage, or adoption, and sharing a common residence.

Oedipus complex The unconscious desire of the male to marry his mother.

Orderly replacement The notion that successive generations are duplicates of or similar to preceding generations.

Ordinal position in birth order One's position of birth among siblings, such as being the oldest or youngest child.

Pacific Islanders Categories of people residing on islands in the Pacific such as Hawaii, Samoa, Guam, or Fiji.

Parallel marriage A marriage in which the husband and wife perform similar tasks on an equitable basis; both are employed and both share child care and domestic tasks.

Patriarchal family A family in which the husband rules or has dominance over the wife.

Patrilineal system A family system that traces descent and inheritance through the father's line.

Patrilocal residence A family system in which a newly married couple is expected to live with the husband's family.

Peer group A group of people with similar or equal status and usually of similar age.

Perinatal Occurring near the time of birth.

Pluralism Many and varied forms of family and marital organization.

Polyandry The marriage of one woman to more than one man at the same time.

Polygamy The marriage of one man or one woman to more than one wife or more than one husband at the same time.

Polygyny The marriage of one man to more than one woman at the same time.

Postparental period The stage of the family life cycle in which children typically leave home and are legally and socially recognized as adults; the conjugal family returns to a two-person, married-couple household and the single parent to a one-person household.

Poverty level A classification of families below a specified income, based on a sliding scale of money income that is adjusted for factors such as family size, composition, and farm/nonfarm residence.

Power The ability to control or influence the behavior of others, even without their consent.

Primary group A small group of people who interact in personal, direct, and intimate ways.

Principle of least interest The notion that the partner with the least interest in a relationship is in a position to exploit the other.

Progressive Denoting groups and persons who view families as pluralistic and accept change and nontraditional life-styles as legitimate.

Proletariat The class, or social group, of people who labor and serve as the instrument of production for the bourgeoisie.

Propinquity Proximity; with regard to marriage, the notion that persons who live close to one another are more likely to marry.

Proposition A statement of the relationship between two or more concepts.

Race A socially defined group distinguished by selected physical characteristics.

Random sample A group of persons selected in such a way that every member of the population had an equal chance of being chosen.

Rape Sexual intercourse by force or threat of force without the consent of the victim; involving vaginal, anal, or oral penetration. *Marital rape* refers to the same conditions occurring between spouses. *Acquaintance rape* is where the assailant is personally known to the victim.

Reciprocity The two-way exchange of goods or services; basic to a social exchange frame of reference.

Reconstituted family A family, including a man and a woman, at least one of whom has been previously married, and the children from one or both prior marriages; a stepfamily.

Reference group A group with which persons psychologically identify and to whom people refer when making evaluations of themselves and their behavior.

Remarriage Marriage by anyone who has previously been married.

Role The social expectations or behaviors that accompany a particular status.

Role conflict The situation in which incompatible expectations or behaviors accompany a given status or set of statuses.

Role taking The ability to assume the status of persons with whom one interacts and to see the world from their perspective.

Secondary group A group whose members interact in an impersonal manner, have few emotional ties, and come together for a specific, practical purpose.

Sequential or serial monogamy Marriage to a succession of partners but only one at a time.

Sex The biological condition of being male or female.

Sex control The ability to control the sex of an unborn offspring.

Sex ratio The number of males per one hundred females in a population.

Sex roles Learned and expected patterns of behavior associated with being biologically of one sex or the other.

Sexual harassment Deliberate and unwanted sexual behavior, such as propositioning, abusive or suggestive language, physical attacks, or gestures such as body language, whistles, and stares; serves to annoy, intimidate, or threaten the person to whom it is directed.

Sexualization Sexual socialization; the process by which individuals acquire their sexual self-concepts, values, attitudes, and behaviors.

Sexual script The learned designation of the who, what, when, where, and why of one's sexuality.

Sibling One's brother or sister.

Significant other A person with whom one psychologically identifies and whose opinions are important.

Single parent Generally used in reference to a mother/child or father/child nuclear family unit.

Social class An aggregate of individuals who occupy a broadly similar position on a scale of wealth, prestige, and power.

Social conflict frame of reference A perspective of society that views conflict as natural, permanent, and inevitable and as a significant source of social change.

Social exchange frame of reference A perspective that seeks to explain personal and social behaviors based on reciprocity of rewards and costs.

Socialization The process of learning the rules of and expectations for behavior for a given society.

Social mobility The extent to which it is possible for an individual or family to move from one social class to another.

Social self The organization of internalized roles developed in interaction with others.

Social stratification The ranking of people into positions of equality and inequality; the arrangement of social classes.

Social structure The parts or components of a social system and the way it is organized; the network of interrelated statuses.

Social system A set of interrelated social statuses (positions) and the accompanying expectations (roles) that accompany them.

Society A group of interacting individuals sharing the same territory and participating in a common culture.

Sociology The study of human society and social behavior.

Sororal polygamy The marriage of one man to two or more women, all of whom are sisters.

Sororate The marriage of a widower to the sister of his deceased wife.

Status A socially defined position occupied by a person; may be ascribed (age, race, sex) or achieved (husband, father, teacher).

Stem family An extended-family type consisting of two families in adjacent generations joined by economic and blood ties.

Stepchildren The children by a former marriage of one's husband or wife (stepmother, wife of one's father by remarriage; stepbrother, son of one's stepparent by a former marriage; etc.).

Stepfamily A family including a man and a woman, at least one of whom has been previously married, and often including children from that previous marriage. *Simple stepfamilies* include children from just one remarried parent; *complex stepfamilies* include children from both remarried parents.

Stressor events Crisis-provoking events and situations for which families have little or no preparation.

Structural-functional frame of reference A perspective that emphasizes the units of organization plus the consequences of that particular structural arrangement.

Subculture A group of persons that shares in the overall culture of a society but also has its own distinctive values, norms, and life-styles.

Surrogate mother A woman who conceives, carries, and bears a child for another couple.

"Swinging" A type of extramarital coitus in which the couple openly and willingly engages in sexual relationships with other married persons; sometimes referred to as *co-marital sexual mate sharing* or *consensual adultery*.

Symbolic interaction frame of reference A perspective that stresses interaction among people as well as the social processes that occur within individuals made possible by language and internalized meanings.

Symmetrical family A family as a consumption unit rather than a production unit in which marital roles based on gender are eliminated.

Theory A set of logically and systematically interrelated propositions that explain some particular process.

Traditional family The pattern of family organization, customs, life-styles, and behaviors passed down from prior generations and maintained or valued because of an idealized image of how things once were and should be today.

Underclass The group of families within the U.S. population characterized by persistent poverty and a variety of associated problems, such as welfare dependency, joblessness, substance addiction, and crime.

Unilineal system A family system that traces descent and inheritance through either the male line or the female line.

Universal permanent availability The notion that any individual is a potential mate, available for marriage, with any other individual at any time.

Values Ideas and beliefs about what is worthwhile and important; a value theory of mate selection suggests that people select partners who share similar values.

Variable A concept that represents degree or value; a characteristic such as age, class, or income that can vary from one person or context to another.

Vertical mobility Social mobility that involves movement toward a higher or lower social status.

Violence Any act carried out with the intention of physically hurting someone else; family violence focuses on behaviors among parents, spouses, children, siblings, and people who are elderly.

Virginity The state of not having ever engaged in sexual intercourse.

White-collar families The middle-class category of professionals, clerical workers, salespeople, and other employees who have traditionally worn white shirts in their work; often differentiated from blue-collar, or working-class, families.

Widowhood The state of having lost one's spouse through death.

Name Index

Subject Index

Photo Credits

Chapter 1: Page 2, Harvey Finkle/Impact Visuals; Page 15, Robert Harbison; Page 26, Rhoda Sidney/The Image Works.

Chapter 2: Page 40, Laima Druskis/Stock, Boston, Inc.; Page 60, Robert Harbison; Page 69, Farley Andrews/The Picture Cube, Inc.

Chapter 3: Page 76, Jim Harrison/Stock, Boston, Inc.; Page 83, Jim Mahoney/The Image Works; Page 98, Bob Daemmrich/The Image Works.

Chapter 4: Page 108, Michael Siluk/The ImageWorks; Page 127, Jim Whitmer/Stock, Boston, Inc.; Page 132, Elizabeth Crews/The Image Works.

Chapter 5: Page 142, M. B. Duda/Photo Researchers, Inc.; Page 155, Owen Franken/Stock, Boston, Inc.; Page 162, R. Rowan/Photo Researchers, Inc.

Chapter 6: Page 168, Arvind Garg/Photo Researchers, Inc.; Page 179, Janice Fulman/The Picture Cube; Page 185, Earl Dotter/Impact Visuals.

Chapter 7: Page 194, Will Faller; Page 206, Elizabeth Crews/The Image Works; Page 212, Lionel Delevingne/Stock, Boston, Inc.

Chapter 8 Page 218, Peter Menzel/Stock, Boston, Inc.; Page 229, Peter Menzel/Stock, Boston, Inc.; Page 241, Lionel Delevingne/Stock, Boston, Inc.

Chapter 9: Page 256, Spencer Grant/The Picture Cube, Inc.; Page 264, Deborah Kahn-Kalas/Stock, Boston, Inc.; Page 278, Harvey Finkle/Impact Visuals.

Chapter 10: Page 286, David R. Austen/Stock, Boston, Inc.; Page 294, David S. Strickler/The Picture Cube, Inc.; Page 301, Tony Neste.

Chapter 11: Page 318, M. B. Duda/Photo Researchers, Inc.; Page 326, Gatewood/The Image Works; Page 342, Michael Siluk/The Image Works.

Chapter 12: Page 352, Bruce Rosenblum/The Picture Cube, Inc.; Page 364, Laima Druskis/Stock, Boston, Inc.; Page 371, Marianne Gontarz/The Picture Cube, Inc.

Chapter 13: Page 384, Erika Stone/Photo Researchers, Inc.; Page 393, Evan Johnson/Impact Visuals; Page 412, Spencer Grant/The Picture Cube, Inc.

Chapter 14: Page 420, Elizabeth Crews/The Image Works; Page 434, Alan Carey/The Image Works; Page 448, David S. Strickler/The Picture Cube, Inc.

Chapter 15: Page 452, Rhoda Sidney/The Image Works; Page 461, Mary Ellen Lepionka; Page 470, Jack Rosen/Impact Visuals.

Chapter 16: Page 488, Marilyn Humphries/Impact Visuals; Page 500, Robert Kalman/The Image Works; Page 506, George Cohen/Impact Visuals.

Chapter 17: Page 522, Rhoda Sidney/Stock, Boston, Inc.; Page 541, Bettye Lane/Photo Researchers, Inc.; Page 552, Anna Kaufman Moon/Stock, Boston, Inc.

Chapter 18: Page 562, Mark Antman/The Image Works; Page 568, David Jennings/The Image Works; Page 582, Sarah Putnam/The Picture Cube, Inc.